CISA: Certified Information Systems Auditor Study Guide, 3rd Edition

CISA Exam Objectives

The following table maps each of your study requirements into the eight chapters of this book. We organized the contents of each chapter to be read in sequential order to improve the retention of your study. It's much easier to learn if you follow our logical chapter sequence rather than ISACA's breakout list. For a complete list of the CISA Job Practice Areas and corresponding Knowledge Statements, see the Introduction. Exam Task Statements are listed below.

TASK STATEMENT	CHAPTER
Domain 1: IS Audit Process (14%)	
1.1 Develop and implement a risk-based IT audit strategy in compliance with IT audit standards to ensure that key areas are included.	3
1.2 Plan specific audits to determine whether information systems are protected, controlled, and provide value to the organization.	3
1.3 Conduct audits in accordance with IS audit standards, guidelines, and best practices to meet planned audit objectives.	1
1.4 Communicate emerging issues, potential risks, and audit results to key stakeholders.	1
1.5 Advise on the implementation of risk management and control practices within the organization, while maintaining independence.	1, 2
Domain 2: IT Governance (14%)	
2.1 Evaluate the effectiveness of the IT governance structure to determine whether IT decisions, directions, and performance support the organization's strategies and objectives.	2
2.2 Evaluate IT organizational structure and human resources (personnel) management to determine whether they support the organization's strategies and objectives.	2, 5, 6
2.3 Evaluate the IT strategy, including the IT direction, and the processes for the strategy's development, approval, implementation, and maintenance for alignment with the organization's strategies and objectives.	2, 5, 6
2.4 Evaluate the organization's IT policies, standards, and procedures and the processes for their development, approval, implementation, maintenance, and monitoring to determine whether they support the IT strategy and comply with regulatory and legal requirements.	1, 2, 3, 5, 6, 7, 8

Sybex®
An Imprint of
 WILEY

TASK STATEMENT	CHAPTER
5.4 Evaluate the design, implementation, and monitoring of physical access and environmental controls to determine whether information assets are adequately safeguarded.	7
5.5 Evaluate the processes and procedures used to store, retrieve, transport, and dispose of information assets (e.g., backup media, offsite storage, hard copy/print data, and softcopy media) to determine whether information assets are adequately safeguarded.	6, 7, 8

Sybex®
An Imprint of
WILEY

TASK STATEMENT	CHAPTER

TASK STATEMENT	CHAPTER
2.5 Evaluate the adequacy of the quality management system to determine whether it supports the organization's strategies and objectives in a cost-effective manner.	2, 3
2.6 Evaluate IT management and monitoring of controls (e.g., continuous monitoring, QA) for compliance with the organization's policies, standards, and procedures.	2, 3, 5, 6
2.7 Evaluate IT resource investment, use, and allocation practices, including prioritization criteria, for alignment with the organization's strategies and objectives.	2, 3, 5, 6, 7
2.8 Evaluate IT contracting strategies and policies, and contract management practices to determine whether they support the organization's strategies and objectives.	2, 3, 5, 6
2.9 Evaluate risk management practices to determine whether the organization's IT-related risks are properly managed.	2, 3, 5, 6, 7, 8
2.10 Evaluate monitoring and assurance practices to determine whether the board and executive management receive sufficient and timely information about IT performance.	2, 5, 6
2.11 Evaluate the organization's business continuity plan to determine the organization's ability to continue essential business operations during the period of an IT disruption.	8

Domain 3: Information Systems Acquisition, Development, and Implementation (19%)

3.1 Evaluate the business case for the proposed investments in information systems acquisition, development, maintenance, and subsequent retirement to determine whether it meets business objectives.	5
3.2 Evaluate the project management practices and controls to determine whether business requirements are achieved in a cost-effective manner while managing risks to the organization.	2, 3, 5
3.3 Conduct reviews to determine whether a project is progressing in accordance with project plans, is adequately supported by documentation, and status reporting is accurate.	2, 3, 5, 6
3.4 Evaluate controls for information systems during the requirements, acquisition, development, and testing phases for compliance with the organization's policies, standards, procedures, and applicable external requirements.	5
3.5 Evaluate the readiness of information systems for implementation and migration into production to determine whether project deliverables, controls, and organization's requirements are met.	5
3.6 Conduct post-implementation reviews of systems to determine whether project deliverables, controls, and organization's requirements are met.	5

Exam domains are subject to change at any time without prior notice and at ISACA's sole discretion. Please visit ISACA's website (www.isaca.org) for the most current listing of exam domains.

Sybex®
An Imprint of
WILEY

CISA®
Certified Information Systems Auditor®

Study Guide

Third Edition

CISA®
Certified Information Systems Auditor®
Study Guide
Third Edition

David Cannon

Wiley Publishing, Inc.

Acquisitions Editor: Jeff Kellum
Development Editor: Sara Barry
Technical Editors: Brady Pamplin and Tim Heagarty
Production Editor: Christine O'Connor
Copy Editor: Sharon Wilkey
Editorial Manager: Pete Gaughan
Production Manager: Tim Tate
Vice President and Executive Group Publisher: Richard Swadley
Vice President and Publisher: Neil Edde
Book Designers: Judy Fung and Bill Gibson
Compositor: Craig Woods, Happenstance Type-O-Rama
Proofreader: Publication Services, Inc.
Indexer: Robert Swanson
Project Coordinator, Cover: Katherine Crocker
Cover Designer: Ryan Sneed
Illustrators: Kayla McGee, Aaron Tate
Reviewers: Eric Phifer, Stace McRae, Joseph Shook, Chuck Write, Everette Hubbard, Khan Hamid, and Connie Kerr

Library of Congress Cataloging-in-Publication Data

Cannon, David L., 1962-
  CISA : certified information systems auditor study guide / David L. Cannon. — 3rd ed.
    p. cm.
  ISBN 978-0-470-61010-7 (pbk.)
        978-1-118-03365-4 (ebk.)
        978-1-118-03368-5 (ebk.)
        978-1-118-03367-8 (ebk.)
  1. Computer security—Examinations—Study guides. 2. Information storage and retrieval systems—Security measures—Examinations—Study guides. 3. Computer networks—Security measures—Examinations—Study guides. 4. Management information systems—Auditing—Examinations—Study guides. I. Title.
  QA76.3.C3445 2011
  005.8—dc22
                        2010051405

10 9 8 7 6 5 4 3 2 1

Dear Reader,

Thank you for choosing *CISA: Certified Information Systems Auditor Study Guide, Third Edition*. This book is part of a family of premium-quality Sybex books, all of which are written by outstanding authors who combine practical experience with a gift for teaching.

Sybex was founded in 1976. More than 30 years later, we're still committed to producing consistently exceptional books. With each of our titles, we're working hard to set a new standard for the industry. From the paper we print on, to the authors we work with, our goal is to bring you the best books available.

I hope you see all that reflected in these pages. I'd be very interested to hear your comments and get your feedback on how we're doing. Feel free to let me know what you think about this or any other Sybex book by sending me an email at nedde@wiley.com. If you think you've found a technical error in this book, please visit http://sybex.custhelp.com. Customer feedback is critical to our efforts at Sybex.

Best regards,

Neil Edde
Vice President and Publisher
Sybex, an Imprint of Wiley

This third edition is an ongoing tribute to the students who attended our seminars. Their infinite questions were instrumental in the creation of this Study Guide. I wish to express my appreciation to my past employers and clients for the opportunities that led me down this path.

I have been blessed to work with the best staff on this planet: Joe DeVoss, Kayla McGee, Aaron Tate, Angela Adair, and Jessica Autry.

I would like to express a special appreciation to the following people for their years of encouragement: Carl Adkins, Thomas Carson Jr., Jeff Kellum, Sean Burke, Tarik Nasir, Kris Lonborg, David Bassham, Brady Pamplin, Mark and Kris Herber, Alicia Haskin, Chuck Wright, Eric Phifer, Alicia Haskin, Frank Carter, Chris and Tammy Stevens, Daryl Luthas, Matt and Angelia Gair, Frank Carter, and Gary and Michelle Ames.

I hope reading this little book will help you accomplish your dreams.

Semper Fidelis

Acknowledgments

We would like to thank Acquisitions Editor Jeff Kellum and Development Editor Sara Barry for their vision and guidance. Technical Editor Brady Pamplin was very helpful in providing his expert assistance during the writing of this book. We wish to thank Production Editor Christine O'Connor for keeping the book on track, and for her tireless effort in ensuring that we put out the best book possible. We would also like to thank Bonny Andresen, Copy Editor Sharon Wilkey, Compositor Craig Woods at Happenstance Type-O-Rama, Illustrators Kayla McGee, Aaron Tate, TK, Proofreader Publication Services, and Indexer Robert Swanson for their polished efforts to make certain this third edition became a reality.

About the Author

David L. Cannon, CISA, is President and founder of CertTest Training Center, a leading CISA training provider. David has over three decades of practical experience in management and consulting in business development, compliance, IT operations, security and training in such industries as retail, distribution, healthcare, manufacturing, technology and finance. He regularly teaches CISA, BSC, PMP, CISSP and other management seminars across North America with a holistic approach. He's a long-time pilot surviving major engine failures without even scratching the paint. David is committed to helping provide readers the implementation skills necessary for you to be successful. With his latest edition, CISA candidates can rest assured they have the most current self-study content available to advance their career.

Contents at a Glance

Contents

Chapter   3   Audit Process   131

Introduction

This book is designed for anyone interested in taking the Certified Information Systems Auditor (CISA) exam. The CISA certification is one of the hottest in the market, with annual growth in excess of 28 percent, according to the Information Systems Audit and Control Association (ISACA), the governing organization.

It is a trend worldwide for organizations to have to implement and prove the existence of strong internal controls. You may have heard of a few of these, such as the following:

- International Basel III accord for risk management in banking
- COSO, which includes the Sarbanes-Oxley Act (SOX) for public corporations
- U.S. Federal Information Security Management Act (FISMA)
- Payment card industry (PCI) standards for credit card processing
- Health Insurance Portability and Accountability Act (HIPAA)

These are just five of more than twenty high-profile regulations that demand audited proof of internal controls. Frankly, these result in a long list of opportunities for a CISA. This may be the opportunity that you have been looking for, especially if you come from a background of finance or technology.

What Is the CISA Certification?

ISACA offers the most recognized certification in the world for IS auditors: the Certified Information Systems Auditor (CISA) certification. It is recognized worldwide by all corporations and 153 governments of the World Trade Organization. ISACA has active members in more than 140 countries and is recognized as the de facto leader in IT governance, control, and assurance. This association was founded in 1969 as the Electronic Data Processing Auditors Association, with an objective to develop specific international IS auditing and control standards derived from the worldwide financial controls issued by Committee of Sponsoring Organizations (COSO). As a result, ISACA has created the number one information systems audit certification in the world, the CISA.

ISACA controls and administers the CISA exam worldwide. More than 50,000 professionals have earned their CISA to date. It is one of the most requested credentials in governance and consulting.

What Is the Job Market for Certified IS Auditors?

The CISA world is still moving forward. After the worldwide banking collapse of 2008, corporations are hiring and retaining consultants in an effort to prove compliance before they get caught short. Consulting companies also hire CISA-certified professionals to help service clients. Large and small organizations are finding themselves at a competitive disadvantage if they're unable to demonstrate a stronger level of internal controls. The myth of an organization being "too big to fail" has officially proven to be false. I'll show you examples as evidence of this in Chapter 1.

One of the fundamental rules of auditing is that participating in the remediation (fixing) of problems found during the audit would compromise the auditor's independence. Under the rules of independence, the independent auditor must remain independent to certify the results as valid. A second, unrelated auditor should perform remediation work. The requirements for regulatory compliance are ongoing, and that means remediation at some level will be ongoing too. In other words, the auditor requirement is actually doubled. The opportunity for you is available right now.

For many years, organizations have undergone the scrutiny of financial audits. As financial systems have become more and more complex, computer automation has introduced new concerns over the integrity of electronic financial records. In the past, an organization would simply hire a certified public accountant to review their financial records and attest to their integrity. Larger organizations would hire certified internal auditors to assist with reviewing internal controls of the business to help reduce the ongoing cost of external audits. Now, the long list of regulations requiring internal controls has focused attention on the information systems. Computers are now the house in which the financial records live. The CISA is the top credential for auditing IS and related internal controls. If you can't prove integrity of the computer environment, you can't trust the integrity of electronic records either.

Why Become a CISA?

So, why become a CISA? The answer: credibility and opportunity. Many people proclaim themselves to be IS auditors. The majority of uncertified auditors are no more than well-meaning individuals who habitually violate the official audit standards. Here is a short list of the benefits associated with becoming a CISA:

Demonstrates Proof of Professional Achievement   The CISA certification provides evidence that you have prior audit experience and are able to pass a rigorous certification exam. The exam tests your knowledge of auditing practices related to information systems. The test itself is loaded with technical challenges that require a significant understanding of technology. Your CISA certification shows that you understand the fundamentals of applying audit concepts to the abstract world of information systems. A CISA is expected to lead an audit in accordance with widely accepted audit practices. Being certified demonstrates to the world that your experience represents a significant value.

Provides Added Value to Your Employer   Today's employers are savvy to the value of training. Your CISA study is expected to illuminate new methods to improve your skills on the job. It's fairly common for individuals to start their career by mimicking a more senior person performing a similar job (as the saying goes, monkey see, monkey do). Our goal is to shine the light on specific practices that you should have been following, even if you never heard of them before. Your job performance will improve after you learn the proper foundation and CISA resources.

Provides an Assurance of Quality to Your Clients   Audit clients are a demanding breed of individuals. The fate of the client's organization may rest on the findings detailed in the auditor's report. There is little room for mistakes. The CISA credential indicates that you are a person who would be trustworthy to deliver accurate results. Who would you trust to represent you: a person with no proof, or someone who can demonstrate an independent measurement of credibility? The person reading the audit report needs to understand that your work is accurate. Clients will direct capital and resources to be expended according to the report you provide. The CISA certification represents a third-party audit of your basic audit knowledge. It helps prove your credibility.

Increases Your Market Value   The CISA credential helps separate you from the mass of self-proclaimed auditors. Many organizations regard the CISA as the hallmark of professionalism. There is no better way to attract the favorable attention of management. It does not matter whether you're internal or external to the organization—the credential speaks for itself. Government regulations with more-intrusive requirements are becoming a growing concern for executives. Your customer may not understand all the details necessary to describe the job of an auditor; however, your client will recognize that an experienced auditor with the CISA certification is usually the best choice to fulfill their needs. In addition, audit firms can bill more money for certified professionals.

Provides a Greater Opportunity for Advancement   Every organization strives for good people who are motivated. What does the lack of certification say about someone? Is it that they are unmotivated? Could it be that they are not capable? Or is it simply that they are afraid to try? No manager in their right mind would promote an individual who has not proven their value. Taking the time to get trained and certified shows the world that you are motivated, that you are somebody who wants to get things done. That trait alone can get you promoted. Instead of using words to describe your ability, you can prove it with your CISA credential. People will know that you're serious about your job and will treat you accordingly.

Builds Respect and Confidence from Other People   The world today is extremely specialized. Consider that many things of premium value in today's world are certified. We have certified used cars, certified mail, certified public accountants, certified travel agents, certified lawyers, and even certified Subway sandwich artists. The people you meet may not completely understand what is involved in being a CISA. However, they will understand that you have expended time and energy to obtain the certification. You will gain their respect because of the effort you've demonstrated. If given the choice, almost everyone would choose to use a person who is certified. The CISA is a major step toward the widespread credibility that you desire.

Who Should Buy This Book?

If you're serious about becoming a professional CISA auditor, this is the book to study for your exam. If you're curious about becoming an auditor, in this book you will learn how the auditor's job is actually done.

The people entering the CISA profession are usually one of the following:

- IT professionals with a desire to expand into the lucrative world of consulting
- Financial professionals looking for upward mobility with new challenges
- Internal auditors seeking to demystify the control issues within IT

This book is unique in the field of IS auditing. You will benefit by learning the workflow, methods, and decision points necessary to be a successful auditor. Each chapter builds step-by-step toward obtaining your goal. Inside this book are important details about how to accomplish your job, the exam objectives for each chapter, and all of the most important auditing concepts.

Why Is This Book My Best Choice?

This book is specifically designed to help you become a well-respected CISA. No jumbled brain dumps or answer cramming in here. We have been teaching very successful CISA seminars for several years with outstanding career results. This book will not replace a $1,000 seminar, but it will help you pass the exam. Your CISA exam alone is just a small steppingstone in your professional life. Passing the exam does not prove you will be a good auditor. It simply gives your client a reason to listen to you for another 15 seconds. Now you have 15 seconds to prove you know what you are talking about.

Imagine telling someone that you are a certified juggler of flaming swords. You can bet their next comment would be, "Light up the swords and start juggling"—show me your skill. Clients are impressed when they see the results, not by you passing an exam. Our goal is to take you through the CISA material better than anyone else by showing you the "how and why" of performing IS audits:

- If you are familiar with technology, this book will help you understand how the auditor must act to be successful.

- If you come from a financial background, we're going to take you through an introductory tour of technology. The CISA is *not* a technician's test. Our explanations in this book are technically correct and designed to be simple to understand.

Many opinions exist about how the information systems audit should be performed. This book covers a combination of the official auditing standards of COSO, ISO, and ISACA. These are necessary for you to be successful. Rest assured that these standards are not in conflict with each other. You'll find that this book contains the valuable information necessary to operate an internal audit or a successful consulting practice. Initially our focus is on helping you pass your exam. However, you will discover that this information can help you earn a great deal more than a paper certificate, if you apply it.

Each chapter in this book has been arranged in a logical sequence focusing on a practical application. ISACA produces fine materials written by committees of authors, each contributing a handful of their own pages. We have chosen to take a different route. The material in this book is written in a complete logical sequence of application that we would use to teach our own staff prior to an audit engagement. Every point you read will build your knowledge through to the subsequent pages of this Study Guide. The analogy is comparable to building a pyramid. You'll start with gaining a firm understanding of the basics and build your way up to the advanced material with almost no duplication. We strongly suggest that you read the book in sequence, without skipping ahead.

How to Become a CISA

The CISA designation is given to individuals who have demonstrated their ability to fulfill the following five requirements:

Pass the CISA Exam The CISA examination is offered two times a year, once in June and again in December. You have to register for the test three months before it is administered. You can register online at www.isaca.org or by mail. You take the test with pencil and paper in front of a live test proctor. The examination is 200 multiple-choice questions, and there is a 4-hour time limit. A grade equal to 75 percent is required to pass the CISA examination, and you must be in the top 1/3 of ISACA's grading curve.

Professional Experience in Information Systems Auditing, Control, or Security To qualify for certification, you must demonstrate five years of IS auditing experience. ISACA will accept up to two years of substitution toward the work experience requirement, as follows:

Related Experience Substitution You can substitute a maximum of one year of experience from financial or operational auditing, or from information systems experience.

College Credit Hour Substitution The equivalent of an associate or bachelor's degree can be substituted for one or two years, respectively (60 hours or 120 hours).

University Instructor Experience Substitution A full-time university instructor can substitute two years of on-the-job experience toward one year of the IS auditing control or information security experience.

Your CISA test results are valid for five years from the examination date. Even without any experience at this time, you can take the examination. Certification will be awarded only after you have provided verification of desired work experience (of five years or the equivalent). ISACA limits acceptable experience to that which has occurred within 10 years prior to your application date.

Continuous Adherence to ISACA's Code of Professional Ethics Trust and integrity are paramount to the auditor's profession. You will be required to pledge your ongoing support for adherence to the IS auditor's code of professional ethics.

Continuing Education in the Audit Profession You are required to continuously improve your skills. Continuing education is the best method of maintaining an individual's competency. Learning new skills with new certifications will improve your professional abilities. Demonstrating a commitment to continuing education differentiates qualified CISAs from those who have not fulfilled their professional responsibilities. You will be required to demonstrate a minimum of 20 contact hours of training each year, which must total 120 contact hours in a three-year period.

Adherence to Well-Established IS Auditing Standards The purpose of auditing standards is to ensure quality and consistency. Auditors who fail to meet these standards place clients, themselves, and the profession in peril. ISACA provides excellent information to guide auditors through their professional responsibilities. The auditing standards are based on well-recognized professional practices applied worldwide. The auditor's job is to apply these standards while providing excellent notes so others can independently reproduce the exact same results. Good work is proven when evidence testing is verified through matching identical results from other auditors.

How to Use This Book and CD

This book is organized into eight chapters. Each begins with a list of chapter objectives that relate directly to the CISA exam.

An "Exam Essentials" section appears near the end of every chapter to highlight the topics that you're likely to encounter during your exam. These exam essentials are intended to provide guiding thoughts rather than a laundry list of details. Our goal is to help you focus on the higher-level objectives from each chapter as you move into the next chapter.

At the end of every chapter are approximately 25 basic review questions with explanations, and more questions are available online. You can use these basic review questions to help gauge your level of understanding and better focus your study effort. As you finish each chapter, you should review the questions and check whether your answers are correct. If not, you should really read the section again. Look up any incorrect answers and research why you may have missed the question. It may be a case of failing to read the question and properly considering each of the possible answers. It could also be that you did not understand the information. Either way, going through the chapter a second time would be valuable.

We have included several testing features in the book and on the companion CD. Following this introduction is an assessment test that will help you gauge your study requirements. Take this test before you start reading the book. It will help you identify areas that are critical to your success. The answers to the assessment test appear after the last question. Each question includes a short explanation with information directing you to the appropriate chapter for more information.

Included on this book's CD are two bonus exams of 80 questions each. In addition, there are more than 300 flash cards. You should use this Study Guide in combination with your other materials to prepare for the exam.

Take these practice exams as if you were taking the real exam. Just sit down and start the exam without using any reference material. We suggest that you study the material in this book in conjunction with the related ISACA references on IS auditing standards. The official CISA exam is very challenging. Most individuals will barely finish the exam before time runs out. Fortunately for you, our students have a high success rate. You have it within you to become the next certified CISA.

You are ready for your CISA exam when you score higher than 90 percent on the practice examinations and chapter reviews.

A copy of this book is on the CD in Adobe Acrobat PDF format for easy reading on any computer, iPad, or Kindle.

The practice exams included on the CD are timed to match the pace of your actual CISA exam.

What to Expect on the CISA Exam

Certainly you are curious about the types of questions you will encounter on the exam. ISACA is very protective of the actual test questions. Let's look at how the test is designed:

- The CISA exam is *not* an IT security test. Candidates will be expected to understand the basic concepts and terminology of what they will be auditing. However, security knowledge alone will not help candidates pass the test.

- The CISA exam is *not* a financial auditor exam. Candidates are not expected to be accounting technicians nor to perform complex financial transactions.

- The CISA exam is *not* a computer technician exam. Candidates are not expected to build computers nor to configure network devices. They are expected to understand the common terminology.

- The entire focus is on how to apply the structured rules of financial auditing to the abstract world of managing information technology.

By properly studying this book, you will better understand the hows and whys of being a successful CISA. Just remember, the IS auditor is a specially trained observer and investigator. We don't actually fix problems; we report findings after using a structured process of investigation. Understanding how to get the right evidence is the key.

How to Fail Your CISA Exam

The CISA exam is based on ISACA's auditing standards and the application of the Statement on Auditing Standards (SAS). Abstract concepts of IT require the auditor to use a different approach to auditing. Adults learn by direct experience or by speaking with other people. Here are the two ways to fail your exam:

Rehearsing Practice Questions More Than Twice   One bad habit is to rehearse by using practice questions. Studies have proven the brain stops learning after the second pass over the same question, and then it starts memorizing the wording. This causes the brain to record the answer as rote memory rather than to learn the information. As a result, you will likely miss the correct answer on your exam because of the different way ISACA presents the questions and answer choices. Another problem is using questions from the Internet that cannot be traced to an official reference source Bad questions still make the seller money while programming you with the wrong information. Beware of ghostly sellers hiding behind websites without full contact information prominently displayed. I suggest you stick to the questions provided with this book or use the ISACA official practice questions. Stop rehearsing the same question after two passes. Instead, reread the corresponding section in the book.

Improper Study Preparation   The CISA exam is designed to prevent cram study. You will discover that the structure of the exam questions is rather convoluted. Some of the answer choices will barely fit the question. Just select the best choice that honors the spirit and intent of our audit objectives. It's possible that the best answer is only 51 percent correct. Go with the 51 percent answer if that is the best choice available. This confusion is intentional, to prevent the test taker from using rote memory. The best study technique is to read about

1 hour per night while taking manual notes. Be sure to read all the sections—every page in the order presented. Previous CISA candidates were quite perturbed to discover that the area they assumed to be their strongest was instead where they scored poorly. You may have many years of experience in the subject, but what matters is that your view agrees with ISACA's exam. I have not heard of a single person getting a better score after protesting an official exam question. ISACA uses a professional testing company to run their exam. Protest a question if you must, but I'll wager that you lose the protest and your protest fee in the end.

The Best Way to Pass Your CISA Exam

Be prepared to answer questions about what the *auditor* should be doing. Correct answers are not focused on technical details, as you might expect from an IT equipment support person. An auditor is an executive position. Senior auditors can meet with the audit committee, composed of the board of directors, each quarter to candidly discuss issues without other executives present. Auditors hire, manage, and directly supervise technical experts who do detailed work for us (audit standards: using the work of others). COSO, ISO, and ISACA standards specifically state that the technical expert is not qualified to function in auditor duties on the audit team.

Always remember, the exam is all about how to implement ISACA audit standards. Relying on what you do at work or practicing rote memory is an excellent path to failure. The purpose of a standard is to represent a uniform unit of measure. Auditors are expected to help executives understand how controls in specific standards function at various levels. Compensating controls use an alternative method that creates the same equivalent effect. Because life requires risk-versus-reward decisions, we know everyone will have to compromise and live with some risk present. Hopefully, their preferences are not based on stupid decisions. As auditors, we look at the risks and then decide whether the controls are effective through testing and analysis. We get paid to observe, analyze, and decide. Think about how CSI detectives work on the TV show, and you are on the right track. This is the focus of your exam. We listen to evidence via test results. Without enough solid evidence and proper testing, we might issue a qualified opinion, which means we are limiting how the client will use our report.

Never forget that an audit is simply a review of history. Audit opinions are actually scores based on specific audit objectives, collecting enough evidence samples, testing, analysis of results, and reporting. The auditee is the target subject who starts with a score of zero and builds points based on supporting evidence. As auditors, we are expected to use accredited audit procedures. The standards say that auditors simply test the evidence to determine whether a management claim of compliance is supported (possibly true) or unsupported (false). COSO, ISACA, and ISO standards say auditors are *not* responsible for detecting all the problems nor are we responsible for subsequent acts. If another auditor comes up with different results, it's due to procedural problems, evidence issues, or the weak skills of one of the auditors.

Test Taking and Preparation

The CISA examination is quite difficult unless you are prepared. Preparation requires good study habits and a well-planned schedule. You should review your notes at least 30 minutes per night, but never more than 2 hours per day. As we said, cramming for this examination will not work.

Let's discuss preparations leading up to test day—specifically, the best method to arrange your schedule for that ace grade.

30-Day Countdown

Review each chapter in your Study Guide. Remember, this book was written to build your understanding successively with a minimum of duplication. Each chapter elaborates on information in the preceding chapter. Give extra attention to the subjects that you may have skimmed over earlier. The test is written from the viewpoint of an auditor, using directives from ISACA's world.

 NOTE Number one hint: Make sure you are reading from the auditor's perspective.

You should review the electronic flash cards on the accompanying CD. It is also an excellent technique to make your own flashcards by using 3″×5″ index cards. Take a dozen or two dozen to the office each day for random practice between meetings.

Be sure to run through the bonus exams on the CD. They are less difficult than the real test, but still a good resource to see where you stand. The value of these tests is in improving your resilience and accuracy.

Be sure to request a day of rest. Ask your boss for personal time. Use vacation time if necessary. Most employers will understand after you remind them of the limited testing dates.

10-Day Countdown

The exam location may be in a hotel, college, or convention center. It will save you a great deal of time and stress to drive over to visit the test site. You should do this even if you have been there recently. The room number for your test will be printed on your exam acceptance letter. Make it a point to locate the meeting room and physically walk up to touch the door. In colleges, it is possible that room 300 is a significant walk away from room 302. Arriving at the wrong building can ruin your day if it makes you late to the exam.

Convention centers are worse. Unknown to you, there may be a big trade convention over the same weekend. Such an event will change the availability of parking in the area. It will also affect the long route you may have to walk in order to enter the examination room.

The best suggestion is to scout the area for a nearby place to eat breakfast. Plan to eat healthily before the exam begins.

3-Day Countdown

The best aid to a high score is to take off early on Friday. Remember, the exam is early on Saturday morning. Make a pact with your friends and family to leave you alone all day Friday. You may consider limiting your diet to simple foods, avoiding anything that is different from usual. This is not the time to experiment.

Make a pact with yourself: There are no errands or chores more important than passing the exam.

Go to bed earlier than usual. Do whatever it takes. You will need to be up and totally focused by 6 a.m. Try to go to bed by 10 p.m. Set two alarm clocks to get up on time. Put your favorite study materials together in a carrying bag. You will take them with you to the exam for a final glance before being seated for the test. The exam is a "closed book" test.

Do not attempt to cram on Friday night; it will work against you in a long test like the CISA. Just review your notes again. Be sure to run through the flash cards and chapter review questions.

We suggest people with a technical background review Chapter 2, "Managing IT Governance," and Chapter 3, "Audit Process" twice. If you have a financial background, the best advice is to reread Chapter 4, "Networking Technology Basics," and Chapter 7, "Protecting Information Assets." Practicing drawing the diagrams and models on a separate sheet of paper will help you understand the specific wording of questions and make it easier to select the correct answer. Be prepared to redraw the models from memory during your exam.

Dress for Comfort

This is not a fashion show. It's a long exam, and you need to plan for comfort. Regardless of the season, the testing room is usually one of two extremes: either hot and stuffy or cold and breezy. It does not matter whether the problem is caused by an Arctic snowstorm, overactive heating system, or super strong air conditioner blowing icy snow in your face. You should dress in layers of clothing so you can add a sweater or strip down to a T-shirt for comfort. I took my CISA exam during a Texas summer and froze my buns under the icy blast of the university's air conditioner. I went back to the same room a few years later for my CISM exam, and the room was sweltering hot. It's better to dress prepared for anything.

Test Morning

Time to get up and get yourself moving. Be sure to arrive at the exam early. Test room locations have been known to change overnight, especially at college locations.

After arrival, you can sit in the hallway while you wait. This is an excellent time to make a final review of your notes. There is no advantage to being seated before 7:30 a.m. Just park yourself within a few feet of the door to ensure that you are not forgotten or missed. You can expect a long line at some test locations. Major cities may have 200–300 people sitting in different rooms.

Upon entering the room, ask if you can draw inside the test booklet. Tell the proctor you like to make longhand notes when solving problems. Usually the booklet will never be reused, so you can mark in it all day long.

You can make notes to yourself in the booklet and mark your favorite answer, and then just transfer the answer from the test booklet to the answer sheet. This technique really helps if you start jumping around or choose to skip a question for later. Consider drawing useful diagrams such as the OSI separate of duties model on the inside back cover of the booklet. The proctor will tell you that only answers on the answer sheet will count toward your score.

Plan on Using All 4 Hours

You should expect the test to take the entire 4 hours. Manage your time carefully to avoid running out of time before finishing the test. It is advisable to plan ahead for both pace and breaks. The exam proctor will usually allow you to take restroom breaks as long as you do not talk to anyone about the exam while out of the room. You might find it helpful to reduce fatigue by just taking a walk to the restroom and then splashing water on your face. One trip per hour seems to work fine. Most test takers will finish in the last 10 minutes before time is called by the proctor.

Read the Question Carefully

Read each question *very* carefully! The questions are intentionally worded differently from this Study Guide. For overly confusing questions or ones that you are not sure of, try reading them twice or even three times.

On the first pass, circle the operative points in the question, such as the words *not*, *is*, *best*, *and*, *or*, and so on. Next, underline the nouns or the subject of the question. For example, if the question is "The purpose of controls is to...," you would underline *purpose* and circle the word *is*.

On the second pass, ensure that you understand the implied direction of the question and its subject. Is the question a positive (*is*) or negative (*is not*) implication? Watch for meanings that are positive, negative, inclusive, or exclusive. A common technique used for writing test questions is to imply terminology associations that should not exist or vice versa. Do not violate the intent of the question or answer. Most people fail a question by misreading it.

On the third pass, dissect the available answers by using a similar method. Watch for conflicting meaning or wrong intent.

Place a star next to any question in the booklet when you have doubts about your answer. You can return to the question before turning in your answer sheet. (This keeps your answer sheet clean of any stray marks.)

For your final check, you can compare the answers marked in the test booklet to your answer sheet. Remember that there is no penalty for wrong answers. Do not leave any blank. Just take a guess if you must.

Done! The Exam Is Over

Plan for a relaxing activity with your family or friends after the exam. We suggest you plan something that is fun and doesn't require mental concentration; you will be mentally worn out after the exam. Do not punish yourself by looking up the answers for a particular test question. The test is over. Now it's time to enjoy yourself.

We wish you all the best. Good luck on your exam.

Getting Your CISA Awarded

A notice of your official letter with overall score will be mailed or emailed to you five to eight weeks after the exam. You should expect the mailed letter to be only two pages stating that you either failed or passed. ISACA will inform you of your score. Contesting a score is usually a waste of effort.

After you pass, the next step is to download and complete ISACA's application to be certified. You will need to provide contact names for your references, complete with email addresses and phone numbers. Each reference will need to sign a form indicating your experience and checking the box stating you would be an asset to the audit profession. It's your job to mail these forms back to ISACA along with your application for certification. ISACA will verify your claim prior to awarding you the CISA credential. No reference = no credit. Inform your references in advance so they are ready to respond to ISACA's reference check. It's a good idea to have lunch with your references in advance. Give them a copy of your CISA application to discuss together in person. You can expect to be an official CISA 10 to 12 weeks after the exam—*if* you are prompt in filing the application and do a good job of managing the timely response of your references.

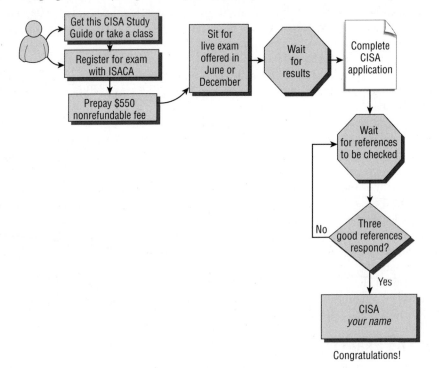

Related Professional Certifications

Although this book focuses on ISACA's CISA certification, there are many more certifications you should consider for your professional advancement. This section offers a sampling of the commonly known professional certifications that cover many of the same topics related to the CISA. This list is not inclusive of all certifications. It focuses on vendor-neutral certification, which provides an unbiased view of the issues facing all vendors and customers.

It is important to be able to separate performance claims (smoke) from truly effective function (results). Results are measured by highest effect on the ultimate need and not by the use of a particular computer software package. There is a big difference between managing and just operating software. Persons with the following certifications should be versed in the basics for success in their field.

Information Systems Security Practices

The following certifications are focused on IS security topics:

Certified Information Security Manager (CISM)   The CISM is a manager's certification. It provides a holistic manager-level view of practices when compared to the CISSP. The CISM certification and exam are administered by ISACA. CISM covers the more advanced areas of setting up and running an ISO 27000 information security management system (ISMS), staffing to sustain operations, risk management reviews, specific management controls, and governing IS security. Certification requires passing the exam plus five years of experience in IS auditing, control, or security. Your CISA experience can count toward the work experience requirement.

Certified Information Systems Security Professional (CISSP)   This certification is governed by the International Information Systems Security Certification Consortium, or (ISC)². The CISSP is a general awareness certification for technicians that covers 10 of the 15 international knowledge areas of information security. Certification requires passing the CISSP exam plus five years of IS security experience. Studying for the CISSP does not prepare you for the CISA. The CISSP exam has about 30 percent of the technical references in common but leaves out the audit information necessary to pass the CISA.

Systems Security Certified Practitioner (SSCP)   This certification is also administered by (ISC)². It covers 7 of the 15 international knowledge areas of information security with a focus on individual systems. Certification requires passing the exam plus two years of IS security experience. SSCP is a subset of the CISSP subject material. CertTest recommends that you attend the CISSP course to ensure that you receive all the training necessary for your future.

Security+   This entry-level certification is administered by the Computing Technology Industry Association, or CompTIA (www.comptia.org). It covers a very basic overview of the topics. Security+ is not intended to be a prerequisite for CISM or CISSP. Security+ is good starter for beginners on the junior staff who would not be able to meet the work experience of the other certifications. Security+ is a good start for help-desk service positions.

Auditing

In addition to the CISA, a few of the other certifications focus on auditing, including the following:

Certified Internal Auditor (CIA)   This certification, is administered by The Institute of Internal Auditors (www.theiia.org). It requires passing four separate exams in stages. These exams may be taken separately or combined in any order. Each exam is 125 multiple-choice questions. In addition, candidates must have a bachelor's degree or equivalent, plus 24 months of internal auditing experience. It's refreshing not to be forced to sit through a single exam like an endurance contest.

Certified Fraud Examiner (CFE)   This certification is for professionals with two years of fraud detection–related work experience in the areas of accounting, auditing, fraud investigation, criminology, loss prevention, or law. It's administered by the Association of Certified Fraud Examiners (www.acfe.org). It requires a bachelor's degree and passing the exam.

Certified Information Technology Auditor (CITA)   CITA is a relatively new certification administered by the American Institute of Certified Public Accountants (www.aicpa.org). CPAs in good standing with a valid CISA certification will qualify to receive the CITA certification by AICPA (CPA + CISA = CITA). I know, it sounds like a land grab to me, too.

Supply Chain

The following certifications focus on supply chain management:

Certified Professional in Supply Management (CPSM)   This is a newer certification administered by the Institute of Supply Management (www.ism.ws). It requires a bachelor's degree with three years of full-time, professional supply management experience. Clerical and support experience does not count. The exam is offered in 230 countries worldwide through your local Pearson VUE testing center.

Certified Purchasing Manager (CPM)   This is the original ISM certification, which does not require a college degree. It requires five years of full-time, professional supply management experience or a bachelor's degree plus four years of work experience. Clerical and support experience does not count. The exam is offered in 230 countries worldwide through your local Pearson VUE testing center. The last day to apply for CPM certification is Dec 1, 2013. All applicants after the cutoff are required to apply for CPSM with a recognized college degree.

Disaster Recovery and Business Continuity

The following certifications focus on disaster recovery and touch on business continuity topics. Keep in mind that disaster recovery is focused on rebuilding and emergency actions, while true business continuity is an evolution of ongoing scenario planning focused on generating revenue 365 days a year with or without an emergency. Money buys time; without it, your organization is dead.

Fellow of the Business Continuity Institute (FBCI)   This international certification covers a multiphase program management approach to disaster recovery topics and continuity of operations (COOP). BCI does not cover continuity of government (COG), has nothing useful on business unit priorities, and has no coverage on the generation of revenue, aka funding in government circles. The exam is administered by the Business Continuity Institute (www.thebci.org). Training is available worldwide, and testing is available through your local Prometric testing center.

Certified Business Continuity Professional (CBCP)   This certification is based on U.S. FEMA guidelines. It covers 10 practice areas of disaster recovery and continuity of operations using a project-based approach. It does not cover continuity of government (COG). It does not cover business unit priorities or generation of revenue, aka funding in government circles. The CBCP certification is administered by the Disaster Recovery Institute International, or DRII (www.drii.org). It requires two years of experience in disaster recovery plus passing the CBCP exam.

Associate Business Continuity Professional (ABCP)   The Associate covers the same material as the CBCP, but does not require any work experience. This certification is administered by the Disaster Recovery Institute International, or DRII (www.drii.org).

Master Business Continuity Professional (MBCP)   After getting your CBCP certification, you can apply to participate in the DRII Masters program. This certification is administered by DRII and focuses on the FEMA approach to disaster recovery and rebuilding. Unfortunately MBCP provides nothing in ultra hot topics of improving business unit revenue, emergency revenue generation, gaining or keeping investors, holding market share, revenue priorities, business aquistion, or divestiture. Becoming a MBCP requires passing a qualifying exam, writing a master's thesis, and then passing the MBCP exam. You must also have five years of practical experience to qualify for the application.

Project Management

The following certifications focus on project management:

Project Management Professional (PMP)   This certification is focused on best practices for the project manager. The focus is techniques used by the project manager. It's administered by the Project Management Institute (PMI). The best practice body of knowledge reference is updated with changes in four-year cycles. Currently the 2008 update covers 42 processes in project management using an abstract grouping of techniques. Certification requires 35 hours of formal PMI training with two and a half years of project management–related work experience (4,500 hours) with a four-year college degree. Alternatively, you can qualify with a high school diploma and four and a half years of experience (7,500 hours). PMI frequently checks work references. The PMP exam is a 4-hour computer-based test at your nearest Prometric testing center. You are officially a PMP after passing your exam.

Certified Associate in Project Management (CAPM)   This junior-level certification is a great start for persons who would not qualify for PMP. It's administered by the Project Management Institute (www.pmi.org). Requirements are 23 hours of formal PMI training or 1,500 hours of project management–related work experience plus passing the CAPM exam. The CAPM test covers a reduced version of the PMP content areas. CertTest recommends that all CAPM candidates follow the complete PMP study curriculum to ensure that you receive the full training necessary for a leadership role. The secret is to show your boss that you have been trained with as much knowledge as a PMP. This will help you advance your career, even though you are still building experience.

PRINCE2 Practitioner (Projects In a Controlled Environment, version 2)   This certification was developed for guiding a workflow of interaction between the organization and project managers. It's intended for project managers and team members. The exam covers organizational workflow and is more complex than a simple multiple-choice exam. There is no work experience requirement. It's is administered internationally by UK Office of Management in Government and in the United States by APMG (www.apmg-us.com). Exams are administered by live proctors through PRINCE2-approved training companies or occasionally through cooperation with recognized test proctors at your local library or university. *Author's note: I hold both PMP and PRINCE2 Practitioner certifications. I have found they complement each other in a very nice manner, like yin and yang for project managers. I use this and teach it as a leadership model for other executives' governing projects.*

PRINCE2 Foundation (Projects In a Controlled Environment, version 2)   This is the entry level for project managers and team members. The exam covers organizational workflow. There is no work experience requirement. The certification is administered internationally by OMG and APMG (www.apmg-us.org). You must pass the PRINCE2 Foundation exam before being able to take the Practitioner exam.

Project+   This entry-level certification for junior staff is administered by CompTIA. Certification is obtained by passing a computer-based multiple-choice exam at your nearest Prometric test center. No work experience is required. Project+ is never intended to be a prerequisite for other certifications such as CAPM, PMP, or PRINCE2. It's a good starting point for basic orientation, to help beginners gain an understanding of how a person might run simple daily operational projects.

Physical Building Security

The following certifications focus on physical building security topics:

Certified Protection Professional (CPP)   This certification is focused on the physical side plus various technical methods. Certification requires nine years of verified security-related work experience with a bachelor's degree and passing the exam. A minimum of three years of your experience must be in security management. The exam is administered internationally by the American Society of Industrial Security (www.asisonline.org).

Physical Security Professional (PSP)   Certification requires passing the exam plus a high school diploma and five years of verified security-related work experience. This certification is also administered internationally by ASIS International (www.asisonline.org).

CISA Job Placement Areas

Domain 1—IS Audit Process (14%)

To Provide IS audit services in accordance with IS audit standards, guidelines, and best practices to assist the organization in ensuring that its information technology and business systems are protected and controlled.

Domain 1—Task Statements:

1.1 Develop and implement a risk-based IT audit strategy in compliance with IT audit standards to ensure that key areas are included.

1.2 Plan specific audits to determine whether information systems are protected, controlled and provide value to the organization.

1.3 Conduct audits in accordance with IS audit standards, guidelines and best practices to meet planned audit objectives.

1.4 Communicate emerging issues, potential risks, and audit results to key stakeholders.

1.5 Advise on the implementation of risk management and control practices within the organization, while maintaining independence.

Domain 1—Knowledge Statements:

1.1 Knowledge of ISACA IT Audit and Assurance Standards, Guidelines and Tools and Techniques, Code of Professional Ethics and other applicable standards

1.2 Knowledge of risk assessment concepts, tools and techniques in an audit context

1.3 Knowledge of control objectives and controls related to information systems

1.4 Knowledge of audit planning and audit project management techniques, including follow-up

1.5 Knowledge of fundamental business processes (e.g., purchasing, payroll, accounts payable, accounts receivable) including relevant IT

1.6 Knowledge of applicable laws and regulations which affect the scope, evidence collection and preservation, and frequency of audits

1.7 Knowledge of evidence collection techniques (e.g., observation, inquiry, inspection, interview, data analysis) used to gather, protect and preserve audit evidence

1.8 Knowledge of different sampling methodologies

1.9 Knowledge of reporting and communication techniques (e.g., facilitation, negotiation, conflict resolution, audit report structure)

1.10 Knowledge of audit quality assurance systems and frameworks

Domain 2—IT Governance (14%)

To provide assurance that the organization has the structure, policies, accountability, mechanisms, and monitoring practices in place to achieve the requirements of corporate governance of IT.

Domain 2—Task Statements:

2.1 Evaluate the effectiveness of the IT governance structure to determine whether IT decisions, directions and performance support the organization's strategies and objectives.

2.2 Evaluate IT organizational structure and human resources (personnel) management to determine whether they support the organization's strategies and objectives.

2.3 Evaluate the IT strategy, including the IT direction, and the processes for the strategy's development, approval, implementation and maintenance for alignment with the organization's strategies and objectives.

2.4 Evaluate the organization's IT policies, standards, and procedures, and the processes for their development, approval, implementation, maintenance, and monitoring, to determine whether they support the IT strategy and comply with regulatory and legal requirements.

2.5 Evaluate the adequacy of the quality management system to determine whether it supports the organization's strategies and objectives in a cost-effective manner.

2.6 Evaluate IT management and monitoring of controls (e.g., continuous monitoring, QA) for compliance with the organization's policies, standards and procedures.

2.7 Evaluate IT resource investment, use and allocation practices, including prioritization criteria, for alignment with the organization's strategies and objectives.

2.8 Evaluate IT contracting strategies and policies, and contract management practices to determine whether they support the organization's strategies and objectives.

2.9 Evaluate risk management practices to determine whether the organization's IT-related risks are properly managed.

2.10 Evaluate monitoring and assurance practices to determine whether the board and executive management receive sufficient and timely information about IT performance.

2.11 Evaluate the organization's business continuity plan to determine the organization's ability to continue essential business operations during the period of an IT disruption.

Domain 2—Knowledge Statements:

2.1 Knowledge of IT governance, management, security and control frameworks, and related standards, guidelines, and practices

2.2 Knowledge of the purpose and the essential elements of IT strategy, policies, standards and procedures for an organization.

2.3 Knowledge of organizational structure, roles and responsibilities related to IT

2.4 Knowledge of the processes for the development, implementation and maintenance of IT strategy, policies, standards and procedures

2.5 Knowledge of the organization's technology direction and IT architecture and their implications for setting long-term strategic directions

2.6 Knowledge of relevant laws, regulations and industry standards affecting the organization

2.7 Knowledge of quality management systems

2.8 Knowledge of the use of maturity models

2.9 Knowledge of process optimization techniques

2.10 Knowledge of IT resource investment and allocation practices, including prioritization criteria (e.g., portfolio management, value management, project management)

2.11 Knowledge of IT supplier selection, contract management, relationship management and performance monitoring processes including third party outsourcing relationships

2.12 Knowledge of enterprise risk management

2.13 Knowledge of practices for monitoring and reporting of IT performance (e.g., balanced scorecards, key performance indicators - KPI)

2.14 Knowledge of IT human resources (personnel) management practices used to invoke the business continuity plan

2.15 Knowledge of business impact analysis (BIA) related to business continuity planning

2.16 Knowledge of the standards and procedures for the development and maintenance of the business continuity plan and testing methods

Domain 3—Information Systems Acquisition, Development, And Implementation (19%)

To provide assurance that the management practices for the development/acquisition, testing, implementation, maintenance, and disposal of systems and infrastructure will meet the organization's objectives.

Domain 3—Task Statements:

3.1 Evaluate the business case for the proposed investments in information systems acquisition, development, maintenance and subsequent retirement to determine whether it meets business objectives.

3.2 Evaluate the project management practices and controls to determine whether business requirements are achieved in a cost-effective manner while managing risks to the organization.

3.3 Conduct reviews to determine whether a project is progressing in accordance with project plans, is adequately supported by documentation and status reporting is accurate.

3.4 Evaluate controls for information systems during the requirements, acquisition, development and testing phases for compliance with the organization's policies, standards, procedures and applicable external requirements.

3.5 Evaluate the readiness of information systems for implementation and migration into production to determine whether project deliverables, controls and organization's requirements are met.

3.6 Conduct post-implementation reviews of systems to determine whether project deliverables, controls and organization's requirements are met.

Domain 3—Knowledge Statements:

3.1 Knowledge of benefits realization practices, (e.g., feasibility studies, business cases, total cost of ownership [TCO], ROI)

3.2 Knowledge of project governance mechanisms (e.g., steering committee, project oversight board, project management office)

3.3 Knowledge of project management control frameworks, practices and tools

3.4 Knowledge of risk management practices applied to projects

3.5 Knowledge of IT architecture related to data, applications and technology (e.g., distributed applications, web-based applications, web services, n-tier applications)

3.6 Knowledge of acquisition practices (e.g., evaluation of vendors, vendor management, escrow)

3.7 Knowledge of requirements analysis and management practices (e.g., requirements verification, traceability, gap analysis, vulnerability management, security requirements)

3.8 Knowledge of project success criteria and risks

3.9 Knowledge of control objectives and techniques that ensure the completeness, accuracy, validity and authorization of transactions and data

3.10 Knowledge of system development methodologies and tools including their strengths and weaknesses (e.g., agile development practices, prototyping, rapid application development [RAD], object-oriented design techniques)

3.11 Knowledge of testing methodologies and practices related to information systems development

3.12 Knowledge of configuration and release management relating to the development of information systems

3.13 Knowledge of system migration and infrastructure deployment practices and data conversion tools, techniques and procedures.

3.14 Knowledge of post-implementation review objectives and practices (e.g., project closure, control implementation, benefits realization, performance measurement)

Domain 4—Information Systems Operations, Maintenance And Support (23%)

To provide assurance that the IT service management practices will ensure the delivery of the level of services required to meet the organization's objectives.

Domain 4—Task Statements:

4.1 Conduct periodic reviews of information systems to determine whether they continue to meet the organization's objectives.

4.2 Evaluate service level management practices to determine whether the level of service from internal and external service providers is defined and managed.

4.3 Evaluate third party management practices to determine whether the levels of controls expected by the organization are being adhered to by the provider.

4.4 Evaluate operations and end-user procedures to determine whether scheduled and non-scheduled processes are managed to completion.

4.5 Evaluate the process of information systems maintenance to determine whether they are controlled effectively and continue to support the organization's objectives.

4.6 Evaluate data administration practices to determine the integrity and optimization of databases.

4.7 Evaluate the use of capacity and performance monitoring tools and techniques to determine whether IT services meet the organization's objectives.

4.8 Evaluate problem and incident management practices to determine whether incidents, problems or errors are recorded, analyzed and resolved in a timely manner.

4.9 Evaluate change, configuration and release management practices to determine whether scheduled and non-scheduled changes made to the organization's production environment are adequately controlled and documented.

4.10 Evaluate the adequacy of backup and restore provisions to determine the availability of information required to resume processing.

4.11 Evaluate the organization's disaster recovery plan to determine whether it enables the recovery of IT processing capabilities in the event of a disaster.

Domain 4—Knowledge Statements:

4.1 Knowledge of service level management practices and the components within a service level agreement

4.2 Knowledge of techniques for monitoring third party compliance with the organization's internal controls

4.3 Knowledge of operations and end-user procedures for managing scheduled and non-scheduled processes

4.4 Knowledge of the technology concepts related to hardware and network components, system software and database management systems

4.5 Knowledge of control techniques that ensure the integrity of system interfaces

4.6 Knowledge of software licensing and inventory practices

4.7 Knowledge of system resiliency tools and techniques (e.g., fault tolerant hardware, elimination of single point of failure, clustering)

4.8 Knowledge of database administration practices

4.9 Knowledge of capacity planning and related monitoring tools and techniques

4.10 Knowledge of systems performance monitoring processes, tools and techniques (e.g., network analyzers, system utilization reports, load balancing)

4.11 Knowledge of problem and incident management practices (e.g., help desk, escalation procedures, tracking)

4.12 Knowledge of processes, for managing scheduled and non-scheduled changes to the production systems and/or infrastructure including change, configuration, release and patch management practices

4.13 Knowledge of data backup, storage, maintenance, retention and restoration practices

4.14 Knowledge of regulatory, legal, contractual and insurance issues related to disaster recovery

4.15 Knowledge of business impact analysis (BIA) related to disaster recovery planning

4.16 Knowledge of the development and maintenance of disaster recovery plans

4.17 Knowledge of types of alternate processing sites and methods used to monitor the contractual agreements (e.g., hot sites, warm sites, cold sites)

4.18 Knowledge of processes used to invoke the disaster recovery plans

4.19 Knowledge of disaster recovery testing methods

Domain 5—Protection Of Information Assets (30%)

To provide assurance that the security architecture (policies, standards, procedures, and controls) ensures the confidentiality, integrity, and availability of information assets.

Domain 5—Task Statements:

5.1 Evaluate the information security policies, standards and procedures for completeness and alignment with generally accepted practices.

5.2 Evaluate the design, implementation and monitoring of system and logical security controls to verify the confidentiality, integrity and availability of information.

5.3 Evaluate the design, implementation, and monitoring of the data classification processes and procedures for alignment with the organization's policies, standards, procedures, and applicable external requirements.

5.4 Evaluate the design, implementation and monitoring of physical access and environmental controls to determine whether information assets are adequately safeguarded.

5.5 Evaluate the processes and procedures used to store, retrieve, transport and dispose of information assets (e.g., backup media, offsite storage, hard copy/print data, and softcopy media) to determine whether information assets are adequately safeguarded.

Domain 5—Knowledge Statements:

5.1 Knowledge of the techniques for the design, implementation, and monitoring of security controls, including security awareness programs

5.2 Knowledge of processes related to monitoring and responding to security incidents (e.g., escalation procedures, emergency incident response team)

5.3 Knowledge of logical access controls for the identification, authentication and restriction of users to authorized functions and data

5.4 Knowledge of the security controls related to hardware, system software (e.g., applications, operating systems), and database management systems.

5.5 Knowledge of risks and controls associated with virtualization of systems

5.6 Knowledge of the configuration, implementation, operation and maintenance of network security controls

5.7 Knowledge of network and Internet security devices, protocols, and techniques

5.8 Knowledge of information system attack methods and techniques

5.9 Knowledge of detection tools and control techniques (e.g., malware, virus detection, spyware)

5.10 Knowledge of security testing techniques (e.g., intrusion testing, vulnerability scanning)

5.11 Knowledge of risks and controls associated with data leakage

5.12 Knowledge of encryption-related techniques

5.13 Knowledge of public key infrastructure (PKI) components and digital signature techniques

5.14 Knowledge of risks and controls associated with peer-to-peer computing, instant messaging, and web-based technologies (e.g., social networking, message boards, and blogs)

5.15 Knowledge of controls and risks associated with the use of mobile & wireless devices

5.16 Knowledge of voice communications security (e.g., PBX, VoIP)

5.17 Knowledge of the evidence preservation techniques and processes followed in forensics investigations (e.g., IT, process, and chain of custody)

5.18 Knowledge of data classification standards and supporting procedures

5.19 Knowledge of physical access controls for the identification, authentication and restriction of users to authorized facilities

5.20 Knowledge of environmental protection devices and supporting practices

5.21 Knowledge of the processes and procedures used to store, retrieve, transport and dispose of confidential information assets

Domain 6—Business Continuity and Disaster Recovery (14%)

To provide assurance that in the event of a disruption the business continuity and disaster recovery processes will ensure the timely resumption of IT services while minimizing the business impact.

Domain 6—Task Statements:

6.1 Evaluate the adequacy of backup and restore provisions to ensure the availability of information required to resume processing.

6.2 Evaluate the organization's disaster recovery plan to ensure that it enables the recovery of IT processing capabilities in the event of a disaster.

6.3 Evaluate the organization's business continuity plan to ensure its ability to continue essential business operations during the period of an IT disruption.

Domain 6—Knowledge Statements:

6.1 Knowledge of data backup, storage, maintenance, retention, and restoration processes, and practices

6.2 Knowledge of regulatory, legal, contractual, and insurance issues related to business continuity and disaster recovery

6.3 Knowledge of business impact analysis (BIA)

6.4 Knowledge of the development and maintenance of the business continuity and disaster recovery plans

6.5 Knowledge of business continuity and disaster recovery testing approaches and methods

6.6 Knowledge of human resources management practices as related to business continuity and disaster recovery (e.g., evacuation planning, response teams)

6.7 Knowledge of processes used to invoke the business continuity and disaster recovery plans

6.8 Knowledge of types of alternate processing sites and methods used to monitor the contractual agreements (e.g., hot sites, warm sites, cold sites)

The official and most up-to-date CISA Job Placement Areas can be found at ISACA's website at www.isaca.org/Certification/CISA-Certified-Information-Systems-Auditor/Prepare-for-the-Exam/Job-Practice-Areas/Pages/default.aspx.

Assessment Test

1. Which is *not* a purpose of risk analysis?
   A. Assists the auditor in identifying risks and threats
   B. Assists the auditor in determining audit objectives
   C. Supports risk-based audit decisions
   D. Ensures absolute safety during the audit

2. Which of the following functions should be separated from the others if segregation of duties cannot be achieved in an automated system?
   A. Authorization
   B. Reprocessing
   C. Correction
   D. Origination

3. What is the purpose of the audit committee?
   A. To provide daily coordination of all audit activities
   B. To challenge and review assurances
   C. To govern, control, and manage the organization
   D. To assist the managers with training in auditing skills

4. What are the qualifications of the incident commander when responding to a crisis?
   A. Trained crisis manager
   B. First person on scene
   C. Member of management
   D. First responder

5. Which of the following is required to protect the internal network when a wireless access point is in use?
   A. Wireless encryption
   B. Wired equivalent protection
   C. Wireless application protocol
   D. Network firewall

6. How should management act to best deal with emergency changes?
   A. Emergency changes cannot be made without advance testing.
   B. The change control process does not apply to emergency conditions.
   C. All changes should still undergo review.
   D. Emergency changes are not allowed under any condition.

7. Which of the following would be a concern that the auditor should explain in the audit report along with their findings?

   A. Detailed list of audit objectives

   B. Undue restrictions placed by management on evidence use or audit procedure

   C. Communicating results directly to the chairperson of the audit committee

   D. Need by the current auditor to communicate with the prior auditors

8. What are the different types of audits?

   A. Forensic, accounting, verification, regulatory

   B. Financial, compliance, administrative, SAS-74

   C. Information system, SAS-70, regulatory, procedural

   D. Integrated, compliance, operational, administrative

9. Which of the following management methods provides the most control rather than discretionary flexibility?

   A. Distributed

   B. Centralized

   C. In-house

   D. Outsourced

10. What indicators are used to identify the anticipated level of recovery and loss at a given point in time?

    A. RPO and RTO

    B. RTO and SDO

    C. RPO and ITO

    D. SDO and IRO

11. What is the principal issue surrounding the use of CAAT software?

    A. The capability of the software vendor

    B. Documentary evidence is more effective

    C. Inability of automated tools to consider the human characteristics of the environment

    D. The possible cost, complexity, and security of output

12. Digital signatures are designed to provide additional protection for electronic messages in order to determine which of the following?

    A. Message read by unauthorized party

    B. Message sender verification

    C. Message deletion

    D. Message modification

13. What is the primary objective of the ISACA audit standards and professional ethics publication?

    A. Provide consistency without embarrassing you or our profession

    B. Explain the professional duties you could follow when building your practice

    C. Provide a comprehensive audit toolkit

    D. Provide a sample reference the auditor may use during their audit without copyright restrictions

14. What does the third layer of the OSI model equate to in the TCP/IP model?

    A. Network

    B. Internet

    C. Data-Link

    D. Transport

15. Which of the following statements is true concerning asymmetric-key cryptography?

    A. The sender encrypts the files by using the recipient's private key.

    B. The sender and receiver use the same key.

    C. The sender and receiver have different keys.

    D. Asymmetric keys cannot be used for digital signatures.

16. Who is responsible for designating the appropriate information classification level?

    A. Data custodian

    B. Data user

    C. Data owner

    D. Security manager

17. At which layer of the OSI model does a gateway operate?

    A. Layer 3

    B. Layer 4

    C. Layer 5

    D. Layer 7

18. What is one of the bigger concerns regarding asset disposal?

    A. Residual asset value

    B. Employees taking disposed property home

    C. Standing data

    D. Environmental regulations

19. What is the primary purpose of database views?

   A. Restrict the viewing of selected data

   B. Provide a method for generating reports

   C. Allow the user access into the database

   D. Allow the system administrator access to maintain the database

20. Which step is necessary before moving into the next phase when using the System Development Life Cycle?

   A. Phase meeting

   B. Change control

   C. Formal approval

   D. Review meeting

21. Which of the following indicates why continuity planners can create plans without a business impact analysis (BIA)?

   A. Management already dictated all the key processes to be used.

   B. They can't because critical processes may change monthly or annually.

   C. Business impact analysis is not required.

   D. Risk assessment is acceptable.

22. Which of the following answers contains the steps for business process reengineering (BPR) in proper sequence?

   A. Diagnose, envision, redesign, reconstruct

   B. Envision, initiate, diagnose, redesign, reconstruct, evaluate

   C. Evaluate, envision, redesign, reconstruct, review

   D. Initiate, evaluate, diagnose, reconstruct, review

23. Segregation of duties may not be practical in a small environment. A single employee may be performing the combined functions of server operator and application programmer. The IS auditor should recommend controls for which of the following?

   A. Automated logging of changes made to development libraries

   B. Procedures that verify that only approved program changes are implemented

   C. Automated controls to prevent the operator logon ID from making program modifications

   D. Hiring additional technical staff to force segregation of duties

24. Which of the following is true concerning reporting by internal auditors?

   A. Results can be used for industry licensing.

   B. The corresponding value of the audit report is high.

   C. Results can be used for external reporting.

   D. The corresponding value of the audit report is low.

25. The auditor is permitted to deviate from professional audit standards when they feel it is necessary because of which of the following?

   A. Standards are designed for discretionary use.

   B. The unique characteristics of each client will require auditor flexibility.

   C. Deviating from standards is almost unheard of and would require significant justification.

   D. Deviation depends on the authority granted in the audit charter.

26. What does the principle of auditor independence mean?

   A. It is not an issue for auditors working for a consulting company.

   B. It is required for an external audit to prevent bias.

   C. An internal auditor must undergo certification training to be independent.

   D. The audit committee would bestow independence on the auditor.

27. What is the best definition of *auditing*?

   A. Review of past history using evidence to tell the story

   B. Forecasting compliance generated by a new system preparing to enter production

   C. Precompliance assessment based on management's intended design

   D. Certification testing of the system benefits or failures

28. Which of the following is the most significant issue to consider regarding insurance coverage?

   A. Premiums may be very expensive.

   B. Insurance can pay for all the costs of recovery.

   C. Coverage must include all business assets.

   D. Salvage, rather than replacement, may be dictated.

29. What are the five phases of business continuity planning according to ISACA, for use on the CISA exam? (Select the answer showing the correct phases and order.)

   A. Analyze business impact, develop strategy, develop plan, test plan, implement

   B. Analyze business impact, write the plan, test strategy, develop plan, implement

   C. Analyze business impact, develop plan, implement, test plan, write the plan

   D. Analyze business impact, develop strategy, develop plan, implement, test plan

30. Using public-key interchange (PKI) encryption, which key is used by the sender for authentication of the receiving party?

   A. Sender's private key

   B. Recipient's private key

   C. Recipient's public key

   D. Sender's public key

31. Which the following statements is true concerning a software worm?

   A. Uses authentication defects to freely travel to infect other systems

   B. Is a synonym for a malicious virus appending itself to data files

   C. Must be executed by opening a file

   D. Attaches itself to programs and data by the opening and closing of files

32. What are three of the four key perspectives on the IT balanced scorecard?

   A. Business justification, service-level agreements, budget

   B. Organizational staffing, cost reduction, employee training

   C. Cost reduction, business process, growth

   D. Service level, critical success factors, vendor selection

33. Which sampling method is used when the likelihood of finding evidence is low?

   A. Discovery

   B. Cell

   C. Random

   D. Stop and go

34. Which of the following would represent the greatest concern to an auditor investigating roles and responsibilities of the IT personnel?

   A. An IT member is reviewing current server workload requirements and forecasts future needs.

   B. An IT member monitors system performance, making necessary program changes and tracking any resulting problems.

   C. An IT member tests and assesses the effectiveness of current procedures and recommends specific improvements.

   D. An IT member works directly with the user to improve response times and performance across the network.

35. When auditing the use of encryption, which of the following would be the primary concern of the auditor?

   A. Management's control over the use of encryption

   B. Strength of encryption algorithm in use

   C. Key sizes used in the encryption and decryption process

   D. Using the correct encryption method for compliance

36. Which of the following represents the hierarchy of controls from highest level to lowest level?

   A. General, pervasive, detailed, application

   B. Pervasive, general, application, detailed

   C. Detailed, pervasive, application, detailed

   D. Application, general, detailed, pervasive

37. What is the primary objective in the third phase of incident response?

    A. Containment

    B. Lessons learned

    C. Eradication

    D. Analysis

38. What is the purpose of using the ACID principle with database applications?

    A. Write the entire transaction to the master file or discard without making any changes.

    B. Environmental protection to safeguard the server to ensure maximum uptime.

    C. Each data transaction is step-linked to ensure consistency.

    D. Unnecessary data is removed from the database for better performance.

39. Which key is used for decryption in public key cryptography to provide authentication of the person transmitting the message?

    A. Sender's private key

    B. Recipient's private key

    C. Sender's public key

    D. Recipient's public key

40. What is the principle purpose of using function point analysis?

    A. Verify the integrity of financial transaction algorithms in a program

    B. Estimate the complexity involved in software development

    C. Review the results of automated transactions meeting criteria for the audit

    D. Provide system boundary data during the Requirements Definition phase

41. Which of the following is the best way to protect encryption keys from being compromised?

    A. Limiting the use of individual keys

    B. Using a physically isolated system to generate the keys

    C. Storing the keys in a key vault-rated server

    D. Changing the encryption keys every four months

42. Which of the following is not one of the three major control types?

    A. Preventative

    B. Deterrent

    C. Detective

    D. Corrective

43. Which method of backup should be used on a computer hard disk or flash media prior to starting a forensic investigation?

   A. Full

   B. Logical

   C. Differential

   D. Bitstream

44. After presenting the report at the conclusion of an audit, the lead auditor discovers the omission of a procedure. What should the auditor do next?

   A. Log on to www.careerbuilder.com and change their current employment status to available.

   B. Cancel the report if audit alternatives cannot compensate for the deficiency.

   C. File an incident disclosure report with the audit association to minimize any liability.

   D. No action is required as long as the omitted procedure is included in the next audit.

45. Executing the verify function during a tape backup is an example of which type of the following controls?

   A. Corrective

   B. Administrative

   C. Preventative

   D. Detective

46. In regards to the IT governance control objectives, which of the following occurrences would the auditor be most concerned about during execution of the audit?

   A. Using the practice of self-monitoring to report problems

   B. Using proper change control

   C. Conflict in the existing reporting relationship

   D. Production system without accreditation

47. What is the purpose behind the system accreditation?

   A. Hold management responsible for fitness of use and any failures

   B. Provide formal sign-off on the results of certification tests

   C. Improve the accuracy of forecasting in IT budgets

   D. Make the user responsible for their use of the system

48. Which of the following is *not* one of the primary methods used to implement physical controls, detective controls, and corrective controls?

   A. Legal

   B. Logical

   C. Physical

   D. Administrative

49. Which of the following techniques is used in the storage and transmission of a symmetric encryption key?

    A. Key rotation

    B. Generating a unique encryption key

    C. Key wrapping

    D. Generating a shared encryption key

50. Which of the following situations should the auditor consider if the auditee has implemented six phases of the System Development Life Cycle (SDLC)?

    A. The auditee is probably doing a good job with no concerns at this time.

    B. The IT governance model has been implemented.

    C. The auditee may be missing a critical function.

    D. There are only five phases to the System Development Life Cycle.

51. Which backup method will copy only changed files without resetting the archive bit (archive flag)?

    A. Physical

    B. Incremental

    C. Full

    D. Differential

52. What is the purpose of a digital signature?

    A. Electronic marker showing the recipient that a sender actually sent a document

    B. Provides a copy of the sender's public key along with the document

    C. Cyclic redundancy check to prove document integrity

    D. Provides the recipient with a method of testing the document received from a sender

53. What is the functional difference between *identification* and *authentication*?

    A. Authorization is a match; identification is only a claim until verified.

    B. Authentication is only a claim; identification is a verified match.

    C. Identification is only a claim until verified; authentication is a match.

    D. Identification is only a claim; authorization is a match.

54. Select the best answer to finish this statement: A _____ is strategic in nature, while the _____ is tactical.

    A. policy, procedure

    B. standard, procedure

    C. procedure, standard

    D. policy, standard

55. What is the primary objective for using a system with a Redundant Array of Independent— or Inexpensive—Disks (RAID)?

   A. Prevent corruption

   B. Increase availability

   C. Eliminate the need for backups

   D. Increase storage capacity

56. What function does the auditor provide?

   A. Second set of eyes, which are external from the subject under review

   B. Independent assurance that the claims of management are correct

   C. Assistance by fixing problems found during the audit

   D. Adapting standards to fit the needs of the client

57. Which of the following situations does *not* represent a reporting conflict?

   A. Information security manager reporting to internal auditors.

   B. Employee reporting violations to their boss, who is also in charge of compliance

   C. IT security reporting to the chief information officer

   D. Self-monitoring and reporting of violations

58. Complete the following statement with the best available answer: The _____ file is created when the system shuts down improperly. It usually contains _____ that is/are useful in forensic investigations.

   A. dump, contents from RAM memory

   B. abend, a history of all the user transactions processed

   C. diagnostic, system startup settings

   D. abort, all user account information

59. In using public-key interchange (PKI) encryption, which key is *not* used by the recipient for decrypting a message?

   A. Sender's private key

   B. Recipient's private key

   C. Sender's public key

   D. Recipient's public key

60. Where should the computer room be located?

   A. Secure basement

   B. First floor

   C. Middle floor

   D. Top floor

61. What is the primary purpose of using the root kit?

   A. System administration tool used by the super user, also known as the server agent

   B. Method for tracing source problems in determining cause-and-effect analysis

   C. Camouflage technique designed to hide certain details from view

   D. Covert method of remotely compromising the operating system kernel

62. Complete the following statement: A _____ must be used to prevent _____ of the hard-disk evidence during the collection phase of forensic investigations.

   A. forensic specialist, analysis

   B. write blocker, contamination

   C. immunizer, corruption

   D. data analyzer, destruction

63. Which of the following statements is true concerning the role of management and the role of the auditor?

   A. Management uses the auditor's report before making their assertions.

   B. Management must make their assertions prior to the auditor's report.

   C. The auditor is able to view only evidence that has been predetermined by management.

   D. The auditor's opinion will be based on the desire of management.

64. Which of the following is the best way for an auditor to prove their competence to perform an audit?

   A. Prior experience working in information technology

   B. Citing each point in a regulation with an audit objective and specific test

   C. Obtaining auditor certification with ongoing training

   D. Prior experience in financial auditing

65. Which of the following processes would be the best candidate for business process reengineering?

   A. Excluded process

   B. Nonworking process

   C. Working process

   D. Marginal process

66. Which of the following statements is true concerning the auditor's qualified opinion?

   A. The auditor has reservations about the findings.

   B. The auditor is professionally qualified to give an opinion.

   C. The auditor has no reservations about the findings.

   D. The auditor has prior experience working in the IT department.

67. Which of the following statements is true regarding use of the Rapid Application Development (RAD) methodology in software programming?

　　A. Still requires the use of traditional project management techniques

　　B. Eliminates the need for using traditional planning techniques for project management

　　C. Automates the entire software development process, starting from phase 1

　　D. Automates the software development process from feasibility through implementation

68. During a business continuity audit, it is discovered that the business impact analysis (BIA) was not performed even through an initial feasibility review of the financial statement was performed. What would this indicate to the auditor?

　　A. The customer was able to get their plan in place without using the BIA technique.

　　B. The business continuity plan is likely to be a failure.

　　C. Risk analysis and their selection of the strategy fulfill their most important objectives.

　　D. It's not necessary to perform a business impact analysis because financial feasibility was performed.

69. Which of the following systems uses heuristic techniques to make decisions on behalf of the user?

　　A. Associate decision mart

　　B. Expert system

　　C. Decision support system (DSS)

　　D. Data warehouse

70. Which of the following is the best representation of a soft token used for two-factor authentication?

　　A. Digital signature

　　B. Digital identity

　　C. Digital certificate

　　D. Digital hash

71. Which of the following is the best example of implementing a detective control via administrative methods?

　　A. Auditing of system configuration and log files

　　B. Running a verification of the backup tape for integrity

　　C. Using an intrusion detection and prevention system (IDPS)

　　D. Restoring a damaged file using a copy from the vendor's installation CD

72. Which of the following nonstatistical audit samples is also known as a judgmental sample?

　　A. Haphazard

　　B. Attribute

　　C. Unstratified mean

　　D. Random

73. A member of the auditee staff offers to loan you an unauthorized copy of software that you need for a short time. What should you, as the auditor, always remember?

   A. It's okay to borrow the software for one-time use.

   B. The auditee is not acting in an ethical manner.

   C. The auditee will usually get amnesty for turning in the auditor or discrediting the auditor.

   D. Odds of getting caught on this are very low.

74. What is the primary purpose of the agile programming methodology?

   A. Automate the tedious administrative portions of the System Development Life Cycle

   B. Rapidly create prototypes within a very short time

   C. Create flexible internal controls that are easy to keep up-to-date

   D. Improve the quality of traditional planning with better documentation of requirements

75. Which of the following firewall setups would *not* be a concern to the auditor?

   A. Firewall not backed up nightly

   B. Backup media left in the drive

   C. Source routing enabled

   D. Remote login or file sharing enabled

76. Who should the auditor notify if an illegal or inappropriate act involves the persons responsible for governance of controls?

   A. Law enforcement

   B. Audit committee

   C. Federal regulators

   D. Whistle-blower hotline

77. What is the primary purpose of the audit charter?

   A. Specify the scope of the audit

   B. Serve as a record for the agreed-upon terms of the engagement with external auditors

   C. Specify the mutually agreed-upon procedures that will be used during the audit

   D. Grant the auditor responsibility, authority, and accountability

78. Complete the following statement: A Certified Information Systems Auditor will lose their certification if they _____.

   A. advise and educate the auditee about what the auditor is looking for

   B. continue to participate in professional education

   C. share blank audit checklists with the auditee

   D. possess or use materials for which they do not hold a valid copyright license

79. Portfolio management includes all of the following, except:

    A. Selection of projects based on the best return on investment

    B. Centralized control of priorities across the projects

    C. Management of concurrent projects

    D. Method of controlling changes in the work breakdown structure

80. Which of the following audit tools incorporates dummy transactions into the normal processing on a system?

    A. Continuous and intermittent simulation (CIS)

    B. Integrated test facility (ITF)

    C. Program audit hooks

    D. Snapshot

Answers to Assessment Test

1. D. The risk analysis does not ensure absolute safety. The purpose of using a risk-based audit strategy is to ensure that the audit adds value with meaningful information. For more information, see Chapter 3.

2. A. Authorization should be separate from all other activities. A second person should review changes before implementation. Authorization will be granted if the change is warranted and the level of risk is acceptable. For more information, see Chapter 3.

3. B. The purpose of the audit committee is to review and challenge assurances made and to maintain a positive working relationship with management and the auditors. For more information, see Chapters 2 and 3.

4. B. The first person on the scene is the incident commander, regardless of rank or position. The incident commander may be relieved by a person with more experience or less experience, according to the situation. The incident commander will change throughout the crisis. For more information, see Chapter 8.

5. D. A firewall is still required to protect the internal network even if the wireless network is using Wired Equivalent Privacy (WEP). The WEP design has been broken and is considered insecure under all conditions. See Chapter 7 for more information.

6. C. All emergency changes should still undergo the formal change management process after the fact. The review determines whether the change should remain in place or be modified. For more information, see Chapter 6.

7. B. Undue restrictions on scope would be a major concern as would a lack of time or the inability to obtain sufficient reliable evidence. For more information, see Chapter 3.

8. D. All of the audit types are valid except procedural, SAS-74, verification, and regulatory (which are all distracters). The valid audit types are financial, operational (SAS-70), integrated (SAS-94), compliance, administrative, forensic, and information systems. A forensic audit is used to discover information about a possible crime. For more information, see Chapter 1.

9. B. Centralized management always provides the most control. Distributed management is also known as discretionary because the decision is made locally and is based on a variety of factors. Distributed methods provide the lowest overall control. For more information, see Chapter 7.

10. A. The recovery point objective (RPO) indicates the fallback position and duration of loss that has occurred. A valid RPO example is to recover by using backup data from last night's backup tape, meaning that the more recent transactions would be lost. The recovery time objective (RTO) indicates a point in time that the restored data should be available for the user to access. For more information, see Chapter 8.

11. D. Computer-assisted audit tools are able to perform detailed technical tasks faster than humans and produce more accurate data during particular functions such as system scanning. Cost, training, and security of output are major considerations. For more information, see Chapter 3.

12. B. Digital signatures provide authentication assurance of the email sender. Digital signatures use the private key of the sender to lock (encrypt) and the sender's public key to verify the sender's identity (by unlocking). Message hashing provides assurance the message was not modified. For more information, see Chapter 7.

13. A. ISACA audit standards of professional ethics are intended to provide consistency. We do not want you to cast any disgrace upon our profession. We hope that by following the standards, you will not embarrass yourself or fail to understand the duties of an auditor. For more information, see Chapter 1.

14. B. The third layer of the OSI model is the Network layer. Use the memory tool of "No Interest Having Anchovies" to remember the layers of the TCP/IP model. The "Interest" layer of the TCP/IP model is the Internet layer. For more information, see Chapter 4.

15. C. The sender and receiver each have their own public and private (secret) key-pair. All the other statements are false. Asymmetric keys are definitely used for creating digital signatures. The sender would never use the recipient's private key, only the recipient's public key. For more information, see Chapter 7.

16. C. The data owner is responsible for designating the appropriate information security level and appointing the custodian. The data owner is usually a vice president or higher, up to an agency head. The data owner also specifies the controls to be used. The audit committee and management can change the security level if the data owner fails to properly classify the data. For more information, see Chapter 7.

17. D. According to ISACA, the gateway operates at application layer 7 in the OSI model. The function of the gateway is to convert data contained in one protocol into data used by a different protocol. An example is a PC-to-mainframe gateway converting ASCII to mainframe Extended Binary Coded Decimal Interchange Code (EBCDIC). For more information, see Chapter 4.

18. C. Any standing data should be purged from the equipment prior to disposal. Standing data refers to information that can be recovered from a device by using any means. For more information, see Chapter 6.

19. A. Database views are used to implement least privilege and restrict the data that can be viewed by the user. For more information, see Chapter 7.

20. C. Formal approval is necessary before moving into the next phase. A review meeting is held with the stakeholders, project manager, and executive chairperson. All of the projections and open issues are discussed. Each item is approved, rejected, or cancelled. The project may advance to the next stage with formal approval. The auditor should look for evidence of formal approval and how the decision was made. For more information, see Chapter 5.

21. B. It is not possible to create business continuity plans without a current business impact analysis (BIA). The BIA identifies critical processes and their dependencies. The critical processes will change as the business changes with new products and customers. For more information, see Chapter 8.

22. B. According to ISACA, the general steps in business process reengineering are envision the need, initiate the project, diagnose the existing process, redesign a process, use change management to reconstruct the organization in transition, and evaluate the results. For more information, see Chapter 2.

23. B. Procedures should be implemented to ensure that only approved program changes are implemented. The purpose of separation of duties is to prevent intentional or unintentional errors. A logical separation of duties may exist if a single person performs two job roles. The ultimate objective is to ensure that a second person has reviewed and approved a change before it is implemented. For more information, see Chapter 6.

24. D. Reports by internal auditors have a low corresponding value due to the built-in reporting conflict that may exist. This is why external independent audits are required for regulatory licensing. For more information, see Chapter 3.

25. C. Standards are mandatory, and any deviation would require justification. Exceptions are rarely accepted. For more information, see Chapter 2.

26. B. The auditor must be independent of personal and organizational relationships with the auditee, which could imply a biased opinion. The auditor is not permitted to audit a system for which they participated in the support, configuration, or design. An auditor may not audit any system that they helped to remediate. For more information, see Chapter 1.

27. A. Auditing is a review of past history. We use evidence and testing to determine the story. It's not possible to use an audit to forecast compliance benefits before entering production. Every system creates unforeseen consequences that can be fully realized only after that system enters production. You can audit the system attributes during design and development, not the unrealized operating issues impacting its compliance. Compliance requires an audit after it enters production to include the way the system is actually used and managed. For more information, see Chapters 3 and 5.

28. D. The insurance company may dictate salvage to save money. Salvage will increase the delay before recovery. Any replacement purchases by the organization may not be covered under reimbursement. For more information, see Chapter 8.

29. D. Notice that analyzing the business impact is always the first step. Then criteria are selected to guide the strategy selection. A detailed plan is written by using the strategy. The written plan is then implemented. After implementation, the plan and staff are tested for effectiveness. The plan is revised, and then the testing and maintenance cycle begins. For more information, see Chapter 8.

30. C. The sender uses the recipient's public key to encrypt a file that only the recipient can read (decrypt). The sender's private key provides authenticity. The sender's public key provides integrity. The role of the keys is based on the direction of the transaction. The roles reverse when the original recipient replies with another message, thereby assuming the sender's role. For more information, see Chapter 7.

31. A. Unlike a virus, a worm can freely travel across network connections to infect other systems. Worms exploit authentication failures in other programs to copy themselves between systems. Worms can infect files without the file being opened or closed by the user. For more information, see Chapter 7.

32. C. The four perspectives on the IT balanced scorecard are the customer perspective, business process perspective, financial perspective, and the growth perspective. Each of these seek to define the highest return by IT. For more information, see Chapter 2.

33. A. Discovery sampling is known as the 100 percent sample. All available sources are investigated to find any evidence that may exist. Discovery sampling is commonly used in criminal investigations. It's also the best way to find possible correlations when an event cannot be explained. For more information, see Chapter 3.

34. B. The separation of duties is intended to prevent an individual from monitoring their own work or authorizing their own changes. Self-monitoring and self-authorization would be a problem warranting serious concern because it violates the intention of IT governance. The auditor would want to investigate whether changes were formally reviewed and approved by the change control board prior to implementation. For more information, see Chapter 6.

35. A. The most important concern is how management controls the use of encryption. Is the encryption managed under a complete life cycle from creation to destruction? The management of keys should govern creation storage, proper authorization, correct use with the appropriate algorithm, tracking, archiving or reissuing, retiring, and ultimately the destruction of the encryption keys after all legal obligations have been met. For more information, see Chapter 7.

36. A. General controls represent the highest class of controls that apply to everyone within the organization. Pervasive controls represent the protection necessary when using technology. IS controls are pervasive in all departments using computers. No matter who is in charge, the IS controls must be used to ensure integrity and availability. Detailed controls specify how a procedure will be executed. Application controls are the lowest-level controls that are usually built into the software or that govern its use. Application controls will be compromised if the higher-level controls are not present. For more information, see Chapter 3.

37. A. The phases in incident handling are 1) preparation, 2) detection and analysis, 3) containment eradication and recovery, and 4) post-incident activity, including lessons learned. For more information, see Chapter 6.

38. A. The ACID principle says to write the entire transaction or back it completely out. A stands for atomicity (all or nothing), C for consistency (restore data if the write fails), I for isolation (separation between transactions), and D for durability (retain the data). For more information, see Chapter 5.

39. C. The sender's public key provides authentication that the message came from that specific individual. For more information, see Chapter 7.

40. B. Function point analysis is used by highly experienced programmers to estimate the complexity involved in writing new software. It starts by counting the inputs, outputs, inquiries (searches), data structure, and external interfaces. For more information, see Chapter 5.

41. A. Limiting the use of encryption keys is the best available choice to protect them from compromise. Separation of duties also applies to encryption keys. Each encryption key should have a special purpose without reusing the same key on different tasks. For more information, see Chapter 7.

42. B. The major control types are physical (stops), detective (finds), and corrective (fixes). A deterrent control is simply a very weak form of preventative control. For more information, see Chapter 3.

43. D. Bitstream imaging is the only backup method that records the deleted files along with the contents of the swap space and slack space. Bitstream backup is also referred to as physical imaging. All of the other choices would miss these important files that are necessary as evidence. For more information, see Chapter 6.

44. B. The auditor needs to review the audit alternatives to determine whether the alternatives could sufficiently compensate for the omission. The auditor should cancel their report if the omitted procedures would change the outcome and if audit alternatives cannot compensate for the deficiency. For more information, see Chapter 3.

45. D. Creating a tape backup is a preventative control to prevent the loss of data. However, the verify function is a detective control intended to detect any discrepancies between the tape and the hard disk. It's a detective control because it still requires the operator to manually fix the problem after it is found. Verification and audits are always detective controls. For more information, see Chapter 3.

46. B. Use of proper change control would represent the most concern for the auditor. Auditors want to see change control procedures being used for separation of duties. All of the other choices represent violations warranting further investigation. For more information, see Chapters 2 and 6.

47. A. System accreditation is a formal sign-off witnessing management's acceptance of fitness for the system's intended use and full responsibility for any failures. System accreditation is for a period of 90 days, 180 days, or 365 days (annual). The system must be reaccredited by the expiration date. For more information, see Chapter 5.

48. A. Legal is not one of the primary implementation methods. Controls are implemented by using physical methods, logical methods (technical), and administrative methods. Administrative methods include laws, policies, procedures, and contracts. The combination of physical, logical, and administrative methods is used to obtain legal compliance. For more information, see Chapter 3.

49. C. Key wrapping is used to protect encryption keys during storage and transmission of the keys. Encryption keys should never be directly accessible to the user. For more information, see Chapter 7.

50. C. The complete System Development Life Cycle contains seven phases, not six. The auditee may have a control failure because the postimplementation (phase 6) or disposal process (phase 7) may not have been formally adopted. Using fewer than seven phases would indicate that shortcuts have been taken. For more information, see Chapter 5.

51. D. The differential backup method will copy all files that have changed since the last full backup but will not reset the archive bit. Files can be restored in less time by using just the last full backup with the last differential backup tape. For more information, see Chapter 8.

52. D. An electronic signature is worthless unless the recipient actually tests the signature by decrypting it. Electronic signatures should never be trusted by their presence. Digital signatures must be tested by the recipient to verify their authenticity. For more information, see Chapter 7.

53. C. Identification is simply a claim that must be verified. Authentication is when the claim matches the reference, thereby indicating that the identity is correct. For more information, see Chapter 7.

54. D. A policy is strategic, standards are tactical, and procedures are operational. For more information, see Chapter 1.

55. B. Using a system with a Redundant Array of Independent—or Inexpensive—Disks (RAID) will increase availability. RAID does not prevent data corruption; therefore, backups are still required. RAID systems use more disk space for redundancy but provide less available storage capacity. For more information, see Chapter 4.

56. A. Whether conducting an internal or external audit, the auditor is a paid impartial observer. None of the other statements are true. The auditor never takes ownership of problems found. Standards are either met by the client (compliant) or not met by the client (not compliant). For more information, see Chapter 1.

57. A. IT security managers should report problems to internal auditors. It's a reporting conflict if an IT-related employee is required to make violation reports directly to their manager. There may be job pressures to cover up problems. A built-in reporting conflict exists when your job requires you to report violations to your superior, when the same person is responsible for ensuring compliance. For more information, see Chapter 6.

58. A. A crash dump file is created when the system crashes abruptly. This file contains the contents of working memory (RAM) and a list of tasks that were being processed. This special diagnostic file is extremely helpful during forensic investigations. For more information, see Chapter 6.

59. A. The sender's private key is never used by the recipient. It takes only three keys to decrypt the message: the sender's public key, the recipient's public key, and the recipient's private key. For more information, see Chapter 7.

60. C. Middle floors. ISACA states that the computer room should never be in the basement because of the risk of flooding. The first floor is susceptible to break-ins. The top floor is susceptible to roof leaks and storm damage. In this book, we discuss the details of how the basement decision occurred. For more information, see Chapter 6.

61. D. Root kits are used by hackers to remotely subvert the operating system security and compromise the kernel. Root kits can be installed without the knowledge of the user and use stealth techniques to hide their existence from monitoring software. For more information, see Chapter 7.

62. B. A write blocker is used to prevent any changes from being written to the hard disk during the collection of evidence. The simple act of booting up the computer will cause changes that taint the evidence. Any changes, no matter how small, will be used by defense lawyers to prove that evidence tampering occurred. Any claim of evidence tampering that cannot be disproved will destroy the value of the evidence. For more information, see Chapter 6.

63. B. Management must make their assertions independent of the auditor's report. The role of the auditor is to determine whether management claims can be verified as correct by the available evidence. For more information, see Chapter 1.

64. B. Every auditor should build a list of all the individual points contained in a regulation, citing each point by page, paragraph, and line number. This detailed specification will be used to explain how the audit meets the objective. Specific tests should be created for each item. If the audit test must be rerun, the subsequent auditor should always find similar results by using your documentation. For more information, see Chapter 3.

65. B. A nonworking process would be the best candidate for reengineering. The actual decision is based on the best return on investment. There is no need to reengineer something that fails to generate a positive return. For more information, see Chapter 2.

66. A. A qualified opinion means the auditor has reservations about the scope of the audit, concerns with the available evidence, or concerns that the findings may not represent the true story. Audit reports containing a qualified opinion will have limitations on the use of the report. For more information, see Chapter 3.

67. A. Rapid Application Development (RAD) methodology automates only a portion of phase 2 requirements, phase 3 design, and phase 4 development. RAD does not provide the planning and documentation necessary in feasibility, requirements, implementation, and postimplementation. For more information, see Chapter 5.

68. B. The business continuity (BC) plan is likely to fail. It would be nearly impossible for a BC plan to work without first performing a business impact analysis (BIA). Nobody can protect business processes that they were unable to define in a formal specification (BIA report). For more information, see Chapter 8.

69. B. Expert systems make decisions for the user by using weighting rules against data points in the database (heuristics) to build correlations. Expert systems frequently contain more than 100,000 discrete points of data. All the other choices expect the user to make their own decision based on available information. For more information, see Chapter 5.

70. C. Digital certificates (also known as soft tokens) can be used for two-factor authentication. The key fob is also known as a hard token because of its physical nature. Passwords do not provide for two-factor authentication unless coupled with hard tokens, soft tokens, or biometrics. For more information, see Chapter 7.

71. A. Auditing of the system configuration and reading system logs are examples of detective controls implemented by using administrative methods. Auditing is always a detective control. Auditors may use computer-assisted audit tools, but auditing is still an administrative process. For more information, see Chapter 3.

72. A. A haphazard sample is also known as a judgmental sample. For more information, see Chapter 3.

73. C. The auditee will usually get amnesty for turning you in. Copyright violations are always illegal and unethical. You can bet that the auditee will later boast about how they helped you, or blast you for issuing an unfavorable report after they did you a favor. Never use unauthorized software under any condition; besides breaking the law, it will make you look bad. No honest person or organization wants to use an auditor who violates the law. For more information, see Chapter 1.

74. B. Agile programming is used to create prototypes via time-box management techniques to force new iterations within short periods of time. Traditional administrative planning and documentation is forfeited in favor of the undocumented knowledge contained in a person's head. For more information, see Chapter 5.

75. A. Firewalls do not need to be backed up except after changes to the system. Backups of the firewall must be full backups on stand-alone devices, also known as a zero-day restore. An auditor should be seriously concerned if source routing is enabled (major hazard), backup media is left in the drive (covert storage for attackers), remote login or file sharing is enabled (open to remote access). For more information, see Chapter 7.

76. B. The auditor should contact the audit committee, never law enforcement or the regulators. If necessary, the auditor's lawyer will handle contacting the authorities. For more information, see Chapter 3.

77. D. Audit charters are high-level documents used to grant authorization to the auditor responsible for conducting an audit, and to specify that the auditor will be accountable for their behavior. For more information, see Chapter 3.

78. D. CISAs can lose their credentials by possessing or using materials for which they do not hold a valid copyright license. Violating copyright restrictions is a violation of law and ethics. For more information, see Chapter 1.

79. D. Portfolio management is similar to trading stocks or baseball cards. The objective is to get the highest possible value for your collection of projects. Each project is judged on which ones represent the best return on investment; all other projects are cancelled or ignored. Changes to the work breakdown structure (list of project tasks) will occur within the project itself. For more information, see Chapter 2.

80. B. The auditor can use an embedded audit module, also known as an integrated test facility, to create a set of dummy transactions that will be processed along with genuine transactions. The auditor compares the output data against their own calculations. This allows for substantial testing without disrupting the normal processing schedule. For more information, see Chapter 3.

Chapter 1

Secrets of a Successful Auditor

THE OBJECTIVE OF THIS CHAPTER IS TO ACQUAINT THE READER WITH THE FOLLOWING CONCEPTS:

- ✓ Understanding the foundation of IS audit standards

- ✓ Understanding the auditor's professional requirements

- ✓ Familiarity of auditor skills necessary for a successful audit

- ✓ Understanding mandatory versus discretionary wording of regulations

- ✓ Knowing the various types of audits

- ✓ Knowing how to communicate with the auditee

- ✓ Understanding auditor leadership duties, including planning and setting priorities

- ✓ Understanding the organizational structure of corporations and consulting firms

Welcome to the world of information systems (IS) auditing. We congratulate you for having the foresight and ambition to enter one of the most challenging careers in the world. The business issues in our global economy have created tremendous opportunities for individuals such as yourself.

Imagine what the world would be like without the Internet. A world without electronic systems would feel prehistoric. The days of manual systems of bookkeeping are gone.

All organizations, regardless of size, are being driven toward increasing levels of automation. This increasing dependency on electronic information systems has created the need for a new type of auditor: the information systems auditor.

Just as financial auditors verify monetary balances and bookkeeping practices, the IS auditor verifies the integrity of the electronic system. Information systems are used to maintain customer data, company files, inventory, and records of transactions. IS auditing can provide a fabulous opportunity for people with financial or information technology backgrounds.

In this chapter, you will study the foundation of IS audit standards. The Certified Information Systems Auditor (CISA) certification establishes professional requirements and defines the auditor skills necessary for a successful audit.

The CISA candidate is expected to know the different types of audits. There is an established process for communication with the auditee. Every successful auditor must understand their leadership duties, including planning and setting priorities. Every IS auditor is expected to recognize the difference between mandatory versus discretionary wording in regulations.

We will discuss the organizational structure of corporations and consulting firms. The auditor will need to evaluate the organization's governance structure to determine whether IT objectives are aligned to organizational goals. This chapter reviews methods for managing projects, including audit projects.

This chapter is a foundation for the next chapter, which is about the IS governance process. That in turn is followed by a chapter on the auditing process. Each concept we discuss will be in effect from now through the end of this Study Guide to progressively build your knowledge. Do not skip ahead.

Understanding the Demand for IS Audits

For decades, the dominant control placed upon an organization was the financial audit. Although theft and fraud have always existed, the general expectation was that almost all organizations could be trusted without additional regulations. We expected management to be honest. Well, those naive days are over. Welcome to the new world, which has a growing number of intrusive regulations. Modern business culture is moving rapidly to less trust with more testing to reduce the chances of insider corruption. Greed is a powerful motivator to some individuals in authority.

Executive Misconduct

Let's reflect on some of the great people who created this wonderful job opportunity for us. Mom always said to give special recognition to those deserving people who help you further your career opportunities:

- Italy's Parmalat dairy scandal occurred in 2003, when executives admitted that an account that was supposed to be holding 4 billion Euro dollars of assets in the Cayman Islands did not exist. According to industry news, four of the world's leading banks were indicted for their participation. This triggered creation of ISO 15489 as the new standard of records management.

- One of the wealthiest men in America, Raj Rajaratnam, was arrested for insider trading in October 2009. His net worth is estimated at $1.3 billion. Charges allege his $21 billion hedge fund scheme caused the Sri Lanka stock market to drop 4 percent.

- Bernie Madoff pled guilty to architecting a $65 billon Ponzi scheme that almost collapsed Wall Street. He admitted to depositing his clients' money while never making any legitimate investments on their behalf. Madoff created false paperwork to convince clients and U.S. Securities Exchange (SEC) regulators that he was engaged in legitimate trading. Several SEC auditors suggested that Madoff's practices should be investigated. Unfortunately, SEC management ignored the auditors' warnings, possibly because of Madoff's former role on the SEC executive board.

- Allen Stanford from Antigua is charged with running a fraudulent investment scheme similar to Madoff's. Charges allege he cheated 50,000 customers out of $8 billion by promising investors dramatic returns that are unlikely, if not impossible, to achieve. Industry reports claim that the investment derivatives market is so complex and poorly regulated, it's been relatively easy to hide fraud.

- American International Group (AIG) former CFO Howard Smith overstated income by $3.9 billion (10 percent of income) and loss reserves by $500 million to quiet analyst complaints about AIG's declining financial reserves. The SEC agreed to settle after AIG agreed to pay over $1.6 billon in damages.

- Arthur Andersen executive David Duncan violated his independence with his client, CFO Andrew Fastow of Enron. Duncan participated in improper, biased activities for Enron by ordering his staff to shred documents to obstruct the Enron investigation.

- Cendant Vice Chairman E. Kirk Shelton was convicted of fraud in an accounting scandal for falsely inflating income to drive up the stock price.

- Former U.S. Congressman William J. Jefferson was sentenced to 13 years in prison for accepting hundreds of thousands of dollars in bribes while in office. Jefferson was convicted on 16 counts of bribery, racketeering, and money laundering related to brokering business deals in Africa.

- Comverse Technology CEO Jacob "Kobi" Alexander was captured by federal authorities after fleeing the country in an attempt to avoid prosecution for orchestrating a fraudulent scheme of backdating options while running a secret stock options slush fund.

- Enron executives Ken Lay, Jeffrey Skilling, Andrew Fastow, Lea Fastow, Ben Glisan Jr., and Dan Boyle were proven guilty for running the world's largest scam of off-balance-sheet (OBS) transactions.

- International Product Investment Corp. (IPIC) CEO Gregory Earl Setser was convicted of conspiracy, securities fraud, and money laundering. Setser has been sentenced to 40 years in prison without parole and ordered to pay approximately $62 million in restitution for running an investment pyramid scam.

- Tyco International ex-CEO Dennis Kozlowski is serving 8–25 years in prison for stealing $134 million from the company. Ex-CFO Mark H. Schwartz was given the same prison sentence. The scheme involved grand larceny, conspiracy of falsifying business records, and inflating statements of operating income by at least $500 million by using improper accounting practices.

- Lincoln Savings and Loan Association CEO Charles Keating was found guilty of causing the $2.6 billion collapse of the savings and loan industry in 1988. So far the estimated cost of the bailout is said to be over $110 billion. Keating accused the auditor of having a vendetta against him for bringing the evidence to the attention of regulators.

- WorldCom ex-CEO Bernard Ebbers is serving 25 years for securities fraud and filing false reports concerning an $11 billion accounting fraud. WorldCom triggered the creation of the U.S. Sarbanes-Oxley Act of 2002 (a corporate governance law for internal controls). CFO Scott Sullivan testified against Ebbers to get a reduced sentence. Controller David Myers admitted he told the accounting staff to make billions of dollars in adjustments to financial statements so the company's stock price would rise. Former accounting director Buford Yates went to prison for following the orders of his superiors to make billions of dollars of unexplained adjustments in financial records.

We could continue with more examples of executive misconduct, including insider trading by ImClone Systems CEO Samuel D. Waksal, embezzlement of $77 million by Patterson-UTI Energy CFO Jonathan D. Nelson, fraud by former HealthSouth CFO Weston Smith, and securities fraud plus bank fraud with embezzlement by executives John Rigas and son Timothy Rigas of Adelphia Communications Corporation.

The U.S. Securities and Exchange Commission reported more than 1,000 successful corporate fraud convictions from 2002–2005, including the following:

- 92 corporate presidents
- 86 chief executive officers (CEOs)
- 40 chief financial officers (CFOs)
- 14 chief operating officers (COOs)
- 98 vice presidents (VPs)
- 17 attorneys (lawyers serving as corporate council)

Times are rapidly changing worldwide. These global businesses were damaged by bad executive decisions. Even some common business practices that were acceptable five to ten years ago are now illegal. More organizations are adding *back-claw* provisions obligating executives to repay salary and bonus money if they are found guilty of misrepresentation. But it's still not enough to stop corruption.

More Regulation Ahead

Our world continually bears witness to repetitive leadership failures. New regulations for more-stringent financial and internal controls are driving business into a control frenzy. Executives have shunned new attempts by government because the purpose of any regulation is to eliminate choice. Many organizations are run using two philosophies: charge clients whatever you can get away with (what the market will bear) and take as many shortcuts as possible. Regulation is intended to prevent shortcuts while putting a minimum limit on control. The common effect of more regulation is lower profits. You may have already heard of the following regulations in the news or at work. Knowing these regulations isn't necessary for the test, but it can help grow your career.

Committee of Sponsoring Organizations of the Treadway Commission (COSO)   This United Nations committee of world governments created a series of regulatory laws uniquely tailored by each country for the same purpose of governing banking and financial operations. The most common financial integrity controls under COSO are known by the following names:

- U.S. Sarbanes-Oxley Act (SOX) for NYSE publicly traded corporations, similar to the U.S. government's own internal controls in the Office of Management and Budget Circular A-123
- Canada's Ontario Securities Exchange (OSX) for publicly traded corporations
- Australian Securities Exchange Corporate Governance Council (ASX-10)
- Japanese Financial Instruments and Exchange Law (J-SOX), a version of Sarbanes-Oxley
- International Financial Reporting Standards (IFRS), which includes the European Union, Australia, Canada, Japan, Russia, and the United States

Banking Regulations   New regulations in banking are being added each year to support the increase in world trade. The focus is to improve risk management, record keeping and data security. Samples of these include the following:

- Basel Accord for Bank Capital Measurement and Standards (international)
- Payment Card Industry (PCI) Data Security Standard (international)
- Gramm-Leach-Bliley Financial Services Modernization Act (United States)
- Federal Financial Institutions Examination Council regulations (FFIEC, United States)
- Fair and Accurate Credit Transactions Act (FACTA, credit processing, United States)

Other Important Regulations   It's worth mentioning just a few more regulations from other industries, including medical records management, security of government information processing, and security of automated controls. Here are just some of over 20 more regulations:

- Health Insurance Portability and Accountability Act (HIPAA, United States)
- Federal Information Security Management Act (FISMA, United States)
- Supervisory control and data acquisition (SCADA, for utilities)
- Numerous privacy laws worldwide

Basic Regulatory Objective

All of these regulations require government offices and business enterprises to possess two simple components:

- Evidence of operational integrity
- Evidence of internal controls to protect valuable assets

An *asset* is defined as anything of value, including trademarks, patents, secret recipes, durable goods, data files, competent personnel, and clients. Although people are not listed as corporate assets, the loss of key individuals is a genuine business threat. We can define a *threat* as a negative event that would cause a loss if it occurred. The path that allows a threat to occur is referred to as *vulnerability*. Your job as an IS auditor is to verify that assets, threats, and vulnerabilities are properly identified and managed to reduce risk. Let's take a moment to review Table 1.1 comparing the differences between assets, threats, and vulnerabilities.

TABLE 1.1 Comparing differences between asset, threat, and vulnerability

	Asset ($$)	Threat (Event)	Vulnerability (Pathway)
Knowledgeable people	X		
Clients and contacts	X		
Taking risks in business	X		X
Data	X		
Cost of compliance kills profit		X	
Lack of executive governance			X
Competitor wins our clients		X	
Loss of market (sales decline)		X	
Bad decisions		X	
Unique know-how	X		
Lack of training (not knowing how or why)			X
Special equipment	X		
Software licenses	X		
Regulatory failure or contact breach		X	
Documentation, forms, procedures	X		
Hacker attack is successful		X	
Subcontractor takes shortcuts			X
Don't read event logs			X

In the past, organizations were allowed to operate with fewer restrictions. The problem with past regulation (or lack thereof) was that many organizations were taking risks that would have been unacceptable to investors and business partners had they been fully informed of corporate actions. Financial auditors were focused on reviewing bank balances and verifying that transaction totals proved to be correct. Increasing use of automation enables little mistakes to cascade into massive catastrophes. Stockholders, customers, and the government are looking for reassurance that management has taken the necessary precautions to prevent loss or corruption.

Our economy is founded on banking and investment. The majority of our global economy invests directly or indirectly in stock and financial markets. You may be an indirect investor through pension funds or bank investment portfolios. Unfortunately, there exists a group of individuals who view stock as their own private monetary system. How wonderful it must be to have our money at their disposal, without any terms of repayment, without interest or consideration, and without the requirement to ever pay the money back. Sounds ridiculous, doesn't it? But frankly, that is exactly how the stock market operates. A large number of bank investment derivatives work the same way. You invest money with the hope that one day you will see something in return, knowing that you could lose it all.

One of the purposes of a controls audit is to ensure that there is reason to believe investors' money is protected from stupid mistakes. Our free enterprise strives to prevent another market collapse and protect the world banking system from crashing. We expect management to specify policies and to create procedures, processes, and safeguards to prevent loss and corruption. It is the job of management to design a solution that effectively protects corporate assets.

Governance Is Leadership

To lead an organization is what governance is all about. Executive management is expected to use its position to set operating rules, which becomes the organization's culture. Is that culture built on candid honesty, or omission and deceit? Do other executives and employees ask permission first or undertake unauthorized actions with the expectation of amnesty (forgiveness) later? In poorly governed organizations, management usually fails to lead, while individual executives fail to accept responsibility. As a result, the organization experiences a breakdown of trust. Without leadership and trust, employees stuck in the middle will take self-directed chances without authorization. That is a dangerous culture lacking governance, lacking trust, and obviously not being led by their executives. Being risk averse indicates a lack of leadership. Real leaders blaze a path to persevere, adapt, and overcome challenges.

To govern is to lead by position of authority, set the rules, designate the priorities, and exercise good decisions. Every organization must undertake risks in order to move forward and survive. A primary objective in auditing is to determine if these actions are formally authorized and controlled to reduce unnecessary risk, or if they occur haphazardly.

Audits are used to measure the success of organizational governance. As an IS auditor, you must be familiar with the various policies, standards, and procedures of any organization that you are auditing. Auditing principles are essentially the same for government and commercial business. In addition, you must understand the purpose of your audit. You will look at those topics in this section.

Audit Results Indicate the Truth

What does the auditor do? We make a living by listening to management assert their claim. The next step is to find enough meaningful evidence and then test that evidence to prove or disprove the claim. We then issue final results in our report of findings. The following simple flowchart illustrates the basic process.

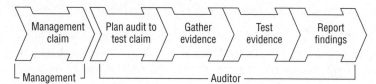

We are looking for evidence of the truth. Does the auditee perform their work as claimed by management? *Governance* exists if the right people of authority looked at the issue, made an intelligent decision, and took appropriate action. Governance is proactive leadership. One of the most acceptable methods of governing is through issuing policies, with supporting standards, guidelines, and easy-to-follow procedures for the staff to follow. Results are tested through audits. Comparing written procedures and observing a person performing the tasks will indicate the truth. It's not hard to audit correctly.

Understanding Policies, Standards, Guidelines, and Procedures

A plethora of documentation exists in the operation of any organization. Management uses this documentation to specify operating and control details. Consistency would be impossible without putting this information into writing.

Organizations typically have four types of documents in place:

Policies   Simply stated, a policy is an executive mandate to identify a topic containing particular risks to avoid or prevent. Policies are high-level documents signed by a person of significant authority with the power to force cooperation. The policy is a simple document stating that a particular high-level control objective is important to the organization's success. Policies may be only one page in length.

- Compliance is *mandatory* when a policy is officially mandated.
- The authority of the person mandating a policy will determine the scope of implementation.

The highest level of authority are people holding top management positions. Principal issuers of policies that receive widespread support are elected officials, agency heads, board members of corporations, chief executive officers, financial officers, operating officers, and upper vice-level management. Policies issued at lower levels are often ignored outside of a particular department or project.

Standards   These are mid-level documents containing *measurement control points* to ensure uniform implementation in support of a policy. After management identifies "what to protect" by issuing a policy, the next step is to specify a standard containing a list of specific measurement points to obtain compliance. Management reviews, peer reviews, testing, and audits are used to compare a subject to the standard with the intention of certifying that a minimum level of uniform compliance exists.

- Standards identify specific control points necessary for compliance.

- Standards *do not* contain the workflow for compliance.

- Management's job is to use individual points from each standard to create appropriate procedures in a complete workflow in order to obtain compliance within the organization.

No doubt a standard is implemented with different levels of influence. The authority level of the person mandating a policy will have a profound effect on implementation. Authority makes a noticeable difference in the scope of implementation including level of effort used. All standards can be grouped into four basic categories from highest influence to lowest:

Regulatory Standard   It's a regulatory control when mandated by a government law or government agency to protect the economy, society, or our environment.

Industry Standard   Rapid progress during development of new technology will always outpace official standards. Specifications developed by the inventor usually become de facto standards until widespread adoption of a ratified standard. Consensus necessary to ratify, adopt, and implement a new official standard is usually measured in years of delay.

Organizational Standard   Executive management at various organizations will set their own standards to help obtain their goals. The organization may be an association, agency, cooperative nonprofit organization, or for-profit business. CISA is a professional standard set by the ISACA organization; it's not a license nor mandate for anyone else to adopt. Clients and management can choose to accept it or look elsewhere to other organizations. Management chooses to apply its own standard or follow the standards created by another organization. The primary purpose of the International Organization for Standardization (ISO) was to eliminate confusion by providing a universal definition of what needed to be accomplished.

Personal Standard   A person's own internal standard will govern everyday life. These unofficial standards may change with our age, education, or life experiences.

- A person of high standards will uphold virtues of honor and integrity by respecting people, doing the right thing without misleading, and remaining vigilant against causing harm.

- A person of low standards is often without ethics, ignores consequences, shows no concern over intellectual property, or ignores ownership of distilled information.

Every auditor needs to be on the lookout for persons willing to violate personal standards of honor, integrity, and honesty. Improper actions foretell of bigger trouble.

Guidelines   These are intended to provide advice pertaining to how organizational objectives might be obtained in the absence of a standard. The purpose is to provide information that would aid in making decisions about intended goals (should do), beneficial alternatives (could do), and actions that would not create problems (won't hurt). Key points to remember about guidelines are as follows:

- Guidelines are *discretionary* because the directions provided are usually incomplete.
- The user has to adapt or discard portions of the information to fit the intended use.

Procedures   These are "cookbook" recipes providing a workflow of specific tasks necessary to achieve minimum compliance to a standard. Details are written in step-by-step format from the very beginning to the end. Good procedures include common troubleshooting steps in case the user encounters a known problem. On occasion a procedure may be deemed ineffective. The correct process is to update ineffective procedures by using the change control process described later. Valuable information to remember about procedures include these points:

- "Best practices" represent information suggested to help users develop their own procedures.
- The purpose of a procedure is to maintain the highest possible control over the outcome.
- Compliance with established procedures is mandatory to ensure consistency and accuracy.

Figure 1.1 illustrates the hierarchy of a policy, standard, guideline, and procedure.

Understanding Professional Ethics

Ethics is about knowing what is right verses wrong and doing the right thing each time. Ethical professionals will place the client's interest ahead of their own provided the client is acting in a forthright, honest manner. Auditors are usually bound by more than one set of professional standards. An auditor is expected to honor the laws plus abide by the rules of their professional certification. Every CISA is required to follow ISACA's code of ethics in addition to those of any other organization to which the Auditor belongs.

Following the ISACA Code

The Information Systems Audit and Control Association (ISACA) set forth a code governing the professional conduct and ethics of all certified IS auditors and members of the association.

As a CISA, you are bound to uphold this code. The following eight points represent the true spirit and intent of this code:

- Auditors agree to support the implementation of appropriate policies, standards, guidelines, and procedures for information systems. They will also encourage compliance with this objective.

FIGURE 1.1   The relationship between a policy, standard, guideline, and procedure

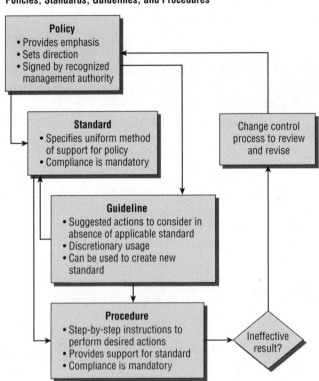

Policies, Standards, Guidelines, and Procedures

Policy
- Provides emphasis
- Sets direction
- Signed by recognized management authority

Standard
- Specifies uniform method of support for policy
- Compliance is mandatory

Change control process to review and revise

Guideline
- Suggested actions to consider in absence of applicable standard
- Discretionary usage
- Can be used to create new standard

Procedure
- Step-by-step instructions to perform desired actions
- Provides support for standard
- Compliance is mandatory

Ineffective result?

- Auditors agree to perform their duties with objectivity, professional care, and due diligence in accordance with professional standards implementing the use of best practices.

- Auditors agree to serve the interests of stakeholders in an honest and lawful manner that reflects a credible image upon their profession. The public expects and trusts auditors to conduct their work in an ethical and honest manner.

- Auditors promise to maintain privacy and confidentiality of information obtained during their audit except for required disclosure to legal authorities. Information they obtain during the audit will not be used for personal benefit.

- Auditors agree to undertake only those activities in which they are professionally competent and will strive to improve their competency. Their effectiveness in auditing depends on how evidence is gathered, analyzed, and reported.

- Auditors promise to disclose accurate results of all work and significant facts to the appropriate parties.

- Auditors agree to support ongoing professional education to help stakeholders enhance their understanding of information systems security and control.

- The failure of a CISA to comply with this code of professional ethics may result in an investigation with possible sanctions or disciplinary measures.

Ethics statements are necessary to demonstrate the level of honesty and professionalism expected of every auditor. Overall, your profession requires you to be honest and fair in all representations you make. The goal is to build trust with clients. Your behavior should reflect a positive image on your profession. All IS auditors are depending on you to help maintain the high quality and integrity that clients expect from a CISA.

Every CISA should have a strong understanding of these objectives and how each would apply to different audit situations.

Preventing Ethical Conflicts

Auditors are bombarded by certain people attempting to sway us from our straight and narrow course of honesty. Seemingly simple violations can become uncontrollable career killers. Do not allow yourself to participate in any situation that could tarnish your image as an auditor. Just having a false reputation of dishonest activity will quash your career like a black plague.

Let's look at a few common examples of unethical or criminal behavior that you need to avoid:

Theft of Intellectual Property   Intellectual property includes the assembly of data from the public domain and proprietary sources into a distillation of comprehensible answers, creating a unique original work. The creator who expended the resources becomes the owner entitled to legally benefit from the resulting work. Persons of low standards will ignore effort, money, time, and resources expended by developers during countless hours of careful research. Another telltale sign of low standards is callous discounting of family sacrifices made by the developer (programmer, inventor, researcher, or author) to balance expenses until ultimately distilling their final work. Repayment for all their effort occurs after the hard work.

Copyright Violations   Written works including specially prepared information, books, musical works, and computer programs are protected by copyrights. Dishonest persons will take, steal, or redistribute unauthorized bootleg copies of computer software knowing it defrauds the developer of a paycheck for their relentless effort in making quality software. The same issues apply to unauthorized copies of music, movies, books, and standards documentation.

The possession, purchase, or distribution of any bootleg materials will lead to forfeiting your CISA certification along with all other certifications requiring an ethics statement. You don't have to be convicted of a crime to lose your certification. COSO requires violators be removed from any positions of control or management because they are known to be untrustworthy. Trafficking in bootlegs provides an excellent route to unemployment and a future of living in jail.

Failing to Follow Your Own Rules   Make sure that you uphold the spirit and intent of the audit profession. The best way to kill your career is to give the perception that you violate the rules yourself. It's necessary to "walk the talk" by doing everything right, just as you expect from your customer. By doing this religiously, you will become almost bulletproof.

Violating the Law   Being associated with a suspected scam is nearly as damaging as being convicted in the courtroom. The best way to stay out of trouble is to avoid questionable deals. Never accept a free or loaner copy of software from IT workers. It's a trap that usually involves someone bragging about how they helped you out by violating the law, ethics, or company policy. Always be prepared to show the purchase receipt and original product to prove you are honest and ethical. Lack of evidence implies guilt and destroys any chance of defending yourself. Vendor shipping records are an excellent source of proof.

Not Reporting Violations Promptly   Remember, the person reporting (in this case, you) will usually get amnesty, unless someone else turns you in first. You need to be prepared to turn over evidence unless you want to join others in their convictions. Honest auditors always report the truth. It's what keeps us in business.

Never underestimate an individual possessing interest to steal marketing research, client lists, or business plan data to use for their own improper gain. Be wary of individuals willing to do whatever the boss or a friend requests while overlooking how their actions are unethical, irresponsible, or possibly illegal. Trouble is brewing with those who base reasoning on greed or willingly accept the wrong actions for fear of losing employment. Review the beginning of this chapter again if you need any examples of executives and auditors being "burned at the stake" for violating the public's trust.

Guilty people get amnesty for turning you in. It's unfair, but the guiltiest will typically get amnesty for turning someone else in for participation. So the person who says, "don't worry" is not worried. They secretly know that you will become their scapegoat at the first sign of trouble. Beware of any special deal or exception that can be used against you. The truth never stays secret.

Understanding the Purpose of an Audit

An *audit* is simply a review of past history. The IS auditor is expected to follow the defined audit process, establish audit criteria, gather meaningful evidence, and render an independent opinion about internal controls. The audit involves applying various techniques for collecting meaningful evidence, and then performing a comparison of the audit evidence against the standard for reference.

If the assertions of management and the auditor's report are in agreement, you can expect the results to be truthful. If management assertions and the auditor's report do not agree, that would signal a concern warranting further attention.

Your key to success in auditing is to accurately report your findings, whether good or bad or indifferent. A good auditor will produce verifiable results. No one should ever come in behind you with a different outcome of findings. Your job is to report what the evidence indicates.

Classifying Basic Types of Audits

We can classify audits into three basic categories. Each of these represents a slightly different level of trust and unique objectives. The purpose is always to determine the truth.

Internal Audits and Assessments   This involves auditors within their own organization looking to discover evidence of what is occurring inside the organization (self-assessment). These audits have restrictions on their scope, and the findings should not be shared outside the organization. The findings cannot be used for licensing.

External Audits   In an external audit, a customer audits their vendor/supplier to verify integrity of transactions, internal controls, compliance, or the entire relationship. In other words, the business audits its customer or supplier, or vice versa. The goal is to ensure the expected level of performance as mutually agreed upon in their contracts.

Independent Audits   Independent audits are outside of the customer-supplier influence. Third-party independent auditors are relied on for licensing, certification, or product approval. A simple example is independent consumer reports.

So what will the CISA be asked to look at during an audit? Auditors are called to audit products, processes, and systems.

Determining Differences in Audit Approach

IS auditors are expected to apply the discipline of financial audit standards to a variety of abstract situations. Each of these requires a different approach. Let's review the basic approach required for each of these audits to be successful:

Product audits check the attributes against the design specification (size, color, markings). The 2007 hazardous toy recall of over a million Chinese-manufactured toys for Mattel is an example of using a product audit. The lead-based paint used on the toys was in violation of the design specifications. You can expect that CISAs will audit more software products than toys.

Process audits evaluate the process method to determine whether the activities or sequence of activities meet the published requirements. Business Impact Analysis (BIA) and Business Process Reengineering (BPR) discovery projects are prime examples. We want to see how the process is working. This involves checking inputs, actions, and outputs to verify the process performance.

System audits seek to evaluate the management of the system, including its configuration. The auditor is interested in the team members' activities, control environment, event monitoring, how customer needs are determined, who provides authorization, how changes are implemented, preventative maintenance, and so forth, including incident response capability.

Financial audits verify financial records, transactions, and account balances. This type of audit is used to check the integrity of financial records and accounting practices compared to well-known accounting standards.

Operational audits verify effectiveness and efficiency of operational practices. Operational audits are used frequently in service and process environments, including IT service providers. An operational audit is detailed in Statement on Auditing Standard 70 (SAS-70).

Integrated audits include both financial and operational controls audits. An integrated audit is detailed in SAS-94.

Compliance audits verify implementation of and adherence to a standard or regulation. This could include ISO standards and all government regulations. A compliance audit usually includes tests for the presence of a working control.

Administrative audits verify that appropriate policies and procedures exist and have been implemented as intended. This type of audit usually tests for the presence of required documentation.

Information systems certification and/or accreditation usually involves formal system testing against a reference standard, whereas accreditation represents management's level of acceptance.

Surveillance audits verify that the auditee is continuing to follow the correct procedures. This type of audit is a routine checkup occurring between the certification and recertification audits.

Now we need to move on to the different roles people play in the audit.

Understanding the Auditor's Responsibility

As an auditor, you are expected to fulfill a fiduciary relationship. A *fiduciary relationship* is simply one in which you are acting for the benefit of another person and placing the responsibilities to be fair and honest ahead of your own interest. An auditor must never put the auditee interests ahead of the truth. People inside and outside of the auditee organization will depend on your reports to make decisions.

The auditor is depended on to advise about the internal status of an organization.

Comparing Audits to Assessments

As stated earlier, the audit is a formal process performed by a qualified independent auditor. Audits are different from inspections or assessments because the individual performing the audit must be both objective and impartial. This is a tremendous responsibility. To clarify, the following provides a comparison of an audit and assessment:

Audit   In legal terminology, an *audit* is defined as a systematic inspection of records involving analysis, evidence testing, and confirmation. An audit generates a report considered to represent a high assurance of truth. Audits performed by an outside independent auditor have the highest assurance because the degree of assurance is proportional to the independence of the auditor. Audits are used in reporting engagements.

Assessment   An assessment is less formal and frequently more cooperative with the people/objects under scrutiny. Its purpose is to see what exists and to assess value based on its relevance. The assessment report is viewed to have moderate-to-low value when compared to an audit.

The primary goal of an assessment is to help the user/staff work toward improving their score. However, the more formal external audit is the score that actually counts for regulatory compliance purposes.

Internal audit departments frequently conduct "internal use only" audits, which are of lower assurance. The goal is to help guide the organization to pass an external audit at a lower overall cost. Internal audits provide key support to executive governance.

Always remember that the basic control requirement is to separate the worker from the person providing *authorization*. This separation of duties is applicable across the entire organization in determining sales price concessions, setting credit limits, determining finance terms, processing deposits, maintaining inventory control, purchasing, legal contracts, and daily I.T. operating duties. Risk of failure or corruption is reduced by removing authority from the worker and redistributing smaller authority for decisions between multiple managers. Assessments are considered biased because the separation is not clean as it would be under a formal independent audit.

Differentiating Between Auditor and Auditee Roles

There are only two titles for persons directly involved in an audit. First is the *auditor*, the one who investigates. Second is the *auditee*, the subject of the audit. A third role exists that is normally outside of the audit, known as the *client*. ISACA refers to these as audit roles versus nonaudit roles.

Let's clarify the titles and basic roles of these people by their relationship to the audit. We can refer to them as members of the following categories:

Auditor   The auditor is the competent person performing the audit.

Auditee   The organization and people being audited are collectively called the auditee.

Client　The client is the person or organization with the authority to request the audit. A client may be the audit committee, external customer, internal audit department, or regulatory group. If the client is internal to the auditee, that client assumes the auditee role.

Everyone else is considered outside of the audit roles. Audit details should be kept confidential from persons not directly involved as auditee or the client.

Your purpose as an auditor is to be an independent set of eyes that can delve into the inside of organizations on behalf of management or can certify compliance on behalf of everyone in the outside world. *Independent* means that you are not related professionally, personally, or organizationally to the subject of the audit. You cannot be independent if the audit's outcome results in your financial gain or if you are involved in the auditee's decisions or design of the subject being audited.

When determining whether you are able to perform a fair audit, you should conduct an independence test. In addition, you must remain aware of your responsibility as an auditor under the various auditing standards.

Applying an Independence Test

Here is a simple self-assessment to help you determine your level of independence:

INDEPENDENCE SELF-TEST	YES	NO
Are you auditing something you helped to develop?		
Are you free of any conflicts, circumstances, or attitudes toward the auditee that might affect the audit outcome?		
Is your personal life free of any relationships, off-duty behavior, or financial gain that could be perceived as affecting your judgment?		
Do you have any organizational relationships with the auditee, including business deals, financial obligations, or pending legal actions?		
Do you have a job conflict? Does the organizational structure require your position to work under the executive in charge of the area being audited?		
Did you receive any gifts of value or special favors?		

If any answer is yes, you are not independent. Any conflicts will place a shadow of doubt on the objectivity of the audit findings. Only internal auditors (whose aim is to improve internal performance) can answer yes and still possibly continue the audit. External auditors are required to remain independent during an independent audit. Any potential conflicts should be disclosed immediately to the lead auditor. You may be reassigned to eliminate the conflict. The lead auditor may determine that the impact is low enough that you can remain in the role as long as the client sponsor is aware of the situation. Attempting to hide the truth is a bad idea. No conflict means you are cleared to proceed.

Real World Scenario

Being Fair and Objective

Early in my career, I learned a slogan that helped guide me through some difficult decisions: "The truth is the truth until you add to it." As an auditor, you are expected to report findings that are fair and objective. It is presumed that the auditor will ask the right questions during the audit. In this book, we intend to teach you a practical application of the audit standards, including the right questions to ask.

What if the client asks you to provide advice to the company's design staff while you are engaged as the external auditor? The unknowledgeable auditor could create a conflict or lose the client's respect. A good auditor would remind the client of the need for auditor independence. Imagine the power of the following statement that you, as a professional auditor, could make:

> *Sir/Madam, In my role as external auditor, I must remain independent of design decisions; otherwise, I would not be able to provide you the independence and objectivity required. Providing design advice would be a violation of several standards governing auditor independence, including public corporation audit standard AS-1, IFRS audit practices, ISACA professional standards, and Statement on Auditing Standards 1, 37, and 74 (SAS-1, SAS-37, and SAS-74).*

> **NOTE** You are encouraged to explain what an auditor looks for during an audit. You must be careful not to participate in design decisions, detailed specification, or remediation during your role as the auditor. You may be hired to help with remediation; however, you will be disqualified from auditing any related work. The same principle applies to design work and system operation.

Implementing Audit Standards

Auditors have the luxury of being able to rely on well-known accounting standards that have been accepted worldwide. The standards were originally developed for financial audits, but their spirit and intent also apply to IS auditing. Frequently, a minor adaptation will provide the foundation and detail necessary for use in IS audits. These standards allow you to render a fair opinion without fear of retribution or liability.

Where Do Audit Standards Come From?

IS security professionals and auditors may refer to a variety of applicable standards when planning or auditing controls. Every professional needs to recognize that two classes of standards usually exist:

Parent Class with Broad Application across a Variety of Industries   Examples include the ISO 27002 information security management standard, NIST 800-53 controls, and NIST 800-26 (Security Self-Assessment Guide for Information Technology Systems). Older versions of ISO standards frequently bear lower ID numbers.

Industry Specific with a Limited Scope   Examples include the FFIEC regulation and portions of HIPAA, which may incorporate only select portions of the parent class standards.

All governance controls exist for the purpose of managing money, protecting assets, safeguarding information, providing process handling, and/or managing people. Modern commerce controls in world trade are determined by the members of COSO, ISO, and the Organization for Economic Cooperation and Development (OECD). Only governments can be members of these international control organizations. So your vendor, your company, and your association can never be full members—at best, only followers eligible for discounted purchases of meeting minutes or publications. Figure 1.2 shows the relationship of world trade organizations to the creation of parent class controls.

FIGURE 1.2   World Trade Organization creates parent class controls

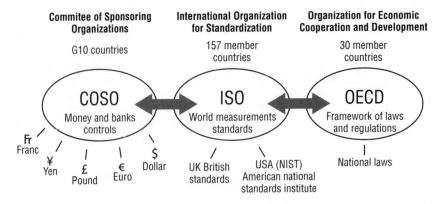

Financial controls and financial audits are based on following the COSO controls. Therefore, auditing standards are underneath COSO directives for how to control money. With money to spend, it's inevitable that the next step is to trade for something of value such as food, machinery, or raw materials. COSO sets the standards involving monetary transactions.

The ISO is responsible for determining the measurement of products by attributes. Common examples include imperial miles to metric kilometers, weight from pounds to grams, and the number of bushels of corn into metric tons. The ISO sets the standards involving measurement. The ISO also defines IS security, operation of IT systems, and certification testing for both products and people.

Now the only component missing is governing law. That's where the OECD steps in to solve the dilemma. The OECD provides a United Nations forum for countries to incorporate legal objectives into the local laws of another country. The goal is closing loopholes across international laws. The OECD is making it harder for people to escape prosecution. It also enabled the U.S. Sarbanes-Oxley act to be adapted to become Japan's Financial Instruments and Exchange Law (J-SOX) along with other laws. The OECD publishes standards on privacy, antispam, and data usage crossing borders. The purpose of OECD is to establish a shared definition of acceptable conduct, define criminal offenses, and encourage prosecution and oversight.

 Real World Scenario

Where Does ISACA Fit?

ISACA standards, guidelines, procedures and the ISACA COBIT framework provide an IT-only view. The association uses portions of COSO standards blended with a handful of ISO IT standards. Volumes of other material is not incorporated. Therefore, a smart auditor will help clients understand that ISACA does not include other important controls necessary for governing critical business areas of the enterprise such as the following:

- Sales/marketing

- Manufacturing

- Engineering/development

- Human resources

- Logistics

- Finance

- Legal filings for contracts

- Government-mandated filings

This means ISACA compliance does not meet regulatory standards by itself. ISACA exists to help the auditor understand where to focus in terms of IT-specific controls.

NOTE   Government-mandated filings include public disclosure with the SEC of enterprise operating exceptions. These filings provide public notice of major problems, hacking attacks, ERP failures, service outages, and other conditions bearing a possible impact on the organization's financial viability. The government wants to alert stockholders and provide an opportunity for investors to dump their stock or reconsider investing. This is popular with COSO member countries because the government's shared goal is to protect the investor stock market, not the enterprise. The U.S. version is part of the SEC 8-K exception reporting system. A great way to keep your job is to never be responsible for crashing the ERP servers at month-end, because more than a few hours of outage may result in a mandatory public disclosure.

Understanding the Various Auditing Standards

You need to understand the two basic categories of audit testing: audits either verify that an item necessary for compliance exists (*compliance test*) or check inside for the substance and integrity of a claim (*substantive test*). Just how does an auditor know what to do in these audits? As an IS auditor, you are fortunate to have several credible resources available to assist you and guide your clients.

Among these resources are standards and regulations that direct your actions and final opinion. It would be quite rare to depart from these well-known and commonly accepted regulations. In fact, you would be in an awkward situation if you ever departed from the audit standards. By following known audit standards, you are relatively safe from an integrity challenge or individual liability. By adhering to audit standards, a good auditor can operate from a position that is conceptually equal to Teflon nonstick coating. Nothing negative or questionable could stick to the auditor.

You can learn more about auditing standards by reading and then implementing information provided by the following:

- American Institute of Certified Public Accountants (AICPA) and International Federation of Accountants (IFAC).

- Financial Accounting Standards Board (FASB) with Statement on Auditing Standards (SAS), standards 1 through 114, which are referenced and applied by the AICPA and IFAC.

- International Financial Reporting Standards (IFRS), which replaced the Generally Accepted Accounting Principles (GAAP) after all the corruption scandals you read about in the beginning of this chapter. The United States and the United Kingdom are no longer using GAAP because of wide-spread mis-representation found during investigations of executive corruption. IFRS is now required because of changes in regulatory law to reduce chances of financial misrepresentation.

- COSO, providing the COSO internal control framework that is the basis for standards used in global commerce. COSO is the parent for the standards used by governments around the world.

- U.S. Public Company Accounting Oversight Board (PCAOB) of the Securities and Exchange Commission, issuing audit standards AS-1, AS-2, AS-3, AS-4, and AS-5. PCAOB is the standards body for Sarbanes-Oxley, including the international implementation by the Japanese government and European Union (US-SOX, J-SOX, and E-SOX).

- OECD, providing guidelines for participating countries to promote standardization in multinational business for world trade.

- ISO, which represents participation from the member governments.

- U.S. National Institute of Standards and Technology (NIST), providing a foundation of modern IS standards used worldwide. When combined with British Standards/ISO (BS/ISO), you get a wonderful amount of useful guidance.

- FISMA, which specifies minimum security compliance standards for all systems relied on by the government, including the military and those systems operated by government contractors. (The U.S. government is the world's largest customer.)

- ISACA and the IT Governance Institute (ITGI) issue the Control Objectives for Information and Related Technology (COBIT) guidelines, which are derived from COSO with a more specific emphasis on information systems.

- Basel Accord Standard, which is currently using Pillar III (Basel III) for governing risk reduction in banking.

Although this list may appear daunting, it is important to remember that all these examples are in fundamental agreement with each other. Each standard supports nearly identical terms of reference and supports similar audit objectives. These standards will have slightly different levels of audit or audit scope. ISACA and its new IT Governance Institute have developed a set of IT internal control standards for CISAs to follow. These incorporate several objectives of the COSO internal control standard that have been narrowed to focus on IT functions. Let's look at a brief overview of the ISACA standards.

ISACA IS Audit Standards

The members of ISACA are constantly striving to advance the standards of IS auditing. CISAs should check the ISACA website (www.isaca.org/standards) for updates on a quarterly basis. The current body of ISACA Audit Standards is organized using a format numbered from 1 to 16:

S1 Audit Charter   The audit charter authorizes the scope of the audit and grants you responsibility, authority, and accountability in the audit function.

S2 Independence   Every auditor is expected to demonstrate professional and organizational independence.

S3 Professional Ethics and Standards of Conduct   The auditor must act in a manner that denotes professionalism and respect.

S4 Professional Competence   The auditor must have the necessary skills to perform the audit. Continuing education is required to improve and maintain skills.

S5 Planning   Successful audits are the result of advance preparation. Proper planning is necessary to ensure that the audit will fulfill the intended objectives.

S6 Performance of Audit Work   This standard provides guidance to ensure that the auditor has proper supervision, gains the correct evidence to form conclusions, and creates the required documentation of the audit.

S7 Audit Reporting   The auditor report contains several required statements and legal disclosures. This standard provides guidance concerning the contents of the auditor's report.

S8 Follow-up Activities   The follow-up activities include determining whether management has taken action on the auditor's recommendations in a timely manner.

S9 Irregularities and Illegal Acts   This standard outlines how to handle the discovery of irregularities and illegal acts involving the auditee.

S10 IT Governance   This standard covers the authority, direction, and control of the information technology function. Technology is now pervasive in all areas of business. Is the auditee properly managing IT to meet their needs?

S11 Use of Risk Analysis in Audit Planning   This standard provides guidance for implementing a risk-based approach in audit planning. Risk planning is used to determine whether an audit is possible. Auditors always weigh our level of competency to conduct the audit. Audit plans should be structured for the maximum return on investment when designing specific audits, aka *impact for the dollar spent.*

S12 Audit Materiality   Auditors must use evidence that portrays the most accurate story. The absence of controls or a potential weakness may cumulatively result in unacceptable risk to the organization. Ineffective controls, absence of controls, and control deficiencies should be disclosed in the audit report.

S13 Using the Work of Other People   It's impossible for the auditor to perform all the work alone. The work of other experts may be included in the audit, provided the auditor is satisfied with their competencies, relevant experience, professional qualifications, independence, and quality control. A scope limitation may be required in the final audit opinion if the other experts do not provide appropriate and sufficient evidence. An expert working in the same area as the one being audited should not be relied on.

S14 Proper Audit Evidence   Appropriate evidence includes the written procedures performed by the auditor, source documents, corroborating records, samples, and corresponding test results. Reliable evidence is based on its source, natural state, and authenticity. Audit evidence must be specifically identified, cataloged, and cross-referenced in the audit documentation, via auditor notes and working papers.

S15 Effective IT Controls   Working IT controls represent an integral foundation in the organization's overall internal control environment. IS auditors should monitor and evaluate the effect or absence of IT controls. It's necessary to help management understand the IT controls' design, implementation, and methods of improvement. The level of effective controls provided by outsourcing, or their absence, may help or hurt the organization.

S16 Electronic Commerce Controls   E-commerce allows the business to conduct electronic transactions with other businesses (business-to-business, or B2B) and directly to consumers (business-to-consumer, or B2C) over the public Internet. E-commerce requires the auditor to implement risk-based audit plans with data-gathering techniques for continuous assurances regarding the security and integrity of the environment. ISACA standard S16 excludes non-Internet-based private networks such as Electronic Data Interchange (EDI) and Society for Worldwide Interbank Financial Telecommunication (SWIFT).

 This chapter, as well as Chapter 3, "Audit Process," will thoroughly discuss all the objectives contained in ISACA's audit standards.

During the audit process, auditors will find clients are more receptive when your audit goals are linked to specific citations in the audit standards. You should aim to fill a known and defined point of compliance rather than provide a vague statement relating to something you may have read in a textbook. Don't make the mistake of trusting your job to misinformation, rumors, or free advice on the Internet. Each audit point should be listed in a requirements register citing the exact regulation (or contract) with a fully traceable reference to the exact page, paragraph, and line number of each item necessary for compliance. The lack of this level of detail indicates shoddy work or the likelihood of misrepresentation.

Most of the IT controls originated from demands imposed by a government agency. Security started in the military. Budgets and financial tracking were introduced by the banking industry. In fact, the first internal control in business was the budget. Since 1998, additional internal controls have been added each year. Figure 1.3 demonstrates the relationship of these various sources.

Specific Regulations Defining Best Practices

Let's review the basic purpose of several major regulations (see Figure 1.4). These are predominantly U.S. regulations with worldwide compliance implications due to global outsourcing.

Every regulation is designed to mandate the minimum acceptable requirements when conducting any form of business within that specific industry. The auditor must remain aware of two types of statements contained in all regulations:

Recommended (Discretionary)   These are actions that usually contain statements with the word *should*—for example, suggested management responsibilities, staffing, control mechanisms, or technical attributes.

FIGURE 1.3 Where IT control standards originate

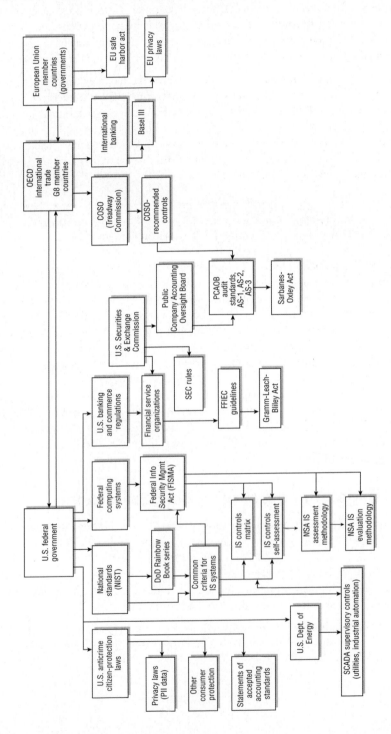

FIGURE 1.4   Sample of regulations defining best practices

Sample of Regulations	Intended Purpose	Application
SOX U.S. Sarbanes-Oxley Act of 2002	• Integrity in public corporations. • Mandates full disclosure of potential control weaknesses to audit committee. • Creates officer liability.	• 906 Act, signed attestation of integrity in financial statement. • 302 Act, signed attestation of full disclosure to audit committee every 90 days of any potential control weaknesses. Management commitment to find and remediate weaknesses. • 404 Act, recommended internal controls.
GLBA U.S. Gramm-Leach-Bliley Act 2002	• Minimum processing performance requirement for financial institutions, collection agencies, mortgage and real estate companies. • Privacy & data protection controls in banking. • Creates officer liability.	• Sets maximum service outages at 59 minutes for basic account functions. • Public disclosure of security breaches. • Mandatory verification of continuity plans by quarterly testing.
Basel III Basel Accord Standard III	• Risk management controls in banking.	• World banking consortium of the G-10 member countries to safeguard international banking.
PCI Payment Card Industry Security Act of 2005	• Information security requirements for merchants and card processors to reduce fraud and identity theft.	• More-restrictive data retention. • Prohibit storage of account numbers. Violation if IT system fails to comply. • Data destruction requirements.
FFIEC U.S. Federal Financial Institutions Examination Council	• Multiple government authorities. • Uniform principles, standards, and report forms. • Mandatory federal examination of financial institutions.	• Financial institutions. • Banks. • Non-banks, credit unions, & thrifts. • Subsidiaries. • Holding & edge companies. • Foreign banks and non-banks operating in U.S. jurisdictions. • Officers, employees, and certain individuals.
HIPAA U.S. Health Insurance Portability and Accountability Act of 1996	• Privacy for records in healthcare organizations and benefit managers. • Combat fraud, waste and abuse in healthcare.	• Insurance companies. • Insurance processors. • Healthcare providers. • Custodian of records. • Patient record handling.
FISMA U.S. Federal Information Security Management Act of 2002	• Security controls in all systems and information relied upon by the U.S. government. • Designed to unite Federal Information Processing Standards (FIPS).	• All U.S. government federal systems including military. • IT systems for U.S. critical. • Infrastructure in commerce.
SCADA U.S. Supervisory Control and Data Acquisition	• Security for automated control systems in U.S. critical infrastructure.	• Utility industry, power generation & transmission, water, gas, communications. • Research facilities. • Traffic control. • Manufacturing. • Other automated control.

Required (Mandatory)   These are actions that contain the word *shall*. *Shall* indicates the statement is a commandment of compliance. *Shall* is not optional. The auditor must remember that failing to meet a required Shall objective is a real concern. The regulations serve to protect the citizens at large.

Incredible justification would usually be required to prove the organization's actions do not fall under the jurisdiction of the regulation. The regulator will accept no excuses without a major battle, and on almost every occasion will win any potential disputes. Most juries are composed of individuals who will interpret claims by using a basic commonsense approach without detailed knowledge of a particular industry. Almost all excuses for violating the regulatory objective have failed in court battles.

Each organization in that market is required to meet the objective in spite of cost or revenue issues. In other words, the organization must comply even if it means that compliance will cause the organization to lose money. Failure to make a profit is not a valid exception from the law. The organization must strive to obtain compliance or can be forced to exit the industry with fines and sanctions. The auditor may need to consult a lawyer for advice upon discovery of significant violations.

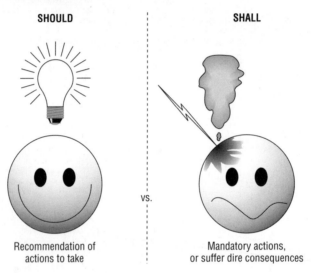

SHOULD

SHALL

vs.

Recommendation of
actions to take

Mandatory actions,
or suffer dire consequences

Audits to Prove Financial Integrity

IS auditors may be engaged in a variety of audits. The only fundamental difference between internal and external audits is auditor independence. Although the focus and nature of the audit may vary from time to time, your audit function and responsibilities will remain constant.

Government interpretation of laws and regulations has determined that financial audits and internal controls are interrelated. Medium-to-large businesses undergo a quarterly audit for their financial statements. The goal is to ensure that the executives are held accountable for the accuracy of financial reports. IS auditors are called upon to determine whether the systems used for financial reporting are secure and trustworthy. This connects the integrity of the financial statement to the integrity of the IS environment. You could not ensure the integrity of one without verifying the other.

If financial integrity problems are discovered, a common legal strategy is to claim someone else committed any offenses creating misrepresentation. However, a well-managed IS environment prevents and detects unauthorized modifications. It takes a series of strong controls to help prove who to hold accountable.

As an example, consider the requirements specified under SOX for public corporations. There are two critical reporting functions that management must fulfill under SOX:

- SOX Act section 906 statement, in which management attests to the integrity of financials and indicates that no hidden or questionable transactions exist

- SOX Act section 302 statement, in which management attests that full disclosure of the section 401–404 internal controls has been made to the audit committee, and that no deficiencies or weaknesses were withheld

Management must make their assertions of compliance without reliance on the auditor. The intention of these two statements is to bind management with liability. SOX is essentially a disclosure law. Its purpose is to provide government authorities with a method of ensuring criminal prosecution of corporate officers if management misrepresents the truth.

Auditor Is an Executive Position

Many people are envious of the CISA's position. They see nice cars, lunches with important people, expensive suits, and comfortable expense accounts. Nobody seems to pay attention to the humorous situation of six auditors sharing one folding table while sitting in a closet, balancing laptop computers with only one network jack and one telephone to share. Frankly, the auditor position grants you the luxury of being well-paid observers with professional benefits. Occasionally, your office and travel accommodations may not be the best. However, the reality is that most people look up to auditors with respect.

Your clients expect you to be authoritative and professional regardless of the circumstances. Your office is mobile, so you are depended on to handle decisions in the field. Your clients include the highest levels of management within an organization. Those clients expect you to assist them with your observations and occasional advice. You will deal with the challenges of providing advice in a manner that does not interfere with the independent audit. Remember the independence question raised earlier in this chapter?

Personnel at every level of your client's organization have an expectation of your appearance. You are going to be judged by your speech, mannerisms, clothing, and grooming. You should always wear professional attire to a level more formal than the attire of your client. Your neat and pressed appearance instills respect and confidence. Your courtesy of manner and speech dictates that you should use reassuring words. Any humor by the auditor should always be restrained and professional.

Understanding the Importance of Auditor Confidentiality

The client entrusts the auditor with sensitive information. A good auditor would never betray that confidence nor allow sensitive information to be revealed at any time. Any breach of confidentiality would be unforgivable. It is conceivable that during your audit, you may discover information that could cause some level of damage to the client if disclosed. You should prepare for the possibility of detecting irregular or even illegal acts that have occurred.

To protect yourself, you must exercise caution and least privilege in all activities. The concept of *least privilege* refers to providing only the minimum information necessary to complete a required task. It is the auditor's responsibility to implement security controls to maintain confidentiality. Auditors use working papers composed of reports, checklists, and spreadsheets that contain details plus secrets that need to be protected. The information you're privy to may be alarming to some, damaging to others, or trigger additional actions by a perpetrator.

To ensure confidentiality, the auditor should adopt the following operating principles:

- Sensitive information is the property of the owner and should not be removed from the owner's office by the auditor.

- The auditor should contact legal counsel for advice concerning confidentiality and laws that would dictate disclosure to authorities. You should follow basic principles of confidentiality at all times.

- Many auditors use automated *working papers (WPs)* during an audit. Spreadsheets and report-writing templates are common tools to increase efficiency. We refer to audit checklists, procedures, computer-generated output, templates, and databases as working papers. The next level of automation is entering our workplace to aid even the smallest auditor. This includes more-advanced database automation, evidence tracking, and report-generation tools. The data must be protected with access control and regular data backup. Make sure to back up your work. It would be unforgivable to lose your audit work and client data by failing to implement your own recommended controls.

- Every auditor should seriously consider using locking security cables and privacy viewing screens for laptops. You will gain respect by demonstrating your concern for maintaining confidentiality while protecting assets. The laptop could still be stolen with broken parts lying on the floor, but at least you would have some evidence that the theft was not completely your fault. At prior audit firms where I worked, these controls were mandatory for continued employment.

- A document file archive is created during each audit. The archive is subject to laws governing records retention. Every auditor is advised to leave all records in the custody of the client unless criminal activity is suspected. The client shall maintain sole responsibility for the safe retention of the archive.

Working with Lawyers

There is much discussion concerning who should hire the auditor. Should it be the client or the client's lawyer? At stake is the legal argument of confidentiality under attorney-client privilege. Most communication between lawyers and the client may be exempt from legal discovery (disclosure). But there is no such legal protection to hide fraudulent activities or conspirators involved.

We suggest that you ask the client. If necessary, the lawyer could issue a letter authorizing the auditor's work on the client's behalf. As an auditor, you have to be able to do your job without intimidation in order for it to be fair and honest work. This should be spelled out in the audit charter or your engagement letter. A good auditor will leave the legal issues to the lawyers and focus on performing a good audit. Truth often serves as an excellent defense.

Working with Executives

New auditors will notice that pressing attitudes in executive management may be different from what you expect. Executives are usually very concerned about the following basic issues:

Current Sales   This is the primary indicator of the health of a business. (In government circles, the same concern would be funding.) In a down economy, executives will be seriously focused on how to restore revenue. In executive circles, we regard our jobs as temporary—the job lasts only as long as we report good financial gains. It takes only a few months or two quarters of poor financials before investors will seek to replace the executives in charge, depending on the organization.

Operating Costs   Executives keep a watchful eye on operating expenses, capital purchases, payroll, and anything else that has a major effect on financial reporting.

Opportunity   Executives are watchful of the present market. What opportunities lay ahead that we should focus on exploiting? These opportunities will create interest in reorganizing the business, adding or reducing staff, and repurposing product lines or services to gain market share.

 Executive interest in compliance is based on supporting needs in the preceding three concerns: opportunity, sales, and reducing operating costs.

Most executives understand that legal interpretations usually immunize executives for business decisions made within the power of the organization charter, with proper authority and in good faith, using whatever information was available at the time, indicating due care was used. It is highly unusual to find any deep research was used in the initial decisions.

Working with IT Professionals

Most IT professionals can be divided into two categories: supporting roles (IT) or programmers (IS). Let's take a moment to focus on their viewpoints and concerns:

IT Supporting Roles   These individuals include help desk, user support, server administrators, and network administration. Their scope of influence is on purchasing, installing, and supporting off-the-shelf products. Therefore, the solutions they propose may follow a specific vendor's product line rather than consider other options. In the media business,

99 percent of all solutions will be based on using Apple computers because of the well-known advantages in the complex media production workflow. Generally, Microsoft users work in an office environment, where productivity is based on a simpler workflow of independent tasks: email, word processing, spreadsheets, and less-sophisticated presentations such as PowerPoint. Whether it's Apple or Microsoft Windows users, we are usually referring to commercial off-the-shelf software.

The IT viewpoint of system security is limited to functions such as enabling/disabling settings, running system scanners (antivirus, port, or services analyzer), loading vendor patches, making data backups, and following physical security procedures. IT support systems are primarily geared toward detecting attacks through "known" system vulnerabilities. Utterly rare is any defense in place against attacks on middleware. *Middleware* is every program or driver existing between the user interface and their data. Actually changing a complete series of default settings when installing programs is extremely rare by IT staff for fear of creating support headaches. IT people almost never run the custom installation nor should the auditor expect IT operations to delete unnecessary lines of program code from an open source software package. The highest security impact rests on the programmers.

IS Programmers Programmers actually decide on the security architecture while designing and writing the software application. This applies to both end-user applications as well as to operating systems. Building in-depth security can be a real pain to developers because the user may never even see it. For programmers, the security is predicated on the services and protocols they choose to use, port numbers, add-in functions by embedding smaller programs, and logic procedures. Advanced yet required security functions such as encrypted databases are dependent on complex key management, often requiring skills beyond the typical programmer.

Today the vast majority of breaches occur through exploiting design faults in software applications. Common hacker targets include embedded login ID with passwords stored in scripts for the programs to interact with other programs. These new attacks against overlooked or ignored program weaknesses are referred to as *zero-day* attacks because they use specialized types of circumvention not previously known to IT support staff.

Retaining Audit Documentation

In most cases, the archive of the integrated audit may need to be kept for seven years. Each type of audit may have a longer or shorter retention period, depending on the regulations identified during audit planning. If the client loses the files, that would be their problem and not yours.

When I hear that a client does not have a complete archive, the first sound in my head is *chi-ching*! I get to charge them extra money for re-creating the missing documentation.

During an audit, you will be preparing reports and documentation on laptops belonging to members of your audit staff. All members of the audit team should practice good physical security, including using physical cable locks on the laptops and locking up sensitive files each evening or when not in use. You must be wary of prying eyes and big ears. It is advisable for the audit team to implement a designated "war room" as a secure work location. Meetings and interviews with all other persons should occur in a different location that is also safe from prying eyes and ears.

Providing Good Communication and Integration

Have you ever felt nervous, threatened, or intimidated? What are your own feelings when you're told an auditor is coming to visit? Nothing launches a person's defensive attitude faster than the threat of an audit. A good auditor understands client expectations and realizes it is necessary to take time to speak with customers who may be curious or nervous.

It is a good idea to alleviate fear and anxiety by implementing the following objectives with your client:

- Establish a mutual understanding of the auditor's role. The auditor's job is to be a second set of eyes and ask the right questions.

- Establish mutual respect. To be successful, mutual respect must exist between the auditees and auditor. When you find a problem, do not place blame on a specific individual, because the very person you are speaking with could be the one who made the poor decision. Do not insult your client; just stick to the facts. You could say the following: "Based on the information available at the time, it may have looked like an acceptable idea; however, it is time for you to consider…" A good auditor is always respectful of other people and their feelings.

As a former auditee, I always appreciated an auditor who took the time to explain to me what the audit would entail. Please keep in mind that the auditee feels at a disadvantage. It will be helpful to simplify your explanations. You can measure your own performance by the general attitude toward you at the auditee site. You are doing a good job if the client shows interest and is forthcoming with truthful answers.

Understanding Leadership Duties

A good auditor spends time planning and setting priorities before commencing an audit. You will need to make plans on how you will be working with your own team. Develop the leadership style you want to implement. The days of Captain Bligh shouting orders "lest ye be flogged" are gone.

Let's look at the characteristics of good leadership:

- Your leadership style needs to clearly identify when your directions are mandatory and when they are open to feedback and comments. Team members should feel comfortable making comments and asking questions.

- A good leader will develop specific requirements for success and then share those plans. A good leader will strive for the buy-in and cooperation of the staff. You cannot lead those who do not want to be led or those who do not understand the objectives.

- An old and still valuable leadership lesson states that the staff holds the fate of their manager in their hands. The manager will be promoted or disgraced by the performance of their staff. If your people believe the work is good, you will usually get good results. If they do not believe in what you're doing, it will become a failure. Your personal opinion of good or bad is not the pinnacle factor. What matters is what the staff believes. True believers can generate exceptional results. Making time to educate your staff and demonstrating a willingness to take criticism are traits of a good leader.

The audit manager is responsible for creating clearly defined responsibilities and authority. There can be only one boss in order to prevent confusion. It is the responsibility of this one boss to make the hard decisions and answer for the choices made.

A regular schedule of briefings for both the auditee and the audit team are required. All client communication should be vetted before it is shared. *Vetting* is the process of evaluating and editing words to obtain the desired outcome.

Planning and Setting Priorities

Good auditing is the result of proper planning, not magic or luck. Every audit starts with an audit charter or engagement letter. The customer will define the focus and scope of the audit. It is the auditor's responsibility to gather pre-audit information and develop a schedule integrating the audit team functions with the customer's schedule. To be successful, a project management methodology should be used.

Let's look at a few of the auditor's responsibilities during the planning phase:

- Gaining an understanding of the customer's business

- Respecting business cycles (monthly, quarterly, seasonal, and annual)

- Establishing priorities

- Selecting an audit strategy based on risk and information known or observed

- Finding the people for your audit team

- Coordinating the logistics prior to the audit for resources, work space, and facilities

- Requesting documents (discovery requests)

- Scheduling people's time and availability

- Arranging travel and accommodations

- Planning for delays or nonperformance

- Considering rescheduling if recent downtime or risks warrant it
- Developing alternative strategies
- Developing a briefing schedule

NOTE   We will be spending a significant amount of time on the subject of audit planning in Chapter 3.

A professional auditor provides the auditee with a list of basic requirements and necessary resources well in advance of the audit team arrival. A good auditor also gives plenty of notice as to what they need to perform their job. This includes documentation requests for manuals, policies, and procedures that will be included in the subject of the audit.

NOTE   We are astounded by how many times auditors fail to request sufficient desk space and access to IT resources prior to an audit team's arrival. Never forget that it's the auditor's job to convey work requirements in advance. Proper planning is the hallmark of a professional.

Providing Standard Terms of Reference

The auditor needs to remain fair and objective when executing an audit. As an auditor, you should be consistent and courteous to your clients. *Standard terms of reference* can be developed to promote respectful and honest interpretation. As an auditor, you should try using the following terms, or something similar:

- Auditee claim/statement
- Present
- Not present
- Planned
- Tested (how)
- Not tested (why)
- Observed
- Verified (how)
- Not verified
- New requirement
- Requirement changed
- Requirement cancelled
- Failed to meet requirement

- Resource not available
- Insufficient evidence
- Access denied
- Personnel unavailable
- Lack of time

 Real World Scenario

What Exactly Does *Addressed* Mean?

A genuine pet peeve of many practitioners is the term *addressed*. Just what does it mean? Does it mean that someone is working on it? Does it mean that the client scheduled it for a future meeting and nothing is happening at this time? Does it mean that they wrote down the details and put it in an envelope with the name of the person who should look at it? Imagine how satisfied a mortgage company would be if you told them your payment has not been made yet, but it's in an envelope and addressed. That envelope is in your pocket, and you intend to mail it someday, but it's been addressed! A more specific explanation is required. Auditors should dig for better answers than the word *addressed*.

Dealing with Conflicts and Failures

A good auditor recognizes that some degree of conflict is inevitable and failures are always possible. IS auditors face the challenges of time, money, resources, and attitudes. These challenges may be with the client or with the auditor. The auditor must always demonstrate professionalism. An exceptional auditor will exercise common sense with a quick response. An exceptional auditor uses past experiences and makes the job look effortless, especially when dealing with change or conflict.

Identifying the Value of Internal and External Auditors

This Study Guide may imply an external auditor position. This is intentional in order to emphasize auditor independence. However, substantial opportunities exist for both internal and external auditors.

External auditors are paid to be independent reviewers for an organization. *Internal auditors* can add enormous value to an organization by providing ongoing efforts that help prepare the organization for an external audit. The internal auditor could approach the situation with an attitude of independence even though they will be unable to certify or attest to final results. Their expert audit skills could help guide design and remediation efforts at a substantially lower cost than that of their external counterparts.

In the internal auditor position, I would focus my efforts on reducing a four-week external audit to only ten days. Depending on the organization, it may take a few years to reach this noble objective. In the meantime, my auditing services will definitely be adding value to the organization through emphasis and cost reduction. Internal auditors can aid every organization by improving evidence collection.

Understanding the Evidence Rule

The audit world revolves around the collection and review of reliable evidence. Without evidence, a claim or assertion is unverifiable and an auditor cannot separate fact from fiction. Good evidence is intended to substantiate a claim or prove the existence of something you have interest in knowing.

A good auditor will use sufficient evidence to formulate their *auditor's opinion.* No opinion can be formed when you lack evidence of acceptable quantity, relevance, and reliability. Your job is to be a professional skeptic and demand proof in the form of evidence you can verify. The best evidence will need little explanation to interpret. When more judgment is required to understand the evidence, that evidence has decreased value. Your job is to render a score based on the evidence captured during the audit. Having no evidence would warrant a zero score.

Let's suppose you are looking for evidence concerning an existing corporate policy. First, you would look for the policy itself. Is it a paper or electronic document? Documents that cannot be located within a couple of hours could be assumed not to exist. Inability to find the policy would indicate it is not actively used. Now assume the client has found a copy of the policy. Was it easily accessible or covered with dust?

The next step is to verify that you have the current edition. Your audit charter may or may not ask you to review (test) the contents of the policy. Either way, you will need to verify that the policy is actually in use by the client's organization. You might conduct a random survey of workers, asking whether they can show you a current copy of the policy.

Next, you would ask questions to see whether the workers had actually read the document. However, existence of the policy alone does not meet the evidence rule. The auditee's score would improve as more persons demonstrate that they actually read the document.

It is not uncommon for an auditee to respond that the policy is on their website. You should ask the person to show you the link and open the page. You want to know if the client can successfully demonstrate an ability to find the document.

Another method would be to look for notes containing the minutes of meetings where the policy was discussed. It is rare for a policy to exist without some form of questions being raised or argued. Challenges to the policy may exist in emails. You may also ask for a person to perform the tasks related to the policy and observe their actions. Direct observation is powerful evidence. Simply ask the client to reperform a task whenever you want to cut to the heart of a claim. The words *show me* can invoke either fear or pride depending on the truth of the situation. Once again, no evidence equals no score.

We will discuss evidence again throughout this Study Guide.

Stakeholders: Identifying Who You Need to Interview

As an IS auditor, it is important for you to be cognizant of whom you should be interviewing, and how long those interviews should take. Every auditor will frequently face a time crunch due to the customer's schedule or other issues. You will need to pay particular attention to the value of the others' time. Consider the work outage created when you take someone out of their job role to spend time with you. Will it be necessary to backfill their position by providing a substitute during this time away?

Think for a moment of what it would cost the organization for a key executive to spend 15 minutes with you. This executive's time may be measured in personal compensation or by the revenue they generate for the organization. Top executives, such as the CEO, will have compensation packages that include both money and substantial shares of stock. Based on total compensation, the CEO may be receiving several thousand dollars per hour or more.

Former Walt Disney CEO Michael Eisner received total compensation equal to $27,000 per hour, which was equivalent to approximately 0.18 percent of the revenue generated under his leadership during the same time period.

The moral is that to justify 15 minutes of somebody's time, you better have something to discuss that is of greater value than that person's prorated value to the organization (greater than prorated revenue + compensation). Consider the cost for a meeting of high-level executives. You need to ensure that the time spent is relevant and remains focused on the audit objectives. The savvy auditor respects the value of a person's time.

Every system will have an inherent need for controls. The auditor needs to ensure that discussions occur with the correct individuals concerning appropriate controls. Three basic IT-related roles exist for every system: owner, user, and custodian. Table 1.2 shows examples of individuals with their associated roles and responsibilities.

TABLE 1.2   Responsibilities of data owner, user, and custodian

Role	Example	Basic Responsibilities
Data owner	Vice president	Determine classification Specify controls Appoint custodian
Data user	Internal business user Business partner Business client (web)	Follow acceptable usage requirements Maintain security Report violations
Data custodian	Database administrator Production programmer System administrator	Protect information Ensure availability Implement and maintain controls Provide provisions for independent audit Support data users

These individuals don't have to work in the IT department. On the contrary, these roles exist regardless of the individual department boundaries. If someone performs the function, the responsibility of the role applies to that person. No exceptions. If a person performs two roles, two sets of responsibilities apply. If someone performs all three roles, either it's a one-person operation or you need to have a talk about separation of duties and the value of their data.

Understanding the Corporate Organizational Structure

It is always helpful for the auditor to clearly understand the relationships and responsibilities at different levels of an organization. The auditor needs to understand who holds the authority. Let's focus on some basics that will be pervasive throughout this book.

Identifying Roles in a Corporate Organizational Structure

Businesses are focused on generating money for investors. There will always be some type of management hierarchy in order to maintain control. Government and nonprofit organizations will use a similar control hierarchy; however, the titles will be different. For government and nonprofit organizations, the term *mission objectives* would be substituted for the term *revenue*.

Figure 1.5 illustrates a typical business *corporation*.

FIGURE 1.5   A typical business organizational chart

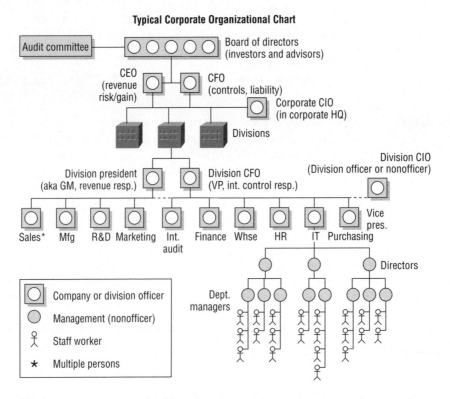

Let's start at the top of the diagram and work our way down:

Board of Directors   The board of directors usually comprises key investors and appointed advisers. These individuals have placed their own money at stake in the hopes of generating a better return than the bank would pay on deposits. Board members are rarely—usually never—involved in day-to-day operations. Some members may be retired executives or run their own successful businesses. Their job is to advise the CEO and the CFO. Most organizations indemnify board members from liability; however, government prosecutors will pursue board members if needed.

Audit and Oversight Committee   The members of the board will have a committee comprising directors outside of the normal business operations. Executives from inside the organization can come to the committee for guidance and assistance in solving problems. This committee has full authority over all the officers and executives. They can hire or fire any executive. Each audit committee has full authority with a charter to hire both internal and external auditors. Auditors are expected to discuss their work with the audit committee. An auditor has the right to meet in private to discuss issues with the audit committee once a year without the business executives present. If auditors discover certain matters that stockholders should be informed about, the auditor shall first bring it to the attention of the audit committee. Regulations such as SOX require that all significant weaknesses be disclosed to the audit committee every 90 days.

Chief Executive Officer (CEO)   The CEO is primarily focused on generating revenue for the organization. The CEO's role is to set the direction and strategy for the organization to follow. The CEO's job is to find out how to attract buyers while increasing the company's profits. As a company officer, the CEO is liable to government prosecutors. Corporate offi cers have signing authority to bind the organization.

Chief Operating Officer (COO)   The COO is dedicated to increasing the revenue generated by the business. This is a delegate in charge of making decisions on behalf of the CEO with assistance from the CFO. COOs are often found in larger organizations. As a company officer, the COO is liable to government prosecutors.

Chief Financial Officer (CFO)   The CFO is in charge of controls over capital and other areas, including financial accounting, human resources, and IS. Subordinates such as the CIO usually report to the CFO. As a company officer, the CFO is liable to government prosecutors.

Chief Information Officer (CIO)   The CIO is subordinate to the CFO. The CFO is still considered the primary person responsible for internal control. A CIO might not be a true company officer, and this title may bear more honor than actual authority, depending on the organization. An exception may be a CIO in corporate headquarters. The CIO has mixed liability, depending on the issue and the CIO's actual position in the organization.

President/General Manager   The president, sometimes referred to as the general manager, is the head of a business unit or division. As a company officer, the president/general manager is usually liable to government prosecutors. Regulations such as SOX encourage management to require all divisional presidents and controllers to sign integrity statements in an effort to increase divisional officer liability.

Vice President (VP)   The vice president is the second level of officer in a business unit or division. As a company officer, the vice president is usually liable to government prosecutors.

Department Directors (Line Management Position)   Typically directors are upper-level managers supervising department managers and do not have company officer authority. In large organizations, you may encounter a major-level director and minor-level director.

Managers and Staff Workers   Managers are responsible for providing daily supervision and guidance to staff members. Staff members may be employees or contractors working in the staff role. Managers and staff members are seldom held responsible for the actions of a company unless they knowingly participate in criminal activity.

Identifying Roles in a Consulting Firm Organizational Structure

Now we will look at the structure of a typical consulting firm. A *consulting firm* is a hybrid organization. Internal clerical and support functions are similar to those in a typical business. The consulting side of the firm uses functional management positions. The staff is allocated according to temporary project assignments. At the end of each engagement, the staff will be reallocated by either returning to the available resource pool or by becoming unemployed until the next engagement.

Figure 1.6 illustrates the organizational structure of a typical audit firm.

FIGURE 1.6   A typical auditing firm organizational chart

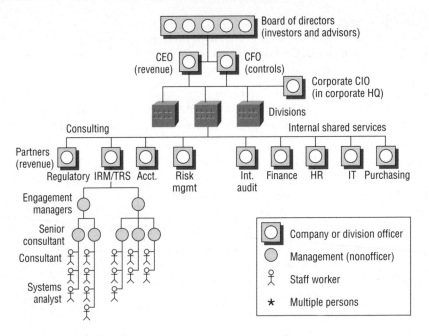

We'll review the structure here:

Managing Partner   A managing partner refers to a C-level executive in the consulting practice. This could be a position equal to a corporate president. Managing partners have the responsibility and authority to oversee the business divisions. Various partners in the firm will report to the managing partner.

Partner   A partner is equivalent to a divisional president or vice president and is responsible for generating revenue. Their role is to represent the organization and provide leadership to maximize income in their market segment. Partners are required to maintain leadership roles in professional organizations and to network for executive clients. Most partners have made financial commitments to produce at least $15 million in annual revenue along with supporting other business management functions. The partner and all lower managers are responsible for professional development of the staff.

Engagement Manager   This is a director-equivalent position with the responsibility of managing the client relationship. The engagement manager is in charge of the audit's overall execution and the audit staff. The engagement manager is responsible for facilitating the generation of new income opportunities from the client.

Senior Consultant   This is a field manager whose responsibilities include leading the daily onsite audit activities, interacting with the client staff, making expert observations, and managing staff assigned to the audit.

Consultant   This is a lead position carrying the responsibility of interacting with the client and fulfilling the audit objectives without requiring constant supervision. A consultant is often promoted by demonstrating an ability to fulfill the job of senior consultant or supporting manager.

Systems Analyst   This is usually an entry-level position. Often the individual is selected for their ambition and educational background and may be fresh out of college. Systems analysts perform some lower-level administrative tasks as they build experience.

Summary

In this chapter, we covered the pervasive foundation of knowledge necessary for you to be a successful IS auditor. Our goal is to provide basic auditor knowledge to help guide your decisions. The secret of a successful auditor is to understand who to believe and their motivation. A successful IS auditor will follow industry-accepted practices while dealing with conflict and change in a manner that generates admiration from their clients. It is your responsibility as an IS auditor to demonstrate effective leadership skills in the pursuit of your work. A good leader will take control of the situation to direct all effort toward fulfilling the desired objective.

In the next chapter, we will discuss proper organizational governance before diving into the audit process in Chapter 3.

Exam Essentials

Know the purpose of policies, standards, guidelines, and procedures.   Policies are high-level objectives designated by a person of authority, and compliance to policies is mandatory. Standards ensure a minimum level of uniform compliance to a policy, and compliance to standards is mandatory. Guidelines advise with preferred objectives and useful information in the absence of a standard. Guidelines are often discretionary. Procedures are a cookbook recipe of specific tasks necessary to implement a standard. Compliance to procedures is mandatory.

Know the ISACA standards governing professional conduct and ethics.   The auditor is expected to perform with the highest level of concern and diligence. Each audit should be conducted in accordance with professional standards and objectivity, and should implement best practices.

Understand the general purpose of the audit and the role of the IS auditor.   The purpose of auditing is to challenge the assertions of management and to determine whether evidence will support management's claims.

Understand an audit role versus a nonaudit role.   There are only two roles in an audit. The first role is that of the auditor who performs an objective review, and the second is the role of everyone else. A person cannot be an auditor and also involved in the design or operation of the audit subject.

Understand the importance of IS auditor independence.   It is unlikely that an auditor could be truly independent if the auditor were involved with the subject of the audit. Auditor independence is an additional assurance of truth.

Know the difference between discretionary and mandatory language.   In regulatory language, the word *shall* designates a mandatory requirement. The word *shall* indicates that there is no excuse for failing to meet the stated objective, even if compliance would cause a financial loss. The word *should* indicates a recommendation that could be optional, depending on the circumstance.

Know the different types of audits.   The types of audit are financial, operational (SAS-70), integrated (SAS-94), compliance, administrative, and information systems.

Understand the importance of IS auditor confidentiality.   The IS auditor shall maintain confidentiality at all times to protect the client. Sensitive information should not be revealed at any time. Your client expects you to protect their secrets whenever legally possible.

Understand the need to protect audit documentation.   The data must be protected with access controls and regular backup. Sensitive information is the property of the owner, and its confidentiality shall be protected by the auditor. A document archive is created during the audit and is subject to laws governing record retention.

Know how to use standard terms of reference.   The auditor should communicate by using standardized terms of reference to avoid misunderstanding or confusion. The standard terminology should be defined through a mutual agreement at the beginning of the audit.

Understand application of the evidence rule.   Audit evidence needs to be confirmed or verified to ensure that it is actually used in the production process.

Identify who the auditor may need to interview.   The IS auditor needs to consider the roles of data owner, data user, and data custodian when selecting persons to interview. Data owners specify controls, data users are to follow acceptable usage requirements, and custodians protect the information while supporting data users.

Understand the organizational structure.   Officers of an organization are usually persons with the title of vice president or higher, up to the board of directors. Department directors, managers, and staff workers are seldom liable for the organization, unless criminal activity is involved.

Review Questions

1. What is the difference between a policy and a procedure?

    A. Compliance to a policy is discretionary, and compliance to a procedure is mandatory.

    B. A procedure provides discretionary advice to aid in decision making. The policy defines specific requirements to ensure compliance.

    C. A policy is a high-level document signed by a person of authority, and compliance is mandatory. A procedure defines the mandatory steps to attain compliance.

    D. A policy is a mid-level document issued to advise the reader of desired actions in the absence of a standard. The procedure describes suggested steps to use.

2. What does *fiduciary responsibility* mean?

    A. To use information gained for personal interests without breaching confidentiality of the client.

    B. To act for the benefit of another person and place the responsibilities to be fair and honest ahead of your own interest.

    C. To follow the desires of the client and maintain total confidentiality even if illegal acts are discovered. The auditor shall never disclose information from an audit in order to protect the client.

    D. None of the above.

3. What are common types of audits?

    A. Forensic, accounting, verification, regulatory

    B. Integrated, operational, compliance, administrative

    C. Financial, SAS-74, compliance, administrative

    D. Information systems, SAS-70, regulatory, procedural

4. What is the difference between the word *should* and *shall* when used in regulations?

    A. *Shall* represents discretionary requirements, and *should* provides advice to the reader.

    B. *Should* indicates mandatory actions, whereas *shall* provides advisory information recommending actions when appropriate.

    C. *Should* and *shall* are comparable in meaning. The difference is based on the individual circumstances faced by the audit.

    D. *Should* indicates actions that are discretionary according to need, whereas *shall* means the action is mandatory regardless of financial impact.

5. Which of the following is *not* defined as a nonaudit role?

    A. System designer

    B. Operational staff member

    C. Auditor

    D. Organizational manager

6. Why is it necessary to protect audit documentation and work papers?

    A. The evidence gathered in an audit must be disclosed for regulatory compliance.

    B. A paper trail is necessary to prove the auditor is right and the auditee is wrong.

    C. The auditor will have to prove illegal activity in a court of law.

    D. Audit documentation work papers may reveal confidential information that should not be lost or disclosed.

7. What is the purpose of standard terms of reference?

    A. To meet the legal requirement of regulatory compliance

    B. To prove who is responsible

    C. To ensure honest and unbiased communication

    D. To ensure that requirements are clearly identified in a regulation

8. What does the term *auditor independence* relate to?

    A. It is not an issue for auditors working for a consulting company.

    B. It is required for an external audit.

    C. An internal auditor must undergo certification training to be independent.

    D. The audit committee bestows independence upon the auditor.

9. Which of the following is true concerning the roles of data owner, data user, and data custodian?

    A. The data user implements controls as necessary.

    B. The data custodian is responsible for specifying acceptable usage.

    C. The data owner specifies controls.

    D. The data custodian specifies security classification.

10. What is the definition of a *standard* as compared to a *guideline*?

    A. Standards are discretionary controls used with guidelines to aid the reader's decision process.

    B. Standards are mandatory controls designed to support a policy. Following guidelines is discretionary.

    C. Guidelines are recommended controls necessary to support standards, which are discretionary.

    D. Guidelines are intended to designate a policy, whereas standards are used in the absence of a policy.

11. Who should issue the organizational policies?

    A. Policies should originate from the bottom and move up to the department manager for approval.

    B. The auditor should issue the policies in accordance with standards and authorized by the highest level of management to ensure compliance.

    C. The policy should be signed and enforced by any level of management.

    D. The policy should be signed and enforced by the highest level of management.

12. The auditor's final opinion is to be based on which of the following?

    A. The objectives and verbal statements made by management

    B. An understanding of management's desired audit results

    C. The audit committee's specifications

    D. The results of evidence and testing

13. What is the purpose of ISACA's professional ethics statement?

    A. To clearly specify acceptable and unacceptable behavior

    B. To provide procedural advisement to the new IS auditor

    C. To provide instructions on how to deal with irregularities and illegal acts by the client

    D. To provide advice on when it is acceptable for the auditor to deviate from audit standards

14. How does the auditor derive a final opinion?

    A. From evidence gathered and the auditor's observations

    B. By representations and assurances of management

    C. By testing the compliance of language used in organizational policies

    D. Under advice of the audit committee

15. What is the difference between a threat and a vulnerability?

    A. Threats are the path that can be exploited by a vulnerability.

    B. Threats are risks and become a vulnerability if they occur.

    C. Vulnerabilities are a path that can be taken by a threat, resulting in a loss.

    D. Vulnerability is a negative event that will cause a loss if it occurs.

16. Which of the following statements is *not* true regarding the audit committee?

    A. Executives inside the organization oversee the audit committee and are responsible for keeping the committee busy working on compliance programs.

    B. Executives can be hired and fired by the audit committee because this committee is responsible for management oversight.

    C. The audit committee is composed of members from the board of directors. This committee has the authority to hire external auditors, and external auditors may meet with the committee on a quarterly basis without other executives present.

    D. The audit committee provides senior executives a method of bringing problems into a confidential discussion for the purpose of exploring a resolution.

17. The _____ type of audit checks attributes against the design specifications.

    A. Process

    B. System

    C. Compliance

    D. Product

18. Assessments and audits have several points in common. Which of the following statements provides the best description of an assessment compared to an audit?

A. Audits are more formal than assessments.

B. They are similar in nature; the difference is in wording.

C. Both provide reports that can be used for licensing purposes.

D. Assessment reports provide a high assurance of the situation.

19. The audit may uncover irregularities and illegal acts that require disclosure. The auditor is obligated to promptly disclose this information to the authorities.

A. True

B. False

20. Which of the following statements is true?

A. The auditee is the person running the audit, and the client is the subject of the audit.

B. The auditor is the person running the audit, and the client is the subject of the audit.

C. The client is the person setting the scope for the audit, and the auditor performs the work.

D. The client pays for the audit, and the auditor sets the scope of the audit that will follow.

21. How should the auditor assist in the remediation of problems found during the audit?

A. Take ownership of the issue and participate in designing the plan for fixing the problem.

B. The auditor should decide whether the problem is major or minor, and then advise the auditee with a specific solution after considering the impact to the business.

C. The auditor should help the auditees. The auditor can add value by defining the specific steps necessary for remediation of the problem.

D. The auditor should never take ownership of problems found. Auditors are encouraged to provide general advice to the auditee, including an explanation of what to look for during the audit.

22. Which of the following in a business organization will be held liable by the government for failures of internal controls?

A. President, vice presidents, and other true corporate officers

B. Board of directors, president, vice presidents, department directors, and managers

C. All members of management

D. Board of directors, CEO, CFO, CIO, and department directors

23. Which of the following is the best description of an ongoing audit program for regulatory compliance?

A. An audit is performed once for the entire year, and then repeated by using the same information for each successive year.

B. An audit may be automated by using audit program software.

C. An audit is a series of unique projects of short duration that add up to cover all the steps necessary for annual compliance.

D. An audit is a series of assessments performed by the auditee for the purpose of licensing and regulatory compliance.

24. What term simply means the right people of authority looked at the issue, made an intelligent decision, and took appropriate action?

A. Leadership

B. Corporate responsibility

C. Chain of command

D. Governance

25. Which of the following assurance methods is acceptable for external use, including licensing?

A. Independent audit

B. Assessment

C. External audit

D. Internal audit

Answers to Review Questions

1.   C. A policy is signed by the person of highest authority to ensure compliance by the members of the organization. Compliance to policies, standards, and procedures is mandatory.

2.   B. Accountants, auditors, and lawyers act on behalf of their client's best interests unless doing so places them in violation of the law. It is the highest standard of duty implied by law for a trustee and guardian.

3.   B. All of the audit types listed are valid except procedural, SAS-74, verification, and regulatory. The valid audit types are financial, operational (SAS-70), integrated (SAS-94), compliance, administrative, forensic, and information systems. A forensic audit is used to discover information about a possible crime.

4.   D. *Should* represents discretionary information in a regulation. *Shall* indicates that compliance is mandatory regardless of profit or loss.

5.   C. Every role except an auditor is a nonaudit role. Anyone in a nonaudit role is disqualified from being an independent auditor.

6.   D. The auditor may discover information that could cause some level of damage to the client if disclosed. The information could trigger additional actions by a perpetrator. In addition, the auditor shall implement controls to ensure security and data backup of their work.

7.   C. Standard terms of reference are used between the auditor and everyone else to ensure honest and unbiased communication. Without standard terminology, it would be difficult to know whether we were discussing the same issue or agreed on the same outcome.

8.   B. The auditor must be independent. Having a personal relationship with the organization being audited could result in a biased opinion. The business relationship is also an issue if the organization has influence over the auditor. The goal is to be fair, objective, and unrelated to the subject of the audit.

9.   C. The data owner specifies controls, is responsible for acceptable use, and appoints the data custodian. The data users will comply with acceptable use and report violations. The data custodian will protect information and ensure its availability. The custodian will also provide support to the users.

10. B. A standard is implemented to ensure a minimum level of uniform compliance. Guidelines are advisory information used in the absence of a standard. Compliance to standards is mandatory; compliance to guidelines is discretionary.

11. D. Policies should be signed, issued, and enforced by the highest level of management to ensure compliance by the organization. It is the responsibility of management (not the auditor) to implement internal controls.

12. D. The auditor is to be a professional skeptic who tests assertions of management and renders an opinion based on the evidence discovered during the audit.

13. A. This statement specifies that IS auditors are expected to fulfill their duties with the highest standards of honest and truthful representation. It is unacceptable to violate the fiduciary relationship with your client.

14. A. A final opinion is based on evidence gathered and testing. The purpose of an audit is to challenge the assertions of management. Evidence is gathered that will support or disprove claims.

15. C. Assets are anything of value. Threats are negative events that cause a loss if they occur. Vulnerabilities are paths that allow a threat to occur.

16. A. All of the answers except A are true. The audit committee is responsible for management oversight of the executives. The audit committee is usually composed of board members who provide executives a forum to discuss problems in order to rectify the situation. The audit committee can hire or fire anyone in the organization, usually focusing their attention on external auditors and senior executives.

17. D. Product audits compare design specifications (feature, size, color, markings, and so forth) against the attributes of the finished product. The CISA may use this type of audit during certification of custom-built software programs or prior to software release from a development company.

18. A. An assessment is less formal than an audit. The purpose of an assessment is to determine value based on relevance. Assessments have a lower value because they are not independent or a regimented independent audit.

19. B. False. The auditor should contact one level of management above where the suspected activity took place. If the problem involved managers responsible for internal controls, the auditor should report it to the highest level of management available, which is usually the audit committee. Auditors should never contact the authorities directly unless advised to do so by their own attorney.

20. C. The client sets the scope of the audit. The auditee is the target (subject) of the audit. The auditor designs the audit plan according to the client's scope and then performs the audit in accordance with published audit standards and procedures.

21. D. The auditor must never take ownership of the problems found. The auditor may provide general advice to the auditee and demonstrate what they are looking for during the audit. The auditee needs to design their own remediation plan. Auditors who participate in detailed remediation planning are no longer objective nor independent.

22. A. Officers of the organization will typically hold the title of vice president or higher. A CIO might not be a corporate officer, unless the position is located in the parent organization. A division-level CIO may or may not be a true corporate officer. Those holding the position of department director and below are seldom held liable by the government for internal control failure. A department director is a supporting manager to the vice president.

23. C. Projects are unique and usually of limited duration, for a fixed period of time with a definite start and stop date. The projects may be coupled together into a series of projects in order to fulfill an ongoing operational need, such as an annual audit program or perpetual quality program.

24. D. Governance means the right people of authority made a decision. Governance occurs at the top level of management to prevent anarchy. Decisions made at too low a level below the executives may be an indicator of lack of governance.

25. A. An independent audit is the only one acceptable for external use, including licensing. Internal audits usually lack the independence required because the internal auditor may be overly concerned about their job. Assessments are less formal than an actual audit. External audits could be limited in scope to only what the customer or vendor wants to see.

Additional CISA practice questions are available on the author's website at www.CertTest.com.

Chapter 2

Managing IT Governance

THE OBJECTIVE OF THIS CHAPTER IS TO ACQUAINT THE READER WITH THE FOLLOWING CONCEPTS:

- ✓ Defining governance and IT governance

- ✓ Known issues in the scope and implementation of controls

- ✓ Understanding how the reference standards are used to enhance governance

- ✓ Identifying who is responsible for implementing governance

- ✓ The fiduciary responsibility and security requirements that every organization must exercise to protect assets and information

- ✓ Defining the executive strategy, direction, and objectives

- ✓ Understanding the differences between Portfolio, Programs, and Projects Accepted management practices that are in use to optimize allocation of available resources

- ✓ How management establishes adequate internal controls for the IT organization

- ✓ What management needs to do to protect the critical dependencies of information systems in economic transactions

- ✓ How an organization demonstrates that it has exercised the best available management options to protect itself

- ✓ Using business process reengineering to fix missing and nonworking processes

For this chapter, we need to start with basic definitions of politics versus truth and ethical behavior. *Politics* is effectively defined as an agenda and often includes using deceit, lies, or willful omission. Self-serving personal agendas may be pushed ahead of the best interests of society or an organization. In contrast, truth represents honest and candid details without bias. Ethics are overriding principles for behavior in a moral, honest manner, doing the right thing for someone else ahead of your own agenda.

Now let's tackle the definition of *governance* by using truth and ethics as our foundation.

To govern means to direct and control the actions or conduct of others by using rules and controls set by an authority. Those persons in charge of governance are executive officers. This governing body of an institution, an organization, or a territory is held responsible for determining its policies and controlling its activities. These officers will decide the rules, precedent, law, or guiding principles to define acceptable conduct. Governance is no different for leaders of state (executive government) or leaders of business organizations (top industry executives). Each top executive leader is personally tasked with the responsibility of setting rules, communicating protective policies, establishing sanctions (penalties) for noncompliance, and specifically delegating explicit authority to someone responsible for enforcement of the policy. Although these leaders may delegate portions of work to achieve enterprise governance, they cannot delegate their responsibility for liability of failure.

Governance issues are proportional to the size of the organization. In a small organization, workers can easily communicate directly with the executives in charge. There is little doubt who is responsible for getting work done or any errors in judgment. Executives in small organizations seldom hesitate to accept responsibility. As an organization grows in size, the odds of misunderstanding or being disconnected from problems will increase. Unscrupulous executives might deny or attempt to dodge their responsibilities by claiming they are someone else's problem. The entire governance push primarily targets midsized to larger organizations, in which it can be difficult to tell exactly who to hold responsible or whose job is it to prevent, detect, and correct specific problems. The world is fed up with corruption and ineptitude of executive management, as mentioned in the examples in Chapter 1, "Secrets of a Successful IS Auditor."

Information Technology (IT) governance is a subordinate control mechanism. Business unit executives are the true leaders of the organization because of their ability to generate direct revenue. They specify the business rules to be used by their organization. Executive enterprise governance occurs at the level above the IT department.

Non-IT executives specify the level of integration and control an organization has over its information technology investment. No doubt information technology is pervasive in business today because software cuts costs by replacing people. Software is the new modernized work force operating without sick days, pay increases, or holidays. Without enterprise governance, it's impossible for IT to fulfill its portion of the control responsibilities. The intrinsic value of information technology must be fully incorporated into every aspect of the business, rather than separated into a distinct IT function. IT fulfills a role as the new domestic servant, no different from a house maid or gardener, performing the underlying tasks to keep things neat and orderly.

The level of IT integration will have a dramatic effect on how the organization defines its mission, achieves strategic goals, and communicates its fulfillment of the executive's vision of growth.

It's undoubtedly true a typical IT department is unable to explain the detailed operating priorities in the workflow of the business unit. This is why there's so much preaching by ISACA to gain an in-depth understanding of the business itself. Auditors can test this statement with a handful of simple questions:

- What are the top three revenue-generating products by actual name?

- What is the specific problem each product solves for the buyer?

- Who are the top five buyers for each of these top products?

- What is the average gross and net profit margin on each sale?

- What is the typical order size and delivery time for each of these top buyers?

- Can you identify the specific fulfillment role of each individual across all of the departments?

Now the maid/gardener analogy fits. Most domestic servants don't know the details of how their boss makes money either. Without a tool such as the balanced scorecard technique to define the specifics, it would be impossible for IT to deliver the proper support of step-by-step objectives in the detailed business unit workflow. This is why the non-IT executive level has to clearly understand details of the direction, objectives, and priorities for their business unit and then help their IT executives follow the details of this workflow to create a unified direction with an overarching list of IT objectives. The business unit workflow should define the IT scorecard.

The auditing of IT governance will include the highest levels of organizational management and must cross internal boundaries between divisions and departments.

Strategy Planning for Organizational Control

To be successful, management must define a strategy and provide for effective corporate governance. *Strategy* is defined as "an adaptation of behavior or structure with an elaborate and systematic plan of action." Another more specific definition of strategy is "to create a fundamental change in the way the organization conducts business." Obviously, the Second definition indicates that there are only a handful of people with that much authority. *Corporate governance* is often defined by ISACA as "ethical behavior of corporate executives toward shareholders and stakeholders to maximize the return of a financial investment." To clarify who is responsible for corporate governance, we could use this definition: "to lead by position or authority."

Three high-level management objectives to be verified by the auditor are as follows:

- A strategic alignment between IT and the enterprise objectives (formal strategy). Proper planning is required to deploy resources in the right place for the right reason. Management is always responsible for getting it done (corporate governance, preventive controls).

- A process of monitoring assurance practices for executive management. The senior executives need to understand what is actually occurring in the organization (staying involved by using detective controls).

- An intervention as required to stop, modify, or fix failures as they occur (corrective action). Everyone has some kind of problem. Management should be working to resolve the issue immediately rather than covering it up by hiding the truth.

Each organization needs to develop their directional strategy. What direction should the business take to fulfill its goals? The strategy selected progresses to focus on client needs and how to fulfill that market. Critical success factors are selected. Marketing initiatives are designed to generate revenue with plans for fulfillment to the buyer. Figure 2.1 demonstrates the path of organizational requirements in conjunction with the IT requirements.

FIGURE 2.1 IT alignment with organizational objectives

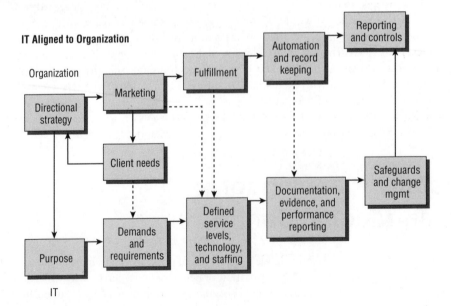

The revenue process entails a significant amount of administrative overhead and record keeping. The expectation in every business is to make money and not be hampered by a particular technology nor tied to a particular vendor.

The IT department is looking for a clearly stated purpose that IT is expected to fulfill. The department looks at the demands and requirements necessary to be successful. A structured service-level agreement can be generated with this data, complete with staffing and technology growth plans.

Technology plans have to fulfill a business objective. For instance, take Amazon.com. This very successful bookseller isn't necessarily hung up on using Microsoft Windows, Macintosh, or Unix. What the executives want to know is that all the money is processed and the product arrives on time to fulfill their customers' expectations. Systems management and auditing on the back end will verify that all their bookkeeping and internal controls are functioning effectively. In an industry-leading move, Amazon added same-day shipping as a $5 option on select stock for customers geographically located near the Amazon warehouses. The bookseller downloads the daily courier route schedules and then compares the pickup and delivery schedule to the buyer's address. Orders placed in the morning can arrive the same afternoon in select major cities. A same-day delivery option is automatically added to the shopping cart for eligible purchases. Amazon demonstrates excellent integration of the business and IT strategy.

The top side of Figure 2.1 is motivated by gains in revenue. Executives take calculated risks to exploit new opportunities for their business to make more money. Conversely, IT is expected to prevent service failures that hurt revenue. IT may also be expected to focus on activities that enable revenue and concurrent activities to prevent loss based on risk management planning. This can make it difficult to determine which problem or goal is the priority.

Auditors can gain insight by looking into the IT reporting structure. The CEO is solely responsible for revenue-generating functions, and other revenue functions may be delegated to an underlying chief operating officer (COO). IT functions reporting to the COO provide services that generate revenue. If the IT operation does not generate revenue, it's a support function (aka cost center) reporting to the chief financial officer (CFO). Refer to Figure 2.2.

The principal mechanism for ensuring IT alignment is an IT steering committee. The business unit executives identify operating challenges in their workflow, priorities, and desired technical direction.

FIGURE 2.2   Reporting structure demonstrates IT's purpose

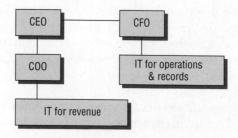

Overview of the IT Steering Committee

Most organizations use an IT strategy committee or IT steering committee. An *IT steering committee* is used to convey the current business requirements from business executives to the IT executive. The name of the committee is not as important as the function that it performs; a committee may perform more than one function. What's important is that the job of steering operations to business requirements is occurring.

Steering committees should have a formal charter designating the participation of each member. This charter grants responsibility and authority in a concept similar to an audit charter. An absence of a steering committee charter would indicate a lack of formal controls—a condition warranting management oversight review.

The steering committee is also discussed in Chapter 5, "Information Systems Life Cycle." Figure 2.3 shows the basic organizational structure of a steering committee.

The steering (or strategy) committee is made up of quite a few individuals. Each individual is required to have the authority to act on behalf of their department. These members are vice president–level or higher in the organization so they can help align the IT efforts to specific business requirements.

FIGURE 2.3   Organizational structure of a steering committee

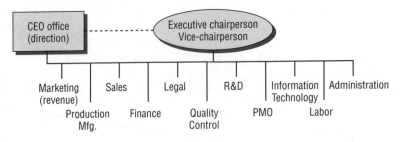

The committee is managed by an executive chairperson. The CEO is expected to provide directional guidance in person or via a representative, such as the COO, to identify targeted sources of revenue. Each member of the committee is expected to participate in focus discussions concerning business issues. On occasion, the committee may invite trusted observers or presenters to the meeting to increase awareness of a particular area.

After the business objectives are identified, the next step is to determine the business objectives for IT to fulfill. The steering committee sticks to high-level objectives rather than dictating technical detail.

Let's look at the representation necessary on the steering committee:

Marketing   Marketing should be represented on the steering committee. The purpose of all marketing is to attract buyers for the organization's product or service. Even if the organization builds the world's finest product, it will not matter unless a steady stream of buyers make a purchase.

Manufacturing/Software Development   The input from manufacturing or software development is required to align production efforts to sales efforts.

Sales   The sales function is to convert interested prospects from marketing campaigns into closed sales. Sales executives are interested in using technology to facilitate more sales. The cooperation of manufacturing and technology is necessary to assist the sales effort.

Finance   Financial guidance and budgeting skills are essential to optimize the organization's investment. Obtaining funding approval for projects would be difficult without the cooperation of the finance comptroller.

Legal   The executive from the legal department should ensure compliance to the law. Qualified legal counsel advises management in areas of uncertainty. Expert legal counsel should help protect the company from excessive liability or undue risk as a result of a control failure.

Quality Control   The quality process provides consistency in operations, manufacturing, and risk mitigation. A well-run quality process is a major contributor to the organization's survival. Failures in quality control can damage market image or lead to liability problems.

Research and Development (R&D)   The Research and Development staff is constantly working on creating new products and improving existing products. The R&D effort is focused on developing products that will generate revenue six months to two years in the future.

> Depending on the organization, R&D may be suspended during times of financial shortfall. The planned R&D budget would be applied to projects with a faster return or to pay past-due obligations. But never forget that R&D is your future; without new products, the organization will lose market share and die (or be sold off to a competitor).

Program and Project Management Office (PMO)   The head of the project management office, if one exists, should be on the committee to advise members using the organization's master list of all current and proposed project commitments across every department (aka master project register). Ideas presented by customers may require changes, causing the need for new projects to modify existing programs. Change is required to be successful in business. Remember that projects are temporary, while programs are ongoing for multiple years or even perpetual. We will talk more about this later in the chapter.

Business Continuity   The head of business continuity planning should always be in attendance. Business continuity is about supporting new product rollouts, maintaining revenue of high-profit areas, helping to shut down low-profit activities, and finally, aiding disaster-recovery efforts to salvage what's left over after a calamity. This person *must* be from the business unit with the authority of a vice president or major director and may possess the title of continuity manager or program manager. This person's job is to assess positive impact or help exploit opportunities presented in support of the organizational strategy. IT is never suited for this role because business continuity is about the business unit first and foremost. It's important not to sacrifice revenue continuity, investor continuity, client continuity, and continuity of key personnel in favor of shortsighted decisions.

Information Technology   The chief information officer (CIO) or vice president of IT listens to business ideas and objectives raised by committee members. This person acts as a liaison to facilitate the involvement of IT. The IT member may delegate planning and research activities to members of the IT organization. The CIO is expected to bring back observations and suggestions based on input from their technical staff.

Human Resources   The management of personnel grows more complex each week. Compliance with federal labor standards is mandatory. International organizations require special assistance that is beyond the expertise of most non-HR executives. Noncompliance can carry stiff penalties.

Labor Management   An executive representative from any labor organization, such as a labor union, may need to be involved in decisions concerning labor. This can be a touchy subject depending on the organization. Labor unions are losing power due to competitive pressure of globalization.

Administration   Office administration functions include bookkeeping, record keeping, and the processing of paperwork. Every executive would be handicapped without an administrative assistant.

The steering committee reviews ideas and opportunities to make recommendations. Those recommendations go to the board of directors for review. If the idea receives preliminary approval, resources are allocated for project planning. The steering committee executives perform a final review of comparing the total cost and benefit to determine whether the project is a "go" or "no-go."

If a go decision is reached, the organization specifies details, charters the project, allocates funds, commits resources, and moves the plan into execution. If the project is scheduled to be a repeating event, the project is assigned to program status. Otherwise, it is managed as a project with fixed time duration, and the assigned project team members will disband after project completion.

Figure 2.4 is a flowchart of the IT steering process.

FIGURE 2.4   The IT steering committee process

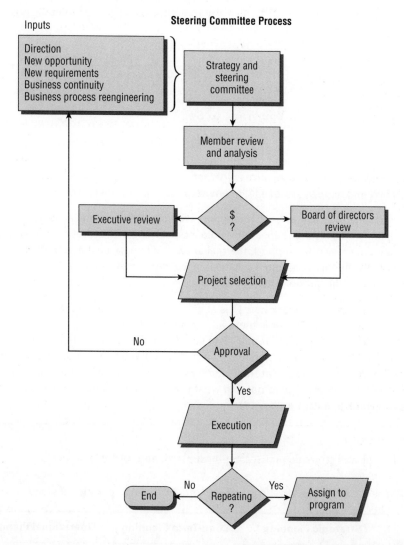

In strategic planning, plans generally run in a time frame of three to five years. A tactical plan is going to be carried out over six months to a year and may last two years. Monthly plans are no more than steps in the tactical plan. When an organization projects three to five years, it is really developing a strategy. Examples of successful strategies include the following:

- Run a streamlined, low-cost, and profitable airline operation like Southwest Airlines

- Offer the best market reach like eBay, connecting buyers and sellers with better advertising services than newspapers

- Provide competitive rate marketing like Progressive insurance

- Take over the music/movie rental distribution like Apple with iTunes
- Use the shipping model of FedEx to ensure that your package is absolutely, positively delivered overnight

---

 Real World Scenario

How Many Hamburgers Do You Want to Sell?

One of our famous awareness questions aims to help people understand the issues of strategy and focus: If someone wanted to be in the hamburger business, *what is the number one critical success factor that would be necessary for the hamburger business to be successful?* Interestingly enough, we have heard a lot of answers, and none of them were correct.

Claude Hopkins, the original master of marketing, would tell you that the answer would not be menu, nor would it be location, nor would it be staffing, nor secret recipe. Although each of those points may offer support, the real answer is hungry customers. If we could establish where the hungry customers are located, we could make money reselling cold cheeseburgers out of the back of a station wagon.

In that regard, it is important to ask how IT is aligned to the organization. Does IT seek to satisfy the hungry customers, or is there an expectation for the customer to wander over on their own? Does IT provide repair-level support or is it truly strategic, carrying the company to their most noble objective? The reality is that when you build the world's best mousetrap, customers don't naturally come knocking at the door. The reality is that someone will need to find the customer and what the customer wants. Value is simply a perception of benefit and desire.

Table 2.1 compares strategic plans, long-term plans, and operational plans.

TABLE 2.1 Differences between strategic, long-term, and operational plans

	Strategic Planning	Long-Term Planning	Operational Planning
Time frame	3 years +	1–3 years	1 year or less
Who does this?	Board of directors, CEO, COO, CFO	CEO, COO, CFO, VP, departmental director	Departmental director, manager, technical lead
Question	What business trends should we be exploiting? Should we expand or contract?	What are the major business components? What should we concentrate on now? What products and services are planned?	What specific tasks must be done to meet the long-term plan?

TABLE 2.1   Differences between strategic, long-term, and operational plans *(continued)*

	Strategic Planning	Long-Term Planning	Operational Planning
Output	General broad statement of what business the company is in	Financial goals Market opportunities Management organization Next review period	Assumptions for the period Changes needing to be made Production times Responsibilities Budget

Now that we have discussed the definition of strategic planning, it is time to get specific about the content of the executive strategy.

Using the Balanced Scorecard

To set forth a strategic goal without proper planning and meaningful definitions would be both negligent and reckless. One of the most powerful executive planning tools available is the *balanced scorecard (BSC)*. The BSC is a strategic methodology designed for senior executives.

Originally, the balanced scorecard was designed in a university environment to be used by business executives for reporting metrics. A very smart person once said, "The product's actual use will be invented at the customer site," meaning you can build what you want, but the customer will determine how it's used to solve their problem. It turns out that the most successful executives are using the BSC to define internal cause-effect relationships of smaller plans that run their business, not just to report metrics as originally conceived.

The scorecard approach converts organizational objectives of customer perception, business processes, employee growth and learning, and financial goals into a series of defined actions. We typically call these actions either *projects* or *programs*, but the BSC doesn't care. The BSC refers to projects and programs as *initiatives* (what you are doing).

Eight years ago, after a less-than-successful board meeting, I set a personal goal to learn how to apply the BSC tool. I searched all websites in the first 200 Google results and read every book available from Barnes & Noble. Plenty of people claimed knowledge of the BSC, yet consistently failed to demonstrate how the inner details actually worked. Frankly, none provided enough direction to make it work. I fell into the same trap as everyone else. It takes special training with firsthand experience to receive the benefits that this type of advanced planning tool offers. My biggest realization has been that the BSC is unique to each organization. The BSC reflects the objectives and desires of your CEO. ISACA just wants you to know it exists. I teach my students in our seminars how to use it, exceeding the exam study requirement. So this section is my short brochure-level introduction on how it works. I use the BSC constantly each week and stand behind all my statements with supporting evidence.

When properly implemented, the scorecard concept enforces better alignment by defining details of strategic business objectives. Overused terms such as *world class* and *customer driven* are broken down into low-level definitions that the staff can actually implement. Using the scorecard should eliminate activities of little or no strategic value.

The scorecard methodology is common outside the IT environment. However, information technology can benefit from using the balanced scorecard if it is implemented by the CEO or CFO. To be effective, the scorecard must be driven from the top down.

Table 2.2 illustrates the four scorecard perspectives and matching emphasis area of the BSC methodology. For example, the finance perspective will place emphasis on cost control and company profits.

TABLE 2.2   Balanced scorecard methodology

Perspective	Emphasis
Customer	What is our market image?
	What makes us different?
	How should the organization appear to the customer?
	Why would a client want to do business with us?
Business process	What is our mission?
	How can we create a genuine competitive advantage?
	What are our critical success factors?
	What are the key performance indicators?
Financial	What are the financial goals?
	What are the shareholder goals?
	Are we a cash cow or a pioneer?
Growth and learning	What information do we need to beat our competition?
	What are the organization's growth plans?
	How will we keep or obtain the knowledge and workers necessary to support the organization's plans?

A small number of organizations are successful at using the balanced scorecard approach, while many fail. The BSC will fail if run by anyone under the title of CEO or COO because it's all about integrating functions of the business unit workflow. Remember, your top leader sets the business rules, and everyone else follows.

BSC is considered an exceptional tool for conveying objectives with cross functional dependencies. Several executives referred to BSC as old news. Implementation failure, resistance or flawed adoption, is due to one of two scenarios:

- Division executives could not agree on the business direction or priorities. Their self-directed business interest is separated from the organization's common goal.

- The executives had a lack of BSC training, misunderstood the objective of breaking department boundaries or reallocating department budgets to other areas, and possessed little BSC experience.

The advantages and disadvantages of using the scorecard methodology are as follows:

Scorecard Advantages   The BSC promotes a focus on the specific if-then linkage between different objectives and their budgets. The goal is direct support of organizational objectives. If you change funding or strategy on a linked initiative (project or program), the effect can be seen rippling through the scorecard. We are actually using the BSC to create well-defined articulated strategies.

All the initiatives (project or programs) are linked into a complete process flow that ignores departments and traditional boundaries. Never again will strategy be determined in one meeting and budget determined somewhere else.

When fully implemented, none of the departments will have their own budget to spend. The result is project-based, program-based staffing. It does not matter whether the department function is internal or external.

Each department pledges its level of support to a defined strategy initiative. The corresponding budget money is issued to the department, provided it is meeting its delivery goals. No support of the linked project means no money, no people, and no job. This blocks waste and uncovers personal agendas.

Each employee works from a personal scorecard created by cascading the BSC down into specific execution tasks. The combined effect of the personal scorecards will achieve their department's objective. Achievement of the departmental objectives will help fulfill the organizational objectives.

Scorecard Disadvantages   The scorecard requires a careful selection of initiatives by the CEO or CFO. It is reported in executive trade journals that metrics derived from a committee will consistently fail. Interestingly, observations indicate that executives unwilling to adapt to the scorecard methodology may lack a genuine interest in being a team player or may possess more interest in building their own empire within the organization. Politics can kill the BSC unless the sponsor eliminates the people creating political conflict. Strong sponsors will not hesitate to remove obstacles.

The balanced scorecard can contain whatever you need to define. It is flexible in having three, four, or five perspectives depending on what your executives decide is needed. The typical approach of four perspectives is shown in Figure 2.5. Notice how the different initiatives are linked into a complete process.

There are several secrets involved in making the scorecard generate true results. Every balanced scorecard is unique to the organization. Beginners and politically motivated executives using a BSC will most likely encounter at least 20–30 failed attempts, which end in frustration, before it begins to show a glimmer of success. The detailed notes of the balanced scorecard will uncover mistakes, overlap, and errors just as writing out math problems in longhand did when you were in grade school. Keep trying, because the benefits will far outweigh the effort. Each failed attempt is simply an indicator of an existing relationship problem or definition problem. Problems need to be fixed one by one before you can build an effective linkage. Often this includes retreating a few steps to adapt for changes as they are discovered. That's part of the magic in using BSC. The strategy becomes more defined with each pass, forcing each problem to be fixed before it can effectively function inside the overall strategy plan.

FIGURE 2.5   Balanced scorecard with four perspectives

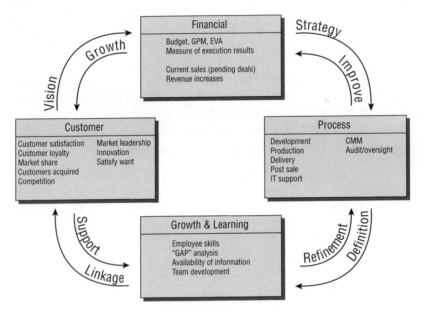

Every planning exercise brings more clarity as you roll the linkages forward and backward to fine-tune the details. It's like using algebra to solve a problem and then using calculus to prove you actually did solve the problem by returning back to zero where you started. Now once the strategy works forward and backward, you will have an incredibly valuable diagnostic tool with excellent definitions exploding all the details into specific action items. Initiatives (projects or programs) are now selected, scoped, and funded based on which ones generate the highest return on investment (ROI).

What if your project or program doesn't generate revenue? Simply put, it would be linked with a function that is generating revenue and used to calculate the combined operating costs. For example, security costs in a bank are coupled with the profits the bank generates. The final ROI estimate is used to decide whether that area of the business is expanded or shut down. What if you make more money from brokering mortgages? You may switch from being a full-service bank into focusing on mortgages. The final goal is to find the highest-earning ROI and quit wasting resources on marginal or losing activities. Consider two examples of changes in priorities to pursue a better ROI:

- Executives at AMR operate American Airlines and spun off Sabre reservations as a separate company. One reporter asked which was more profitable. The response was that American Airlines' business need created Sabre, yet Sabre's reservation system is more profitable with a better ROI.

- Blockbuster video rentals had to change its business direction as revenue fell off because of stronger competitors. The younger generation considers it outdated to drive to a Blockbuster store. iTunes or Netflix online delivery is now viewed as the better choice in our highly connected Internet world. Blockbuster is trying everything to stay in business, including game rentals, and closing as many stores as possible while switching to online video distribution. No doubt this upset old business priorities.

During my travels to teach this course, I have heard countless stories of failed BSC initiatives, often stemming from executives of different divisions not being able to agree on the primary strategy nor objectives. Inevitably, there is a disagreement concerning the future direction of the organization. This often leads to each group leaving to write their own dysfunctional BSC, which inevitably fails. Without the chief executive to set crystal-clear direction, the politics of which division to acquire, expand, sell off, or shut down will block any progress. A single BSC will have only one, two, or possibly three defined mission objectives. The second or third objective will be a supporting subset of the top objective. The best BSC will not be politically popular with everyone, and it's not supposed to be a popularity contest. The objective is to cut costs by eliminating everything outside of primary workflow, kill political empire building in departments, maximize efficiency, and increase profits.

The balanced scorecard fundamentally changes how employees prioritize and report their work. Activities and projects are selected on the basis of the value created under established metrics. This also results in a change in how the employee is evaluated. It is essential that management and staff receive proper training prior to implementation. Just remember, without full buy-in at all levels, the balanced scorecard is likely to fail.

 A strong sponsor can drive successful BSC implementation by removing or replacing anyone who is an obstacle.

IT Subset of the BSC

The IT balanced scorecard should be a subset of the organization's overall balanced scorecard. IT is a critical follower, not a business unit leader. Therefore IT must follow the business unit scorecard first, then fill in the supporting points which relate to IT functions. When properly implemented, the scorecard methodology supports the highest-level business objectives.

As a CISA, you need to understand how the balanced scorecard can be applied specifically to information technology. ISACA describes the scorecard by using three layers that incorporate the more common four perspectives (customer, business process, financial, and growth and learning). The three layers for IT scoring according to ISACA are as follows:

Mission   Develop opportunities for future needs. Become the preferred supplier of IT systems to the organization. Obtain funding from the business for IT investments. Deliver effective and cost-efficient IT services. Often the mission statement sounds like an advertising slogan. In reality, the mission statement should be less of a political statement and more specific in definition. Therefore, each mission statement needs supporting details contained in the strategy definition. The goal of the BSC is to convert vague mission statements into clear-cut action items that the staff can understand and then implement.

Strategy   Common platitudes include the following: Attain IT control objectives. Obtain control over IT expenses. Deliver business value through IT projects. Provide ongoing IT training and education. Support R&D to develop superior IT applications. All these sound great, but they need significantly more detail before they can be implemented.

The only objective that matters is IT contribution to bottom-line profitability through reduction of operating costs or increasing marketing speed and accelerating product delivery. Using the BSC can help define the lower-level initiatives necessary to make the mission functional. Far too many executives fail to provide a well-defined, articulate strategy. A definition is needed that maps detailed cross-coordination rolling across departmental boundaries. Strategy should put the user's workflow ahead of technology.

Metrics   Develop and implement meaningful IT metrics based on critical success factors and key performance indicators. We'll cover more about metrics in Chapter 6, "System Implementation and Operations."

The balanced scorecard method is a wonderful tool for the auditor to gain invaluable insight into the organization. A simple BSC exercise will uncover the organization's critical path while illuminating its ROI dependencies.

Decoding the IT Strategy

Executive management usually provides a vague objective for their IT strategy, hopefully to fulfill their business objectives. It's a familiar story of two possible outcomes. One occurs because the executives do not actually understand the complete details in their workflow but have seen bits and pieces of what they desire through news articles, vendor briefings, and spotty advice. IT is left to cobble all the bits and pieces into some type of disjointed Frankenstein monster with a never-ending series of control problems, spiraling costs, and user dissatisfaction. Ongoing user headaches will persist through various workaround contortions necessary to get the job done. But it doesn't have to be this way.

The second outcome involves a more detailed approach, but frankly it's still rare to find. Although everyone claims to do this, in reality exceptionally few do it right. Done correctly, executives will charter a special project outside of the normal organizational structure. The project mission is to analyze the end-to-end workflow necessary to fulfill their business objective. The project would produce an accurate record of the following details:

- Complete step-by-step business unit workflow for each individual revenue item (product or service)
- Written identification of the most likely, specific risk associated at each step in the workflow (step 1, risk 1,2,3)

- Written identification of known event triggers (step 1, risk 1, contingency trigger for risk 1)

- Written identification of known contingency alternatives (step 1, risk 1, trigger, contingency)

- Reduction of steps or alternatives to produce bottom line profits with less overhead, less handling

No job is sacred, and no department is essential. The focus is on identifying the absolute minimum steps necessary to get the job done in the correct order and how the system software should be doing it without regard to current technical capabilities.

This is where true strategy lives, because the purpose of any long-term strategy is to specify the future direction and identify specific obstacles to conquer. This is where business process reengineering and the balanced scorecard fit. But the auditor's real question is whether the client accomplished the hard work of discovery or just took a shortcut into a commodity product offered by vendors such as Microsoft or Oracle.

 Out-of-the-box enterprise software usually turns into a costly, disjointed nightmare unless a complete fitness-of-use study is conducted before entering into a letter of intent or contract. This study should focus on your unique business workflow.

The IT strategy should be specified from the top down by the CEO or COO. Remember, the goal of governance is to hold the executives at the top responsible for decisions and all of the consequences. The strategy is then formalized into a policy and communicated throughout the organization by the highest-ranking executive of the organization. Figure 2.6 shows the executives involved at the strategy level (in policy making).

You should assume that the executives have already gone through an informal process of gathering requirements. Their strategy may be to insource or to outsource. However, one of their most important questions is to determine how the strategy will be funded. Each of the following methods of funding bears unique advantages and disadvantages:

Shared Cost   It is common for the bulk of IT costs to be allocated as a shared cost across all members of the organization. This method is relatively easy for the finance department to implement. Unfortunately, it may lead to user dissatisfaction. Some users and their managers may feel that they are paying for a service that is not received.

Charge-Back   Individual departments receive a direct charge for system use. This is designed to be a pay-as-you-go style of accounting for IT expenses. Charge-back schemes are quite effective if properly implemented. Mainframe charge-back schemes are particularly effective for usage billing.

Sponsor Pays   This last type can present a significant challenge to IT governance. The project sponsor pays all the bills. Unfortunately, it creates two common problems. The first problem is that the sponsor purchases extra capacity that is not sanctioned or guarded by IT. As a result, another project effectively steals the extra capacity investment without paying for it. The second problem is that in exchange for funding the project, the sponsor may demand more authority over decisions. This method is notorious for creating shadow support organizations.

Additional conflicts usually occur with IT management in disputes over budget responsibilities, not implementing all the proper controls, lack of effective monitoring, and improper reporting of failures. The best way to solve the conflict is by fully enforcing separation of duties. The sponsor still pays for the project, while the operating decisions will be shared between the project owners, users, custodians, internal audit, and executive oversight. Authority of the sponsor is reduced.

FIGURE 2.6   Executives involved at the IT strategy level

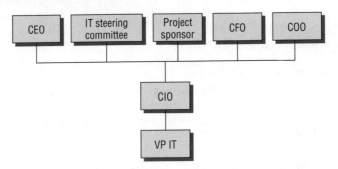

The auditor should remain aware that a shadow organization (duplicate function under a different manager) represents a genuine control failure. This lack of integration represents an ongoing concern in the areas of cost control, duplication of effort, or a political difference in both direction and objectives. The proper solution would be assignment of dedicated resources coordinated and reporting to the same functional manager serving the entire enterprise. Allowing shadow organizations to exist should be reported as failure in executive governance against the top executives (CEO, COO, CFO).

Shadow organizations indicate willful distrust between executives. Usually the basis of shadow groups is a self-centered agenda that creates a design contributing toward a functional control failure.

Specifying a Policy

Executive management has the responsibility of setting goals. Each goal should be supported with a defined set of objectives. A strategy should be in place to achieve those objectives. The next step is to specify a policy to communicate management's desires to the subordinates.

Every policy should be designed to define a high-level course of action. The purpose of the policy is to inform interested parties of a chosen solution. A well-designed policy is based on a statement by management of the policy's importance. The statement explains how this particular policy supports a business objective. The policy is signed by the most senior person available to prove authorization.

We discussed the role of policies, standards, and procedures in Chapter 1. Table 2.3 should serve as a memory refresher concerning the role of policies, standards, and procedures.

TABLE 2.3   Strategic role of a policy

	Strategic	Tactical	Operational
Goal objective	X		
Policy	X		
Standard		X	
Procedure			X

Successful policies are issued from the top down to all subordinates. The policy may designate a department director to create a standard in support of the policy. The final procedures are generated from the workers at the bottom of the hierarchy. Common procedures are intended to be implemented from the bottom up. The procedure is a lower-level person's response in support of the executive's policy.

Types of Policies

Policies are designed to inform interested parties about a particular situation. The policy may be advisory, regulatory, or informational:

Advisory Policy   An advisory policy explains the condition to be prevented by the policy and provides notice as to the consequences of failure. The interested party may be an employee. The subject could be acceptable use of the Internet. In the Internet example, the advisory mandate is to either comply or be fired.

Regulatory Policy   The term *regulatory* indicates that this policy is mandated by some type of law. All organizations under the jurisdiction of the regulation are expected to comply. Failure to comply will result in criminal liability.

Informational Policy   Informational policies inform the public of the organization's operating policies. Examples include the customer privacy policy, the customer refund policy, and the customer exchange policy.

IS auditors should be aware that undefined policies indicate a lack of control.

After the strategy is selected and the goals are set and the policy is created, it's time to begin the planning process. In planning, the strategy is broken down into usable definitions to move it closer to reality. Let's start by looking at the difference between portfolio management, program management, and project management.

Portfolio Management

A collection of assets of value (aka investments) is known as a portfolio. Examples include real estate property, treasury bonds, corporate stock ownership, gold bullion, title to patent rights, and other intellectual property. In the movie business, a studio's portfolio might include their own helicopters with cameras, contracts with some of the biggest celebrities on the planet, private sets with streets lined with full-size buildings to look like a picturesque town, and cable distribution contracts with Sony, HBO, and DirecTV. Just remember, a portfolio is a collection of assets even if it's no more than a shoebox full of Mickey Mantle baseball cards. These assets may be traded when deemed necessary by executive management in response to changes in the market.

Program Management

Program management (aka programme management) refers to ongoing activities necessary to support continuous operation. Programs are intended to last for as long as the organization is interested in doing business. The program is usually managed by an executive vice president (EVP) who will be responsible for sustaining its operation. A few examples of sustaining programs include the following:

- Marketing
- Human resources, including payroll
- Bookkeeping
- Facility maintenance
- Regulatory compliance (via continuous audit)

A continuous challenge to program management is the constant change that naturally occurs. Programs are intended to last longer than a person's career. This means the program is constantly trying to adapt to new circumstances. The program will have an ongoing need of hiring, training, and retaining personnel to keep it running. As a result, the program will usually generate the need for several projects. For the last two decades, project management has replaced middle management as the agent of change.

Project Management

Projects are temporary endeavors that operate outside of the normal organizational structure. The project manager brokers any request that crosses the boundary of normal business. The project is a set of activities that will be used to create, adapt, or destroy assets of the organization. Modifying a computer program to be Payment Card Industry (PCI) compliant in its credit card handling is good example of an adaptation project. Demolishing an old building to make room for a new project such as a parking lot is an example of destroying former assets. The same could be said for shutting down and dismantling an outdated computer system. Examples of common projects include the following:

- Development of new products
- Construction
- Repairs
- Updates
- Individual audits

Project management is a risk-reduction method. There are substantial differences in the effort and rigor of planning large enterprise capital projects versus the smaller operational projects of departments such as IT and internal audits. Most of the IT projects are small, within the same department, and their project manager really doesn't have much authority. A department-based project manager is usually expected to also perform the work; therefore, the emphasis is on how fast the work can be performed. It's not about full planning if the project manager is also the worker. Conversely, enterprise capital projects will normally be run by an executive project manager or project management office (PMO) who direct others to perform the work.

Project Management Office

Higher stakes in business include greater risk of failure with bigger benefits for success. Most professionals in operational roles do not have the specialized training necessary for complex cross-departmental planning. The role of the project management office is to provide mature services in support of individual project managers. A good analogy would be to consider the services of FedEx Office or a well-equipped executive suite. These types of facilities have specialized equipment, expert personnel available, and reference material a typical professional would not have on hand at their desk.

Let's say you have received a project to relocate a branch office across the country. The project requirements include a time estimate and the proposed budget for review by the finance department for presentation to the board of directors. So where would you begin? This is where the project management office comes into play. Within a mature PMO will be a pool of technical specialists available to work on your project for an internal charge-back fee. These specialists will know how to run advanced project-planning software, including how to set up a chart of accounts for accruing costs to the correct cost center of each individual item.

Mature PMOs have a *master project register* of all projects in the organization, plus access to historical data of other projects to aid in estimating realistic forecasts of both time and cost. One of the PMO managers or quality assurance assessors will help you walk through the details of your plan to increase the odds of success. A well-run, mature PMO will even have sets of professional presentation templates you can use to really look good.

Table 2.4 provides a quick comparison of the differences between using a PMO and doing it all yourself.

TABLE 2.4   Comparison of PMO to DIY project planning

	Mature PMO	DIY
Centralized reporting (across departments)	✓	
Advanced project-planning software	✓	Maybe
Planning software expertise and assistance	✓	Rarely
Certified budgeting software with chart of accounts for cost accrual/billing	✓	
Historical performance data from variety of past projects	✓	Unlikely
Industry estimating database	✓	
Skilled personnel to use, borrow, or rent	✓	
Trained and experienced project managers	✓	Maybe
Planning assistance	✓	
High-quality presentation templates	✓	
Access to executives and managers across departments	✓	Unlikely
Master project register: Coordination of all projects across the enterprise (planned, running, completed)	✓	
Frustration level	Low	High
Size and complexity of projects	All	Department only

Usually the PMO is staffed with personnel holding certification as either a project management professional (PMP) or PRINCE2 practitioner. I hold both certifications at the instructor level and will attest they are quite beneficial to each other. PMP is focused on the activities of the project manager, while PRINCE2 targets the organizational aspects of the executive board and project sponsor. Obviously. as shown in Table 2.4, a mature, well-equipped PMO is a fantastic organizational asset.

Project Management versus Quality Models

A typical IS audit has many elements in common with projects and project management. These two disciplines are definitely related. To excel in auditing, you must excel at project management. Your success lies in the ability to define all the abstract components necessary for the project to be successful. Several of the common management models are shown in Table 2.5. The table includes the focus levels of the Capability Maturity Model (CMM), which is discussed later in this chapter.

TABLE 2.5 Project management and quality-control models

Source	Focus	Structure
Project Management Institute (PMI)	Projects (international) Unique or repeating (Targets CMM levels 0–3)	42 process areas Focus on PM duties and techniques, is abstract not a methodology
PRINCE2 (P2)	Projects (APMG-UK) Unique or repeating (Targets CMM levels 0–3)	9 process areas Focus on organizational process methodology
Total Quality Management (TQM)	Quality control Repeating process control (Targets CMM levels 3–5)	Zero-defects program Statistical process control Walter Shewhart (1931) also associated with Phillip Crosby and W. Edwards Deming
Six Sigma	Quality control Repeating process control (Targets CMM levels 4–5)	Reduce defects from 16,000 to 3.4 per million Motorola derivative of TQM for commodity-based mass production
ISO 9001	Quality control Repeating process control (Targets CMM levels 3–5)	Latest revision combines all ISO 9000 quality standards International derivative of TQM

Now let's get into managing a project. For simplicity, we will use a summary reflecting the Project Management Institute processes. This brief overview should be more than enough to fulfill your CISA study requirements. I will caution that PMI identifies 42 processes but still lacks a true step-by-step implementation methodology. If you execute all of these techniques in the singular manner, the project planning will take forever or just won't get done right. A project manager with any real authority will be dedicated solely to planning and supervision of work, while hands-on activities will be performed by workers assigned to the project.

In this section, you will learn some basic information about using the *PMBOK* Guide Fourth Edition standard to help you manage your audit. It would be a very good idea to acquire additional knowledge about project management and how to manage specialized projects. We suggest two sources for additional information:

- CertTest Training Center (www.certtest.com)—the company we work for—offering training courses in project management. CertTest is a PMI global Registered Education Provider (REP). In addition to CISA training, we are expert specialists teaching you a complete step-by-step implementation recipe including the complex interdependencies in a pragmatic workflow. CertTest's objective is about getting the best possible job results with a consistent implementation method, not just passing an exam.

- PMI (www.pmi.org) for additional information about the project management standard known as the *PMBOK Guide*, or information about becoming a certified PMP.

Projects are progressively elaborated. Every project starts out with simple high-level ideas that are polished and becomes defined into more and more detail during planning. Each successive version of the plan adds additional details concerning the definition of work and purpose of each activity. This helps define and control details of the project.

A simple definition of project management is to balance competing demands while trying to accomplish your goal. These demands are called the *triple constraint*. We can define them as these competing values:

- Scope

- Resources (cost, time)

- Quality

Think about it: Could you ever satisfy all the items on your to-do list within the budget and available time? Maybe, if the scope is small or you win the lottery. Specific needs within a project can change before completion. A good project manager embraces and adapts to the change. A novice or soon-to-be-ex project manager may not. So after all your planning is done, a change control plan is necessary to keep up with reality.

The PMBOK Process Groups

The PMI *PMBOK* Guide provides a reference for defining the project life cycle. Your organization may decide to modify this life cycle to meet the unique challenges facing your needs. Five process groups for running a project are shown in Figure 2.7 to illustrate the relationship.

Initiating   This process starts the project or a new phase of the project. It's all about the sponsor defining the objective, putting up the money, and authorizing the project to begin.

- A project is not going anywhere until the official project charter is signed to prove authority and assigned responsibility (just like an audit charter).

- The objective of the project is usually time and cost sensitive. If it arrives late, the client or sponsor will miss the opportunity they wanted to exploit. So a project has to achieve targeted financial rewards outlined in the business case, not just work or be "made to work" by staff. It must perform the original intent to be called successful. The sponsor's viewpoint of success is not what the project costs but instead a measure of financial gains for the sponsor (that is, it generates revenue 10 or 20 times the combined overall cost).

- A critical step during initiation is to identify each stakeholder (anyone with a positive gain or negative loss if the project is successful). These are the people you must work with to be successful as project manager. Write down everyone into a stakeholder register.

FIGURE 2.7 Overlapping project process groups

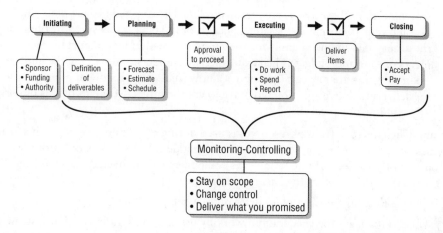

 The Monitoring-Controlling (MC) process starts immediately after we have a project definition, during the Initiating process. A common misconception is that MC is a fourth or fifth phase. The MC process continues in parallel with every activity until the project is completed.

Planning This process group represents almost half of the 42 PMI processes. Planning is where the project scope, goals, and objectives are detailed. The focus of planning is to estimate, organize, and sequence all activities. The finished plan becomes a performance baseline; your project is going to be expected to operate within an 8 percent to 10 percent variance of this forecast. The major activities in planning are as follows:

- Collect requirements.
- Plan communications (to stakeholders).
- Define the scope to identify the boundaries of this project.
- Take all the planned activities and group like activities into work packages. The combined list of work packages will create the overall work breakdown structure (WBS).
- Define the activity, put it in proper sequence, and then forecast the dates for each to start and finish.

- Smart project managers are prepared to cut less-essential items as the project runs. To cut or not to cut is based on overall impact from the sponsor's viewpoint. There are always things that will be left out until a later upgrade or improvement project.

- Estimate costs to determine a budget.

- Estimate resources to be used to develop an HR plan.

- Define quality and how quality will be achieved.

- Create a risk register (list) of likely risk the project will encounter. Don't waste time on anything but the top risks. Then plan your responses to the known risks. Contingency plans provide a benefit only for known risks.

- Combine all of these into a procurement plan. The finished project plan will become your performance baseline. Success of the plan is measured by obtaining the anticipated financial gains for the sponsor, ahead of less-important measurements of time and budget. The key to success is understanding how the anticipated financial gains are measured along with how small the window of opportunity is for delivering this result. You will have to cut the project scope to fit this opportunity window or cancel it.

Executing   The largest portion of resources is used during executing activities. This group of activities comprises the major work to create project deliverables. As work progresses, each promise of the project will materialize as components are delivered for a working product or service. Let's look at the basic steps in executing:

- The baseline (aka project plan) determines what gets done.

- The PM manages the execution of work by using a work authorization system. Nobody does anything until it's the right time in planned sequence.

- Different project members may be added to the team according to the work being performed at any given time. This means that the PM is going to acquire team members, train or develop the people for the task, and manage their work performance.

- Simultaneously, the project manager will be responsible for distributing information to manage the stakeholders' expectations and for conducting the procurements.

- Quality assurance is performed while the work is getting done to ensure that the deliverables (product, service, result) meet the requirement.

Closing   As each work package (activity) is completed, it's time to pay vendors and put the files in an archive to close out that individual item in the project.

- The closing process runs throughout the entire project because vendors want to get paid for each delivery.

- Closing involves auditing invoices to approve which ones will be paid and which ones will not be paid because of nonconforming deliverables or not paid because items are shipped ahead of schedule.

- The project is closed when all the sponsor's required items have been delivered and accepted.

Early payment may affect the ability to return or exchange items for full credit if the requirements change as the project evolves. Early payment can also cause premature expenditure of budget funds and can create storage or staging headaches. Far too many times as auditors we have heard, "The product is already paid for, and it's nonreturnable, so (the buyer) has no choice but use it."

Some of the most valuable project information will come out of lessons learned during the project. During the closing step of each activity or deliverable, it is necessary to capture those lessons learned in writing. Otherwise, we're doomed to duplicate mistakes. If something works better than expected, we want to know how we did it for next time.

Monitoring-Controlling (Keeping It Real)   This is where you have control over the project. Monitoring-Controlling starts at the very beginning of the project, from the initial objective, and lasts until everything is delivered and the project is closed. As the project runs, changes will be discovered that create a revision in the Planning and Executing phases. These processes are used to measure performance and control changes. Examples include review meetings, dealing with substitutions, and schedule changes. The Project manager might fire a vendor and hire a replacement. Monitoring-Controlling includes the following:

- Monitoring work being performed.

- Performing integrated change control to approve, reject, or retire requirements in the project. This is usually accomplished by comparing the current risk, proposed risk, and expected benefit.

- Performing quality-control reviews to determine whether the product is going to meet all the stakeholder requirements.

- Controlling and reverifying scope and project schedule.

- Authorizing payments to vendors while managing any outstanding claims.

- Reporting project performance against the original baseline from the earlier planning. Show where you match and where you missed in the projections comparing actual performance.

The ultimate goal is to ensure that if your project was supposed to deliver a solar-powered car with three wheels colored orange, that is exactly what was produced (delivered), unless you have a signed change order for the variance.

Changes in scope or poor results will force the project manager to loop backward to the sponsor for revisions to the Initiating phase. Sometimes a project exceeds the scope or needs revision before it can continue. Your sponsor may help or decide to cancel the project.

Implementation Planning of the IT Strategy

IT strategy plans must be created to aid the organization in the fulfillment of long- and short-term business objectives. Each IT plan should correlate to a specific organizational goal. The business goal may be to improve customer contact management, expand e-commerce services, or improve operating speed with better software integration. The supporting IT plan could define implementation and support for a new Customer Relationship Management (CRM) system. IT's role is that of a requirements facilitator and custodian. The true strategic value will be determined in the minds of the business executives. There should be a concern if IT's influence is overriding other non-IT business objectives. The IT strategy will be composed of plans for data, software applications, technology, personnel, and facilities.

Data Plan

IT data plans are created in support of the organization's intended use of the data. An example is the creation of a new customer survey system, database marketing system, or financial record-keeping system. The key is to determine what data you really need and how you will protect it. This is accomplished by implementing an information classification program with administrative policies and procedures. Well-run businesses and governments have been doing this for hundreds of years to explain how each piece of data should be handled. After the intended use of the data is recognized, the next step is to define the application to manipulate the data.

Application Management Plan

Computer software applications are actually methods of accomplishing work. Therefore, a software management plan is necessary to define the type of work to be performed. A consumer bank may be in the same industry as a debt collection company, for example. However, both organizations use different software applications. Computer software applications need to be tailored to fit the client's needs.

 Computer software is not an advantage if the competitor uses the same software, unless the implementation is unique and highly customized. Devolving to an out-of-the-box solution will usually kill the client's value-added advantage over competitors.

It is possible to gain a competitive advantage by using a different product than the competitor uses. The advantage is attaining a higher level of business integration and/or lower operating costs. The cost argument is the very reason why some software applications use open source SQL (OpenSQL) for a database rather than a commercial vendor. Both are fine products. The cost difference may allow for a significant investment in specialized customization by a guru to build highly integrated software, which can create a competitive advantage with a lower overall operating cost. The resulting integrated software may perform a unique function that the competitor will have difficulty obtaining because of required knowledge, lead time needed, or additional capital investment.

It is the kiss of death is to allow a vendor's technical assistance manager (TAM) or technical implementation manager to determine the assessed value of work accomplished. The vast majority of vendor TAMs are well paid to avoid providing custom fitness-of-use. Never, never accept justification that a TAM can be trusted because they work for a bigger organization or work for the vendor. TAMs are notorious for selling buyers on using out-of-the-box installations while billing 15–30 percent more. These predatory practices bleed the buyer.

Cost avoidance can be a competitive advantage. The application risk is that the integration does not occur or the intended application usage is flawed.

Computer application software represents a substantial investment in capital. Computer software creates business risks that must be managed. The risks include process failure, increased operating risk, ineffective results, waste of capital resources, lost time, and increased operating cost for the same effective output.

Technology Plan

Technology plans address an organization's technical environment by indicating the types of hardware and software that will be used. Unfortunately, some organizations start with the hardware technology first and attempt to force the data and application requirements into their desired technology. Putting the technology plans first may hinder the results.

Organizational Plan

The IT organizational structure needs to be designed to support the business strategy. Information technology is usually regarded as a function of internal administration. This would place IT under the head of internal controls (the CFO, VP of finance, or the comptroller). Figure 2.8 illustrates a typical IT organization. We will discuss the individual positions as we proceed through this chapter.

Figure 2.8 can serve as a road map if you're unsure about the authority of positions we discuss in this chapter.

Facilities Plan

Finally, the strategy needs to incorporate a facilities plan. Where will the data applications and technology reside? Who will manage the environment? The final decision will be based on the desires of management. These desires can include increased control, insourcing, outsourcing, or a hybrid combination.

FIGURE 2.8 Typical IT organizational structure

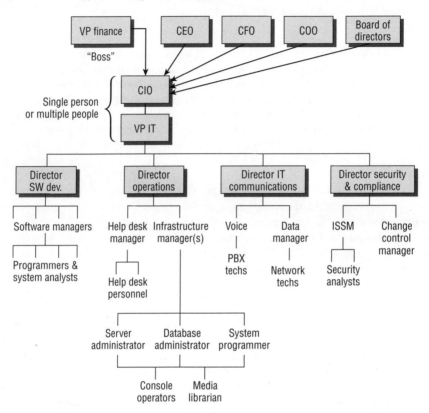

Using COBIT

Knowing what to do is a challenge for all auditors. Discussions were occurring on this subject long ago in the old Electronic Data Processing (EDP) audit association, before it was renamed ISACA. One of the goals of every association is to add value by improving the performance of its members. ISACA has definitely delivered on this goal. The definitive framework for IS auditing is called the Control Objectives for Information and Related Technology, also known as COBIT.

This control framework contains a complete set of strategies, processes, and procedures necessary for executives to lead the IT organization. COBIT is now in its fourth edition. Within the supporting manuals, you will find the guidance provided in the audit toolkit invaluable. COBIT is protected under copyright, so it's a good idea not to lose your CISA certification by doing something stupid like having a bootleg copy.

The audit guideline section contains more than enough questions necessary for a first-class audit. It covers the entire spectrum from executive strategy down to device settings. BSC properly combined with COBIT would make a phenomenal audit practice.

Now let's get back to the auditing plan. We have discussed strategy, so the next step is to figure out the work location.

Identifying Sourcing Locations

The next step in governance is to identify sourcing locations. The sourcing decision may be based on the operating cost for particular geographic locations. Operating cost is a combined factor of facilities, labor, regulations, and available resources. Organizations may choose to perform functions on site, in their facility. Alternatively, there may be an advantage to performing functions off site, at other offices or with an outside vendor. This is a common practice for customer support, employee payroll, and manufacturing. Cheap labor may influence management's decision to move the location offshore, to another country.

 Three popular offshore locations include China, India, and Russia. The expected benefits include cheaper labor or lower standards for environmental compliance. The effective cost of steel, concrete, and materials to construct an office is approximately the same worldwide.

Performing functions offshore introduces both opportunities and burdens. The opportunities include a potentially lower production cost. There is also an advantage for an organization to operate 24 hours a day in order to lower turnaround times. Consider the effect when the day shift identifies a problem, and the night shift in another country fixes it before the day shift returns in the morning.

Disadvantages include the potential loss of control or the disclosure of proprietary intellectual property. In some countries, the culture, language, or level of education presents unique challenges. Cultural examples of potential conflicts include India's caste system, and Africa's ongoing tribal wars and gender-based discrimination. Consider attitudes in some societies toward a woman in an authoritative role.

 Real World Scenario

The "Follow the Sun" Concept

Executive management may choose to service its customers by using a *follow the sun* concept, which in simple terms means that the organization moves daily support functions to an *offsite* location 8 to 12 hours away. The second (or third) office is starting their morning when the current office is closing at the end of the day. Each day, as one office closes, another office located in a different time zone takes over support (each time traveling to the west with the new day). Customers could always have a full staff available to help, regardless of the time of day.

A company might instead choose to schedule multiple shifts within the same office. As an auditor, you should inquire how the client retains full control with multiple shifts of personnel. What management controls are in place? Frequently the late-night staff has less supervision or greater access to shared work areas without detection.

Sourcing Practices

The world is growing smaller as transportation and communication services improve. Many of the old cultural barriers have been reduced by the global economy. This global economy also has increased the number of competitors in the fierce battle for revenue. An organization at one time worried only about servicing clients in a small number of local time zones. Now customers depend on businesses 24 hours a day, worldwide.

Most administrative and technical support functions can be performed from alternate locations. Some of the services that could be fulfilled from remote locations include the following:

- Accounting and bookkeeping
- Accounts payable (AP) and accounts receivable (AR)
- Data entry and transcription
- Live telephone support (including IT, customer service, order taking)
- Legal and medical records management and processing
- Human resources and benefits administration
- Creative advertising production
- Printing
- Software development
- Systems administration

In the following section, you will look at the various types of sourcing methods, what factors go into choosing a sourcing method, and why it is important for you as an IS auditor to be familiar with them.

Sourcing Methods

The decision of location is usually based on the cost of operation, market pressures, or a centralization versus decentralization strategy. Management may choose to hire personnel by using a combination of insourcing and outsourcing. Services provided by internal staff are referred to as *in-house* (*insourced*). Services provided by an external vendor are referred to as *outsourced*. The insourced versus outsourced decision may be based on a case-by-case or project-by-project requirement.

On occasion, an opportunity may present itself that exceeds the capability of the existing service provider. *Hybrid sourcing models* may be effective under a joint venture or to provide additional capability. The hybrid model combines insourcing and outsourcing on a function-by-function basis.

The advantage of outsourcing is that someone else may be able to perform the work better or cheaper, or frankly may know how to do something others don't. Insourcing provides more control. The hybrid method retains control in selected areas and uses the outsource contractor for collateral work. Outsourcing may allow the client to focus on what they do best, their core revenue generator. A potential disadvantage is losing control under the contract. Maybe the methods used by a subcontractor will cost less because they are cutting corners that, if known, a company might find unacceptable.

The basic decision may result from an executive thinking about the following:

- Is this something that the organization wants to do in-house?
- Is this something the company should outsource?
- Is there an advantage to sending this offshore?
- Is the organization bringing it back from offshore?
- Will local processing be a competitive advantage?
- Is the location here, in this building, or is it in another building?

Globalization Issues

Businesses may encounter a variety of globalization issues, including international regulation, local laws, tribal rivalries, or cultural class or caste systems. As an organization begins to look at opportunities for global outsourcing, they have to keep in mind the controls and the total costs related to that decision.

A business looks for inexpensive operating facilities with a high-quality labor pool willing to work for lower wages. If the business is going to decide whether to outsource, it needs to look at all the practices and strategies that are in place.

A business can run into problems over the differences in legal regulations between governments. Additional concerns can arise in different currency exchange rates and government taxation methods. Some of these requirements may indicate that foreign outsourcing would not provide any advantage.

Competitive advantage should be a factor in the sourcing decision. For example, American Apparel manufactures clothing exclusively inside the United States and pays better-than-average wages for their industry. Their advantage is a shorter cycle time from market idea to delivery and sale in their stores. American Apparel touts a one-day turn-around from a finished idea. Their competition has to contend with manufacturing and shipping delays measured in months.

In the last few years, Russia and the Baltic states have benefited from increased popularity, as companies reconsider India or choose to outsource for the first time. Increasing operating costs and U.S. consumer rejection are troublesome to companies outsourcing to India. The cost of real estate in India is skyrocketing. China is reeling backward after a virtual tidal wave of product recalls. Additional reasons cited for Russian sourcing include a more convenient proximity to Western Europe, more positive consumer attitudes of acceptance, a well-educated population, financial savings in real estate prices, and the competitive low cost of labor.

Legal Compliance Issues

When dealing with outsourcing issues, companies need to be aware that what is legal in one country might not be legal in another. Examples include the European Union (EU) privacy laws, which are much stricter than those of the United States, or the shortfall of intellectual-property laws in China, which frankly don't exist. In China the attitude is that if someone has a copy, they own it. Therefore, business management needs to understand: How does that country or culture see it?

As a primitive example, just compare the religious holidays and lifestyles that different countries observe. For example, the flow of harmony in the office is considered upset in Japan if everyone does not go to lunch at the exact same time, and return within a couple of minutes of one another. In Mexico, the lunch hour is two hours and often includes drinking alcohol followed by a siesta (nap). It is not uncommon for employees to drink alcohol during the office lunch hour in the United Kingdom (referred to as having a few pints or getting pissed over a few drinks).

While management plans their labor strategy, there should be a provision ensuring continuity of operations for both in-house and outsourced activities.

Subcontractor Liability Trap

The biggest downside of outsourcing is liability. Outsourcing permits an organization to reassign the tasks to be performed but not the liability. It's not possible to transfer the actual liability for failure. Insurance may help cover some of the expenses but not the damage to your reputation, the cancelled sales, or the costs of defending a lawsuit.

Consider the situation of ValuJet Airlines. A subcontractor violated cargo-loading procedures when it placed a hazardous container in the cargo bay. The container exploded, causing the airplane to crash. A massive media circus was spawned by the event. ValuJet held their subcontractor liable. The public held ValuJet responsible. The public didn't pick the subcontractor; ValuJet did. ValuJet was expected to spend extra time and money to supervise the subcontractor. The airline folded and assets were sold to Airtran. This broke the chain of liability to protect the investors.

Let's consider the long-term effects of the following well-publicized examples of food contamination:

- In 2007-2008, problems surfaced worldwide in many well-known brands of canned pet food. A supplier of ingredients shipped tainted flour, which led to the death of many beloved family pets. Other pet owners reported paying expensive medical bills for emergency care by veterinarians. Retailers trashed their entire inventories of pet food and asked for refunds to cover the losses. Some pet owners are pursuing lawsuits against the brands for the harm to their pets and their own emotional strain.

- ConAgra Foods is still involved in legal battles over a bad batch of ingredients used in Peter Pan peanut butter. One lawyer advertised on television to "keep the jar and call attorney Loncar," thus promoting possible monetary awards for the consumer to sue ConAgra. Wal-Mart sold the same ConAgra peanut butter under its own house brand.

- Several products manufactured in China are now banned from the United States and other countries because of unacceptable chemicals in foods or illegal hormones used to grow vegetables and fish.

Outsourcing does not relieve the company's responsibility to test products or services for compliance. In fact, the outsourcer should be trusted less and tested more. The auditor is always interested in how the process of governing all outsourced services is handled.

In-House Operations Return

It's interesting how some vendors can perform the task cheaper than in-house. Unfortunately, the cost and benefit structure might not be telling the whole story. Outsourcing is frequently an option when the organization

- Is unable to get the right result
- Considers the process is too much work
- Fails to define their actual needs
- Attempts to circumvent legal requirements

As time goes by, it may be discovered that the outsource provider is taking unacceptable shortcuts or charging higher prices than expected. Additional issues to consider include turnaround time plus increased costs of supervision necessary to maintain the desired results.

WARNING   Using outsourcing to circumvent legal requirements is based upon assigning the work to external contractors. The subcontractor is financially encouraged to take potentially dangerous shortcuts to reduce operating expenses. The reduction may be based on using unlicensed labor, using hazardous products, paying wages below minimum standards, or something else. A number of major corporations have been accused of this unethical and even illegal practice. Most of the accused are either sentenced or plea bargain to pay fines.

We have discussed strategy and sourcing. Next, we'll discuss the performance of the executives in delivering results.

Conducting an Executive Performance Review

The executive staff is subject to review by the audit committee. As you recall, it is this committee's job to challenge the assumptions and assurances in the organization. The audit committee is expected to provide management oversight and allow executives the opportunity to discuss confidential issues about the business. An effective audit committee will advise individual executives with an opinion for possible solutions to internal problems.

Independent auditors are hired by the audit committee to provide an impartial (independent) opinion as to the status of internal controls. Audit committees are frequently the client of external audit engagements.

Understanding the Auditor's Interest in the Strategy

As an IS auditor, you need to find evidence of management governing IT and the enterprise. The composition and performance of the steering committee could be a powerful source of evidence. You may be able to review the plans and meeting minutes from the committee. The auditor's goal is to assess the performance of the CEO and executive management in developing and leading a successful strategy based on business objectives.

Overview of Tactical Management

By using tactical management, an organization selects a maneuver or technique that will render a better result. The goal of tactical management is to manage the return on investment for information systems. The successful manager will need to establish a requirement for the collection of performance metrics. The performance metrics are used to determine whether the results are improving or deteriorating against a baseline. The same metrics are used to demonstrate management success to the executives and stakeholders.

Figure 2.9 illustrates the tactical level in the organizational chart.

Individuals at the tactical level should be providing support to the strategic objectives. The majority of planning work accomplished at the director level is tactical in nature. Strategic plans are handed down from top management. The director level is expected to fulfill the strategic goals by providing solutions without the authority to make changes in other areas of the organizational structure. A director's authority outside of their own department is limited to requesting and negotiating.

FIGURE 2.9   Tactical level in the organization

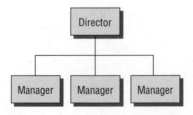

Planning and Performance

Every IS organization has a number of functions that it should implement to fulfill its strategic plan, its tactical plan, and its daily plan. An auditor looks at any industry-standard benchmarks for performance optimization that have been adopted. Several are available, including the National Institute of Standards and Technology's controls matrix and the Federal Information Security Management Act (FISMA). In addition, the organization may use an organizational planning maturity model such as the Organizational Project Management Maturity Model (OPM3) by the Project Management Institute.

It is possible that the organization benchmarks its business continuity plans and disaster plans after the public domain version of the Business Continuity Maturity Model (BCMM). The organization may have an information assurance program and be using the ISO 27002 or Capability Maturity Model (CMM).

The value of benchmarking is to determine the organization's position and progress as compared to a recognized reference. There are several competitive advantages to benchmarking, the first of which is the ability to attract respect and more-favorable terms from stakeholders. Every IS organization has an issue regarding financial management.

These questions come up:

- What does IS pay for?
- What does the department pay for?
- What does the project pay for?

Individual departments may be operating a shadow IT group funded by department budgets. This condition usually indicates some type of failure to align to the business objectives in the strategic plan.

Management Control Methods

All levels of management are responsible for providing leadership. Good leaders generate better performance from individual employees. To manage is to create an unnatural result. If the same result would naturally occur by itself, you are not managing it. The objective of management is to get a better result. Every organization needs to plan for how to collect continuous evidence of performance. The minimum requirements of good management include the following:

- Performance reporting
- General record keeping
- Safeguards and implementation details of controls

The auditor needs to review a variety of documents, including the organization's strategic plan, policies, IT plans, and operating procedures. These include plans for training, system mitigation, system certification, disaster recovery, continuity, and the inevitability of change. As an auditor, you will need input from people besides IT management to ensure alignment with the enterprise objectives.

Performance Review

Performance review refers to the identification of a target to be monitored, tracked, and assigned to a responsible party, and the resolution of any open issues. Existing systems require a regular review to determine the ongoing level of compliance to internal controls and the next steps to take.

The Capability Maturity Model (CMM) is a method for evaluating and measuring the maturity of processes in organizations. A rating scale from 0 to 5 is used. A score of zero indicates that nothing is occurring. Level 1 maturity indicates that the initial activity was successful and may later progress up to level 5, when the activity is statistically controlled for continuous improvement. The CMM rating scale was developed by the Software Engineering Institute at Carnegie Mellon University and has been widely used for rating business process capabilities.

 The Capability Maturity Model is also discussed in Chapter 5.

Levels of the CMM are as follows:

Level 0 = Nothing Yet   The level of zero is implied in the CMM but may not be noticed. This is important when evaluating process maturity. Missing processes and controls without evidence will be rated as zero. Many individuals assume that all controls are present when, in fact, some may be missing. A process or control must have occurred in order to reach a level of maturity (1–5).

Level 1 = Initial   Processes are unique and chaotic. The organization does not have a stable environment. Success is based on individual competencies and heroics. This level often produces products and services that work. However, output may exceed the available resources or be dependent on specific individuals. At level 1, people have the most freedom and flexibility to make their own decisions.

Level 2 = Repeatable   Processes are repeatable. The organization uses project management to track projects. The project status is communicated by using milestones with a defined work breakdown structure. The basic standards, processes, descriptions, and procedures are documented.

Level 3 = Defined   Processes are well documented and understood. Level 3 is more mature and better defined than level 2. Processes have objectives, measurements, improvement procedures, and standards. The results in level 3 are predictable by qualitative measure.

Level 4 = Managed   Management can use precise measurement criteria to control the processes and identify ways to adjust the results. Processes at level 4 are predictable by quantitative measure.

Level 5 = Optimized   This is the highest level, with continuous improvement of processes. Objectives for improvement are defined and continually revised to reflect business needs and objectives. Products at CMM level 5 have been so well defined that they are effectively converted into a commodity.

Level 5 is the ideal maturity for the maximum level of control in outsourcing. It allows the company to switch to using less-skilled people who are told what to do, receive less pay, and they demand workers don't question management's authority. Workers have the absolute least authority with the fewest possible decisions at level 5.

 ISACA's COBIT uses the CMM approach to rate auditee performance by the maturity of their control environment.

Figure 2.10 shows the five maturity levels of the CMM in a lateral view.

FIGURE 2.10 Capability Maturity Model

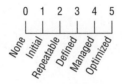

Frankly, attaining higher levels in the maturity model increases the likelihood that internal controls are successful. A higher CMM grade indicates a definition of maturity with a higher degree of control.

Consider the typical hooks in an outsource contract. The buyer is hooked to it, and so the following questions should be investigated:

- Did the client/auditee give away resources, intellectual-property knowledge, or procedures of value that will not be recoverable?

- Has the client/auditee given away highly qualified personnel who will no longer be in-house?

- What will a contract change cost, if desired?

- Can the contract be cancelled?

- If a decision is made to cancel, what will it take to get the replacement function online?

This should be enough information for the prospective CISA. Let's take a look at sources of governance models.

Auditors may refer to a variety of applicable standards when planning or auditing controls. First, we need to mention that controls exist for the purpose of managing money, protecting assets, safeguarding information, handling processes, and/or managing people. In fact, one of the first controls in business was a budget.

World trade dictates the use of modern commerce controls. Do you know what it takes to be a member of the World Trade Organization (WTO)? First you would need to be a government, because only governments can be members of the WTO. Standards in world trade are determined by the member countries participating in the Committee of Sponsoring Organizations (COSO = money), International Organization for Standardization (ISO = measures), and Organization for Economic Cooperation and

Development (OECD = laws). Only governments can be members of these international control organizations.

Let's look at how standards originate and how these standards relate to trade controls.

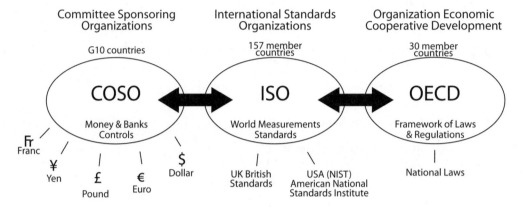

Committee of Sponsoring Organizations

COSO sets the controls for monetary and banking systems. These controls include the foundation of worldwide audit policies, standards, and guidelines. Accountants and auditors worldwide use COSO controls to develop best practices and implementation guides. ISACA's COBIT is an IT-only derivative mixing COSO objectives with American Institute of Certified Public Accountants (AICPA) and International Federation of Accountants (IFAC) practices into an IT-specific control model.

International Organization for Standardization

The next step after we've determined the value of the dollar, yen, or dinar is to agree on weights and measures for product trade. The specialty of ISO is determining weights and measures, including technical measurement of IT systems. Nowadays everyone relies on the worldwide ISO standards for reference. ISO standards contain numerous points that are identical to the U.S. and British standards working in concert. Let's look at six out of the more than twenty-three major standards an auditor could use as reference to IT management and security:

- ISO 9001 Quality Management Standard (QMS)
- ISO 15489 Records Management which applies to everyone
- ISO 15408 Common Criteria for System Security Assurance
- ISO 27002 Information Security Management Standard (ISMS)
- ISO 27006 ISMS Security Techniques Auditing
- ISO 19011 Guidelines for Management Systems Auditing

ISO 27002 is actually functioning quite well as the executive summary for implementing the U.S. NIST 800-53 technical standard. For your CISA exam, it's only important to understand how the various standards are integrated into auditing. You will not need to know the details to pass your CISA exam. The ISBOK Successful Practitioner's Guide to Implementing Information Security is a good source for future reference on integrating the details found in the various standards.

Just a reminder: ISO standards are protected by international copyright. Each country sells a single-user copy for the equivalent of $1 per page. That's how ISO gets funding. CISAs should not have bootleg copies under any condition. Besides the legal issues, it violates your certification. Remember, the person who turns you in will usually get amnesty.

With so much attention on internal controls, the most important step an organization can take is the first—to implement controls. Any one of these best practices models should already be implemented.

National Institute of Standards and Technology

The U.S. government has set forth standards for engineering, weights and measures, and even computer processing. Management of the standards is assigned to the *National Institute of Standards and Technology (NIST)*. The NIST technical standards for information technology management are mandatory for government agencies and optional for nongovernmental organizations. Many of the IT best practices were derived from NIST.

The U.S. government passed new internal control regulations under FISMA to unify the former Federal Information Processing Standards (FIPS). The U.S. internal control rating requirements for compliance are posted on the NIST website under the heading for special publications (`http://csrc.nist.gov`). NIST is an excellent technical resource for governance models that implement the CMM.

Quality Management

Every organization should have processes in place to ensure that people are taking steps to do the right job at the right time. Quality management is a pervasive requirement.

We discuss quality further in Chapter 3, "Audit Process," and Chapter 5.

Risk Management

Risks occur at all levels. There are strategic risks, tactical risks, operational risks, and inherent risks. Now let's look at one of the more common risk management formulas.

The first step in risk management is to calculate how much a single loss event would cost. This formula multiplies an asset value (expressed in dollars) by the percentage of loss for a particular event. For example, the percentage of loss of a stolen purse is likely to be 100 percent. In that example, the loss would be 100 percent of purse value. The loss due to data-entry errors may be equal to 0.007 percent of labor cost. This first formula is expressed as follows:

Asset value (AV) $ × exposure factor (EF) % = single loss expectancy (SLE)

The single loss expectancy can be multiplied by the number of related events that are likely to occur for the year. The final result would be the estimated annual loss, as shown in the following formula:

Single loss expectancy (SLE) × annual rate of occurrence (ARO) = annual loss expectancy (ALE)

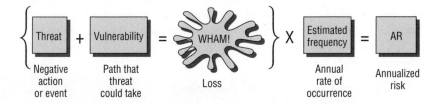

Risk management should be pervasive in all areas of business, including the IT department. Two types of risk always exist:

Positive risk: Opportunity of exploit, gain, and reward

Negative risk: May result in loss

The choices are to avoid, mitigate, transfer, or accept. You can eliminate the risk only through avoidance, but the typical goal is to reduce the level of risk to something acceptable.

When developing a risk management program, the auditor wants to find evidence that the risk management function has been implemented with an established purpose—in other words, that someone has been assigned responsibility, and risk management is a formal ongoing process, not just a review by lawyers.

Auditors should beware of persons primarily focused on negative risk management. Commerce thrives on exploiting positive risk opportunities. A well-balanced control framework will provide for increasing exploitation of positive risk (growth opportunity) and still offer an equal balance of negative risk (loss protection). Otherwise, revenue will fall as the negative control framework chokes off profitability. Or worse, the controls won't be used at all.

Risks can involve many areas of the business. Impacts can be direct or indirect, positive or negative. Positive risk includes expansion, new products, new jobs, and acquisition to gain market share. Negative risk will damage the organization's position or capital, cause layoffs or the loss of key personnel, or impair future opportunities. Typical assets include the organization's key personnel, proprietary methods or recipes, customer list, general information about marketing or development, data records, user files, hardware, and software. Assets could also include the facility, a particular document, or services rendered. The risks, or threats, could be terror acts, malicious fraud, executing the wrong procedure, theft, or failure of controls. It's interesting that criminals do not look at vulnerabilities the same way as an upstanding individual. To a criminal mind, a window becomes an entry or exit point to a building with the aid of a brick.

Risk management operates at a variety of levels: Management at the strategic level focuses on whether going forward with a particular strategy over a period of years is a good idea. Management could be at a project level—is the project on track? Or it could be at a daily or hourly or by-the-minute operational level to ensure that personnel are doing what they are supposed to do. Frankly, most major disasters are caused by a domino effect of a tiny failure multiplying into numerous failures that become catastrophic.

Overall, situations of high risk—where high loss, high consequence, or high impact is possible—require a method to ensure that the problem receives adequate consideration and the appropriate level of effort to prevent an unfortunate outcome. It is extremely common for IT staff to execute poor change control when dealing with interruptions, failures, theft, fraud, or just general risk while under pressure.

Personnel Risk

Determining the requirements related to hiring or terminating outsourced personnel can be challenging. Several companies have discovered way too late that certain organizations in the European Union have some rather stout requirements for expatriation and repatriation. The company may be liable for future employee benefits and the individual's cost of relocation. The requirements could also include severance plans that provide advance pay of up to about a year, the company's purchase of the former employee's home because that person did not have time to sell it, and payment of medical expenses for six months to a year. These requirements can make a huge difference if a company is planning changes such as layoffs or is trying to determine whether hiring a contractor is a good idea.

Information Security Risk

Every organization communicates sensitive data over delicate communication lines, which are not necessarily secure. In fact, every government has mandates to conduct surveillance for foreign intelligence in order to provide trade advantages for their citizens. News articles indicate that government organizations from competing countries are attempting to bring foreign technology to domestic organizations. It's the old game of economic espionage and political advantage. Data security is the number one concern when planning for communication crossing the border. We refer to this as *transborder communication*. One of the challenges is determining whether the data is legal or regulated across the border. The next concern may be that infrastructure issues impede delivery or quality of service from a geographically remote location.

 France was the first country to implement an organized system of spying on foreign nationals, beginning in the 14th century. The United States was one of the later countries to follow this initiative. Surveillance is mandated in the United States under the Foreign Intelligence Surveillance Act of 1978 (USC Title 50, Chapter 36, FISA).

Implementing Standards

IT governance is founded on the implementation of formal policies and standards. Each standard is supported by a matching procedure. The purpose of IT governance is to ensure that the risks are properly managed by mitigation, avoidance, or transfer. Let's review a short list of the policies required to address issues faced by IT governance:

Intellectual Property   The term *intellectual property* refers to data and knowledge that is not commonly known. This information possesses a commercial value. The IS auditor should understand how the organization is attempting to protect its intellectual property. There is no method for registering a trade secret. The owner has to undertake all control measures necessary to keep it secret. The rights of intellectual property can be destroyed by a failure of the organization to take preemptive action.

Data Integrity   What mechanisms have been put in place to ensure data integrity? Does the organization have input controls? How is the data validated for accuracy? Are the systems formally reviewed in a certification and accreditation process? What level of security management and access controls are present? Internal controls for data integrity are required by most industries and government regulation. The goal of data integrity is to ensure that data is accurate and safely stored.

>**Backup and Restoration**   What are the plans and procedures for data backup and restoration? The number one issue in IT is loss of data due to faulty backup. The failures can be procedural or technical.

>**Security Management**   Without security controls, ensuring data integrity is impossible. Internal controls prevent unauthorized modifications. The Sarbanes-Oxley Act (SOX) and FISMA mandate strong security controls.

Mandatory versus Discretionary Controls   Every control is based on the human implementation. The organization needs to clearly identify its management directives for implementation of controls. Every control will be one of two fundamental types:

>**Mandatory Control**   This is the strongest type of control. The implementation may be administrative or technical. A mandatory control is designed to force compliance without exception. Mandatory controls are managed from a centralized authority.

>**Discretionary Control**   The weakest type of control is discretionary. In a discretionary control, the user or delegated person of authority determines what is acceptable.

Monitoring   The IT systems should be monitored throughout the entire life cycle and in daily operations. The monitoring process provides valuable metrics necessary to compare alignment to business objectives. The purpose of governance is to lead. It would be impossible to lead without understanding ongoing conditions. Monitoring may prove that the organization is well run or a ticking time bomb. Without monitoring, determining whether an incident needs attention would be impossible.

Incident Response   A response is required for skilled individuals to deal with technical problems or the failure of internal controls. An incident may be major or minor depending on the circumstances. It is necessary to have an established policy, standard, and procedure for handling the incident response. At the beginning of an incident, it is impossible to accurately foretell the full impact of possible consequences. An incident response team should be in place to investigate suspicious situations. Care and diligence is necessary because it may later be determined that the initial response area is a crime scene. The mishandling of evidence could lead to forfeiture of the organization's damage claims. Unproven allegations against an individual or organization will frequently result in financial liability by the accuser.

 We discuss the details of monitoring and incident response in Chapter 6.

Human Resources

IT governance is conjoined with requirements to properly manage people. Good management is founded on human resource management that is well defined, fair, and consistent. Let's take a look at a few of the HR-related policies that affect IT management:

Hiring   What are the organization's policies for selecting the best candidate? How should the interview process be handled? Quality management is required during the hiring process to ensure that the organization is in compliance with equal opportunity standards.

Termination   Personnel may be terminated via either friendly or unfriendly procedures. The requirements for layoffs are relatively clear. What are the procedures for terminating personnel over extended periods of time? A special procedure may be necessary in the case of an upcoming personal retirement. A different procedure may apply to an employee who will be returning as a contractor on the same project. A hostile termination could stem from workplace violence, a criminal act, fraud, or a dispute with other personnel.

Employee Contracts   Many organizations use employee contracts to specify terms of employment. This technique is typically in effect in states with a Right to Work law. Right to Work laws are primarily about *union versus nonunion employment*—that people have a right to decide whether they want to be part of a union, that union membership can't be a condition of employment. The use of employment contracts is invaluable for identifying the ownership of new discoveries. The employment contract details that the individual is performing work for hire, to the benefit of the employer organization.

Confidentiality Agreement   A standard practice is for employees and contractors to sign a confidentiality agreement. The purpose is to ensure that strategic, tactical, and operational details are not divulged outside the organization. Operating without a confidentiality agreement is usually a significant risk.

Noncompetition Agreement   The employer may implement a noncompete agreement to prevent the employee from working for a competitor until after a specific period of time. The terms of this type of agreement may be successful as long as they are not overly restrictive for the amount of money paid to the employee.

Ethics Statements   The organization should provide a statement of what is acceptable and unacceptable behavior. The best method for preventing a problem is to explain to an individual what actions are acceptable. Unacceptable behavior includes any activities for personal gain at the expense of the organization.

Performance Evaluation   A standardized process should be in place for reviewing an employee's performance. Each employee in the same basic role should be judged by their manager on defined criteria, pertinent to their organizational role. A quarterly or annual review is customary. More-progressive organizations may conduct reviews on a weekly or monthly basis. The morale of hard-working employees is damaged if the boss fails to notice their good work. The results of each review fall under HR record retention requirements for several years.

Promotion Policy   What is the organization's promotion policy? Is it based on job performance, education, or something else? The organization is required to demonstrate a fair and objective promotion policy in order to meet equal opportunity compliance.

Work Schedule   Work schedules and vacation schedules should be clearly defined. In some financial organizations, the vacation schedule is implemented as a detective control. An individual is forced to take vacations in one- or two-week increments. During that employee's absence, another individual performs that job, and a discovery audit may take place to ensure that no irregular or illegal acts have been committed by the employee.

Corrective Counseling   What are the organization's policies for corrective counseling after poor performance from the employee? Care must be taken to prevent discrimination. An improper termination can create a financial liability. An employee may collect monetary damages if able to prove wrongful termination.

These are just a few of the many policies and procedures necessary to manage human resources. The IS auditor should be concerned about activities that increase the organization's level of risk. This includes Human Resources activities.

System Life-Cycle Management

All computer systems need to be managed through their entire life cycle. Each system will go through a series of phases starting with a feasibility study. Next, requirements are generated and followed by system design. Systems are tested for integrity, and their fitness of use is determined. The life cycle continues into system implementation. After successful implementation, the system can migrate into production use. Each year of production, the system should undergo a review. The annual postimplementation review focuses on the system's present condition compared to the more current requirements. A system may be upgraded to the new requirements or retired. This is just a summary.

The CISA is interested in understanding how the organization manages each phase of this process. Evidence should be obtained to support the auditor's conclusions.

We cover the system life cycle in more depth in Chapter 5.

Continuity Planning

Information technology systems are so pervasive today that most organizations would cease to operate if their computers were unavailable. IT governance requires continuity planning for systems and data. Auditors need to be aware of multiple continuity objectives besides disaster recovery. While IT is just the records keeper, executives in the business units are worried about far greater continuity challenges which can threaten organizational survival 365 days of the year. In the business unit, a whole series of continuity decisions occur through normal executive scenario planning without involving IT. These decisions include the following:

- Executive continuity (who's in charge)

- Investor continuity (money)

- Brand/organization continuity (image/resizing)

- Continuity of key personnel (living assets)

- Product line continuity (product image)

- Client continuity (revenue)

Any disruption to IT operations could have far-reaching negative effects. Members of the media can be merciless in their quest to report an interesting story. The damage to an organization's reputation and brand can be fatal. ISACA wants every CISA to be aware of the need for disaster continuity planning. We have expanded coverage of business continuity in Chapter 8, "Business Continuity and Disaster Recovery."

Insurance

Adequate insurance is the minimum response for asset protection. This is a corrective administrative control. There are issues concerning insurance, including the cost versus actual benefits received. Insurance does not replace lost market share, nor damage from unauthorized disclosure of confidential information. Acts of God, war, and terrorism are exempt from coverage in most insurance policies. Proper risk management reduces the organization's exposure. Risk reduction efforts, combined with insurance, are a good practice. The CISA should be aware that there is a difference between real insurance and self-insurance.

 Normally, the term *self-insurance* implies a level of protection that does not exist. Self-insurance means the organization is accepting the risk with full liability for any consequences. If a loss occurs, the organization will pay everything out of its own pocket.

Performance Management

Performance management serves to inform executives and stakeholders as to the progress of current activities. A fair and objective scoring system should be used. Scores may be based on a current service-level agreement. Another method is to use key performance indicators (KPIs), which tend to represent a historical average of monitored events. Unfortunately, a key performance indicator may indicate a failing score too late to implement a change. A perfect example of a KPI is the high-school report card. By the time the score is reported, the target child may not be eligible to graduate.

A process should exist to report the performance of IT budgets and noncompliant activities. Executive management should encourage the reporting of issues without punishing the messenger. Some effort is necessary to ensure the accurate and timely flow of information upward to the executives. False information can be very damaging.

Instead of just having a qualitative assessment of good or bad, or high, medium, or low, this should be an accounting exercise using a quantitative measure. It could be semiquantitative, using a ranking scale similar to scoring in a school: 70 to 79 is a C, 80 to 89 is a B, 90 to 100 represents an A, and then percentages such as A– or A+. This technique will convert a subjective decision into a more objective review. The Capability Maturity Model is very effective for communicating performance metrics.

Figure 2.11 shows a brief glimpse of the CMM used to report metrics.

FIGURE 2.11   Excerpt of CMM to report metrics

Metric	CMM process maturity	Change	% Compliance
Help desk support	0 — 3.9 — 5	▲	100%
Laptop security plan	0 — 2.9 — 5	▲	73%
Laptop data encryption	0 — 3.4 — 5	●	67%
New user security training	0 — 3.4 — 5	▲	58%
Existing user security training	0 — 1.5 — 5	▼	19%
Vulnerability scan users	0 — 1 — 5	▲	8%

Managing Outsourcing

When an organization decides to consider outsourcing, one of the concerns is that the organization may lose the visibility necessary to effectively operate the processes. The outsource contract should require a *right to audit* the service provider. Occasionally the response is that they cannot be audited by everyone because they do not have the time or the money, but will give you a copy of the SAS-70 service provider's audit report, which is a standard audit format. Unfortunately, the report may be insufficient to management needs, because the report is probably vetted and groomed to ensure it states the level of information the service provider wants to convey, not necessarily what may be observed during your own audit.

Our suggestion is that if a company is considering outsourcing, the auditor could ask, "Why not run a controls audit and a service-level agreement (SLA) audit using the client's auditor, or a full audit before signing the contract?" The goal is to determine whether the service provider is fulfilling their entire obligation before signing a contract. Why risk the time and money to sign a contract while silently hoping and praying that the requirements are met?

An excellent idea is to implement a business process review before outsourcing.

Overview of Business Process Reengineering

One of the principles in business that remains constant is the need to improve your processes and procedures. Most trade magazines today contain discussions of the detailed planning necessary for implementing change in an organization. The concept of change must be accepted as a fundamental principle. Terms such as *business evolution* and *continuous improvement* ricochet around the room in business meetings. It's a fact that organizations which fail to change are destined to perish.

As a CISA, you must be prepared to investigate whether process changes within the organization are accounted for with proper documentation. All internal control frameworks require that management be held responsible for safeguarding all the assets belonging to their organization. Management is also responsible for increasing revenue. Let's discuss why business process reengineering (BPR) review is important.

Every IS auditor is required to choose sides. An IS auditor's independence would be compromised by participating in a nonaudit role on the BPR project. You can't audit your own work. If an IS auditor has participated in the design of systems, processes, or procedures as part of the BPR team, that auditor is required to refuse the audit of those functional areas. Therefore, it's common to have two sets of auditors during BPR projects. One set works on the BPR team to help steer the project, and auditors from a second firm perform verification audits. *Cha-ching!*

Why Use Business Process Reengineering

Times change. People change. Needs change. It is said that change is the only constant in life. BPR is used to improve process performance by removing, combining, or replacing steps that are no longer important. BPR is concerned with reducing costs of the existing process while increasing performance. BPR includes three major areas for improvement:

Business Efficiency Efficiency will increase as the proficiency of workers increases (as they gain experience). In the very beginning, work is slow with multiple test inspections to ensure that results will be acceptable. Workers will progress through the *learning curve*. With more experience, the workers' technique will become more refined. Eventually, the number of inspections may be reduced after the quality becomes consistent.

Improved Techniques   New improvements in the existing techniques will be discovered with more experience. An updated technique may eliminate previous steps that become unnecessary because of higher consistency. Improved methods and advances in technology can change how a process is performed. Several steps may be combined into a single step; eliminating the unnecessary steps increases efficiency. It may be necessary to add extra steps in the process if quality begins to decline.

New Requirements   New requirements may be added in response to a regulation, business need, or customer. The existing business process will be reworked to comply with the updated requirements.

BPR activities are performed as a unique project. The BPR project will design a new process or improve existing processes to replace the outdated, inefficient processes.

BPR Methodology

Every good methodology specifies a basic vision to illustrate its strategy, and recommends standards to follow and procedures to use. There is more than one version of the BPR methodology available for businesses. For clarity, we are going to focus on the views representative of ISACA and the COBIT framework of management guidelines. These are considered an excellent resource in the industry.

The key to governance is for management to take responsibility as the leader for implementing change, while establishing an adequate system of internal control. This would include implementing a culture of continuous monitoring to fuel continuous improvement. There is a saying: "You can't fix what you can't prove." It would be ridiculous to charge off on a whim under the guise of BPR without supporting evidence. Yet some companies do it all the time. BPR is often coupled with an enterprise resource planning (ERP) implementation. It would be a reckless misuse of company resources to switch to a particular ERP system just because it sounds cool, makes you look important, or aids your political agenda because it's the same system used at a former employer.

Consider for a moment that many of us are members of the general public. Stock-holding investors are on the outside of the business without full knowledge of the internal processes. We expect you as the auditor to investigate the supporting evidence and tell us whether management is making good, solid decisions based on intelligent facts. We hold you, the auditor, responsible for telling the truth. Please keep this fiduciary responsibility in mind when working on BPR-related projects.

Genius or Insanity?

It is a commonly held belief that there is a fine line between genius and insanity. The secret is to know which side of the line you're on. The latter is beyond the scope of this book, so let's focus on the genius side. True genius is grounded in a logical progression of intelligent thought.

History is loaded with the names of famous people regarded as the inspired genius in their fields. One characteristic is pervasive: Every great accomplishment was based on lessons learned from careful observations. These observations provided the facts necessary to fuel a progression of ideas into an intelligent hypothesis. The next step was to determine an objective method for testing the hypothesis. Useful metrics were created to help measure results. If the hypothesis failed, it was back to the drawing board to check their work and revise their ideas. Each test simulation yielded additional data to steer their thoughts.

Even Leonardo da Vinci's ideas were considered wild hallucinations until it was realized he had collected evidence indicating a crystal-clear thought process involving observation, hypothesis, and testing. Discipline to keep detailed records is essential for successful BPR projects.

Goal of BPR

All BPR projects are intended to be strategic in nature. We are going to change the way the business operates. Service organizations and manufacturers need a mechanism to support their evolution. Continuous improvement is necessary to survive the challenges of increasing competition with the constant pressure of rising costs. Any change to a running business introduces new magnitudes of risk. Thin profit margins leave little tolerance for bad ideas or inadequate implementation. Proper reengineering will involve comprehensive changes affecting the design structure of management, people in support roles, information systems, and operating policies.

One of the auditor's duties is to impress upon management that controls are necessary. You may need to correct their view that controls appear to slow the process by explaining how controls are necessary to offset the risks that would be difficult to manage or to measure. The most damaging risks are those whose likelihood or effect you cannot calculate. Repeated answers of "I don't know" may indicate that you're on the wrong side of the genius-insanity line.

Guiding Principles for BPR

Let's instill a few guiding principles for your BPR activities. The purpose is to lend a structure to support the innovative thinking necessary for you to be successful. Reengineering projects are founded on specific situations and require creative ideas to generate the appropriate solution. Let's look at three possible approaches:

Think Big   This is an unconstrained top-down approach. The focus is on determining how the organization's strategy can be implemented without being restrained by existing processes. Many of the details in the current processes are ignored. All emphasis is placed on the future process to be (end state). Ideas are generated to answer the question, what will it ultimately be? This is consistent with the change philosophy presented by Jim Collins's famous research on why some companies are more successful than equal competitors in *Good to Great* (HarperCollins, 2001) and by authors Michael Hammer and James Champy in *Reengineering the Corporation* (HarperCollins, 2003). Donald Trump is famous for using the think big approach because people naturally want to be involved in big projects.

Tom Peters illustrates the power of thinking big in his fabulous book *Re-imagine!* (Dorling Kindersley, 2006). The risk is bigger and so are the rewards.

Incremental   This is a bottom-up approach that models existing processes to gain deeper understanding. Metrics are created and compared to identify what can be changed to streamline the process. The focus is on making incremental changes to the current process by identifying opportunities for improvement. The downside of the bottom-up approach is the tendency for BPR teams to spend too much time documenting the current process. By focusing so hard on the current process, their innovative thoughts and ideas are stifled. Overall gains are small because creative genius is lost. This tends to fit the stereotype of detail-oriented accountants spending too much time counting the beans while ignoring the potential that could be realized by exploiting a broader strategy.

Hybrid Approach   The most practical application is a mixed approach. Planning begins with a top-down view of the big-picture strategy. Bottom-up research is performed to understand the current functionality and define the processes in use. The process starts by grading what you have as good, average, or poor (GAP), and then comparing it to what you want. This GAP analysis is used to identify the differences between what is getting done and what needs to occur. The GAP will provide valuable insight for determining the best transition path. This will result in an initial recommendation that may require relatively small changes to remove bottlenecks. Alternatively, it could yield a series of more-complex projects, thus charting a course that places the organization ahead of its competitors. This is a noble route that the auditor is advised to undertake.

Knowledge Requirements for BPR

To be competent in BPR requires a working knowledge of auditing standards and the control frameworks such as COBIT. The competent auditor must possess the following skills before undertaking a BPR project:

- Up-to-date information systems auditing skills
- Specialized CISA audit standard knowledge
- Specialized knowledge of the company processes and procedures
- Specialized knowledge of the functional area being audited
- General management knowledge and skills
- Interpersonal "people" skills

The IS auditor can make an important contribution to their knowledge of internal controls and systems. Frequently the auditor will have to reengineer their own skills and audit approach to deal with the radical changes created by BPR. When auditing BPR, the CISA complements the other auditors on the BPR team who will be representing the special needs of finance and regulatory compliance.

BPR Techniques

ISACA expects every CISA to understand the operating techniques used in BPR projects. There are some conflicting viewpoints by different BPR experts; however, most of the suggested techniques include the following:

- Revising the logical order of individual processes to simplify the process of improving overall quality

- Reviewing a logical diagram of an existing process to determine whether multiple jobs can be combined into fewer steps

- Giving workers additional authority to make operational decisions while maintaining an acceptable level of control

- Eliminating superfluous or overlapping processes

- Standardizing processes, procedures, methods, products, and tools across the organization

- Using the most effective controls to ensure governance

- Converting manual processes into automated methods

- Establishing parallel processes for business continuity

BPR projects should be undertaken only when the business value can be demonstrated. Three simple methods to demonstrate business value are to increase capability, to reduce operating cost, or to obtain compliance with a new requirement. The BPR project may commence after the steering committee has reviewed the ROI evidence, agreed with the scope, and granted formal approval to proceed.

BPR Application Steps

ISACA cites six basic steps in their general approach to BPR. These six steps are simply an extension of Shewhart's Plan-Do-Check-Act model for managing projects:

Envision   Visualize a need (envision). Develop an estimate of the ROI created by the proposed change. Elaborate on the benefit with a preliminary project plan to gain sponsorship from the organization. The plan should define the areas to be reviewed and clarify the desired result at the end of the project (aka *end state objective*). The deliverables of the envision phase include the following:

- Project champion working with the steering committee to gain top management approval

- Brief description of project scope, goals, and objectives

- Description of the specific deliverables from this project

With a preliminary charter to evidence management's approval, the project may proceed into the initiation phase.

Initiate   This phase involves setting BPR goals with the sponsor. Focus on planning the collection of detailed evidence necessary to build the subsequent BPR plan for redesigning the process. Deliverables in the initiation phase include the following:

- Identification of internal and external requirements (project specifications)
- Business case explaining why this project makes sense (justification) and the estimated return on investment compared to the total cost (net ROI)
- Formal project plan with budget, schedule, staffing plan, procurement plan, deliverables, and project risk analysis
- Level of authority the BPR project manager will hold and the composition of any support committee or task force that will be required
- Identification of the profit and loss (P&L) statement's line-item number that money will be debited from to pay for this project and the specific P&L line number that the financial return will later appear under (to provide strict monitoring of the ROI performance)
- Formal project charter signed by the sponsors

It's important to realize that some BPR projects will proceed to their planned conclusion and others may be halted because of insufficient evidence. After a plan is formally approved, the BPR project may proceed to the diagnostic phase.

Diagnose   Document existing processes. Now it's time to see what is working and identify the source of each requirement. Each process step is reviewed to calculate the value it creates. The goal of the diagnostic phase is to gain a better understanding of existing processes. The data collected in the diagnostic phase forms the basis of all planning decisions:

- Detailed documentation of the existing process
- Performance measurement of individual steps in the process
- Evidence of specific process steps that add customer value
- Identification of process steps that don't add value
- Definition of attributes that create value and quality

Put in the extra effort to do a good job of collecting and analyzing the evidence. All future assumptions will be based on evidence from the diagnostic phase.

Redesign   Using the evidence from the diagnostic phase, it's time to develop the new process. This will take several planning iterations to ensure that the strategic objectives are met. The formal redesign plans will be reviewed by sponsors and stakeholders. A final plan will be presented to the steering committee for approval. Here's an example of deliverables from the redesign phase:

- Comparison of the envisioned objective to actual specifications
- Analysis of alternatives (AoA)

- Prototyping and testing of the redesigned process
- Formal documentation of the final design

The project will need formal approval to proceed into the reconstruction phase. Otherwise, the redesign is halted pending further scrutiny while comparing the proposed design with available evidence. Insufficient evidence warrants halting the project.

Reconstruct   With formal approval received, it's time to begin the implementation phase. The current processes are deconstructed and reassembled according to the plan. Reconstruction may be in the form of a parallel process, modular changes, or complete transition. Each method presents a unique risk and reward opportunity. Deliverables from this phase include the following:

- Conversion plan with dependencies in time sequence
- Change control management
- Execution of conversion plan with progress monitoring
- Training of users and support personnel
- Pilot implementation to ensure a smooth migration
- Formal approval by the sponsor.

The reconstructed process must be formally approved by management to witness their consent for fitness of use. IT governance dictates that executive management shall be held responsible for any failures and receive recognition for exceptional results. System performance will be evaluated again after entering production use.

Evaluate (Post Evaluation)   The reconstructed process is monitored to ensure that it works and is producing the strategic value as forecast in the original justification. It's necessary to establish performance, what was learned in the process, and how the proposed changes will be managed.

- Comparison of original forecast to actual performance
- Identification of lessons learned
- Total quality management plan to maintain the new process

A method of continuous improvement is implemented to track the original goals against actual process performance. Annual reevaluation is needed to adapt new requirements or new opportunities.

These steps are easier to practice if you can relate them to something meaningful. Let's compare the BPR process steps with similar objectives in PMI project management and the System Development Life Cycle (SDLC). An excellent way to get buy-in is to communicate by relating BPR steps to other methodologies already in use. Table 2.6 provides an illustration of the objectives in common.

TABLE 2.6   Comparison of common objectives

BPR Process Areas	PMI Project Management Phases	System Development Life Cycle (SDLC)	Objectives in Common
Envision	Initiating	Feasibility	Determine scope, get a strong sponsor, target a process, set goals
Initiate		Requirements definition	Obtain stakeholder buy-in, identify external customer needs
Diagnose	Planning		Identify process attributes, possible benchmarks, activities, resources, roles, cost estimates, and communication needs
Redesign		System design	Devise solutions and alternatives through brainstorming and creative techniques
	Executing	Development	Build prototypes to test the new design
Reconstruct		Implementation	Install IT systems, train users and support staff, begin transition
Evaluate	Monitoring-Controlling	Postimplementation	Monitor and review the new process to see whether goals were attained
	Closing		Document lessons learned, archive files, assign the process to a quality program (TQM)

Now we need to clarify the role of information systems in the BPR effort. Just how does IS help make this project successful?

Role of IS in BPR

ISACA has identified four distinct roles to be delivered by information systems within the BPR projects. IT is a key supplier of tools necessary for the business to be successful. The four roles of IS are as follows:

- Enable the new processes by improving automation.
- Provide IT project management tools to help analyze the process and defined requirements.

- Provide IT support for collaboration tools, teleconferencing, and specialized software supporting the business users.
- Help business unit managers to integrate their business process with ERP systems. This may include integrating business partners through online transaction processing.

Business Process Documentation

When looking at changes to business processes or when implementing these changes, the CISA should consider the use of the following tools to help define and document the processes being changed:

Process Maps   Diagram business processes by using flowcharts, influence diagrams, and fish-bone diagrams to assist in the definition and documentation of the process.

Risk Assessment   Look at the process by using the preceding risk categories as well as other categories. External risk and organizational risk should be assessed. Tools for risk identification, such as interviewing experts, brainstorming, holding risk identification roundtable sessions, and using the Delphi technique, should be considered. The Delphi technique uses a blind interaction of ideas between members of a group. Each member provides suggestions without knowledge of the suggestions by other participants. The exercise continues until a consensus is reached. We cover some of the other methods of performing a risk assessment in Chapter 3.

Benchmarking   Compare your process to another process that is the same or similar.

Roles and Responsibilities   Define and document who is responsible for what process or what portions of the process. Many times the auditor will discover through interviews that several people know a portion of the process but no one knows the whole process.

Tasks and Activities   Define tasks and activities in conjunction with defining roles and responsibilities. The purpose is to define who performs what work and how it affects the overall process. The results may be documented in a project work breakdown structure (WBS). All the tasks in the project are grouped into related work packages. Each task is assigned with its predecessor and successor dependencies identified. The list of tasks is referred to as the WBS.

Process Controls and Data Process Restrictions   Document the current process with clearly defined checkpoints and/or checklists to ensure that the entire process is being performed. Define the data available for the process. This includes defining contributory sources and defining all data available from the process being considered for review.

Now it's time to discuss the types of planning tools available for BPR projects.

BPR Data Management Techniques

High-quality data can be assembled into information that will create significant power. Several planning tools and techniques have been developed to capture the data. We need good tools to combine this data into meaningful information. Let's look at a few of the available options:

- Traditional project management such as PMI
- Analysis tools such as Critical Path Method (CPM) or Program Evaluation Review Technique (PERT) charting
- Presentation using graphical flowcharts (process flow diagrams) with decision trees
- Manual process of setting goals, and performing root cause analysis and risk analysis

The right tools will harness the power necessary for your BPR project to be successful. Let's start with the manual process of setting goals through benchmarking. Later we will discuss the manual process of risk analysis in the Business Impact Analysis project.

Benchmarking as a BPR Tool

Benchmarking is the process of comparing performance data (aka *metrics*). It can be used to evaluate business processes that are under consideration for reengineering. Performance data may be obtained by using a self-assessment or by auditing for compliance against a standard (reference standard). Evidence captured during the diagnostic phase is considered the key to identifying areas for performance improvement and documenting obstacles. ISACA offers the following general guidelines for performing benchmarks:

Plan   Identify the critical processes and create measurement techniques to grade the processes.

Research   Use information about the process and collect regular data (samples) to build a baseline for comparison. Consider input from your customers and use analogous data from other industries.

Observe   Gather internal data and external data from a benchmark partner to aid the comparison results. Benchmark data can also be compared against published standards.

Analyze   Look for root cause-effect relationships and other dependencies in the process. Use predefined tools and procedures to collate the data collected from all available sources.

Adapt   Translate the findings into hypotheses of how these findings will help or hurt strategic business goals. Design a pilot test to prove or disprove the hypotheses.

Improve   Implement a prototype of the new processes. Study the impact and note any unexpected results. Revise the process by using controlled change management. Measure the process results again. Use preestablished procedures such as total quality management for continuous improvement.

The benchmarking process is a valuable first step toward self-improvement. Figure 2.12 illustrates the benchmarking process.

Another excellent tool is the Business Impact Analysis (BIA). This would be more involved than benchmarking, yet a properly executed BIA will yield extremely valuable information.

FIGURE 2.12   Benchmarking process

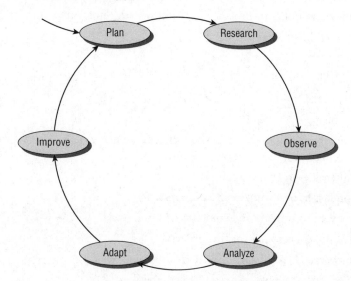

Using a Business Impact Analysis

The *Business Impact Analysis (BIA)* is a discovery process. Its purpose is to uncover the inner workings of any production related process. The BIA will answer questions about actual procedures, shortcuts, workarounds, and the types of failure that may occur. Armed with this knowledge, it is possible to assess priorities.

Part of the BIA is to determine what the process does, who performs the process, and what the output is. The BIA also determines the value of the process output to the organization. The BIA interviewer will ask key managers and key workers a series of questions to discover the low-level details of current processes. Some sample BIA questions that might be asked of key personnel in a BPR process review include the following:

1. What processes do you perform?

2. Who do you perform these actions for?

3. What tools, equipment, and systems do you use?

4. What request, event, or system provides an indication for you to start work on the subject (input)?

5. Get/show examples of the work the person performs (processes). Do multiple processes exist? If so, be sure to document each process for later review.

6. Who is the key vendor and the alternate vendor?

7. What is the time sensitivity of the process?

8. What is the basic priority of the process?

9. Where do you record your work (output)?

10. Who uses the output of your process next, and who depends on your output?

11. What happens if the process is
    - Not used
    - Not available
    - Not performed
    - Not accepted

12. What other methods could you use to accomplish the process? Are there workarounds or alternate processes that might already exist?

13. Would the alternate procedure really work?

14. How can you test it, or has it already been tested?

15. Who else knows this process and could do this in a crisis?

16. Who is the ultimate customer for this process?

17. How much revenue does this process create or support?

18. Is documentation on this process readily available?

19. Is documentation on the technical requirements for the process readily available?

20. Are there previous audit reports about this process that can be examined?

21. What is the projected lifetime of this process? Will the process continue to be used, or is this process being made obsolete by a future process or projected change in business?

Questions 17 and 21 provide key information for determining the true value of the process. Determining how much revenue the process creates or supports helps define its true value to the enterprise. Another measurement for value is to determine how long the process will remain in use.

For example, an organization can afford to spend $50,000 to reengineer a shipping process if they intend to use the process in perpetuity. The cost savings or cost avoidance saved each year will be used to pay for this effort. Processes expected to end within one year will need to be carefully evaluated to determine whether the payback is worth the effort. Practical advice suggests that processes selected for reengineering should have a lifetime in excess of one year, or be nonworking processes, to provide enough return value for the time and effort expended to reengineer them.

Proper planning of the process reengineering project requires documentation of the process to be modified. If the process has been correctly documented with all outputs and all interrelated activities, the chances of having "leftover parts" is minimized.

BPR Project Risk Assessment

Radical improvements are not possible without increased risk. BPR projects are known to have a high rate of failure. Risks associated with changing an existing process must be identified. The *ISACA Audit Standards, Guidelines, and Procedures* identify several risk areas to consider when planning a BPR project. The risks can be broken down into three broad areas of design risks, implementation risks, and operational risks:

Design Risks   A good design can improve profitability while satisfying customers. Conversely, a design failure would spell doom to any BPR project. It would be reckless to undertake new projects without dedicated resources capable of committing the time and attention necessary to develop a quality solution. Often this type of detailed planning may consume more money and time than is available from key personnel. ISACA wants all CISA candidates to recognize the risks that may occur in the BPR design:

Sponsorship Risks   C-level management is not supportive of the effort. Insufficient commitment from the top is just as bad as having the wrong person leading the project. Poor communication is also a major problem.

 Real World Scenario

BIA Improves Awareness

Consider the example of a multinational company that owns a division manufacturing radios. During the BIA process, it is determined that 31 percent of the overall net retained revenue for this organization is generated by the small group manufacturing radios in the United States. Their number one customer is the U.S. military, which favors products made in this country.

This tiny division represents only 7 percent of the multinational company. Therefore, the results bring up an interesting question regarding the net performance from the other 93 percent of the company. The radio division is definitely a top asset. A smart person would wonder whether the executives should implement a BPR project to reproduce the similar results in the other 93 percent of the business or sell off less-profitable divisions. To outsource manufacturing overseas would compromise their advantage of supplying U.S.-made products.

Overall, internal awareness was improved by spotlighting the outstanding profitability of the radio division. Additionally, the analysis sparked conversations that overseas manufacturing would remove the company's market advantage by throwing its product into an import price war.

Scope Risks   The BPR project must be related to the vision and the specifications of the strategic plan. Serious problems will arise if the scope is improperly defined. It's a design failure if politically sacred processes and existing jobs are excluded from the scope of change.

Skill Risks   Absence of radical "out of the box" thinking will create a failure by dismissing new ideas that should have been explored. Thinking big is the most effective way to achieve the highest return on investment. Participants without broad spatial skills will experience serious difficulty because the project vision is beyond their ability to define an effective action plan.

Political Risk   Sabotage is always possible from people fearing a loss of power or resistant to change. Uncontrolled rumors lead to fear and subversion of the concept. People will resist change unless the benefits are well understood and accepted.

Implementation Risks   The implementation risks represent another source of potential failures that could occur during the BPR project. The most common implementation risks include the following:

Leadership Risks   C-level executives may fail to provide enough support for the project to be successful. Leadership failures include disputes over ownership and project scope. Management changes during the BPR project may signal wavering needs that may cause the loss of momentum. Strong sponsors will provide money, time, and resources while serving as project champions with their political support.

Technical Risks   Complexity may overtake the definition of scope. The required capability may be beyond that of prepackaged software. Custom functions and design may exceed IT's creative capability or available time. Delays in implementation could signal that the complexity of scope was underestimated. If the key issues are not fully identified, disputes will arise about the definitions of deliverables, which leads to scope changes during implementation.

Transition Risks   The loss of key personnel may create a loss of focus during implementation. Personnel may feel burned out because of workload or their perception that the project is not worth the effort. Reward and recognition are necessary during transition to prevent the project from losing momentum.

Scope Risks   Improperly defined project scope will produce excessive costs with schedule overruns (variance from schedule). Poor planning may neglect the human resource requirements, which will lead team members to feel that the magnitude of effort is overwhelming. The reaction will cause a narrowing of the scope during implementation, which usually leads to a failure of the original BPR objectives.

Operation/Rollout Risks   It's still possible for the BPR project to fail after careful planning. Common failures during production implementation include negative attitudes and technical flaws. These problems manifest in the form of management risks, technical risks, and cultural risks:

Management Risks   Strong respected leadership is required to resolve power struggles over ownership. Communication problems must be cured to prevent resistance and sabotage. Executive sponsors need to provide sufficient training to prevent an unsuccessful implementation.

Technical Risks   Nothing kills a rollout faster than insufficient support. Inadequate testing leads to operational problems caused by software problems. Data integrity problems represent a root problem capable of escalating into user dissatisfaction. Perceptions of a flawed system will undermine everyone's confidence.

Cultural Risks   Resistance in the organization is a result of failing to achieve user buy-in. Resistance will increase to erode the benefits. Effective training is often successful in solving user problems. Dysfunctional behavior will increase unless the new benefits are well understood and achieved.

Practical Application of BPR

BPR projects require the use of all the principles found in project management. It is advisable to consider project management as the framework for your BPR project. Many of the PMI processes will be utilized to manage the project inputs, tools (techniques), and outputs necessary for the project to be successful. By following a recognized standard, the project manager can prevent most of the errors and common omissions inherent in almost any project.

Let's discuss some practical ground rules for BPR projects:

- Don't fix an existing process unless it's broken.
- Calculate the ROI before investing any resources.
- Make sure you fully understand the process before you try to fix it.
- Make sure you don't have any "leftovers" after reengineering the process. All the original components should be reused, modified, or formally retired.

The following points illustrate how each of these ground rules applies to planning a BPR project.

Don't Fix an Existing Process Unless It's Broken

The return on investment is usually very small unless the existing process is already broken. Small improvements can be gained at lower cost by using the normal change control process. There is no need to implement a BPR project unless dramatic changes are required. The highest return on your investment will be realized by collective brainstorming to fix a missing or broken process.

Calculate the Return on Investment before Investing Any Resources

There is never enough money for all the proposed projects. Opportunity is synonymous with the availability of resources. Businesses must change and evolve to remain competitive. It would be both reckless and negligent to charge off on a new project without having first calculated the potential return on your investment. So ask, "What will we actually get back for our money?" Resources should be spent using the principles of *highest and best use*, also known as *portfolio management*.

If you had only $10,000, what would be the best use of that money? Where should you invest your thoughts and time? You might consider only those ideas that have a profound or life-changing effect rather than just paying some outstanding bills. For example, is the money best spent on a minor system upgrade or by investing in additional staff training? Choose the solution that best improves your bottom-line profits. Don't waste money on something with no return or a low return.

Make Sure You Fully Understand the Process before You Try to Fix It

Even if the process is suspected to be faulty, it's important to have proper evidence before making any changes. The fastest way to failure is to start making changes based on incorrect assumptions.

The BIA is an efficient method for collecting high-quality data. The BIA process involves interviewing subject matter experts to determine what the process does and tracing the root sources of process specifications. A well-run BIA will uncover a complete blueprint of the entire process flow in sequence with influential dependencies and some of the known alternative methods to accomplish the desired results. BIAs are frequently used in organizational acquisitions, divestitures, business continuity planning, and business process reengineering. The value of the BIA is the ability to make decisions factoring in all of the low-level details indicating overreliance, untapped capacity, and alternative sources with the potential to increase net revenue.

 Real World Scenario

Example: USAA Insurance Converts to 100% Digital Imaging

The United Services Automobile Association (USAA) offers insurance and banking services to military and former military personnel. The insurance side of the business needed to fix the problem of files being misplaced. A suggestion was made to switch to document imaging. This would require a complete change in the way the business operates. After careful study, it was determined that USAA could reduce the number of administrative steps in processing claims from 36 to just 6 steps. To accomplish this, their mailroom needed to scan every piece of paper arriving from customers. The benefit was that incomplete claims could be processed through the system while the company simply waited for a final signature or missing evidence to finish the process. The new system went live in 1990 and has been successful. Subsequent BPR projects have expanded the scope to include USAA's other financial services.

Make Sure You Don't Have Any "Leftovers" after Reengineering the Process

Everything in the current process exists for a reason. This is why it's necessary to discover the specifications for inputs, actions, and outputs of the process before making any changes. Some specifications will be new, whereas others may be eligible for retirement. Each specification needs to be thoroughly investigated, no matter how small. The purpose and relationship of every specification needs to be considered before you can determine its disposition.

At one particular organization, the inventory manager misunderstood the reason why the factory needed to warehouse more than 100,000 product labels. It turned out that the label was a custom-made warning label that cost almost nothing if ordered in very large quantities.

The labels had a moderate delay from ordering until shipping to the factory. It turned out to be an extremely serious violation of government law if the product shipped without the required warning label. In fact, it was better to halt production than to ship without the mandated warning label.

Every hour spent in research and planning should be focused on tracing the most current specifications. Each specification will either be reused, modified, or formally retired.

Practical Selection Methods for BPR

The BPR selection process looks for areas with the greatest return on investment. The needs of each organization are unique. Executive governance dictates that the executives must define unique selection criteria and a selection process. Each process under consideration for reengineering must be evaluated and generally fits into one of the following categories:

- Nonworking process
- Marginal process
- Working process
- Excluded process

In addition to these categories, the overall value needs to be considered in the equation. Is there a reasonable ROI for reengineering each process under consideration? Using a report in the format of Table 2.7 is helpful for organizing the discussion of investment, return, and priority.

TABLE 2.7   BPR return on investment and priority

Category	No ROI Anticipated (Probably Not Selected for BPR)	ROI Anticipated	Priority for BPR
Nonworking process	*Insert your process names without ROI*	*Insert your process name having ROI*	1
Marginal process	"	"	2
Working process	"	"	3
Excluded process	"	"	4

You should remember that your goal during BPR is to ensure that the organization is properly managing the entire process.

Let's summarize each of these categories with a little more detail:

Nonworking Process   Some elements of the process are simply not working. It may be a manual or an automated process that can't deliver to the expectations of the user. This is an ideal target for process reengineering. Nonworking processes are usually the highest priority if their business value can be justified. Priority will be based on the anticipated financial return that the process can generate.

Marginal Process   This type of process seems to work yet fails to generate any tangible benefit. Something about the design may be preventing it from generating its full potential. It may be a control issue or design failing to deliver to a specific need. The output of the process needs to be closely reviewed to determine what need it was intended to solve and whether there is any value created by reengineering it. Otherwise, the process might be discontinued.

Working Process   This process is currently in use and generating some type of meaningful benefit. You should have existing documentation of how the process works and its related specifications. Working processes are expected to have a support staff and the necessary controls to achieve compliance with their business objective.

Excluded Process   An excluded process might be exempt from BPR because of its special nature or limited frequency of use. Politics is never a valid reason for exclusion. A process nearing retirement may be excluded because BPR would not generate any increase in value.

Troubleshooting BPR Problems

Without excellent leadership, the BPR project can become a convoluted mess. Even the simplest of objectives may wander aimlessly into failure. We want to take a few minutes to diagnose some of the more common BPR problems you may encounter as an auditor:

Problem: Reengineered Process Resembles the Existing Process   Compare the process to its current objectives and specifications. It will not be identical unless the initiation and diagnostic phases were compromised. If the diagnostic phase was objective, the best solution is to rethink the redesign by using a higher-level approach. Too much emphasis was placed on duplicating the attributes of the old process if the redesign occurred at too low a level or protected a politically sacred area. Approach it again with a "think big" philosophy.

Problem: Business Process Does Not Fit All the Customers   Unserved customers may be outside the target market. Analyze the intended audience to determine whether it represents your most profitable clients. If so, there is no problem in the BPR design. Use the Pareto principle (aka 80/20 rule) to evaluate the net revenue created by the unserved customers. Stick to those clients who generate the highest return in net profits. Times change; everyone else may not be your target customer.

Problem: Implementation of the New Process Is Stalled or Slowing   Failure to implement indicates problems in reconstruction or political blocking. Implementing a smaller pilot project may work to smoke out the problem. Extra effort may be needed to resell the concept and to train the users. A strong leader is usually willing to remove political obstacles (or the person obstructing progress) as long as the effectiveness of the new process has been proven.

Problem: New Process Is Not Performing as Expected or Generates Hidden Incompatibilities   Business processes have informal relationships that may have been missed during BPR planning. Perform a stakeholder analysis to identify missing stakeholders or underrepresented dependencies. The problem can be rooted in leadership failure during initiation, inadequate diagnosis, missed material specifications, or poor planning during reconstruction. This is a frequent problem found in outsourcing arrangements after the impact of total costs are calculated. It may occur during initial implementation or postevaluation.

Additional information on business process reengineering can be found under the BPR guideline G-26 in the *ISACA* Audit Standards, Guidelines, and Procedures.

Understanding the Auditor's Interest in Tactical Management

Tactical management involves the departmental director and manager. Tactical performance reporting should occur during weekly and monthly status meetings with senior-level executives. Tactical performance is frequently included during a regular audit.

As an IS auditor, you will be interested in learning the scope and extent of project management methodologies in use. Your interest will include gaining an understanding of the management tools in use and application of management controls. Tactical management should be using a change control process that exercises advance planning, risk management, and due diligence. The auditor should seek materially relevant evidence demonstrating management's efforts in support of the strategic objectives. The auditor's opinion should include a determination of the effective level of IT integration with various stages of project management. Is tactical management well integrated with measurable performance?

Operations Management

We start the discussion of operations management with a simple definition. An *operation* is a procedure to set forth or produce a desired result.

The objective of operations management is to promote consistency with an effective response to the user requests. Operations management represents support for issues faced in day-to-day business. The operations support is sometimes referred to as firefighting or user support. This section briefly covers the IT goals and operations management.

Sustaining Operations

Every organization faces the program level challenges of sustaining operations. You will investigate whether the IT staff has the capability to sustain current operations. Three areas of interest are immediately identifiable. The auditor should seek evidence to discover whether the following five sustaining factors are met:

- Effective leadership
- Adequate staffing
- Written procedures
- Constant monitoring
- Level of staff integration

It would be practically impossible to sustain regular operations without documented procedures executed by an adequate number of well-trained IT staff members. The staff members must be able to interact and communicate effectively inside the IT organization and with the business organization. To ensure these objectives, each member of the IT team will need to have specified roles and responsibilities.

Tracking Performance

Performance of all operations should be tracked and reported by using metrics developed for the user's needs. These metrics should be based on best practices of NIST, COSO, ISACA's COBIT, and other industry standards. It is the responsibility of tactical management to develop the metrics. Operations management is required to report the detail necessary to generate a score.

Chapter 6 covers operations and metrics in more detail.

Controlling Change

Change control is an organized process for making sure that the best possible decision is reached. The reality is that any change introduces new variables. A person can execute a minor change that does what it intended, but then also has unintended consequences such as disabling or invalidating a previous control setting or a processing method. So change control must be a methodical process.

The change process should be evidenced by supporting policies and procedures. One employer, for example, had a policy that IT server and network changes would occur only on Tuesdays and Thursdays in the evening. Users were required to provide their work-acceptance test procedures along with a competent user from their department. The user would run their own tests to prove whether the evening change had an impact. Positive impacts were desired.

Negative impacts signaled the need to rerun the intended change procedure or restore the system to its earlier condition. Management allowed changes over the weekend if the requirement was so broad as to exceed an 8-hour window. Their preference was to avoid scheduling changes that would result in the next workday being on Monday. Problems occurring on Monday tend to set a negative tone for the entire week.

Internal auditors should be involved in change control meetings. The visibility and experience of the internal auditor present a valuable opportunity for the client. An internal audit should review requested changes to ensure that each change complies with the best practices of change management. You can bet that the staff will become more alert when they realize that the internal auditors are watching.

Understanding the Auditor's Interest in Operational Delivery

The auditor will need to evaluate whether the organization has provided effective daily support in accordance with the IS strategy. What is IT expected to deliver? Taking that into consideration, what are the issues considering fulfillment and capacity to supply this need? There should be a systematic decomposition of how each business objective is translated down into specific needs, which are fulfilled by specific tasks. If there is no stated requirement in a business objective, there should be no specific need, only a request. The IT alignment concept is to dedicate all efforts toward bona fide goals identified in the business strategy, not requests. The auditor's job is to ensure that proper controls are in place and are appropriate to the unique risks of each source and location.

Summary

In this chapter, we have reviewed the authority levels in the organization and controls used for IT governance. A short definition of IT governance is to effectively lead and monitor performance of the information technology investment. IT governance exists at three levels: strategic, tactical, and operational management. Top executives are responsible for providing the strategic guidance with policies and decisions to define objectives; department directors provide tactical management with standards and plans for their subordinates. The operational functions and procedures are controlled by the managers with execution by staff workers.

Exam Essentials

Know how to evaluate the performance and effectiveness of the IT governance structure.   Does IT support the organizational objectives? You will investigate how the IT management decisions are made. After a decision is reached, it is important to understand how the directions are communicated to ensure that the decision supports the desired outcome. Does evidence indicate that management is leading the activities necessary to fulfill the business strategy?

Understand that the organizational structure must be designed to support the business strategy and objectives.   Does the client have a well-documented organizational chart with accurate job descriptions? How does the client handle problem reports, user complaints, and staff member concerns? Is there a mechanism for management oversight?

Be aware that the IT policy, standards, and procedures must be developed under the supervision of management.   A formal process should exist to ensure that each policy is in support of legal requirements and fulfills a business objective. You need to understand how the client determines policies and standards. Who approves the adoption and implementation? Do the policies and standards directly support the business strategy? Do the standards and procedures support the resulting IT strategy?

Know that management is responsible for ensuring compliance with policies and standards.   Operating procedures must be developed to promote compliance and consistency. Have policies, standards, and procedures been formally implemented? How does management monitor compliance? How are violations detected, corrected, and prevented?

Understand that risk management practices should be in use at all times.   Risk management applies to the decision-making process concerning projects, vendors, and operational support. Is an effective risk management practice in use? Does the evidence show that risks are properly managed?

Know that quality management requires the use of generally accepted IT standards.   A benchmarking process should be in use, with a control framework such as COBIT, ISO 17799, the COSO control framework, and the OECD security guidelines. A maturity model such as CMM should be in use to show progress or regression in regard to internal controls.

Understand that IT performance and IT vendors should be tracked by using key performance indicators.   The goal of IT governance is to align IT resources to support the business strategy. The role of IT is to solve support problems faced by business users. The IT steering committee is designed to identify business support issues to be resolved by IT. Key performance indicators are based on business needs and used to determine the IT return on investment.

Review Questions

1. What is the primary purpose of the IT steering committee?
   A. Make technical recommendations
   B. Identify business issues and objectives
   C. Review vendor contracts
   D. Specify the IT organizational structure

2. Which of these strategies is used in business process reengineering with an incremental approach?
   A. Bottom-up
   B. End-state
   C. Unconstrained
   D. Top-down

3. The Software Engineering Institute's Capability Maturity Model (CMM) is best described by which of the following statements?
   A. Measurement of resources necessary to ensure a reduction in coding defects
   B. Documentation of accomplishments achieved during program development
   C. Relationship of application performance to the user's stated requirement
   D. Baseline of the current progress or regression

4. What would be the area of greatest interest during an audit of a business process reengineering (BPR) project?
   A. The steering committee approves sufficient controls for fraud detection.
   B. Planning methods include Program Evaluation Review Technique (PERT).
   C. Risk management planning with alignment of the project to business objectives.
   D. Vendor participation including documentation, installation assistance, and training.

5. What is the correct sequence for benchmark processes in business process reengineering (BPR) projects?
   A. Plan, research, observe, analyze, adapt, improve
   B. Research, test, plan, adapt, analyze, improve
   C. Plan, observe, analyze, improve, test
   D. Observe, research, analyze, adapt, plan, implement

6. Which of the following statements is true concerning the steering committee?

    A. Steering committee membership is composed of directors from each department.

    B. The steering committee focuses the agenda on IT issues.

    C. Absence of a formal charter indicates a lack of controls.

    D. The steering committee conducts formal management oversight reviews.

7. Which of the following is *not* an advantage of a mature project management office (PMO)?

    A. Advanced planning assistance

    B. Master project register

    C. Coordination of projects across departments

    D. Independent projects

8. The Capability Maturity Model (CMM) contains five levels of achievement. Which of the following answers contains three of the levels in proper sequence?

    A. Initial, Managed, Repeatable

    B. Initial, Managed, Defined

    C. Defined, Managed, Optimized

    D. Managed, Defined, Repeatable

9. The organization's _____ is focused on exploiting trends forecast in the next three to five years.

    A. Strategy

    B. Long-term planning

    C. Operational plan

    D. Managerial plan

10. Which of the following is the best example of mandatory controls?

    A. User account permissions

    B. Corporate guidelines

    C. Acceptable use policy

    D. Government regulation

11. During the selection of a BPR project, which of the following is the ideal target with the highest return?

    A. Marginal process

    B. Nonworking process

    C. Working process

    D. Excluded process

12. Who sets the priorities and objectives of the IT balanced scorecard (BSC)?

   A. Chief information officer (CIO)

   B. Chief financial officer (CFO)

   C. Chief executive officer (CEO)

   D. IT steering committee

13. Which of the following business process reengineering (BPR) risks are likely to occur during the design phase?

   A. Transition risk, skill risk, financial risk

   B. Management risk, technical risk, HR risk

   C. Technical risk, detection risk, audit risk

   D. Scope risk, skill risk, political risk

14. Which of the following answers contains the steps for business process reengineering (BPR) in proper sequence?

   A. Diagnose, envision, redesign, reconstruct

   B. Evaluate, envision, redesign, reconstruct, review

   C. Envision, initiate, diagnose, redesign, reconstruct, evaluate

   D. Initiate, evaluate, diagnose, reconstruct, review

15. What is the name of the decentralized control method enabling someone to make a decision based on their own options?

   A. Executive

   B. Discretionary

   C. Detailed

   D. Mandatory

16. What is the primary purpose of employee contracts?

   A. Define the relationship as work for hire

   B. Prevent individuals from ever working for competitors

   C. Enforce the requirement to join a union

   D. Specify the terms of employee benefits

17. Which of the following is a governance problem that may occur when projects are funded under the "sponsor pays" method?

   A. Deliverables are determined by the sponsor.

   B. The definition of quality may be insufficient.

   C. The sponsor may not implement the proper controls.

   D. The sponsor may not have enough funding.

18. Which of the following is not a reason cited in the text that balanced scorecard (BSC) implementations could fail?

A. Politics of losing the department budget

B. Top management provides full support

C. Lack of BSC training and awareness

D. Empire building by the department head

19. *Shadow organization* refers to two groups performing similar functions under different departments. What does the presence of a shadow organization indicate?

A. Twice the support coverage

B. A relationship of trust and proper delegation of authority

C. Executive distrust or failure to integrate

D. A sponsor who is cooperating as a team player with separation of duties

20. Which type of charge-back scheme is notorious for violating separation of duties or for attempting to exceed authority?

A. Sponsor pays

B. Actual usage billing

C. Charge-back

D. Budgeted cost

21. What is the advantage of using PERT analysis during projects for business process reengineering (BPR)?

A. It charts a detailed sequence of individual activities.

B. It is a critical path methodology.

C. It is used to perform root cause analysis.

D. It enables the use of decision tree reporting.

22. Which statement about the Capability Maturity Model is *not* true?

A. Level 3 provides quantitative measurement of the process output.

B. Level 3 processes have published objectives, measurements, and standards that are in effect across departmental boundaries.

C. Level 5 provides maximum control in outsourcing because the definition of requirements is very specific.

D. Level 5 maturity converts a product into a commodity and allows a company to pay less and demand unquestionable adherence to management's authority.

23. Which of the following statements has the best correlation to the definition of *strategy*?

    A. Defines the techniques to be used in support of the business objective

    B. Defines the necessary procedures to accomplish the goal

    C. Defines guidelines to follow in a recipe for success

    D. Defines what business we are in for the next three years

24. Why is change control considered a governance issue?

    A. It forces separation of duties to ensure that at least two people agree with the decision.

    B. Change control increases the number of people employed and therefore provides a valuable economic advantage.

    C. It allows management to hire less-skilled personnel and still get the same results.

    D. Proper implementation of governance saves money by reducing the need for change control.

25. Which of the following is *not* considered a control failure?

    A. Using a policy that lacks a detective mechanism to identify violations

    B. Modifying an ineffective procedure outside of change control

    C. Testing to discover how many policy violations have occurred

    D. Implementing a policy or standard without consequences of failure

Answers to Review Questions

1. B. The purpose of the steering committee is to bring the awareness of business issues and objectives to IT management. An effective steering committee will focus on the service level necessary to support the business strategy.

2. A. The incremental approach uses bottom-up modeling of the existing process. Overall gains tend to be small because this method focuses so hard on current processes. All the other choices represent a think-big (top-down) approach without limitations. Top-down looks at what it could be, not what it is (end-state).

3. D. The Capability Maturity Model provides a baseline measurement of process maturity. The CMM begins with no process defined and progresses through five phases of documentation and controls. The fifth phase represents the highest level of maturity.

4. C. The steering committee provides guidance to IT concerning business objectives. A risk management plan must be in use for every BPR project. The purpose of risk management is to determine whether the project can actually fulfill a business objective. The second part of risk management is to determine whether the organization will be able to complete the project and generate the desired results.

5. A. The business process reengineering sequence is to plan for change, research possible implications, observe the current process, analyze potential opportunities for improvement and verify key performance indicators, adapt to the new/updated process, and work to improve the results.

6. C. The steering committee should be authorized by a formal charter. The lack of a steering committee indicates that IT is not governed by formal alignment to business objectives. The technology investment is not properly managed as an investment portfolio should be managed. The purpose of the steering committee is to convey business issues that IT should consider and objectives to fulfill. Membership of individuals on the steering committee should be formally designated.

7. D. The PMO provides governance to coordinate and oversee all projects across the organization. This provides historical data for estimating, and success and failure criteria. PMO provides maturity to the process of managing projects.

8. C. The five levels of achievement in the Capability Maturity Model (CMM) are level 1—Initial, level 2—Repeatable, level 3—Defined, level 4—Managed, and level 5—Optimized.

9. A. A strategy provides answers to "what business" the organization wants to be in. This strategy is based on scenario planning and forecasting to alter the organization's structure, priorities, locations, and staffing. It could result in the decision to buy, sell, or consolidate.

10. D. A government regulation is a mandatory control that forces compliance. Mandatory controls are the strongest type of control. Permission is explicit or it must be denied.

11. B. Nonworking processes, whether manual or automated, are usually the highest priority if their business value can be justified.

12. C. The BSC is intended to provide a unifying approach on how the CEO expects the business process to interact across the organization. IT's scorecard is a subset of the CEO's overall enterprise scorecard. The BSC's objective is to break down management barriers and convert department budgets into an entire cross-function workflow. The CEO or COO will control decisions to eliminate waste and prevent self-directed decisions by department managers.

13. D. The primary risks during the BPR design phase are improper scope, lack of necessary skills, political resistance, and a failure by management to support the project.

14. C. The steps are as follows: Visualize a need (envision); the sponsor sets BPR goals (initiate); document existing processes (diagnose); develop the new process (redesign); implement changes (reconstruct); provide postmonitoring to improve the results (evaluate).

15. B. Discretionary control is usually the choice selected in business. Its weakness is that someone decides rather than uses a formal centralized authority. Auditors should investigate how decisions are made and who makes each decision. This is usually a good place to look for control failures.

16. A. Employee contracts provide evidence of the work relationship: that the employee is providing "work for hire" to the company. All of the employee's discoveries and development become the intellectual property of the employer.

17. C. The auditor needs to recognize that the sponsor may attempt to exceed their authority or fail to implement proper controls. Project scope should be controlled and verified to include separation of duties with preventative, detective, and corrective controls. It would be a failure in governance to allow a project to occur otherwise.

18. B. The major goal of using a BSC is to ensure that everyone under the CEO's, COO's, and CFO's management understands a primary unified direction. BSC is designed to kill empire building by division heads, vice presidents, and department-level directors. The number one deliverable is cutting waste by eliminating self-directed decisions below the C-level and returning control to the CEO or highest executive.

19. C. Shadow organizations indicate an integration failure caused by executive distrust or similar conflict. This creates additional conflict with inefficiencies of scale. Problems include conflicting strategies, and the sponsor violating separation of duties or exceeding their normal authority. Shadow organizations are known for duplication of effort, creating a high combined cost to the organization.

20. A. Sponsor pays is notorious for problems of exceeding authority, violating separation of duties, and failing to implement all the governance controls. Sponsors tend to pay for only what they want. Exceptionally good sponsors consider everyone's needs ahead of their own agenda.

21. B. PERT analysis shows the critical path to illustrate the minimum specific tasks necessary to complete the project's objective. The CPM technique is a valuable tool for demonstrating what must be accomplished versus what was requested. High-dependency tasks get performed, while low-dependency tasks may be cancelled from the project.

22. A. Qualitative measurement (opinion based) occurs at level 3, and quantitative measurement (counting based) is at level 4. Level 5 effectively converts the product into a commodity with the intent to squeeze out every last percentile of improvement. All workers are expected to just do what they are told and have no authority. At level 5, the company has the most control and may decide to outsource with lower-paid workers.

23. D. Strategy defines the primary business we are in for the next three to five years. Using this information, the business can develop or adopt supporting standards and then create low-level procedures to accomplish the strategic objective.

24. A. Change control is a foundation of good governance. The purpose is to reduce questionable decisions. Benefits of change control include no longer wasting resources on low-profit tasks and preventing failure by reducing the risk (risk mitigation).

25. C. All of the available options except testing indicate that a control failure was present. The minimum effective control must include a preventative, detective, and corrective action.

Additional CISA practice questions are available on the author's website at www.CertTest.com.

Chapter

3

Audit Process

THE OBJECTIVE OF THIS CHAPTER IS TO ACQUAINT THE READER WITH THE FOLLOWING CONCEPTS:

- ✓ Understanding management of the overall audit program
- ✓ Developing and implementing a risk-based audit strategy
- ✓ Understanding how to structure an audit
- ✓ Implementing the principles of quality into audit activities
- ✓ Planning required for specific audits
- ✓ Implementing risk management and control practices while maintaining independence
- ✓ Understanding qualifications and competence requirements
- ✓ Conducting audits in accordance with standards, guidelines, and best practices
- ✓ Knowing the types of controls and how they are implemented
- ✓ Understanding the effect of pervasive controls on audits
- ✓ Acquiring and using proper audit evidence
- ✓ Understanding the new challenge of electronic discovery
- ✓ Dealing with conflict, potential risks, and communicating to stakeholders
- ✓ Preparing audit documentation and reports

This chapter covers the entire audit process, using the ISO audit standards with additional detail from ISACA. As you will recall, the ISO standards rank superior, and it's good that ISACA is working diligently to keep up. Every client seeking assistance from a CISA is interested in obtaining annual certification or compliance for their organization. To be successful will require a series of individual audits to encompass all of the little bits and pieces necessary to reach that coveted letter of compliance. Once the organization is certified, a series of surveillance audits are required to ensure that the client is still performing the right tasks and still following their own procedures.

Understanding the Audit Program

An *audit program* is a ongoing series of smaller audits to ensure that the organization is taking necessary steps to remain compliant to the evolving changes in regulations or market conditions. Let's look at the difference between program management and running a project:

Program Management   Programs are a series of ongoing activities usually managed by an executive vice president. Program leaders operate within the normal organizational structure while providing progress and status reports for as long as the organization or program exists. The program will outlive the careers of the workers, so it is necessary to recruit and train replacements to continue the work. Programs include quality management, financial accounting, human resource management, asset management, marketing and sales, and maintenance, to name a few. A program can charter temporary projects such as individual audits to support short-term program objectives. Big goals are broken down into a series of small projects, like movements in a ballet or acts in a theatrical play. The completed series of projects are sequenced to fulfill the objective of the program.

Project   A project is a short-term set of activities managed by a project manager operating outside of the normal organizational structure. The project manager will report to the sponsor paying for the project or an assigned manager. All formal orders and reporting by the project manager will be brokered through this liaison to reduce confusion and increase the sponsor's control. The project manager may be an internal resource, consultant, or vendor depending on the situation. The scope of the project is limited, and objectives are clearly defined with a fixed ending date for completion. The objective could be to move a group of workers from one building to another, convert to a different ERP system, cancel outsourced services to bring back in-house operations, raise money for charity, and so forth. After the task is completed, the project is over. Everyone on the project will have to find work elsewhere in another project or for another client.

It's important to understand that the audit program incorporates all of the requirements across the organization into one overall compliance plan. Each individual regulation is listed in detail on a requirements register and becomes part of ongoing surveillance monitoring for the current year. The internal audit group will receive its charter from the audit program. Frequently, the audit program will possess the authority to hire third-party independent auditors for annual certification.

Audit Program Objectives and Scope

Every audit program will contain a list of objectives. High level objectives may come from executive mandate, regulations, or industry standards. The auditor should expect audit program objectives to vary according to department tasks, the subject matter, or a particular step in their process workflow. Larger organizations have more audit objectives, and smaller organizations usually have fewer because management has better control with fewer communication problems in a smaller organization.

Let's consider the example of a midsize consulting business that accepts credit cards for payment. Table 3.1 demonstrates a simplified view of some audit program objectives that this consulting house would likely encounter.

TABLE 3.1   Example of audit program objectives

Objective	Regulation/Standard	Departments	Desired Audit Frequency
PCI 1.2	Payment card industry	Sales, Finance, IT	Monthly
EEOC	Equal Employment Opportunity Commission	HR	Quarterly
Personnel security clearances	Government contract eligibility (detailed)	HR	Quarterly
ISO 14001	Environmentally friendly: LEED, GoGreen	Facilities	Annually
ISO 27002	Information Security Management System	IT, Quality	Quarterly
ISO 15489	Records management	Finance, Quality	Quarterly
ISO 27006	Audit certification	HR, Internal Audit	Quarterly

TABLE 3.1   Example of audit program objectives *(continued)*

Objective	Regulation/Standard	Departments	Desired Audit Frequency
IFRS	International Financial Reporting Standard (Replaced GAAP)	Finance	Monthly
Personnel certification	Individual retraining to maintain credentials relied upon by clients	HR	Annually

Notice how the audit program objectives span into different departments, each with its own specialized technical experts. Information technology (hardware) and information systems (programming) will probably have a bit part in compliance for every one of these objectives. This means that because of the subject matter, a CISA auditor may serve in a junior member role participating on the audit team for finance or ISO audits.

In several of these examples, the lead auditor will need to be a certified accountant, an ISO certified in quality, an ISO certified in environmental systems, or certified by the Society for Human Resource Management. The auditor competence provision in the auditing standard is intended to remind us to limit activities to our area of proven expertise or get additional training to expand our skills. We cover more detail on audit team roles and responsibilities later in this chapter. At this stage, my goal is to demonstrate how an organizational audit program manages multiple compliance requirements while ignoring departmental boundaries.

Audit Program Extent

Size and complexity of an auditee organization will have a direct influence on the audit program. As auditors, our goal is the same, but scale and volume become the challenge. Larger organizations will require a more involved audit approach because of the volume of people and diversity of job roles. Proving governance is a challenge in larger organizations, where it may be difficult to pinpoint exactly who is responsible for a specific activity. Then you have to find enough evidence to test in support of the audit conclusion. In a large organization, staff members may wonder if they have the authority to make decisions that have not been previously encountered.

Small organizations have significantly lower audit requirements simply because fewer people are involved and management has the benefit of more day-to-day visibility. In a small business, the majority of workers usually know what is going on and why decisions are made.

Let's look at the audit planning issues you need to consider regardless of the size of the organization:

- Number of geographic locations
- Diversity of products
- Activities outsourced to third party (subcontract)

- Needs for certification, accreditation, or registration
- Concerns raised from interested parties
- Complexity of regulations or contracts to be audited
- Type, scope, and number of activities to be audited
- Participation required by external subcontractors
- Audit frequency
- Follow-up on recommendations in previous audits
- Cost, resource, and time requirements
- Discontinuation of low-profit activities, layoffs, failing products

Organizations will change in response to economic market situations. The costs of compliance are wrapped into the overhead cost of a product or service. Regardless of the industry, there are only two possible outcomes: If it is profitable, the product or service will continue; if it is not profitable or costs too much to be compliant, the product offering will be shut down with offices closed and workers laid off.

In reality, many executives realize there is no profitable return on investment for compliance. Compliance is a burden cost of overhead. Compliance eats profits. If you're compliant, you may continue in business while attempting to make a profit. An organization will be forced out if they are noncompliant or quit the market if unable to make a profit after all the costs are incurred. One of the primary objectives of the audit program is to produce enough dependable evidence through internal auditors to reduce the full burden cost of using external auditors.

Don't quit your job at a big company to offer consulting services to small business. Most small businesses are not able to financially support ongoing governance and auditing consultants.

Audit Program Responsibilities

An ongoing audit program is part of the risk-mitigation strategy. As mentioned previously, its goal is to combine the overall requirements into one centrally managed plan. It is very important to ensure proper record keeping of all audit activities in order to realize the expected benefit. Audit program management will usually include a commercially produced audit management system (AMS) with the following functions:

- Database of individual elements within the compliance objectives (COBIT, NIST 800-53, ISO 27002, SOX)
- List of audit tasks (open, completed, closed)
- Approved audit procedures
- Approved templates and working papers

- Skills matrix for audit team members
- Resource scheduling features
- Budget estimating
- Performance tracking system
- Historical records of prior audits for comparison

Without this type of centralized control of the audit program, the auditor's performance would be haphazard at best. Individual audit teams will rely on the AMS to ensure consistency between audit projects. In organizations with low maturity, the AMS provides a good starting point. In larger organizations, it is essential to accomplish the auditor's mission.

Audit Program Resources

While the planning and tracking mechanisms of the AMS represent a tremendous value, it takes money and skilled personnel to run an audit program. Financial resources need to be allocated to properly develop, implement, and manage the ongoing audit function. Let's consider a few of the basic resource requirements:

Financial Commitment   Money is required with the authority to spend it on everything that supports the audit program. This includes personnel, tools, travel, training, administrative support, and other expenses. In well-run organizations, these basic costs of auditing are pre-approved to reduce overhead expense.

Competent Auditor   Training and maintaining the auditor skill level is an ongoing struggle. It will take more than the minimum two weeks of annual training to stay current with the proliferation of vendor software upgrades and changes in various regulations. Auditors will also rely on technical experts.

Technical Expert   A technical expert is a nonauditor providing specific knowledge or expertise to the audit team. This person assists with special skills related to the organization, process, or activity to be audited. Consider the *CSI: Crime Scene Investigation* television show. CSI uses experts in weapons, forensics, psychology, and so forth. As CISAs, we might use technical specialists with vendor skills in Java, Unix, SAP, Oracle, or PeopleSoft, for example. Maybe the audit needs forensic skills or requires assistance with language and cultural issues. In Arabic culture, men interviewing women will be a problem. Technical experts perform specific tasks while the auditor supervises to evaluates the results. Technical experts usually need additional training on how to work with the auditor because the auditor is still in charge of all decisions and interpreting the relevance of results.

Audit Tools   It takes more than a book of auditing techniques to properly manage the audit process. Funds will need to be allocated to purchase auditing tools along with the necessary training in their use. Never forget, the best way to select audit software is to attend training *first* for two or three different vendors; then decide if the software actually fits your intended workflow. Some vendors will discourage training first because it shifts power to the buyer.

Administrative Support Resources   Great presentations do not write themselves. They are usually the work of several dedicated individuals. Those individuals represent a significant asset. Low-quality work done in a hurry because of a rushed deadline is still crappy work. The audit program manager is responsible for ensuring sufficient travel time, proper accommodations, resource availability, scheduling, and other needs.

Managing the audit program takes a commitment to do the right thing at the right time. It takes money, commitment, and performance tracking to ensure quality. Without the full support of executive management in time, wide-scale visibility, and money, your audit program will fail. Once you have sufficient support, the next step is to ensure that the correct procedures are being used for consistency.

Audit Program Procedures

As you will recall from Chapter 1, "Secrets of a Successful Auditor," the audit program policy informs everyone that the overall auditing program is important. We use standards as a uniform rule of measurement, and each standard is supported by a set of procedures. The audit program is run in the same manner as an ISO 9001 quality management program. Every auditor needs to ensure that the following procedures are in their toolkit:

- Audit planning
- Scheduling audits
- Assuring competence of auditors and audit team leaders
- Selecting appropriate audit teams
- Assigning roles and responsibilities
- Conducting audits
- Maintaining audit program(me) records
- Monitoring performance and effectiveness
- Complaint tracking
- Reporting to top management on overall achievements

In larger organizations, these are included in the AMS database. In a small organization, all these activities can be addressed in a single combined procedure. It is the auditor's job to ensure that each is accomplished with the appropriate degree of rigor based on the risk or consequences of failure.

Audit Program Implementation

It's important to communicate the audit program and objectives to relevant parties including executives, clients, staff workers, and vendors. The audit program manager must be actively participating in all three aspects of running the administrative audit program (programme).

Management Control   The audit program manager needs to be visible to relevant parties in order to effectively communicate issues and objectives. This individual is a spokesperson for the auditors. The audit program manager's goal is to ensure that individual audits are conducted according to the overall program objectives.

Centralized Record Keeping   Audit records provide evidence in the form of information relevant to proving compliance to audit criteria or deficiencies that need to be fixed. This valuable data contains sensitive information that requires safeguards to protect from loss or unauthorized disclosure. A centralized record-keeping system provides significantly more control than a distributed system. Consistency is critical in order to realize the cost-saving benefits. Audit program managers are responsible for ensuring the review and approval of audit records. Audit records should be kept within an ISO 15489–compliant records management environment.

Distribution Control   Records kept locked away provide no real benefit to the users. Therefore, distribution control is necessary to get the appropriate records to clients and other specific parties. This is part of the overall workflow to ensure proper follow-up after the audit.

Now that the control basics have been accomplished, it is time to look at the contents of the audit program records.

Audit Program Records

External auditors will be very interested in how the records of prior audits are maintained. A highly organized system of records management instills confidence because it proves that the audit program is being followed with a high degree of rigor. A disorganized mess would indicate an implementation failure of the audit program. A short list of the audit records we expect to find includes the following:

Auditing Program Schedule   This should include an annual schedule of individual audits including dates and duration. There should be some indication of the planned date and the actual date completed.

Records of Individual Audits   We should find an audit plan with records indicating auditing team personnel, auditee, sampling plan, evidence testing procedures, and results. Every audit file should include a copy of the correspondence and reports issued. These include the following:

- Nonconformity reports
- Corrective and preventative action reports
- Audit follow-up reports
- Results of audit program review

Audit Team Personnel Records   Reports and findings are only as good as the auditors who produced them. Records are necessary to indicate how the audit team was selected and individual attributes for each team member. Some examples include the following:

- Skills matrix
- Team selection criteria

- Auditor training records (competence)
- Auditor performance evaluation
- Recommendations to improve performance

All this great information would be worthless unless record retention safeguards are properly implemented. One of the best safeguards is to conduct an ongoing monitoring interview process.

Audit Program Monitoring and Review

Great results do not happen automatically. In fact, it would be reckless negligence to set up an audit program unless the results are tracked to ensure that everybody's doing the job right. From a quality control perspective, it is important to verify the audit procedures in use are conforming to the stated objectives. Let's revisit three of the requirements in order to have a continuous improvement process. The first metric we need is the goal, followed by a performance measurement, and then by reporting the results with trend analysis. Let's look at the difference between a goal indicator and a performance indicator:

Key Goal Indicator (KGI)   Just think of the KGI as a scoreboard. Each KGI indicates that a specific goal has been reached. Its purpose is to show that you achieved your overall goal. Examples of personal KGIs may include paying off your home mortgage, your children being accepted to a fine university, graduating from university, saving enough money for retirement, and having grandchildren. For CISA work, the KGI might be PCI compliance, SOX section 400 related to "off book transactions," compliance for projects or contracts not listed in financial reports, ISO 9001 certification, and other major initiatives.

Key Performance Indicator (KPI)   These metrics are like percentages you can find in sports. In baseball, a player's batting average (30.06 percent), homerun average (06.91 percent), and bases stolen (05.33 percent) represent the athlete's historical performance. Metrics are also used to record the performance of personnel, time, and accuracy during the audit. These metrics are the foundation of continuous improvement. As auditors, we are interested in monitoring several important components necessary for a successful audit program. Here are just a few:

- Evolving needs and expectations of interested parties (scope changes)
- Implementation of alternatives or new procedures in audit planning
- Conformity with audit procedures and schedules
- Consistency between audit teams
- Improvements in record keeping
- Feedback from audit clients and auditees
- Improvement observations from auditors
- Audit results and trends

Every audit should undergo a series of performance reviews with the expectation of recording lessons learned from each audit. This should include a pre-audit review to ensure that the auditor is prepared to execute the audit. A second performance review occurs during the audit, followed by postaudit review to ensure quality. Let's start with the preplanning of an individual audit.

Planning Individual Audits

The auditing process is based on a series of generally accepted auditing procedures. An audit is simply a systematic review of historical data. It involves defining a realistic objective, capturing applicable evidence (sampling plan), testing the evidence (verification), comparing test results to audit criteria (evaluation), and generating a report of findings (audit results). The person responsible for managing the audit program will appoint a team leader for each specific audit. Your job as an IS auditor is to provide reasonable assurance that audit objectives are accomplished using applicable professional auditing standards. Let's review a few basics in scope planning:

Audit Scope   Think of the audit scope as boundaries described by processes to be reviewed, within specific physical locations of the organization. Keep it simple by describing location, units to measure, specific activities, and a particular process with an applicable time period measured in days, weeks, or months. Compliance *never* happens in one giant audit. Our goal is to break down the big, complex workflow into a series of small and manageable audits executed on different days or different months.

Audit Criteria   Identify a set of policies the client wants to be measured against. Then specify the procedures or requirements to compare against the evidence collected.

Audit Team   It's rare for the audit to be done by only one person. Audit teams conduct the audit with support of technical experts as needed. One senior auditor is appointed as the lead auditor, and the team may include auditors in training. This group operates just like the investigative team of specialists featured as crime solvers on the *CSI* TV shows. Depending on the objectives, the audit can be performed by internal staff, vendors, or external third parties. Here are some possibilities:

Internal Audits (or First-Party Audits)   These represent a self-declaration of conformity. A moderate level of independence may be demonstrated by the auditor having no responsibility in the activity being audited. This would be someone with no operational responsibility auditing in a different area unrelated to their own job.

External Audits (or Second-Party Audits)   Customers, vendors, or someone with interest in the activity being audited will conduct the audit.

Independent External Audits (or Third-Party Audits)   This is the highest level of trust because the auditors are not related to the organization being audited. The conclusions for this audit can be used for licensing or industry certification.

Integrated Audit (or Combined Audit)   This occurs when two or more functions are being audited at the same time for the sake of efficiency.

Joint Audit   In a joint audit, two or more auditor organizations cooperate to audit a single auditee. This might occur because of the complexities of scope or tight deadlines. Special consideration should be given to the formal division of labor between the different organizations and reviewed before the audit commences.

During an audit, it is important to remember that all decisions and opinions will need to be supported by evidence and documentation. It is the auditor's responsibility to ensure consistency in the audit process. An *audit quality control plan* should be adopted to support these basic objectives.

There are 10 audit stages to be aware of when performing an audit. CISAs need to be aware of their duties in each of these stages:

- Approving the audit charter or engagement letter
- Preplanning the audit
- Performing a risk assessment
- Determining whether an audit is possible
- Performing the actual audit
- Gathering evidence
- Performing audit tests
- Analyzing the results
- Reporting the results
- Conducting any follow-up activities

In this chapter, you will look at each of these stages in detail along with various procedures used during the audit. Figure 3.1 illustrates a simple flowchart of the audit process. The actual execution of the audit will be more complex.

We will begin with the process of establishing an audit charter in order to gain the authority to perform an audit. You can follow the process by using the following bar graphic to stay in sync as we go through the 10 stages.

Establishing and Approving an Audit Charter

The first audit objective is to establish an *audit charter*, which gives you the authority to perform an audit. The audit charter is issued by executive management or the board of directors.

When we refer to management, we are referring to the auditee unless stated otherwise.

FIGURE 3.1   Overview of the audit process

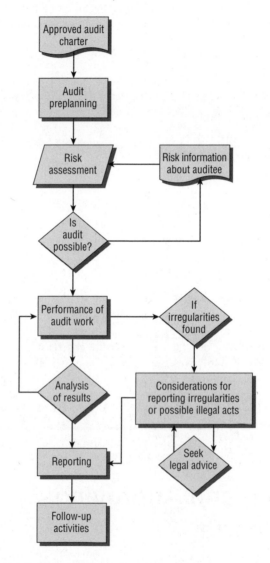

The audit charter should clearly state management's assertion of responsibility, their objectives, and delegation of authority. An audit charter outlines your responsibility, authority, and accountability:

Responsibility   Provides scope with goals and objectives

Authority   Grants the right to perform an audit and the right to obtain access relevant to the audit

Accountability   Defines mutually agreed-upon actions between the audit committee and the auditor, complete with reporting requirements

Role of the Audit Committee

Each organization should have an *audit committee* composed of business executives. Each audit committee member is required to be financially literate, with the ability to read and understand financial statements including balance sheets, income statements, and cash flow statements. The audit committee members are expected to have past employment experience in accounting or finance, and hold certification in accounting. A chief executive officer with comparable financial sophistication may be a member of an audit committee.

The purpose of the audit committee is to provide advice to the executive accounting officer concerning internal control strategies, priorities, and assurances. It is unlikely that an executive officer will know every detail about the activities within their organization. In spite of this, executive officers are held accountable for any internal control failures. Audit committees are not a substitute for executives who must govern, control, and manage their organization. The audit committee is delegated the authority to review and challenge the assurances of internal controls made by executive management.

The audit committee is expected to maintain a positive working relationship with management, internal auditors, and independent auditors. The committee manages planned audit activities and the results of both internal and external audits. The committee is authorized to engage outside experts for independent assurance. Both internal auditors and external auditors will have escalation procedures designed to communicate significant weaknesses that have been identified. The auditor will seek to have the weaknesses corrected in order to give a positive assurance that the risk is appropriately controlled and managed. The head of the internal audit and the external audit representative should have free access to the audit committee chairperson. This ensures an opportunity to raise any concerns the auditor may have concerning processes, internal controls, risks, and limitations. This reporting relationship is shown in the following graphic.

The audit committee should meet on a regular basis, at least four times a year, to fulfill this requirement. The Sarbanes-Oxley Act of 2002 (SOX) requires executives to certify that

all internal control weaknesses have been discovered, with full disclosure to the audit committee provided every 90 days.

The audit committee is responsible for issuing the audit charter to grant the authority for internal audits. The audit charter should be approved by the highest level of management as well as the audit committee. Authority also needs to be granted for an independent audit. A document called an engagement letter grants authority for an independent external audit.

Preplanning Specific Audits

The audit charter allows the delegation of an audit to an external organization via an engagement letter. The *engagement letter* helps define the relationship to an independent auditor for individual assignments. The letter records the understanding between the audit committee and the independent auditor.

> The primary difference between an engagement letter and an audit charter is that an engagement letter addresses the independence of the auditor.

Engagement letters should include the following:

- All points outlined in the audit charter
- Independence of the auditor (responsibility)
- Evidence of an agreement to the terms and conditions (authority)
- Agreed-upon completion dates (accountability)

Now that we have the authority, it is time to move into preplanning everything we're going to do in the audit. The first step in preplanning is to ask, "What is the objective of this particular audit?" The objective may be compliance to a particular standard, surveillance auditing as follow-up to determine if the staff is still following their own procedures, or something that is new. An excellent method for determining the scope is to start a discussion asking questions about six key areas. Remember, scope is defined as a boundary of what is included and what is not. So let's start with these questions and topics:

Management What are the business rules and objectives? Has management formally adopted a standard to be followed? Does management require their systems to be certified? Does executive management provide accreditation of the complete hardware/software system before entering production?

Data What data is involved? Is this customer data, engineering data, financial data? Are there any regulations governing data restrictions, acceptable or unacceptable use?

Intended Usage   How is this data used? What is it for? Possibly a manual operation? Is it part of a software application?

Technology Platform   Is this data in a computer program? In a file cabinet? Transmitted wirelessly on cell phones? Will you have an impressive multimedia presentation leveraging the combined workflow advantages of Apple Macs? Is the objective basic office spreadsheets and word processing for a PC? Does the user require their LCD display in a pair of sunglasses? Is the goal to reduce end-user support? Will you be switching from Microsoft to Unix servers for cost savings in user licensing?

Facilities   Where does the work get done? Are the main systems located here or somewhere else? How much space is required to accommodate the staff? Where are the customers located? Where are the subcontractors located for the work that is outsourced? How many facilities are involved? Do we need special security clearance to gain access?

People Involved   Who are the people we will work with on the client side? Who are the people on the auditee side? Using the skills matrix for reference, who is available to be on the audit team? Do we have the appropriate technical experts available? Who are the observers and auditors in training on this project? Do any of the participants have a travel conflict or schedule restriction?

The next audit objective is to plan the specific audit project necessary to address the audit objectives. Analysis of your audit planning method should occur at least annually to incorporate the constant stream of new developments in both the industry and the auditing field.

Understanding the Variety of Audits

Each audit is actually an individual project linked to an ongoing audit program. The IS auditor may be asked to perform a variety of audits, including the following:

Product or Service   Efficiency, effectiveness, controls, and life-cycle costs

Processes   Methods or results

System   Design or configuration

General Controls   Preventative, detective, and corrective

Organizational Plans   Present and future objectives

To be successful, the auditor needs to engage in a fact-finding mission. You will need to take into consideration business requirements that are unique to the auditee or common to their industry. Each business has its own opportunities, challenges, and constraints. Remember, the purpose of an audit is to help management verify assertions (claims). Proper planning is necessary to ensure that the audit itself does not disrupt the business or waste valuable resources, including time and money.

Your audit objectives will include compliance to professional auditing standards and applicable laws. The IS auditor needs to be prepared to justify any deviation from professional audit standards. Deviation is a rare event.

As an auditor, you will need to consider the impact of the audit on the business operation. You will need to gain an understanding of the business, its purpose, and any potential constraints to the audit. Let's look at the questions an auditor could ask to gain insight of the business operation:

Knowledge of the Business Itself   What are their specific industry regulations? For example, are they governed by the U.S. Occupational Safety & Health Administration, any financial securities regulations, or the Health Insurance Portability and Accountability Act because of offering employee medical benefits?

- What are the business cycles? The retail industry operates on a schedule that begins Christmas holiday activities in September. Their busy season is at the end of the year, whereas the construction industry is busy from March through August.
- What are the reporting cycles? Is their year-end on September 30 or December 31?
- What are the critical business processes necessary for survival?
- Are reports available from prior audits?
- Will the auditors be able to tour the facilities? Which location and when?
- Who should be interviewed? Will those people be available?
- What are their existing plans? Are any new products, clients, or significant changes planned?

Strategic Objectives   The top executive sets a strategy with supporting definitions for the entire organization. This strategy defines what the business will be doing over the next three to five years. It answers the question of what the business will be engaged in. Is it the same industry or is it branching out into another market?

- What is the direction and structure going forward?
- What is the organizational plan for integrating IS?
- What are the business objectives that IS will be expected to fulfill?
- What are the defined IS goals?
- What is the strategic plan for the next two to three years?
- What are the supporting tactical plan steps during the next one to two years?
- What work is occurring from now to the end of the year?

Financial Objectives   Businesses use a portfolio approach to manage their investments, keeping those with the highest return and discarding underperformers. What is the return on investment (ROI) goal for the current capital investment and related expenses?

- How are assets managed?
- How are costs allocated to departments and projects?
- What is the budget and forecasting process?
- What are the financial reporting objectives? Will the client need an integrated audit for SOX reporting?
- What are the business continuity plans?

Operational Objectives for Internal Control   Operational activities focus on running the business within a budget period, usually within a 12- to 14-month window. The focus is on what should be done today and this year.

- Should any policies or procedures be tested?
- Will this be an administrative audit?
- How is system administration managed?
- How are performance metrics managed?
- What is the method used for capacity planning?
- How have access controls been implemented?
- What is the strategy and status of business continuity and disaster recovery plans? How many exercise tests have occurred this year?
- What controls exist for managing network communications?
- What is the nature of the last system audit? Are self-assessments used?
- What are the staffing plans?

Figure 3.2 shows four basic areas related to the organization's business requirements.

FIGURE 3.2   Understanding the business requirements

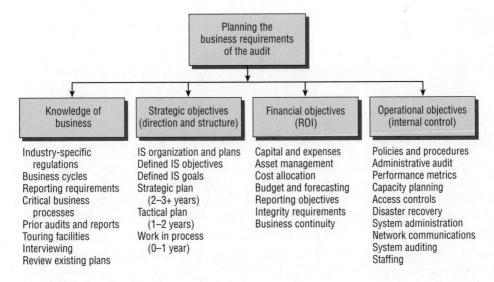

Identifying Restrictions on Scope

Every IS auditor will need to provide details when significant restrictions are placed on the scope of an audit. You will need to review your audit objectives and risk strategy to determine whether the audit is still possible and will meet the stated objectives. The audit report should explain specific restrictions and their impact on the audit. If the restrictions preclude the ability to collect sufficient evidence, you should render no opinion or no attestation in the audit.

Examples of restrictions include the following:

- Management placing undue restrictions on evidence use or audit procedures that could seriously undermine the audit objective
- Inability to obtain sufficient evidence for any reason
- Lack of resources or lack of sufficient time
- Ineffective audit procedures

Auditors have been known to terminate an engagement if the client places restrictions that are too severe on the audit. It is not unheard of for a client to discharge an auditor after receiving accurate findings that are distasteful to the client. The replacement auditor may need to inquire why a prior auditor is no longer being used by the auditee.

In some instances, the auditee will need to establish a level of communication between the previous auditor and replacement auditor. The purpose of this communication is to ensure that the client is not trying to obstruct truthful findings. Blackouts, or missing audit periods, would be a concern shared by more people than just the auditor. Statement on Auditing Standard 84 (SAS-84) provides additional details if you ever encounter this situation.

Audits are intended to provide relevant information that is meaningful to the client. Everything stated in the audit working papers and your report should represent the verified truth. The best way to show that you have done an excellent job is to list each item from the audit criteria along with the matching finding when you are finished. Keeping good notes will alleviate disputes about the accuracy of your work.

Gathering Detailed Audit Requirements

Every audit should have a set of requirements and objectives in support of the ongoing program—for example, the controls and efforts necessary to comply with regulations such as SOX. It is not possible to test all the requirements in one monolithic audit, so we break down (*decompile*) the larger compliance requirements into a series of smaller audits (*modular stages*):

Client Duties   Every audit has a client who sets the scope, grants authority, and agrees to pay for the project. The client's duties include the following:

- Set the scope
- Specify the audit objectives
- Grant access to the auditee and resources
- Define the reporting structure and confidentiality requirements

Auditee Duties   The auditee is responsible for working with the auditor to do the following:

- Confirm purpose and scope
- Identify critical success factors (CSFs) and measures of performance
- Identify personnel roles and responsibilities
- Provide access to information, personnel, locations, and systems relevant to the audit
- Cooperate with the gathering of audit evidence
- Provide access to prior audit results or to communication with prior auditors if necessary
- Specify reporting lines to senior management
- Make their assertion of controls and effectiveness independent of the auditor

Auditor Duties   The auditor is responsible for the following:

- Plan each audit to accomplish specific objectives necessary for annual compliance.
- Identify specific standards used for the audit (such as PCI section 11, NIST 800-53 controls, ISO 27002 management objectives, SOX section 401 or 404, FIPS 142, and so forth).
- Use a risk-based audit strategy.
- Identify special requirements of confidentiality, security, and safety. The information encountered by the auditor may be sensitive because of competitive value or possible legal repercussions.
- Identify specific procedures to be used for the audit. All procedures must be in writing.
- Document how the audit procedures are linked with specific audit objectives.
- Create a list of the evidence needed to review in order to prepare the audit findings.
- Create a written project plan.
- Identify resources required, including people, areas for access, hardware, and software.
- Develop time and event schedules with estimated start and end times.
- Provide audit cost estimates.
- Specify a date when the auditee and client can expect to receive a final report.

Scheduling should be mutually agreed upon so there are no surprises. Surprise requests tend to damage the relationship rather than build confidence. Your auditee will wonder whether you are just an incompetent planner or if you have an ulterior motive. Surprises make the auditee leery, if not downright distrustful, of your intentions.

As an auditor, you need to understand the nature of the systems that your client desires to be audited. It would be nearly impossible to audit systems whose mission you do not understand.

During preplanning, it's important to review the capabilities of each member of the audit team. Is each member of the audit team up to the task? The engagement manager or lead auditor should be made aware if a member of the team is missing a certification or a clearance rating necessary to conduct the audit.

In addition, audit plans can change depending on whether the client is using a centralized or distributed system design. The location of IS facilities and personnel will need to be considered.

The auditor needs to demonstrate due care as a professional in both planning and execution. There are a number of definitions for the word *care*:

Basic care is defined as the bare minimum necessary to sustain life without negligence.

Ordinary care is better than basic and provides an average level of customary care in the absence of negligence.

Extraordinary care is defined as that which is dramatically above and beyond what a normal person would offer or a situation would entail.

Various degrees of care could fall under the definition of *due care*. The degrees of care are proportional to the level of risk or loss that could occur. *Negligence* is the absence of care. A conscientious person will exercise due care in the performance of their job. Failure to exercise due care would be negligence.

Using a Systematic Approach to Planning

Every audit is a systematic approach of testing samples of evidence to measure compliance against a designated standard. Anyone with the correct attitude has the potential to be a good auditor after proper training. Let's start with two foundation-level audit objectives:

- To test control implementation to see whether the auditee has implemented adequate safeguards
- To comply with legal requirements that specify procedures necessary to remain legal

It is not unusual to discover missing controls or the absence of formally documented legal requirements. Auditors may discover that the auditee's understanding of the requirements is quite vague—but no need to fear, because you can be the super auditor. You can use a special method called the *process technique*, published by Walter Shewhart. Shewhart taught the quality techniques later used by W. Edwards Deming and Philip Crosby.

The purpose of the process technique is to guide a repeating cycle of constant improvement for a process or system. It can be used to identify specific action items necessary to accomplish vague requirements, such as "maintain adequate security." Let's implement the four basic steps used to perform Shewhart's process technique (Plan, Do, Check, Act):

Plan   Is there a plan or a method?

Did management convey the importance of this objective by sponsoring a policy?

Has the auditee established what needs to be done by identifying specific tasks or procedures?

The auditor may find evidence including outlines, procedures, flowcharts, specifications, or notes.

Do   Now you look to see whether the plan, procedure, or method is being followed according to their plan. Is the work output matching their plan?

Look for the existence of status reports, meeting records, employee training, or other documentation used in their work area.

Check   Is anyone monitoring the process? Is there a quality control check or peer review being used? If so, what is the acceptable criterion?

How are problems discovered and reported? Look for compliance testing and evidence of noncompliance, such as rework or discards. What metrics are used? Look for deviation reporting.

Act   Inevitably, there are differences between what was expected in the plan and the actual outcome. The Act step refers to analyzing the differences, and then taking action to adjust the process so the problem is corrected. Action should always be taken to fix the problems as they are found.

Shewhart's famous graphic is shown to illustrate the Plan-Do-Check-Act cycle. Using this cycle made Deming famous. It will help you too.

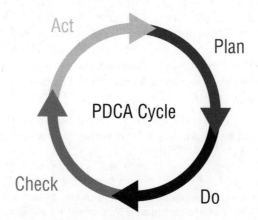

A really smart auditor will focus on situations that are not normal to determine how decisions are made. Auditors should always be curious about how a decision was reached. What evidence is available to justify the decision? Whose approval was required?

Comparing Traditional Audits to Assessments and Self-Assessments

A discussion of the audit process would not be complete without mentioning the specific differences between audits and assessments or control self-assessments. The auditee can work to improve their audit score between audits by using assessments and self-assessment techniques:

Traditional Audits   To employ the formal skills of a professional auditor is considered a traditional audit. In a traditional audit, the auditor manages the audit through the entire audit process and renders a final opinion.

Audits are used to specifically measure auditee claims against a reference standard. The audit generates a report viewed to represent a high assurance of truth. Audits are used in attest reporting engagements (when the auditor attests that the auditee claims are true).

The audit results may be used for regulatory licensing and external reporting.

Assessments   Assessments are less formal and frequently more cooperative processes that scrutinize people and objects. A client may employ a professional auditor to work with the auditee. The goal is usually to "see what is out there." Assessments implement informal activities designed to determine the value of what may already exist. Value is based on relevance and fitness of use. An assessment report is viewed to have a lower value (moderate-to-low value) when compared to an audit. Assessments are excellent vehicles for training and awareness. The goal of an assessment is to help the staff create a sense of ownership while working toward improving their score.

Results of the assessment remain internal to the organization and are not eligible for use in regulatory licensing.

Control Self-Assessments (Internal)   A control self-assessment (CSA) is executed by the auditee. With a CSA, the auditor becomes a facilitator to help guide the client's effort toward self-improvement. The auditee uses the CSA to benchmark progress with the intention of improving their score. A great deal of pride can be created by the accomplishment of CSA tasks and learning the detail necessary to succeed in a traditional audit. Therefore, the CSA process can generate benefits by empowering the staff to take ownership and accountability.

Control self-assessment will not fulfill the independence requirement, so a traditional audit is still required. CSAs can be used to identify areas that are high risk and may need a more detailed review later.

Know the difference between audits and assessments. *Audits* are formal activities that are conducted by a qualified auditor and generate a high assurance of the truth. Audits can be used for licensing and regulatory compliance. *Assessments* are less-formal activities designed to determine the value of what may already exist. Value is based on relevance and fitness of use. The assessment is excellent for instilling a sense of ownership in the staff. Assessment results should remain internal to the organization.

As auditors, our goal is to report the truth and to educate our clients. Using traditional audits with a combination of lower-cost assessments will help our client become more successful. Now it's time to move forward into risk management.

Performing an Audit Risk Assessment

Performing a risk assessment is the next step after the audit objectives have been identified. The purpose of a risk assessment is to ensure that sufficient evidence will be collected during an audit. We will add a new term to your auditor vocabulary: *materiality*. Materiality refers to evidence that is significant and could change the outcome.

While searching for evidence, it is important to remember that you are not looking for 100 percent of all conceivable evidence. You are interested in material evidence that will be relevant to the outcome of your audit. Please keep in mind that it is easy to be distracted during an audit. You should focus your efforts on material evidence that either proves or disproves your specific audit objective. Your findings and opinion will be based on this material evidence.

An audit risk assessment should take into account the following types of risks:

Inherent Risks   These are natural or built-in risks that always exist. Driving your automobile holds the inherent risk of an automobile accident or a flat tire. Theft is an inherent risk for items of high value.

Detection Risks   These are the risks that an auditor will not be able to detect what is being sought. It would be terrible to report no negative results when material conditions (faults) actually exist. Detection risks include sampling and nonsampling risks:

> **Sampling Risks**   These are the risks that an auditor will falsely accept or erroneously reject an audit sample (evidence).

> **Nonsampling Risks**   These are the risks that an auditor will fail to detect a condition because of not applying the appropriate procedure or using procedures inconsistent with the audit objective (detection fault).

Control Risks   These are the risks that an auditor could lose control, errors could be introduced, or errors may not be corrected in a timely manner (if ever).

Business Risks   These are risks that are inherent in the business or industry itself. They may be regulatory, contractual, or financial.

Technological Risks   These are inherent risks of using automated technology. Systems do fail.

Operational Risks   These are the risks that a process or procedure will not perform correctly.

Residual Risks   These are the risks that remain after all mitigation efforts are performed.

Audit Risks   These are the combination of inherent, detection, control, and residual risks.

These are the same risks facing normal business operations. In the planning phase, an IS auditor is primarily concerned with the first three: inherent risk, detection risk, and control risk. All of the risks could place the business or audit in jeopardy and should be considered during some level of advance planning.

An auditor should create plans to allow for alternative audit strategies if an auditee has recently experienced an outage, service interruption, or unscheduled downtime. It would be unwise to pursue an audit before the business has ample time to restabilize normal operations. Plans should include an opportunity to reschedule without violating a legal deadline.

Determining Whether an Audit Is Possible

A good auditor remembers that setting priorities is their responsibility. You will need to assess the risk of the audit and ensure that priorities have been fulfilled. If you are unable to perform the necessary audit functions, it is essential that the issues be properly communicated to management and the audit committee. An audit without meaningful evidence would be useless.

The auditor will need to work with the auditee to define specific requirements and identify any third-party providers. You will need to review the auditee's organizational structure and to identify persons in areas of interest that are material to your audit.

Management has the ultimate responsibility for internal controls and holds the authority for delegation. Management may choose to delegate tasks to a third party (*outsource*). The outsource organization must perform the daily tasks as designated, but unfortunately management will still retain liability that cannot be delegated. Executive management will still be held responsible for any failures that occur with or at the outsource organization. The federal government has gone to great lengths to ensure that the decision maker (management) can be held fully accountable for their actions and liable for any loss or damage.

Organizations with outsourcing contracts and labor unions could be particularly difficult unless you have sufficient cooperation. In the case of labor unions, it is often necessary for the shop steward to be present and involved in all plans and activities. Failure to do so may result in an operational risk of the union workers walking off the job.

Outsourced activities will present their own challenges with potential restrictions on access to personnel and evidence. It would not be uncommon for a service provider to decline your request for an audit. Most outsource providers will attempt to answer such requests by supplying you with a copy of their latest SAS-70 report, which is a standard report format for service providers. Occasionally, when a client requests and receives the SAS-70 report from a service provider, the value of content in the SAS-70 report may be overstated because there is usually a shady accountant or auditor somewhere willing to misstate or overlook problems in exchange for a generous fee.

The purpose of the SAS-70 is to eliminate multiple organizations from individually auditing the service provider. You can expect that several points of detailed evidence you requested will have been filtered or masked in the SAS-70 report. Your client's original outsource contract should have included a provision for the right to audit along with the service-level agreement. It must be clearly stated whether the SAS-70 is acceptable or if an individual audit is required. Performing your own audit adds cost but offers high levels of control. Be advised that some outsource providers run on a different business schedule than their clients.

 Real World Scenario

Working in Labor Union Environments

We are acutely aware of how seemingly trivial actions can have significant consequences in a labor union environment. Plugging in our own computers to a client's network resulted in a complete work stoppage after our actions were observed by an unhappy union worker. Every union worker in the plant stopped what they were doing. We were immediately summoned by management to explain our actions. After several agonizing minutes of us begging forgiveness, the shop steward agreed that everyone could return to work. Your illustrious author received a dire warning not to do this again. Fortunately, the client agreed to cover the cost of the work stoppage, and we did not have to take money out of our own pocket.

Identify the Risk Management Strategy

After identifying a methodology for risk evaluation and control, the auditor will need to identify potential risks to the organization. The auditee will assist by providing information about their organization.

To properly identify risks, the auditor also needs to identify the following:

- Assets that need to be protected
- Exposures for those assets
- Threats to the assets
- Internal and external sources for threats
- Security issues that need to be addressed

Part of documenting risk data is for the auditor to identify potential risk response strategies that can be used in the audit with each identified risk. The four risk responses are as follows:

Accept (de facto)   Take your chances. Ignoring a risk is the same as accepting it. The auditor should be concerned about the acceptance of high-risk situations. By not taking action, the management team has automatically accepted the risk. Not making a decision and taking action means management has already accepted the risk.

Mitigate (Reduce)   Do something to lower the odds of getting hurt. The purpose of mitigation is to reduce the effect of the potential damage. Most internal controls are designed to mitigate risk.

Transfer   Let someone else take the chance of loss by using a subcontractor or insurance. You can transfer the risk but not the liability for failure. Blind transfer of risk would be a genuine concern. This applies to outsourcing agreements and the reason for a *right to audit* clause in the contract.

Avoid   Reject the situation; change the situation to avoid taking the risk.

An assessment of risk will usually include a list of all possible risks that threaten the business and your evaluation of how imminent they are.

Toy manufacturer Mattel experienced the problem of inherited liability for distributing toys manufactured with hazardous lead paint (2007). Mattel was held responsible in the eyes of the public for failing to manage their subcontractor effectively. Unknown to Mattel, their subcontractor chose to ignore specifications in favor of using a lead-based paint. Mattel was scrutinized for failing to detect the violation prior to shipping their toys. Other examples of inherited liability include the pet food recall caused by tainted flour in the ingredients. The U.S. Food and Drug Administration placed a widespread ban on fish from Chinese suppliers because of questionable practices by the subcontractors using illegal growth hormones. A quick Google search will yield many more examples of liability inherited from subcontractors. When you transfer risk, you still own the liability.

Figure 3.3 shows the basic process of responding to risks. A CISA is expected to understand the different types of responses. Risk management principles will apply to your audit planning. Your client will select from similar choices in their decisions about the risks faced by their organization.

Is This Audit Feasible?

Every auditor hears some unusual and even unrealistic audit requests during their career. One of the biggest challenges is to produce a meaningful audit with findings that make a difference for the client. The real value of performing an audit is to help the client. Findings and evidence from the audit will motivate the organization to fix deficiencies. Audit reports help justify costs to improve work performance. A good audit relies on sufficient information. It would be impossible to do a quality job without adequate cooperation from the auditee. We need answers that are appropriate, for planning all the way through execution. It takes time and resources to get the job done.

Review the client's expectation along with the level of cooperation you're receiving from the auditee. Ask yourself these questions:

- Do you think you can get the job done to produce meaningful audit results?

- Are the goals of this audit realistic?

- Does the audit team have the skills necessary to perform this audit?

- Do you have enough time to do a quality job, even if the schedule is tight?
- Is the auditee willing to cooperate?

If you answered no to any of the questions, this audit is not ready. You need to investigate alternatives or find another client, because the audit is a train wreck waiting to happen. However, if you answered yes, it's time to proceed and make your boss proud.

FIGURE 3.3   Risk analysis process flowchart

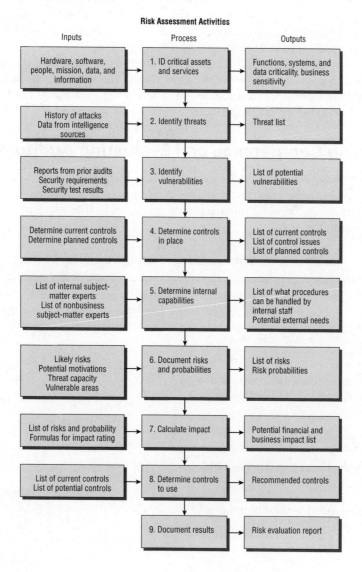

Performing the Audit

The next objective in auditing is to perform the actual audit. Here you will need to make sure you have the appropriate staff, ensure audit quality control, define auditee communications, perform proper data collection, and review existing controls.

Selecting the Audit Team

You will need to have personnel for the audit and to define the audit's organizational structure. You also will need to create a personnel resource plan, which identifies specific functions and skill sets necessary to complete your audit objectives. Individual skills and knowledge should be taken into consideration while planning your audit. Remember, it's impossible for the auditor to be an absolute expert in everything.

You will need to rely on the work of others, including your own audit team members, subcontractors, and possibly members of the client's staff. You should create a detailed staff training plan that is reviewed at least semiannually and before each audit. The time to train or retrain personnel is before the audit begins.

Determining Competence and Evaluating Auditors

It's amazing how many individuals claim the title of IS auditor. We can use the ISO standards to clarify what it takes to be a competent auditor in terms of prerequisite education, work experience, and training. Table 3.2 summarizes the minimum qualifications for IS auditors as compared to technical experts.

TABLE 3.2 Competence of auditors and technical experts

	Audit Team Leader	Competent Auditor	Technical Expert
Auditor with experience in at least three complete audits.	X		
Capability to communicate effectively in writing and oral presentations. Should possess good negotiating skills.	X		
Secondary-level education.	X	X	X
4+ years of full-time practical work experience in related to IT.	X	X	X
Successfully completed 5+ days of training covering the subject matter of the audit.	X	X	

TABLE 3.2 Competence of auditors and technical experts *(continued)*

	Audit Team Leader	Competent Auditor	Technical Expert
Experience in the entire audit process of assessing IT and information security prior to assuming responsibility as auditor.	X	X	
Experience performing software programming-code reviews to assess fitness of use and risks in implementation.			X
Technician-level certifications (RCDD, MCSE, CCIE).			X
Experience that is reasonably current through continual professional development.	X	X	X

As mentioned in Chapter 1, the auditor role is an executive-level position. The auditors manage the process of providing an accurate evaluation while assessing the whole situation and making formal recommendations. Technical skills are nice attributes; however, project management skills are even better because every audit is a project in need of a leader to get it completed on time. A good method for getting the right people working together is to create a skills matrix.

Creating a Skills Matrix

The auditor will lead persons with specialized skills, including the use of database scanners and other automated audit tools. A *skills matrix* should be developed, which indicates areas of knowledge, proficiency, and specialized training required to fulfill the audit. You use the skills matrix to identify members of the audit team according to the specific tasks each will perform. The purpose of the skills matrix is to ensure that the team has the right people with the right qualifications working on the right task. You use the matrix to demonstrate gaps and training needs. This discourages management from assigning you an unskilled "warm body." Table 3.3 shows a sample skills matrix.

TABLE 3.3 Sample skills matrix

Audit Task	Person	Training or Certification	Related Work Experience
# 8: Review of existing policies and records for PCI user training, all security, system configuration, and incident response.	M. Anderson	IA, CISA	Internal auditor

TABLE 3.3   Sample skills matrix *(continued)*

Audit Task	Person	Training or Certification	Related Work Experience
# 9: PCI section 11 network perimeter analysis.	J.T. Jennings	CISA, Network+, CCNA	PCI and PCI section 11 testing
# 10: Conduct enumeration scan of network hosts and open ports. Exclude "Zeus" server and customer service computers.	R. Martin	CISA	XP admin, BSD Unix admin
# 14: Select logs for review. Supervise and assist in review with B. Goldfield performing task.			
# 15: Catalog system log file data for analysis of past events to forensic-test the incident response.	B. Goldfield	BS computer science	Intern, system analyst

Using the Work of Other People

Occasionally, finding a competent independent expert in database administration for a particular vendor on your project may prove difficult. However, you might be able to retrain a member of the client's support staff to provide sufficient assistance to complete the audit.

Auditors frequently use the work of others as long as the following conditions are met:

- Assess the independence and objectivity of the provider.

- Determine their professional competence, qualifications, and experience.

- Agree on the scope of work and approach used.

- Determine the level of review and supervision required.

If these conditions are met, the auditor may choose to use the work of others. A CISA should have serious concerns if the work does not meet their audit evidence requirement for any reason. You can use only evidence of sufficient quality, quantity, and relevance. Failure to meet this requirement may require a change in the audit scope or canceling the audit.

Competence means having the right training, related experience, discipline, and qualifications for the job. Qualifications include recognized certification with the proper clearance for the job. Clearance may include having both permission to work the audit and a valid security clearance, especially in government auditing.

Ensuring Audit Quality Control

Quality does not happen automatically. It is a methodology that must be designed into your process and not just inspected afterward. Quality control is necessary in every audit.

Let's take a moment to define what quality is and how to recognize quality. We can do this by using three easy-to-remember points:

- *Quality* is defined as conformance to specifications.

- Planning and prevention create quality. Quality does not occur postappraisal.

- The standard of performance is zero defects, not by just getting "close enough." Sixth and seventh sigma do not reach zero defects. Quality can be measured by the price of failure (nonconformance).

Audit standards, guidelines, and procedures were developed to promote quality and consistency in a typical audit. The ISACA audit standards were developed to assist CISA auditors in performing audits. Additional guidance can be obtained by reading the ISACA audit guide at www.isaca.org/standards.

Your audit will need a variety of quality performance metrics to ensure success. When designing a quality control process, an auditor should consider doing the following:

- Use an audit methodology (documented plan and procedures).

- Gain an understanding of the auditee needs and expectations.

- Keep a checklist of the tasks to be accomplished.

- Respect business cycles and deadlines.

- Hold client interviews and workshops.

- Use customer satisfaction surveys.

- Agree to terms of reference used by client, auditee, and auditor, as discussed in Chapter 1.

- Establish audit performance metrics.

- Measure the audit plan against actual performance.

- Respond to auditee complaints.

Quality can vary according to the requirements set forth by management. The auditor must take all the necessary steps to ensure that audit work is performed with very high standards of quality to generate a high assurance of the truth. Anything less will make you and the images of our profession appear questionable. High standards always bring respect.

Establishing Contact with the Auditee

The auditor must work with management to define the auditee communication requirements. As discussed in Chapter 1, the auditee often feels at a disadvantage to the auditor. Without effective communication, the auditee will feel disillusioned, confused, or disconnected from the audit. Each of these conditions would be undesirable; audits without client buy-in would be a major disaster.

> Occasionally, the auditee may request to see information concerning the audit plan. Depending on your assignment, it may be acceptable to allow the auditee to view your blank checklists; however, the auditor's notes should remain confidential during the audit. It is usually not a good idea to give the auditee copies of your blank forms because doing so could provide the foundation for disputes or engineered answers.

It is your job as the auditor to be a "second set of eyes" in reviewing the present condition at the organization. You are responsible for reporting accurate findings to senior management and the audit committee. The audit charter may assist you by defining the required level of auditee communication.

Remember to be effective in your communication, and to be diligent about several points, including the following:

- Describing the audit's purpose, service, and scope

- Dealing with problems, constraints, and delays

- Responding to client questions and complaints

- Dealing with issues outside the scope of this particular audit

- Understanding timing and scheduling—knowing when the client expects the work to occur

- Following the reporting process—knowing when and how the client wants to hear from you

- Obtaining an agreement of your findings with your client

- Implementing confidentiality, implementing the principle of least privilege (need to know)

- Providing special handling for evidence of irregularities or possibly illegal acts

Nothing will replace the simple act of asking the client what level and frequency of communication they expect. The preceding points are simply a starting position. You should synchronize the auditee communication plan with your own internal audit team communication plans.

During the planning process, the auditor will need to gain approval from management for access to the appropriate staff personnel. A member of the audit team may be assigned to coordinate everyone's schedule.

Making Initial Contact with the Auditee

Your initial contact with the auditee may occur as an introduction by phone, as an informal greeting in their office, or during a formal meeting. Never forget that the auditee is someone that your client values. It is imperative to show your respect by using your very best manners. Savvy auditors will dress a little nicer than the other attendees without being overly stuffy or flamboyant. I always wear a suit for the first meeting to visually reinforce my position as executive manager. In the military I learned that the extra effort to dress in formal attire demonstrates our respect for the other person. There is nothing wrong with keeping a nice shirt and slacks in the car for a quick change. After the initial meeting, you can change into something a little more casual in case the client wishes to take you on a tour of their dirty warehouse or gritty machine shop.

When you establish communication with the auditee, it's a good idea to make sure you're speaking with the correct representative. Be friendly and politely confirm your authority to conduct the audit. You can say something like this: "Well, Mr. Sayed, I appreciate you taking the time to speak with me about the upcoming PCI compliance audit. Miriam Seth has hired our firm to conduct the audit. I will be your contact person during this engagement. My role is to work with you to ensure that everything is done right with minimum disruption." The auditee will also be interested in the proposed timing of the audit activities and kickoff meeting. It will help if you identify the date your final audit report is due.

Smart auditors will provide an initial presentation about the proposed audit schedule and team composition. This doesn't have to be a long presentation, but it should be enough to give them an understanding of when the major activities occur and who will be involved. The initial presentation should include a checklist of the items necessary to perform the audit. The request should be sent well in advance of any onsite activities and include at least the following components:

- Request access to relevant documents and records.

- Provide a list of the items the auditor is looking for, using common titles and a brief description (for example, a copy of the records management policy, security classification procedure, system certification procedure, organizational chart, and prior audit reports of software code reviews).

- Determine applicable site safety rules.

- Make arrangements for the audit resources.

- Agree on attendance of observers and a guide for the audit team.

- Request audit team workspace needs with technology services to support the audit workflow.

Communications Schedule

The best way to prevent misunderstanding is to publish a communications schedule. Rumors can kill even the best audit unless everyone is kept informed of the truth. Professional auditors will publish a communications schedule identifying dates and times of status meetings, progress updates, reports, and everything else necessary to keep everyone informed. By using the basics of project management, we can publish a short list of objectives, which will help you look good.

Identify Stakeholders   Make a quick list of everyone who is an interested party on this audit. This will be the audit team members, your own boss, individuals representing the client, and individuals who are representing the auditee. Make sure each of the stakeholders receives a schedule relevant to their level of participation. Don't forget to include administrative support personnel who help you with security access, accommodations, travel schedules, and other valuable aid. We may not send everyone the same information, but we don't want to leave anyone out.

Communication Requirements   Spend a little bit of time analyzing the requirements for each of the stakeholders. Remember, a stakeholder is anyone who has a positive or negative interest in the audit. Think about what they may want to know in regard to activities, issues, or progress. It helps to discuss this directly with the client and auditing management to alleviate any disputes.

Message Content   Consider the types of messages you will be communicating. Status updates and meeting announcements may be simple messages. However, the content of exception logs and reports is best delivered in a printed format with some form of distribution control.

Confidentiality Requirements   Be absolutely religious about providing the necessary security controls to protect confidentiality of sensitive information. Do not place your client's information or reputation at risk.

Communication Technology   Identify the communication preferences for each of the stakeholders. What is the best way for the message to get delivered and still be convenient for the recipient? Keep in mind that how recipients will react varies depending on the message content. There are some messages that are best delivered in person rather than by voice mail or text.

Complaint Process   A simple, easy-to-use complaint process will provide the auditor an outstanding source of information. Of course, we always expect you'll have a few nuisance complaints. As auditors, we look for complaints in historical records including e-mails, status reports, and help-desk tickets. It is safe to say that if a process is being used, someone will have a question or complaint about specific details. If there are no complaints, either the process is very old or nobody is using it. It is imperative to be extremely polite in dealing with complaints because this may be your one opportunity to hear about an exception before it's reported to the big boss and blows up in your face. The best rule of thumb is to always give amnesty to the messenger, even if that person is the one responsible for the mistake. Although amnesty may be used as one-time situation, it is not applicable to forgiving repetitive mistakes.

Now is a good time to communicate some of the data collection techniques that auditors use in audits.

Using Data Collection Techniques

As part of the planning process, the auditor needs to determine how data will be gathered for evidence to support the audit report. To collect useful data, the savvy auditor will use a combination of techniques, including the following:

Staff Observation   You can observe staff in the performance of their duties. Auditor observation is a powerful form of evidence.

Document Review   Remember, the evidence rule will apply as you review existing documentation. Presence of a document does not mean it is actually in use. You should review the auditee documentation and any related legal documentation. Legal documentation may be either contracts or regulatory laws.

Interviews You can interview selected personnel appropriate to the audit. Be sure to structure the timing and questions for the interview. You need to ensure that the questions are consistent and to allow extra time to discuss any interesting points raised.

Workshops Workshops can generate awareness and understanding. The audit committee may be a good audience for a workshop. Well-executed workshops can save time compared to individual interviews.

Computer-Assisted Audit Tools (CAAT) Newer auditing software does a fabulous job of checking configuration settings, user account parameters, system logs, and other time-consuming details.

Surveys Conducting surveys is a tried-and-true method of obtaining cheap and easy answers. Unfortunately, the truthfulness of individual responses raises questions about the survey's consistency and resulting trustworthiness. People may answer the question by using a skewed perspective, or just respond with answers they believe you want to hear, regardless of the truth. Overall reliability of the survey remains an ongoing concern.

Each technique has its advantages and disadvantages. For example, surveys offer an advantage of time but have the disadvantages of inconsistency and limited response. A survey cannot detect a personal mannerism such as hesitancy, surprise, or restlessness. Surveys may execute quickly but carry extra administrative support burdens. It will take time and resources to create the survey, distribute it, track responses, provide answer assistance, ensure quality control, and tally the results. Because of human nature, people will seldom answer a survey in a manner that reduces their agenda and perceived value to an organization.

An auditor can observe an auditee during an interview and ask additional probing questions based on the auditee response. The auditor weighs each response in an attempt to create consistent scoring of answers by multiple interview subjects. Interviews consume more time but can gather additional information.

Most clients will be impressed if you demonstrate genuine interest and take very good notes. It will help you obtain auditee buy-in and make them feel the audit report will contain statements of value. Just be sure to avoid the perception of an interrogation.

One of the best techniques to prepare for an interview is to conduct a document review. This provides the evidence an auditor needs to uncover the truth about an organization.

Conducting Document Review

One of the first stages in auditing is to conduct a document review. The purpose is to obtain an understanding of the available information the auditor can use to help guide the audit. The auditor is interested in gaining a better understanding of the auditee's environment. Nothing will end your career faster than a bad audit with nebulous results.

Familiarize Yourself with the Auditee's IT Environment

That old saying about "getting to know a person by walking in their shoes" certainly applies to IS auditing. You have to depend on the auditee to show you the design strategy and purpose of their IT environment. Their IT structure is supposed to be aligned to their business objectives.

Before you can determine whether that alignment exists, auditors will need to tour their facility with a walk-through. You should expect the client to provide a current network diagram. We prefer a schematic-level diagram rather than a high-level overview. The view from 3 feet away is a zillion times more informative than from 100 thousand feet. It does not matter whether the diagram is in digital format or hand drawn. What matters is that the diagram is accurate. We would accept a computer diagram with small hand-written changes, on the condition that the original document is updated before we finish the audit. Good detail would indicate that the auditee is actively working to manage their systems. We would ask the auditee to sign the document to certify that it is current and correct.

Auditors should be particularly interested in understanding how transactions flow through the auditee's IS environment. You need to identify how transactions are authorized along with any potential routes for physical and logical access. Integrity cannot exist without access controls. A good auditor will take plenty of notes during a walk-through and will follow up with questions. Areas of significant interest to the auditor include the following:

- Hardware systems.

- Operating systems.

- Applications, database software, and special utilities.

- Monitoring and control systems (at the server, network, and application level).

- Relevant documentation, especially diagrams, flowcharts, and process diagrams.

- Personnel roles and specific duties. Job descriptions and a copy of the organizational reporting relationship will be helpful (*org chart*). Hopefully, a skills matrix or training plan will exist.

- Relationship of the IT design to their higher-level business objectives. Is the design driven by strategic business requirements or technology favorites?

- Separation of duties pertaining to transaction authorization. This would apply to all significant transactions in the IT environment and within applications. The auditor would want to know who authorizes system access, changes, new transactions, deletions, and updates.

Auditees should have documentation on their day-to-day workflow. Always request copies of prior audit reports to understand past issues and whether the problems have been resolved. It is relatively common for there to have been so many changes that workers are no longer following their printed documentation. One of the primary objectives of the document review is to quickly determine whether the auditee actually follows the procedures. This is an issue of conformity.

If the documentation is out-of-date or inadequate, your audit team leader needs to inform the client. It would be a waste of money and time to automatically fail an audit. The audit team leader and the client need to reach a decision on whether the audit should be suspended until the documentation concerns are resolved or if the audit should be allowed to continue.

Understanding the Hierarchy of Internal Controls

Every auditor should consider two fundamental issues concerning internal control:

Issue 1: Management Is Often Exempt from Controls   Management has the responsibility of installing controls for the organization, yet some of the executives are exempt from their own controls. An excellent set of examples is noted at the beginning of Chapter 1, where multiple executives fraudulently altered records. One of the fundamental purposes of an audit is to determine whether executives are providing an honest and truthful representation based in fact.

Issue 2: How Controls Are Implemented Determines the Level of Assurance   Implementing strong controls contributes to the level of assurance, which may be confirmed by the auditor. Strong assurance means it represents a 95 percent or greater degree of truth. Unsatisfactory implementation of controls compromises the overall objectives. No auditor can provide a satisfactory report if the controls are improperly implemented or insufficient for their objective.

Let's review the basic framework of controls according to the ISACA standards. ISACA based these standards on common auditing guidelines for financial audits as well as government guidelines for auditing and for computer environments. Information systems controls are composed of four high-level controls: general controls, pervasive IS controls, detailed IS controls, and application controls. This clarification is required because portions of the financial audit techniques may not be appropriate for some IS audits. Computer environments can be rather complex and abstract. A summary of the controls is as follows:

General Controls (Overall)   This is the parent class of controls governing all areas of the business. Examples of general controls include creating accurate job descriptions and separating duties to prevent employees from writing their own paychecks. We expect management to implement administrative controls to govern the behavior of their entire enterprise. General controls also include defining an organizational structure, establishing HR policies, monitoring workers and the work environment, as well as budgeting, auditing, and reporting.

Pervasive IS Controls (Technology)   A pervasive order or pervasive control defines the direction and behavior required for technology to function properly. The concept of a pervasive control is to permeate the area by using a greater depth of control integration over a wide area of influence. Internal controls are used to regulate how the business operates in every area of every department.

The IS function uses pervasive controls in the same manner as a manufacturing operation, bank, or government office. Pervasive controls are a subset of general controls, with extra definition focused on managing and monitoring a specific technology. For example, pervasive IS controls govern the operation of the information systems no matter what, even if the topic is about using your BlackBerry, iPhone, or laptop for business. Anyone using these electronic aids or other IT aids will have duties to follow, including acceptable use, backups, data sync, and security issues.

Pervasive IS controls are used across all internal departments and external contractors. Proper implementation of pervasive IS controls improve the reliability of the following:

- Overall service delivery
- Software development
- System implementation
- Security administration
- Disaster recovery
- Business revenue continuity

The lack of pervasive IS controls, or weak controls, indicates the possibility of a high-risk situation that should draw the auditor's attention. Lower-level detailed controls will be compromised if the pervasive controls are ineffective.

At the pervasive-control level, the auditor needs to consider the experience level, knowledge, and integrity of IS management. Look for changes in the environment or pressure that may lead to concealing or misstating information. This problem is prevalent when users manage their own departmental systems separate from the IT department. External influences include outsourcing, joint ventures, and direct relationships. Internal influences include flaws in the organizational structure or reporting relationship, where a built-in conflict may exist.

Detailed IS Controls (Tasks)   Specific procedures require additional detailed controls to ensure that workers perform the job correctly. Detailed controls refer to specific steps or tasks to be performed. In the finance department, a specific set of controls is practiced when creating a trial balance report. Detailed IS controls work in the same manner to specify how system security parameters are set, how input data is verified before being accepted into an application, or how to lock a user account after unsuccessful logon attempts. Detailed IS controls specify how the department will handle acquisitions, security, implementation, delivery, and support of IS services.

An auditor investigating the IS controls should consider findings from previous audits in the subject area. Give consideration to the amount of manual intervention required, the activities outside the daily routine, and the susceptibility of bypassing the IS controls. A smart auditor will always consider the experience, skills, and integrity of the staff involved in applying the controls.

Application Controls (Embedded in Programs)   This is the lowest subset in the control family. All activity should have filtered through the general controls, and then the pervasive controls and detailed controls, before it reaches the application-controls level. The higher-level controls help protect the integrity of the application and its data. Leaving an application exposed without the higher-level controls makes as much sense as leaving a child defenseless in the woods to fend for itself. Just like children, the application needs to be sheltered and protected from harm.

Management is responsible for having applications tested prior to production through a recognized test method. The goal is to provide a technical certification that each system meets the requirements. Management has to sign a formal accreditation statement granting their approval for the system to enter production based on fitness of use and accepting all responsibilities of ownership. Accreditation makes management accountable for system performance and liability of failure (who to blame or who to reward).

Reviewing Existing Controls

The next step in the planning process is to review the existing internal controls that are intended to prevent, detect, or correct problems. Management is responsible for designating and implementing internal controls to protect their assets. You can obtain initial information about existing controls by reviewing current policies and procedures, and later by interviewing managers and key personnel. The purpose of internal controls can be classified into one of three categories:

Preventative   Controls that seek to stop (prevent) the problem from occurring. A simple example is prescreening job applicants for employment eligibility. Synonyms for preventative controls include words such as *proactive* or *deterrent activities* designed to discourage or stop a problem.

Detective   Controls that are intended to find a problem and bring it to your attention. Auditing is a detective control for discovering information.

Corrective   Controls that seek to repair the problem after detection. Restoring data from a backup tape after a disk drive failure is a corrective control. *Reactive control* is a synonym of *corrective control.*

Controls from the three mid-level categories are implemented by using one of the following three methods:

Administrative   Using written policies and procedures (people based)

Technical   Involving a software or hardware process to calculate a result (special technology)

Physical   Implementing physical barriers or visual deterrents (building design)

The auditor should be concerned with the attitude and understanding demonstrated by the auditee. An excellent exercise is to ask the auditee to which category their control would best apply. You may hear some unique and often incorrect responses. The process of reviewing the controls to prevent, detect, or correct is an excellent awareness generator with your auditee.

Table 3.4 lists some examples of these control types.

TABLE 3.4 Controls and methods of implementation

Control Type	Implementation Method	Some Examples
Preventative "stops"	Administrative	Hiring procedures, background checks, segregation of duties, training, change control process, acceptable use policy (AUP), organizational charts, job descriptions, written procedures, business contracts, laws and regulations, risk management, project management, service-level agreements (SLAs), system documentation
	Technical	Data backups, virus scanners, designated redundant high-availability system ready for failover (HA standby), encryption, access control lists (ACLs), system certification process
	Physical	Access control, locked doors, fences, property tags, security guards, live monitoring of CCTV, human-readable labels, warning signs
Detective "finds"	Administrative	Auditing, system logs, mandatory vacation periods, exception reporting, run-to-run totals, check numbers, control self-assessment (CSA), risk assessment, oral testimony
	Technical	Intrusion detection system (IDS), high-availability systems detecting or signaling system failover condition (HA failure detection), automated log readers (CAAT), checksum, verification of digital signatures, biometrics for identification (many search), CCTV used for logging, network scanners, computer forensics, diagnostic utilities
	Physical	Broken glass, physical inventory count, alarm system (burglar, smoke, water, temperature, fire), tamper seals, fingerprints, receipts, invoices
Corrective "fixes"	Administrative	Termination procedures (friendly/unfriendly), business continuity and disaster recovery plans, outsourcing, insourcing, implementing recommendations of prior audit, lessons learned, property and casualty insurance
	Technical	Data restoration from backup, high-availability system failover to redundant system (HA failover occurs), redundant network routing, file repair utilities
	Physical	Hot-warm-cold sites for disaster recovery, fire-control sprinklers, heating and AC, humidity control

When you exercise this awareness game of preventative, detective, and corrective controls, it is interesting to notice how technology-oriented people will provide an overt emphasis on technology, while nontechnology-oriented people will focus on administrative and physical controls. If your background is technology, you will need to consider administrative or physical solutions to approach a reasonable balance of controls. Nontechnology-oriented people will need to force their emphasis to include technical controls and achieve a similar level of balance.

The Secret of Strong Controls

The secret to achieving strong controls is to implement layers. The minimum for an effective control is to have at least one point in each of the three areas: preventative, detective, and corrective. For example, a policy without a detective mechanism or a corrective mechanism is not enforceable. The strongest controls implement all nine layers (preventative, detective, and corrective implemented by using administrative methods, physical methods, and technical methods).

The preventative control, for example, would include an administrative policy with technical protection and physical signs or barriers. A corresponding detective control would be implemented with authorization to audit proper job descriptions and procedures. The detective control would include technical methods, such as intrusion, and detection and physical indicators, such as a video recording of people's activity in secure areas. The control would be coupled with corrective actions—such as manual procedures for isolation, and technical recovery using data restored from backup tapes or physical replacement. This is referred to as *depth of controls*.

Strong control = multiple preventative controls + multiple detective controls + multiple corrective controls

Weak control = shallow, bare-minimum control + implementation or no implementation

Now that we have covered the basic preventative, detective, and corrective controls, it is time to move on to preparing the audit plan.

Preparing the Audit Plan

All auditors are required to prepare a thorough set of audit documentation at the start of each audit. This includes copies of the charter and scope, audit plans, policies, and specific procedures used during the audit. You should record both handling and test procedures. Audit reports are frequently used as evidence in lawsuits and criminal cases of embezzlement or fraud. As you recall, in Chapter 1 we mentioned several cases involving corruption perpetuated by dishonest executives. Professional auditors will need to demonstrate the extent to which they have complied with IS auditing standards.

Your job as an auditor is to provide consistency. All your findings should be repeatable by another auditor. Documentation should include the auditor's working notes and evidence necessary to reperform the audit. The key to building a successful practice is to map each of your planned tasks and corresponding findings to a specific point of compliance in the standard or regulation. This mapping may require you to identify the page, paragraph, and line number in the regulation—and for each item you will show as compliant or noncompliant. During the audit, you should be preparing records to answer the following questions:

- Who was involved?

- What was audited, how was the evidence obtained, and what specific test procedure was used?

- When did it occur?

- Where did it occur?

- Why (the purpose of the audit)?

- How were the audit plan and procedures executed?

Later, the auditor's final working papers should be placed into an audit documentation archive, including copies of any reports that were issued.

The auditor should always remember that records of each audit may be needed again in the future. Integrated audits such as SAS-94 will have documentation retention requirements equal to the financial statement, typically at least seven years. Financial and internal control records for an integrated audit serve as a matched pair that should not be separated. Records for certain systems or processes may have a retention requirement specified in their service-level agreement or contract. Very specialized systems used in aerospace, life safety, hazardous materials, or the military may be retained for decades.

 Audit team leaders should prepare the audit plan including scheduling and coordination of activities. The detail should match the scope and complexity of the audit with flexibility for changes. The finished audit plan should be reviewed and accepted by the audit client and presented to the auditee before onsite activities commence.

Assigning Work to the Audit Team

Your audit team is composed of experienced auditors, newbie auditors in training, and technical experts able to guide you through the complexities of the system you will be auditing. It is not realistic for the auditor to be an expert in everything, so we rely on the assistance of technical experts. It is important to realize that the technical experts do not function in the auditor's role, but simply provide assistance to help gather evidence and support the auditor during the testing process. Table 3.5 illustrates the work responsibilities for various members of the audit team.

TABLE 3.5   Work responsibilities for members of the audit team

	Lead Auditor	Auditor	Technical Expert	Auditor in Training	Guide
Manage audit team	X	X			
Communicate issues to client or auditee	X			Observe	
Facilitate access to personnel and resources					X
Manage technical experts		X		Observe	
Facilitate escalation assistance	X	X			X
Collect samples		X	Assist	Observe	
Perform testing		X	Assist	Observe	
Analyze results		X	Assist	Observe	
Determine findings		X		Assist	
Prepare reports		X		Assist	
Perform quality control	X			Assist	

After the audit team is in place, it's time to dive in to preparing the working documents. The auditors' working documents provide a road map of activities to be performed and the historical record of work accomplished in the ultimate pursuit of our findings.

Preparing Working Documents

Auditors thrive on printed procedures and quality control checklists. Working documents include hard-copy forms and electronic templates to record information, document records of meetings, catalog supporting evidence, ensure consistency during evidence testing, and record our audit findings. It is very important not to leave out material elements during the audit. I've included one of my checklists to help you understand what is involved in producing the working papers.

Working Papers Checklist

- Audit objectives

- Audit criteria and reference documents

- Audit scope (identifies organizational and functional units and specific processes to be audited)

- Dates and places where onsite activities are to be conducted

- Expected time and duration of onsite audit activities, including meetings with auditee and audit team meetings

- Roles and responsibilities of audit team and accompanying persons

- Allocation of resources to critical areas of audit

- Identification of auditees representative for the audit

- Working and reporting language if different from language of auditor or auditee

- Audit report topics

- Logistic arrangements (travel, onsite facilities, and so forth)

- Matters related to confidentiality

- Any audit follow-up actions

Audit team leaders are responsible for having the working papers reviewed for quality control. This review may be performed as a peer review or manager review. The ongoing review of the auditors' working papers is an excellent risk reduction technique.

Conducting Onsite Audit Activities

As auditors, we have performed a significant amount of planning before starting the onsite auditing activity. Our best efforts may be wasted if the auditee or client feels uncomfortable about our actions. It is very important for the auditee and client to feel involved and comfortable during the audit. Otherwise, we may not hear what we need to hear or see what we need to see to reflect the truth in our report. The auditor has an excellent opportunity to win friends and influence people during the opening meeting. This may be the first time the auditee gets to meet us in person.

The opening kickoff meeting needs to be well planned. It should be scheduled with plenty of consideration for the attendee to make necessary arrangements in their calendar. The agenda should be distributed in advance in a letter along with an email to all the involved parties. Our objective is to allow the client and auditee's management an opportunity to ask basic questions about who should attend. It is best if the persons responsible for the functions being audited are present at this opening meeting. The following is a sample agenda:

Sample Agenda

- Confirm the audit plan objectives

- Identify the authority to perform the audit (charter)

- Identify location, access level, and resources required

- Provide a short summary of how the audit activities will be undertaken
- Confirm the communication channels (liaison, reporting structure, methods)
- Confirm the meeting schedule (interviews, all meetings during audit, reviews, date and time of the closing meeting)
- Provide the auditee an opportunity to ask questions

The best way to ensure proper attendance is a polite courtesy call immediately following the email announcement. A follow-up reminder is helpful the day before the meeting is scheduled to take place. Effective communication is essential to successful audits.

Gathering Audit Evidence

Every good auditor understands the necessity of collecting tangible and reliable evidence. You read an introduction to the evidence rule in Chapter 1. Although you may really like or admire the people who are the subject of the audit, your final auditor's report must be based on credible factual evidence that will support your statements.

Consider for a moment something not related to IS auditing: police investigations or famous television courtroom dramas. Every good detective story is based on careful observation and common sense. A successful detective searches for clues in multiple places. Witnesses are interviewed to collect their versions of the story. Homes and offices are tirelessly searched for the minutest shred of relevant evidence. Detectives constantly ask whether the suspected individual had the motive, opportunity, and means to carry out the crime. The trail of clues is sorted in an attempt to determine which clues represent the greatest value and best tell the story. Material clues are the most sought after. From time to time, the clues are reviewed, and the witnesses reinterviewed. The detective orders a stakeout to monitor suspects. Ultimately, the suspects and clues of evidence are brought together in one place for the purpose of a reenactment. Under a watchful eye, the materially relevant portions of the crime are re-created in an attempt to unmask the perpetrator. In the movies, the detective is fabulously successful, and the criminal is brought to justice.

Unfortunately, IS auditing is not so dramatic or thrilling to watch. A CISA candidate needs to possess a thorough understanding of evidence, because IS auditing is centered on properly collecting and reviewing evidence. Let's start with a short discussion on the characteristics of good evidence.

Using Evidence to Prove a Point

Evidence will either prove or disprove a point. The absence of evidence is the absence of proof. In spite of your best efforts, if you're unable to prove those points, you would receive zero credit for your efforts. An auditor should not give any credit to claims or positive assertions that cannot be documented by evidence. No evidence, no proof equals no credit.

 All auditees start the audit with zero points and have to build up to their final score.

Understanding Types of Evidence

There are two primary types of evidence, according to legal definition:

Direct Evidence   This proves existence of a fact without inference or presumption. *Inference* is when you draw a logical and reasonable proposition from another that is supposed to be true. Direct evidence includes the unaltered testimony of an eyewitness and written documents.

Indirect Evidence   Indirect evidence uses a hypothesis without direct evidence to make a claim that consists of both inference and presumption. Indirect evidence is based on a chain of circumstances leading to a claim, with the intent to prove the existence or nonexistence of certain facts. Indirect evidence is also known as *circumstantial evidence*.

An auditor should always strive to obtain the best possible evidence during an audit. Using direct evidence is preferable whenever it can be obtained. Indirect evidence represents a much lower value because of its subjective nature. An auditor may find it difficult to justify using indirect evidence unless the audit objective is to gather data after detecting an illegal activity. An audit without direct evidence is typically unacceptable.

Selecting Audit Samples

Audit samples are selected for the purpose of collecting representative evidence to be subjected to either compliance testing or substantive testing (which is defined later in this chapter). The auditor should consider a selection technique that will provide the most relevant evidence supported by appropriate analytical procedures.

Two basic types of audit samples can be designed by the auditor to fulfill their requirements: statistical and nonstatistical. Figure 3.4 shows the various audit samples, as well as their testing methods. Care is given to the selection process in order to avoid drawing the wrong conclusion from the wrong sample. This is referred to as a *sampling risk*. Let's look at each of these samples more closely.

Statistical Sampling

Statistical sampling uses mathematical techniques that result in an outcome that is mathematically quantifiable. Statistical samples are usually presented as a percentage. The purpose of statistical sampling is to gain an objective representation. Samples are selected by an objective mathematical process. The auditor should be aware that if the client has strong internal controls, the sample sizes may be smaller because the odds of fraud or failure will be lower.

FIGURE 3.4   Audit samples

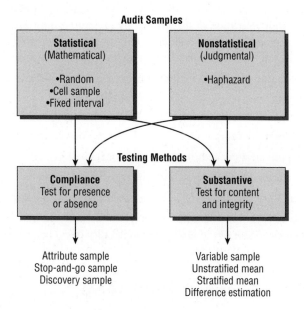

Examples of statistical sampling include the following:

Random Sampling   Samples are selected at random.

Cell Sampling   Random selection is performed at predefined intervals.

Fixed Interval Sampling   The sample existing at every n + interval increment is selected for testing.

Nonstatistical Sampling

Nonstatistical sampling is based on the auditor's judgment (also referred to as *judgmental sampling*). The auditor determines the sample size, the method of generating the sample, and the number of items to be analyzed. The results of judgmental sampling are unlikely to represent the actual population. This is a subjective process usually based on elements of risk or materiality. An example of nonstatistical sampling includes *haphazard sampling*, in which the samples are randomly drawn for testing.

Every good audit plan contains both collection plans and sampling plans. Be sure you know what you want to see and what samples you will need to test. A good sampling plan is required unless you want to conduct a 100 percent examination.

Recognizing Typical Evidence for IS Audits

You will attempt to gather audit evidence by using techniques similar to those used by a detective. Some of the data you gather will be of high value, and other data may be of low value. You will need to continually assess the quality and quantity of evidence. You may discover evidence through your own observations, by reviewing internal documentation, by using CAAT, or by reviewing correspondence and minutes of meetings.

Examples of the various types of audit evidence include the following:

- Documentary evidence, which can include a business record of transactions, receipts, invoices, and logs
- Data extraction, which uses automated tools to mine details from data files
- Auditee claims, which are representations made in oral or written statements
- Analysis of plans, policies, procedures, and flowcharts
- Results of compliance and substantive audit tests
- Auditor's observations of auditee work or reperformance of the selected process

All evidence should be reviewed to determine its reliability and relevance. The best evidence will be objective and independent of the provider. The quality of evidence you collect will have a direct effect on the points you wish to prove.

Using Computer-Assisted Audit Tools

Computer-assisted audit tools (CAAT) are invaluable for compiling evidence during IS audits. The auditor will find several advantages of using CAAT in the analytical audit procedure. These tools are capable of executing a variety of automated compliance tests and substantive tests that would be nearly impossible to perform manually. These specialized tools may include multifunction audit utilities, which can analyze logs, perform vulnerability tests, or verify specific implementation of compliance in a system configuration compared to intended controls.

Understanding CAAT Techniques and Limitations

CAAT includes the following types of software tools and techniques:

- Host evaluation tools to read the system configuration settings and evaluate the host for known vulnerabilities
- Network traffic and protocol analysis using a sniffer
- Mapping and tracing tools that use a tracer-bullet approach to follow processes through a software application using test data
- Testing the configuration of specific application software such as a SQL database
- Software license counting across the network
- Testing for password compliance on user login accounts

Many CAATs have a built-in report writer that can generate more than one type of predefined report of findings on your behalf.

Numerous advantages may exist, but they come at a cost. These expert systems may be expensive to acquire. Specialized training is often required to obtain the skills to operate these tools effectively. A significant amount of time may be required to become a competent CAAT operator.

Some of the concerns for or against using CAAT include the following:

- Auditor's level of computer knowledge and experience

- Level of risk and complexity of the audit environment

- Cost and time constraints

- Specialized training requirements

- Speed, efficiency, and accuracy over manual operations

- Need for continuous online auditing

- Security of the data extracted by CAAT

 WARNING A CISA may encounter individuals who are self-proclaimed auditors based solely on their ability to use CAAT software. You should consider this when using the work of others. The ability to use CAAT alone does not represent the discipline and detailed audit training of a professional auditor.

Using CAAT for Continuous Online Audit

The new audit tools offer the advantage of providing continuous online auditing. You should be aware of the six types of continuous online auditing techniques:

Online Event Monitors   Online event monitors include automated tools designed to read and correlate system logs or transaction logs on behalf of the auditor. This type of event monitoring tool will usually generate automated reports with alarms for particular events. A few examples include software that reads event logs, intrusion detection systems, virus scanners, and software that detects configuration changes, such as the commercial product Tripwire. (Low complexity.)

Embedded Program Audit Hooks   A software developer can write embedded application hooks into their program to generate red-flag alerts to an auditor, hopefully before the problem gets out of hand. This method will flag selected transactions to be examined. (Low complexity.)

Continuous and Intermittent Simulation (CIS) Audit   In continuous and intermittent simulation, the application software always tests for transactions that meet a certain criteria. When the criteria is met, the software runs an audit of the transaction (intermittent test). Then the computer waits until the next transaction meeting the criteria occurs. This provides for a continuous audit as selected transactions occur. (Medium complexity.)

Snapshot Audit   This technique uses a series of sequential data captures that are referred to as *snapshots*. The snapshots are taken in a logical sequence that a transaction will follow. The snapshots produce an audit trail, which is reviewed by the auditor. (Medium complexity.)

Embedded Audit M(EAM)   This integrated audit testing module allows the auditor to create a set of dummy transactions that will be processed along with live, genuine transactions. The auditor then compares the output data against their own calculations. This allows substantive integrity testing without disrupting the normal processing schedule. EAM is also known as *integrated test facility*. (High complexity.)

System Control Audit Review File with Embedded Audit Modules (SCARF/EAM)   The theory is straightforward. A system-level audit program is installed on the system to selectively monitor the embedded audit modules inside the application software. Few systems of this nature are in use. The idea is popular with auditors; however, a programmer must write the modules. (High complexity.)

Table 3.6 summarizes the differences between these CAAT methods.

TABLE 3.6   Summary of CAAT methods

CAAT Method	Characteristics	Complexity
Online event monitors	Reads logs and alarms.	Low
Embedded program audit hooks	Flags selected transactions to be examined.	Low
Continuous and intermittent simulation (CIS)	Audits any transaction that meets preselected criteria, waits for the next transaction meeting audit criteria.	Medium
Snapshot	Assembles a sequence of data captures into an audit trail.	Medium
Embedded audit module (EAM)	Processes dummy transactions along with genuine, live transactions.	High
System control audit review file with embedded audit modules (SCARF/EAM)	System-level audit program used to monitor multiple EAMs inside the application software. This is a mainframe class of control.	High

CAAT simplifies the life of an auditor by automatically performing the more menial, repetitive, detail tasks. The auditor needs to consider the CAAT reports while tempering them with some basic commonsense observations.

Understanding Electronic Discovery

New developments are occurring in legal procedures for courts. The increased use of computers has led to widespread reliance on electronic data records. In the old days, evidence could be discovered by rummaging through printed mail, business records, file cabinets, and the dusty storage warehouse. Electronic record keeping is a wonderful tool for automation, yet it can also perpetuate fraud, intentional omissions, or misrepresentation. *Electronic discovery* is the investigation of electronic records for evidence to be used in the courtroom.

The legal standard for electronic discovery is referred to as *e-discovery*. These rules were created to aid auditors and investigators by requiring owners of electronic records to disclose their existence and to provide the data in a simple, easy-to-read format (unencoded). Under e-discovery rules, the party who owns or possesses the data is required to perform the conversion and to certify that the contents are truthful and complete in their representation of the content. Put simply, the data owner is no longer permitted to use unintelligible or secret codes to keep database contents a secret from investigators.

State and federal courts are still debating the final rules for e-discovery. The law recognizes two parties: the producing party, which provides the evidence, and the receiving party, which receives the evidence. Here's what the auditor can expect until a final ruling is ratified:

- Discovery starts with a conference between the parties to plan the discovery process. Any issues related to disclosure of electronically stored information should be identified.

- The conference sets the scope to identify possible sources of information. The judge may be asked to include the decisions of the meeting in a court order.

- Limitations on scope may be identified based on undue cost or undue burden of production. Limitations will be determined by the judge after considering assertions of both parties and the nature of the case. Discovery may be ordered if the requesting party shows good cause in support of a claim or defense.

  - The scope may include data available online on any system.

  - The scope may include recovering deleted data.

  - The scope may include searching standing data from backup media and other offline sources.

  - The scope may include discovery of email and email records.

  - A search protocol will be agreed upon by the parties or ordered by the judge.

  - Unless the parties agree otherwise, the format shall be PDF or TIFF images without alteration of format or removal of revision history.

  - The judge may order the costs to be allocated equally, or unequally if good cause is shown why the other party should bear the cost.

- Sometimes portions of data, such as formulas and lawful business secrets, are protected by a claim of privilege. If privileged information is produced in discovery, it may be recalled for return, sequester, or destruction after notification is given to the receiving party with an explanation of the basis for privilege. The information may not be disclosed after notice is given, and the producing party must preserve the information until the claim is resolved.

- Under U.S. Federal Rules of Civil Procedure rule 37, the court may not impose sanctions on a party for failure to provide electronically stored information that was lost as a result of routine good-faith operations, if the records preservation was not mandated by regulation or exceptional circumstances.

E-discovery applies to criminal cases and civil lawsuits. The courts have determined that using encryption to hide or to cover illegal activities will result in multiple criminal penalties. Failure to cooperate with e-discovery requests can result in fines or prosecution. E-discovery requests include access to audit company records, HR files, database files, financial systems, and email correspondence.

 The management of every organization, as well as auditors, needs to learn more about the impact of e-discovery on their business activities. Awareness can prevent future legal headaches.

Grading of Evidence

All evidence is graded according to four criteria. This grading aids the auditor in assessing the evidence value. It is important to obtain the best possible evidence. The four characteristics are as follows:

Material Relevance   Evidence with material relevance influences the decision because of a logical relationship with the issues. Materially relevant evidence indicates a fact that will help determine that a particular action was more or less probable. The purpose of material evidence is to ascertain whether the same conclusion would have been reached without considering that item of evidence. Evidence is irrelevant if it is not related to the issue and has no logical tendency to prove the issue under investigation.

Evidence Objectivity   Evidence objectivity refers to its ability to be accepted and understood with very little judgment required. The more judgment required, the less objective the evidence. As you increase the amount of judgment necessary to support your claims, the evidence quickly becomes subjective or circumstantial, which is the opposite of objective. *Objective evidence* is in a state of unbiased reality during examination, without influence by another source. Objective evidence can be obtained through qualitative/quantitative measurement, and from records or statements of fact pertaining to the subject of the investigation. Objective evidence can be verified by observation, measurement, or testing.

Competency of the Evidence Provider   Evidence supplied by a person with direct involvement is preferred. The source of this person's knowledge will affect the evidence value and accuracy. A secondhand story still holds value by providing information that may lead to the evidence the auditor is seeking.

An *expert* is legally defined as a person who possesses special skill or knowledge in a science or profession because of special study or experience with the subject. An expert possesses a particular skill in forming accurate opinions about a subject; in contrast, a common person would be incapable of deducing an accurate conclusion about the same subject.

Evidence Independence   Evidence independence is similar to auditor independence, meaning the provider should not have any gain or loss by providing the evidence. Evidence supplied by a person with a bias is often questionable. The auditor should ask whether the evidence provider is part of the auditee's organization. Qualifications of the evidence provider should always be considered. A person with a high degree of detailed understanding is vastly more qualified than an individual of limited knowledge. Evidence and data gathered from a novice may have a low value when compared to data gathered by an expert. A person who is knowledgeable and independent of the audit subject would be considered the best source of evidence.

Table 3.7 lists examples of evidence grading. An IS auditor should always strive to obtain the best evidence, which is shown in the far-right column.

TABLE 3.7   Example of evidence grading

	Poor Evidence	Good Evidence	Best Evidence
Material Relevance	Unrelated	Indirect (low relation)	Direct (high relation)
Objectivity	Subjective (low)	Requires few supporting facts to explain the meaning	Needs no explanation
Evidence Source	Unrelated third party with no involvement	Indirect involvement by second party	Direct involvement by first party
Competency of Provider	Biased	Nonbiased	Nonbiased and independent
Evidence Analysis Method	Novice	Experienced	Expert
Resulting Trustworthiness	Low	Medium	High

Evidence is analyzed by using a structured test method to further determine the value it represents. The audit process itself represents a major portion of preparation work to support the analysis of actual evidence.

Every test procedure must be documented in writing to ensure that a duplicate test for verification will yield the same result. Tests may need to be repeated quarterly or annually to measure the auditee's level of improvement. Each test execution should be well documented with a record of time, date, method of sample selection, sample size, procedure used, person performing the analysis, and results.

It is often a good practice to use video recording to document the test process when the execution of the test method may be challenged—for example, to videotape a forensic computer audit if the results may be subject to dispute by individuals who are unfamiliar with the process.

The evidence grading effort aims to improve the resulting trustworthiness of the evidence. A competent IS auditor who can gather evidence and provide expert analysis with a high evidence trustworthiness rating is quite valuable indeed.

Timing of Evidence

An additional factor to consider in regard to evidence is timing. *Evidence timing* indicates whether evidence is received when it is requested, or several hours or days later. In electronic systems, the timing has a secondary meaning: Electronic evidence may be available only during a limited window of time before it is overwritten or the software changes to a new version.

We have discussed the character of evidence, evidence grading, and timing. The next section explains the evidence life cycle relating to the legal chain of custody.

Following the Evidence Life Cycle

The evidence will pass through seven life-cycle phases that are necessary in every audit. Every IS auditor must remain aware of the legal demands that are always present with regard to evidence handling. Failure to maintain a proper chain of custody may disqualify the evidence. Evidence handling is just as important for SOX compliance as it would be for suspected criminal activity. Evidence handling is crucial for compliance to most industry regulations.

WARNING   Mishandling of evidence can result in the auditor becoming the target of legal action by the owner. Mishandling evidence in criminal investigations could result in the bumbling auditor becoming the target of both the owner and the alleged perpetrator of a criminal activity.

The seven phases of the evidence life cycle are identification, collection, initial preservation storage, analysis, postanalysis preservation storage, presentation, and return of the evidence to the owner. The entire set of seven phases is referred to as the *chain of custody*. Let's go down the list one by one:

Identification   The auditor needs to identify items that may be objective evidence lending support to the purpose of the audit. The characteristics of the evidence location or surroundings should be thoroughly documented before proceeding to the collection stage. All evidence shall be labeled, dated, and notated with a short description about its purpose or discovery. From this point forward, the evidence movements must be logged into a tracking record. Your client will not be happy if evidence is misplaced.

It may be important to demonstrate how the evidence looked when it was discovered. Identification includes labeling and can include photographing physical evidence in an undisturbed state at the time of discovery.

Collection   The collection process involves taking possession of the evidence to place it under the control of a custodian. Special consideration should be given to items of a sensitive nature or high value. The IS auditor needs to exercise common sense during the collection process. Client records need to be kept in a secure location.

For most audits except criminal investigations, the IS auditor should be cognizant of the liability created by taking the client's confidential records out of the client's office. We strongly advise that all records remain within the client's facility to relieve the auditor of potential liability. The best way to prevent accusations is to ensure that you never place yourself in a compromising position. Allow the client to remain responsible for evidence security. Just be sure to lock up each evening before you leave.

Evidence of compliance is required for regulations such as SOX. A smart auditor recognizes that storage of any evidence in their own office is not acceptable. Records should be placed in a bonded record storage facility with the cost paid by your client. Consider the liability created by exposing records in your office to theft, destruction, or disclosure by a search order from an unrelated court subpoena.

Criminal evidence should not be disturbed until after proper identification and labeling. It may be beneficial to have a nonbiased observer present as a witness to attest to the investigator's actions as observed during the collection activity.

Initial Preservation Storage   A major problem with evidence is the challenge of preserving it in its original state. The preservation and storage process is a vital component in the chain of custody. The custodian of the evidence must be able to prove that the evidence has been protected and no alteration has occurred. The slightest change will transform the evidence without changing its identity. Electronic evidence requires special handling procedures to overcome future claims that the evidence has been altered (evidence tampering).

The chain of custody must remain unbroken to prevent evidence from being disqualified. In legal proceedings, a common method of disqualifying evidence is to argue that the custodian has failed the chain-of-evidence requirements. A related accusation is that evidence has been tampered with, which is often a plausible argument unless it can be proven that mishandling never occurred.

Analysis   In this phase, the evidence samples are examined by observation, scientific test, and qualitative and quantitative measurement. The entire process and results should be well documented. Individual tests may need to be rerun if errors are discovered with the test procedure, sample, or personnel executing the test.

In some instances, the test results may need to be duplicated by a second independent tester to validate the initial finding.

As you may recall, regulatory compliance is an ongoing requirement. The same internal controls will need to be tested at least once each year. The auditor should ensure that the testing process produces a reasonable degree of consistency in each subsequent audit.

Postanalysis Preservation Storage   After testing, the evidence and samples must be returned to preservation and secure storage. The evidence will continue to stay in storage except during presentation or retesting.

The auditor should be aware that proper handling is paramount for success in legal proceedings. Evidence used in legal trials may be retrieved and returned multiple times for use in court presentations prior to final release for return to the owner. The U.S. legal process allows for trials in at least three separate courts as the case progresses through to final appeal.

> A bonded evidence storage facility might be used for storage when the evidence is used in legal cases lasting several years. An example would be a case of corporate fraud or theft.

Management may decide that the evidence used in routine compliance audits should be copied and bound into storage binders. Selected copies of those documents would be sent to storage with the client's financial records. This ensures the ability to demonstrate the evidence in a near original state for any future investigation by industry regulators. Initial evidence collection is a time-consuming process that might be difficult to duplicate in the future.

Presentation   The evidence and findings are to be presented in support of the auditor's report. A variety of details may be included or omitted depending on the nature of the report. Reports of system performance offer little detail when compared to reports of criminal activity.

Return to Owner   The evidence is returned to the owner after the audit test results are successfully evaluated, or after legal proceedings are officially concluded by order of the final court. It is important to notice the distinction. In noncriminal activity, the evidence is promptly returned when the audit is concluded. Evidence may be held in preservation storage for several years if situations of suspected criminal activity exist.

Figure 3.5 demonstrates the logical flow through the entire chain of custody. A CISA is required to be competent in this evidence life cycle.

FIGURE 3.5   The evidence life cycle

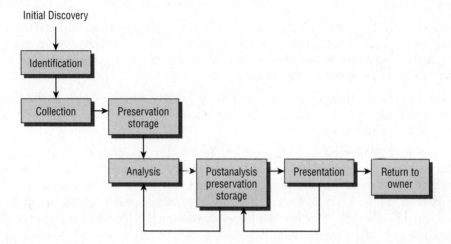

Now we will discuss examples of evidence that an IS auditor will typically use during an audit. After the evidence is gathered, the next step is to perform compliance tests or substantive testing.

Conducting Audit Evidence Testing

As stated earlier, the basic test methods used will be either compliance testing or substantive testing. It's important that audit samples appropriate for the test method selected by the auditor have been collected.

Compliance Testing

Compliance testing tests for the presence or absence of something. Compliance testing includes verifying that policies and procedures have been put in place, and checking that user access rights, program change control procedures, and system audit logs have been activated. An example of a compliance test is comparing the list of persons with physical access to the data center against the HR list of current employees.

Compliance testing is based on one of the following types of audit samples:

Attribute Sampling   Generally popular in compliance testing, the objective of attribute sampling is to determine whether an attribute is present or absent in the subject sample.

The result is specified by the rate of occurrence—for example, the presence of 1 in 100 units would be 1 percent.

Stop-and-Go Sampling   Used when few errors are expected, stop-and-go allows the test to occur without excessive effort in sampling and provides the opportunity to stop testing at the earliest possible opportunity. It is a simple form of testing to reinforce any claim that errors are unlikely in the sample population.

Discovery Sampling   This 100 percent sampling is used to detect fraud or when the likelihood of evidence existing is low. Forensics is an excellent example of discovery sampling. This is an attempt to discover evidence.

Precision, or Expected Error Rate   The precision rate indicates the acceptable margin of error between audit samples and the total quantity of the subject population. This is usually expressed as a percentage, such as 5 percent. To obtain a very low error rate, it is necessary to use a very large sample in testing. Auditors are justified in using a smaller sample size when the total population is expected to be error-free. A larger sample is required when errors are expected to be present in the population. The larger sample can yield a higher average. When errors are expected, the auditor must examine more data to determine whether the actual errors are within a tolerable error rate (maximum errors you would accept).

Error levels may be determined by reviewing the findings of a prior audit and by considering changes in the organization's procedures. Use the risk-based audit strategy to determine whether your samples and tests are telling the truth about the auditee.

Substantive Testing

Substantive testing seeks to verify the content and integrity of evidence. Substantive tests may include complex calculations to verify account balances, perform physical inventory counts, or execute sample transactions to verify the accuracy of supporting documentation. Substantive tests use audit samples selected by dollar value or to project (forecast or estimate) a total for groups with related characteristics.

    Substantive testing is based on one of the following types of audit samples:

Variable Sampling   Used to designate dollar values or weights (effectiveness) of an entire subject population by prorating from a smaller sample. Consider the challenge of counting large volumes of currency by its weight. Variable sampling could be used to count currency by multiplying the physical weight of one unit by the total weight of the combined sample, and then multiplying by the face value printed on the bill or coin. A demonstration is a single $50 bill weighing 1.0 gram, with the entire sample of $50 bills weighing 61 grams altogether. The combined sample weight would indicate a total quantity of 61 bills for an estimated dollar value of $3,050. This is a common technique for forecasting quantity and value of inventory based on particular characteristics.

Unstratified Mean Estimation   Used in an attempt to project an estimated total for the whole subject population.

Stratified Mean Estimation   Used to calculate an average by group, similar to demographics, whereby the entire population is divided (stratified) into smaller groups based on similar characteristics. Examples are teenagers from the ages of 13 to 19, people from the ages of 20 to 29, people from the ages of 30 to 39, and those who are male or female, smokers or nonsmokers, and so on.

Difference Estimation   Used to determine the difference between audited and unaudited claims of value.

Tolerable Error Rate

A tolerable error rate is used to indicate the maximum number of errors that can exist without declaring a material misstatement.

- For compliance tests, a tolerable error rate is the maximum deviation from a procedure that the auditor is willing to accept. Hint: If you want to remain an auditor, it had better be a very small deviation.

- In substantive testing, the auditor uses their judgment concerning material relevance and concludes whether the audit objective has been achieved. The test procedure and results should indicate a truthful pass or fail. A smart auditor will always lean toward the conservative side for safety in their measurement.

Regardless of the audit sample and test method used, the auditor is presumed to have a high degree of confidence when the audit coefficient is 95 percent or higher. The *audit coefficient* represents your level of confidence about the audit results. It is also referred to as a *reliability factor*.

Record Your Test Results

Just like Leonardo da Vinci and Louis Pasteur, every auditor needs to keep logs documenting their tests, samples, results, and observations. The auditor must trace all findings of conformity and nonconformity in their documentation of test results. Always remember that your audit test results must be repeatable by another auditor.

Each finding of evidence can be classified into one of these common reporting statements, presented in order of most desirable to least desirable:

Noteworthy Achievement   The auditee has demonstrated that some aspect in the process or system is being done very well. The auditee's efforts are very effective, and the auditor wants to bring recognition where credit is due. The auditee has exceeded the requirements.

Conformity   The testing of evidence proves that the auditee is accomplishing their stated objectives. Minimum requirements have been met.

Opportunity for Improvement   A specific item found is not in violation but should be targeted as an opportunity for improvement. For example, if the level of work integration is low, fixing this issue could reduce waste or the amount of manual effort required.

Concern   The evidence and auditor's observations indicate the possibility for future problems that need to be understood by management. Examples include overreliance, inefficiency, cascading problems, and the likelihood of failure.

Nonconformity   Testing indicates that a violation exists, which needs to be corrected. The violation found may be of minor or major significance. Nonconformities include system defects or missing control capabilities.

Let's begin the move toward testing samples and generating the preliminary report of audit findings.

Generate Audit Findings

Using your audit plan as a road map, it's time to analyze the evidence samples. The goal is to determine whether the samples tested by the auditor indicate conformity (meets requirement) or nonconformity (fails requirement).

We have two concerns as auditors related to testing: sufficiency of evidence and contradictory evidence. Let's look into this further:

Sufficiency of Evidence   Is there enough evidence of sufficient quantity and quality to fulfill the intended purpose and scope of the audit? If not, the auditor will not be able to prove conformity. The auditor should continue working the audit and report the limitations. Unless enough evidence can be found, the auditee will fail to meet compliance or substantive goals.

Contradictory Evidence   Let the evidence tell the story. Contradictory evidence suggests that either the auditor is doing something wrong or you have discovered evidence proving a problem actually exists (nonconformity). The auditor needs to perform additional quality assurance checks and recheck the test results to determine the reason that this nonconformity has been detected.

Detecting Irregularities and Illegal Acts

It is management's responsibility to implement the controls and supervision necessary to detect irregularities and potentially illegal acts in their environment. Management is responsible for making written assertions as to their representation of internal controls. Audit plans should include provisions and procedures in the event an auditor encounters irregularities or possibly illegal acts.

Examples of illegal activities include the following:

Fraud   Any act of deception used to gain an advantage. Misrepresentation is a type of fraud. Examples include posting transaction records that are intentionally false and without genuine merit.

Theft   Taking or acquiring resources that are not rightfully yours. The legal term *conversion* is another name for theft. Embezzlement is a form of theft.

Suppression   Suppressing data or records and their effects in business transactions. This is related to *obstruction* and *willful omission*.

Racketeering   The process of repeated (pervasive) fraud or other crimes. Racketeering is governed by the Racketeer Influenced and Corrupt Organizations (RICO) Act, which carries dire consequences to those parties alleged to have participated.

Regulatory Violations   Intentionally or unintentionally violating the law.

Indicators of Illegal or Irregular Activity

The IS auditor should understand that an organization's internal controls will not eliminate the possibility of irregular or illegal activity. Although it is not the auditor's job to detect these conditions, it is important to be alert to potential indicators. The auditor should be on the lookout for the following symptoms:

Questionable Payments   Examples include fees that appear to be excessively high or low, failed account reconciliation, payments to government officials, and payments for unspecified services.

Unsatisfactory Record Control   Examples include poor record keeping in general, proper controls not in use, evidence of falsified documents, missing documentation, and the untimely shredding of documents in advance of corporate retention guidelines.

Unsatisfactory Explanations   Examples include large or unusual transactions, and especially transactions with related companies at the end of the financial reporting period such as month-end or quarter-end. Other examples include overbooked or underbooked sales, unexplained or unusual items, or unexplained funds held in suspense accounts.

Other Questionable Circumstances   These might relate to the lifestyles of the organization's executives and employees.

Responding to Irregular or Illegal Activity

If you discover any potentially irregular or illegal activity, the next step is to attempt to determine whether management is aware of the situation or has participated in the suspected activities. The auditor should document all information, evidence, findings, and conclusions that led to the discovery of the suspected activities:

- The auditor should consider any unusual or unexpected relationships that could lead to material misstatements or misrepresentations.
- The auditor should maintain a position of professional skepticism.
- Upon learning of material irregularities or illegal acts, the auditor should promptly notify one level of management higher than where the suspected activities may have taken place.
- If the activities involve a person charged with internal controls or governance, reporting should take place at the highest level possible.

- The auditor should not contact law enforcement or regulators until advised to do so by the auditor's legal counsel. Special handling procedures are usually required to protect the auditor.

- The auditor should never become a party to the suspected activity. The auditor should seek competent legal advice if unsure about what actions to take. You may be advised to prepare for termination of the audit.

Findings Outside of Audit Scope

Don't be surprised to discover something outside the scope of your audit; it happens all the time. Smart auditors recognize their obligation to stay within the mutually agreed-upon scope of their client. No respectable auditor would ignore problems found outside the original scope. The first objective is to determine whether the problem is major or just a minor nuisance. Here's what to do:

Minor Problem   Report the discovery to the auditee and continue the audit within the original scope.

Major Problem   Report the finding to your lead auditor or engagement manager. The audit team leader is responsible for reporting the discovery to the auditee's management. In addition, a decision needs to be made regarding whether this situation warrants additional investigation, and whether the audit should stop or continue within the original scope. Major problems outside of scope should be listed in your audit report. Be sure to ask your lead auditor whether the problem warrants reporting as a nonconformity within this particular audit or just mentioning it without marking it as a nonconformity. The most successful auditors understand that the highest level of professionalism is necessary to handle this type of situation. Well-mannered professionals may gain additional audit work if the situation is handled correctly.

Report Findings

After performing your audit, the next step is to prepare a presentation to report your findings. Reporting is the process by which the auditor conveys to management their findings, including the following:

- Audit scope

- Audit objectives

- Methods and criteria used

- Nature of findings

- Extent of work performed

- Applicable dates of coverage

In addition, the final report should state any restrictions, reservations, or qualifications (concerns) that the auditor holds in relation to the audit. The auditor may provide a final opinion or no opinion based on these potential limitations. Auditors may issue qualified or unqualified opinions:

A qualified opinion means there are restrictions on the nature or the content of the findings.

An unqualified opinion has no restrictions on its use because the findings have no reservations.

Statement on Auditing Standards (SAS), the COSO internal controls framework, and the IT Governance Institute (ISACA-ITGI) publish several points of information that should be included in the final report. You should consult their publications for specific details. In summary, the recommendations include the following:

- A title that includes the word *independent* (for an external audit)
- The applicable date of the report
- Identification of the parties and subject matter
- An executive summary
- Any visual representations, charts, graphs, or diagrams
- A statement of the standards followed during the audit
- A statement of the procedures performed, and whether they were agreed to by the specified parties
- Any necessary disclaimers
- A statement of additional procedures, if performed
- A statement of restrictions on the use of the report
- A statement of any auditor concerns, reservations, or qualifications to the audit
- Detailed findings and the auditor's opinion
- Auditor signature and contact information

The IS auditor's signature attests that the audit report and stated findings are true and correct. *Attestation* is the act of providing your assurance via a signature that the contents of a document are authentic and genuine.

 You should keep your report easy to read. Simple graphics, tables, and color coding will be appreciated by your client.

After producing the final report, you will need to meet with the auditee and management to review the findings. The primary purpose of this meeting is not to change your findings, but to obtain acceptance and agreement by the auditee. This is the final quality-control check before issuing your final report. You want to ensure that the facts are correctly presented in your report. A final copy of this report and of your working notes will need to be placed into the audit archive for document retention.

Approving and Distributing the Audit Report

A draft of the audit report should be distributed to the auditee personnel who participated in the audit. Many details may be relatively confidential or sensitive. The audit team leader may determine that the best course of action is to share only portions of the report with the person responsible for that specific area. Auditees and clients should be given the opportunity to agree or disagree with the auditor's draft report. Their comments should politely be recorded for incorporation to the auditor's final report. This is a very important quality control process that must occur in every audit. It is not necessary for the auditor to agree, but it is necessary to give the auditee an opportunity to voice concerns over discrepancies or complaints. Many times the issue is simply political wording rather than a disagreement of the findings. However, in the end, the audit report needs to match the truth as verified by the auditor.

Identifying Omitted Procedures

On the rare occasion that an auditor determines after issuing a draft or final report that one or more auditing procedures have been omitted, it may be necessary to review some of the audit alternatives to compensate for the omission. If the omitted procedures present material bearing on the outcome, and the audit alternatives cannot compensate for the deficiency, canceling the report and reissuing a new report (if appropriate) may be necessary. If the omitted procedures have tangible bearing on the outcome, the auditor should consult with their lawyer for advice concerning any possible avenues or potential legal actions.

Conducting Follow-Up (Closing Meeting)

After issuing a report, the auditor is required to conduct an exit interview with management to obtain a commitment for the recommendations made in the audit. Management is responsible for acknowledging the recommendations and designating whatever corrective action will be taken, including the estimated dates for the action.

In subsequent audits, you will check whether management honored their commitments to fix or remediate deficiencies found in a prior audit. Occasionally, the deficiencies are left uncorrected because changes in the organizational design or practice have eliminated the conditions of the prior control's weakness. Particular findings may apply to events that are no longer relevant. Otherwise, you expect management to act in a timely manner to correct the deficiency as originally reported.

The auditor should never take ownership of any problems found. This would violate your independence. All issues raised in your findings should be regarded as owned by the auditee. It's the job of their management to fix it.

Sometimes events of concern are discovered, or occur, after an audit has been completed. You would be concerned about the discovery of subsequent events that pose a material challenge to your final report. Accounting standards recognize these events and classify them as follows:

Type 1 events refer to those that occurred before the balance sheet date.

Type 2 events are those that occurred after the balance sheet date.

Depending on the type of audit, you may have additional reporting requirements or activities. These may require additional disclosures or adjustments to your report based on the nature of the event that was recently discovered or occurred.

 It is not the auditor's responsibility to detect subsequent events.

Summary

This concludes our review of the IS audit process. A CISA is expected to have a thorough understanding of the entire audit process. You will be expected to understand the issues and motivation behind each step.

A violation of the audit process would be a concern and would likely indicate that the outcome is meaningless. As an IS auditor, you should always strive to honor the spirit and intent of the audit process. Conduct audits in accordance with recognized audit standards, guidelines, and best practices. It is your job to plan the audit around the business requirements by using a risk-based approach and to collect meaningful evidence. You are expected to produce an objective report based on the evidence you obtained during the audit. The final report will be communicated to management with the goal of gaining their commitment to resolve any weaknesses found. Your actions should be well documented and reproducible by another auditor.

Chapter 1 covered how the auditor should look, act, and think. Chapter 2, "Managing IT Governance," presented the techniques used for IT governance. This chapter discussed how the auditor should perform the audit.

Exam Essentials

Know how to develop and implement a risk-based audit strategy. The auditor should focus on areas of high value. The risk assessment will help to determine whether the audit will yield meaningful information. Certain types of conditions may be difficult to audit. It is important that the audit is based on meaningful evidence that is materially relevant.

Understand how to conduct IS audits in accordance with published standards, guidelines, and best practices. The auditor is expected to follow published audit standards to ensure thoroughness and consistency. Deviations from standards and guidelines is rare. Any deviation must be well documented, but results may not be accepted by the audit community. The purpose of best practices is to aid the auditor by identifying useful procedures and techniques. Every audit should be designed to adhere to standards.

Be familiar with how to plan for specific audits. The CISA needs to understand the constraints and requirements of individual audits. It is the auditor's job to identify the resource requirements, sampling requirements, test methods, and procedures to be used. The auditor will identify appropriate personnel to be interviewed. The interview process must be scheduled and must implement predefined questions for the purpose of gathering data. An audit involving third-party personnel will present its own unique challenges.

Know the auditing practices and techniques. Well-established IS auditing procedures ensure thoroughness and consistency necessary for a successful audit. Good audits will implement a well-thought-out sequence of procedures to evaluate materially relevant samples. ISACA provides the auditor with foundation knowledge that should be implemented during your audit. Effective sample selection of meaningful tests should yield materially relevant results.

Be familiar with IS control objectives and performing control assessment. High-level controls are categorized as general controls, pervasive controls, detailed controls and application controls. Internal controls are intended to be preventative, detective, and corrective. Each control may be implemented using administrative methods, physical methods, and technical methods. The purpose of the controls is to prevent harm and protect an asset. The IS auditor is responsible for evaluating the effectiveness of controls.

Know some of the various types of computer-assisted audit tools (CAAT). Computer-assisted audit tools are software tools that can provide detailed analysis of computer systems configuration, vulnerability, logs, and other information. The CAAT output should be kept confidential because of the potentially sensitive nature of its contents.

Understand the continuous auditing methods. Continuous audit methods such as audit hooks or SCARF with embedded audit modules (SCARF/EAM) are used in environments where it is not possible to interrupt production.

Know the techniques to gather information and manage the evidence life cycle. The auditor can collect information through traditional sources of business records, computer data files, and CAAT. Meaningful information can be obtained through personal interviews, workshops, and surveys. All information and evidence should be recorded and tracked. The evidence life cycle comprises identification, collection, preservation, analysis, safe storage, and finally its return to the owner. Evidence used for criminal prosecution must be handled with the highest degree of care. Evidence that is mishandled will void legal claims and may result in punitive legal action.

Know the types of evidence and evidence grading. The best evidence will tell its own story. The best evidence will prove or disprove a point. The best evidence is both objective and independent. The timing of evidence must be considered when calculating its useful value. Evidence that is late and subjective will be of low value. Material evidence will have a bearing on the final outcome. Irrelevant evidence will not affect the final decision.

Familiarize yourself with the types of audit tests and sample selection. Audit tests can be substantive or compliance based. It is important to select an appropriate sample in order to generate data to reflect the actual situation. Audit test procedures and sample selection methods must be well documented to ensure verifiable and reproducible tests. The sample may be selected based on physical characteristics, value, or size of population.

Understand how evidence is analyzed for reporting conformity or nonconformity. The auditor must have sufficient evidence of quality and quantity in order to report a conformity. Test results are usually reported as noteworthy for special achievement, conforming to minimum requirements, opportunity for improvement, concern that's not a violation yet, and nonconformity.

Know how to deal with irregular and illegal acts. It is possible that you could encounter evidence of irregular or illegal acts. The discoveries should be communicated to the next level of management higher than where the act occurred. Such a discovery involving persons responsible for internal controls must be reported to the absolute highest level of management. The auditor should consult their attorney for legal advice.

Know how to advise clients on implementing risk management and control practices while maintaining independence. The auditor is encouraged to educate their client and help increase awareness of control issues. It is important that the auditor does not participate in specific discussions of design or architecture. The auditor must not work on fixing problems if the auditor is expected to be independent. A client may hire an auditor for remediation and use a separate, unrelated auditor for the audit. The auditor cannot be independent if they participated in the audit subject.

Be able to communicate issues, potential risks, and audit results. The auditor is expected to communicate materially relevant issues to management through the audit reporting process. Issues of high significance should be communicated directly to the audit committee. The final results of each audit should be verifiable and reproducible. All communication must convey the facts without placing blame on individuals.

Understand the role of traditional audits compared to control self-assessment (CSA). Control self-assessments are designed to empower the customer's staff. The intention is to generate awareness and ownership of problems. A control self-assessment is an excellent way to improve the performance of an organization between traditional audits. The traditional audit is still necessary to the independence requirement.

Review Questions

1. Which term best describes the difference between the audit sample and the total population?

    A. Precision

    B. Tolerable error rate

    C. Level of risk

    D. Analytic delta

2. Which is *not* a purpose of risk analysis?

    A. Support risk-based audit decisions

    B. Assist the auditor in determining audit objectives

    C. Assist the auditor in identifying risks and threats

    D. Ensure absolute safety during the audit

3. Failing to prevent or detect a material error would represent which type of risk?

    A. Overall audit risk

    B. Detection risk

    C. Inherent risk

    D. Control risk

4. Which of the following is *not* a type of quantitative sampling model?

    A. Difference estimation

    B. Stratified mean per unit

    C. Unstratified mean per unit

    D. Qualitative estimation per unit

5. The two types of tests are referred to as _____ and _____ using _____ sampling methods.

    A. Substantive tests, compliance tests, variable and attribute

    B. Compliance tests, substantive tests, variable and discovery

    C. Predictive tests, compliance tests, stop-and-go and difference estimation

    D. Integrity tests, compliance tests, stratified mean and unstratified mean

6. What is the purpose of the audit charter?

    A. To engage external auditors

    B. To grant responsibility, authority, and accountability

    C. To authorize the creation of the audit committee

    D. To provide detailed planning of the audit

7. Which of the following is false concerning a control self-assessment (CSA)?

    A. Empowers the user to take ownership and accountability

    B. Eliminates the need for a traditional audit

    C. May be used to identify high-risk areas for later review

    D. Will not have the level of independence provided by an external auditor

8. Which of the following would be a concern of the auditor that should be explained in the audit report along with their findings?

    A. Detailed list of audit objectives

    B. The need by the current auditor to communicate with the prior auditor

    C. Communicating results directly to the chairperson of the audit committee

    D. Undue restrictions placed by management on evidence use or audit procedures

9. What is the purpose of the audit committee?

    A. To assist managers with training in auditing skills

    B. To govern, control, and manage the organization

    C. To challenge and review assurances

    D. To provide daily coordination of all audit activities

10. Which type of audit may be used for regulatory licensing or external reporting?

    A. Qualified audit

    B. Independent assessment

    C. Control self-assessment

    D. Traditional audit

11. What is the best data collection technique the auditor can use if the resources are available?

    A. Surveys that create a broad sample

    B. Review of existing documentation

    C. Auditor observation

    D. Interviews

12. Which of the following types of risk are of the most interest to an IS auditor?

    A. Control, detection, noncompliance, risk of strike

    B. Inherent, noninherent, control, lack of control

    C. Sampling, control, detection, inherent

    D. Unknown, quantifiable, cumulative

13. Which of the following describes the relationship between compliance testing and substantive testing?

    A. Compliance testing checks for the presence of controls; substantive testing checks the integrity of internal contents.

    B. Substantive testing tests for presence; compliance testing tests actual contents.

    C. The tests are identical in nature; the difference is whether the audit subject is under the Sarbanes-Oxley Act.

    D. Compliance testing tests individual account balances; substantive testing checks for written corporate policies.

14. What is the principal issue surrounding the use of CAAT?

    A. The capability of the software vendor.

    B. Possible cost, complexity, and the security of output.

    C. Inability of automated tools to consider the human characteristics of the environment.

    D. Documentary evidence is more effective.

15. Auditors base their report on findings, evidence, and the results of testing. It's more of a score than an opinion. Which of the following types of evidence sampling refer to a 100 percent sample?

    A. Attribute

    B. Stop-and-go

    C. Cell

    D. Discovery

16. An IS auditor is performing a review of an application and finds something that might be illegal. The IS auditor should do which of the following?

    A. Disregard or ignore the finding because this is beyond the scope of this review

    B. Conduct a detailed investigation to aid the authorities in catching the culprit

    C. Immediately notify the auditee of the finding

    D. Seek legal advice before finishing the audit

17. The auditor is permitted to deviate from professional audit standards when they feel it is necessary; which of the following is true regarding such deviation?

    A. Standards are designed for discretionary use.

    B. Deviation is almost unheard of and would require significant justification.

    C. Deviation depends on the authority granted in the audit charter.

    D. The unique characteristics of the client will require auditor flexibility.

18. Which is the best document to help define the relationship of the independent auditor and provide evidence of the agreed-upon terms and conditions?

   A. Audit charter

   B. Annual audit plan

   C. Engagement letter

   D. Auditor's report

19. Who has the responsibility of setting the scope of the audit?

   A. Auditor

   B. Client

   C. Audit manager

   D. Auditee

20. What is the biggest issue with the decision to transfer risk to an outsourced contractor?

   A. There is potential for uncontrollable increase in operating cost over time.

   B. Outsourcing shifts the entire risk to the contractor.

   C. The company still retains liability for whatever happens.

   D. Outsourcing shields the company from intrinsic risks.

21. Audits are intended to be conducted in accordance with which of the following ideals?

   A. Specific directives from management concerning evidence and procedure

   B. Reporting and communication

   C. Assessment of the organizational controls

   D. Adherence to standards, guidelines, and best practices

22. During audit planning, several documents are produced in support of the project. Which of these is used to identify the person responsible for specific tasks in order to gain funding and ensure quality?

   A. Skills matrix

   B. Procurement matrix

   C. Task matrix

   D. Activities matrix

23. Which of these types of computer-assisted audit tools (CAAT) is designed to process dummy transactions during the processing of genuine transactions?

   A. Continuous and intermittent simulation

   B. Embedded program audit hooks

   C. Embedded audit module

   D. Online event monitor

24. Which of the following conditions is *false* in regard to using the work of other people during your audit?

    A. Ensure independence of the provider.

    B. Accept the work based on job position.

    C. Use agreed-upon scope and approach.

    D. Provide supervision and review.

25. ISACA refers to testing for strong controls. What is the best description of a strong control?

    A. Effective implementation of multiple controls targeting the same objective

    B. Preventative controls that stop the problem from ever occurring

    C. Using at least one control in each of the three categories of preventative, detective, corrective

    D. Implementing comprehensive pervasive controls inside of an ERP application

Answers to Review Questions

1.   A. The compliance test uses precision to describe the rate of occurrence out of the sample population. The compliance testing uses precision to describe the expected error rate of the sample compared to total population. Precision is usually expressed as a percentage.

2.   D. Risk analysis is used to determine whether the audit has any chance of representing the truth. Nothing in the realm of IS auditing is absolute because of the abstract nature of technology implementations.

3.   B. A detection risk is that you would fail to detect that a material error has occurred.

4.   D. Difference estimation, stratified mean, and unstratified mean are valid sample types for substantive testing. Qualitative estimation is just a distractor.

5.   A. Answer B is incorrect because compliance testing uses discovery sampling to detect fraud. C and D are distractors.

6.   B. he audit charter's purpose is to grant the right to audit and delegate responsibility, authority, and accountability.

7.   B. All of the statements are true except B. A CSA is not a substitute for a traditional audit.

8.   D. Undue restrictions on scope would be a major concern as would the lack of time or the inability to obtain sufficient reliable evidence.

9.   C. The audit committee's purpose is to review and challenge assurances made, and to maintain a positive working relationship with management and the auditors.

10. D. Traditional independent audits are conducted with formality and adherence to standards necessary for regulatory licensing and external reporting. It's true that there is always a shady auditor ready to lie for a client. The world expects an independent audit to be conducted by a qualified auditor representing a high degree of truth. Assessments are too informal and therefore can be used only internally in the organization.

11. D. Interviewing selected personnel is the best technique. Surveys, document review, and observations generate a lower yield.

12. C. The answers including risk of strike, lack of control, and unknown are distractors.

13. A. Substantive testing checks the substance or integrity of a transaction. Compliance testing looks for presence of controls or control attributes.

14. B. CAATs are able to perform faster than humans and produce more-accurate data in functions such as system scanning. Cost, training, and security of output are major considerations.

15. D. Discovery sampling is used to find 100 percent of everything possible when fraud is suspected or the likelihood of finding evidence is low. All the other possible choices are valid sampling methods used in compliance testing.

16. D. Seek competent legal advice. It is not the auditor's job to detect potentially illegal acts; however, the auditor should seek the aid of a lawyer concerning liability and reporting requirements.

17. B. Standards are mandatory, and any deviation would require justification.

18. C. The engagement letter is used with independent auditors to define the relationship. This letter serves as a record to document the understanding and agreement between the audit committee and the independent auditor. It provides the independent auditor the responsibility, accountability, and authority to conduct the audit.

19. B. Every audit is paid for and requested by a client, who is responsible for setting the scope, granting authority, and providing access to the auditee.

20. C. The work can be outsourced; however, the liability for failure remains with the company. One example is the Firestone tire failure affecting Ford Motor Company. Another is the lead paint used by subcontractors forcing the giant toy recall of 2007. Liability cannot be outsourced.

21. D. Audits should adhere to standards, guidelines, and best practices. Answer A represents a restriction on scope. B and C are components of answer D.

22. A. A skills matrix is used to identify the skills of each person and to ensure that the right person is performing the task. Using a skills matrix in planning is an excellent method to justify proper funding for training or additional personnel.

23. C. Embedded audit module (EAM) processes dummy transactions during the processing of genuine transactions. The intention is to determine whether the system is functioning correctly.

24. B. The auditor should never base the decision on the job position of the other person. All of the other choices are vague but truthful. Always assess the independence of the provider, check their qualifications, agree on scope and procedures used, and supervise and review their work. Don't use it if the results are questionable or fail to follow very high adherence to audit standards.

25. A. Strong controls will implement multiple types of preventative, detective, and corrective controls using a combined approach of administrative methods, physical methods, and technical methods. This is referred to as depth of control, hopefully using all nine layers. Using the bare minimum would be a weak control.

Additional CISA practice questions are available on the author's website at www.CertTest.com.

Chapter

4

Networking Technology Basics

THE OBJECTIVE OF THIS CHAPTER IS TO ACQUAINT THE READER WITH THE FOLLOWING CONCEPTS:

- ✓ Computer hardware terms, and advantages of different types of system architecture

- ✓ Functional introduction to the OSI model and its relationship with TCP/IP

- ✓ Methods of creating different types of area networks (LAN, WAN, PAN, WLAN)

- ✓ Network addressing and methods for routing data communications

- ✓ Different types of networking equipment and their purposes

- ✓ Network services including DHCP, Domain Name System, and firewalls

- ✓ An introduction to network management

In this chapter, you will study networking technology equipment and concepts. As mentioned in Chapter 1, "Secrets of a Successful Auditor," and Chapter 3, "Audit Process," one of the first priorities for the auditor is to gain an understanding of the auditee's environment. ISACA expects every auditor to understand the functionality of the IT infrastructure. The infrastructure comprises a unique architecture of computer hardware and special-purpose software. You will study the advantages of implementing different types of system architecture. Technology-savvy IT professionals need to study this entire chapter just as much as everyone else. The objective is to understand how ISACA views the use of networking technology rather than how your favorite vendor views it.

A functional introduction of the OSI model is presented along with its relationship to the TCP/IP model used in the real world. Using the OSI model as the backdrop, we discuss the functions of different types of network equipment. It is important for CISAs to understand the purpose and capabilities presented by the operating systems, routers, switches, firewalls, and other peripherals. The goal of this chapter is to provide a general understanding of how the infrastructure could be assembled in a manner that fulfills most of the internal control requirements.

We wrap up the chapter with a discussion on network management because auditors are expected to understand network analyzers, capacity planning, and monitoring techniques. Several of the points regarding network security are covered again in Chapter 7, "Protecting Information Assets." The purpose of this chapter is to provide you a firm foundation in networking technology.

Understanding the Differences in Computer Architecture

All computers are not created equal. The differences in architecture have a substantial impact on performance and system security. However, every computer has three basic types of components:

Central Processing Unit   The first component group centers around the central processing unit, also known as the *CPU*. The CPU performs mathematical calculations with the assistance of an internal arithmetic logic unit, a high-speed memory cache, and working memory space known as random access memory (RAM). Data stored in RAM is erased when power is turned off.

Input/Output   The second component group provides input and output to peripheral devices such as keyboards, monitors, and disk drives. This input and output channel is used to transmit data to and from the CPU for processing. Computers with a simple architecture may use a common channel for all communication with the CPU. This channel may be an individual connector or a shared data bus of several devices.

Data Storage   The third component group is data storage. Every computer requires additional storage space, such as a hard disk. Data storage may be fixed in a semipermanent location or removable. When a computer is turned on, the initial startup process is executed from internal programmable chips and data storage disks. This startup function is called *boot strapping (boot)* or *initial program load (IPL)*. The operating system is loaded from data storage, along with device driver information for the basic input/output system (BIOS). The system is available for use after completion of the boot, or IPL, process.

Figure 4.1 is a general diagram illustrating the architecture of a computer. Notice the CPU on the upper left. The CPU is the brains of the system and is attached to all of the other components with a string of electrical conductors. This string of conductors is called the system *data bus*, which is represented as the lines drawn across the middle of the diagram. *Bus* is an electrical term that means a shared electrical path. The CPU could not run effectively without the support of solid-state memory, known, as indicated earlier, as *random access memory (RAM)*. Random access memory is not as fast as the CPU. A special type of superfast memory is used to buffer between the CPU and RAM to help the CPU run at maximum speed. This high-speed CPU buffer memory is known as *cache*. The heart of computer processing occurs between the CPU, cache, and RAM. Other devices are attached to the data bus through computer expansion slots and interfaces. The disk drives and network each have their own electronic interface or add-in card connected to the data bus. This is how the information flows to and from the electronic components.

Integrated circuits (ICs) of the CPU can perform mathematical calculations faster than we can think or act. In fact, a computer with a single CPU will spend a great deal of time waiting for human input. The CPU can therefore support light processing for several users at one time with little delay. The process of CPU sharing for multiple users is called *time-sharing* (see Figure 4.2). Each user or system process receives a tiny segment of time for processing their request. Only one request is processed at a time. All other processing requests are parked in memory, awaiting their turn. Each processing request is serviced by generating a system interrupt. The CPU halts on interrupt and swaps processing with the task stored in memory. This process is similar to how you handle interruptions when the telephone rings. The computer is presumed to be running so fast that the other users do not notice any significant delay.

Computers with single processors have two major drawbacks. The first issue is related to *separation of duties* (SoD) for system security. Each system interrupt halts any security software that is running and allows the task to be processed before restarting the security software. The second drawback is the CPU bottleneck created by processor-intensive activities of database and graphics-rendering software.

FIGURE 4.1 Computer hardware architecture

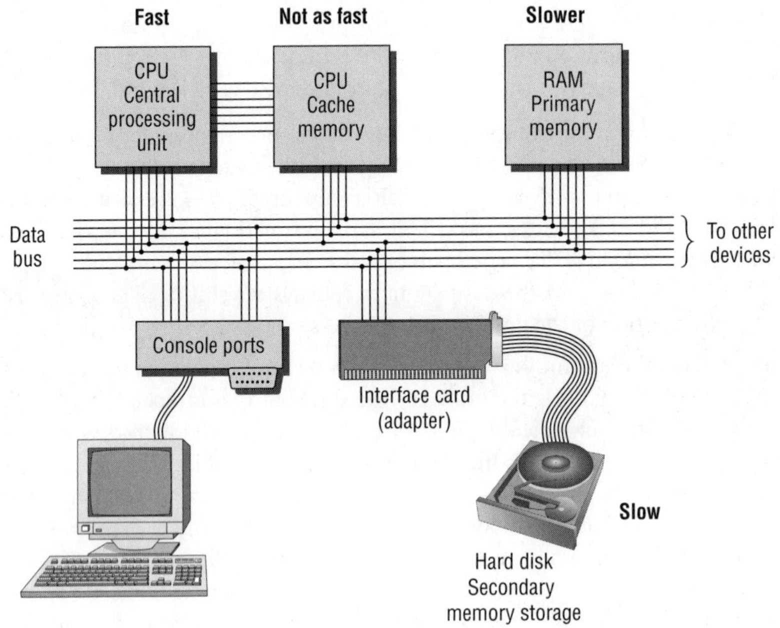

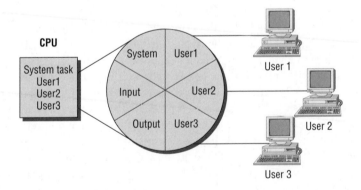

FIGURE 4.2 Single-CPU system with multiple users (time-sharing)

Multiprocessor computers and computers based on multicore CPUs are designed to deal with the demands of process-intensive applications. Multiprocessor systems are ideal for high-security environments because the security software will be able to run without any interruption. The processor may still perform time-sharing functions for multiple users; however, the load is allocated across multiple CPUs. Figure 4.3 shows a typical multiprocessor architecture.

FIGURE 4.3   Multiple-processor architecture

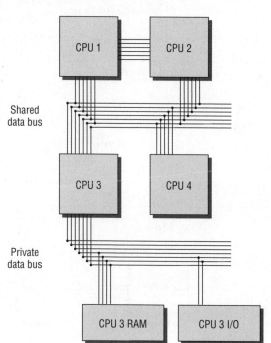

Security software on a computer with a single CPU is halted during each system interrupt request to allow the next task to be processed. The security software is then restarted and halted again between each request by another program to run on the single CPU chip. Computer interrupts occur in normal operation hundreds or thousands of times per second.

When the multiprocessor system is booted, the first processor accepts the responsibility of running system functions for control, input, and output. The first CPU schedules processing tasks across the other CPUs. These tasks include the dedicated servicing of requests from programs such as *Structured Query Language* (SQL) database on CPU 2, running dedicated monitoring software without any interruptions on CPU 3, and off-loading miscellaneous user requests to CPU 4.

The operating system becomes a resident on CPU 1 and performs hardware checks for input and output. The second processor loads as a task processor only. Each additional processor does the same. This allows the first CPU to have uninterrupted control of the system operations, including security, while the other CPUs perform problem-solving tasks in response to user requests.

Figure 4.4 shows how the workload is stacked and processed through the CPUs. Notice that each CPU has a small stack of tasks that are each in different phases of processing.

This stacking of tasks is referred to as *pipelining*. Think of it as a pipeline full of people standing at your door and wanting you to do work for them.

FIGURE 4.4 Multitasking systems (single-processor and multiprocessor workload)

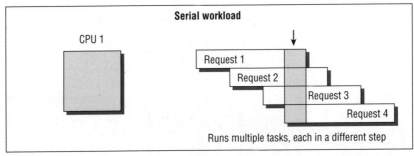

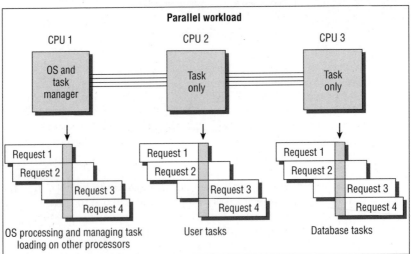

A single CPU would be maxed out with a small pipeline. The multiprocessor system, on the other hand, designates one CPU to be the equivalent of a manager, while the other CPUs each process their own pipeline full of requests. In the real world, this could look like a room full of people talking on the phone, eating a snack, drinking coffee, and answering email all at the same time. As you're aware, a group of people can drink a lot more coffee and process a lot more email than one person. The same can be said about computers with multiple processors.

Multiprocessor systems can perform high-security processing with a separation of duties. Individual processors could be dedicated to perform security functions without interruption. The CPU can be programmed to ignore interrupt requests. Ignoring a processing request is referred to as *interrupt masking*. Interrupt masking is useful for ensuring that high-priority tasks are not interrupted.

Selecting the Best System

In this section, you will look at various computer operating systems, as well as how to determine the best computer for you. In addition, you will compare some of their capabilities and look at supervisory versus problem states. Finally, you will look at data storage and port controls more closely.

Identifying Various Operating Systems

Every computer uses some sort of operating system (OS) to control the hardware. Each make and model of computer hardware is slightly different. For example, the processor type might be different, or the computer might use a specialized disk drive subsystem.

Computer programs of the 1950s and 1960s were not as portable as they are today. The old computers required the programmer to write a unique program for each model of system. As time progressed, computer software evolved with the development of new programming languages and then new operating systems.

Rocket to the Moon

The Unix operating system was created by Ken Thompson to run a computer program called Space Travel. The more advanced operating system used in the 1960s was the Multiplexed Information and Computing Service (Multics). This is why you may encounter references to Multics in older Unix documentation. Thompson noticed two problems while trying to run the Space Travel program.

First, the time-sharing design of running Multics on the available hardware did not give Thompson's program the dedicated speed necessary for it to run fast enough. So Thompson decided to delete the Multics time-sharing functions. The revamped single-user operating system was named the Uniplexed Operating and Computing System (Unics). It was later renamed Unix after some multiuser capabilities were re-added.

The second problem was software portability across hardware. Each time Thompson attempted to move the Space Travel program from one computer to another, it was necessary to rewrite the program to accommodate differences in hardware. Dennis Ritchie joined Thompson to work on projects for software portability across different hardware. They created a series of programming languages known as B, and then C. This is the same C programming language that you hear about today. All later additions to the original C programming language bear the designators C+, C++, and C# (also known as C Sharp). Chapter 5, "Information Systems Life Cycle," covers more details on programming.

Portable Software Systems

Modern computers use a more refined operating system. You will typically use an operating system designed for the type of hardware you intend to use. IBM's z/OS (formerly MVS) is common in the IBM mainframe world, whereas Unix is run on a variety of systems. Microsoft Windows is popular for its relatively low initial cost and widespread availability. The Apple

Mac OS has a smaller, yet growing, market share with a devoutly dedicated following in the graphics and motion picture industry.

Each of these operating systems shares common traits. The operating system vendor works with the hardware manufacturer to create specialized hardware support within the operating system. The application programmer simply compiles the program for a particular operating system. All the user needs to do is to match their desired application software to the operating system, and then match the operating system to the available hardware.

Figure 4.5 shows what a common computer operating system looks like.

FIGURE 4.5 Computer operating system

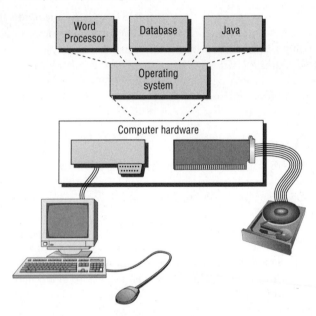

Every commercial-grade computer OS provides at least the following functions:

- Provides a user interface to the computer. The interface is often called a *shell*. This is the command-line or graphical interface supporting the directions to the computer.

- Manages security and event logging during the interaction between a user and the computer hardware.

- Provides a common software platform to run application programs. Computer programs run on top of the operating system. The operating system acts as a translator between the program and the hardware. Application programs no longer need to be rewritten for hardware changes if using the same OS.

- Provides an organized file system to store and retrieve data.

- Provides a method of input and output to various devices, including disk drives, network connections, printers, and video displays.

- Coordinates internal communications between programs and processing of tasks by the CPU.

- May provide no security, primitive login security, or advanced security to protect the data and programs from harm.

Operating systems can be designed to support a single user or multiple users. You can run software slowly in a batch of requests (set of requests, also known as *batch mode*) or in smaller and faster batches to simulate real-time transactions.

Computers can function in an ever-increasing variety of roles. Some computers are designed for special-purpose functions—for example, the iPhone, Blackberry or newer 4G handhelds or new 3G integrated wireless phones. Many computers are designed for general-purpose use as a desktop or laptop computer. Table 4.1 lists some of the typical functional roles that computers fulfill.

TABLE 4.1   Typical computer roles

Role	Function	Examples
User workstation	Runs applications to solve problems and can access data on network servers	Microsoft Office, personal spreadsheets, email client, web surfing. Usually desktop or laptop.
File server	Stores data files for shared user access	Microsoft and Novell shared network drives (usually labeled F: through Z:), Unix file mounts (/usr/home/~your_name), mainframe file share to PC using drive letters or links.
Website server	Performs the same function as the file server	www.certtest.com
DNS server	Converts server domain names into their matching IP addresses	Domain Name System is a program to find the IP address matching the name you entered. DNS works like an automated phone book. You type easy-to-remember names such as www.certtest.com and DNS tells your computer the corresponding IP address.
Database server	Stores raw data and organizes it in tables for authorized users to access	Accounting software, sales automation, and online shopping carts. Can exist on a file server, web server, or dedicated machine. May be internally developed or built using a commercial product such as Oracle SQL, MySQL, IBM Informix, or IBM DB2.

TABLE 4.1   Typical computer roles *(continued)*

Role	Function	Examples
Appliance or special-purpose device	Performs dedicated processing	Web cache, proxy server, email server, network router, or gateway. *Appliance* refers to a preconfigured computer designed to support a single need. Built from a general-purpose computer or unique hardware and configured to run a special-service program. Your home satellite receiver for the Dish Network or DirecTV is a PC hardware appliance running Linux.

Determining the Best Computer Class

Computers come in a variety of sizes and prices, based on their processing power and throughput. (*Throughput* is a measure of how much information passes through the system in a specific period of time.) There are four major classes of computer systems: supercomputers, mainframe computers, minicomputers, and personal computers.

Supercomputers

Supercomputers are designed for intense scientific calculations. A supercomputer would be used to calculate the incredible details of a nuclear reaction and to trace the particles through their life cycle, for example. Supercomputers are not measured in size, but instead by the lightning speed at which transactions can occur. They tend to be specialized systems running large-scale simulation and analysis programs. The mission of supercomputers is to solve complex mathematical calculations. Supercomputers are not used for processing a business database or corporate financial records.

Mainframe Computers

Mainframe computers are large, scalable, general-purpose systems designed to support incredible volumes of data. These are the large boxes you would see in a traditional data center. A single mainframe computer could be as small as a filing cabinet or as large as a roomful of refrigerators, all depending on its configuration.

Mainframes have the advantage of being able to process massive amounts of data in parallel, with incredible throughput. These systems are capable of multithreading thousands of programs simultaneously. *Multithreading* allows programs to be executed in parallel to minimize idle time within the processors. Mainframe computers have provided the control-based role model for other systems to follow. Mainframes implement an excellent separation of duty (SoD) framework.

Prices range from $50,000 to tens of millions of dollars. A mainframe offers several advantages to those who can afford one, including the following:

Rock-solid virtual machine that can partition resources into smaller environments. You can easily set up one mainframe to act as 300 to 5,000 PC servers, without the administrative headache.

Outstanding security. The internal system-partitioning controls have built-in segregation of duties with multiple layers of security. Internal system control reporting is excellent.

Lower software licensing costs. Software licenses are based on the physical machine or CPU. The mainframe software-licensing model provides a wonderful economy of scale with the added ability to share the license across multiple users inside the virtual machine (VM) feature. This can save hundreds of thousands of dollars.

Excellent financial-reporting controls. Most mainframes were designed to bill individual usage as a profit center. You can practically charge the user for each electron in the processing of their job across each device used.

Very high throughput with stability that is measured in years.

Mature 40-year arsenal of system support programs. Mainframes are highly respected for their vast libraries of programs designed for advanced internal control.

IBM is the dominant vendor in the mainframe market, with 90 percent of the market share. Sales of mainframe systems are increasing in response to issues of control and economies of scale. For large operations, the mainframe is proving again to be an economical choice. Its high-volume parallel throughput cannot be matched by smaller systems.

Midrange Computers

Midrange computers, also referred to as *minicomputers*, are designed to be operated by individual departments or smaller organizations. The upper end includes the IBM iSeries and newer System z9 class, which are designed to be either a mainframe or midrange computer, depending on the configuration selected by the buyer. PC-style superservers with multiple processors from IBM, Dell, Hewlett-Packard, and Sun/Oracle represent the most common midrange systems.

Unix is also popular as a midrange operating system. Unix lacks several of the partition and security controls of a mainframe environment, but it does have many of the important job-processing features at a lower overall operating cost. Microsoft's operating system is used by organizations operating without system programmers. The latter customers let Microsoft control their system's design, security, and overall cost structure.

Microcomputers

Microcomputers are small systems that can be implemented as a PC, notebook, or personal digital assistant (PDA). Most microcomputers are designed to service the needs of an individual user. The operating system may have multiuser capability if running on sufficient hardware to support the requirement. Unfortunately, separation of duties on micro systems is lacking in scope and depth of control when compared to the control framework implemented on mainframe systems.

Microcomputers can run a variety of general-purpose operating systems, including Unix, Microsoft Windows, and the Apple Mac OS X. Microcomputers were invented to meet users' demands for more control over their individual processing needs. At the time, mainframes were dedicated to large-volume batch processing and ignored many of the user requests for processing.

The explosion of microcomputers has created a growing awareness of all the internal security controls that are missing. The biggest problem with microcomputers is the lack of mainframe-grade controls.

As an IS auditor, you may hear the term *MIPS*. MIPS is an acronym for *millions of instructions per second*. It is often used as a numerical claim of system performance with little regard for the real-world environment. MIPS is actually a highly subjective number used to hype a particular computer. The true measure of performance is system throughput, measured in the total volume of transactions processed from end to end.

Comparing Computer Capabilities

It is your job as an auditor to determine whether the IT environment is aligned to the business requirements. Figure 4.6 is a simple graphical representation of the differences in capabilities among mainframes, minicomputers, and microcomputers.

FIGURE 4.6   Comparing mainframes, minicomputers, and microcomputers

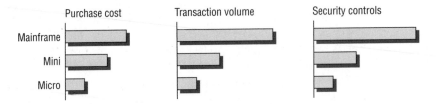

The dominant criteria used for system selection is the desired throughput. Another area of interest is the level of internal control required by the user.

Chapter 6, "System Implementation and Operations," covers capacity and workload management issues.

Figure 4.7 demonstrates the simple hierarchy of the classes of computer systems and their market share.

At the top of the pyramid is a mainframe, which has the highest level of capability. Mainframes are not as numerous because of initial purchase cost. In the middle is the mid-range computer for individual departments or a smaller organization. Midrange-processing computers are extremely popular for running databases such as Oracle Financials, SAP Manufacturing, or Oracle's PeopleSoft. At the bottom are the vast numbers of PC work-station users with a lower-end processing requirement.

FIGURE 4.7   Computer processing market share

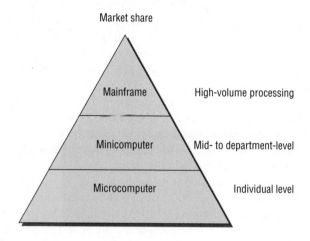

Ensuring System Control

With all this computer processing, it is necessary to ensure adequate management controls.

The first level of control in the computer is the privileged *supervisory user*. Every computer needs a special user account representing the highest level of authority, for the purpose of controlling change. This supervisory user is also known as the *superuser, root user,* or *administrator*. The names may be different, but the purpose is the same. This privileged user is responsible for configuration, maintenance, and all ongoing administrative tasks. The supervisory user is often exempt from the internal controls imposed on other users. This exemption gives the administrative user much more power and poses a unique challenge to system control.

The typical user spends their day trying to get the computer to solve problems. This common user has limited access and is subject to a variety of system controls. All office workers fall into this second category.

The technology world has created simple terminology to illustrate the differences between the supervisory user and everybody else. All computers operate in these four basic operating states:

Supervisory State   The system security front-end is not loaded. All processing requests are run at the highest level of authority without any security controls.

General User, or Problem, State   Security is active, and the computer is supposed to be solving problems for the user.

Wait State The computer is busy working to service other tasks and unable to respond to another user request.

Halt State All processing has stopped due to a command by the administrator, user or program processing exception. In secure trusted environments it may be better for the system to be halted rather than allow an invalid transaction to be processed.

The goal of a computer hacker is to gain problem state access (general user access) and convert it into supervisory state access (supervisor access). After gaining access to the system, the hacker will use a variety of attempts to break into supervisory control. The hacker may use invalid parameters to cause a supervisory-level program to fail. Some programs, such as password-change utilities or print queue management, may default to a supervisory-level command prompt upon failure. This allows the hacker to bypass the normal security front-end. An attacker or poorly written software program can trigger an overload of processing requests, which creates an extended series of wait states. When the computer is overloaded with requests, the condition is called a *denial of service*. The computer is too busy to help the user.

Software parameter control is important for multiple reasons. As stated, invalid software parameters may be used by a hacker. Another risk is valid software parameters that should be run only for a special administrative purpose. Access to the command line should be restricted. It is much safer to design menus or restricted user interfaces to ensure security.

Dealing with Data Storage

Adequate data storage is an important issue in a production environment. Controls need to be in place to ensure safe storage of data. The auditor is concerned with how many copies of the data exist and the controls that are in use. It is amazingly easy to lose control over electronic data. As an auditor, you would be concerned about both the integrity and security mechanisms in use by the client.

Tape management systems (TMSs) and disk management systems (DMSs) are used to help retain control over data files. These automated systems can provide label and tracking management. The security of the data is always an issue. Good media management practices include the ability to rapidly identify every version of data under the organization's control with the label, location, and status of each piece of media that data is stored on. This is the job function of a good tape or media librarian.

The following are some of the common types of data storage media:

Magnetic Hard Disk These rigid, metal disks mounted inside a sealed disk drive are high-speed devices that are designed for permanent installation. Capacity can go from gigabytes to terabytes. Hard disks are the most common method of online data storage. By using special software, you can cluster drives into high-availability storage arrays. An example is RAID. The definition is either *Redundant Array of Inexpensive Disks* or *Redundant Array of Independent Disks*. A vendor might use the latter to facilitate a higher sales price.

Let's talk about capacity planning for a RAID system. RAID level 0 (zero) offers no protection, but RAID level 1 provides full redundancy using total duplication. Full duplication is referred to as *disk mirroring.*

The initial issue for RAID-1 was cost and capacity sizing. If you had a total of 500 gigabytes of disk and installed RAID-1, the result was a maximum of 250 usable gigabytes. RAID-1 used twice the disk space for half the capacity. Next you had to subtract room for the 20 percent minimum free disk space needed to run the operating system, so now the RAID-1 usable capacity was only 200 gigabytes out of 500 gigabytes. Some customers liked the idea, but others were confused. This led to creating other methods for RAID in an attempt to accomplish redundancy equivalent to RAID-1 at a lower cost. Lower cost meant using fewer disk drives.

RAID levels 2, 3, and 4 are considered operational failures. The time to rebuild damaged data took too long after a single disk failure. RAID uses multiple disks connected into *disk strings.* The failure of a single disk is not supposed to be a problem. Two or more disk failures in the same disk string would kill the RAID system.

RAID level 5 is considered a successful alternative. It uses fewer disks than RAID-1 with more usable space. Most drive arrays sold in the market feature a RAID-5 design.

RAID level 6 was another operational failure. The next design was more successful. RAID level 7 uses independent disks with a very high transfer rate. In RAID-7, it's possible to combine multiple disks into a single spanning partition operating at much higher speeds.

Hybrid RAID systems have also entered the market. These crown jewels implement two different RAID methods into one system:

Hybrid RAID 0+1 systems implement two sets of RAID-0 disks into two mirrored strings running under RAID-1.

Hybrid RAID 5+1 systems put two RAID-5 disk strings into a fully duplicated pair. The pair is extra redundant because two RAID-5 disk arrays are duplicated as two RAID-1 sets for a double redundant approach.

Depending on your system hardware capabilities, you can have single mirror, double mirror, or triple mirror disks:

Single mirror is two disks (or sets of disks, also known as disk arrays) holding two mirror-image copies of the same data. The disks function independently if one fails. This is the typical RAID-1 implementation.

Double mirror has three disk sets holding three copies of the same data. Each disk set functions independently for extra redundancy.

Triple mirror uses four sets of disks offering quadruple copies of data. IBM has offered this feature for about two decades. The extra disk set can be unpaired to allow live backups during the peak usage time in your workday. System administrators refer to this type of backup process as *unmounting, breaking the mirror,* or *remounting* disk to tape. Triple mirror ensures that you never have fewer than three copies of live data online, and you have an incredibly low risk of disk failures. After backup is completed, the fourth set is remirrored to make the data current.

You are expected to understand a few basic differences between RAID levels. Table 4.2 covers these basic differences. You could copy and then cut out the table to be used as flash cards for memorization.

TABLE 4.2 Description of RAID operating levels

RAID Level	Operating Mode	Description
RAID-0	Striping across multiple disks	Not fault-tolerant. This design simply makes several small disks appear as one big disk.
RAID-1	Mirroring	Excellent way of creating two live copies of the data. Most expensive to implement; cuts disk space in half.
RAID-2	Hamming error-correcting code (ECC)	Interweaves data across multiple drives with error-correcting parity code. Too resource intensive.
RAID-5	Block-level distributed parity	This method is commonly used in disk arrays. The design uses less disk space than RAID-1 for the same amount of usable storage.
RAID-7	Optimized asynchronous	Uses independent, asynchronous transfer mode of very high transfer rates. Rather expensive.
RAID 0+1	High transfer rate	Combines two sets of RAID-0 disks with a RAID-1 mirroring design. The objective is to increase performance. Unfortunately, a two-drive failure can cause major data loss.

Figure 4.8 is a basic diagram of the different RAID systems. Notice that individual disks are attached to form *disk strings*.

Magnetic Soft Disk This includes floppy, Zip, Jaz and Iomega drives. They are designed with a soft read-write disk inside a hard shell. This highly portable media is available in capacities from 500 MB to more than 32 GB.

Magnetic Tape Available in reel or cartridge design, magnetic tape is the most common method of long-term data storage. Its original use was in 2,400 bpi (bits per inch) tape mounted on a reel. Capacities have grown dramatically. With higher capacity came the cartridge version. Cartridge tapes can have an internal design similar to a reel-to-reel cassette or a single-reel design like the old eight-track tape. Examples include Digital Linear Tape (DLT), 4–8 mm Digital Data Storage (DDS), nine-track reel, 3480 and newer 3590 cartridge, VHS video, DVD video, and others. High-quality tapes can be expensive when you buy the hundreds of blanks necessary to properly stock a backup library. Different backup vendors require very particular hardware devices with special software for backups. Frequently, tape media is portable only to identical tape drives with identical software from the same manufacturer. A malfunctioning tape drive can permanently destroy the tape and all the data it contains.

FIGURE 4.8   Graphical diagram of RAID disk systems

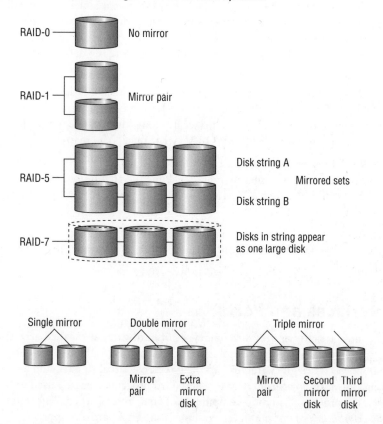

Tapes offer the luxury of allowing the administrator to back up 100 percent of the operating system, its invaluable configuration data, complete programs, and user data in one process. Individual files or the whole system can be fully restored from tape to match a specific point in time from years ago.

Read-Only Memory   Programmable read-only memory (ROM) is used to permanently record software programs on integrated circuits (chips). The advantages are lightning-fast program loading and solid-state nonvolatile storage without moving parts. Programming is accomplished by using specialized equipment to burn or fuse microscopic links inside the semiconductor chip. Once programmed, the software becomes permanent and cannot be changed or erased. This can be either a product limitation or security advantage depending on the intended purpose. To upgrade, you must physically replace the ROM chip. These chips are not portable between devices.

Flash Memory   A special type of electronically erasable programmable read-only memory (EEPROM) is used in computers for flash BIOS, video cameras, USB handheld removable memory sticks, and newer portable devices. These are designed to supplement or replace magnetic disks. Unfortunately, the flash devices are easily lost or stolen. The small size and high capacity can be a real security concern. Some of these devices are bootable and can bypass your security controls. They have limited portability but are improving daily. Flash memory is great for forensic discovery since the data is never really deleted; it's always recoverable unless the flash chip is physically destroyed.

Optical CD-ROM   Used to store read-only data or music, optical CD-ROMs have a typical capacity of 80 minutes of audio or 700 MB of data. This is an excellent method for archiving files or data backup when using a CD disk burner. It is a highly portable media. Blank disks are inexpensive and may be referred to as WORM (write once, read many).

Optical CD-RW   A rewriteable version of the old CD-ROM design, these disks can be erased and rewritten just like all other magnetic disk media. If you used the old WORM nomenclature, this would be called a WMRM disk (write many, read many). Today nobody calls them anything but CD-RW.

Optical DVD   This is a newer variation of the optical CD with higher capacity measured in gigabytes. The DVD is commonly used for video or data storage. This is a highly portable media.

Using Interfaces and Ports

Computers use interfaces to connect different types of hardware, also called accessories. According to the Institute of Electrical and Electronics Engineers (IEEE), an *interface* is a combination of physical design characteristics, voltages, electrical signals, and a protocol for communicating. The term *protocol* refers to a standard procedure or rule used to organize the communication process. Common computer slang may refer to the physical interface connector as a *computer port*. A common example is the USB hardware port.

    Hospitals refer to standard procedures for treating a patient as the *protocol*. This definition is similar in meaning to the procedures a computer uses to process communication requests.

Protecting Hardware Port Controls and Port Access

Every security professional is acutely aware of how physical access can bypass logical security controls. Physical input/output (I/O) ports provide an avenue for an individual to gain a higher degree of system access. The simultaneous connection of a modem and network card creates an unregulated pass-through opportunity that can circumvent perimeter defenses. As an auditor, you would want to see what controls have been implemented regarding physical access to input/output ports.

Microcomputers are particularly susceptible to port access via the keyboard, USB, RS-232, or network connection.

The ISACA COBIT contains a section covering physical security controls for IT servers, routers, and other high-value network devices.

Figure 4.9 shows the basic computer ports. Notice the PC ports for keyboard, video, printer, and serial attached devices. The mainframe has similar ports that are distributed between several large equipment chassis. No matter where they're located, all of the ports must be protected.

Computers communicate over these I/O ports to a variety of storage devices. Physical security controls are intended to protect the physical ports. Logical controls are used to protect data communications. A logical control is usually implemented as a software program control.

FIGURE 4.9   Hardware input and output ports

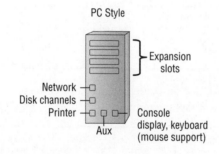

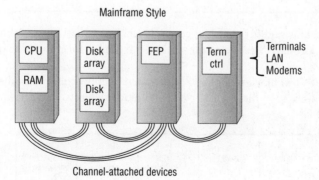

Using Software Ports

A second type of computer interface is the software operating system port. These are commonly referenced in discussions about data communication, programming, and networking. *Software ports* (or *sockets*) function similarly to hardware ports. The software port does not have any physical hardware. Instead, it exists as simply a reference location, or *buffer*, for software to send data during transmission. As data arrives at the designated software port, another program is waiting for it. The program detects new data and processes it by using whatever set of rules have been designated within its protocol. Different requests will be processed by using different rules as specified in their unique protocol.

Each software port has a designated function assigned to it by its programmer. To promote compatibility, IEEE designated the usage (protocol) for the first 1,023 software ports used in the Transmission Control Protocol/Internet Protocol (TCP/IP). Visualize these as post office mailboxes. Each mailbox represents a different destination. The protocol in business is for people to pay bills after an invoice arrives in their mailbox. The payment is sent back using a return address. A computer using the File Transfer Protocol (FTP) sends data on port 21, as per its protocol standard. Terminal login (telnet) uses port 23 for its communications. This port design provides an orderly method of flow control between programs.

Let's look at the way the Internal Revenue Service (IRS) communicates with taxpayers. Consider the following types of forms the IRS expects a taxpayer to use. If you have the wrong form, your request is denied or ignored.

W-4 Estimated tax withholding	1099-Misc Reporting non-employee income	W-2 Year-end taxable income	4868 Request for extension to file 1040 tax return

Now we can use that analogy to demonstrate how the same concept applies to computers sending electronic service requests across the network.

TCP-23 Terminal access	TCP-20 Transfer file	TCP-21 File transfer flow control	TCP-25 Electronic mail server	UDP-53 Domain name lookup service

Computer programs and firewalls expect each service request to occur on a specific port number, just as the IRS expects you to use a particular form to make different types of requests.

Network firewalls can block requests. UNIX system administrators can disable ports in the computer's configuration file /etc/services to block requests. In the following example, only FTP is allowed.

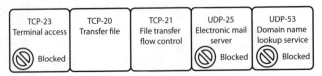

TCP-23 Terminal access 🚫 Blocked	TCP-20 Transfer file	TCP-21 File transfer flow control	UDP-25 Electronic mail server 🚫 Blocked	UDP-53 Domain name lookup service 🚫 Blocked

Software ports have to be protected too. The most common methods involve making detailed settings in the software configuration. Unfortunately, it's common for a software vendor to set the factory default, which uses insecure promiscuous settings. The vendor's intention is to eliminate calls for installation assistance to their help desk. This is why vendors often compromise your safety by requiring new software to be installed with the unrestricted access privileges of the root user or system administrator. It ensures that their software installs while leaving the remaining security consequences for someone else to deal with.

WARNING Beware of default settings. Richard Feynman is a bright physicist who worked at the secretive Los Alamos research labs during the development of the first atomic bomb. Using his brilliant powers of observation, Feynman deduced how to discover portions of safe combinations by detecting the tumbler's position after the safe's lock was opened by someone else. One day, a locksmith opened a safe within minutes after everyone thought the combination was lost. Feynman set out to discover the locksmith's secret. He spent several weeks building rapport with the locksmith. Then one day he asked the big question, "How did you open the safe?" The locksmith replied, "I called the manufacturer and asked for the default combination used when the safe was originally shipped." You can read more fascinating stories in the book *Surely You're Joking, Mr. Feynman!* (W.W. Norton & Company, 1997). Computer software vendors publish their default settings in technical books and training manuals and on the Internet for the whole world to see.

A second level of protection is provided by blocking access to software ports via a firewall. Chapter 7 discusses firewalls.

One of the best methods of illustrating software communication is the Open Systems Interconnect (OSI) model. The model is intended to demonstrate the activities that occur by using a method of hierarchal layers.

Introducing the Open Systems Interconnect Model

In the early 1980s, the International Organization for Standardization (ISO) was busy creating a new data communications model. Its intention was to build the next generation of communications protocols to replace both proprietary protocols and the de facto TCP/IP. In the end, the cheaper TCP/IP won the battle.

Many customers had no interest in paying for the cost of developing the Open Systems Interconnect (OSI) protocol. The OSI model is still used as a training tool. As an auditor, you need to recognize that the OSI model is designed to facilitate separation of duties (SoD). This model stratifies data communication into seven distinct layers. Each layer provides a unique function in support of the layer above. Each layer is controlled by different people operating in different roles. We use the OSI model to identify and correct SoD violations. The OSI model also helps identify weaknesses in policies, missing standards, and problems in procedures. OSI is one of 23 SoD models used in governance, especially for information security. But don't worry, because the CISA exam covers only a handful.

The OSI model is one of over two dozen separation of duties (SoD) models savvy auditors can use to identify control failures.

For example, the physical layer includes all the ISP subcontractors, telephone company and facility personnel. Therefore, formal policies (including contract terms) with matching procedures are necessary to enforce SoD on the physical layer. The same issue applies to the other OSI layers.

We are going to walk through the OSI model layer by layer and compare each function to the TCP/IP protocol model. The seven layers of the OSI model are as follows:

- Physical layer (1)

- Data-Link layer (2)

- Network layer (3)

- Transport layer (4)

- Session layer (5)

- Presentation layer (6)

- Application layer (7)

Let's start with a simple memory trick to remember each of the OSI layers in proper order from 1 to 7 (see Figure 4.10). My favorite mnemonic is *Please Do Not Throw Sausage Pizza Away (PDNTSPA)*.

We have been using this mnemonic for two decades. This mnemonic holds a unique association with a TCP/IP memory aid.

FIGURE 4.10   Mnemonic for seven layers of the OSI model

OSI memory aid

Away	= (Application)	Layer 7
Pizza	= (Presentation)	Layer 6
Sausage	= (Session)	Layer 5
Throw	= (Transport)	Layer 4
Not	= (Network)	Layer 3
Do	= (Data-Link)	Layer 2
Please	= (Physical)	Layer 1

Each of the first letters relates to the first letter of an OSI layer, working your way up from the bottom. It is in your best interest to learn how to draw the OSI model and these layers from memory. You will find it helpful on your CISA exam. You will also find it helpful during discussions, when you're trying to uncover the details about a particular product. It will impress clients.

The second, related mnemonic (see Figure 4.11) is *No Interest Having Anchovies (NIHA)*. Once again, each letter refers to a layer of the official Department of Defense (DoD) TCP/IP model, working up from the bottom.

FIGURE 4.11   Mnemonic for TCP/IP layers

OSI		TCP/IP memory aid	
Application	Layer 7		
Presentation	Layer 6		
Session	Layer 5	(Application)	Anchovies
Transport	Layer 4	(Transport)	Having
Network	Layer 3	(Internet)	Interest
Data-Link	Layer 2	(Data-Link)	
Physical	Layer 1	(Network)	No

Let's review the basic OSI process for handling data. The top layer is where your application is running. The lower layers process the request and prepare the data for transmission as it works its way down to the bottom. When it reaches the bottom of the OSI model, the data has been broken down into electrical signals.

These electrical signals will be received by the other computer. Upon receipt, the transmission headers are stripped off. The remaining data message is passed to the application software running on the other computer. Figure 4.12 shows how this looks.

FIGURE 4.12   OSI processing of headers and data

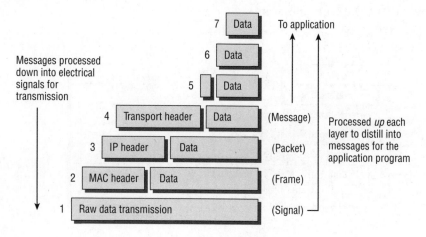

Now that you understand in general how data is transmitted when using the OSI and TCP/IP models, let's go inside the individual layers, one by one.

Layer 1: Physical Layer

The Physical layer defines physical requirements in the cables and voltages (see Figure 4.13). This layer indicates functional specifications for creating, maintaining, and deactivating an electrical link between systems. Wireless transmitters substitute radio signals for the physical cable connection. Similarly, lasers substitute flashes of light to simulate electrical signals over fiber-optic cable.

FIGURE 4.13   OSI Physical layer

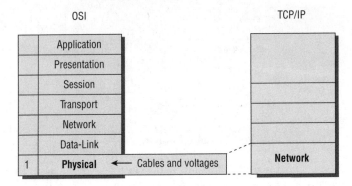

Layer 2: Data-Link Layer

The Data-Link layer (see Figure 4.14) focuses on establishing data communications via hardware device drivers and their transmit/receive function. Layer 2 provides flow control, error notification, and the order sequence during transmission.

FIGURE 4.14   OSI Data-Link layer

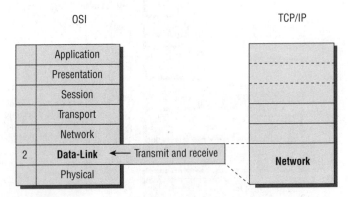

Communication in layer 2 is established between each network card's Media Access Control (MAC) address. A *MAC address* is a burned-in serial number that is unique to every network card ever manufactured. The address is unique because it uses the manufacturer's ID and the board serial number. Each computer uses the MAC address for "to" and "from" communications within the same broadcast domain (layer 2). You can view the MAC address on your computer by using the following software commands:

For Microsoft Windows, type **`ipconfig /all`** at the command line in the DOS command box.

In Unix, type **`ifconfig -al`** at the command-line prompt.

The computer will display something like what you see in Figure 4.15.

FIGURE 4.15 Viewing your MAC address

```
C:\> ipconfig /all

IP Configuration
      Host Name...............................: CertTest54
      Primary DNS Suffix.....................:
      IP Routing Enabled....................: No
      WINS Proxy Enabled...................: No
      Appletalk Enabled.......................: No

Ethernet adapter Local Area Connection:
      Description..............................: Intel(R) PRO/100
      Physical Address.......................: 00-80-3F-AA-D6-82 YOUR MAC ADDRESS
      DHCP enabled...........................: No
      IP Address...............................: 209.43.221.35
      Subnet Mask............................: 255.255.255.0
      Default Gateway.......................: 209.43.221.1
      DNS Servers............................: 206.199.8.4
                                                101.2.253.11
```

Every device on every network is supposed to have a unique MAC address. Imagine in the office how two people with the exact same name or exact same email address would create a communication conflict. The same is true of MAC addresses. In OSI layer 2, the computers communicate by sending messages to each other's MAC address.

The combined group of MAC addresses on the same network is referred to as a *broadcast domain. Domain* refers to scope boundaries of items located under the same controlling influence. Domains indicate relationships within the same general space. Computers in the same broadcast domain will hear (or see) all the traffic of the other computers.

Broadcast domains are no more than a noisy shouting match between computers on the same subnet. Every computer in that segment will hear every conversation from all the computers. For example, Microsoft NetBIOS is a layer 2 protocol. Dynamic Host Configuration Protocol (DHCP) is also a layer 2 protocol. Figure 4.16 helps illustrate how layer 2 is used.

We talk about DHCP later in this chapter.

FIGURE 4.16   Layer 2 communicates by MAC address.

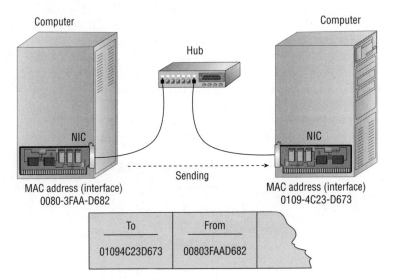

If too many computers were talking at the same time, we would have a congestion problem. This is referred to in Ethernet as a *collision.* Upon detecting a collision, the computers will stop to listen to the traffic, wait a few microseconds, and then attempt to transmit again. Too many collisions will render the data link unusable. Consider the analogy of two people talking over each other on a cell phone.

 Ethernet networks can rarely sustain traffic loads over 45 percent. The rule of thumb for Ethernet is that you budget for network upgrades at 35 percent sustained utilization, and get out the boss's credit card to place an order for overnight delivery at 50 percent sustained bandwidth utilization. Ethernet will not run dependably over 50 percent. The 100 percent mark is both theoretical and unattainable.

Layer 3: Network Layer

The Network layer defines networking (see Figure 4.17). Computers are stupid. The computer simply follows the directions of the person who programmed its settings or loaded the detailed list of instructions (a program). Your network administrator uses a numeric grouping of addresses to identify systems within the network.

Networks can be administratively divided into logical groups, or segments. (Dividing services is also called *provisioning* in the telephone industry.) The purpose is to create a logical hierarchy to facilitate easier management. We refer to this grouping as IP *subnetworks (subnets).*

FIGURE 4.17   OSI Networking layer

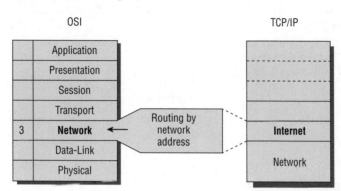

Each subnetwork has its own individual network address that is unique on the network. Separating similar traffic into subnets provides better performance and promotes logical separation of duties for better security.

The number one weakness of internal networks is a lack of separation. Simple traffic filters could be installed to prevent Finance department users from accessing computers in the research labs, for example. Would the Finance employees ever need to access the research computers, or better yet, would the Research employees ever need direct access to the company financial data? No, they would not in the normal course of business. Subnetworks support the concept of least privilege.

Every system requires its own unique IP address to prevent communication conflicts. IP addresses can be divided into smaller groups of addresses to create a smaller subnetwork. This is accomplished by using hexadecimal overlays to parse the address into smaller pieces—this is known as *netmasking*. Each time the IP address range is subdivided, the result must be of equal size. Subnetworks can turn one large network into two smaller networks that are equal in size—or into 4, 8, 16, 32, or even 64 tiny subnets.

Several of the usable IP numbers will be lost in the overhead of subdividing. This is because every subnet must have four specific addresses allocated to function:

The **numeric name** (for example, 192.0.0.0) is used in the router to identify the network path to each system on the network.

The **starting IP address** is the first available IP address you can assign to a device on the network.

The **ending IP address** is the last available IP address you can assign to a device on the network. You can use every address in the range between the starting IP address and the ending IP address. The range of usable IP addresses in a network or subnet is called the *IP address space*.

The **broadcast IP address** is the default method used to send traffic to all the devices on the same subnet. Think of it as the computers' version of a public address system with loudspeakers paging information over the intercom. This layer 3 *broadcast domain* is composed of IP addresses. (Layer 2 uses MAC addresses for its broadcast domain.)

Every time an IP address is subdivided, these two IP addresses are consumed in overhead to create the subnet (numeric network name, IP, and broadcast IP). The IP address reserved for the network name and the broadcast IP address cannot be assigned to any devices. Figure 4.18 helps illustrate how IP addresses are subdivided into smaller networks (aka subnets).

FIGURE 4.18   Dividing IP addresses into subnets

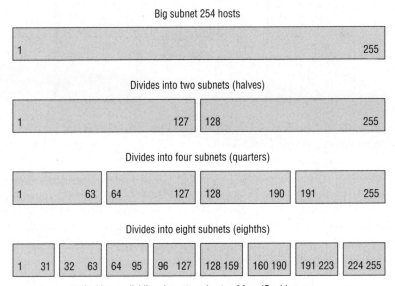

Big subnet 254 hosts

Divides into two subnets (halves)

Divides into four subnets (quarters)

Divides into eight subnets (eighths)

And keeps dividing down to subnets of four IP addresses

Your computer acquires an IP address from either a static configuration setting or a dynamic configuration by using DHCP based on the older Boot Protocol (BOOTP). The computer ties the IP address to its layer 2 MAC address. We refer to this as *binding* an IP address. Routing decisions are based on the IP address.

The computers and routers implement the Address Resolution Protocol (ARP) to match the IP address with the correct MAC address. Each IP address and corresponding MAC address is stored on computers and routers in tables used during lookup, just like a telephone book. Figure 4.19 illustrates how ARP works.

FIGURE 4.19   Using IP address resolution to find a MAC address (ARP)

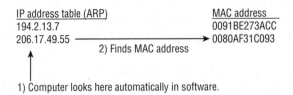

IP address table (ARP)
194.2.13.7
206.17.49.55

MAC address
0091BE273ACC
0080AF31C093

2) Finds MAC address

1) Computer looks here automatically in software.

The system uses Reverse ARP (RARP) with a MAC address to find the corresponding IP address. Some systems can determine their own IP address by sending their own MAC address to a RARP server, as in the case of DHCP. For example, there are two kinds of telephone books: one is sorted by name order (like ARP), and the other is reverse sorted by street address (RARP). Figure 4.20 shows RARP using the MAC address to find the corresponding IP address. Later in this chapter, we discuss an additional method called Domain Name System (DNS) to assign human-friendly alphabetic names to IP addresses.

FIGURE 4.20   Using the Reverse Address Resolution Protocol (RARP) to find the IP address

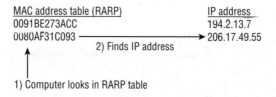

As you may you recall, the problem in layer 2 is that all the systems are transmitting so much that noise is created across the subnet. The issue is similar to noise in a school cafeteria. Some conversations are broadcast with everyone listening, while a few are discreet between a couple of users. With a layer 3 network address, it is possible to reduce traffic noise by unicast transmission to an individual address. *Unicasting* makes a point-to-point communication to only one device (a private call). So what if you need to send a message to more than one address, but not everyone? You could use *multicasting* to deliver the same data transmission to a group of addresses very efficiently. A multicast is similar to a conference call and is the basis of virtual networking and webcasts.

 Real World Scenario

Technical Trivia

Internet Protocol (IP) uses a four-position numerical address. This IP address structure is similar to your postal mail routing address in reverse. If you used your mailing address in IP format, the result would look like State.City.Street.House number. IP version 4 uses addresses that are 8 bytes, or 32 bits, long. The new IP version 6 is designed for 16-byte, or 128-bit, addresses to give the expanding world more addresses. Computers use a method of grouping IP v4 addresses, starting with 000.000.000.000 through 255.255.255.254.

Finding a Path across the Network

Network routing is the process of directing traffic to the intended destination. This can be accomplished by using static settings or by allowing the computer to follow instructions provided by a *routing protocol*. Routing protocols have been used for centuries to help ships navigate the globe, trains to switch tracks while heading to their destinations, and airplanes to safely navigate the clouds.

Static routing uses specific to-from mappings of IP addresses created by the network administrator. This is similar to following highway road signs. When driving to New York from Texas, for example, the driver gets on Interstate 20 and just follows the signs for turns and exits until reaching New York. The router's static mapping is quite similar. To-from settings are manually typed into the router and stored in the routing table of each router. The user's computer is set to use the router as their *default gateway* for every IP address located outside their subnet. Their default gateway is like an electronic on-ramp to the information superhighway. Each router on your journey points you to the next router (like a turn or exit ramp sign) until you reach your destination. Return traffic is routed back the same way. So both ends need to have their own set of directions to form a complete path for communications. These route settings will not change unless the network administrator manually changes them. Static routes are good for security and are used when the network traffic is both predictable and relatively simple. Figure 4.21 illustrates the analogy of the network routing protocol compared to a driver following highway road signs.

FIGURE 4.21 Static routing analogy to highway signs

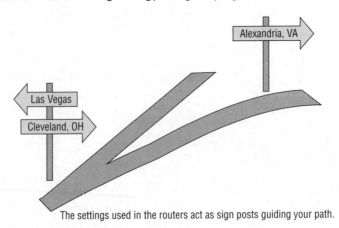

The settings used in the routers act as sign posts guiding your path.

Larger or more-complex networks may have multiple paths to the same destination. The network might even have redundant connections for better fault tolerance. This could make static routing rather difficult to maintain. The routers get confused, just like people, if duplicate routes exist. Which route should we take? Routing tables contain a set of metrics such as cost, speed, and number of links to cross. The administrator can set these manually to help the computer use the best available route. An automatic *split-horizon* feature in the routing protocol blocks any loops that may occur by forcing travel in only one direction (path).

Dynamic routing uses a protocol algorithm to automatically adjust the path to the intended destination. This method uses special router information protocols to signal available paths (routes), dead routes (unroutable), and other changes. The routers will monitor routing updates and signal other routers to reconfigure their routing tables as changes occur. Dynamic routing is easy to enable. It removes the complexities of building an advanced configuration. To some individuals, this seems like the best answer; however, dynamic routing can be both beneficial and dangerous. Dynamic routing changes can be initiated by the following:

- Router equipment failure
- Addition of new networked devices
- Incorrect configuration of a network-attached device, including a common workstation

Figure 4.22 shows how a false network route can be accidentally created through a user's PC. The user's computer software caused the problem by transmitting a route that should not exist.

FIGURE 4.22   False network route via user PC

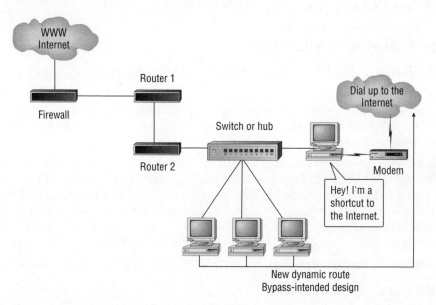

By default, all network devices will listen to route updates. This can create a nightmare if left to default settings. Poor administration of computers and routers can cause traffic to be misdirected into a dead-end route or bandwidth bottleneck. Common examples of the dynamic routing protocols include the following:

- Routing Information Protocol (RIP), which is a primitive method with few control safeguards. RIP is enabled on computers by default. RIP updates generated from a user's computer can inadvertently change the route path for everyone on the network (see Figure 4.22).
- Open Shortest Path First (OSPF), which uses manually configured reference tables. OSPF is popular in larger networks.

- Interior Gateway Protocol (IGP), which routes traffic within the same organization.
- Border Gateway Protocol (BGP), which communicates between separate networks.

Proper design of the network usually includes implementing both static and dynamic routing. Static routes can provide a designated *router of last resort* if prior dynamic routes fail. Using a router of last resort is similar to saying, "Honey, I think we are lost; would you please pull over and ask this nice router for directions?"

For higher security, the routers should be configured to accept updates from only a trusted router—one the network administrator knows and indicates we can trust. The trusted router is authenticated by its MAC address, digital certificate, or access control list (ACL). Trust is established by forcing in-depth testing using detailed challenges. Each test result provides a determination of the degree of trust. Trust is always temporary. Trust does not exist by a leap of faith, nor by legal contracts. Trust is measured per transaction. Constant unrelenting challenge-response continues the trust until a single failure kills the trust. This helps prevent route corruption. Chapter 7 covers more details of security.

Layer 4: Transport Layer

The Transport layer specifies the transport delivery method (see Figure 4.23). There are two basic methods:

Confirmed delivery uses a TCP connection to the destination. This is similar to requesting a return receipt and sending certified mail from the post office. TCP is slower and provides error correction.

Unconfirmed delivery operates on a User Datagram Protocol (UDP) connectionless datagram, which is typically broadcast across the network like a shout in a dark room. UDP is faster with less overhead. Even if transmissions are unicast between two stations, the higher-level software application would have to confirm delivery, because UDP does not offer delivery confirmation. There is no guarantee of the data being received on the other end. It is the responsibility of the recipient program to detect errors.

Next comes the Session layer, where we get a login screen or other type of access.

FIGURE 4.23   OSI Transport layer

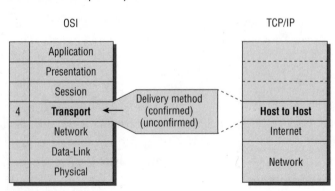

Layer 5: Session Layer

The Session layer governs session control between applications (see Figure 4.24). This is where you initiate communications to a system and establish, maintain, and terminate a communication session. Examples include Network File System (NFS), SQL*Net for remote database sessions, and Remote Procedure Call (RPC).

FIGURE 4.24 OSI Session layer

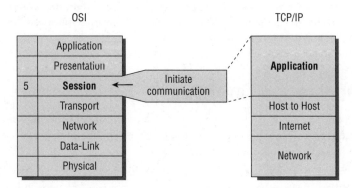

Layer 5 functions of session and error control are handled in TCP/IP by the user's application software. Under TCP/IP, it is the responsibility of the user's application to manage the functions of session, presentation, and application.

Layer 6: Presentation Layer

The Presentation layer defines the presentation format (see Figure 4.25). This is where you specify the format and data structure to be used for programs. Layer 6 will specify the differences between a PDA, VT100 terminal, or workstation with What-You-See-Is-What-You-Get (WYSIWYG) display capabilities.

FIGURE 4.25 OSI Presentation layer

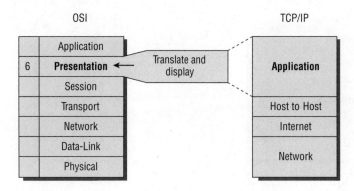

Layer 6 converts data received from the Session layer into an electronic format that can be handled by the upper-level Application layer (layer 7). It also works in the opposite direction, receiving application data from layer 7 and reformatting it for the underlying layer 5. For TCP/IP, the presentation function is combined into the TCP/IP Application layer.

 Layer 6 provides screen formatting. The purpose of encryption is to prevent layer 6 from displaying your secrets. The encryption-decryption process occurs in OSI layer 7 through a custom software application or inside a layer 7 gateway process.

Layer 7: Application Layer

The Application layer is where the problem-solving calculations of the computer software program run (see Figure 4.26). Various types of computer application software execute in the Application layer, including the following:

- Systems Network Architecture (SNA) gateways, which convert the ASCII 7-bit data structure into an IBM Extended Binary Coded Decimal Interchange Code (EBCDIC) 8-bit data structure for the mainframe.

- Domain Name System (DNS), which is the program that associates a domain name to the matching IP address (for layer 3).

- File, print, and web servers.

- Databases and office automation software (such as OpenOffice.org and Microsoft Office).

- User's data encryption, such as Pretty Good Privacy (PGP) using variables (keys) to encrypt and decrypt the output. We explore encryption methods in Chapter 7.

FIGURE 4.26   OSI Application layer

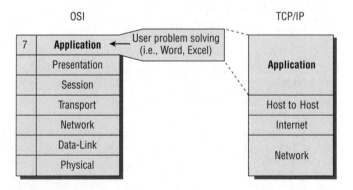

It's best to remember that layer 7 is the problem solver of work automation. User programs and workflow automation occur here. To help alleviate confusion, the seven layers are commonly referred to as the full *protocol stack*. A basic off-the-shelf router may have only parts of the OSI protocol stack to run just layers 1–3, which indicates that a layer 7 process such as a IBM System Network Architecture (SNA) gateway is beyond the device's capability. Common network switches have only layer 1 and layer 2 stacks, while combination switch-routers have layers 1, 2, and 3 implemented. All-in-one network appliances may have the full protocol stack implementing all seven layers with different degrees of capability. Servers and workstations have all seven layers in use.

It is important to remember that a gateway will run at the Application layer, which is the highest level of the OSI model.

Understanding How Computers Communicate

Now that we've covered all seven layers of the OSI model, let's take a finished look at the communication between two computers across the network by using the OSI model. We will assume that a router is being used in the communication path.

First, the user makes a request in their application software on layer 7. That request is passed down through each layer on its way to the bottom. Along the way, each layer performs its function to ultimately transform the request into a series of electrical signals or light flashes for transmission on layer 1 (the Physical layer of cable and voltages).

Next, the network hub (or network switch) on layer 1 passes the signal up to the layer 3 network router. The packet is routed through one or more routers directing the user's request to the intended destination computer. It helps to remember that network routing is similar to routing airline flights through particular cities, or railroad trains switching tracks as they travel across the country.

Finally, the request is received as a series of electrical signals (or light flashes) on layer 1 of the other computer. The request is passed up through each layer of the OSI model and processed accordingly. The request is then received in its Application layer, where it is executed. The response is packaged and sent back through the OSI model in reverse, until it reaches the application program on the other computer.

An example of how this looks is displayed in Figure 4.27.

Congratulations, you have now learned the SoD secrets of the OSI model. You'll need to be sure to review its relationship with the TCP/IP model. The OSI model will be used as a discussion tool, while the TCP/IP model is the de facto standard of the real world.

Now we will move into discussing the physical side of networking. We will begin with a simple illustration of physical networks.

FIGURE 4.27   OSI communication between systems

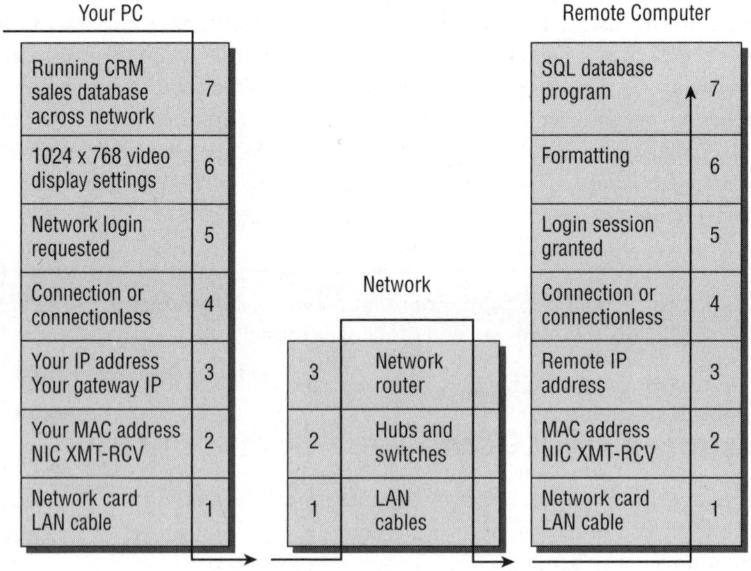

Your PC			Network			Remote Computer	
Running CRM sales database across network	7					SQL database program	7
1024 x 768 video display settings	6					Formatting	6
Network login requested	5					Login session granted	5
Connection or connectionless	4					Connection or connectionless	4
Your IP address Your gateway IP	3		3	Network router		Remote IP address	3
Your MAC address NIC XMT-RCV	2		2	Hubs and switches		MAC address NIC XMT-RCV	2
Network card LAN cable	1		1	LAN cables		Network card LAN cable	1

Understanding Physical Network Design

The first computer networks were created by connecting serial ports between two or more computers. This primitive design used modem software to handle file transfer between systems.

Networks evolved with the invention of token passing and broadcast transmissions. The invention of the hub, or shared media access unit, created the opportunity to connect multiple computers together on the same segment (again, referred to as a subnet). The concept of a network *bridge* was created to connect two subnets into the same, single subnet. A layer 2 bridge allows all traffic to pass from one side to the next. The bridge could be configured to allow broadcast across it or configured to filter broadcasts and reduce noise—it depended on the bridge manufacturer's design.

Later, it became apparent that it would be necessary to connect two separate networks together without merging them into a single subnet as a bridge would. Many people complained that too many systems were creating too much traffic when all the computers were located within one giant subnet.

Thus came the development of the *router*. Early routers were simply computers with two interface cards. Interface 1 serviced a connection to LAN 1, and interface 2 provided a connection to LAN 2. A software-routing program was then loaded to be run on the computer's CPU.

The routing program basically determines whether individual traffic requests need to cross to the other side. If so, the router passes the request through the other LAN interface to reach its destination. If the destination is within the same subnet (LAN 1 to LAN 1), the router ignores the traffic. This protects the other subnet from unnecessary data transmission noise (LAN 2). That is the basic function of a router. Routers forward data traffic when necessary and insulate users on other subnets.

Figure 4.28 shows what some of the first networks looked like.

FIGURE 4.28   First computer networks

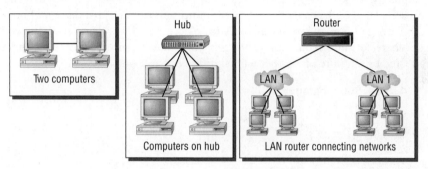

In modern networks, the routing function can be loaded onto a router card installed in the network switch chassis. Traditional routers are usually a dedicated device in their own chassis.

Understanding Network Topologies

As networks grew, creating a standardized topology for all the connections became necessary. Early networks were very proprietary. It was difficult to mix equipment from different vendors. Although this was good for the manufacturer, it drove computer users nuts. Over the years, three basic network cable topologies have become widely accepted: bus, star, and ring. Let's look at the design of these three topologies.

Identifying Bus Topologies

One of the first topologies to become accepted was the *bus topology* (see Figure 4.29). This presented a relatively inexpensive method for connecting multiple computers.

FIGURE 4.29   Bus topology

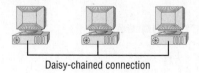

In a bus topology, each computer is daisy-chained to the next computer. A single coaxial cable passes through the connector on the back of each computer on the network. This cable runs through the office like a single rope, which ties all the systems together.

The design has one major drawback: A break in the bus cable would interrupt transmission for all the computers attached to that cable. Cabling a bus topology can also be cumbersome.

Identifying Star Topologies

The star topology is the most popular topology in use today (see Figure 4.30). In a *star topology*, each computer has a dedicated cable connection running to a network hub (or switch). This design offers the most flexibility for placement of workstations. It also offers the highest degree of cable redundancy. The cable redundancy ensures that other computers are not affected by a failure of another workstation's connection.

FIGURE 4.30   Star topology

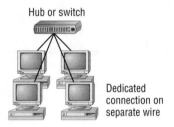

This is the design of most data networks. It is also used by the PBX telephone switch to connect individual telephone stations. The primary drawback to the star topology is the cost of all the additional cable required to make connections for each station.

Figure 4.31 demonstrates the practical application of the star topology. Notice that each workstation has a connection to a nearby wiring closet. This design ensures that you do not exceed the maximum recommended cable length. The acceptable length of cable varies depending on the cabling type used. Normally it is 100 meters on unshielded twisted-pair (UTP). The star topology helps reduce the cabling cost by shortening the cable distance to reach each user. The hubs and switches are located in the wiring closet to connect users to the network.

Every cable is terminated at the wall plate near the user and at a patch panel in the wire closet. A patch cord connects the building cable from the patch panel to the ports of the hub/switch. A backbone connection is then run from the data center to the wiring closet to establish a complete path for network communication. Figure 4.31 shows the real-world implementation of a star topology, complete with wiring closet and backbone to the data center.

Identifying Ring Topologies

The most famous token-passing LAN protocol is IBM's ring topology, known as Token Ring (see Figure 4.32). Each LAN computer is connected to a media access unit (MAU). Each MAU is connected to both an upstream MAU and downstream MAU to form a backbone loop. Network traffic can be transmitted in either direction. This bidirectional loop is referred to as the *ring*.

A network ring topology has the advantage of built-in redundancy. If the ring breaks, all traffic will travel through the ring in the opposite direction, thereby avoiding the break point. The individual workstations are then connected into the ring by using a star topology.

The telecommunications companies use the ring technology in their fiber-optic networks. This design allows the redundant path necessary to create a fault-tolerant network.

FIGURE 4.31   Practical application of the star topology

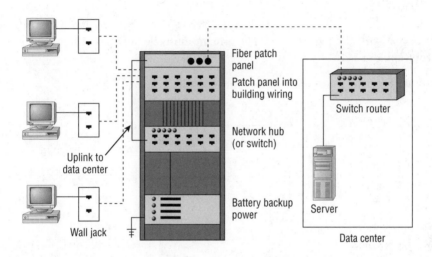

FIGURE 4.32   Ring topology

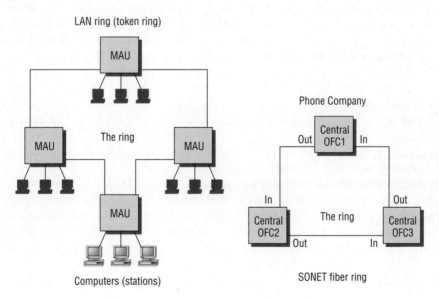

Identifying Meshed Networks

The important network links can have alternate path connections to increase redundancy. The meshing of star networks is a common method of providing redundancy similar to the approach used by a ring topology. The principal difference is that a meshed network is a series of point-to-point connections between critical backbone connections. The router determines which link to use based on predefined routing criteria. A network administrator defines the best link and the alternate path link to use if the best link is down.

There are essentially two types of meshed networks:

Full Mesh   A fully meshed network has alternate connections for every major backbone point on the network (see Figure 4.33). The primary obstacle to this design is the cost of implementation.

FIGURE 4.33   Full mesh network (N -1 design)

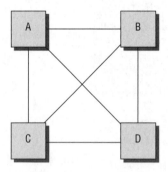

Partial Mesh   When you cannot afford a full mesh network, you may decide to implement a partial mesh for the most critical links (see Figure 4.34). Occasionally, the critical link may not be determined by the overall value of traffic. The additional link may be determined by the ability of the sponsor to pay the additional cost. A partial mesh is better than no redundancy at all.

 Real World Scenario

N -1 = Full Mesh Networks

Network designers refer to full mesh networks as the *N -1* design. This design gives the highest possible redundancy. *N* stands for the number of points to be connected, and the *-1* refers to a hub and spoke design with the total number of additional connections necessary to achieve a fully redundant mesh. The number of full mesh network connections required = N x (N – 1) / 2. As you can see, the number of connections grows very rapidly—with 45 links required for 10 sites, and 190 links for only 20 sites. Full mesh networks are rare.

FIGURE 4.34   Partial mesh network

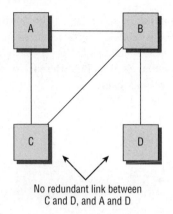

No redundant link between
C and D, and A and D

Differentiating Network Cable Types

IS auditors are fortunate to have the guidance of industry cable standards provided by the IEEE and the Electronic Industries Alliance/Telecommunications Industry Association building wiring committee (also known as EIA/TIA). Several methods have been developed to use a variety of cables to create a network. Each type of cable has its own unique characteristics of construction or transmission capability. Some cables are better suited for voice, for example. Others are designed for the high demands of data.

You are not expected to design the cabling system used in a network. That is the job of a Registered Communications Distribution Designer (RCDD), a certified expert in the layout of cable systems. Industry reports verify that 97 percent of network problems are related to the cabling design, cable quality, cable implementation, or connector failure. Design services of an RCDD are usually affordable when justified against cumulative cost of downtime. IEEE and EIA/TIA standards specify more than 100 details for operating stability, safety, and building-code compliance. Details of proper design will far exceed the capability of a Microsoft Certified Systems Engineer (MCSE) or Unix administrator for all but the smallest of networks.

Cable installations are commonly referred to as *cable plants*. The cabling system for data and voice can be complex, depending on the requirement. A CISA is required to have a basic understanding of the three most common cables used to build a network. You should understand the description and limitations of each type.

Coaxial Cable

Early networks used a form of *coaxial* (or *coax*) cable with mesh shielding to prevent electrical interference. The wire is similar to antenna cable or the cable for your television set. Coax has been replaced by unshielded twisted-pair (UTP) for most indoor environments. You can still use coaxial cable in areas prone to electrical interference or for outdoor connections. Figure 4.35 shows an illustration of coax cable.

FIGURE 4.35   Coaxial cable

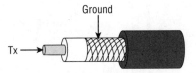

Coaxial cable is an older and slower design than UTP. It contains two electrical conductors (copper center, metal outer shielding covered with PVC plastic sheathing). It is commonly used for Ethernet networks with a bus topology. It's often used in distances up to 185 meters, but can be extended by using a repeater.

Unshielded Twisted-Pair (UTP) Cable

Unshielded twisted-pair (UTP) cable is the most popular for connecting computers to a network. *Unshielded* means that the wire does not have any protection from electrical interference. The twisting creates an electrical cancellation to prevent the wire from broadcasting like an antenna. Untwisted wire will create magnetic fields of interference that can swing a compass needle, whereas twisted wire will be invisible to the same compass.

UTP is an inexpensive, twisted, four-pair wire used for 10/100 Mb Ethernet. Pairs are twisted to reduce electromagnetic interference (EMI). Each wire is run directly to a hub/switch in the wiring closet. Figure 4.36 illustrates the twisted wire-pair construction.

FIGURE 4.36   Twisted-pair wiring

Notice how each connector has two transmitting wires (send) and two receiving wires, which give UTP the ability to carry more data than coaxial cable. There are four common categories of UTP:

- CAT-3 (Category 3) for voice only
- CAT-5 (Category 5) for voice and data

- CAT-5e (enhanced) for 1 GB, 100 Mhz data
- Higher-rated CAT-6 and CAT-7, available for transmission up to 1,000 Mhz

Fire codes in commercial buildings specify that one type of jacket be used for twisted-pair cabling. The cheaper twisted-pair cabling uses PVC as the covering jacket. Unfortunately, PVC burns like a fuse when lit and produces toxic fumes. Fire codes call for plenum-grade Teflon jacketing to be used in plenum spaces to prevent the spread of fire.

UTP is used in distances of less than 200 feet and is commonly used in star topologies. Special types of UTP are used for distances of up to 100 meters. Coaxial is used for longer runs or where some electrical interference may be an issue.

Fiber-Optic Cable

A *fiber-optic* cable is constructed of tiny strands of glass fiber. Lasers or light-emitting diodes (LEDs) are used to flash signals through the glass strands. Fiber-optic cable is commonly used for backbone connections and long-haul installations. You can send multiple streams of data concurrently through the same strand of glass by using different-color wavelengths. The process is called *dense wave multiplexing*. The drawbacks are price and the fragile glass strands, which break easily when stressed.

Fiber-optic cable has an extremely wide bandwidth. It can support concurrent transmission of voice, video, and data traffic by using multiple lasers to transmit light. Each laser color is a separate channel, allowing 12, 24, and 64 lasers to share one fiber without degradation. Higher-end equipment can have even more lasers sharing the same stand of glass fiber. Speed, based on equipment used, is between 1 gigabit (Gb) and 100 terabits (Tb). Fiber-optic cable is also difficult to tap. Figure 4.37 shows the basic concept of a fiber optic cable multiplexing light into separate streams of traffic.

FIGURE 4.37   Fiber-optic cable

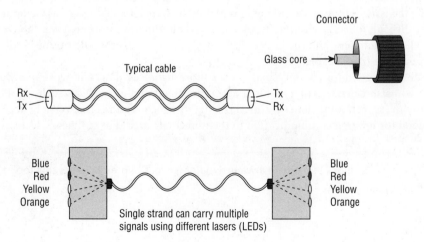

It is important to understand when you would use copper twisted-pair and when you would use fiber-optic cable.

Connecting Network Devices

Now that you understand the OSI model and cabling, it is time to discuss the various devices necessary to build a network. Every CISA is expected to understand the purpose of common networking equipment.

Let's begin from the bottom up. The first thing you need is customer requirements. What does the customer intend to connect to the network? The next question is, what is their intended usage while on the network? We are constantly amazed at how many times the client expects a network to magically be all things to all people. Proper identification of requirements will go a long way toward aligning the network to the organizational objectives.

We can start with the number of user connections. Each user will need to plug into a network hub or switch. A *network hub* is an electrical connection box that amplifies and retimes the electrical signals for transmission. A hub is similar to an electrical junction box. All traffic is shared across each port.

A *network switch* performs the functions of a hub and contains an intelligent processor capable of running logic programs. Switches separate traffic between ports to create the appearance of a private communications line. This is the same design that is in PBX telephone switches and in LAN switches.

The network architect may encounter a problem with the distance between network devices. The solution may be to use a special cable type for that run, or to add another device to compensate for the distance. A *network repeater* can amplify the tiny electrical signals to drive longer distances. Repeaters receive a signal and then repeat the transmission down the next link. We could also use fiber-optic cable from that particular leg of the run. Fiber-optic cables are popular for use in long runs across the building or across the globe.

Maybe the issue is that wires are not acceptable for your intended usage. For example, it would be difficult to use a wire-line connection for counting inventory in a warehouse. The users would be unhappy, and the heavy steel wheels of the forklift would not be kind as they ran over the fragile cable.

Wi-Fi radio is good for communication over short distances. This will work in a warehouse. It will also work within a building for connecting handheld devices such as a PDA. Another wireless method includes infrared (IR) light, which requires line-of-sight access. This is good for limiting communication to the immediate area, but still needs security.

Wireless security is always a major issue. Chapter 7 covers this topic.

There may be a need to divide a network into small sections because of the sheer number of systems. Maybe you want to divide the network to put each group into their own subnet. Subnetting could protect the Accounting department from the Research and Development traffic, for example. This is performed by segmenting the big network into smaller groups of subnetworks (subnets).

You can subnet by using a *router* to provide access across the subnets while eliminating unnecessary traffic on each subnet. As you will recall, a router will insulate subnets from traffic conversations that do not involve their systems. Just connect the router to the switch/hub for each subnet and set up the router configuration.

You can also implement virtual subnets known as *virtual LANs (VLANs)* to divide the users. A VLAN is like an automatic conference calling list configured on the network switch (layer 2). A VLAN will simulate one subnet for all the target computers (that's where the term *virtual* comes into the name). The VLAN methods vary depending on the comprehension of the installer and the capability of the manufacturer. The basic methods of creating a VLAN are to use specific ports, to associate MAC addresses into a VLAN, or to create policy rules if the switch hardware has that capability. Let's discuss each of these methods here:

Port-Based VLAN (Layer 1)   The administrator manually configures a specific port into a specific VLAN. This works well for uplinks, systems that don't move, and small networks.

MAC-Based VLAN (Layer 2)   This ties the MAC address into a VLAN by reading the network traffic and then automatically reconfiguring the network port on your switch.

Policy- or Rule-Based VLAN (Layer 2 Supporting Layer 3 Routing)   A high-quality network switch reads the IP header in your traffic and executes an administrator's rule to join a VLAN based on protocol or by IP address. When correctly implemented, the process is automatic and does not require any software on the workstation. Switch ports will reconfigure automatically when the system is moved.

No matter what, every VLAN needs a router to access the other subnets. This router may be a physically separate device or a router CPU inside the same chassis. Now add the network servers and you will have a working computer network. Just be sure to include enough network-attached printers to make everyone happy.

Table 4.3 provides a summary of the various local area network devices that you will encounter.

TABLE 4.3   Local area network equipment

LAN Equipment	Purpose
Router (layer 3)	Connects to separate subnetworks or adapts a connection to different transmission media. Routers decide whether the traffic needs to pass along another route or should just stay in the original subnetwork. This relieves traffic congestion across the network. Examples include LAN 1–to–LAN 2 and LAN-to-WAN circuits. Routers can also convert between Ethernet, Token Ring, and telephone company communication protocols.

TABLE 4.3   Local area network equipment *(continued)*

LAN Equipment	Purpose
Switch (layer 2)	Provides an intelligent process of creating discreet communication on each port. Same function as the PBX telephone switch, which creates the illusion of private communication lines for each user. Network VLANs are similar to administrator-designated group conference calling. Requires a router (layer 3 router function) to communicate with a different subnetwork or between VLANs.
Bridge (layer 2)	Connects two separate networks by using the same network addressing in one subnet. Intelligent bridge is the same as layer 2 switch.
Hub (layer 1)	Connects individual cables to share data between ports. Amplifies and retimes the tiny electrical signals. Similar to an electrical junction box for networking cables.
Repeater (layer 1)	Designed to boost the signal strength across a cable to overcome distance limitations.
Wi-Fi transmitter (layer 1)	Short-range wireless transmitter/receiver to connect laptops and PDA devices to the LAN. (May be integrated into an all-in-one router offering both layer 1 and layer 3 functions.)

 To connect different networks, you need a router.

Routers provide intelligent decisions about routing traffic down particular links. The router is like a cop directing traffic in the direction it needs to travel. Routers come in a wide variety of shapes, sizes, and capabilities. An Internet router needs at least one Internet port and one LAN port. The type of router port depends on the type of circuit you need to connect.

Using Network Services

Several pages ago, we discussed the OSI model with examples of network services running on layer 7. In the example, we mentioned network servers with a few of the services they provide. Let's discuss two common network support services that relate to everyone using a network: DNS and DHCP.

You will also need a firewall to protect your network. We discuss firewalls in depth in Chapter 7.

Domain Name System

Computers like to use binary numbers, network administrators like to use IP addresses, and all of us who run computers like to refer to machines by name. Names are so much easier to remember. Even names can get confusing, so the Internet is designed to allow fully qualified domain names. A *fully qualified domain name (FQDN)* is what you see on the left side in the URL portion of the browser as you surf the Internet. Have you ever wondered how the web browser finds the website you typed? The answer is: by using the Domain Name System (DNS).

Routers have tables of IP addresses, along with the routes to take to reach those addresses. DNS servers are a layer 7 software application that contains a list of alias names and their associated IP addresses. DNS is how you end up reaching a website without knowing its IP address.

DNS offers additional flexibility. You can change the IP address without having to tell everyone about the address change. Just keep the DNS server updated with your new IP address. If DNS fails, you will not be able to access the target or you will resort to typing the IP address (if known).

Figure 4.38 shows the process of DNS looking at the company name and responding to your request.

FIGURE 4.38   DNS name service (address lookup)

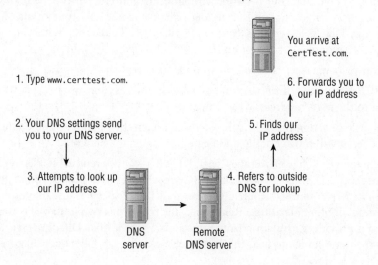

A major problem with traditional DNS is the lack of security. Network productivity is essentially shut down if the DNS server is lost or attacked. Attackers can poison DNS by using fake servers or injecting fake DNS updates. This is the same problem discussed with layer 3 routing-table updates. The preferred method is to implement Secure DNS (S-DNS) by using ACLs and digital certificates. Name-lookup services and DNS updates would be accepted only from DNS servers able to continually verify their identity. Trust is destroyed upon the first failure in an ongoing challenge-response process.

Dynamic Host Configuration Protocol

For years, the job of a network administrator entailed the tedious task of configuring IP addresses on each computer. Manual settings are still the best choice for network servers; however, the user workstation is another matter.

Dynamic Host Configuration Protocol (DHCP) can automatically configure the IP address, subnet mask, and DNS settings on a computer. DHCP is an improved version of the original BOOTP using RARP. Both DHCP and BOOTP have the same operational design.

The theory of operation is simple. Figure 4.39 shows how DHCP works. Here are the steps:

1. A computer on your network is set up as the DHCP server. For remote dial-up, the better access servers will have this ability built in to support the modems. The DHCP server will be configured by your network administrator with a pool of IP addresses eligible for dynamic allocation.

2. The DHCP server listens on the network for an IP packet containing a type 67 code in the header. (Don't worry, that level of detail is not on your exam.)

3. A computer is booted on your network without an IP address. During the boot process, the computer recognizes that an IP is needed. The computer sends out a type 67 request asking for any DHCP server to assign it an IP address. The request contains the MAC address of the computer asking for an IP.

4. The requesting computer waits several seconds for a response.

5. Your DHCP server recognizes the type 67 request and responds with a type 68 reply addressed to the MAC address of the sender.

6. If the reply is received in time, the computer will accept the IP address and configuration settings. Then it will finish bootup and begin talking on the network.

Every idea in the world has its Achilles' heel. DHCP is no different. DHCP is implemented on OSI layer 2. This means that the DHCP mechanism is dependent on making a broadcast with its MAC address. Routers will not pass broadcasts because the resulting traffic is undesired on all other occasions. Remember, the router has two jobs: one is routing, and the second is providing insulation from unnecessary traffic. The DHCP server needs to be located on the same subnet to hear the computer making a DHCP request. Figure 4.40 shows how DHCP is blocked by the router.

FIGURE 4.39   How DHCP works

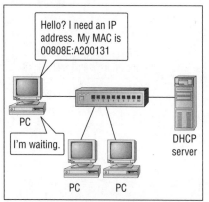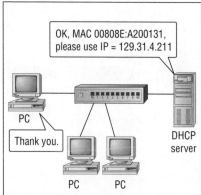

FIGURE 4.40   DHCP and the router issue

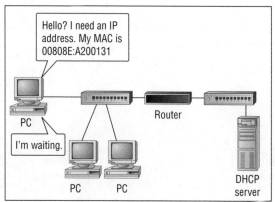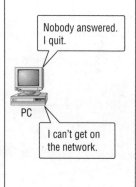

The DHCP Router Solution

Rather than building a bunch of DHCP servers, you can make a simple change to the router configuration. The router will still perform its normal functions; however, it can be set to forward DHCP requests to another subnet. The router command setting is called a bootup-helper-address or DHCP-helper-address.

This helper address setting will forward both the initial request and the associated DHCP server reply. The process is simple, as shown in Figure 4.41.

Dynamic IP addressing under DHCP is quite convenient for users. However, unsecured implementations of DHCP could grant an intruder easier access into the network. We discuss this security issue further in Chapter 7.

FIGURE 4.41   Router with DHCP helper address

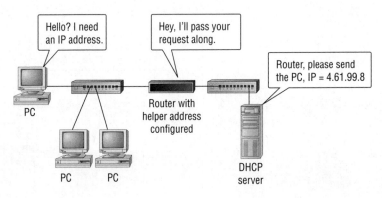

Expanding the Network

Modern routers can connect high-speed LANs to remote places for the purpose of creating a wide area network (WAN). Figure 4.42 shows what a WAN might look like.

FIGURE 4.42   Expanding the network

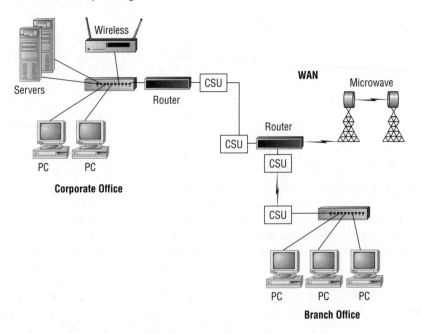

Remote access is a popular feature. WANs are similar to a LAN; however, the implementation is different. Special equipment is necessary to adapt the transmission signal to telephone and radio equipment. Figure 4.42 shows the basics of expanding a network.

Setting up a WAN requires planning. Let's start with the most important component, which is information. The first thing you need is the customer requirements. What does the customer intend to connect to the network? Questions should be asked about who will be connecting to the network. Will the users be employees, business partners, or clients? Once again, you ask questions about their intended usage while on the network. What controls are planned? Hopefully, the client will be able to impress the auditor with answers that are well thought out.

Your client might want to have dial-in access to the network for their users. This can be accomplished in two ways:

Individual Modems   An individual modem can be connected to a computer on the network. This is a simple method that is adored by every hacker in the world. Individual modem connections bypass the majority of network security controls. Your monitoring tools may think this is just an ordinary internal computer with free rein over the attached subnet—or worse, the whole network. A hacker can easily find modems by using automated dialing tools or checking a list of known modems posted at hacker sites. Insecure modems are still a threat to security. A sharp auditor will investigate the compliance of dial-in modems to their security policy.

Network Access Server   An access server can be used with a modem pool. It can be a slick product from Cisco or a PC configured with special software such as Microsoft Remote Access Service (RAS). The access server should have special monitoring and security controls.

It is safe to assume that the remote connection will be attached to one of the routers. You should encourage the practice of separating remote connections into their own subnet. This promotes separation of duties with the benefit of simplifying the implementation of security controls. Remote router connections will probably need a firewall if the connection is wireless or could involve someone besides the organization's employees.

Using Telephone Circuits

High-speed telephone circuits such as T1 (1.54 Mbps) and T3 (44.5 Mbps) use a channel service unit (CSU) instead of a regular modem. The CSU is a special device used by the telephone company and designed for connection to their equipment. Telephone circuits like this can be divided or combined by using a multiplexor. A *multiplexor* converts one high-speed telephone port into many lower-speed ports, or combines several lower-speed lines to appear as one high-speed line. Multiplexors are invisible to the user.

Table 4.4 summarizes the various types of equipment you might use when connecting to a WAN.

TABLE 4.4 Networking equipment

Device	Purpose
Router with WAN port	Connect LAN to remote WAN via telephone circuits.
Modem	Low-speed telephone dial-up connection to the access server for users, or attached to the router for remote administration.
Channel service unit (CSU)	Similar to a very special modem. Designed to connect a router port to a high-speed telephone company circuit. Fast transmission speeds from 1 MB to 44 MB per line. Common in WANs.
Multiplexor	Combines multiple lower-speed telephone circuits to appear as a single fast circuit, or splits a fast circuit into multiple lower-speed connections. It has a function similar to that of any splitter or combiner.

The telephone company will provide whatever service the client is able to afford. In some areas, the services may be limited. High-speed services such as Digital Subscriber Line (DSL) are available in only limited areas. The limitation is based on cost: Your telephone company will invest in areas that have enough demand to warrant the business cost. In rural areas, people have few choices. These are known as last-mile service areas, where the phone company will lose money.

The world of telephone circuits is based on several generations of telephone company equipment. The older generation is based on the Integrated Services Digital Network (ISDN). The newest generation is built by using Dense Wave Multiplexing (DWM) with multiple lasers over fiber optics with Asynchronous Transfer Mode (ATM). Each generation of technology has intrinsic advantages and disadvantages.

Let's run down the list. We suggest you pay attention because these details may be of value during audits and discussions on network planning. The following are various ways you can connect to your network via a wired route.

Dedicated Telephone Circuits

Dedicated telephone circuits are billed by location with actual usage billed by distance. The user is charged a monthly fee plus any long-distance charges.

Plain Old Telephone Service (POTS) POTS is available almost everywhere. This is the regular telephone line capable of data transmission up to 56 Kbps. POTS is based on using half of an ISDN circuit. POTS is the only circuit that is considered to be "off" when not in use. Transmission is halted when you hang up the phone. All the other telephone circuits we discuss are always live and transmitting.

Integrated Services Digital Network (ISDN)   ISDN is the foundation of POTS. Therefore, you should be able to get ISDN almost anywhere. The basic rate interface (BRI) bandwidth starts at 128 Kbps per line. It can be used as one 128 Kbps channel or divided into two 56 Kbps circuits. Optional ISDN speeds on a primary rate interface (PRI) can go up to 1.544 Mbps. You can run up to 23 channels of data, voice, and video over ISDN. In Europe and Australia, the PRI speeds are 2.048 Mbps, equal to 30 channels. Most video conference sets use ISDN. The ISDN circuit is always on and live.

Digital Subscriber Line (DSL)   DSL is usually the least-expensive high-speed circuit using a higher frequency over a standard telephone line. This allows your standard voice telephone line to simultaneously carry DSL higher-speed traffic without conflict. DSL is substantially limited by distance. It is available only in high-density areas where the phone company can make a profit. Speeds range from 368 Kbps to 20 Mbps depending on your area. The DSL circuit is always on and live. If you turn off DSL equipment, the phone company disables your circuit.

Primary Trunk Line (T1)   T1 is a dedicated trunk line equal to 24 POTS circuits. The user is charged by the mile for basic T1 service. Telephone PBX systems are usually connected by one or more T1 trunks running back to the telephone company's central office. The administrator can provision (divide) the trunk into whatever variety of fractional service they desire for voice, video, or data. T1 lines never shut down. In North America, T1 speeds are 1.544 Mbps each, and 2.048 Mbps in Europe.

Trunk Line (T3)   One T3 circuit is made up of 28 T1 circuits offering a combined speed of 44.736 Mbps. This type of connection is usually reserved for wholesale customers and higher-volume buyers. The T3 circuit can be provisioned (divided) into fractional speeds, multiple T1s, or up to 672 64 Kbps channels for voice, video, or data. T3 circuits dedicated to data services are referred to DS-3 circuits.

Each of the circuits in the preceding list represents a dedicated connection that is either between the telephone company and the buyer's office, or installed as a private line between the buyer's offices. Figure 4.43 shows the relationship of the different telephone circuits.

FIGURE 4.43   Usage of the different telephone circuits

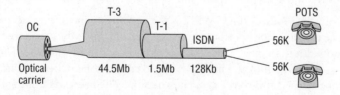

Packet-Switched Circuits

Packet switching evolved to eliminate the need for everyone to set up expensive dedicated lines. The Internet is a packet-switched network. Transmissions can route anywhere without regard to distance. This means that the path from Los Angeles, California, to Mexico City, Mexico, might pass through Atlanta, Georgia, depending on the carrier and the time of day.

Similarly, using a special diagnostic tool, we noticed our downloads from Dell were routed from Grapevine, Texas (near Dallas), to Parsippany, New Jersey, and then to Austin, Texas (a journey of more than 2,700 miles). Interesting, because our Grapevine office is only 229 miles from Dell in Austin, Texas. In packet switching, the source and destination are known, but the path automatically changes (it is variable). One of the first packet switching methods is X.25.

International Telecommunication Standard X.25 (X.25)   X.25 was an early 1970s digital packet-switching protocol designed to create WANs over public data networks run by the telephone company. It's considered the foundation of modern switched networks. X.25 contained three major advances:

- A field for handling special transmission parameters called the facility code. This allowed you to specify a quality of service.

- Ability to create permanent virtual circuits (PVCs). This administrative configuration setting allowed the administrator to specify a fixed path for all communication. PVCs were created to replace the leasing of dedicated telephone lines.

- Ability to create switched virtual circuits (SVCs). The source and destination were specified, but the path was temporary, dynamic, and constantly changing. SVCs were not dedicated.

X.25 is now used primarily as a reference model, except for a few old die-hard customers. The lessons learned in X.25 created new technology for communications.

Frame Relay   Frame Relay (FR) is an inexpensive packet-switching system using the same type of interface protocol as X.25 with PVC and SVC capability. Frame Relay is different from X.25 in format and functionality. The FR data packets may arrive out of sequence. Therefore, it is important to have equipment capable of caching enough data in memory for reassembly sequencing before use by the user. Frame Relay works great for data/voice applications, but some video transmissions may appear choppy to the viewer unless adequate memory caching is used. End connection points are specified by using data link connection identifiers (DLCI numbers). The DLCI specifies the destination, similar to a phone number. Frame Relay speeds range from less than 1.544 Mbps up to 44.5 Mbps. The Frame Relay circuits are always on and live unless you want the telephone company to disable your circuit for several days.

Asynchronous Transfer Mode (ATM)   ATM is the new backbone of the telecommunications industry. The transmission speeds are very high, from 155 Mbps to more than 1 GBps. That is more bandwidth than most companies could ever use in this decade. The ATM design implements cell switching and multiplexing to ensure solid delivery. Data is sent down multiple concurrent paths to the same destination. The first data cell to arrive will be used, while later duplicates will be discarded. ATM can use 132 switched paths (SVCs) during transmission. It is very reliable. The ATM circuit is always on and live unless you want the telephone company to shut down your circuit for several days.

Switched Multimegabit Data Services (SMDS)   This is a very high-speed data communications service. I doubt it would ever be mentioned on your exam. It's included to demonstrate where public data networks are going. The first ATM services offered speeds of only 1.5 Mbps, and SMDS was 3.4 Mbps. Advances in technology raised the speeds 100 times.

SMDS is available on a limited basis at 340 Mbps to 3.4 Gbps (3,400 Mbps). It's designed for transmitting over a dual bus in metropolitan networks. The SMDS payload is big enough to encapsulate (carry) entire LAN traffic (Ethernet 802.3, 802.4, and Token Ring/ FDDI 802.5).

SMDS has two interesting features: security and group addressing. Source addresses are verified by the network to ensure that the assigned interface is legitimate. The user is protected from *address spoofing* (fraudulent devices). Source and destination addresses can be screened to prevent delivery of unwanted traffic. Group addressing allows multicasting of a single transmission to a specific group of addresses without sending to anyone else. The private virtual network features add additional security and efficiency.

WARNING   We have discussed several communication circuits that are always on and live. This can allow a hacker to attack you 24 hours a day, every day. High-speed circuits can support high-speed attacks or high-speed theft of your data. Think firewalls!

Using Wireless Access Solutions

The basic network concepts are identical for developing a network solution sans wire. Wireless is used when the wiring costs are prohibitive or the wires would defeat the intended purpose.

Each wireless system requires a minimum of two antenna systems. The antenna stations have both transmitting and receiving capabilities.

The following are various ways you can connect to your network via wireless access:

Wi-Fi Radio   This is the most common type of wireless access. The design uses a layer 1 transmitter/receiver to support a signal range of up to 1,500 feet. It uses digital spread spectrum or frequency hopping over a private radio channel. It is commonly used by the military and private companies operating mobile fleets. Large-scale Wi-Fi may use cellular service. Smaller-scale use includes Wi-Fi hot spots.

It's relatively simple to construct a wireless LAN. Several vendors offer low-cost wireless access points (APs), which are similar to a wireless hub or router. The AP is connected to a wired network and broadcasts connectivity to handheld devices. Usually the range of an AP is 300 feet, equivalent to 100 meters. Users can move freely within the 300-foot broadcast range without losing any connectivity. The individual broadcast area (range) is also known as a *cell*. This is comparable to the design of cellular telephone networks. The effective range can be increased by combining APs and their multiple cells (service range). Wireless LANs (WLANs) are based on the IEEE 802.11 standard.

Station (STA)   The station, or Independent Basic Service Set (IBSS), is a wireless device on the end of the network, such as PDA, laptop, or mobile phone.

Access Point (AP)   This is a wireless transmitter/receiver that provides basic network services, usually within 300 feet, equivalent to 100 meters. Higher-power transmitters with longer ranges are entering the marketplace. The AP and STA compose a basic WLAN.

Cell   The individual AP broadcast range is known as the cell, or span of coverage. Multiple AP cells are linked together to increase the range and allow roaming within the building or between buildings. The relationship is shown in Figure 4.44.

FIGURE 4.44   Basic wireless network

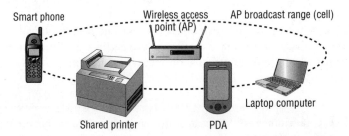

A group of wireless devices uses an ad hoc arrangement when communicating directly with each other in a peer-to-peer relationship without an AP. The terminology *ad hoc* is based on the dynamic master-slave relationship between devices. Ad hoc networks have a short broadcast range, which is also referred to as the piconet, or personal area network (PAN). Bluetooth is the most common ad hoc network for providing connectivity between a cell phone and a wireless headset.

Pico means one trillionth, or very small. Bluetooth technology creates an ad hoc network of one master and one to seven slaves, up to a total of eight devices. This teeny network provides short-range direct-link interconnectivity.

WARNING   The lack of effective security is an enormous drawback in wireless networking. Implementation of Wired Equivalent Privacy (WEP) and Wireless Protected Access (WPA) proved to be practically worthless because of static passwords (aka Wireless Pre-Shared Keys (PSK). As of 2005, wireless networks using 802.11a, 802.11b, 802.11g, and 802.11n have been officially deemed unsafe. Those unsafe implementations represent the majority of wireless LAN equipment installed worldwide. In response, IEEE issued a revised wireless standard in 2005 called 802.11i Robust Security Networks (RSNs). A third-party security VPN must be used when RSN is not available. We discuss RSN in Chapter 7.

Satellite Radio   This is the next most common method. The signal is bounced off a low-orbit satellite in space. Obviously, the service area is huge. Very popular for remote communications or linking to numerous field locations, satellite is heavily used in trucking fleets, ships, and retail chain operations. The transmission speeds are lower, and cost is an issue unless you buy a large volume of air time. Private uplinks are available for telephone, data, fax, and video applications. Satellite data-phones are common for emergency response. Transmission speeds are 9.6 bps to 4 MBps, with specialized hardware required. Satellite communication has a 2- to 5-second transmission delay due to signal propagation delay. For example, the Iridium satellites are less than 500 miles up compared to 23,000 miles for geosynchronous satellites.

Microwave   Microwaves are used in short-distance runs—1 to 30 miles—across cities and over mountain ranges. Microwave service has been around for 50 years. The only drawbacks are the clear line of sight required for transmission and the construction cost. Connection speeds range from 1 MBps to 100 MBps. The primary advantage is no recurring transmission costs aside from equipment purchase and regular maintenance. Severe weather and fog can disrupt signals.

Laser   Lasers are being used as an alternative to microwaves. Lasers also work to connect two offices by using the unobstructed aerial space to cross above public roads. It is similar to fiber optics without the fiber cable. Transmission speeds from are from 1 MBps to 100 MBps. Severe weather and fog can disrupt signals.

It is strongly recommended that every land-based wireless connection have a firewall installed between the wired network and the wireless equipment. Many implementations of wireless encryption still contain holes in security. Motivated hackers can access radio connections by using technology available in the amateur radio community. Laser access may be more difficult, but hackers have proven it is possible.

It is important that we address the subject of short-range wireless networking for use with radio frequency identification tags. This is an area that will increase as more organizations attempt to implement automated tracking.

Wireless RFID Systems

Radio frequency identification (RFID) is a hot topic. RFID uses a tiny tag, which contains silicon chips and antennas that enable the tag to be detected by scanners. The original purpose was to protect inventory from department store shoplifters. Later RFID was expanded to include planting tags in boxes for better warehouse control.

The security and privacy issues regarding RFID are increasing every day. As an IS auditor, you are expected to have a basic understanding of RFID. You will encounter an increasing number of issues regarding RFID implementations. Citizens are growing more concerned about their privacy.

Passive RFID tags are regularly used in inventory control and for implant in live animals. These tags may be covertly read at a distance. Newer tags are built into the product and are not detectable. The user could be scanned as they walk through a building. RFID tags in adult products or medical prescription packages could lead to interesting conversations about privacy.

Under President Bill Clinton's administration, the U.S. Food and Drug Administration and other government agencies approved the use of RFID tags for human implant. There are multiple human implant vendors on the market today. The ads for human implant claim RFID tags are safe and nonremovable. One vendor claims that the intended purpose is to protect newborn infants by tracking your baby in the hospital. Other advertised uses include prisoner identification or the identification of elderly individuals unable to provide information for themselves. This new RFID situation poses an increasing variety of privacy concerns.

Another type of RFID uses a transponder to transmit a signal. The RFID transponder uses an internal power source to respond to queries by an antenna in the area. A common example is the toll tag used by a toll road authority for the electronic collection of usage fees. A variety of organizations including law enforcement collect surveillance data on common citizens by using active RFID toll tags along with automobile satellite services and cell phone records.

Government researchers have determined RFID tags can be easily cloned without the user's or recipient's knowledge. Any RFID signal you can read can be duplicated. The implications may be either good or evil depending on the desire of individuals. You can expect more controversy as the issues develop.

Summarizing the Various Area Networks

The IT management may choose to maintain a network administration staff at each site or use remote access. Either choice has its advantages and disadvantages.

Routers can use a modem for individual low-speed telephone connections of 56 Kbps. This would be intended for remote support of the router itself. (Turn off the modem when not in use to keep out the hackers.)

We have discussed both LAN and WAN networks. The discussion would not be complete without mentioning the multitude of variations. In the beginning, the LAN was the focus. Then the need arose to connect to remote users. Supporting remote connections became rather involved, and the whole idea was termed a WAN. Since that time, the world has continued to generate new products with a combination of need, politics, and marketing. The LAN-WAN naming convention has brought us new terminology for other types of area networks, including personal area networks (PANs), campus area networks (CANs), metropolitan area networks (MANs), and storage area networks (SANs).

Table 4.5 introduces you to the types of area networks that the CISA is expected to encounter. You need to know the descriptive features of each one.

TABLE 4.5   Common networking acronyms

Network Acronym	Description
Local area network (LAN)	Connecting computers within the building by using hubs, switches, and routers. Usually very fast connection speed of 100 to 1,000 MBps.
Virtual local area network (VLAN)	Artificial grouping of disparate workstation ports across various LAN switches to appear as if all were connected to a common subnet. Similar to a PBX conference-calling group. Primitive VLANs use fixed ports. Advanced VLANs use dynamic rules to automatically assign ports without user/administrator intervention. The user can plug in anywhere, and the switch reconfigures the port within fractions of a second. Moves are automatic using IP address rule, protocol rule, or MAC address rule.

TABLE 4.5   Common networking acronyms *(continued)*

Network Acronym	Description
Storage area network (SAN)	A cluster solution for interconnecting different kinds of file storage for server farms. Often use Ethernet, SCSI, ATM, or fiber-optic connections.
Personal area network (PAN)	Coverage is within 10 feet of the immediate area. Used for connecting PDA and handheld personal devices to synchronize with your computer. Also known as a piconet.
Campus area network (CAN)	Connecting computers between buildings in a school or corporate campus by using cable, fiber optics, or wireless transmitters.
Metropolitan area network (MAN)	Connecting computers between different buildings located in the same city.
Wide area network (WAN)	Multi-city connection over longer distances. Connection speeds range from under 1 MB on cheap telephone circuits to over 1 GBps on optical carrier circuits (OC*x*).

Political battles over authority will exist regarding the control over most networks. The basic operation of local and wide area networks is quite similar. The principal difference is the area of coverage and who is in charge of that area.

Using Software as a Service (SaaS)

Since the beginning of the computer industry, software providers have operated service bureaus to process data for users. Early service bureaus were outsource vendors hosting applications on the vendor's large mainframe computer located in a remote data center. Subscribers would submit their requests via printed forms, keypunch cards, or terminals on dial-up lines. Examples included CompuServe, electronic data processing for payroll, and bulletin board services (BBS).

The Internet changed the way we connect to the vendor, but the operating concept is still the same. Over the years, a smart salesperson introduced the term *application service provider* (ASP) and *software as a service* (SaaS) to make this service bureau concept sound newer. Users still rely on someone else's server to process their data. As auditors, we recognize the increased risks of using remote third-party services for processing proprietary and confidential data.

Almost anyone can set up a networked server with commercially licensed software and call themselves an SaaS vendor. Customers may pay a per-user or subscription fee in exchange for processing their data remotely on the vendor computer.

Advantages

Let's look at some of the reasons people use SaaS vendors:

Lower Initial Cost   The vendor provides the infrastructure.

Instant Scalability   The user can expand or upgrade for more money.

Security   Hopefully, the vendor is providing controls and monitoring with full liability. Beware of limited liability clauses indicating that the buyer can't recover damages for breach.

Cheaper Support   The user can use only a portion of the service as needed. No full-time employees or personnel on-call expenses are required.

Disadvantages

There are, of course, disadvantages, too:

Expense   Pay-as-you-go billing can get expensive as processing volume increases.

Control of Data   The vendor has control over the subscriber data. The subscriber can be locked out if the bill isn't paid or out of luck if the vendor fails.

Liability   Most vendor service agreements contain liability exclusions. Subscribers may be on their own if a data breach, loss, or system failure occurs. The vendor is usually not liable for consequential losses.

It's very difficult, if not impossible, to be sure that subscriber data is properly destroyed after deletion. Deleted data is still resident and recoverable on the vendor's storage disks.

The subscriber of the ASP/SaaS vendor will usually retain the liability for any failures unless a special contract is negotiated. Clients and regulators will always hold the subscriber responsible for their decision to use the SaaS vendor.

SaaS became very popular in Customer Relationship Management (CRM), sales force automation, and stock exchange trading. Popularity grew to include human resources, inventory control, help desk management, and client billing.

The principal motivation for using SaaS was to lower the expense of infrastructure and ongoing operating costs. For some customers, the draw was rapid deployment of applications without involving the IT department. Another variation of the SaaS business model is cloud computing.

Cloud Computing

This has become the generic reference for processing data across the Internet on a remote server operated by a vendor. The Internet itself is referred to as the cloud because all the details are hidden from the user. Just as in the ASP/SaaS operating model, the vendor provides use of computing resources for a fee to the subscriber. Auditors need to be aware of four basic variations of cloud computing currently being offered. These include private cloud services, public cloud services such as Google Docs, cooperative cloud services for an association of subscribers, and hybrid cloud services:

Private Cloud Services   An organization can lease exclusive use of the servers and communication equipment run by an internal service provider or external vendor. Terms of service usually include specialized contracts negotiated with service-level agreements to guarantee security, penalty clauses, right to audit, liability for breaches, and specific details on availability of services. The subscriber selects the authorized users and specifies the operating rules. Clients who care about the confidentiality, regulatory data requirements, and usage of their data use private cloud services.

Public Cloud Services   Subscribers pay a fee or may get free starter usage as with Google Docs, LinkedIn, Myspace, Twitter, or Facebook. This subscriber has no way of verifying where their data is actually stored or accessed or how it is being handled. Usually the service agreement exempts the vendor from any direct liability for data loss or breach. All the users share the same resources. There may be no compensation for the loss of use. Subscribers may be told privacy exists while the actual terms of service exclude any guarantees of privacy. The vendor may sign up anyone as a subscriber. Individuals and small groups of users without liability for breaches of confidentiality use public cloud services to initially save money.

Cooperative Cloud Services   Professional associations and community groups may have their own private-label computing cloud service. This should be considered a variation of the public cloud because it's doubtful the group spent much money or negotiated any tangible service levels.

Hybrid Cloud Services   One of the advantages of cloud computing is the ability to mix and match services from different vendors across the Internet. The subscriber retains the majority of, if not all, liability for data breaches, service failures, and outages. The hybrid cloud design may be popular with subscribers who believe they are circumventing the cost of using their own IT department or private cloud services. The auditor should investigate the type of data being used, appropriate protection based on data classification, and the consequences of failure should a breach, loss, or outage occur.

Now we need to take a few minutes to wrap up with an overview of managing the network before we conclude this chapter.

Managing Your Network

Networks are constantly increasing in complexity. A network outage can cause significant impact to an organization's business activities. It would be naive to assume that the systems could run without supervision. The network administrator holds the duty of monitoring network performance and is the first line of defense for detecting security violations. This is possible only with specialized tools designed to manage network assets. Let's take a look at the basic tools used to manage the network.

Syslog

Today almost all computers and network devices have the capability for centralized system logging, known as *Syslog*. The design sends audit log messages to a centralized server for aggregation of event logs and alerts. Syslog is a common and simple utility that requires little processing power.

It is an excellent tool to aid the monitoring efforts of system administrators. This form of centralized logging is excellent for security monitoring and audit log retention. Syslog can be enabled on an individual system within a few minutes.

Syslog has some disadvantages. Unfortunately, it does not contain message authentication. There is still no mechanism for providing message integrity. The Syslog design also lacks the mechanism to verify delivery of a message.

The principal advantage of Syslog is that audit logs can be automatically transmitted to another server for safe storage. This assists in providing evidence for the auditor. It can also be a compensating control in environments where the logs may be deleted. Figure 4.45 shows how Syslog collects logs from servers and other network devices.

FIGURE 4.45   How Syslog works

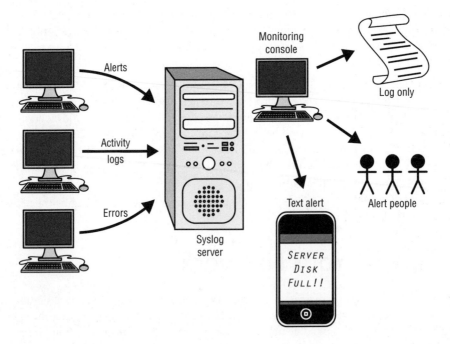

Automated Cable Tester

Cable industry studies report that 97 percent of all network problems are related to faults in the physical cable plant (layer 1). Advanced handheld cable testers are used to certify the quality of network wire runs. These handheld scanners test individual data cables by automatically running a series of electrical tests and transmission tests. The tests check a variety of conditions, including compliance to recommended length, signal strength, transmission cross talk, electrical noise interference, and electrical pin connections. Cables that pass these tests are certified as compliant. Once certified, the cable is ready for production use.

Protocol Analyzer

A computer can be configured with special software designed to record and analyze network transmissions. This software is often referred to as a *packet sniffer*. Network administrators use this as a tool for troubleshooting network performance problems. The sniffer operates in promiscuous mode and records transmissions of every packet traversing the segment. The sniffer can see only traffic within the segment to which it is attached. It cannot see traffic across the routers or switches unless the traffic is passing down the segment where the computer is attached. The sniffer will show you communication between systems and the passwords used.

Hackers can use a sniffer to capture user IDs and passwords in clear text, and to map the network. This is why sniffers are considered a tremendous threat in the wrong hands.

Simple Network Management Protocol

Networks can be monitored and controlled by using the Simple Network Management Protocol (SNMP). The network administrator usually runs an SNMP network management program such as OpenNMS or the practically ancient HP OpenView software to monitor servers and routers. A Network Management System (NMS) gives you the capability to check the up/down status of individual network devices.

You can use SNMP to monitor almost any network device, including servers, routers, gateways, hubs, and workstations. By default, SNMP provides the capability to do the following:

- Read: Monitor a device with notification of possible error conditions
- Write: Reconfigure limited system parameters
- Use SNMP to reboot or shut down the network device

The SNMP security mechanism is extremely weak and relies on simple passwords transmitted in clear text that are easy to read. As an auditor, you should be concerned about SNMP being allowed to travel unregulated across the network. All SNMP-managed devices need to use unique passwords rather than the default passwords *public* and *private*.

Vendor documentation will refer to the passwords of *public* and *private* by using the term *community strings*. A community string is actually a simple password used to gain control of the target system. All that is needed is the target system IP address and matching SNMP password (community string). Many organizations are not properly educated about the *public* and *private* password risk. It is the network administrator's job to define SNMP access control lists and to manage the implementation of unique SNMP passwords for each device. Failure to do so would grant anyone control of any system using the same SNMP password (community string). Otherwise, SNMP is a good internal monitoring tool.

Remote Monitoring Protocol Version 2

The Remote Monitoring Protocol version 2 (RMON2) is a major improvement over version 1, offering data beyond basic network health via up/down status. RMON2 gives you the ability to monitor all seven layers of the OSI model, including application performance. You can view the performance of a single application running across the network or select a stratified view of the combined bandwidth allocation. Figure 4.46 shows the basic design of how RMON2 works, using sensors to collect a wide sample of performance data for enterprise-level reporting.

FIGURE 4.46   How RMON2 works

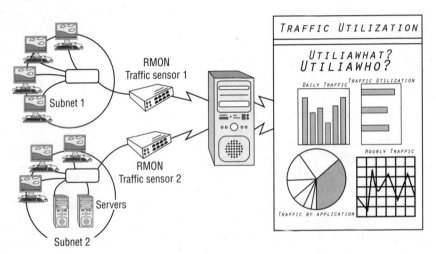

Twenty-one layers of RMON performance data are available. By comparison, a network packet sniffer can record only a snapshot containing a few minutes or hours of layer 1, 2, and 3 data. RMON2 can provide a broader range of nonstop performance while recording tremendous levels of detail covering a time span of hours, days, months, and even years. Most RMON2 implementations write the records to an SQL database for reporting and long-term retention. This is a true enterprise-class monitoring system.

It is important to remember that useful administration tools also make good hacker tools. Every administrative tool needs to be governed by the organization's internal controls.

Summary

The information systems auditor is expected to understand common networking technology. You should know the name of each piece of equipment and its role in the computer network. Occasionally, you may encounter systems that are filling an all-in-one role. In that event, you should remember computer architecture limitations: It is not possible for single-processor systems to perform all functions without a momentary interruption of the security software. Both single-user systems and multiuser systems have design vulnerabilities that can be exploited.

It is the job of the CISA to evaluate the auditee's technology implementation. Despite advancements in technology, common problems will usually be rooted in fundamental errors of design or implementation. Security is best implemented in multiple layers to provide compensating control for design vulnerabilities. The purpose of this chapter has been to familiarize you with the basic concepts. The world depends on the CISA to review the client's design for the purpose of identifying vulnerabilities or failure points. You should always ask yourself whether the technology truly fulfills the objectives of the business and the objectives of security controls. If not, it might just be a superfluous investment in way-cool technical junk. Technology without proper internal controls is a bomb waiting to explode.

Exam Essentials

Understand the basics of computer architecture.   Computer architecture comprises a central processor unit with high-speed cache memory and solid-state random access memory (RAM). All the computer's components communicate by using a shared data bus, constructed of electrical wires. Interfaces connect the data bus to the electronic components such as the video display or the hard disk drive. There are different classes of computers based on size and capability, including the personal computer, midrange computer (mini), mainframe, and supercomputer.

Remember that computers may use single CPUs or multiple CPUs.   In either case, the system can be running in time-sharing mode to support multiple users (multiuser mode). With multiple CPUs, it is possible to assign each processor to a particular task. Multiple-CPU architecture provides a way for security software to run completely uninterrupted. Otherwise, the computer security software will be interrupted in the normal course of servicing processing requests.

Know that the computer operating system manages communications between the hardware and user programs.   The operating system provides services for scheduling, dispatching, security, and input and output functions. All operating systems are not equal in their implementation of internal controls. The mainframe represents a role model for the highest level of system controls. Security controls are lacking while the system is in supervisory state during maintenance or initial program load (IPL).

Understand that system ports must be protected from physical access and logical access.   Examples of system ports include interface ports, the console or master terminal, and all network communication ports.

Know that computer networking is accomplished by using a variety of devices.   Network cables are joined together by hubs or network switches to form a network. Smaller networks are known as subnets. Multiple subnets can be joined together by using a router. The purpose of the router is to direct traffic between different networks. A firewall is a specially configured device that selectively routes traffic between two networks. The firewall's method depends on its internal architecture.

Remember that wide area networks are created by using wired telephone circuits or wireless transmitters to connect LANs.   Network security at external access points is always a concern. Every network access point presents an opportunity to motivated hackers. High-speed communications circuits allow for high-speed attacks. Modern telephone circuits, except for POTS, are always on and present a 24-hour attack opportunity. The first wide area networks were created by using circuit-switched telephone lines that were billed by distance traveled. Newer packet-switching technology charges for the data sent, not the distance traveled.

Understand that the OSI model provides a simple reference for explaining the functions occurring in computer networking.   Nobody actually runs the OSI protocol; in the real world, most communication is performed over the Internet Protocol (IP). A CISA must demonstrate an understanding of how OSI relates to IP.

Remember that computer networks can be complex and require constant monitoring.   Typical monitoring tools include the packet sniffer to analyze communications, Syslog to transmit system logs to a safe location for review, and Simple Network Management Protocol (SNMP) to alert administrators about conditions impacting network operations. SNMP can feed a network management system, such as OpenNMS or Remote Monitoring Protocol (RMON2).

Review Questions

1. Which RAID level does not improve fault tolerance?

   A. RAID level 0

   B. RAID level 1

   C. RAID level 2

   D. RAID level 5

2. Which type of network device directs packets through the Internet?

   A. Hubs

   B. Routers

   C. Repeaters

   D. Modems

3. Which of the following is a list of OSI model levels from the top down?

   A. Application, Physical, Session, Transport, Network, Data-Link, Presentation

   B. Presentation, Data-Link, Network, Transport, Session, Physical, Application

   C. Application, Presentation, Session, Transport, Network, Data-Link, Physical

   D. Presentation, Data-Link, Network, Transport, Session, Physical, Application

4. Which of the following is the most popular media for connecting workstations in a corporate environment?

   A. Coaxial

   B. Shielded twisted-pair

   C. Unshielded twisted-pair

   D. Fiber optics

5. What is one of the first priorities for an auditor reviewing security of the client's network?

   A. Checking firewall configuration settings

   B. Understanding details of network architecture and implementation

   C. Verifying the use of strong passwords

   D. Reviewing records to indicate systems are monitored and IDPS systems are working properly

6. At which layer of the OSI model does a gateway operate?

   A. Layer 3

   B. Layer 5

   C. Layer 6

   D. Layer 7

7. Which of the following network topologies provides a redundant path for communication?
   A. Fiber-optic
   B. Star
   C. Ring
   D. Bus

8. What is the purpose of the Address Resolution Protocol (ARP)?
   A. Find the IP address
   B. Find the mailing address
   C. Find the MAC address
   D. Find the domain name

9. What is the security issue regarding packet analyzers?
   A. Viewing passwords
   B. Special training
   C. Purchase cost
   D. Only for auditor's use

10. Which of the following is *not* a function of the operating system?
    A. Filing system for storage and retrieval
    B. Detection of system penetration
    C. User interface (shell)
    D. Security functions with event logging

11. Which of the following protocols is likely to be used for monitoring the health of the network?
    A. OSI
    B. SNMP
    C. SMTP
    D. RIP

12. What is the difference between a router and a switch?
    A. Both operate at layer 2; the router routes traffic, and the switch connects various users to the network.
    B. Both operate at layer 3; the router routes traffic, and the switch connects various users to the network.
    C. They operate at OSI layer 3 and layer 2, respectively.
    D. They operate at OSI layer 2 and layer 3, respectively.

13. Which type of network cabling is relatively immune to interference, difficult to tap, and can run extended distances?

   A. Coaxial

   B. Shielded twisted-pair

   C. Unshielded twisted-pair

   D. Fiber-optic

14. Which type of memory is used to permanently record programs on solid-state chips and retains the data even after power is turned off?

   A. Random access memory

   B. Read-only memory

   C. Flash memory

   D. Optical memory

15. Network switches have frequently replaced the use of network hubs. What is the issue in regard to monitoring when using a network switch?

   A. Hubs will pass all traffic across ports.

   B. SNMP must be configured properly.

   C. Switches operate at OSI layer 2.

   D. Switches filter traffic between ports.

16. Which of the following statements is false concerning the communication circuits used in wide area networking?

   A. Switched virtual circuits (SVCs) may use different routes to reach the destination.

   B. Digital circuit-switched lines are dedicated between locations.

   C. Packet-switched circuits are charged according to distance.

   D. Circuit-switched lines allow the user to transmit any amount of data.

17. The architecture of a computer with a single central processing unit (CPU) contains which of the following points that represents the biggest area of interest to the auditor?

   A. Time-sharing is used to service the different processing tasks one at a time.

   B. An upgrade to a multiprocessor system should be justified to improve response times.

   C. System control software is halted between processing tasks.

   D. A pipeline design should be implemented to minimize system idle time.

18. Which of the following RAID implementations is designed for the disk array to be configured into one large virtual disk partition using high-speed asynchronous data transfer?

   A. RAID-1

   B. RAID-7

   C. RAID-5

   D. RAID-6

19. In network communications, the _____ transmission sends a single data packet to multiple addresses for applications such as Internet-based television.

   A. Broadcast

   B. Multicast

   C. Visicast

   D. Unicast

20. Which of the following network protocols uses the MAC address to find a computer's IP address?

   A. Domain Name System (DNS) protocol

   B. Reverse Domain Name System (RDNS) protocol

   C. Reverse Address Resolution Protocol (RARP)

   D. Address Resolution Protocol (ARP)

21. The Internet Protocol (IP) contains a special feature for separating different types of communication between network addresses. What is this feature called?

   A. Software port

   B. Hardware port

   C. Dynamic Host Configuration Protocol

   D. Virtual Communication Protocol

22. Default settings are used by vendors to help users get the system up and running. What is the auditor's primary area of interest regarding default settings?

   A. Save time and money for the user

   B. Represent the manufacturer's recommended settings

   C. Indicate well-known settings published by the vendor

   D. Reduce support headaches, which increases operational uptime

23. The _____ can be poisoned by a hacker to prevent the computer from converting computer names into network addresses.

   A. Address Resolution Protocol (ARP)

   B. Reverse Address Resolution Protocol (RARP)

   C. Border Gateway Protocol (BGP)

   D. Domain Name System (DNS)

24. Which of the following best describes ad hoc networks?

   A. Dynamic connection of remote devices

   B. Fixed connection of devices

   C. Active Device Host Communication

   D. Wireless connection using a static configuration

25. Except for the older plain old telephone service (POTS) lines, what is the primary issue of remote access over telephone company circuits?

   A. The cost of service may be expensive.

   B. The available bandwidth may be too slow.

   C. A remote-access circuit is always active to accept communication.

   D. Remote access servers (RASs) may be used to create a dial-up modem pool.

Answers to Review Questions

1.   A. RAID level 0 improves performance and can provide large logical drives but it does not increase redundancy. It is often used in combination with other levels to improve performance and redundancy. The purpose of RAID-0 is to combine multiple disks into one giant virtual disk.

2.   B. The function of network routers is to route IP packets throughout the network or the Internet. The router does not know the entire route to the destination. The router holds a routing table that simply provides the address of the next point down the path to the destination. Network routing is like a game of connect-the-dots. The data must travel sequentially from one router to the next router until it reaches the intended destination.

3.   C. It helps to remember the memory tool: Please Do Not Throw Sausage Pizza Away is sequenced from the bottom up.

4.   C. The most popular media is UTP, or unshielded twisted-pair. Coaxial cable is no longer used for connecting workstations. Fiber-optic cable is often used for interconnecting servers.

5.   B. The first priority of the auditor is to gain an understanding of the client's network architecture. This usually begins with a graphic diagram illustrating all of the devices located in the computer room, in wiring closets, and used in remote connections. It's important for the auditor to understand implementation details of each device: physical characteristics, purpose, and configuration. This may require the auditor to use a technical expert in network device configuration.

6.   D. According to ISACA, the gateway operates at application layer 7 in the OSI model. The function of the gateway is to convert data contained in one protocol into data used by a different protocol. An example is an SNA PC-to-mainframe gateway converting ASCII to mainframe Extended Binary Coded Decimal Interchange Code (EBCDIC).

7.   C. The ring topology provides two paths for communication. If the ring is damaged, the data can be transmitted in the other direction through the undamaged segment. The most common implementation of a ring topology is IBM Token Ring and fiber-optic rings used by the telephone company to connect the central office wiring centers for maximum reliability.

8.   C. The Address Resolution Protocol (ARP) is used when you have an IP address and need to find the MAC address.

9.   A. Network protocol analyzers, also known as sniffers, can view clear-text passwords being transmitted across the network. The sniffer can decode packets being transmitted and is useful for troubleshooting network protocol problems.

10.   B. The operating system will not be able to detect a system penetration because it usually can't tell the difference between a service request being made by a legitimate user or program, and an illegitimate request. The job of the operating system is to provide an interface between a computer program and the computer hardware.

11. B. The Simple Network Management Protocol (SNMP) is frequently used to monitor the health of the network in conjunction with a Network Management System (NMS) such as OpenNMS or older HP OpenView. The security of the SNMP configuration on each device can be a concern for the auditor. SNMP can be used in a malicious fashion to paint a picture of the network's design.

12. C. The network router operates at layer 3 for the purpose of directing traffic across the network to other subnets. The network switch operates at layer 2 to provide Data-Link services between the computers in the same subnet. A router connects different subnets.

13. D. Fiber-optic cable can transmit signals for several miles. The primary issue regarding fiber optics is the cost and special handling to prevent damage. Fiber-optic cable can be tapped by using special tools and skills; however, the process is relatively difficult for most individuals.

14. B. Solid-state integrated circuits implementing read-only memory (ROM) will provide permanent storage of data, regardless of electrical power. ROM is programmed by burning electrical connections inside the integrated circuit (IC) chip. Optical memory is not a solid-state process. Flash memory can be erased and reprogrammed. Random access memory (RAM) is volatile and will be erased when power is turned off.

15. D. Network switches are designed to filter unnecessary data traffic between ports, with the objective of making a shared connection appear to be a private line. The switch cannot tell the difference between data traffic you want to monitor and unnecessary traffic. Switches contain monitoring ports that can be configured to relay a portion of the traffic to a monitoring sensor, but it may be difficult for the monitoring port to keep up with enough speed. Hubs operate on layer 1 and will pass 100 percent of the traffic without an issue.

16. C. Circuit-based communication lines such as T1 and T3 are billed according to distance traveled. Almost all high-speed lines in use today are digital. Circuit-switched lines are dedicated connections between locations, with billing based on the distance between the locations. Circuit switching is more expensive but has some security advantages. Conversely, packet-based lines such as frame-relay are billed according to the amount of data sent, without regard to the distance traveled. The Internet uses packet switching to span the globe.

17. C. The computer's central processing unit (CPU) operates in time-sharing mode by using interrupts to start and stop the processing of requests (tasks). In computers with a single CPU, internal system controls such as security software are constantly started and stopped as the CPU switches back and forth between different tasks. A multiprocessor system allows the security software to be run in dedicated mode on a dedicated CPU without any interruptions, which improves overall system security.

18. B. RAID level 7 is designed to allow several high-speed disks (disk array) to be configured as one large virtual drive partition using asynchronous transfer mode.

19. B. Multicasting is used to efficiently send a single transmission to multiple addresses.

20. C. Reverse Address Resolution Protocol (RARP) is used when the computer's MAC address is known (for example, when using BOOTP/DHCP to find the computer's IP address). RARP is used just like a reverse telephone directory using a street address enabling you to look up the owner's name.

21. A. Software ports, also known as sockets or buffers, are used to create an orderly communications flow between programs. These software ports are analogous to individual post office mailboxes; each box has a special destination and purpose.

22. C. Beware of default settings on computers and network devices. Default settings are published on the Internet and in service manuals. The default settings benefit a vendor by reducing customer support and presenting the image that the vendor's product is easy to use. Unfortunately, the use of default settings creates a security nightmare. This information is frequently used by hackers to compromise a system. The most cost-effective technique for providing security is to change the default settings to use a unique setting at every opportunity.

23. D. The Domain Name System (DNS) protocol is used to associate computer names such as magic, development2, and www.certtest.com, to their corresponding IP addresses. The original design of DNS did not include any real provisions for security. Secure DNS (S-DNS) uses access lists and two-factor authentication with digital certificates to help thwart hackers' attempts to poison the DNS server, or substitute a fake DNS server that points to the wrong computers.

24. A. Ad hoc networks are a dynamic grouping of devices in ever-changing configurations. Imagine the wireless devices connecting via Bluetooth when you enter a coffee shop, client's office, or your own automobile. As you move though your activities each day, the configuration of this overall network is changing. Ad hoc means unstructured and ever changing.

25. C. Digital high-speed circuits (for example, ISDN, T1, T3, frame relay, ATM, and DSL) are always on (live) by design. If you attempt to turn off (or disable) a high-speed digital circuit, the telephone company will disable the circuit for several days. The original plain old telephone service (POTS) disconnected your equipment from the hacker's reach when you hung up the phone line. Digital circuits never allow the user to "hang up the receiver" and therefore are never disconnected. Firewalls are required on digital high-speed circuits because the hacker could attack 24 hours a day.

Additional CISA practice questions are available on the author's website at www.certtest.com.

Chapter 5

Information Systems Life Cycle

THE OBJECTIVE OF THIS CHAPTER IS TO ACQUAINT THE READER WITH THE FOLLOWING CONCEPTS:

✓ Implementing all seven phases of the System Development Life Cycle

✓ Understanding how to evaluate the business case for proposed system and feasibility to ensure alignment to business strategy

✓ Impact of international standards relating to software development

✓ Understanding the process of conducting the system design analysis

✓ Understanding the process for developing systems and infrastructure requirements, acquisition, and development and testing to ensure it meets business objectives

✓ Understanding how to evaluate the readiness of systems for production use

✓ Knowledge of management's responsibility for accepting and maintaining the system

✓ Understanding the purpose of postimplementation system reviews relating to anticipated return on investment and proper implementation of controls

✓ Evaluating system retirement and disposal methods to ensure compliance with legal policies and procedures

✓ Basic introduction to the different methodologies used in software development

In this chapter, you will study the methodology of best practices for software development. You will learn an overview of the preferred management techniques for designing, building, and maintaining custom computer software. This is referred to as the *System Development Life Cycle*.

When auditing software development, you will assess whether the prescribed project management, System Development Life Cycle, and change-management processes were followed. You are expected to evaluate the processes used in developing or acquiring software to ensure that the program deliverables meet organizational objectives.

We will discuss software design concepts and terminology that every CISA is expected to know for the CISA exam.

Governance in Software Development

Every organization strives to balance expenditures against revenue. The objective is to increase revenue and reduce operating costs. One of the most effective methods for reducing operating costs is to improve software automation.

Computer programs may be custom-built or purchased in an effort to improve automation. All business applications undergo a common process of needs analysis, functional design, software development, implementation, production use, and ongoing maintenance. In the end, every program will be replaced by a newer version, and the old version will be retired. This is what is referred to as the *life cycle*.

It is said that 85 percent of a business's functions are related to common clerical office administration tasks. The clerical functions are usually automated with commercial off-the-shelf software. Each organization does not need to custom-write software for word processing and spreadsheets, for example. These basic functions can be addressed through traditional software that is easily purchased on the open market. This type of commodity software requires little customization. The overall financial advantages will be small but useful. When purchasing prewritten software, an organization follows a slightly different model that focuses on selection rather than software design and development. Prewritten software follows a life cycle of needs analysis and selection, followed by implementation, which leads to production use and ongoing maintenance.

The remaining 15 percent of the business functions may be unique or require highly customized computer programs. This is the area of need addressed by custom-written computer software. The challenge is to ensure that the software actually fulfills the organization's strategic objectives.

Let's make sure that you understand the difference between a strategic system and a traditional system.

A *strategic system* fundamentally changes the way the organization conducts business or competes in the marketplace. A strategic system significantly improves overall business performance with results that can be measured by multiple indicators. These multiple indicators include measured performance increases and noticeable improvement on the organization's financial statement. An organization might, for example, successfully attain a dramatic increase in sales volume as a direct result of implementing a strategic system. The strategic system may create an entirely new sales channel to reach customers.

Auction software implemented and marketed by eBay is an example of a strategic system. The strategic software fundamentally changes the way an organization will be run. For a strategic system to be successfully implemented, management and users must be fully involved. Anything less than significant fundamental change with dramatic, measurable results would indicate that the software is a traditional system.

You should be aware that some software vendors will use claims of strategic value with obscure results to try to sell lesser products at higher profit margins. The auditor's job is to determine whether the organizational objectives have been properly identified and met. Claims of improvement should be verifiable.

Traditional systems provide support functions aligned to fulfill the needs of an individual or department. Examples of traditional systems include general office productivity and departmental databases. The traditional system might provide 18 percent return on investment, whereas a strategic system might have a return of more than 10 times the investment.

Management of Software Quality

Controlling quality is an ongoing process of improving the yield of any effort. True quality is designed into a system from the beginning. In contrast, inspected quality is no more than a test after the fact. This section covers models designed to promote software quality:

- Capability Maturity Model (CMM)
- ISO Software Process Improvement and Capability dEtermination (SPICE)

Capability Maturity Model

Let's review the Capability Maturity Model and introduce the related international standards. As you may recall from Chapter 2, "IT Governance," the Software Engineering Institute's Capability Maturity Model (CMM) was developed to provide a strategy for determining the maturity of current processes and to identify the next steps required for improvement.

The CMM roots are based in lessons learned from Henry Ford's assembly-line automation during the U.S. industrial age of the early 1900s. Several analogies exist between CMM and the manufacturing process quality concepts of Walter Shewhart, W.W. Royce, W. Edwards Deming, Joseph Duran, and Philip Crosby. Most of the people who understood the analogy relating manufacturing processes to business processes have long since retired. This promotes a false impression that CMM is new, when it's just new to them.

The goal of CMM is to eliminate decision making authority from the department manager and workers. Authority shifts higher and higher up to the executive management level as process maturity increases. Depending on the complexity, in medium to larger organizations it may take months or years of internal improvement to reach the next CMM level. Let's take a quick overview of the levels contained in the CMM:

Level 0 = Nonexistent   This level is implied but not always recognized. Zero indicates that nothing is getting done. Individual managers hold the authority for decisions.

Level 1 = Initial   Processes at this level are ad hoc and performed by individuals. New processes or products are developed for the first time by an individual or small project team. Decision authority resides in the individual workers and is supported by a local manager. Middle managers and supervisors often allow lead workers to make their own self-directed decisions. Typical characteristics are ad hoc activities, prototyping experiments, firefighting problems, unpredictable results, and management activities that vary without consistency.

Level 2 = Repeatable   These processes are documented and can be repeated. The initial project team has created a repeatable recipe (aka a procedure) for duplicating the results. Characteristics are more semiformal methods, tension problems between project managers and line managers, inspected quality rather than quality built in during initial design, and no formal priority system. Decisions are made by individual department managers or project managers. It may work, but there will be coordination problems within the process and between departments. CMM level 2 is the minimum requirement to obtain and maintain ISO 9001 quality certification.

Level 3 = Defined   These are lessons learned and integrated into institutional processes. Standardization begins to take place between departments with qualitative measurement (opinion of quality). Formal criteria is developed for use in selection processes. Decisions are made by formal review committees for the overall good of the business; department managers have less authority.

Level 4 = Managed   This level equates to quantitative measurement (numeric measurement of quality). Portfolio asset management is engrained into all decisions. A formal project priority system is practiced with a project management office (PMO) governing projects universally across all departments. Control is passing up to executives, shifting decision authority away from department managers and project managers.

Level 5 = Optimized   This is the highest level of control, with continuous improvement using statistical process control. At level 5, the workers become a warm-body-style commodity because the rules are so specific that with a little training, almost anyone can perform the tasks. Executives now have the most control, while department managers and workers have almost zero decision authority. A culture of constant improvement is pervasive with a desire to fine-tune the last available percentages to squeak out every remaining penny of profit.

The Software Engineering Institute (SEI) copied process maturity from assembly-line manufacturing. SEI estimates that it may take 13 to 25 months to move up to each successive level. It's just not possible to leapfrog over to the next level because of the magnitude of change required to convert the organization's attitude, experiences, and culture. SEI was one of the first organizations to adapt existing quality models to the evolution of software maturity over 50 years ago. The CMM model has been expanded to cover all types of processes used to run a business or a government office.

The goal of CMM is to reduce, and then eliminate, decision authority from the department managers and workers. Executives gain more control, and decision authority passes upward as maturity increases. By level 5, the workers are a human commodity with a mountain of red tape to prevent any significant variances (no authority, no control, no real changes).

International Organization for Standardization

A significant number of the best practices for quality in American manufacturing have been adopted by the International Organization for Standardization (ISO). ISO is a worldwide federation of government standard bodies operating under a charter to create international standards in order to promote commerce and reduce misrepresentation. One of the functions of the ISO is to identify regional best practices and promote acceptance worldwide.

The work of Shewhart and derivative works of Crosby, Deming, and Duran is focused on reducing manufacturing defects. Their original concepts have been expanded over the last 50 years to include almost all business processes. The CMM represents the best-practice method of measuring process maturity. It makes no difference whether the process is administrative, manufacturing, or software development.

ISO has modified the descriptive words used in the levels of the CMM for international acceptance. As a CISA, you should be interested in three of the ISO standards relating to development and maturity: ISO 15504, ISO 9001, and ISO 9126.

ISO 15504: Variation of CMM

The ISO 15504 standard is a modified version of the CMM. These changes were intended to clarify the different maturity levels across different languages and cultures. Notice that level 0 is relabeled as *incomplete*. Level 1 is renamed to indicate that the process has been successfully performed. Level 2 indicates that the process is managed. Level 3 shows that the targeted process is well established in the organization. Level 4 indicates that individual process output will be very predictable. Level 5 shows that individual process is under a highly supervised continuous improvement program using statistical process control. Table 5.1 illustrates the minor variations between the CMM and the ISO 15504 standard, also known as SPICE.

TABLE 5.1 CMM compared to ISO 15504 (SPICE)

CMM Levels	ISO 15504 Levels
0 = Nonexistent process, so nothing has occurred yet	ISO level 0 = Incomplete
CMM level 1 = Initial	ISO level 1 = Performed
CMM level 2 = Repeatable	ISO level 2 = Managed
CMM level 3 = Defined	ISO level 3 = Established
CMM level 4 = Managed	ISO level 4 = Predictable
CMM level 5 = Optimized	ISO level 5 = Optimized

The purpose of ISO 15504 is identical to the CMM. Variations in language forced the ISO version to use slightly different terminology to express their objectives. Let's move on to a quick overview of two ISO quality-management standards.

ISO 9001: Quality Management

The ISO has promoted a series of quality practices that were previously known as ISO 9000, 9001, and 9002 for design, manufacturing, and service, respectively. These have now been combined into the single ISO 9001 reference. Many organizations have adopted this ISO standard to facilitate worldwide acceptance of their products in the marketplace. ISO compliance also brings the benefits of a better perception by investors. Compliance does not guarantee a better product, but it does provide additional assurances that an organization should be able to deliver a better product.

Within the ISO 9001:2000 and revised ISO 9001:2008 edition, you will find that a formally adopted quality manual is required. The ISO 9001 quality manual specifies detailed procedures for quality management by an organization. The same quality manual provides procedures for strong internal controls when working with vendors, including a formal vendor evaluation and selection process. To ensure quality, the ISO 9001 mandates that personnel performing work shall be properly trained and managed to improve competency. Because an organization claiming ISO compliance is required to have a thoroughly written quality manual in place, an IS audit may request evidence demonstrating that the quality processes are actively used.

It's important to understand the naming convention of ISO standards. Names of ISO standards begin with the letters *ISO*, which are then followed by the standard's numeric number, a colon (:), and the year of implementation. You would read ISO 9001:2008 as ISO standard 9001 adopted using year 2008 revision. The most current version is 2008, so any existing ISO9001:2000 certified organizations are required to get recertified under the revised standard.

ISO 9126: Software Quality

ISO 9126 is a variation of ISO 9001. The ISO standard 9126-2:2003 explains how to apply international software-quality metrics. This standard also defines requirements for evaluating software products and measuring specific quality aspects.

The six quality attributes are as follows:

- Functionality of the software processes

- Ease of use

- Reliability with consistent performance

- Efficiency of resources

- Portability between environments

- Maintainability with regard to making modifications

 You need to know the six major attributes contained in the ISO 9126 standard.

Once again, organizations claiming ISO compliance should be able to demonstrate active use of software metrics and supporting evidence for ISO 9126-2 compliance. You need to remember that no evidence equals no credit.

As a CISA, you should be prepared to identify the terminology used by the CMM and various ISO quality standards. Now that we've reviewed these maturity standards, it is time to mention the matching ISO document-control requirements.

ISO 15489: Records Management

ISO records retention standard 15489:2001 was designed to ensure that adequate records are created, captured, and managed. This standard applies to managing all forms of records and record-keeping policies. It does not matter whether the record format is electronic, printed, or voice. It makes no difference whether the records are used by a public or private organization. The 15489 standard provides the guidance necessary for minimum compliance with ISO 9001 quality standards and records management under ISO 14001. Therefore, an organization must be 15489 compliant to be ISO 9001, ISO 14001, ISO 27002, or ISO 27006 compliant.

Does this standard apply to anyone else? The answer is definitely yes. Records management governs the record-keeping practices of any person who creates or uses records in the course of their business activities. It also applies to those activities in which a record is expected to exist. Examples include the following:

- Financial bookkeeping records

- Contracts and business transactions

- Government filings

- Policies and operating standards

- Payroll and HR records

- Procedures and guidelines
- Records kept in the normal course of business

All organizations need to identify the regulations that have bearing on their activities. Record keeping is necessary to document their actions in order to provide adequate evidence of compliance. Remember that no evidence equals no proof, which demonstrates noncompliance. Business activities are defined broadly by ISO to include public administration, nonprofit activities, commercial use, and other activities expected to keep records. All fundraising campaigns fall under the ISO 15489 standard.

A record is expected to reflect the truth of the communications between the parties, the action taken, and the evidence of the event. Records are expected to be authentic with reliable information of high integrity. Auditors need to be aware of the legal challenges whenever records are introduced as evidence in a court of law. Every good defense lawyer will attempt to dispute the authenticity or integrity of each record by allegations of tampering, mishandling, incompetence, or computer system compromise. Without excellent record keeping, the value of the record as evidence may be diminished or completely lost. This is why the chain of custody actually starts with how records are created in the first place.

ISO 15489 is used by court judges and lawyers as the international standard for determining liability in addition to sentencing during prosecution. All organizations, including yours, should have already adopted a records classification scheme (data classification). The purpose is to convey to the staff how to properly protect assorted records. Consider the different requirements for each of the following types of records:

- Trade secrets
- Unfiled patent applications
- Personal information and privacy data such as HIPAA or bank account numbers
- Intellectual property rights
- Commercial contracts (possibly a confidential record) versus government contracts (a public record)
- Financial data
- Internal operating reports
- Privileged information, including consultation with lawyers
- Customer lists and transaction records (including professional certification)
- Retirement and destruction of obsolete information

Record retention systems should be regularly reassessed to ensure compliance. The corresponding reports also need to be protected because they serve as evidence in support of compliance activities. Most of the fraud mentioned in the beginning of this book, Chapter 1, "Secrets of a Successful IS Auditor," was discovered and prosecuted under ISO 15489 standards.

Let's move on now. It is time to discuss the leadership role of management. We will begin with an overview of the steering committee.

Overview of the Executive Steering Committee

The executive steering committee should be involved in software decisions to provide guidance toward fulfillment of the organizational objectives. We have already discussed the basic design of a steering committee in Chapter 3, "Audit Process."

As you may recall, this steering committee comprises executives and business unit managers. Their goal is to provide direction for aligning IT functions with current business objectives. Steering committees provide the advantage of increasing the attention of top management on IT. The most effective committees hold regular meetings focusing on agenda items from the business objectives rather than IT objectives. Most effective decisions are obtained by mutual agreement of the committee rather than by directive. The steering committee increases awareness of IT functions, while providing an avenue for users to become more involved. In this chapter, we are focusing on the identification of business requirements as they relate to the choices made for computer software.

As a CISA, you should understand how the steering committee has developed the vision for software to fulfill the organization's business objectives. What was the thought process that led the steering committee to its decision? Two common methods are the use of critical success factors (CSFs) and a scenario approach to planning.

Identifying Critical Success Factors

A critical success factor (CSF) is something that must go right every time. To fail a CSF would be a showstopper. The process for identifying CSFs begins with each manager focusing on their current information needs. This thought process by the managers will help develop a current list of CSFs.

Some of the factors may be found in the specific industry or chosen business market. External influences—such as customer perception, current economy, pressure on profit margin, and posturing of competitors—could be another source of factors. The organization's internal challenges can provide yet another useful source. These can include internal activities that require attention or are currently unacceptable.

As an IS auditor, you should remain aware that critical success factors are highly dependent on timing. Each CSF should be reexamined on a regular basis to determine whether it is still applicable or has changed.

Using the Scenario Approach

The *scenario approach* is driven by a series of "what if" questions. This technique challenges the planning assumptions by creating scenarios that combine events, trends, operational relationships, and environmental factors. A series of scenarios are created and discussed by the steering committee. The most likely scenario is selected for a planning exercise.

The major benefit of this approach is the discovery of assumptions that are no longer relevant. Rules based on old assumptions and past situations may no longer apply. The scenario approach also provides an opportunity to uncover the mindset of key decision-makers.

The role of the scenario is to identify the most important business objectives and CSFs. After some discussion, the scenario should reveal valuable information to be used in long-term plans. Remember, the goal is to align computer software with the strategic objectives of the organization, which we will look at next.

Aligning Software to Business Needs

As a CISA, you should understand the alignment of computer software to business needs. Information systems provide benefits by alignment and by impact. *Alignment* is the support of ongoing business operations. Changes created in the work methods and cost structure are referred to as *impact*.

Each organizational project will undergo a justification planning exercise. Management will need to determine whether the project will generate a measurable return on investment. The purpose of this exercise is to ensure that the time, money, and resources are well spent. The basic business justification entails the following five items:

Establish the Need   Business needs can be determined from internal and external sources. Internal needs can be developed by the steering committee and by interviewing division managers. Internal performance metrics are an excellent source of information. External sources include regulations, business contracts, and competitors.

Identify the Work Effort   The next step is to identify the people who can provide the desired results. Management's needs are explained to the different levels of personnel who perform the work. The end-to-end work process is diagrammed in a flowchart. Critical success factors are identified in the process flow. A project plan is created that estimates the scope of the work. This may use traditional project management techniques in combination with the System Development Life Cycle.

Summarize the Impact   The anticipated business impact can be presented by using quantitative and qualitative methods. It is more effective to convert qualitative statements into semiquantitative measurements. Semiquantitative measurements can be converted into a range scale of increased revenue by implementing the system or by cost savings. The CISA candidate should recall the discussion in risk analysis regarding the use of semiquantitative measurement with a range scale similar to A, B, C, D, and F school report card grades.

Conduct Initial Feasibility Analysis   The project may have been selected based on information gathered from operational challenges identified in status reports or complaints. Initial feasibility analysis may be conducted by reviewing financial numbers from the profit-and-loss statement compared to the estimated cost of the project. The second half of feasibility analysis is done to ensure that we have the right resources to implement the proposed system. Feasibility is usually a combination of strategy, time, available products, people, and the anticipated profit.

Present the Benefits   Management will need to be sold on the value of the system. The benefits will typically entail promises of eliminating an existing problem, improving competitive position, reducing turnaround time, or improving customer relations.

In this chapter, we are focusing our discussions on computer software. The steering committee should be involved in decisions concerning software priorities and necessary functions. Each software objective should be tied to a specific business goal. The combined input will help facilitate a *buy* versus *build* decision about computer software. Should the organization buy commercial software or have a custom program written? Let's consider the questions to ask in regard to making this decision. The list presented here is for illustration purposes; however, it is similar to the standard line of questions an auditor will ask:

- What are the specific business objectives to be attained by the software? Does a printed report exist?

- Is there a defined list of objectives?

- What are the quantitative and qualitative measurements to prove that the software actually fulfills the stated objectives?

- What internal controls will be necessary in the software?

- Is commercial software available to perform the desired function?

- What level of customization would be required?

- What mechanisms will be used to ensure the accuracy, confidentiality, timely processing, and proper authorization for transactions?

- What is the time frame for implementation?

- Should building the software be considered because of a high level of customization needed or the lack of available software?

- Are the resources available to build custom software?

- How will funding be obtained to pay for the proposed cost?

The steering committee should be prepared to answer each of these questions and use the information to select the best available option. Effective committees will participate in brainstorming workshops with representation from their respective functional areas. The goal is to solicit enough information to reach an intelligent decision. The final decision may be to buy software, build software, or create a hybrid of both.

The process normally begins with a telephone call asking questions. Initial information is gathered to help compile a written request to solicit offers from vendors. The process of inviting offers incorporates a statement of the current situation with a request for proposal (RFP). The term *RFP* is also related to an invitation to tender (ITT) or request for information (RFI).

RFI/RFP Process

The steering committee charters a project team to perform the administrative tasks necessary to compile a request for information or request for proposal.

Request for information (RFI) is used when the client wants input to see what is available and does not want to give vendors the expectation of any commitment to purchase.

Request for proposal (RFP) indicates that the buyer intends to purchase something from a vendor. Eligible vendors can expect an opportunity to make a sale.

The request is sent to a number of prospective vendors or posted to the public, depending on the client's administrative operating procedure. An internal software development staff may provide their own proposal in accordance with the RFP or participate on the review team. A typical RFP will contain at least the following elements:

- Cover letter explaining the specific interest and instructions for responding to the RFP

- Overview of the objectives and timeline for the review process

- Background information about the organization

- Detailed list of requirements, including the organization's desired service level

- Questions to the vendor about their organization, expertise of specific individuals documented in a *skills matrix*, support services, implementation services, training, and current clients

- Request of a cost estimate for the proposed configuration with details about the initial cost and all ongoing costs

- Request for a schedule of demonstrations and visit to the installation site of existing customers

 All government agencies and many commercial organizations require separation of duties during the bid review process. A professional purchasing manager will become the vendor's contact point to prevent the vendor from having any direct contact with the buyer. The intention is to eliminate any claims of bias or inappropriate influence over the final decision to purchase.

The RFP project team works with the steering committee to formulate a fair and objective review process. The organization may consult ISO 9001:2008 and ISO 9126-2:2003 standards for guidance. The proposed software could be evaluated by using the CMM. In addition, ISACA's Control Objectives for Information and Related Technology (COBIT) provides valuable information to be considered when reviewing a vendor and their products.

As an IS auditor, you should remember that your goal is to be thorough, fair, and objective. Care should be given to ensure that the requirements and review do not grant favor toward a particular vendor. The reviews are actually a form of audit and should include the services of an internal or external IS auditor. It is essential that vendor claims are investigated to ensure that the software will fulfill the desired business objectives.

Reviewing Vendor Proposals

The systematic process of reviewing vendor proposals is a project unto itself. Each proposal has to be scrutinized to ensure compliance requirements identified in the original RFP documents provided to the vendor. You need to ask the following questions:

- Does the proposed system meet the organization's defined business requirements?

- Does the proposed system provide an advantage that our competitors will not have, or does the proposed system provide a commodity function similar to that of our competitors?

- What is the estimated implementation cost measured in total time and total resources?

- How can the proposed benefits be financially calculated? The cost of the system and the revenue it generates should be noticeable in the organization's financial statement. To calculate return on investment, the total cost of the system including manpower is divided by the cost savings (or revenue generated) and identified as a line item in the profit and loss statement.

- What enhancements are required to meet the organization's objectives? Will major modifications be required?

- What is the level of support available from the vendor? Support includes implementation assistance, training, software update, system upgrade, emergency support, and maintenance support.

- Has a risk analysis been performed with consideration of the ability of the organization and/or vendor to achieve the intended goal?

- Can the vendor provide evidence of financial stability?

- Will the organization be able to obtain rights to the program source code if the vendor goes out of business? *Software escrow* refers to placing original software programs and design documentation into the trust of a third party (similar to financial escrow). The original software is expected to remain in confidential storage. If the vendor ceases operation, the client may obtain full rights to the software and receive it from the escrow agent. A small number of vendors may agree to escrow the source code, whereas most would regard the original programs as an intellectual asset that can be resold to another vendor.

Modern software licenses provide only for the right to benefit from the software's use, not software ownership. Escrow does not protect the user from the more common problem of software being discontinued by the vendor.

One of the major problems in reviewing a vendor is the inability to get a firm commitment in writing for all issues that have been raised. There are major vendors that will respond to the RFP with a lowball offer that undercuts the minimum requirements. Their motive is to win by low bid and then overcharge the customer with expensive change orders to bring the implementation up to the customer's stated objective. This makes it necessary to review each bid element line by line to identify what is actually included and what is not.

 A CISA reviews the documentation of business needs and those of the proposed system. The objective is to ensure that the system is properly aligned to business requirements and contains the necessary internal controls.

Change Management

The accepted method of controlling changes to the RFP or application software is to use a change control board (CCB). Members of the change control board include IT managers, quality control, user liaisons from the business units, and internal auditors. A vice president, director, or senior manager presides as the chairperson. The purpose of the board is to review all change requests before determining whether authorization should be granted. This fulfills the desired separation of duties. Change control review must include input from business users. Every request should be weighed to determine business need, required scope, level of risk, and preparations necessary to prevent failure.

You can refer to the client organization's policies concerning change control. You should be able to determine whether separation of duties is properly enforced. Every meeting should include a complete tracking of current activities and the minutes of the meetings. Approval should be a formal process. The ultimate goal is to prevent business interruption. This is performed by following the principles of version control, configuration management, and testing. We discuss separation of duties with additional detail in Chapter 6, "IT Service Delivery."

Management of the Software Project

Let's move on to a discussion of the challenges in managing a software development project. In this section, you'll learn about the two main viewpoints for managing software development. You'll then take a closer look at the role of traditional project management in software development.

Choosing an Approach

There are two opposing viewpoints on managing software development: evolutionary and revolutionary.

The traditional viewpoint promotes *evolutionary development*. The evolutionary view is that the effort for writing software code and creating prototypes is only a small portion of software development. The most significant work effort occurs during the planning and design phase. The evolutionary approach works on the premise that the number one source of failures is a result of errors in planning and design. Evolutionary software may be released in *incremental stages* beginning with a selected module used in the architecture of the first release. Subsequent modules will be added to expand features and improve functionality. The program is not finished until all the increments are completed and assembled. The evolutionary development approach is designed to be integrated into traditional software life cycle management.

 Real World Scenario

An Example of Evolutionary Development

The creation of this Study Guide began with the evolution of study objectives. A prototype outline was created. The outline was refined and later divided into chapters. Each chapter was written as a separate increment. Our technical editor and developmental editor provided independent review of every page. The results of the review were compared to the objectives. Deficiencies were identified for correction and then rechecked. Finally, the finished chapters were assembled to create a working draft. The draft was edited in two more iterations until the final edition was obtained. Each version of this Study Guide will be updated following a similar process until retirement.

The opposing view is that a revolution is required for software development. The invention of advanced fourth-generation programming languages (4GL) empowers business users to develop their own software without the aid of a trained programmer. This approach is in stark contrast to the traditional view of developing specific requirements with detailed specifications before writing software. The *revolutionary development* approach is based on the premise that business users should be allowed to experiment in an effort to generate software programs for their specific needs. The end user holds all the power of success or failure under this approach. The right person might produce useful results; however, the level of risk is substantially greater. The revolutionary approach is difficult to manage because it does not fit into traditional management techniques. Lack of internal controls and failure to obtain objectives are major concerns in the revolutionary development approach.

 The analogy to revolutionary development would be to tell a person to go write their own software. A tiny number of individuals would have the competence necessary to be successful.

Using Traditional Project Management

Evolutionary software development is managed through a combination of the System Development Life Cycle (SDLC) and traditional project management. We covered the basics of project management using the Project Management Institute (PMI) methodology in Chapter 2. The SDLC methodology—which is discussed in detail in the following section—addresses the specific needs of software development, but still requires project management for the nonsoftware business management functions.

When using traditional project management, the advantages include Program Evaluation Review Technique (PERT) with a Critical Path Method (CPM). You will need to be aware of the two most common models used to illustrate a software development life cycle: the waterfall model and the spiral model.

Waterfall Model

Evolutionary software development is an iterative process of requirements, prototypes, and improvement. In the 1970s, Barry Boehm used W.W. Royce's famous waterfall diagram to illustrate the software development life cycle. A simplified version of the *waterfall model* used by ISACA is shown in Figure 5.1.

FIGURE 5.1   Simplified waterfall model (W.W. Royce)

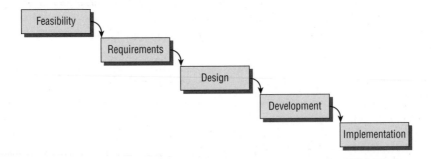

Based on the SDLC phases, this simplified model assumes that development in each phase will be completed before moving into the next phase. That assumption is not very realistic in the real world. Changes are discovered that regularly require portions of software to undergo redevelopment.

Boehm's version of the software life cycle model contained seven phases of development. Each of the original phases included validation testing with a backward loop returning to the previous phase. The backward loop provides for changes in requirements during development. Changes are cycled back to the appropriate phase and then regression-tested to ensure that the changes do not produce a negative consequence. Figure 5.2 shows Boehm's model as it appeared in 1975 from the Institute of Electrical and Electronics Engineers (IEEE).

FIGURE 5.2 Boehm's modified waterfall model

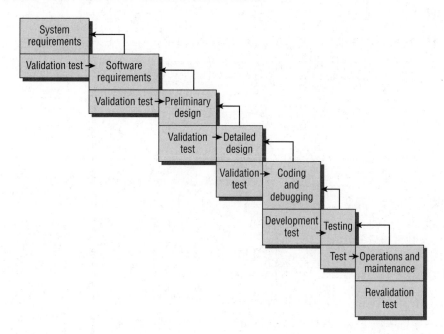

Spiral Model

About 12 years later, Boehm presented the *spiral model* to demonstrate the software life cycle including evolutionary versions of software. The original waterfall model implied management of one version of software from start to finish. This new spiral model provided a simple illustration of the life cycle that software will take in the development of subsequent versions. Each version of software will repeat the cycle of the previous version while adding enhancements. Figure 5.3 shows the cycle of software versions in the spiral model.

Notice how the first version starts in the planning quadrant of the lower left and proceeds through requirements into risk analysis and then to software development. After the software is written, we have our first version of the program. The planning cycle then commences for the second version, following the same path through requirements, risk analysis, and development. The circular process will continue for as long as the program is maintained.

Overview of the System Development Life Cycle

All computer software programs undergo a life cycle of transformation during the journey from inception to retirement. The System Development Life Cycle (SDLC) used by ISACA is designed as a general blueprint for the entire life cycle. A client organization may insert additional steps in their methodology. This international SDLC model comprises seven unique phases with a formal review between each phase (see Figure 5.4).

FIGURE 5.3   Spiral model for software life cycle

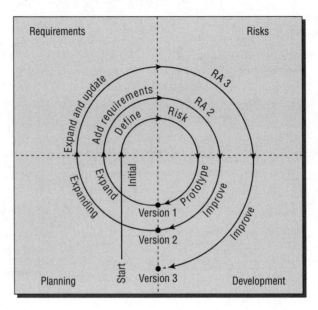

 Auditors will encounter SDLC models with only five or six phases. Upon investigation, it becomes obvious that someone took an inappropriate shortcut, skipping one of the seven phases. A smart auditor will pick up on this lack of understanding to investigate the organization further and discover any additional weakness created by this mistake. Failure to implement all seven phases indicates that a major control failure is present.

Let's start with a simple overview of SDLC:

Phase 1: Feasibility Study   This phase focuses on determining the strategic benefits that the new system would generate. Benefits can be financial or operational. A cost estimate is compared to the anticipated payback schedule. Maturity of the business process and personnel capabilities should be factored into the decision. Four primary goals in phase 1 are as follows:

- Define the objectives with supporting evidence. New policies might be created to demonstrate support for the stated objectives.

- Perform preliminary risk assessment.

- Agree on an initial budget and expected return on investment (ROI).

- Identify the market opportunity that this system is designed to exploit. This opportunity is usually based on the system being live by a particular due date before a competitor can exploit the same opportunity.

FIGURE 5.4   Seven phases of SDLC

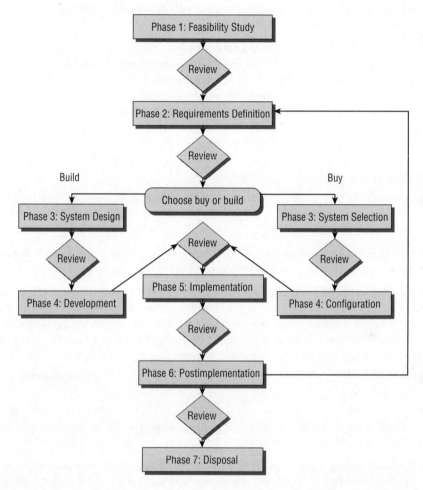

Phase 2: Requirements Definition   The steering committee creates a detailed definition of needs. We discussed this topic a few pages ago. The objective is to define inputs, outputs, current environment, and proposed interaction. The system user should participate in the discussion of requirements. In phase 2, the goals include the following:

- Collect specifications and supporting evidence.
- Identify which standards will be implemented in the specifications.
- Create a quality control plan to ensure that the design remains compliant to the specifications.
- Specify critical due dates for specific functions to be operational.

Phase 3: System Design or Selection   In phase 3, the objective is to plan a solution (strategy) by using the objectives from phase 1 and specifications from phase 2. The decision to buy available software or build custom software is based on management's determination regarding fitness of use. The client moves simultaneously in two possible directions based on whether the decision is to custom build or to just buy components.

Build (Design)   The decision that the best option is to build a custom software program is usually reached when a high degree of customization is required. Efforts focus on creating detailed specifications of internal system design. The function point analysis technique may be used to identify required inputs, external interfaces, data structures, necessary data inquiry capability, and reports. Program interfaces are identified. Database specifications are created by using entity-relationship diagrams (ERDs). Flowcharts are developed to document the business logic portion of design. The initial design is certified by an internal audit against phase 1 and 2 requirements to ensure that all the necessary functionality will be present.

Buy (Selection)   When the decision is to buy a commercial software program, the RFP process is used to select the best off-the-shelf product available based on the specification created in phase 2.

Phase 4: Development or Configuration   The client continues down one or both directions based on the earlier decision of what to build versus available products to buy:

Build (Development)   The design specifications, ERD, and flowcharts from phase 3 will become the master plan for writing the software. Programmers are busy writing the individual lines of program code. Prototypes are built for functional testing. Software undergoes *certification testing* to ensure that everything will work as intended without any surprises or material defects. Component modules of software will be written, tested, and submitted for user approval. The first stages of *user acceptance testing* occur during this phase.

Buy (Configuration)   Customization is typically limited to program configuration settings with a limited number of customized reports. The selection process for customization choices should be a formal project.

Phase 5: Implementation   This phase is common to both buy and build decisions. The new software is installed using the proposed production configuration. Everyone from the support staff to the user is trained in the new system. Final user acceptance testing begins. The system undergoes a process of final certification and management accreditation prior to approval for production use:

- Certification is a technical process of testing the finished design and the integrity of the chosen configuration.

- Accreditation represents management's formal acceptance of the complete system as implemented.

Accreditation includes the environment, personnel, support documentation, configuration, and technology. With formal management accreditation, the approved implementation may now begin production use (go live).

Phase 6: Postimplementation   After the system has been in production use, it is reviewed for its effectiveness to fulfill the original objectives. The implementation of internal controls is also reviewed. System deficiencies are identified. Goals in phase 6 include the following:

- Compare performance metrics to the original objectives.
- Analyze lessons learned.
- Re-review the specifications and requirements annually.
- Implement requests for new requirements, updates, or disposal.

The last step in phase 6 is to perform an ROI calculation comparing cost to the actual benefits received. Over time, the operating requirements will always change.

Phase 7: Disposal   The final phase is the proper disposal of equipment and purging of data. Assets must undergo a formal review process to determine when the system can be shut down for dismantling. Legal requirements may prohibit the system from being completely shut down. In phase 7, the goals include the following:

- Archive old data.
- Mark retention requirements and specify a destruction date (if any). Be aware that certain types of records may need to be retained forever.
- Management signs a formal authorization for the disposal and formally accepts any resulting liability.

If approved for disposal, the system data must be archived, remnants purged from the hardware, and equipment assets disposed of in an acceptable manner. Nobody within the organization should profit from the system disposal.

 Be careful not to confuse the SDLC with the Capability Maturity Model (CMM). A system life cycle covers the aspects of selecting requirements, designing software, installation, operation, maintenance, and disposal. The CMM focuses on metrics of maturity. CMM can be used to describe the maturity of IT governance controls.

Now that you have a general understanding of the SDLC model, we will discuss the specific methods used in each phase. These methods are designed to accomplish the stated SDLC objectives.

Phase 1: Feasibility Study

The *Feasibility Study phase* begins with the initial concept of engineering. In this phase, an attempt is made to determine a clearly defined need and the strategic benefits of the proposed system. A business case is developed based on initial estimates of time, cost, and resources. To be successful, the feasibility study will combine traditional project management with software development cost estimates.

Let's start with the business side of feasibility. The following points should be discussed and debated, and the outcome agreed upon with appropriate documentation:

- Perception of need. Describe the present situation while defining a specific need to be met.

- Link the need to a specific mission objective within the long-term strategy.

- State the desired outcome.

- Identify specific indicators of success and indicators of failure. The best indicators are specific points of functionality along with a due date that this system is expected to exploit a market opportunity before a competitor can do the same.

- Perform a preliminary risk assessment. The outcome should include a statement of the security classification necessary if the decision is to proceed. Will it be common knowledge, or will it involve business secrets, classified data, or the need for other special handling?

- Conduct an analysis of alternatives (AoA). Determine formal and informal criteria in support of the decision for whichever option is selected as the best choice. Document all the answers.

- Prepare a preliminary budget for investment review. Traditional techniques need to be combined with an expert estimation of software development costs.

The most common models for estimating software development cost are the Constructive Cost Model, which uses an estimated count of lines of program code, and function point analysis. Let's begin with the Constructive Cost Model.

Software Cost Estimation

The *Constructive Cost Model (COCOMO)* was developed by Boehm in 1981. This forecasting model provides a method for estimating the effort, schedule, and cost of developing a new software application. The original version is obsolete because of evolution changes in software development. COCOMO was replaced with COCOMO II in 1995.

The COCOMO II model provides a solid method for performing "what if" calculations that will show the effect of changes on the resources, schedule, staffing, and predicted cost. This model deals specifically with software programming activities but does not provide a definition of requirements. You must compile your requirements before you can use either COCOMO model. COCOMO II templates are available on the Internet to run in Microsoft Office Excel.

The COCOMO II model permits the use of three internal submodels for the estimations: Application Composition, Early Design, or Post Architecture. Within the three internal submodels, the estimator can base their forecast on a count of source lines of code or function point analysis.

Source lines of code (SLOC) forecasts estimates by counting the individual lines of program source code regardless of the embedded design quality. This method has been widely used for more than 40 years and is still used despite advances with 4GL programming tools. It is important for you to understand that counting lines of code will not measure efficiency. The most efficient program could have fewer lines of code, and less-efficient software could have more lines. Having a program with few lines of program code typically indicates that the finished software will run faster. Smaller programs also have the advantage of being easier to debug.

Function point analysis (FPA) is a structured method for classifying the required components of a software program. FPA was designed to overcome shortfalls in the SLOC method of counting lines in programs. The FPA method in Figure 5.5 divides all program functions into five classes:

FIGURE 5.5   Concept overview of function point analysis

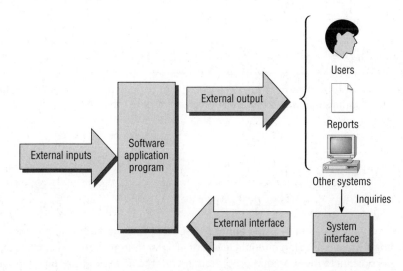

- External input data from users and other applications
- External output to users, reports, and other applications
- External inquiries from users and other applications
- Internal file structure defining where data is stored inside the database
- External interface files defining how and where data can be logically accessed

The five classes of data are assigned a complexity ranking of low, average, or high. The ranking is multiplied by a numerical factor and tallied to achieve an estimate of work required (see Figure 5.6).

FPA is designed for an experienced and well-educated person who possesses a strong understanding of functional perspectives. Typically this is a senior-level programmer. An inexperienced person will get a false estimate. This model is intended for counting features that are specified in the early design. It will not create the initial definition of requirements. Progress can be monitored against the function point estimate to assess the level of completion. Changes can be recorded to monitor scope creep. *Scope creep* refers to the constant changes and additions that can occur during the project. Scope creep may indicate a lack of focus, poor communication, lack of discipline, or an attempt to distract the user from the project team's inability to deliver to the original project requirements.

FIGURE 5.6   Calculating function points

Function Class	Complexity Ranking						
	LOW		MEDIUM		HIGH		Adjusted Weight
Counts per	Count	Multiplier	Count	Multiplier	Count	Multiplier	
External inputs	____	X 3 =____	____	X 4 =____	____	X 5 =____	
External outputs	____	X 4 =____	____	X 5 =____	____	X 6 =____	
External inquiries	____	X 3 =____	____	X 4 =____	____	X 5 =____	
Internal files	____	X 7 =____	____	X 9 =____	____	X 12 =____	
External interfaces	____	X 5 =____	____	X 7 =____	____	X 9 =____	
					Total Adjusted Value =		

  You should acquire formal training and consult a function point analysis training manual if you are ever asked to perform FPA.

Real World Scenario

Getting a Fair Estimate with SLOC and FPA

Estimation of software projects by using either the SLOC or FPA method will render an incorrect estimate if you are using multiple levels of programming languages such as 3GL and 4GL. It is important to mention that programmers refer to each programming language generation as a unique level (third generation equals third level, fourth generation equals fourth level, and so on). We discuss the different levels of programming languages later in this chapter, in the subsection "Writing Program Code." As an auditor, you should simply be aware that the issue does exist and will have a negative effect on the accuracy of an estimate. Each generation level of programming language used will have to be estimated separately to achieve reasonable accuracy.

The overall cost budget should include an analysis of the estimated personnel hours by function. The functions include clerical duties, administrative processes, analysis time, software development, equipment, testing, data conversion, training, implementation, and ongoing support.

Phase 1 Review and Approval

Best practices in software development require a review meeting at the end of each phase to determine whether the project should continue to the next phase. The review is attended by an executive chairperson, project sponsor, project manager, and the suppliers of key deliverables.

The meeting is opened by the chairperson. The project manager provides an overview of the business case and presents the initial assessment reports. Presentations are made to convey the results of risk management analysis for the project. Project plans and the initial budget are presented for approval. Meeting attendees review the phase 1 plans to ensure that the skills and resource requirements are clearly understood.

At the end of the phase review meeting, the chairperson determines whether the review has passed or failed based on the evidence presented. In the real world, a third option may exist: deciding that the project should be placed on temporary hold and reassessed at a future date. All outstanding issues must be resolved before granting approval to pass the phase review.

Formal approval is evidenced by a signed project charter accompanied by a preliminary statement of work (SOW). The project manager is responsible for preparing the project plan documentation. The sponsor grants formal authority by physically signing the documents. Without either of these documents, chances are a dispute will evolve into a conflict that compromises the project. A signed charter and SOW are frequently used to force cooperation by other departments or to prevent interruptions by politically motivated outsiders.

Auditor Interests in the Feasibility Study Phase

In the Feasibility Study phase, you should review the documentation related to the initial needs analysis. As an auditor, you review the risk mitigation strategy. You ask whether an existing system could have provided an alternative solution. The organization's business case and cost justifications are verified to determine whether their chosen solution was a reasonable decision. You also verify that the project received formal management approval before proceeding into the next phase.

Phase 2: Requirements Definition

The *Requirements Definition phase* is a documentation process focused on discovering the proposed system's business requirements. Defining the requirements requires a broader approach than the initial feasibility study. It is necessary to develop a list of specific conditions in which the system is expected to operate. Criteria need to be developed to specify the input and output requirements along with the system boundaries. Let's review the basic steps that can help define the requirements:

- Functional statement of need as described in phase 1.

- Competitive market research. Has the auditee defined what the customer wants? What does the competition offer?

- Identification of legal requirements for data security. Somebody needs to download each regulation and create a list of specific *shall* points referenced by page, paragraph, and line number. This will eliminate scope creep and quell attempts to subvert the project scope. Look at this tiny example relating to compliance under the payment card industry (PCI) laws.

PCI Compliance Mapping Report

Item	Requirement/Specification	Action
6.1	Patch management tracking	Create formal log and pretes
8.3	Implement two-factor authentication	Install digital certificates with
10.2	Develop configuration standards for all components, firewalls, wireless	Implement form configuration m
10.7	Retain audit history for at least one year	Back up and archive Syslog
11.2	Quarterly testing of system	
11.5	Implement file integrity monitoring	

- Identification of the type of reports required for legal filings, both government and customer.

- Formal selection of security controls. Ignorance of the law is a wonderful way to ensure a speedy conviction. The same concept applies to apathy.

- Software conversion study. How will the data be migrated to the new system? When will the switch to production occur?

- Cost benefit analysis to justify selection of features or functionality. It's doubtful that the first version will have all the features that everyone imagined. However, security and controls should never be compromised.

- Risk management plan. A trade-off always occurs in relation to cost, time, scope, and features. An example is to limit internal use to a physical area rather than to violate security by allowing remote access. Later versions may include the additional security controls necessary for safe remote access. The number of uses may be initially restricted. Technical risks must be managed.

- Analysis of impact with business cycles. How could the software be developed, tested, and later deployed without conflicting with the business cycle? Traditional project management plans are created to control the tasks.

In this phase of gathering detailed requirements, the entity-relationship diagram (ERD) technique is often used. The ERD helps define high-level relationships corresponding to a person, data element, or concept that the organization is interested in implementing. ERDs contain two basic components: the entity and the relationship between entities.

An *entity* can be visualized as a database comprising reports, index cards, or anything that contains the data to be used in the design. Each entity has specific attributes that relate to another entity. Figure 5.7 shows the basic design of an ERD.

FIGURE 5.7   Entity-relationship diagram

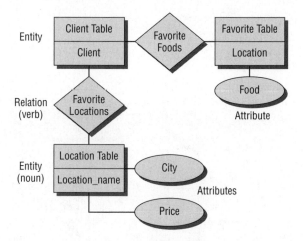

It is a common practice to focus first on defining the data that will be used in the program. This is because the data requirement is relatively stable. The purpose of the ERD exercise is to design the data dictionary. The *data dictionary* provides a standardized term of reference for each piece of data in the database. After the data dictionary is developed, it will be possible to design a database schema. The *database schema* represents an orderly structure of all data stored in the database.

After the ERD is complete, it is time to begin construction of transformation procedures used to manipulate the data. The transformation procedures detail how data will be acquired and logically transformed by the application into usable information. Transformation procedures exceed the capability of fourth-generation (4GL) programming tools. It takes old-fashioned knowledge of the business process and the aid of a skilled software engineer (programmer) to refine an idea into usable logic. Business objectives should always win over the programmer's desire to show off the latest tools, or worse, to subvert a good idea that requires more effort.

High-level flowcharts define portions of the required business logic. A low-level flowchart illustrates the details of the transformation process from beginning to end. The flowchart concept will map each program process, decision choice, and handling of the desired result. The flowchart is a true blueprint of the business logic used in the program. Figure 5.8 shows a simple program flowchart.

The ERD and flowcharts from phase 2 provide the foundation for the system design in SDLC phase 3. Security controls are added into the design requirement during phase 2. You should understand that internal controls are necessary in all software designs.

FIGURE 5.8 Program flowchart

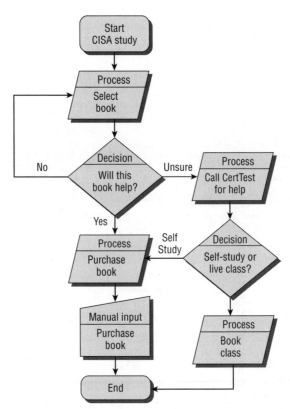

Internal Controls

The internal controls for user account management functions are included in this phase to provide for separation of duties:

Preventative controls such as data encryption and unique user logins are specified.

Detective controls for audit trails and embedded audit modules are added.

Corrective controls for data integrity are included. Features that are not listed in the requirements phase will most likely be left out of the design.

It is important that the requirements are properly verified and supported by a genuine need. Each requirement should be traced back to a source document detailing the actions necessary for performance of work or legal compliance.

A gap analysis is used to determine the difference between the current environment and the proposed system. Plans need to be created to address the deficiencies that are identified in the gap analysis. The deficiencies may include personnel, resources, equipment, or training.

Phase 2 Review and Approval

At the end of phase 2, a phase 2 review meeting is held. This meeting is similar in purpose to the previous phase 1 review. This time, the review focuses on success criteria in the definition of software deliverables and includes a timeline forecast with date commitments. Users need to submit their final feedback assessment and comments before approval is granted to proceed into phase 3. The purpose of the phase 2 review meeting is to gain the authority to proceed with preliminary software design (phase 3). Once again, all outstanding issues need to be resolved before approval can be granted to proceed to the next phase.

Auditor Interests in the Requirements Definition Phase

You should obtain a list of detailed requirements. The accuracy of the requirements can be verified by a combination of desktop review of documentation and interviews with appropriate personnel. Conceptual ERD and flowchart diagrams should be reviewed to ensure that they address the needs of the user.

The Requirements Definition phase creates an output of detailed success factors to be incorporated into the acceptance test specifications. As an auditor, you will verify that the project plans and estimated costs have received proper management approval.

Phase 3: System Design

The System Design phase expands on the ERD and initial concept flowcharts. Users of the system provided a great deal of input during phase 2, which is then used in this phase for in-depth flowcharting of the logic for the entire system. The general system blueprint is decompiled into smaller program modules.

Internal software controls are included in the design to ensure a separation of duties within the application. The work breakdown structure is created for effective allocation of resources during development. Design and resource planning may be one of the longest phases in the planning cycle. Quality is designed into a system rather than inspected after the fact.

The 1-10-100 rule provides an excellent illustration of the costs of quality-related problems. Figure 5.9 shows that for every dollar spent preventing a design flaw in planning, design, and testing, the organization can avoid the additional cost of noncompliance failures:

- $100 to correct a problem reaching the customer
- $10 to correct a problem or mistake during production
- $1 to prevent a problem

According to quality guru Philip Crosby, there are two primary components of quality—the extra expenses known as the price of nonconformance, and the savings in the price of conformance:

Price of Nonconformance (PONC)   This represents the added costs of not doing it right the first time. Think of this as the extra time and cost of rework or uncompensated warranty repair. It's not uncommon for the overall cost of the rework to exceed your original profits.

FIGURE 5.9   1-10-100 rule of quality

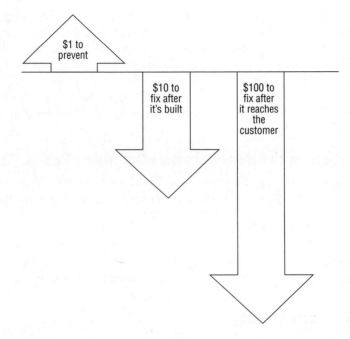

Price of Conformance (POC)   Avoiding the headache by doing it right the first time is known as the price of conformance (POC). Employee training and user training is a POC expense that conserves time and money by avoiding the added cost of nonconformance (PONC).

Quality failures will occur because of variation. Poor planning, flawed design, and poor management are the most frequent sources of failure. We can categorize quality failures as common or specific in nature:

Common Quality Failures   Common failures are the result of inherent variations inside the process, which are difficult to control. Let's consider writing the software programs for a robotic assembly line. Extreme heat affects the finish or adhesion of drying paint. New people may have been hired during production without enough training or experience. This type of common failure is inside the production process, which can affect the quality of a paint job. Management would be held responsible for fixing the problem because it was inside the process. It's management's responsibility to design a solution to prevent the problem.

Special Quality Failures   Special failures occur when something changes outside the normal process. What if the weather was fine, but the paint finish came out wrong? Upon investigation, it was discovered that the problem resulted from using the wrong type of paint or an unapproved substitution. This special failure is something that the workers should be able to fix with their purchasing agent by working with their vendor. It's more of a supply issue than a process problem. Improvements in employee discipline to follow change control for substitution would prevent the defect.

Customer Satisfaction

The best way to create loyal customers is to exceed their expectations. It's important to deliver within the original scope to satisfy customer needs. Failing project managers may make the dangerous mistake of attempting to switch the deliverables by using a bait-and-switch technique referred to as *gold plating*. If you gold-plate doggy poop, it's nice and shiny, but still just fancy poop.

We discussed Deming's planning cycle in Chapter 3 as it related to audit planning. Figure 5.10 shows that the Plan-Do-Check-Act cycle also applies to software design.

FIGURE 5.10   Planning for quality during design (Plan, Do, Check, Act)

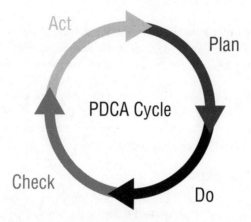

Phase 3 is the best time for the software developer to work directly with the user. Initial designs are created using visual storyboards to portray what the system may look like in production. Creating storyboards without one line of program code is proven to be the least expensive method of developing a system by eliminating costly rework of program code. This is a lesson from the movie industry: Don't bother picking up the movie camera until the entire storyboard sequence flows seamlessly from end to end. The quality of content is king. Making changes on a sheet of paper is vastly cheaper than wasted manpower. You should expect the process to be one of repeated trial and error.

Most professional programmers encourage the progression of meetings necessary to refine the design before a single line of program code is written. This series of meetings is necessary to help convert user ideas and whims into a structured set of deliverables. Never expect users to actually know what they want the first time. Uncovering the actual details of the users' desires is always a learning process. Time should be spent on creating screen layouts, designing formats, and matching the users' desired workflow. Initial plans for developing a prototype in phase 4 are created during this System Design phase.

A significant output during the design phase is to identify how each of the software functions can be tested. Data derived during design provides the base criteria for behavior testing and inspection during phase 4 development testing. Data from user meetings provides a solid basis for user acceptance testing. The documentation created during the design phase initially serves as the road map for programmers during development. Later the phase 3 design documentation will provide a foundation for support manuals and training.

Reverse Engineering and Reengineering

In certain situations, *reverse engineering* may be used to accelerate the creation of a working system design.

 The movie *Paycheck* (2003) starring Ben Affleck was themed around reverse engineering a competitor's product to jumpstart product development for Affleck's employer.

Reverse engineering is a touchy subject. A software decompiler will convert programs from machine language to a human-readable format. The majority of software license agreements prohibit the decompiling of software in an effort to protect the vendor's intellectual design secrets.

An existing system may loop back into phase 3 for the purpose of *reengineering*. The intention would be to update the software by reusing as many of the components as is feasible. Depending on the situation, reengineering may support major changes to upgrade the software for newer requirements.

Software Design Baseline

At the end of the System Design phase, the design documentation is compiled to create a *software baseline*. This baseline incorporates all the agreed-upon features that will be implemented in the initial version of software (or next version in the case of reengineering). The baseline is used to gain approval for a design freeze. A design freeze is intended to lock out any additional changes that could lead to scope creep. Changes will inevitably be proposed that could be incorporated as revisions after the system goes live.

Phase 3 Review and Approval

The phase 3 review meeting starts with a review of the detailed design for the proposed system. Engineering plans and project management plans are reviewed. Cost estimates are compared to the assumptions made in the business case. A comparison is made between the intended features and final design. Final system specifications, user interface, operational support plan, and test and verification plans are checked for completeness. Data from the risk analysis undergoes a review based on evidence. Approval is requested to proceed to the next phase. Once again, all outstanding issues must be resolved before proceeding to the next phase. Each of the stakeholders and sponsors should physically sign a formal approval of the design before allowing it to proceed into development. This administrative control enforces accountability for the final outcome.

Auditor Interests in the System Design Phase

You need to review the software baseline and design flowcharts. The design integrity of each data transaction should be verified. During the design review, you verify that processing and output controls are incorporated into the system. Input from the system's intended power users may provide insight into the effectiveness of the design.

It is important that the needs of the power users are implemented during the design phase. This may include special functions, screen layout, and report layout. You should have a particular interest in the logging of system transactions for traceability to a particular user. You look for evidence that a quality control process is in use during the software design activities. It is important to verify that formal management approval was granted to proceed to the next phase.

WARNING   A smart auditor is wary of systems being allowed to proceed into development without formal approval. The purpose of IT governance is to enforce accountability and responsibility. Even the smallest, most insignificant system represents an investment of time, resources, and capital. None of these should be wasted, squandered, or misused.

Phase 4: Development

Now the time has come to start writing actual software in the *Development phase*. This process is commonly referred to as *coding* a program. Design planning from previous phases serves as the blueprint for software coding. Systems analysts support programmers with ideas and observations. The bulk of the coding work is the responsibility of the programmer who is tasked with writing software code.

Implementing Programming Standards and Quality Control

Standards and quality control are extremely important during the Development phase. A talented programmer can resolve minor discrepancies in the naming conventions, data dictionary, and program logic. Computer software programs will become highly convoluted unless the programmer imposes a well-organized structure during code writing. Unstructured software coding is referred to as *spaghetti bowl programming*, making reference to a disorganized tangle of instructions.

The preferred method of organizing software is to implement a top-down structure. *Top-down structured programming* divides the software design into distinct modules. If top-down program structures were diagrammed, the result would look like an inverted tree. Within the tree, individual program modules (or subroutines) perform a unique function. Modules are logically chained together to form the finished software program. The modular design exponentially improves maintainability of the finished program. Individual modules can be updated and replaced with relative ease. By comparison, an unstructured spaghetti bowl program would be a nightmare to modify. Modular design also permits the delegation of modules to different teams of programmers. Each module can be individually tested prior to final assembly of the finished program.

Adhering to the Development Schedule

The software project needs to be managed to ensure adherence to the planned schedule. Scope creep with unforeseen changes can have a devastating impact on any project. It is common practice to allow up to a 10 percent variance in project cost and time estimates. In government projects, the variance is only 8 percent.

The development project will be required to undergo *management oversight review* if major changes occur in assumptions, requirements, or methodology. Management oversight review would also be warranted if the total program benefits or cost are anticipated to deviate by more than 8 percent for government or 10 percent in industry. The project schedule needs to be tightly managed to be successful. The change control process should be implemented to ensure that necessary changes are properly incorporated into the software development phase.

A *version control* system is required to track progress with all of the minor changes that naturally occur daily during development.

Writing Program Code

The effort to write program code depends on the programming language and development tool selected. Examples of languages include Common Business-Oriented Language (COBOL), C language (C++/C#), Java, the Beginner's All-purpose Symbolic Instruction Code (BASIC), Visual Basic, and Microsoft .NET. The choice of programming languages is often predetermined by the organization. If the last 20 years' worth of software was developed using COBOL, it might make sense to continue using COBOL.

Understanding Generations of Programming Languages

Computer programming languages have evolved dramatically over the past 50 years. The early programming languages were cryptic and cumbersome to write. This is where the term *software coding* originated. Each generation of software became easier for a human being to use. Let's walk through a quick overview of the five generations of computer programming languages:

First-Generation Programming Language   The first-generation computer programming language is machine language. *Machine language* is written as hardware instructions that are easily read by a computer but illegible to most human beings. First-generation programming is very time-consuming but was useful enough to give the computer industry a starting point. The first generation is also known as 1GL. In the early 1950s, 1GL programming was the standard.

Second-Generation Programming Language   The second generation of computer programming is known as *assembly language*, or 2GL. Programming in assembly language can be tedious but is a dramatic improvement over 1GL programming. In the late 1950s, 2GL programming was the standard. Assembly language is still in use today.

Third-Generation Programming Language   During the 1960s, the third generation (3GL) of programming languages began to make an impact. The third generation uses English-like statements as commands within the program, for example, if-then and goto. Examples of third-generation program languages include COBOL, Fortran, BASIC, and Visual Basic. Another example is the C programming language written by Ken Thompson and Dennis Ritchie. Most 3GL programs were used with database functions written separately.

Fourth-Generation Programming Language   During the late 1970s, the fourth-generation programming languages (4GL) began to emerge. These include prewritten database utilities. This advancement allowed for rapid development because of an embedded database or database interface. The fourth-generation design is a true revolution in computer programming. The programmer creates a template of the software desired by selecting program actions within the development tool. This is referred to as *pseudocoding* or *bytecoding*. This development tool will convert bytecode into actual program code. An untrained user could write a program that merely formats reports on a screen and allows a software-generation utility to write the software automatically. Figure 5.11 illustrates the general concept of pseudocoding inside a 4GL development tool.

FIGURE 5.11   Pseudocoding inside a 4GL development tool

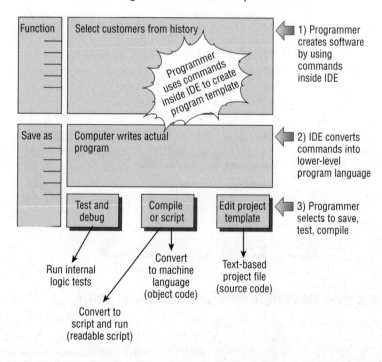

A 4GL is designed to automate reports and the storage of data in a database. Unfortunately, it will not create the necessary business logic without the aid of a skilled programmer. An amateur using a 4GL can generate nice-looking form screens and databases. But the amateur's program will be no more than a series of buckets holding data files. The skilled programmer will be required to write transformation procedures (program logic) that turn those buckets of data into useful information. Examples of commercial 4GL development tools include Sybase's PowerBuilder, computer-aided software engineering (CASE) tools, and YesSoftware's CodeCharge Studio. 4GL is the current standard for software development.

Fifth-Generation Programming Language   The fifth-generation programming languages (5GLs) are designed for artificial-intelligence applications. The 5GL is characterized as a learning system that uses fuzzy logic or neural weighing algorithms to render a decision based on likelihood. Google searches on the Internet use a similar design to assess the relevance of search results.

Figure 5.12 shows the hierarchy of the different generations of programming languages.

FIGURE 5.12   Generation levels of programming languages

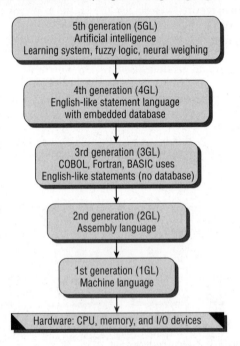

Using Integrated Development Environment Tools

After the programming language has been selected, the next step is to choose the development tool. There are still some programmers able to sit down and write code manually by using the knowledge contained in their head. This type of old-school approach usually creates very efficient programs with the smallest number of program lines.

The majority of programmers use an advanced fourth-generation software code program to write the actual program instructions. This advanced software enables the programmer to focus on drawing higher-level logic while the computer program creates the lower-level set of instructions similar to what a manual programmer would have done. Simply put, a computer program writes the computer program.

The better development tools provide an integrated environment of design, code creation, and debugging. This type of development tool is referred to as an *integrated development environment (IDE)*.

One of the best examples of an IDE is the commercial CASE tool software. You need to understand the basic principles behind CASE tools. CASE tools are divided into three functional categories that support the SDLC phases of 2, 3, and 4, respectively:

Upper CASE Tools   Business and application requirements can be documented by using upper CASE tools. This provides support for the SDLC phase 2 requirements definition. Upper CASE tools permit the creation of ERD relationships and logical flowcharts.

Middle CASE Tools   The middle CASE tools support detailed design from the SDLC phase 3. These tools aid the programmer in designing data objects, logical process flows, database structure, and screen and report layouts.

Lower CASE Tools   The lower CASE tools are software code generators that use information from upper and middle CASE to write the actual program code in phase 4.

You can see the relationship of CASE tools to the SDLC phases in the following diagram.

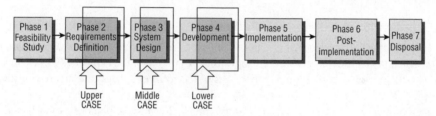

Using Alternative Development Techniques

As a CISA, you should be aware of two alternative software development methods: Agile and Rapid Application Development (RAD). Each offers the opportunity to accelerate software creation during the Development phase. The client may want to use either of these methods in place of more-traditional development. Both offer distinct advantages for particular situations. Both also contain drawbacks that should be considered.

Agile Development Method

Agile uses a fourth-generation development environment to quickly develop prototypes within a specific time window. The Agile method uses time-box management techniques to force individual iterations of a prototype within a very short time span. Agile allows the programmer to just start writing a program without spending much time on preplanning documentation. The drawback of Agile is that it does not promote management of the requirements baseline. Agile does not enforce preplanning. Some programmers prefer Agile simply because they do not want to be involved in tedious planning exercises.

When properly combined with traditional planning techniques, Agile development can accelerate software creation. Executives like the constant pressure to hit a deadline style of Agile management because it forces programmers to deliver visible improvements each day or week. Agile is designed exclusively for use by small teams of talented programmers. Larger groups of programmers can be broken into smaller teams dedicated to individual program modules.

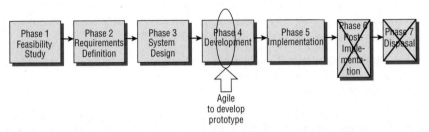

The primary concept in Agile programming is to place greater reliance on the undocumented knowledge contained in a person's head. This is in direct opposition to capturing knowledge through project documentation.

Rapid Application Development Method

A newer integrated software development methodology is *Rapid Application Development (RAD)*, which uses a fourth-generation programming language. RAD has been in existence for almost 20 years. It automates major portions of the software programmer's responsibilities within the SDLC.

RAD supports the analysis portion of SDLC phase 2, phase 3, phase 4, and phase 5. Unfortunately, RAD does not support aspects of phase 1 or phase 2 that are necessary for the needs of a major enterprise business application. RAD is a powerful development tool when coupled with traditional project management in the SDLC.

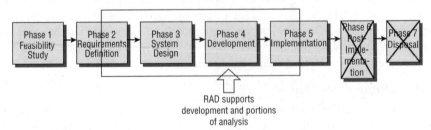

Building Prototypes

During the Development phase, it is customary to create system prototypes. A *prototype* is a small-scale working system used to test assumptions. These assumptions may be about user requirements, program design, or the internal logic used in critical functions. Prototypes usually are inexpensive to build and are created over a few days or weeks. The principal advantage of a prototype is that it permits change to occur before the major development effort begins.

Prototypes seldom have any internal control mechanisms. Each prototype is created as an iterative process, and the lessons learned are used for the next version. A successful prototype will fulfill its mission objective and validate the program logic. All development efforts will focus on the production version of the program after the prototype has proven successful.

WARNING   There is always a serious concern that a working prototype may be rushed into production before it is ready for a production environment. Internal controls are typically absent from prototypes or insufficient for production use.

Compiling Software Programs

A computer program can be written as either a program script or a compiled program. *Program scripts* are written like movie scripts and contain instructions for the computer to follow. The programmer uses a scripting language such as Perl, JavaScript, or Visual Basic. The advantage of scripts is that they are easy to maintain. The program script is stored in human-readable form. The disadvantage is that program scripts are run by using a script interpreter. The script interpreter is slow to execute. A script interpreter compiles a temporary version of the scripted program as it is running on the computer. The scripted program is considered a crystal box, or white box, because a trained human being could read the program script and decipher the structural design of the program. Using scripts also poses a security problem because the program can be easily modified by an unauthorized person.

Compiling programs is a process of converting human-readable instructions into machine-language instructions for execution. The human-readable version of software is referred to as *source code*. A computer programmer will compile programs to increase the execution speed of the software. A simple way to remember the definition is that source code is what the compiler started with. The compiled program is unreadable to humans. This unreadable version of the program is referred to as the *object code*.

Think of object code as the output object created by the compiler. Compiling software provides rudimentary protection of the program's internal logic from inquisitive people. The disadvantage of compiled programs is that reviewing the internal structural design would be practically impossible. The compiled program is essentially a black box. Figure 5.13 shows the different creation paths for compiled programs and program scripts.

Computer programmers will usually compile multiple versions of a program during development and debug testing. Without proper management, this scenario could become a nightmare. How do you ensure that the latest copy is in use? It is the job of configuration and version management to provide a traceable history of multiple versions of computer software.

Implementing Configuration and Version Management

Managing a changing environment is a significant challenge. Constant changes make it difficult to remain organized and coordinated, no matter what you're trying to accomplish. But suppose, for example, that a company wants to release a new software product. During software development, multiple programmers may be working on different modules of the same program. For this example, let's name the program *Report Whiz*. The programming used in the individual modules for Report Whiz may have different levels of maturity to consider. For example, the screen-printing utility might be in version 1.1, while the report-writer module may be in version 6.0. By combining these two modules into Report Whiz, the result will become our finished configuration for Report Whiz version 1.0. Does it sound like this could get confusing?

FIGURE 5.13   Compiled programs versus scripts

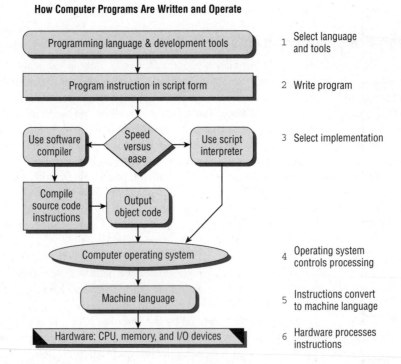

Well, it can. That is the challenge. How will the company manage and track all these different components with the correct versions?

Version control is the tracking of all the tiny details inside both major and minor version changes. By tracking these tiny details, we can understand the internal construction of our finished software configuration. Detailed version control is the foundation of configuration. With version control, we have a detailed configuration that is ready to be managed.

Configuration management is focused on management exercising control over the finished software version. The primary elements of configuration management are control, accounting, and reporting:

Configuration Control   The control of all the design documentation, design changes, all specifications, parts and assemblies, and manufacturing processes. Specifications include the informal notes, observations, and advice written on the documentation.

Configuration Accounting   Timely reporting of any modifications to the originally agreed-upon design documentation that occurs after the initial design release review. It's possible for engineering to design a product that the organization is unable to build. Configuration accounting tracks the compromises and modifications necessary to produce a working product.

Configuration Reporting   This encompasses all the elements of control and accounting, going further to report the configuration as built and delivered to the customer, including any change or maintenance to the product after delivery. This reporting becomes the life history of the product from conception through the useful service life until disposal.

The auditor needs to investigate how the client manages and records changes to a configuration. After obtaining this understanding, you need to ask who authorizes the changes. Finally, you need to ask how the changes are tested and accepted for production use.

Fortunately, there are software tools to assist software developers in managing version control. One of the most common commercial applications for tracking version changes is known as a Polytron Version Control System (PVCS). PVCS software contains a database that manages the tracking of programming changes and revisions of software code. In industry slang, we may refer to the PVCS function as a *Top Copy* or *Latest Copy* system.

The purpose of PVCS is to ensure that each programmer is working with the latest version of the software program code. During the day, the programmer checks out the latest copy of the program code from the PVCS database. The checkout process is similar to the checkout of books from your local library. The PVCS database is designed to synchronize the work of every programmer. A programmer checks out the latest software version, which prevents others from making changes to program code. Each day the programmer returns their finished work to the PVCS-controlled library by using a check-in process. During check-in, the PVCS database informs the programmer with a list of any related changes made by the other programmers. This provides coordination for the team of programmers.

 Real World Scenario

Automated Version Control Tools

Version control software is available from multiple vendors. In addition to the commercial PVCS, other common software options include the Source Code Control System (SCCS), the Concurrent Version System (CVS), the Revision Control System (RCS), and IBM Rational ClearCase tools. There are license versions that are free for noncommercial use. Version control software was written to track revision changes in lines of programming code. The usage has grown to include tracking changes in server configuration, web pages, legal contracts, and complex printed documents.

Debugging Software

A vast assortment of errors occur naturally during the development process. These errors may include syntax errors, inconsistent naming structures, logic errors, and other common mistakes. Most online development tools will assist the programmer by debugging some of the errors. Using top-down structured programming techniques makes it easier to trouble-shoot problems.

Testing the Software

During the Development phase, it is imperative that tests and verification plans are created to debug the software programs. Tests should be performed to validate processing accuracy. Test plans are created to uncover program flaws, manage defects, and search for unintended results. A *logic path monitor* can be used to provide programmers with information about errors in program logic.

During development, software testing occurs at multiple levels. Any deficiencies or errors need to be discovered before the finished program is implemented. There are four basic types of test methods:

White-Box Testing (for Uncompiled Programs)   Also known as *crystal-box testing* because it allows the programmer to view and to test the logic of procedures and data calculations. The intention is to verify each transformation process as data passes through the system. This can be an expensive and time-consuming process. This testing is commonly used for unit and integrity testing of self-developed software. Legal obstacles concerning ownership and proprietary rights may be encountered when attempting to use this type of testing on commercial software. Script-based software is human readable and therefore can be crystal-box tested.

Black-Box Testing (for Compiled Programs)   Intended to test the basic integrity of system processing. This is the most common type of test. The process is to put data through the system to see whether the results come out as expected. You do not get to see the internal logic structures; all you get is the output. Commercial software is compiled into a form that is nonreadable by humans. Black-box testing is the standard test process to run when you buy commercial software. Black-box testing is often used for user acceptance tests.

Functional, or Validation, Testing (for All Programs)   Compares the system against the desired functional requirements. We want to see whether the product has met our objectives for its intended use.

Regression Testing   Tests changes against all the existing software models to detect any conflicts. The purpose of regression testing is to ensure that modifications do not damage existing processes. During regression testing, internal controls are retested for integrity.

All tests should follow a formal procedure in a separate testing environment. Separate testing environment is required for compliance with ISO 9001 and ISO 27002 section 10.1.4. The following types of structured technical tests occur during the Development phase:

- Program module tests (unit test)
- Program interface tests (integration test)

- Internal security control tests

- External security penetration tests (pen-testing)

- Processing volume tests (stress test of maximum workload)

- Performance tests

- Integrity tests (processing accuracy)

- Recovery tests (to verify data integrity after failures)

- Sociability tests (to determine whether the program will have conflicts with another program on the system)

- Preliminary user acceptance testing (to approve the system functionality as delivered)

The test plan and results of each test need to be carefully documented. In environments where strong controls are desired, archiving test records for future reference is necessary. After all the technical tests have been completed to satisfaction, it is time for the most important test of all. The last test in the Development phase is user acceptance testing. This is when the project sponsor determines whether to accept the system. If accepted, the system moves into the Implementation phase.

 Software certification testing in phase 4 development measures the coded software against phase 2 specifications, phase 3 design, effective implementation of internal controls, and fitness of use for production.

Phase 4 Review and Approval

Once again, a phase review meeting is held. The phase 4 review focuses on the software being delivered by the programmers for the users. The Development phase has now concluded. The finished software is compared for compliance against the original objectives, requirements list, and design specifications. Evidence is presented from test results, which should indicate that the software is performing as expected. Plans for ongoing operation are compared to the previous gap analysis to uncover any remaining deficiencies. After all outstanding issues have been resolved, the plan is put before the chairperson for approval to proceed to the Implementation phase.

Auditor Interests in the Development Phase

As an auditor, your prime interest in the Development phase is to verify that a quality control process has been utilized to develop an effective computer program. All internal control mechanisms should be present in the finished program. The programs have undergone debugging with formal testing. Evidence from test results is expected to provide assurance of system integrity. Support documentation has been created in conjunction with an operational support plan for production use. The finished software capabilities have been verified for compliance to the original objectives. The user has accepted the finished computer program. And finally, management has granted formal approval for the software to be implemented.

Phase 5: Implementation

The computer program is fully functional by the time it reaches phase 5. This phase focuses on final preparations for actual production use. Version control is a formal requirement to ensure that the right version of software is running for production.

Software Release and Patch Management

Computer software is authorized for distribution via a release process. Software is released from development and authorized to be installed for production use. Each vendor has their own release schedule.

Computer software releases fit one of the following profiles:

Major Release   A significant change in the design or generation of software is known as a *major release*. Major releases tend to occur in the interval of 12 to 24 months.

Minor Release or Update   *Updates* are also known as *minor releases*. Their purpose is to correct small problems after the major release has been issued.

Emergency Software Fixes   These are known as *program patches*, or *hot fixes*. Emergency fixes should be tested prior to implementation. Every fix should undergo a pretest, even if the test is informal. Emergency software fixes may introduce new problems that are unexpected. Every emergency fix must undergo change control review to determine the following:

- What to remediate
- Whether the change should remain in use

The computer program is now a finished version ready for final acceptance testing and user training. The next step for implementation is to load the client's current data.

Data Conversion

A data conversion plan is developed to migrate existing data into the new system. Great care needs be taken to prevent loading garbage data into the new system. A successful technique to prevent loading garbage is to reload selected portions of shared data directly from the latest source file. An example is reloading a manufacturing kit list directly from the latest engineering design. This would eliminate the migration of outdated information into the new system.

A list of data files eligible for migration is developed. Each file is verified against the system design requirements. If the file is required, procedures would be created to scrub (remove) outdated entries from each file. It is a common practice to hire a data entry service to assist in data conversion. Sometimes it is easier to re-create a file with minimal data, as opposed to the tedious job of grooming existing files. The programmers may write a data conversion utility to reformat existing files, such as a customer list, into the new system. A comprehensive data conversion plan is always required.

System Certification for Production Use

Certification is a technical process of testing against a known reference. The system is tested to ensure that all internal controls are present and functioning correctly. The system certification is based on measuring compliance to a particular requirement. Systems used in the government are required to undergo a certification process before being placed in production use.

Common Criteria (ISO 15408)

The original U.S. computer controls (Trusted Computer System Evaluation Criteria, or TCSEC) have been merged with developments from the European IT security countries (Information Technology Security Evaluation Criteria, or ITSEC) to form an international common criteria for evaluating computer security. This common criteria has been adopted by ISO as Common Criteria standard 15408. CC is the nickname for the complete set of common criteria. Several countries have adopted the CC, including Canada, France, Germany, the Netherlands, the United Kingdom, and the United States. All the ISO member countries are expected to use 15408.

The CC brings the benefits of accumulated wisdom with a flexible approach to standardization and evaluation assurance. Flexibility is provided in this specification of secure products by using seven standardized evaluation assurance levels (EALs). Official testing is provided by an independent lab certified under the ISO 17025 standard for laboratories and testing facilities.

Within the CC is a well-defined set of IT security requirements for prospective products and systems. Here's how it works:

A system to be evaluated is referred to as the *target of evaluation* (TOE). Each TOE has security threats, objectives, requirements, and a summary of functions to be measured. Every TOE contains security functions (TSF) to be relied on in the enforcement of the TOE's desired security policy (TSP).

The grouping of evaluation test objectives is defined as the *protection profile* (PP). A variety of protection profiles have already been created for systems used as workstations, firewalls, network servers, secure databases, and so forth. A PP is intended to be reusable and effective in defining the security requirements for the system.

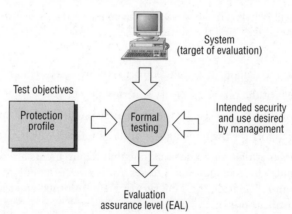

The party requesting evaluation simply picks a PP (protection desired), identifies the TOE (system to test), and pays for the tests to be performed to the appropriate EAL (assurance level 1 through 7). The goal is to make it easier for a vendor to advertise systems appropriate to the client needs. Let's take a brief overview of the elements to be tested:

TOE Security Functionality   The following is a sample list of the components used for security functionality. Each component represents a family of subcomponents required to obtain the EAL:

- Security management features
- Identification and authentication
- User data protection
- Communications with nonrepudiation
- Cryptographic support
- Audit
- Privacy
- Resource utilization
- TOE access (sessions and access parameters)
- Trusted paths/channels
- Protection of TOE security functions

Evaluation of Protection Profiles and Security Targets   All PPs and their associated security target (ST) evaluations contain the following criteria, each with underlying subcomponents of security that must be evaluated. The following list is a quick summary:

- Evaluation assurance.
- Configuration management to verify the TOE's current configuration at the time of testing. Changes would require retesting to maintain the EAL.
- Secure system delivery installation and setup measures to ensure that the system is not compromised during these events.
- Assurance maintenance.
- PP evaluation to demonstrate that requirements are consistent and technically sound.
- Development of the target's security functionality (TSF).
- Guidance documents for use by the users and system administrators.
- Life cycle support for the remediation of flaws found by TOE users.
- Security target evaluation to demonstrate that requirements are consistent and technically sound. This includes the TOE description, security environment, security objectives, and PP claims, the TOE security requirements, and the TOE summary security specification.
- Formal vulnerability assessment to identify vulnerabilities through covert channel analysis, configuration analysis, and examination of the strength of security mechanisms with the identification of flaws introduced during the development of the TOE.
- Tests demonstrating the coverage and depth of developer testing with requirements for independent testing.

Internal control standards require business systems to undergo a certification process. It may be an internal review or a formal review such as the Common Criteria. Every computer system and application should undergo a certification process prior to use in a production environment.

You can find more information on system certification procedures in the U.S. Federal Information Security Management Act (FISMA) guide available through http://csrc.nist.gov and in the ISACA COBIT. Also visit www.commoncriteriaportal.org for information on system certification under the ISO 15408 Common Criteria. System certification is required by most regulations.

As a CISA, you will be required to undergo update and renewal training to keep your certification current. Existing information systems should also go through a recertification process to remain up-to-date. You should be concerned about systems that the customer has not certified for production, or systems for which the certification was not maintained and is now out-of-date.

System Accreditation

The next step after certification for production use is *accreditation*. After passing the production certification test, management determines how or where the system may be used. Accreditation is an administrative process based on management's comfort level with demonstrated performance or fitness of use (management acceptance). Management is responsible for accreditation of systems during the system's useful life cycle. The designated accreditation authority is a senior executive who will accept full responsibility for the consequences of operating the overall system (often the CIO or agency head). Accreditation is by site, type of use, or system.

Accreditation may be in the form of approval to operate in limited use for 90–180 days or (full) annual accreditation. The approved implementation may begin production use. Systems must be recertified and reaccredited annually.

The purpose of system accreditation is to hold a management executive responsible for the system's fitness of use. Every system in production must have accreditation from an executive who can be held responsible for its continued operation, maintenance and annual funding. Lack of current accreditation is scored as a governance failure.

User Training

Now it is time to train the users and system operators. Hopefully, the organization had some of its power users actively involved in prior phases. The new system's power users were usually involved in the phase 2 design. If so, these power users can serve as instructors and mentors to the new system users. A user training plan is necessary to ensure that everyone receives appropriate training for their role. During the training process, each user should receive specific instructions on the new functions of the system. Care should be taken to explain which of the old procedures will no longer be used. The training plan needs to provide for ongoing training of new users.

Special training is required for the system custodians (system administrator, database administrator, and computer console operator). The custodians need to be trained for normal operations and emergency procedures unique to the system. After the people are trained, it is time to move the system into production use.

Go Live and Changeover

The new system has been running separately from production up to this point. A plan is necessary for switching production processing from the old system to the new system. This process is commonly described by the term *changeover*, *cut over*, or *go live*. The changeover can be a substantial challenge depending on the complexity of the environment. A comprehensive migration plan is required in order to be successful. It is imperative that risk management is used to select and sequence changeover plans.

You need to be aware of the following changeover techniques:

Parallel Operation   The old and new systems are run in parallel, usually for an extended period of time. Dual operation allows time to compare the operational differences between the two systems. During parallel operation, software developers can fine-tune any software discrepancies. The primary advantage of parallel operation is the ability to validate the results obtained from the new system against the accuracy of the old system. With parallel operation comes the added burden of simultaneously supporting two major systems. At a future date, the old system will be brought to an idle state while the new system takes over all production processing. Depending on data retention requirements, the field system may still need to be operational for a number of years. The switch from parallel operation to single operation may be performed by using a phase changeover or hard changeover.

 Overall, parallel operation is an excellent technique with the lowest level of risk. Making changes in small doses is always advisable. Major failures during changeover can be a real career killer.

Phased Changeover   In larger systems, converting to the new system in small steps or phases may be possible. This may take an extended period of time. The concept is best suited to either an upgrade of an existing system, or to the conversion of one department at a time. The phased approach creates a support burden similar to that of parallel operation. A well-managed phased changeover presents a moderate level of risk.

Hard Changeover   In certain environments, executing an abrupt change to the new system may be necessary. This is known as a hard changeover, a full change occurring at a particular cutoff date and time. The purpose is to force migration of all the users at once. A hard changeover may be used after successful parallel operation or in times of emergency. One of the biggest concerns about a hard changeover is that it can cause major disruption of normal operations. For this reason, the hard changeover presents the highest level of risk. Risk mitigation activities are of the highest priority whenever the hard changeover technique is chosen.

Phase 5 Review and Approval

This is the last review meeting, and it is concerned with the implementation of a new system. The chairperson opens the meeting with the project sponsor present. The project manager makes a presentation of project updates and achievements. Progress is reported against the plan objectives. Attention then focuses on a review of outstanding engineering issues, system performance as realized in production use, and ongoing service and support plans. The final risk analysis is presented for management approval. After approval is obtained, the system is authorized for production use.

The movie *Man of the Year* (2006), starring Robin Williams with Christopher Walken and Laura Linney, is based on a fictional electronic election. During testing of a new electronic voting machine, a software flaw is discovered in the tally of votes. The development manager ignores the programmer's warning and allows the system to be used in full production. A hidden system flaw results in an unlikely candidate winning the popular vote in error. Ultimately, the truth is discovered, and the voting machine company is ruined and publicly disgraced. Proper certification testing was not performed before the system was placed into production. This fictional story bears striking resemblance to news stories about actual flaws detected in electronic voting machines.

Auditor Interests in the Implementation Phase

The system should be installed and fully operational by the Implementation phase. Support documentation must be in place prior to the system entering production use. All of the appropriate personnel will have been trained to fulfill their roles. The system has completed a final user acceptance test. A production operating schedule should now be in use. The completed system will have undergone a technical certification process. Management reviews the system's fitness of use for a particular task or environment. Management accredits the system for a specified use, based on fitness of use for a particular task or by site location.

You need to verify that appropriate quality control procedures have been executed in support of these objectives. You also need to verify that formal management approval was obtained before the system entered production use. Any deficiencies in management approval should be reported to the audit committee or project oversight.

Phase 6: Postimplementation

The sixth SDLC phase deals with project closure and the administrative process of verifying that the system meets the organizational objectives. A complete project management review is performed. Evidence is checked to verify that the system was implemented as originally designed, with all necessary internal controls present. The results of actual use are compared to the anticipated benefits originally cited in phase 1. The objective is to ensure that these benefits were actually realized by the finished system implementation. Performance measurements are reviewed. A celebration may be in order if the performance exceeded original expectations. Otherwise, a remediation plan may be created to improve current performance.

Additional phase 6 activities will include the following:

Continuous Monitoring   This is to ensure that the controls are still effective. Periodic testing and reporting are necessary.

Annual Review of New Requirements   This includes changes in legal regulations, system connections, and patterns of use. Consider the impact of HIPAA requirements mandating increased confidentiality for protecting access to data by unauthorized internal users. The PCI regulations force truncation of account numbers and mandate use of encryption. It's interesting how Amazon.com changed its software to be compliant, yet most hotels violate PCI regulations by retaining card numbers on file and improperly handling paper records by retaining the full account number plus card identification code (three-digit CID number). The associated hotel operating procedures instruct staff to continue violating PCI in spite of the enormous consequences of the law. Just because it used to be done that way does not mean it should continue to be done that way.

Application System Review   This includes investigating risks related to system availability (uptime, downtime) and to integrity issues such as incomplete or unauthorized transactions. This is a major area of interest for the auditor. Integrity and security are temporary because of the constant changes made by the IT staff and by vendor updates. Whether small or large, a change will always introduce another set of issues. This is referred to as *the law of unintended consequences.*

System Update   Will the newer version of software be installed? Changing versions of the operating system or the application may be a significant project. The updates need to undergo a full certification (recertification) and accreditation process prior to production implementation. Smart CIOs and IT managers have already implemented separate systems for testing and production. The costs were easily justified by comparing the cost of downtime against doing it right the first time.

Environment Changes   Changes in physical controls and personnel can have a major impact on overall control. Administrative policies may need to be added or refined to accommodate changes to the physical area. This could include overtaxing the generator capacity, testing aging batteries on the UPS, or other repairs that have not been performed. More training may be needed to keep the staff up-to-date. Staff rotation is just one manner in which special skills may become stale or lost.

Replacement or Migration to New Systems   It's inevitable that portions of any systems will eventually be replaced or migrated to a newer design. Postimplementation is intended to ensure that nothing important is ignored after the system has gone live. This includes changing hardware, upgrading software, and keeping up with changes in technology.

Phase 6 Review Meetings

Periodic reviews are necessary to verify that the system is maintained in a manner that supports the original objectives and controls. The review should occur at least annually or following a significant change in the business, regulatory climate, or application itself. You may need to utilize the services of a professional expert to conduct the postimplementation review.

> You need to remain aware of the conditions necessary to safely rely on using the work of others. The client will frequently request the auditor to use reports from internal staff in order to reduce audit costs. We discussed this issue in Chapter 1, "Secrets of a Successful IS Auditor," and Chapter 3, "Audit Process."

Auditor Interests in the Postimplementation Phase

As an auditor, you review evidence indicating that the system objective and requirements were achieved. You should pay attention to users' overall satisfaction with the system. You should review evidence indicating that a diligent process of support and maintenance is in use. In this phase, you review system audit logs and compare them to operational reports.

Auditors want to know whether support personnel are actively monitoring for error conditions. A process of incident response and change control should be in use. Management must demonstrate that they are aware of system limitations with regard to the changing requirements of the organization. Management needs to be cognizant of any deficiencies requiring remediation.

In addition, management and the audit committee should remain aware of any external issues that may dictate system modification or removing the application from service. Examples include changes in regulatory law governing minimum acceptable internal controls. A perfect example is the current trend for strong data encryption to be implemented to protect the privacy of individuals. Previously the concerns were focused on using encryption during external data transmission. The latest requirement is for data in databases and on backup tapes to be stored in encrypted form. The loss of unencrypted data carries harsh penalties.

Phase 7: Disposal

This is the last phase of the SDLC life cycle. After the system has been designated to be removed from service, the security manager needs to perform an audit of the system components and remaining data. The goals of this final stage are to prevent accidental loss. Objectives include the following points:

Information Preservation   All data and programs need to be archived for long-term storage.

Media Sanitation   After the standing data has been removed, the system is decommissioned with the intention of shutdown.

Hardware and Software Disposal   Policies and procedures need to exist for the assurance that every disposal is properly managed. No one should profit from the disposal of assets. It's important that the system shutdown does not violate document retention requirements.

A formal authorization from the system owner is required before initiating the disposal phase. Accounting will need to transfer the assets out of inventory. The system owner, accreditation manager, and custodian are to sign the official order moving the system from service. This is the evidence that each has performed their appropriate duties.

Auditor Interests in the Disposal Phase

Evidence should exist to document the disposal process and the records available about prior disposals. The objective is to determine whether the process was correctly followed. A quick check of the asset tags and financial records will help determine the truth. Look to see whether the disposed asset is still shown to hold value in the accounting records.

- Was the disposal formally authorized by an appropriate executive?
- Is the asset still listed as active on the accounting books?
- What are the plans to verify preservation of the old data?
- Did the auditee do a good job?

Last of all, the auditor looks for evidence that the media was properly sanitized before disposal.

Overview of Data Architecture

A chapter on software development would not be complete without a discussion of the different types of data architecture. The selection of data architecture depends on multiple influences, often including the desires and objectives of the system designer. This section focuses on the fundamentals of data architecture.

Databases

A *database* is simply an organized method for storing information. Early databases were composed of index cards. Some of you may recall using the manual card catalog at the local library to look up the location of a particular book. Later, the library's manual card catalog system was automated with a computer database. Data may be organized into a table of rows and columns similar to an Excel spreadsheet.

Databases are designed by using one of two common architectures:

DODB   A data-oriented database (DODB) contains data entries of a fixed length and format. The information entered into a data-oriented database is predictable.

OODB   An object-oriented database (OODB) does not require a fixed length, nor a fixed format. In fact, the object-oriented database was designed for data of an unpredictable nature.

You may find that some people refer to the two common database architectures as a data-oriented structured database (DOSD) and an object-oriented structured database (OOSD).

Let's start the discussion with an overview of the data-oriented database.

Data-Oriented Database

The first type of database is designed around data in a predefined format, that is, numbers or characters of a particular length. A perfect example is the typical web form or Excel spreadsheet. This DODB the simplest type of database to create.

For this example, we would like to start with a simple database for client entertainment. Say that you have a few key clients to entertain. Your firm wants to ensure that you build rapport by inviting the client to join you in their favorite activities whenever possible.

The first step is to define the data to be recorded in the database. In the SDLC model, this would be part of phase 2, the Requirements Definition phase. Follow along by using Figure 5.14 as we explain the key points.

Let's start by defining a database table of rows and columns to hold the clients' contact information. The first table is named `client_table`. This will hold the name, address, phone number, and email address of every client.

Next, build a table for each location where you may take the client to be entertained. This is called `locations_table`. We have added a space to record the average price for this location and a space to record the specialty of the house.

FIGURE 5.14 Example of client entertainment database

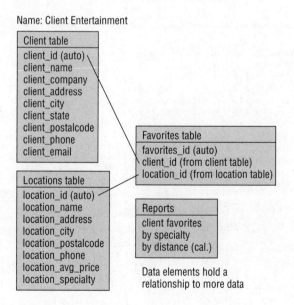

A third table is created to keep track of all of the favorites: `favorites_table` could be used to record favorite food, a game such as billiards, sporting events, and so forth. One of the objectives in the DODB is to divide information into multiple tables that are relatively static. This allows the system to perform a basic search very fast and not have to process all the data at once. The standardization and removal of duplicates is referred to as *database normalization*.

Now you have your tables ready to store information. The next step is to link tables together with a referential link, or relation. This is where the term *relational* enters into the description of the database: an item of data in one table relates to data contained in a separate table. Every entry in the database must have at least one required item to show that the entry actually exists. For example, an account number or a person's name would be required for each entry in the database, even if you don't have all the information. This single required entry is referred to as the *primary key*. Data items used to link to tables are referred to as *foreign keys*. The idea is that other data is foreign to the first table. Data that you can search is called a *candidate key* to the search. The purpose of using the term *key* is to illustrate that it would be impossible to unlock the information unless we know what to use as the key.

To be usable, a database must also have *referential integrity*. This means that data is valid across the linked entries (keys) in two tables. Take a look at Figure 5.15, and you will notice the reference lines drawn between client ID and location ID. This diagram is a primitive ERD.

Another way to view the database is to consider a box of index cards. Each entry is the equivalent of a separate index card. The box of index cards is referred to as the table. A table is made up of rows and columns, like an Excel spreadsheet. Computer programmers may use the term *tuple* in place of the word *row*. Figure 5.16 shows the database rows, or tuples, as they would appear on index cards.

FIGURE 5.15 Example database showing data relationships

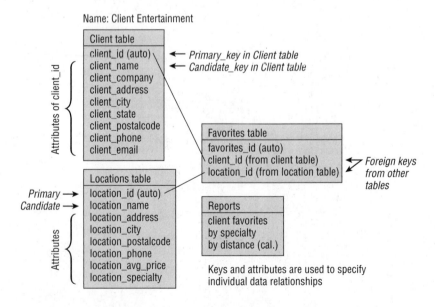

FIGURE 5.16   Database rows, also known as tuples

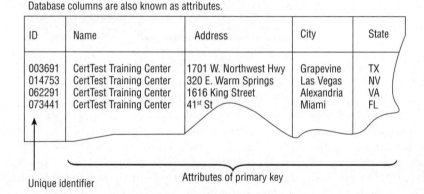

Tuples are the same as rows in a database.

Client: Kelli Jaimson   Address: 3232 Golden Avenue
Client: Jetty Nubonzski   Address: 1244 Main Street
Client: Jessica Landry   Address: 99 Park Place, 11th Floor
Client: James Moore   Address: 35 Lakeside Plaza, Suite 1750

The actual database displays its contents as rows and columns. It is also common to hear the term *attribute* as a synonym for a database column. Figure 5.17 shows the columns, or attributes, as they would appear on the computer screen.

FIGURE 5.17   Database columns, also known as attributes

Database columns are also known as attributes.

ID	Name	Address	City	State
003691	CertTest Training Center	1701 W. Northwest Hwy	Grapevine	TX
014753	CertTest Training Center	320 E. Warm Springs	Las Vegas	NV
062291	CertTest Training Center	1616 King Street	Alexandria	VA
073441	CertTest Training Center	41st St	Miami	FL

Unique identifier

Attributes of primary key

In the illustration, you can see that the ID number is used as a unique identifier (primary key) for each entry. Using a unique ID number allows duplicate names to appear within the database. This is valuable if you have the same company listed with multiple shipping addresses. The unique ID number also permits a name to be updated without any headaches. A common example is to change a maiden name to a married name, or vice versa as the case may be.

In summary, the DODB is designed to be used when the structure and format of your data is well known and predictable. What about data whose structure and format is unpredictable? What about a database that stores documents, graphics, and music files simultaneously? Well, that is the very challenge that led programmers to develop the object-oriented database.

Object-Oriented Database

In a data-oriented database, the program procedures and data are separate. An object-oriented database (OODB) is the opposite. In an OODB, the data and program method are combined into an object. Think of programmed objects as tiny little people or animals with their own way of doing things. Each programmed object has its own data for reference and its own method of accomplishing a required task. Figure 5.18 shows the basic internal design of program objects.

FIGURE 5.18   Concept overview of program objects

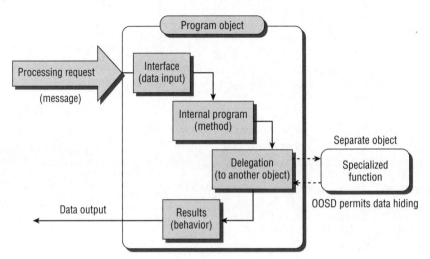

The number one advantage of using programmed objects is that you can delegate work to another object without having to know the specific procedure or characteristics in advance. An example is the computer display settings in the Windows operating system. Microsoft Windows 7 and Office are examples of object-oriented programs. When Microsoft Word was written, for example, the program did not need to know the details of the display screen. The Word program would simply delegate screen output to an object specified by the screen display setting. A configuration file would exist that contains the setting SET DISPLAY=*vendors_ device_driver.* The hardware manufacturer for the display would write an object or driver to paint the image on the screen. The whole object-oriented design lends a great deal of flexibility for modular change.

Object-oriented programming is extremely powerful, and the functional design can be confusing to a novice. Objects are grouped together in an *object class.* An object class is quite similar to a particular class of economy automobiles or class of luxury automobiles, for example. The reference to class indicates the object's position in the hierarchy of the universe. Figure 5.19 shows an example of object classes.

Database Transaction Integrity

Transaction management refers to the computer program's capability to deal with any failure in the logical data update operations used for a particular transaction. Integrity could be damaged if an incomplete transaction was permanently recorded into the database. This is commonly referred to as the ACID model for database integrity. *ACID* stands for atomicity, consistency, isolation, and durability:

- Atomicity refers to the transaction being "all or nothing." On the failure of a transaction, the change is backed out of the database, and the data is restored to its original state of consistency.

- Consistency is required to ensure integrity of the data. Integrity refers to the contents of the database accurately reflecting the truth without error.

- Isolation means that each transaction operates independently of all others. A transaction must finish before another transaction can modify the same data.

- After a transaction is completed, the data must remain. This is referred to as durability.

FIGURE 5.19   Example of object classes

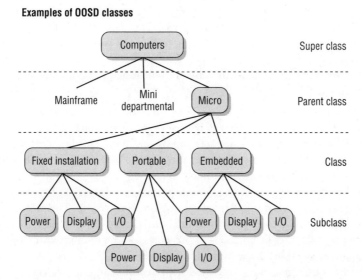

This capability is based on a transaction log used with a *before-image* journal and *after-image* journal. The journals act as a temporary record of work in progress. A version of the database entry before the update is recorded is the before-image. Changes made are held in the after-image. The transaction can be reversed (undone) until the transaction is actually committed (written) to the master file. Once committed, the transaction is then deleted from the journals. A real-world example can be found in the redo and back-out capabilities of the MySQL-Max database. Many databases use a *transaction processing monitor (TP monitor)* to ensure that database activity does not overload the processing capacity of the available hardware.

Decision Support Systems

Advancements in computer programming technology and databases have led to the creation of decision support systems. A *decision support system (DSS)* is a database that can render timely information to aid the user in making a decision. There are three basic types of decision support systems:

Reference by Context   This type of primitive decision support system supplies the user with answers based on an estimated level of relevance. The overall value is low to moderate.

Colleague, or Associate, Level   The colleague level provides support for the more tedious calculations but leaves the real decisions to the user.

Expert Level   It has been reported in graduate studies that the mind of an average expert contains more than 50,000 points of data. By comparison, a colleague or associate might possess only 10,000 points of data. The expert system is usually written by capturing specialized data from a person who has been performing the desired work for 20 or 30 years. This type of information would take a human a significant amount of time to acquire. It is also possible that the events are so far apart that it would be difficult to obtain proficiency without the aid of a computer.

Every decision support system is built on a database. The data in the database is retrieved for use by the program rules, also known as heuristics, to sort through the knowledge base using deductive reasoning techniques in search of possible answers. This is often referred to as the inference engine. The heuristic program rules may be based on a fuzzy logic using estimation, means, and averages to calculate a likely outcome. The programmers refer to the process as *fuzzification* (zoom out) and *defuzzification* (zoom in) depending on whether we are sharpening the average with a stratified mean or derating the average. The meaning of information in the knowledge base can be recorded into a linkage of objects and symbols known as semantic networks. Another technique is to use weight averages in program logic designed to simulate the path of synapses in the human brain.

Let's look at the common terminology used with decision support systems:

Data Mining   After the database and rules are created, the next step in the operation of a decision support system is to drill down through the data for correlations that may represent answers. The drilling for correlations is referred to as *data mining*. To be successful, it would be necessary to mine data from multiple areas of the organization.

Data Warehouse   It is the job of the *data warehouse* to accomplish the feat of combining data from different systems. Data is captured from multiple databases by using image snapshots triggered by a timer. The timer may be set to capture data daily, weekly, or monthly depending on the needs of the system architect.

Data Mart   The *data mart* is a repository of the results from data mining the warehouse. You can consider a data mart the equivalent of a convenience store. All of the most common requests are ready for the user to grab. A decision support system retrieves prepackaged results of data mining and displays them for the user in a presentation program, typically a graphical user interface (GUI).

Figure 5.20 shows the basic hierarchy of the databases loading the data warehouse, which is mined to create a data mart.

FIGURE 5.20   Overview of data warehouse and data mart in DSS

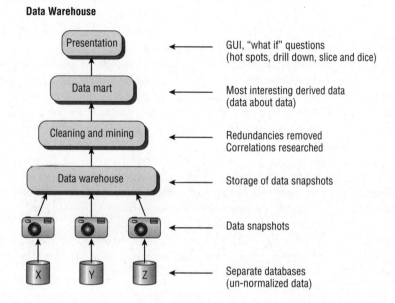

Presenting Decision Support Data

The information presented from the data mart could indicate correlations of significance for the system user. Senior executives may find this information extremely useful in detecting upcoming trends or areas of concern throughout the organization. Keep in mind, the primary purpose of the decision support system is to give the senior-level manager timely information that will aid in making effective decisions.

The next step up from decision support systems is artificial intelligence.

Using Artificial Intelligence

Artificial intelligence (AI) is the subject of many technology dreams and some horror movies. The concept is that the computer has evolved to the level of being able to render its own decisions. Depending on your point of view, this may be good or bad. Artificial intelligence is useful for machines in a hostile environment. The Mars planetary rover requires a degree of artificial intelligence to ensure that it could respond to a hazard without waiting for a human to issue instructions.

Now that the database has been developed, the next concern is to ensure that the transactions are processed correctly. Let's move along into a discussion of program architecture.

Program Architecture

Computer programs may be written with an open architecture or proprietary, also known as closed, design. The software architect makes this decision.

The *open system architecture* is founded on well-known standards and definitions. The primary advantage of open architecture is flexibility. Computer software can be updated and modified by using components from multiple sources. Fortunately, the design promotes the ability to use best-of-breed programs. The disadvantages include having a potential hodgepodge of unstructured programs. For a client, the open system architecture reduces dependence on a particular vendor.

A *closed system architecture* contains methods and proprietary programming that remain the property of the software creator. Most of the program logic is hidden from view or stored in encrypted format to prevent the user from deciphering internal mechanisms. Most commercial software products are a closed, proprietary system with industry standardized program interfaces for data sharing with other programs—in essence, closed architecture with open architecture interfaces. The advantage is that the user can still share data between programs. Another advantage is that the vendor can lock in the customer to their product. The disadvantage is that the customer may be locked in to the vendor's product.

Centralization versus Decentralization

Every organization will face the challenge of determining whether to use a centralized database or a distributed database application. The centralized database is easier to manage than a distributed system. However, the distributed system offers more flexibility and redundancy. The additional flexibility and redundancy of a distributed system carries higher implementation and support costs.

Centralized systems are easier to manage. Centralized systems facilitate mandatory access controls (MAC) by eliminating local decisions on who or what can access the data. Decentralized systems increase the number of support decisions, which increases the likelihood of a security failure.

The decision of centralization versus decentralization would have been addressed by the steering committee and requirements gathered in the SDLC Requirements Definition phase (phase 1). Let's consider the requirements for electronic commerce.

Electronic Commerce

Electronic commerce, also known worldwide as *e-commerce*, is the conducting of business and financial transactions electronically across the globe. This concept introduces the challenges of maintaining confidentiality, integrity, and availability for every second of the entire year. An additional challenge is to ensure regulatory compliance for each type of transaction that may occur over the e-commerce system.

Let's look at a few example transactions:

Business-to-Business (B-to-B, or B2B)   Regular transactions between a business and its vendors. This could include purchasing, accounts payable, payroll, and outsourcing services. This type of transaction is governed by business contracts in accordance with federal law.

Business-to-Government (B-to-G, or B2G)   The online filing of legal documents and reports. In addition, this includes purchasing and vendor management for the products and services used by the government. This type of transaction is governed by a variety of government regulations. An example is the U.S. Central Contractor Registration system (CCR). Vendors doing business with the U.S. government are required to maintain their company profiles in the CCR database.

Business-to-Consumer (B-to-C, or B2C)   Direct sales of products and services to a consumer. B-to-C also includes providing customer support and product information to the consumer. The payment transaction in this type of environment may be governed by banking, privacy, and credit authorization laws. Business-to-consumer applications require additional logging because the normal paper trail does not exist. The auditor will be interested in how the transactions are monitored and reviewed. Authorizations for processing online payments will require special security measures.

Business-to-Employee (B-to-E, or B2E)   The online administration of employee services, including payroll and job benefits. This type of transaction is governed by federal employment regulations and privacy regulations.

Figure 5.21 shows the common e-commerce avenues in use today. Each of these should be the subject of an IS audit.

FIGURE 5.21   E-commerce programs

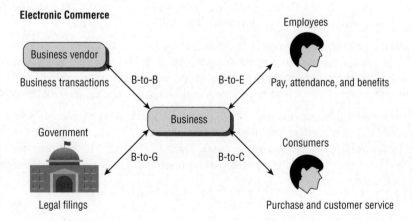

E-commerce poses a number of challenges to security. Because of the level of risk, security should weigh heavily in any considerations of reducing protection for convenience. Strong internal controls are mandatory for e-commerce systems.

 We discuss data security in Chapter 7, "Information Asset Protection."

Summary

This chapter covered IT governance in the System Development Life Cycle. The primary objective of this governance is to ensure that systems are developed via a methodical process that aligns business requirements to business objectives. In this chapter, we touched on standards used in the development of computer software. This chapter also included an introduction to the design of databases, program architecture, and e-commerce.

Throughout the entire System Development Life Cycle are a series of processes to ensure control and promote quality. It is the IS auditor's job to determine whether the organization has fulfilled its duties of leadership and control. The purpose of this chapter is to provide you with a basic understanding of the concepts and terminology used in software development.

Exam Essentials

Evaluate the business case for new systems.   You need to evaluate the requirements for a new system to ensure that it will meet the organization's business goals. You should understand how critical success factors are developed and risks are identified.

Evaluate risk management and project management practices.   You need to review the evidence of the organization's project management practices and risk mitigation practices. The objective is to determine whether the solution was cost-effective and achieved the stated business objectives. A formal selection process should be in use and clearly documented.

Conduct regular performance reviews.   Each project should undergo a regular performance review to verify that it is conforming to planned expectations. The review process should be supported by formal documentation and accurate status reporting. Management oversight review should be in use when plans deviate, assumptions change, or the scope of the project substantially changes.

Understand the practices used to gather and verify requirements.   The organization may use a steering committee with the assistance of various managers to identify critical success factors. Scenario exercises can be used to assist in developing requirements for planning.

Additional requirements may be obtained from the business internal operation, specific business market, customer commitments, and other sources of information.

Know the system development methodology being used.   You need to review the thoroughness and maturity of processes by which all systems (including infrastructure) are developed or acquired.

Know the system development tools, including their strengths and weaknesses.   You need to understand the advantages and disadvantages of traditional programming, Agile, and RAD methodologies. You are expected to understand that 4GL programming languages do not build the necessary business logic without the involvement of a skilled programmer. You are expected to have a basic understanding of the differences between data-oriented programming and object-oriented programming.

Understand quality control and the development of a test plan.   A quality control process should be in use throughout the entire project and system life cycle. Formal testing should occur in accordance with a structured test plan designed to verify software logic, defects, transaction integrity, efficiency, controls, and validation against requirements.

Be familiar with the internal control mechanisms in place and working.   All systems are required to have functioning internal control mechanisms. You need to evaluate the effectiveness of the selected safeguards. Evidence should exist that each control was planned during the system specification phase and that the controls were implemented during development and tested for effectiveness.

Understand the difference between certification and accreditation.   Every system should undergo acceptance testing, followed by formal technical certification testing for production use. After completing technical certification, the system should be reviewed by management for accreditation based on fitness of use. Systems should be recertified on a regular basis to ensure that they meet new demands of evolving requirements.

Be familiar with ongoing maintenance and support plans in use.   You need to evaluate the process of ongoing support and maintenance plans. The intention is to ensure that the plans fulfill the organizational objectives. You verify that the internal control process is in use for authorizing and implementing changes. System changes should undergo a regression test to ensure that no negative effects were created as a result of the change.

Know how to conduct postimplementation reviews.   Every system should undergo a postimplementation review. The purpose is to compare actual deliverables against the original objectives, and to compare performance to the project plan. Regular reviews should occur throughout the system's usable life cycle, preferably on an annual basis.

Know the various programming terms and concepts.   You need to have a working knowledge of the terminology and concepts used in the development of computer software.

Review Questions

1. The advantages of using 4GL software applications include which of the following?
   A. Automatically generates the application screens and business logic
   B. Includes artificial intelligence using fuzzy logic
   C. Reduces application planning time and coding effort
   D. Reduces development effort for primitive functions but does not provide business logic

2. The best definition of database normalization is to
   A. Increase system performance by creating duplicate copies of the most accessed data, allowing faster caching
   B. Increase the amount (capacity) of valuable data
   C. Minimize duplication of data and reduce the size of data tables
   D. Minimize response time through faster processing of information

3. Which of the following statements is true concerning the inference engine used in expert systems?
   A. Makes decisions using heuristics
   B. Contains nodes linked via an arc
   C. Used when a knowledge base is unavailable
   D. Records objects in a climactic network

4. An IT steering committee would most likely perform which of the following functions?
   A. Explain to the users how IT is steering the business objectives
   B. Issue directives for regulatory compliance and provide authorization for ongoing IT audits
   C. Facilitate cooperation between the users and IT to ensure that business objectives are met
   D. Ensure that the business is aligned to fulfill the IT objectives

5. The Software Engineering Institute's Capability Maturity Model (CMM) would best relate to which of the following?
   A. Measurement of resources necessary to ensure a reduction in coding defects
   B. Documentation of accomplishments achieved during program development
   C. Relationship of application performance to the user's stated requirement
   D. Baseline of the current progress or regression

6. Which of the following best describes a data mart?
   A. Contains raw data to be processed
   B. Used in place of a data warehouse
   C. Contains data collected from snapshots
   D. Stores results from data mining

7. Object-oriented databases (OODBs) are designed for data that is _____.

    A. Predictable

    B. Consistent in structure

    C. Variable

    D. Fixed-length

8. What does the term *referential integrity* mean?

    A. Transactions are recorded in before-images and after-images.

    B. It's a valid link between a data entry contained in two tables.

    C. It's a completed tuple in the database.

    D. Candidate keys are used to perform a search.

9. Which of the following statements best explains a program object in object-oriented programming?

    A. It contains methods and data.

    B. Methods are stored separately from data.

    C. It contains 100 percent of all methods necessary for every task.

    D. It does not provide methods.

10. What is the primary objective of postimplementation review?

    A. Recognition for forcing an installation to be successful

    B. Authorize vendor's final payment from escrow

    C. Conduct remedial actions

    D. Determine that its organizational objectives have been fulfilled

11. Which of the following statements is true concerning regression testing?

    A. Used to observe internal program logic

    B. Verifies that a change did not create a new problem

    C. Provides testing of black-box functions

    D. Compares test results against a knowledge base

12. Which of the following migration methods provides the lowest risk to the organization?

    A. Phased

    B. Hard

    C. Parallel

    D. Date specified

13. What are the advantages of the integrated development environment (IDE)?

    A. Simplifies programming and helps debug program code

    B. Eliminates the majority of processes in SDLC phase 2

    C. Prevents design errors in SDLC phase 3

    D. Eliminates the testing requirement in SDLC phase 4

14. What is the difference between certification and accreditation?

    A. Certification is a management process, and accreditation is a technical process.

    B. No difference; both include technical testing.

    C. Certification is a technical test, and accreditation is management's view of fitness for use.

    D. Certification is about fitness of use, and accreditation is a technical testing process.

15. Which of the following development methodologies is based on knowledge in someone's head, as opposed to traditional documentation of requirements?

    A. System Development Life Cycle (SDLC)

    B. Program Evaluation Review Technique (PERT)

    C. Rapid Application Development (RAD)

    D. Agile

16. What is the IS auditor's primary purpose in regard to life cycle management?

    A. To verify that evidence supports the organizational objective and that each decision is properly authorized by management

    B. To verify that all business contracts are properly signed and executed by management

    C. To verify that internal controls are tested prior to implementation by a third-party review laboratory

    D. To verify that a sufficient budget was allocated to pay for software development within the allotted time period

17. Which of the following design techniques will document internal logic functions used for data transformation?

    A. Entity-relationship diagram

    B. Flowchart

    C. Database schema

    D. Function point analysis

18. Which of the following principles includes the concept of all or nothing?

    A. Transaction processing monitor

    B. Atomicity, consistency, isolation, and durability

    C. Runtime processing

    D. Referential integrity

19. Software development uses several types of testing to ensure proper functionality. Which of the following types of testing is used to test functionality on commercially compiled software?

    A. White-box

    B. Code review

    C. Black-box

    D. Crystal-box

20. Programming software modules by using a time-box style of management is also referred to as the _____ method. The purpose is to force rapid iterations of software prototypes by small teams of talented programmers.

   A. Agile

   B. Lower CASE

   C. Rapid Application Development (RAD)

   D. Fourth-generation (4GL)

21. What is the real issue regarding software escrow?

   A. The vendor must use a subcontractor for safe storage of the original development software.

   B. The software contains intellectual value that is conveyed to the client.

   C. The client is entitled to the benefit of only using the software and not owning it, unless they pay more money. Escrow may provide some protection if the vendor goes out of business, but does not prevent software from being discontinued.

   D. Commercial software is kept in escrow in case the vendor sells the rights to another vendor.

22. Which of the following is the best method of reviewing the logic used in software written in program script?

   A. Black-box test

   B. Regression test

   C. Crystal-box test

   D. User acceptance test

23. Which of the software development methods includes planning activities in phase 1 of the SDLC model?

   A. Agile

   B. Rapid Application Development (RAD)

   C. Upper CASE tools

   D. Project management

24. What is the primary purpose of the reviews at the end of each phase in the SDLC?

   A. Approval for the funding to continue development

   B. Approval by management to proceed to the next phase or possibly kill the project

   C. Approval of the final design

   D. Provide the auditor with information about management's decision for regulatory compliance

25. What should be the basis for management's decision to buy available software or to build a custom software application?

   A. Cost savings by switching to a recognized best-in-class application used by others in the industry

   B. Converting from existing internal custom processes to the method new software operates in order to save money by avoiding the cost of customization

   C. Competitive advantage of using the same software as everyone else

   D. Data from the feasibility study and business specifications

Answers to Review Questions

1. D. The 4GL provides screen-authoring and report-writing utilities that automate database access. The 4GL tools do not create the business logic necessary for data transformation.

2. C. Database normalization minimizes duplication of data through standardization of the database table layout. Increased speed is obtained by reducing the size of individual tables to allow a faster search.

3. A. The inference engine uses rules, also known as heuristics, to sort through the knowledge base in search of possible answers. The meaning of information in the knowledge base can be recorded in objects and symbols known as semantic networks.

4. C. The IT steering committee provides open communication of business objectives for IT to support. The steering committee builds awareness and facilitates user cooperation. Focus is placed on fulfillment of the business objectives.

5. D. The Capability Maturity Model creates a baseline reference to chart current progress or regression. It provides a guideline for developing the maturity of systems and management procedures.

6. D. Data mining uses rules to drill down through the data in the data warehouse for correlations. The results of data mining are stored in the data mart. The DSS presentation program may display data from the data mart in a graphical format.

7. C. Data-oriented databases (DODBs) are designed for predictable data that has a consistent structure and a known or fixed length. Object-oriented databases (OODBs) are designed for data that has a variety of possible data formats.

8. B. Referential integrity means a valid link exists between data in different tables. When you follow the link from one table for `first_name`, that links corresponding data we expect to find in the next table, such as *Samantha*, rather than *1109 Milan Ave*. Any error indicates a lack of integrity.

9. A. Objects contain both methods and data to perform a desired task. The object can delegate to another object.

10. D. Postimplementation review collects evidence to determine whether the organizational objectives have been fulfilled. The review would include verification that internal controls are present and in use.

11. B. The purpose of regression testing is to ensure that a change does not create a new problem with other functions in the program. After a change is made, all of the validation tests are run from beginning to end to discover any conflicts or failures. Regression testing is part of the quality control process.

12. C. Parallel migration increases support requirements but lowers the overall risk. The old and new systems are run in parallel to verify integrity while building user familiarity with the new system.

13. A. The integrated development environment automates program code generation and provides online debugging for certain types of errors. It does not replace the traditional planning process. IDE does not alter the testing requirements in SDLC phase 4. Full testing must still occur.

14. C. Certification is a technical testing process. Accreditation is a management process of granting approval based on fitness of use.

15. D. The Agile method places greater reliance on the undocumented knowledge contained in a person's head. Agile is the direct opposite of capturing knowledge through project documentation.

16. A. Evidence must support the stated objectives of the organization. Software that is built or purchased should be carefully researched to ensure that it fulfills the organization's objectives. Each phase of the life cycle should be reviewed and approved by management before progressing to the next phase.

17. B. A flowchart is used to document internal program logic. An entity-relationship diagram (ERD) is used to help define the database schema. Function point analysis is used for estimation of work during the feasibility study.

18. B. The ACID principle of database transaction refers to atomicity (all or nothing), consistency, isolation (transactions operate independently), and durability (data is maintained).

19. C. Compiled software is unreadable by humans. Black-box testing is used to run a sample transaction through the system. The original input is then compared to verify that the output is correct and that it represents what the customer wanted from the system.

20. A. Agile uses time-box management for rapid iterations of software prototypes by small teams of talented programmers. Agile does not force preplanning of requirements and relies on undocumented knowledge contained in someone's head, without complete documentation.

21. C. The client is entitled to the benefit of only using the software, not the right of ownership. Software escrow may be requested by the client to gain full rights to the software if the vendor goes out of business. This would damage the vendor's right to resell intellectual property rights to another vendor. Clients may gain ownership rights to software by paying the vendor for the total cost of development, not just the right to use it. Clients usually decline to pay development costs and will accept the risk of using someone else's software. For example, what would Microsoft charge for the full rights of ownership for Windows Vista? No client would pay it; it's cheaper to accept the risk.

22. C. Crystal-box, also known as white-box testing, is used to review the logic in software written using programming script. The script is still readable by humans until the script is compiled. Compiled programs would be tested using a black-box method.

23. D. Traditional project management is the only methodology that covers all seven phases of the SDLC. Agile is for phase 4 development. Rapid Application Development (RAD) and CASE tools apply only to portions of phase 2 requirements, phase 3 design, and phase 4 development. Everything else requires good old-fashioned project management.

24. B. The review at the end of every SDLC phase is intended to prevent the project from proceeding unless it receives management's approval. The project can be approved, forced to fix existing problems, or killed. In each review, the decision is whether all specifications and objectives are being met or whether the project should be cancelled.

25. D. All the decisions regarding purchasing existing software or building a custom application should be made by using data from the feasibility study and business specifications. More customization or the desire for competitive advantage indicate the need to build a custom application. Using the same software as your competitor may kill your organization profits by putting you into a commodity pricing war. The loss of unique value-added services will damage the business advantage of being different.

Additional CISA practice questions are available on the author's website at www.CertTest.com.

Chapter 6

System Implementation and Operations

THE OBJECTIVE OF THIS CHAPTER IS TO ACQUAINT THE READER WITH THE FOLLOWING CONCEPTS:

- ✓ Knowledge of service-level management practices including operations workload, scheduling, services management, and preventative maintenance

- ✓ Knowledge of the Information Technology Infrastructure Library

- ✓ Knowledge of control functionality in the IT infrastructure

- ✓ Administrative management controls used to protect assets

- ✓ Using data classification schemes to specify appropriate handling of records

- ✓ Physical security protection methods

- ✓ Understanding specific personnel roles and responsibilities

- ✓ Data administration for integrity and optimization of databases

- ✓ Issues facing the use of mobile code, Java, and ActiveX

- ✓ IT performance monitoring using analyzers, system utilization, and log management

- ✓ Understanding of change control management, configuration release management, and emergency changes

- ✓ Knowledge of techniques for problem reporting and incident management

- ✓ Storage, retrieval, transport, and disposition of confidential information

- ✓ Understanding digital forensic techniques

In this chapter, you will focus on the management of information technology (IT) operations designed to support the organization. You will learn about the recommended practices for monitoring service levels and controlling change in the organization. We revisit implementation of administrative, physical, and logical controls specific to daily operations. The best practices of incident management and problem resolution are also discussed.

ISACA expects every IS auditor to understand how to evaluate the techniques and best practices used in IT support.

Understanding the Nature of IT Services

Every time information technology is mentioned, the conversation turns toward operations. IT suffers from the same perceived fate as facilities management, the plumber, or the electrician. People in each of these fields feel that their contribution is invaluable. Yet the truth is that few possess a mastery of the intricate knowledge of how each business unit operates. This common drawback is the principal reason why IT outsourcing is a popular topic with users. Smart IT executives recognize that a fundamental change is necessary. The key to success is conveying how IT operations is a functional servant to its masters in the business unit.

Everyone in the organization is aware of IT operational problems. They may appear as slow response times, systems being unavailable for any reason, problems with data, and ongoing arguments between people who are trying to accomplish their jobs. So how can we improve operations? Let's start with the two most common statements:

Buy More   New product advertisements and dropping prices make it appear as though the solution is to continually buy more until you run out of room, people to implement the product, or money.

Rearrange Priorities   Many organizations continuously fight fires and rearrange the priorities rather than fix the root problem. Changing priorities is more of a workaround to circumvent the problem. The result is lots of work without any real progress.

A third choice gets us closer to the real solution. IT leadership will commit the resources necessary to document and measure the current situation. Time and effort will be expended to determine the root of the real problems. Let's investigate what needs to be accomplished to truly fix the problems:

- Policies will be added or amended.
- Standards will be adopted or modified.

- Job descriptions will be updated to reflect the actual jobs performed to ensure genuine assignment of responsibility and accountability.

- Better procedures will be created and updated.

- Change control will shift from the needs of IT toward the specific business objectives of the users in other departments.

The objective is to change the perception of IT from a bunch of blue-jeans-wearing introverts to organized professionals—sharp-looking individuals able to support the most critical aspects of the business. The vice president of information systems and chief information officer are responsible for creating a corporate culture that recognizes the valuable contributions of a diligent staff.

People strive for recognition. Nobody wants to take a thankless job, especially one that may have long hours. IT governance deals with executives recognizing their responsibility to take control. IT leadership, on the other hand, is focused on only two objectives:

Objective 1   Define IT's mission by using small, simple words, and then set out plans to accomplish it.

Objective 2   Provide the detailed directions and support necessary for your people to succeed.

 Governance refers to the right people in management considering the problem, making an educated decision on how to fix it, and then taking action by getting involved. They spend the appropriate money and time to solve the problem. Anything less is negligent.

Without good management, the nifty technical tools are useless. After leadership is in place and operating, the next step is moving to design the service delivery operation. The majority of this chapter is dedicated to operational measures. Let's begin with a quick reference check of external versus internal measures:

External Measures Are the Customer Viewpoint   Consider what the customer sees in regard to system availability, perception of the help desk, attitudes of the IT staff, response time, and backlog. All of these factors compose customer satisfaction. The user just wants technology to work by calculating something or automating a business task.

Internal Measures Are of Interest to Systems People   The good people in IT will gauge the impact of availability, disk storage capacity, service requests, and all the little technical details about how it will help or hurt their users get the job done. Some IT staff members may be overly concerned with technology itself. That could be a detrimental situation. Technology is not intended as a safe haven for hiding from the hazards of interacting with other people or becoming involved in the challenges and worries of running a business. Internal measures worthy of IT's interest are the details that help or hurt the user in the performance of business duties.

Auditors must remain unbiased and friendly with a helpful attitude. Good people can be hard for employers to find. The auditor should always take care to be respectful and supportive, but does not have to agree with the client or auditee. Without question, the auditor should never make any sarcastic or diminutive comments to anyone because the result may be deemed an unforgivable insult.

Performing IT Operations Management

IT provides a service to business users. Technology is so pervasive that no organization can exist without computers and telephones. IT service represents a commitment to manage technology as efficiently and effectively as possible within the organization. As business needs change, IT services should adapt accordingly. This constant adaptation can be a significant challenge. There's always the possibility of a gap occurring between the IT services delivered and user expectations.

Meeting IT Functional Objectives

In previous chapters, we discussed the requirement for IT services to be aligned with business objectives. Many of the topics we discussed are practically transparent to business users. IT service delivery is different. In this chapter, we discuss the daily activities necessary to support information technology.

Let's begin with a basic review of the functions in IT operations:

Management of the IT Department   The IT department contains managers and staff workers focused on system availability, system integrity, and data confidentiality.

IT Asset Management   Every IT department maintains control over numerous capital assets, including data and software licenses. The organization's total investment in technology, inclusive of all departments, is usually in excess of 4.5 percent of annual gross sales. This makes IT the second-largest custodian of capital assets, following facilities.

Systems Life Cycle   All IT systems are to be maintained in a systems life cycle by using the concepts of the System Development Life Cycle (SDLC) and Capability Maturity Model (CMM).

IT Policies   Executive management and IT management are responsible for developing and issuing policies that support agreed-upon information technology objectives. Examples include a corporate acceptable use policy (AUP), antivirus protection policy, and the designation of information technology as the official custodian for corporate data.

IT Standards   Operating standards are developed by managers and approved by executive management. One such standard is the separation of duties. Other examples include the hours of system availability and system certification prior to production use.

IT Procedures   Operating procedures are developed by staff workers with the assistance of their manager. Operating procedures include the handling of software licenses and escalation procedures for user-reported trouble tickets.

IT Job Descriptions and Responsibilities   To support the operating procedures, the IT department must have job descriptions that reflect the current requirements and responsibilities for each position. Out-of-date or inaccurate job descriptions indicate that nobody is actually responsible for completing the work. It's a control failure because nobody has formal responsibility, formal authorization, or formal authority.

IT Risk Management Process   Risk management is required in all areas of an organization. The IT department is subject to a high level of inherent risk. Failures that occur in information technology have wide-reaching impact. The IT department is required to exercise risk mitigation on a daily basis. The process of change control is one technique used to help mitigate risk.

IT Service to the User   Information technology exists to support business users. The number one representation of value is IT user satisfaction. Attaining high user satisfaction results from a significant effort in back-office systems coupled with a prompt, helpful, and friendly help desk. The typical business user is interested only in how IT solves their individual problem. Customer satisfaction is earned by individual problem-by-problem solutions.

 Real World Scenario

Lights-Out Operations

Based on business requirements and risks, an organization may adopt a policy of running a *lights-out operation*. This term refers to an unmanned facility—although personnel may be in other areas of the building, the control room or data center remains unmanned. Operations are either fully automated or run by remote control. Removing personnel from the data center significantly reduces the risk of environmental contaminants (liquids, debris, food), malicious actions, and human error.

We visited one data center that had so many cables under the raised floor that the floor tiles were bulging under our feet. This was not only unsafe, but also led to communication failures as some brittle cables broke when people walked across the tiles. Fewer problems occur when the servers are physically separate from the workers (physical separation of duties). Service personnel would occupy the computer room only for maintenance.

Now let's look at a common framework of help desk operations that is not a regulation but does represent the best practices in the management of IT services.

Using the IT Infrastructure Library

The number of IT models and frameworks can be confusing. A well-managed organization will implement multiple frameworks, including COBIT for governance, CMM for maturity, SDLC for life cycle, ISO standards, and some type of standard for running the help desk. In reality, each framework or standard is designed as a specific tool for different challenges faced in the overall business. Each has its own audience, which must ultimately function as one team.

The *Information Technology Infrastructure Library (ITIL)* is a collection of management best practices to guide the help desk for delivery of information technology services. ITIL provides a comprehensive and integrated set of service management processes targeted at what it takes to run a successful help desk. The goal of ITIL is to control the delivery of services that will be high quality while remaining cost-effective. Each of the service management processes is technology neutral, scalable, and comprehensive.

ITIL's intended audience is as follows:

- IT service providers
- IT directors
- Managers
- CIOs

Adopting ITIL's guidance could provide such benefits as reduced costs, improved IT services through the use of published best practices, higher customer satisfaction from a more professional approach to service delivery, less wasted effort by following a standard, and improved management of third-party services. ITIL is designed to complement the other IT frameworks, not to replace them. The help desk is usually the front line for the user to report problems; therefore, ITIL has an interface to ISO 27002:2007 information security services. We can use ITIL as one of the triggers for incident response outside of the help desk.

Eleven popular processes are associated with ITIL core functions. These functions and associated processes are as follows:

Service Support

- Service desk, incident management, problem management
- Configuration management, change management, release management
- Interface to connect with ISO 27002 Information Security Management System (ISMS) run separately

Service Delivery

- Service-level management
- Capacity management using ISO 20000 process management
- IT service continuity management
- Availability management
- Financial management for IT services

Functional Planning and Management

- Implementation service management, infrastructure management

- Application management, software asset management

- Business perspective on delivering better IT services to the business user

Several of these points may appear to be overlapping. However, ITIL is complementary, not competing. IT needs to function as a cohesive team rather than as separate groups of people based on individual function. ITIL's framework helps everyone become involved, whether junior or senior, help desk operator or tenured administrator. Implementing this set of practices helps an organization focus their effort to deliver better customer service to people working in the business unit. Figure 6.1 shows an overview of ITIL.

FIGURE 6.1   Overview of ITIL's purpose

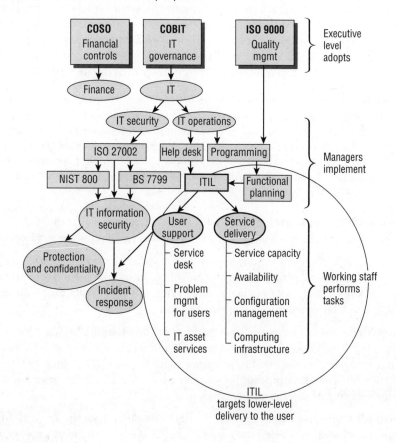

Supporting IT Goals

The goal of operations management is to sustain the business needs of the organization's daily user. Strategy is defined by executive management, technical response is created by middle management, and actual hands-on work is performed by operations managers with their support staff. The work performed should be in direct support of the higher-level business objectives.

As a CISA, you should remain observant of the difference between personnel who are *busy* and those who are *effective*. The volume of work performed is not a single measure of success. IT personnel must be focused on specific business objectives and have the necessary skills to be effective.

Understanding Personnel Roles and Responsibilities

During any dispute over control, it can be challenging to determine who is actually in charge. The client's organizational chart can render a great deal of valuable information. The chart indicates who is in charge at each level, who each person reports to, and what the basic functions are for each job. It's not uncommon to walk into an organization and find that the organization does not have a current copy of their own organizational chart.

> You should recognize that the lack of a current organizational chart is a concern. All positions must have matching job descriptions that are accurate and reflect current responsibilities. Anything more than a small discrepancy in either of these documents indicates a lack of proper internal control. We included a sample organizational chart in Chapter 1, "Secrets of a Successful Auditor."

Let's take a quick look at several of the more common IT positions that should be of interest to you. Each of these roles has a unique degree of authority and influence in IT operations:

IT Director   The IT director has the day-to-day responsibility of managing IS/IT managers and executing the executives' plan. This upper-level manager has the authority to make decisions for their group. IT operations managers receive orders directly from the IT director. The IT director role is similar to the role of a movie director.

IT Operations Managers   IT operations managers direct an IT staff working in software development, on the help desk, in server and network administration, and in information security. These managers are the first line of authority for the users. Each manager is responsible for the creation of effective procedures for their work area. IT operations managers are responsible for handling or delegating any issues that arise.

Systems Architect   This individual reviews the data compiled from the systems analyst and determines the preferred design for new systems. A systems architect's role is to create the overall system layout, whereas the systems analyst works with the end user and creates the ideas of what the business users require to fulfill their job or to align IT to their ultimate objectives. The true objective is to create a system that facilitates the generation of revenue for the organization.

Information Security Manager (ISM)   The information security manager (ISM) should be an individual with training—such as a Certified Information Systems Security Professional (CISSP) from the International Information Systems Security Certification Consortium, an ISACA Certified Information Security Manager (CISM), or someone with an equivalent credential. The ISM specifies security standards to be implemented for all computer systems. The ISM reviews procedures for compliance to security policies. Security management requires special software and tools to perform effective tests and reviews. The ISM specifies control settings to be implemented by the server and network administrators. An ISM should be a very busy person working on security monitoring, security policy compliance, individual system security certification, and systems accreditation. The information security manager is supported by information system security analysts.

It is important to ensure that the ISM function is fulfilled by using a balanced set of security metrics such as NIST 800-53. The auditor likes to see that the organization is paying full attention to internal security controls (instead of management just saying yes and then turning a blind eye toward the implementation). The ISM function is impossible without full management support.

Information Systems Security Analyst (ISSA)   The information security manager leads a group of security professionals known as information system security professionals. This group may be large or small, while always in proportion to the size of the organization and its mission requirements. Security analysts work directly with the business users, IT administrators, and the help desk to improve their security posture. This may include investigating security requirements, conducting awareness training, or helping to test security settings. Security analysts work with every department and participate in key positions on the incident response team.

Change Control Manager   This position is a quality assurance requirement. In small organizations, an individual may fill this role. Larger organizations may use a committee of managers to fill this function. The change control manager ensures that the staff is following proper procedures, controls, and approved plans.

Applications Programmer   Applications programmers write computer programs to solve problems for users. Their role is to create an automated solution for the business end-user. The applications programmer is supported by the systems analyst.

Systems Programmer   The systems programmer writes programs to change the behavior of the operating system or its design. Do not confuse this position with an enhanced operator. An enhanced operator selects settings, whereas a programmer writes software functions from scratch. The systems programmer role varies depending on the environment.

In a Microsoft Windows environment, the systems programmer is Microsoft Corporation unless the client hired a programmer to rewrite functions in the Microsoft operating system. Does the client have programmers to rewrite the internal functions of the Windows 7 operating systems? If not, the client organization is no more than a user, and their systems administrator is a glorified operator of enhanced authority who simply selects predefined options from menus.

In the Unix and mainframe environments, the systems programmer rewrites or modifies the operating system kernel, support utilities, and Job Control Language (JCL). In a nutshell, the systems programmer focuses on modifying or improving the operating system internal functions.

Software Quality Assurance Tester   Somebody needs to continually test program changes, interoperability, and integrity of coding. The software tester performs testing of the application changes, operating system, and functionality between programs. Common duties include white-box and black-box techniques, regression testing, security penetration testing (pen-testing), system certification, and user acceptance testing. This separation of duties promotes high integrity with accuracy.

Network Administrator   This person is the network router technician who handles data communication between devices on the network. The duties include supporting system administrators, managing Internet Protocol (IP) addresses, and monitoring networked devices (usually via Simple Network Management Protocol, or SNMP). The network administrator may be delegated the daily maintenance responsibility of network security devices such as intrusion detection and prevention systems, vulnerability scanners, firewalls, and gateways. A network administrator's primary job is to keep data communications working across the network.

Server Administrator   The server administrator maintains the server hardware and software settings. In a Microsoft environment, the server administrator is an enhanced operator whose role is to select appropriate settings from a GUI interface or predefined menu. The Unix and mainframe administrator counterparts are usually skilled as script programmers or operating system programmers. The Unix or mainframe administrators frequently write their own support utilities or customize the program code of existing utilities to enhance system integration.

Database Administrator   This is the custodian of data, who maintains the database systems. This is usually a role fulfilled by a person with prior experience as senior system administrator or systems programmer.

Computer Operator   This is a junior server technician who assists the system administrator and database administrator. The computer operator functions include starting and stopping software, changing job prioritization, and identifying possible problems during normal processing. A computer operator acts as the eyes, ears, and hands under the direction of the administrator. Computer operators provide clerical assistance on issues of error and log reporting. Operators escalate problems to the attention of more-senior personnel.

Systems Analyst   A systems analyst works with the business end-user to develop requirements. After the requirements are developed, the systems analyst works with the user to define screen layouts and report layouts. The systems analyst then communicates this information to the systems programmer. The systems analyst provides support for business methods to be implemented in technology.

Data Entry Staff   Data could be entered by a professional data entry staff for a large volume of data, or it could be entered by the end user. These days, with web forms and the online atmosphere of IT, data entry by the end user is quite common. If that has been the decision, we of course like to see compensating controls to ensure the integrity of that input.

Media Librarian   A media librarian is a critical role even though it's a junior role. We will refer to this IT position by the short name of *librarian*. The librarian is responsible for keeping track of all media, no matter what type (tape, cartridge, CD, or iOmega or a portable USB memory stick). The librarian is responsible for data storage and its tracking history, including creation date, current storage location, last time accessed, and what data is claimed to be contained on the media. The data may be referred to as a *data set*.

Backup media is sent to an offsite storage company for safe offsite storage. The librarian is required to track when the media was sent and when it arrived at the destination. Every tape and label must be accounted for at all times. Loss of backup media (tape) may constitute a breach of law or require mandatory public disclosure of loss, depending on contents.

The librarian assists with regular self-audits to verify that the property is still in safe storage with the offsite vendor. Media is recalled from storage by the librarian. Media containing old data is recycled by the librarian in accordance with the organization's reuse policy. The librarian is also responsible for proper disposal and destruction of old media.

Help Desk   Every IS organization will have a help desk of some type to support computer hardware or particular software applications. This is where users initially call for first-level support; the caller is asking for IT assistance. The help desk person handles the most basic needs and then escalates problems to the appropriate personnel. The help desk follows the policies and procedures that are specified by management.

Staff on the help desk usually hold a junior role. This support role provides an interface with IT customers. Each help desk person should be trained to recognize problems that need to be referred to more-senior IT staff. The customer interface serves the business person—the end user. The business end-user's job is to make money, and the help desk is intended to help the business user work more effectively. The help desk must keep performance metrics for all requests, including metrics of escalation and problem delegation.

Each of the roles we discussed has a particular function that is necessary to sustain normal operations. It is important that each transaction is properly authorized before it is executed. A physical or logical separation of duties is necessary to provide proper authorization. With separation of duties, you look at who holds custody of the assets and what compensating controls are present.

Figure 6.2 illustrates separation of duties and authorization in the IT department.

The purpose of separation of duties is to segregate authorization so that no individual can execute an action or have direct access to assets by bypassing control. Authorization is the most important element to separate from each job role. Every position should require authorization from another person before changes are made or before sensitive transactions are executed. The separation of duties is a control mechanism that separates the person doing the job from the person who renders authorization. The goal is to prevent stupid mistakes or possibly fraudulent activity.

FIGURE 6.2   Separation of duties

Job Role	Authorize Changes	Production Library Access	Development Library Access	Security Administration Configuration	Execute Production Changes
System user (end user)	Approve	Use	No	No	No
System administration (custodian)	Request	Monitor-Control	No	Implement	When approved
Security administration (custodian)	Approve	No	No	Specify control	No
Programming/ development	Request	No	Create software	No	No
Change testing	Test only	No (use isolated test)	No (use isolated test)	Test only	No
Change control	Approve	No	No	No	No

Using Metrics

The performance of information technology is ultimately interpreted by three fundamental business-performance indicators: IT budget, user satisfaction, and technical indicators. Technical indicators could include a combination of automated and manual metrics. You can gain a reasonable understanding of IT performance by reviewing their chosen indicators and corresponding scores.

Using metrics to measure IT service is required. These service metrics are tools designed to demonstrate the effectiveness of IT operations. Many regulations require the use of IT metrics in general. Each metric should provide a quantifiable measurement corresponding to the organization's internal controls. The IT metrics aid in the evaluation of an organization's performance.

Metrics must be developed for each organization. Each metric should be developed by using the following four principles:

- Data for calculating metrics must be readily obtainable.

- Each process under consideration needs to be repeating and measurable. It must represent a value to the business.

- Each metric must demonstrate a level of performance by using quantifiable information in the form of a numeric total, average, or percentage.

- A metric can be derived by automated or manual means.

The success of IT metrics depends on finding useful measurements that are of value to the organization's stakeholders. Data can be obtained from automated system reports. Data can also be collected manually through self-assessment tools, questionnaires, and user surveys. The metrics may change as new processes and projects are developed in the organization. It is important that each metric selected is realistic and can be used for measuring performance improvement.

Understanding the Types of Metrics

The goal of every metric is to establish a performance target. Performance targets are combined to establish a baseline. Four basic types of metrics can be used to measure IT performance:

Implementation Metric   An implementation metric provides a percentage or comparative count for the quantity of conforming installations—for example, the number of systems with antivirus software installed, or the number of users who have attended IT security orientation training.

Efficiency Metric   An efficiency metric measures the timeliness of service delivery. Examples include resolution time from the help desk or elapsed time for response to an incident.

Effectiveness Metric   This metric evaluates the quantifiable effectiveness of IT service activities. An example is the number of user-reported trouble tickets opened and closed by the help desk with a resolution that was satisfactory to the user. Another example is the number of systems currently maintained in a life cycle program by IT staff.

Impact Metric   An impact metric provides a quantitative measure of incidents by their type—for example, the number of help desk tickets opened and closed for the month. Another example is the number of systems compromised by a virus attack. This metric can be presented as a numeric value, a percentage of the total population, or a dollar value.

Figure 6.3 illustrates the nature of the four basic types of measurement metrics.

The IT department and each major stakeholder need to agree on which metrics to use. It is important to limit the number of metrics to a sustainable quantity. It is recommended that no more than five to ten metrics be collected for each major stakeholder. The metrics are not free; an organization must allocate resources to gather and create meaningful metrics. The data collection and subsequent reporting process must be standardized.

FIGURE 6.3   Basic types of measurement metrics

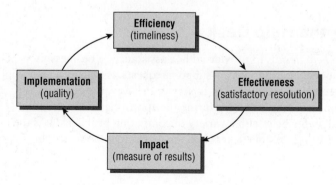

Developing and Selecting a Metric

Every metric developed will contain nine elements of information. ISACA does not expect you to recite each of these points in detail. The objective is to understand how a valid metric is created and managed. Let's look at the nine elements:

Purpose   Describe the overall functional value of this metric. Is this metric for customer measurement, compliance with a regulatory requirement, or internal performance?

Performance Goal   State the desired results of implementation, or the question to be answered by this metric. For example, the goal may be orientation training for new hires or separation of duties on IT servers.

Performance Objective   State the actions that are required to obtain the performance goal. This may be posed as one or multiple questions. For example, are participant-training materials in place for the orientation of new hires? What is the training schedule?

Type of Measurement   Define the quantitative measurement to be used. The measurement is expressed as a percentage, average, number, or frequency—for example, the numeric count and percentage based on attendance.

Data Source   Indicate where the data was captured from. List the specific tools, databases, and personnel that provided the data used in this metric—for example, a Human Resources (HR) employee count, and class attendance records signed upon entry and exit from training.

Available Evidence   List the sources of proof that can document the success or failure represented by this particular metric—for example, an HR roster, invitation list, attendance sheet, or attendee exit examination.

Frequency   State the time period used for data collection. Is this information based on hours, days, weeks, months, or years? For example, data collection may be reported monthly.

Formula Used   State the formula used in the calculation. One example is the number of incidents divided by the total number of systems. Another example is the formula (ratio) = (attendees ÷ total number of employees).

Indicators   Explain the goal of this metric and how it should be interpreted by the reader. For example, if the target for a metric on system certification is 100 percent, a low percentage would indicate a high risk exposure. A higher percentage would indicate a risk reduction by educating users about basic IS security safeguards and high-level notification procedures.

Evaluating the Help Desk

The purpose of a *help desk* is to provide ad hoc assistance to business users. The help desk is the point of origination for new support requests. A help desk may support specific applications or general computer needs. In service delivery, the objective is to provide high-quality and prompt service to the user during the appropriate work hours.

People may call in for help with a variety of computing problems. It is the help desk's responsibility to escalate trouble tickets in a timely manner. Some trouble tickets might be escalated to the system administrator or application support programmer. Other trouble tickets might be escalated to a third party. The help desk provides a single point of contact for the user. Each trouble ticket should be tracked by the help desk until closed or resolved to the user's satisfaction.

The help desk tracks call metrics so that trends can be analyzed. As an IS auditor, you should understand the help desk function. It would be beneficial to conduct a review of the staff on the help desk to determine their level of competency. An audit trail should exist, documenting the process for logging and tracking service requests. You should evaluate the level of documentation for help desk activities and troubleshooting procedures.

Performing Service-Level Management

A *service-level agreement (SLA)* represents an understanding between users and the service provider. The purpose of this agreement is to define performance criteria by specifying the quantity and quality of service desired by the customer.

Let's look at some of the components of the service-level agreement:

System Availability   What are the scheduled hours of system uptime and system downtime for maintenance? How is the processing workload scheduled to prevent conflict? What is the nature and extent of continuity plans?

Service Definition   What are the specific services expected by the user?

Personnel Qualifications   What are the qualifications of the IT support personnel? Will these same personnel be supporting business users? Will the support personnel be trained in the unique requirements of the business?

Security Requirements   What access controls will be implemented? How will physical and logical access controls be implemented? How will the program libraries be protected? How will the data be protected? Will separation of duties be fully implemented?

Data Integrity   What are the data storage and retention requirements? What is the method and frequency of data backup? How will data be protected during transportation?

SLA Performance Reporting   Are all metrics reported against a quantifiable service level? What metrics will be reported? How will the content and format of the metrics be reported? Do the report metrics fulfill actual business objectives? What is the frequency of reporting?

Right to Audit   What level of cooperation and access will a customer have to audit the service provider? Define any schedule or access restrictions in regard to auditing. This was discussed in Chapter 2, "Managing IT Governance."

SLA Change Procedures   What is the process for making changes to the service? What is the cancellation process, and how much would it cost?

Cost of Service   What is the cost of the service offered? How are the charges calculated? How will the service be billed? Are the charges realistic for the level of service provided?

This list is provided as an overview of the components in a service-level agreement. Every service-level agreement should be a formal contract between the vendor and customer. This contract should include the effective period of coverage and renewal options. It is understood that internal service-level agreements will take the form of an agreement of mutual understanding. Either type of agreement must be formally approved by appropriate management, representing both the provider's interests and the user's interests.

Outsourcing IT Functions

The subject of outsourcing can spark an emotional response. Selecting whether to outsource functions or keep them in-house is a decision that should be based on the facts in evidence. It is a common practice for individuals to outsource automobile repair, housecleaning, and lawn maintenance chores. A person purchasing a new home may choose to outsource interior decorating to a professional decorator. Take a look at the reasons why outsourcing may be considered:

- The scope of needs is unknown. Therefore, we need the help of someone more experienced who should know what to do.

- The current staff is not generating the expected results.

- Management decided it would be better to let someone else do it.

- The scope and requirements are extremely well defined—for example, CMM level 5. Now the objective is to reduce operating costs while delivering this well-defined level of service.

The auditor may want to investigate the maturity of the outsourced process, metrics, and user expectations. It is interesting how many times the decision to outsource is later reversed after the true scope is known, the actual requirements are identified, and the shock of the outsourcer's total invoice price is realized. Some processes may be outsourced with the long-term intention of remaining external.

At CertTest, we write two editions of our books, a special expanded edition for our class students plus a general version for Sybex. Both are commercially printed, professionally bound, and shipped by an outsource vendor. Writing the books is a core process we want to do. Printing and binding books internally would cost more money and therefore is not something to undertake. Executives will typically choose to outsource low-profit tasks in order to dedicate all available resources to processes with a high rate of return.

Blindly outsourcing is fraught with hazards. Every outsource agreement requires a contract as evidence of the details agreed upon by both parties. Let's take a moment to look at the minimum contents of a business contract according to ISACA:

Prior to Negotiations   Parties should provide the following:

- Identification of the parties to the contract, usually by company name and address

- Legal name of entity providing service, and legal name of recipient entity (DBA, Inc., LLP, LLC)

- Continuity of service assurances, or lack thereof

- Delivery location and legal jurisdiction

Specific Details   The contract should include these elements:

- General description of services provided
- Duration of the contract with applicable dates
- Description of specific deliverables
- Cost of service changes (fixed price, cost plus, or time and materials)

Performance During Execution   The contract should specify the following:

- Criteria of acceptance or rejection of deliverables
- Anticipated service-level agreement with both qualitative and quantitative measurement
- Security and confidentiality requirements (access levels, nondisclosure, and so forth)
- Frequency of invoicing and payment for service
- Roles of both parties during the contract, with specific points of contact
- Reporting process, report content, distribution, and frequency
- Right to audit
- Dissolution process
- Penalties for nonperformance

Changes and Resolution of Issues   The contract should describe these particulars:

- Cost of changes in service (fixed price, cost plus, or time and materials)
- Modification process to change terms, service, or price
- Problem resolution process
- Recourse

All contracts evidence a formal commitment to purchase and to pay for services or goods. The courts usually regard a contract as the sum total of the agreement between the parties. As a layperson, this means to me that services not specified in the contract should not be expected to occur. If the vendor made a special offer or promise, it should be prominently mentioned in the contract. IT contracts should always be negotiated with the assistance of a professional purchasing manager and legal counsel. A smart auditor allows the legal work to be performed by qualified lawyers. As a rule of thumb, the best lawyer keeps you out of court by preventing the disputes that lead to a lawsuit.

Performing Capacity Management

Capacity management focuses on the monitoring of computing resources and planning for future availability. By using system-monitoring tools, the IT administrator should be able to reasonably estimate the system capacity needed. System utilization reports provide insight into the current processing workload. This workload can be prorated against the operating schedule to forecast future shortfalls.

External changes in the service-level agreements or number of users will have a direct impact on available capacity. During capacity management planning, it is important to assess single points of failure. There will always be a few single points of failure in a system because of the technology selected or the cost of redundancy.

Two Different Outcomes in Redundancy

When available, hardware redundancy may increase or decrease the normal operating capacity. For example, a duplicate disk drive system will never exceed 50 percent of combined total gross capacity. A 1,000 gigabyte (GB) drive array would split into two separate sets of disks with a total capacity of less than 500 GB each. In fact, the usable capacity may be reduced to only 400 GB each after allowing for the minimum free space. So only 400 would be usable from a total capacity of 1,000.

Duplicate firewalls, on the other hand, may double available capacity if they share the workload in parallel. The firewalls would provide two independent communication paths, thereby doubling normal capacity. We discuss this further in Chapter 7, "Protecting Information Assets."

Using Administrative Protection

Throughout this Study Guide, we have discussed the importance of IT governance over internal controls. The first step for a protection strategy is to establish administrative operating rules. Administrative management controls are used to provide written policy and procedure guidance for people. These management controls help overcome shortfalls from the limited implementation of technical controls. You need to be aware of the common administrative controls used in IT service delivery.

Information security management is the foundation of information asset protection. Let's discuss some of the administrative methods used to protect data: information security management, IT security governance, data retention, documenting access paths, and other techniques.

Information Security Management

The objective of *information security management* is to ensure confidentiality, integrity, and availability of computing resources. To accomplish this goal, it is necessary to implement organizational design in support of these objectives. Let's discuss some of the job roles in information security management:

Chief Information Security Office The chief information security office (CISCO) is a role developed to grant the highest level of authority to the senior information systems security officer. Unfortunately, this tends to be a position of title more than a position of real corporate influence. The purpose of the CSO position is to define and enforce security policies for the organization.

Chief Privacy Officer   New demands for client privacy have created the requirement for a chief privacy officer (CPO). This position is equal to or directly below the chief security officer. The CPO is commonly a position of title rather than genuine corporate authority. The CPO is responsible for protecting confidential information of clients and employees.

Information Systems Security Manager   The information systems security manager (ISSM) is responsible for the day-to-day process of ensuring compliance for system security. The ISSM follows the directives of the CSO and CPO for policy compliance. The ISSM is supported by a staff of information systems security analysts (ISSAs) who work on the individual projects and security problems. An ISSM supervises the information systems security analysts and sets the daily priorities.

IT Security Governance

The concept of IT governance for security is based on security policies, standards, and procedures. For these administrative controls to be effective, it is necessary to define specific roles, responsibilities, and requirements. Let's imagine that an information security policy and matching standard have been adopted. The next step would be to determine the specific level of controls necessary for each piece of data. Data can be classified into groups based on its value or sensitivity. The data classification process will define the information controls necessary to ensure appropriate confidentiality.

The federal government uses an information classification program to specify controls over the use of data. High-risk data is classified top secret, and the classifications cascade down to data available for public consumption. Every organization should utilize an information records management system (classification scheme) for their data. International Standard ISO 15489 for records management combined with ISO 27002 for information security management set forth the requirements to identify, retain, and protect records used in the course of business. It's the only method to ensure integrity with proper handling. Let's take a look at the typical classifications used in business:

Public   Information approved for public consumption. It is important to understand that data classified as public needs to be reviewed and edited to ensure that the correct message is conveyed. Examples of public information include websites, sales brochures, marketing advertisements, press releases, and legal filings. Most information filed at the courthouse is a public record, viewable by anyone.

Sensitive   There is a particular type of data that needs to be disclosed to certain parties but not to everyone. We refer to this data as *sensitive*. This data may be a matter of record or legal fact. However, the organization would not want to go about advertising the details. Examples of sensitive information include client lists, product pricing structure, contract terms, vendor lists, and details of outstanding litigation.

Private, Internal Use Only   The classification of data for internal use only is commonly applied to operating procedures and employment records. The details of operating procedures are usually provided on a need-to-know basis to prevent a person from designing a method for defeating the procedure. Examples of private records include salary data, health-care information, results of background checks, and employee performance reviews.

Confidential   This is the highest category of general security classification for proprietary information outside the government. It may be subdivided into confidential and highly confidential trade secrets. Confidential data is anything that must not be shared outside of the organization. Examples include buyout negotiations, secret recipes, and specific details about the inner workings of the organization. Confidential data may be exempt from certain types of legal disclosure.

 Information Classification is a very important preventative control

The overall purpose of using a formal information classification scheme is to ensure proper handling based on the information content and context. *Context* refers to the usage of information.

Two major risks are present in the absence of an information classification scheme. The first major risk is that information will be mishandled. The second major risk is that without an information classification scheme, all of the organization's data may be subject to scrutiny during legal proceedings. The information classification scheme safeguards knowledge. Failure to implement a records and data classification scheme leads to disaster.

Authority Roles over Data

To implement policies, standards, and procedures, it is necessary to identify persons by their authority. Three levels of authority exist in regard to computers and data: owner, custodian, and user.

Data Owner

The *data owner* refers to executives or managers responsible for the data content. The role of the data owner is to do the following:

- Assume responsibility for the data content
- Specify the information classification level
- Specify appropriate controls
- Specify acceptable use of the data
- Identify authorized users
- Appoint the data custodian

As an IS auditor, you will review the decisions made by the data owner to evaluate whether the actions were appropriate.

Data User

The *data user* is the business person who benefits from the computerized data. Data users may be internal or external to the organization. For example, some data is delivered for use across the Internet. The role of the data user includes the following tasks:

- Follow standards of acceptable use
- Comply with the owner's controls
- Maintain confidentiality of the data
- Report unauthorized activity

You will evaluate the effectiveness of management to communicate their controls to the user. The auditor investigates the effectiveness and integration of policies and procedures with the user community. In addition, the auditor determines whether user training has been effectively implemented.

Data Custodian

The *data custodian* is responsible for implementing data storage safeguards and ensuring availability of the data. The custodian's role is to support the business user. If something goes wrong, it is the responsibility of the custodian to deal with this promptly. Sometimes the custodian's role is equivalent to a person holding the bag of snakes at a rattlesnake roundup or the role of a plumber when fixing a clogged drain. The duties of the data custodian include the following:

- Implement controls matching information classification
- Monitor data security for violations
- Administer user access controls
- Ensure data integrity through processing controls
- Back up data to protect from loss
- Be available to resolve any problems

Now we have identified the information classification and the job roles of owner, user, and custodian. The next step is to identify data retention requirements.

Data Retention Requirements

Data retention specifies the procedures for storing data, including how long to keep particular data and how the data will be disposed of. All records follow a life cycle similar to the SDLC model in Chapter 5, "Information Systems Life Cycle." The requirements for data retention can be based on the value of data, its useful life, and legal requirements. For example, financial records must be accessible for seven years. Medical records are required to be available indefinitely or at least as long as the patient remains alive. Records regarding the sale or transfer of real property are to be maintained indefinitely, as are many government records.

Without an information classification scheme, the users and custodians will not know how to handle information. It would be impossible to control leaks, prevent inappropriate destruction, sanction personnel, or survive investigations. Both privileged and public information would become a confused mess, resulting in the wrong information being lost or breached via accidental disclosure.

The purpose of records retention is to specify how long a data record must be preserved. At the end of the preservation period, the data is archived or disposed of. The disposal process frequently involves destruction. We discuss storage and destruction later in this chapter.

After the authority roles and data retention requirements have been identified, the next administrative step is to document the access routes (paths) to reach the data.

Document Access Paths

It would be extremely difficult to ensure system security without recognizing common access routes. One of the requirements of internal controls is to document all of the known access paths. A physical map is useful. The network administrator or security manager should have a floor plan of the building. The locations of computer systems, wiring closet, and computer room should be marked on the map. Map symbols should indicate the location of every network jack, telephone jack, and modem. The location of physical access doors and locking doors should also be marked on the map. This process would continue until all the access paths have been marked. Even the network firewall and its Internet communication line should appear on the map.

Next, a risk assessment should be performed by using the map of access paths. Hackers can injure the facility via the Internet or from within an unsupervised conference room. Special attention should be given to areas with modem access. Modems provide direct connections, which bypass the majority of IT security. Computer firewalls are effective only if the data traffic passes directly through the firewall. A computer firewall cannot protect any system with an independent, direct Internet connection.

The purpose of documenting access paths and performing a risk assessment is to ensure accountability. Management is held responsible for the integrity of record keeping. Guaranteeing integrity of a computer system would be difficult if nobody could guarantee that access restrictions were in place.

The change control process should include oversight for changes affecting the access paths. For example, a change in physical access security may introduce another route to the computer room. Persons entering and leaving through the side door, for example, would have a better opportunity to reach the computer room without detection.

The next step to ensure security is to provide constant monitoring. Physical security systems can be monitored with a combination of video cameras, guards, and alarm systems. Badge access through locked doorways provides physical access control with an audit log. A badge access system can generate a list of every identification badge granted access or denied access through the doorway. Unfortunately, a badge access system will have difficulty ensuring that only one person passed through the doorway at a particular time. A mantrap system of two doorways may be used to prevent multiple persons from entering and exiting at the same time. A *mantrap* allows one person to enter and requires the door to be closed behind the person. After the first door is closed, a second door can be opened. The mantrap allows only one person to enter and exit at a time.

To support the increased security, it will be necessary to train the personnel.

Personnel Management

Everyone in the organization should undergo a process of security awareness training. Education is the best defense. Computer training and job training are commonplace. The organization should introduce a training program promoting IT governance in security to generate awareness. Let's consider the possible training programs:

- New-hire orientation, which should include IT security orientation
- Physical security safeguards and asset protection
- Reeducating existing staff about IT security requirements
- Introducing new security and safety considerations
- Email security mechanisms
- Virus protection
- Business continuity

Every organization should have a general IT security training program to communicate management's commitment for internal controls.

User Training

Proper training of system users can reduce the occurrence of problems. User training may include new-hire orientation, security awareness training, software application training, and refresher programs for existing users. Well-educated users can provide valuable assistance to IT objectives. The educated user will understand when to bring potential concerns to the attention of IT management.

 Real World Scenario

Easy Awareness Training Solution

A good training program can run in 20 minutes or less. The intention is to improve awareness and understanding. Training can occur in combination with normal activities. A favorite technique of ours is to place a 20-minute video presentation on the back end of HR benefits and orientation sessions. This ensures that the audience will be present. HR will provide time and attendance reporting for the participants. Each person on staff will be tracked through a series of presentations, leading to cumulative awareness training. Other methods include a brown-bag lunch event, followed by a contest giveaway to promote attendance.

Physical Access

Physical access is a major concern to IT security. Physical access is based on using barriers to force separation of duties (SOD). It's important even though these protections are limited in computer security since 99% of attacks will come through the Internet. As an IS auditor, you need to investigate how access is granted for employees, visitors, vendors, and service personnel. Which of these individuals are escorted and which are left unattended? What is the nature of physical controls and locking doors? Are there any internal barriers to prevent unauthorized access?

The following is a list of the three top concerns regarding physical access:

Sensitive Areas   Every IS auditor is concerned about physical access to sensitive areas such as the computer room. The computer room and network wiring closets are an attractive target. Physical access to electronic equipment will permit the intruder to bypass a number of logical controls. Servers and network routers can be compromised through their keyboard port or service ports. Every device can be disabled by physical damage. It is also possible for the intruder to install eavesdropping access by using wiretaps or special devices.

Service Ports   Network equipment, routers, and servers have communication ports that can be used by maintenance personnel. A serial port provides direct access for a skilled intruder. Shorting out the hardware can create a denial-of-service situation. Special commands issued through a serial port may bypass the system's password security. When security is bypassed, the contents in memory can be displayed to reveal the running configuration, user IDs, and passwords.

 As auditors, we have observed senior maintenance personnel from the two largest router manufacturers. During one particular crisis, the skilled technicians successfully bypassed security and reconfigured a major set of changes to routers without halting network service and without knowing the actual administrator passwords.

Computer Consoles   The keyboard of the server is referred to as the *console*. Direct access to servers and the console should be tightly controlled. A person with direct access can start and stop the system. The processes stopping the system may be crude and cumbersome, but the outcome will be the same. Direct access also provides physical access to disk drives and special communication ports. It would be impossible to ensure server security without restricting physical access.

Physical Asset Management

Asset management controls are used to provide written policy and procedure guidance for people. These management controls help overcome shortfalls from the limited implementation of technical controls. Three areas often taken for granted are digital assets in the form of electronic work files, software licenses, and storage media tracking.

> ### 🌐 Real World Scenario
>
> #### Ensuring That Personnel Are Honest
>
> Personnel in the organization are expected to be honest. Before access is granted, each person should undergo a formal hiring process complete with background checks. Some individuals in sensitive positions may be bonded to protect the company. The bonding process is a type of insurance that will pay the company for losses caused by the employee. *Fidelity bonding* protects the organization from employee theft. Unfortunately, most fidelity bonds will require the organization to successfully prosecute the accused before any money will be paid out.

Digital Assets

We view data as a capital asset because of the capital investment necessary to create and maintain current data. As a publisher, the labor cost to produce text and original illustrations represents a substantial investment. Building and maintaining a customer list requires substantial investment of capital through marketing campaigns. A list of customers and hot prospects can easily be valued at five to ten times annual gross sales. The effort required to produce contracts, websites, and other materials can be substantial. Digital assets are more than just software.

Software Licensing

Software licenses are an asset of the corporation and need to be controlled and managed. Software licenses represent a major capital investment by the organization. All computer systems are required to have a valid, lawfully obtained software license for the operating system along with a license for each application and each utility installed. A violation of software copyright laws carries substantial penalties and the possibility of public embarrassment. You should observe the client's attitude toward software licenses. Most organizations purchase licenses by a per user count. There should be evidence to indicate that the licenses are managed for copyright compliance. Software Asset Management (SAM) is definitely an area being targeted by ISACA for improvement.

Media Tracking

Technology assets should be inventoried and tracked. Proper ownership labels or property tags should be in use. Tagging and labeling are preventative controls. The audit of inventory tags is a detective control. Media containing software and data should be managed under a physical asset program. This is required under several regulations, including Sarbanes-Oxley, Gramm-Leach-Bliley, HIPAA, Basel I and II, and the EU Data Protection Directive.

All media should be properly labeled. The media librarian is responsible for tracking the location of media. Evidence should exist to indicate that assets and media are properly controlled.

Canadian-based Absolute Software sells a special tracking service designed to recover stolen laptops. Their special utility installs on the laptop as a hidden software program. The laptop can be located by its unique beacon while on the Internet. Absolute's recovery desk notifies law enforcement and automatically provides all the paperwork necessary for search warrants. Absolute can remotely wipe the hard disk clean if necessary to prevent disclosure of the laptop data files.

If there is a problem of shortfall in controlling assets, the alternative method is to assemble multiple controls to create a set of compensating controls.

Terminating Access

Administrative procedures are necessary to ensure that access is terminated when an employee leaves the organization. The access of existing employees should also be reviewed on a regular basis. In a poorly managed organization, the employee will be given access to one area and then to additional areas as their jobs change. Unfortunately, this results in a person with more access than their job requires. Access to sensitive areas should be limited to persons who perform a required job function in the same area. If the person is moved out of the area, that access should be terminated. The IS auditor should investigate how the organization terminates access and whether it reviews existing access levels. The concept of least privilege should be enforced. The minimum level of access is granted to perform the required job role.

Compensating Controls

Compensating controls are alternative methods using a collection of less effective techniques to achieve equivalent levels of protection. The overall goal is to reduce the impact of an error or omission. If you can't implement the preferred control, then it will be necessary to implement several lesser controls working together in unison. As you will recall from previous chapters, controls may be implemented by using a physical method (barrier), technical method (logical), or administrative method (policy and procedure). Compensating controls are used whenever there is a lack of segregation of duties. Examples of compensating controls include the following:

Job Rotation   Rotating individuals between job functions reduces the potential of questionable activities. A person may be asked to take vacation in one- or two-week intervals. During that time, another person performs the job while looking to discover whether anything is out of the ordinary. This is a type of detective control. A collateral benefit is having more than one trained person capable of performing the function.

Audit   Auditing is an essential component of internal control. It is imperative that audit logs are functional and well preserved. The audits may be internal self-assessments or formal independent audits.

Reconciliation   Reconciliation is a type of audit in which records are compared to ensure that a balance exists. Reconciliation is used in financial reporting, project management, scope verification, computer processing batch verification, and other instances where an answer should be verified. Proper reconciliation increases the level of confidence.

Exception Report   On occasion, an error or exception will exist in computer processing and audit logs. All jobs processed should print an automatic exception report to identify the jobs not processed correctly or print a report indicating that no exceptions existed. Exception reporting should be forwarded to the supervisor, escalating up each level until the problem is handled. The supervisor reviews evidence of the event and determines the action required. The goal is to ensure that exceptions are handled properly in accordance with the organizational goals, policies, and standards for internal control.

Transaction Logs   Transaction logs provide audit trails that are designed to alert the user about a particular condition. The IS auditor needs to understand how the client reviews transaction logs, along with what action is taken. The absence of a transaction log would represent a major concern. A similar concern would exist if the transaction logs are not reviewed on a regular basis.

Supervisor Review   The supervisor should review each of the compensating controls through observation and inquiry. Failure to do so may constitute negligence. The supervisory review is the last level of compensating control.

Performing Problem Management

The IT operations staff should have a problem management process in place. Effective problem management provides a timely response by using predefined procedures that include a method for problem escalation.

Situations requiring problem management include the following:

Procedures versus Actual Work   The procedures used in the operation of information technology systems should reflect the actual work performed. The purpose of a procedure is to ensure consistency with the desired result. Actual work that does not match the procedure would indicate a management control failure.

Ineffective and Inefficient Controls   A management review process should exist to deal with ineffective and inefficient controls. Failing controls should be reviewed for merit and potential impact. A compensating control may be implemented to overcome an ineffective control.

Acceptable Use Policy (AUP) Violation   Violation of the acceptable use policy could include the misuse of corporate resources or the presence of nonbusiness materials. The discovery of an AUP violation should trigger the incident-handling process and notification to Human Resources.

Job Accounting   Computer processing is always subject to problems. Conditions of concern include abnormal job terminations and exception handling. Other problems can include jobs that run too fast or excessively slow for the volume of work. Jobs that end too fast may indicate that a portion of the processing was skipped. Consider, for example, a tape backup that appears to complete in record time. An investigation may find that the data written to tape is incomplete or nonexistent. Either condition would indicate a substantial problem.

Training   The training of users and staff is a good response to prevent the recurrence of a problem. Training plans should exist for new-hire orientation, basic user training, and additional awareness training. Test exercises for business continuity also serve to train individuals about their job role during a crisis.

All incidents, problems, and errors are to be recorded. Incidents reported to IT may be either accidental or malicious. An established procedure is required to ensure a thorough investigation.

Incident Handling

Certain events will need to be analyzed by a competent individual with the proper training. Every organization needs an incident response team (IRT) readily available. Whenever someone discovers or suspects that an incident has occurred, this team is quietly notified and called into action. One or more team members begin the investigation by analyzing available data to determine the possible impact. The objective is to limit the damage. A problem should be referred to the appropriate management to ensure that it receives the proper attention. All instances of problems are expected to be resolved in a timely manner. For example, computer security problems should be dealt with immediately. Network printer problems may be a lower priority.

Violation Reporting

Policies and procedures in security plans are ineffective unless management is monitoring compliance. An effective process of monitoring will detect violations. Better control occurs when activity monitoring is separate from the person or activity performing the work. Self-monitoring is a violation of IT governance controls. The built-in reporting conflict of self-monitoring will seriously question the integrity of the reporting process. Separation of duties applies to people, systems, and violation reporting. The IS auditor needs to investigate how violations are reported to management:

- Does a formal process exist to report possible violations?
- Will a violation report trigger the incident response team to investigate?

The role of the IS auditor in personnel management is to determine whether appropriate controls are in place to manage the activities of people inside the organization. Now we will move on to the proper incident-handling process.

Incident-Handling Process

Incident response teams are structured into one of three categories:

- Centralized team
- Distributed team reporting to a central authority
- Coordination team providing guidance and advice to individual responders

Members of the IRT should be formally designated via a written charter. This will help eliminate disputes over members responding versus continuing to work on the tasks of their normal jobs. The staff of the IRT could be employees, outsourced, or a hybrid model. Team members may be needed 24/7, which creates a need for schedule planning. Each response will follow four phases of the incident response life cycle:

Phase 1: Preparation   The basic tasks include appointing team members, getting the team trained, and providing the necessary procedures with appropriate tools to perform the job. Preventative controls can save money by reducing the occurrence of problems. For example, properly maintained antivirus software eliminates many of the virus attacks. Dividing the network with predetermined disconnect points allows undamaged portions of the business to continue near-normal operation after infected areas have been isolated.

Phase 2: Detection and Analysis   System log reports and telephone calls to the help desk are excellent sources of detection. IT's constant monitoring should become the number one source of detection. The team is quietly activated after a problem is detected. In some instances, the incident may be a malicious attack. It is important not to signal the attacker that activity has been discovered. Certain events may require the assistance of outside experts, as in the case of forensic analysis. Test procedures and samples need to be documented. It is possible that the incident is a cyber crime scene containing evidence that must be protected.

Phase 3: Containment, Eradication, and Recovery   Incidents need to be contained as quickly as possible to prevent spreading more damage. Early containment helps keep the situation small enough to manage. Swift decisions are necessary to contain the problem. Acting too late will result in the situation overwhelming the available resources. This means that tough decisions should be preapproved with agreed-upon activation criteria. When the criteria are met, the predetermined action proceeds without any delay. Separate containment strategies should be developed for each major type of incident (fraud, theft, virus attack, server failure, and so forth).

Phase 4: Post Incident Activity   After all the documentation is completed, the next step is to report the incident according to the requirements for your industry. Disclosure is becoming more common for legal compliance. One of the most valuable benefits from incident response is conducting a *lessons learned* meeting. The purpose is to analyze expected results and unexpected consequences in order to improve. Data and records collected from the event may need to be placed in longer-term evidence storage. (See the evidence life cycle in Chapter 3, "Audit Process.")

Auditor's Interest in Incident Handling

Incident handling is an administrative process. Physical damage or an unlocked door at the wrong time should initiate the incident-handling process. Auditors will need to investigate how the organization responds to incidents in regard to security implications.

Auditors need to ask the following questions:

- What are the events necessary to trigger incident response?

- Are the user and the IT help desk trained to know when to call?

- What is the process for activating the IRT?
- Does the IRT have an established procedure to ensure a proper investigation and protect evidence?
- Are members of the IRT formally appointed and trained?

Now, to dispel any misunderstanding, let's take a quick look at forensic computer investigations.

Digital Forensics

Digital forensic investigations target computer data for laboratory analysis. This tiny section on the subject should not be construed as legal advice, because the scope of performing a digital forensic investigation exceeds the capability of this book. Our goal is to provide an introduction to the steps involved in conducting digital investigations related to criminal activity. New electronic discovery laws (e-discovery) are changing the rules and responsibilities in civil and criminal court cases. Auditors and investigators should require a clear, written mandate from the appropriate authority to indicate that they have received lawful authorization before starting a forensic investigation.

There are four basic phases in the forensic life cycle: acquisition, examination, utilization, and review.

Acquisition

The acquisition phase deals with acquiring data from the best possible sources. Data may be recovered from *deleted files*, which are not actually erased by the operating system. The computer simply marks the file as being eligible for overwriting at any time. The actual data is still present.

Computer backups are referred to as *logical backups*. The logical backup copies the directories and files of the volume but ignores deleted files and residual data in *slack space*. The slack is the difference between space actually used by the file and the space allocated. Slack space refers to remnant areas on the hard disk. Physical disk imaging, known as *bitstream imaging*, creates a bit-for-bit copy of the original media, including the deleted files and residual data in slack space. A special *write blocker* is used to prevent the analyzed computer from writing to its storage media.

 Without a write blocker, the evidence becomes altered (tainted), which destroys the chain of custody.

Data may be permanently destroyed on a hard disk by a *wiping utility*, which uses random values to overwrite portions of the media. Security professionals use wiping utilities to clear hard disks for redeployment. Hackers use wiping utilities to destroy evidence, thereby covering their tracks.

Four important points to remember in the acquisition phase are capturing volatile data, retrieving nonvolatile data, avoiding use of the keyboard, and creating multiple images of the files.

- *Volatile data* refers to information in memory that will be lost when the power is shut off. Prematurely shutting off power erases the evidence of an attack, which is stored in computer chip RAM. (We covered this in Chapter 4, "Networking Technology Basics.")

- *Nonvolatile data* is the information contained on the hard disk and flash memory devices. A graceful shutdown causes the operating system to clean up temporary files and clear the swap file before shutting down. A hacker may attach a utility in the shutdown process to erase the trail of their malicious attack. Abruptly removing power from the system can preserve swap files, temporary data, and other information that may have been deleted during a graceful shutdown. Some systems will create an automatic dump of all their contents into a special file, known as a *crash dump*. Unfortunately, a sudden loss of power could also corrupt the data.

 Preplan response procedures by conducting a review by a forensics expert before getting attacked. The best response will be different on different operating systems.

- *Keyboard remapping* allows for individual keys or a combination of keystrokes to perform a very different function than their standard purpose. Hackers frequently remap their keyboard so a simple keystroke such as Ctrl+Alt or F2 will start an automatic wiping of the hard disk to destroy evidence. The best way for the forensic analyst to acquire data is without using the keyboard. Special disk-imaging hardware has been designed specifically for this purpose.

- Multiple copies of the files should be created to avoid working with the originals. Integrity of the files is important. Logical backup is acceptable for informal collection from a live system. Physical bitstream imaging is required if preserving the file times is important.

Examination

Forensic analysts must work with read-only copies of the files, not the originals. Many files contain a header, which can identify the type of data it contains. File extensions are not trustworthy, because the user can assign any extension to a file. Examination should use a toolkit that is well recognized by law enforcement agencies. The de facto standard for prosecution is Guidance Software's EnCase forensic examination software. Examination includes at least the following files:

- Live data files and deleted files that can be recovered

- Contents of memory, network connections, network shares, strings, and directories

- Configuration files for OS, users, passwords, processes run, and jobs

- Log files of system events, audit records, command history, and previously accessed files

- Application files
- System swap files, dump files, temporary files, and hibernation files

Files may be examined from the computer system and the network traffic. Security event management (SEM) software is capable of importing log history from various devices and creating a correlation of events. This allows the reconstruction of events by replaying log and traffic data. Examination of forensic information has been helpful to prosecute espionage, theft of intellectual property, fraud, blackmail, hacking, spamming, murder, and child pornography. Policies and procedures are also needed in case the investigation creates an inadvertent disclosure of sensitive information.

Forensics experts with prior law enforcement experience are preferred as investigators. The special training and experience as a police officer or special agent are well respected by judges.

Utilization

Analysts should review the results of data from individual applications to determine how events will fit together during reconstruction. Correlating events is the most effective way to handle the situation. A detailed, methodical approach is required.

Review

Constant review of the processes can help identify procedural errors, skill gaps, and short-comings in the plans. Changes and updates in the legal process must be incorporated into the process. Failure to prove the case with a successful conviction may backfire with a countersuit for damages.

Monitoring the Status of Controls

Your job as a CISA is to evaluate an organization's internal controls. Internal controls are required during the normal processing at every computer terminal or computer workstation. Without proper controls, a minor error could become a major outage.

We discuss a series of security controls in this Study Guide. In Chapter 7, we discuss specific security controls for protecting information assets. For now, let's visit controls that apply to IT service delivery:

- System monitoring
- Log management
- System access controls
- Data file controls
- Application processing controls

- Antivirus software

- Active content and mobile software code

- Maintenance controls, including change management

- Separate test environment

- Physical and environmental controls (covered later in this chapter)

System Monitoring

Technology systems require continuous monitoring to uncover operational inconsistencies, errors, and processing failures. Managing a system would be impossible if you did not know its present condition.

Let's discuss a few types of monitoring that should be implemented by IT:

Hardware   Electronic hardware should be monitored for workload utilization, errors, and availability. Utilization and errors could indicate an upcoming condition that will affect system availability. The goal is for every system to be usable. The system administrator should always be aware of hardware conditions observed, problems reported, and alerts recorded in system logs.

Software   Most computer software provides event logging. Event logs and audit logs should be enabled and configured to capture information of interest—for example, error conditions, successful logins, unsuccessful login attempts, and configuration changes.

Centralized System Logging (Syslog)   It is a recommended practice for centralized system logging to be installed. This process forwards a copy of each system log to a centralized console for review. The configuration process is relatively simple. A log-reading tool is necessary to convert raw data into meaningful information. System logs contain a lot of duplicate entries. Without a log-reading tool, understanding the priorities would be difficult because of the volume of log entries.

Network Device Monitoring   Servers and routers on the network can be managed by using the SNMP discussed in Chapter 4. One of the older SNMP platforms is HP OpenView although less-expensive management platforms such as OpenNMS are also available. Network-management software provides insight into the overall condition of the networked environment. System alarms are generated before a user calls in to complain. The network-management system is useful only if someone is available to view the alert.

Uptime-Downtime Reporting   SNMP provides an excellent method of tracking uptime and downtime. Some people get very defensive about how this subject is reported. Let's clarify the point for everyone's benefit. There are only two categories, although additional descriptions may exist:

Uptime   The system is available for users to process whatever they desire or need.

Downtime   The system is unavailable for any reason. This may be due to failure or a scheduled outage for service. The word *outage* indicates that the system is effectively down. *Down* means *down*. No matter what the user does, the system will not be available. If this is distasteful, the downtime statistics can be used to justify additional resources. Management may choose to accept the downtime in spite of IT's desire to have 99.999 percent uptime. IT is a humble servant to the business, not the other way around.

> *Downtime* means the system is unavailable for any reason—including failure, maintenance, or while running the backup/restore operations. IT management may refer to downtime as planned maintenance or unplanned outage. Always consider this from the user's perspective. It's counted as downtime if the user is unable to use the system for any reason.

Log Management

Computer logs are an excellent source of information. The only drawback is that without the right tools, computer log files are difficult to read. Assuming you have the right tools, the next question is whether anyone is actually reading the logs. Software logs offer valuable insight into events occurring within systems and throughout the network. The Syslog feature we discussed in Chapter 4 is one of the most powerful tools an organization could use.

Effective log management is based on six easy requirements:

1. Enable logging for security-related events.

2. Enable logging in application software.

3. Enable logging in the operating system.

4. Configure Syslog to export logs from the device to be watched.

5. Configure a Syslog server to receive the log files; this does not require any server license.

6. Read the log files. A simple log-reading utility is used to glean duplicate data.

The devices on the network continually generate log entries on an ongoing basis. Log files present valuable information for telling a story of what is actually occurring across the network. The benefit is obtained by reading the files as part of a regular monitoring procedure. Log files need to be continuously backed up and archived. The information discovered in the log file may be the best trigger for incident response.

System Access Controls

Access to computing resources needs to be controlled. It is imperative that the concept of *least privilege* be implemented with regard to user access of IT computing resources. No individual should be able to log in to the system by using a level of authority higher than their job requires. There are three types of login accounts you need to consider: user login, privileged administrator login, and maintenance login.

User Login and Account Management

New user login IDs are created after Human Resources notifies the IT department of an employee being hired. A similar process should exist when a contractor begins work. Some type of authorization mechanism must exist to control the creation of new accounts.

Each system user is required to have a unique login ID and password. The user login accounts should be given the minimum access rights necessary to perform their job (least privilege). Biometrics or electronic tokens may be implemented on systems with higher levels of security. Every user login should contain the following control attributes:

- A warning banner is displayed prior to login to inform the user that inappropriate access may result in prosecution.

- A minimum password length of six to eight characters is required. The password should be a mix of numbers and letters. The password should not be a printed word found in any dictionary, regardless of language. Automated password-cracking tools start the attack by trying common words and names obtained from dictionaries. (We discuss the details of this in Chapter 7.)

- Unique passwords are forced. The computer system will not allow a password to be reused.

- Passwords are required to be changed at a frequency of 30 to 60 days, depending on the organization's policy.

- A user login ID is suspended after three to five unsuccessful login attempts.

- Unauthorized attempts to access the system are recorded in audit logs.

- The date and time of the last successful login will be displayed to the user upon login. This is to inform the user of when their login ID was last used.

A user login account is suspended or disabled when a notice is received from HR that a particular user is no longer employed by the organization. The disabled account needs to undergo administrative review prior to deletion of the user ID. This review seeks to discover whether the user engaged in any attempts of unauthorized access. If not, the user's data files are archived and forwarded to the appropriate department manager.

Just setting account lockout at three to five failed attempts is not good enough to thwart an attacker. Most hackers will try only one or two login attempts using attack programs that will try again a few minutes later, up to 29,336 times a year, undetected. This type of under-the-radar attack is common. I bet it's already occurring somewhere on your systems. Nobody would be wise to the attack unless they are monitoring every failed login attempt. This type of attack may occur for months, until the hacker gets a successful login. Monitoring should be set to alert on each unsuccessful login attempt that does not conclude with a successful login.

Privileged Login Accounts

Logical access to system administration functions needs to be protected by a separation of duties. Privileged login accounts should not be used for any function other than administration and maintenance. System administrators should possess two separate login accounts. The first login account should be used exclusively for system administration duties. The second login account should have no privileges other than the basic rights of the common user.

The system administrator should perform office administration functions while logged in as a regular user. This reduces the potential impact of errors. In addition, it improves security by reducing the time duration of privileged access. If the administrator walks down the hall to the restroom but is logged in only as a regular user, the risk of another individual gaining physical access to the computer has been reduced. The logical separation of duties can be verified by reading system logs.

All privileged login accounts contain control attributes of a normal user plus the following additional controls:

- Passwords must be changed every 30 days.

- Retired passwords must be written down and stored with backup tapes. Those passwords may be necessary again when older files are restored. Both the tapes and the password lists shall be stored in a fireproof-rated media safe, and also in a secure controlled environment designed for offsite media storage.

- The current passwords should be written down and stored in a safe in case something unforeseen happens to the system administrator. Current passwords will be required for disaster recovery. A second copy of the passwords should be kept in a safe offsite location separate from the data files.

 You may use CertTest's free password generator to help create unique passwords. We grant you limited permission, for nonhostile purposes, to link to our web page. Auditors should encourage the use of stronger passwords. Just visit www.certtest.com/passgen.

Maintenance Login Accounts

All computer systems have default user accounts for system setup and maintenance. The login IDs of these maintenance accounts are often well known and commercially published. Hackers love to use maintenance accounts that have been left open by careless administrators.

Default login accounts should be disabled in a production system. Any valid maintenance accounts should utilize nontypical login names with strong passwords or station restrictions. A station restriction allows login to occur only from a particular system, based on the machine's serial number or address.

The system custodian and network administrator *must* write down all privileged computer passwords for management to distribute without delay or further action. These are the property of the business owners. Reasonable steps are necessary to protect passwords from public disclosure. Good password management dictates privileged passwords change every 30 days. Be sure to keep accurate records for the day you need to restore a 14-month-old backup so you will have matching passwords from that time period. Password lists may be divided up by role and stored separately to support segregation of duties. I will explain why this is a real problem in the next few paragraphs.

The fact is that any failure to comply with maintaining a printed record of system passwords can place the organization in harm's way. Backup tapes may contain data subject to court order or regulatory retention. Any failure to access the data places the organization at serious risk. Hacking your own data will destroy your claims of integrity. Data may not need to be accessed for several years. In addition, the server administrator is a custodian who must follow the directions of management. Privileged passwords cannot be kept secret from a supervisor (manager) because it's their job to verify immediate compliance. This means you either trust your boss or resign immediately to seek employment elsewhere.

Any support person unwilling to cooperate with a password retention policy should be investigated to determine whether the individual or their manager is to undergo a review by the executive oversight committee. Persons unable or unwilling to demonstrate the required level of trust or dedication to perform the necessary work should seek other employment. Termination is the recommended legal action to avoid executive liability.

Just like a plumber or janitor, all support persons are required by their job description to clean up any mess that occurs. These are standard terms of employment for custodians. The concept applies to assembly line workers, building maintenance personnel, security staff, and IT workers. Allowing a support person the ability to hold access codes, data, or resources hostage represents a major breach of governance. Major news stories cite IT/IS workers facing criminal charges for withholding passwords or keycodes belonging to their employer. In each case, the worker fared poorly in front of a judge and was convicted with fines or jail time. Auditors need to remain aware that a lack of executive control over passwords is a serious concern warranting immediate action.

Data File Controls

Access to data files should be controlled to ensure that unauthorized access is effectively impossible. Data access can occur through a perimeter control, direct file access, and middleware. *Middleware* is software that handles data traveling from the user interface to its destination in the database. Each of these types of access requires special controls. It is naive to think that a perimeter control will be completely effective.

Four basic types of data protection controls are required:

Standing Data Controls   *Standing data* refers to information contained in a file or database table. The information should possess controls commensurate with the data value or regulatory requirement. Standing data can be found in file cabinets, on disk drives, and on tape backups. Standing data may require additional controls such as storage in encrypted format within the database.

A significant portion of credit-card-number theft on the Internet is due to unauthorized copying of standing data in shopping cart databases. The U.S. Fair and Accurate Credit Transactions Act of 2003 mandates increased security with truncation of account numbers on receipts and destruction of account numbers after the transaction is processed. The payment card industry (PCI) has its own rules governing credit card data, regardless of whether it's printed or electronic.

System Control Parameters   Data files should be protected from system control parameters that would change the way the files are processed. System control parameters are used to customize the configuration settings and software applications. These settings can alter performance, logging, or file security. Improper implementation can lead to the loss of data, unauthorized access, or undetected errors.

Logical Access Controls   All access to data files should be forced through authentication in a user rights management program (access control program). Direct access to data files through Open Database Connectivity (ODBC) should be prohibited unless controlled by a rights management program with user authentication. It is common for a user to request direct access to the database for the purpose of reading data from another program. This type of uncontrolled direct access should be discouraged.

Transaction Processing Controls   All transactions involving data files should be controlled with authentication and validation checks. The data transformation procedure must be officially approved and managed as part of the system application life cycle. Transaction processing monitors (TP monitors) are frequently used to ensure that database activity does not overload the processing capacity of the available hardware.

Application Processing Controls

System security and integrity are assured through the use of *application processing controls*. Logical access controls require the user to log in with a unique ID and password. The user can begin processing after a successful login. Each application should provide at least three internal processing controls: input, authorized processing, and output.

Input Controls

An *input control* ensures that only valid and authorized information is entered into a transaction. Input controls operate by using a combination of user authorization rights, edit checking, and data entry validation. Sequence checks are used to ensure that each transaction is processed only once. For an excellent analogy, consider how checks and ATM transactions are authorized at a bank.

Input authorization controls include the following:

- Unique login and password
- Signatures on source documents

- Identification of client workstation or terminal
- ReCAPTCHA script to discourage automated input (discussed in Chapter 7)

Processing Controls

The purpose of *processing controls* is to ensure that the data and transactions are valid. Production software programs reside in the production program library. Access to the production program library should be restricted to read-only. There is no reason for the computer programmer or the user to have write access into a production program library.

 Allowing a programmer to have write access to a production program library would be a separation of duties (SOD) violation of change control. The computer operator will move authorized software from the development library to the production library when instructed and authorized by the change control manager. During the move to production, the less-managed or overused encryption keys used during development will be replaced with encryption keys currently used in production. Separation of duties must be enforced at all levels for the cumulative protection controls to work.

Most data processing occurs by using a batch processing mode. The data batch may be small or large. The frequency of processing may be seconds or hours. Regardless of the method, it is necessary to ensure data integrity by using data validation and edit procedures. Without operational processing controls, the database would be no more effective than a garbage can.

Processing controls include the following:

Batch Totals   To compare input against actual processing.

Total Number of Items   To verify that each item was processed.

Transaction Logs   To record activity.

Run-to-Run Totals   To provide verification of the data values during the different stages of processing. This helps ensure the completeness of all transactions.

Limit Checks   To prevent processing of any amount in excess of the expected average. Overly large transactions will not be processed. For example, no employee should receive a paycheck for $50,000. That amount would obviously be excessive outside of executive positions.

Exception Reporting   To identify errors. The exception may hold the batch in suspension until the errors are corrected, or reject individual transactions containing errors, or reject the entire batch of transactions.

Job Cost Accounting   The operating cost of computer processing may be billed to a particular department, project, or application. It is important to observe the effectiveness of job cost accounting when it is used.

Output Controls

Data generated by the system should be protected to ensure confidentiality until it is delivered to the designated user. *Output controls* are just as important for paychecks as confidentiality is for business plans or HR records.

Let's review a few basic output controls:

Report Generation and Distribution   Confidential reports should be output on a printer with restricted access. The report title should indicate that the report is confidential. Exception reports should always generate a page to indicate the exceptions that occurred, or a page to indicate that no exceptions occurred.

Negotiable Instruments   Checks, bonds, and stock certificates are frequently printed on computers. These items should be protected by a combination of logical and physical controls.

Report Retention   Certain types of reports may be required to be controlled under a document retention policy. This applies to records used for regulatory or legal compliance.

Event Logs   Processing logs and audit trails should be protected for integrity and confidentiality at all times. These logs need to be placed under record retention controls.

Antivirus Software

Computers are constantly attacked by malicious software. The attack may be in an email or file attachment. Viruses work by attaching themselves to the end of a file. Antivirus (AV) software will search for the signature (attributes) of known viruses. Without the latest AV updates, the system will be susceptible to attack by new viruses.

Virus   Computer *viruses* are a type of malicious program designed to self-replicate and spread across multiple computers. The purpose of the computer virus is to disrupt normal processing. A computer virus may commence damage immediately or lie dormant, awaiting a particular circumstance such as the date of April Fools' Day. Viruses will automatically attach themselves to the outgoing files. Antivirus software will stop known attacks by detecting the behavior demonstrated by the virus program (*signature detection*) or by appending an antivirus flag to the end of a file (*inoculation*, or *immunization*). New virus attacks can be detected if any program tries to append data to the antivirus flag. Not all antivirus software works by signature scanning; it can also use heuristic scanning, integrity checking, or activity blocking. These are all valid virus detection methods.

Worm   Like viruses, computer *worms* are destructive. Worms are able to travel freely across the computer network by exploiting poorly authenticated system maintenance ports or other known system vulnerabilities. Worms are independent and will actively seek new systems on their own. Most AV software will help you defend against Internet worm attacks.

It's not uncommon for AV updates to cause a conflict with other software on the user's computer. The IT help desk may direct users to download updates from the vendor's website or instruct the users to download updates from only an internal IT server.

Auditors should inquire how the user is to acquire AV updates. Is it directly from the vendor or from IT? The auditor should be interested to see whether the IT staff is actually testing updates on a computer similar to that of the user. If so, what is the delay interval between a vendor releasing AV updates and the time to install this update on all the user computers?

Active Content and Mobile Software Code

Every IS auditor needs to understand the concept of active code and how it affects system security. *Active content* is software that is readily available for download from the Internet. Downloading special drivers, templates, updates, and utilities is a useful function for many people. Anyone who has used the FedEx Office online print service would agree that their software utility makes it easy to get your print job formatted, printed, bound, and delivered without ever leaving your desk. The FedEx programmers did an excellent job of developing downloadable software that helps the user.

Web pages have evolved into multimedia portals capable of delivering live weather maps, streaming news reports, business intelligence, and online education for those without the resources to attend class. Active content provides a useful capability that cannot be ignored. Attackers can abuse the vulnerabilities of active content unless preventative, detective, and corrective controls are implemented:

- IT executives should develop a policy regarding the use of active content (preventative).

- Additional procedures need to be developed to help reduce the associated risk. These include making configuration settings, enabling virus detection, enabling intrusion detection on each system, and linking violations to an incident response mechanism (detective and corrective controls).

Web Browser Functions

When we surf the Internet, the web pages we see are composed of special formatting codes along with embedded function tags. HyperText Markup Language (HTML) handles the screen formatting. Special function tags perform other actions such as retrieving images, playing a multimedia video, playing music, or linking into another program. Programs such as Java and ActiveX extend the browser functionality.

Multipurpose Internet Mail Extensions

Multipurpose Internet Mail Extensions (MIME) was originally designed to be used for electronic mail, although it has evolved for use by all types of multimedia. These extensions include content for the following:

- Audio transmission.

- Video images.

- Embedding text, images, and other data into a file. This is how Portable Document Format (PDF) and email work.

- Support for plug-in applications.

The magic of the Internet is powered by MIME. Benefits of using the Internet are so great that IT has to deal with the situation and be prepared to clean up any mess that occurs. The alternative is to disable Internet access. This strategy of no access may work if the mission data is beyond valuation. Otherwise, the replacement IT staff will be called upon to provide a more palatable solution.

Mobile Software

It's easy to download new programs from the Internet. Sometimes a web page will automatically download a program for the user to increase the functionality of the web page. This is referred to as *mobile software*. It's also known as mobile code or applets. The two dominant leaders are Java and ActiveX. Let's explore the basic characteristics of each:

Java   Java is one of those wonderful programs that runs inside the browser with special security to protect the user's computer. Java uses the *Java Virtual Machine (JVM)* program inside your browser to provide an elaborate level of security. This helps prevent Java programs from damaging your computer. Java permissions can be set to allow digitally signed applications to be run from websites you trust. Unsigned applications can be rejected for security. Three of the most common implementations of Java include the following:

- Small Java programs that download to the user are called *applets*.

- Java programs that run on the server are known as *servlets*.

- JavaScript (or Microsoft's JScript) can be used to perform tasks within the client's browser

Java is object oriented, which provides the delegation capability for applets and servlets to off-load work to another applet or servlet. Untrusted servlets can be executed in a secure JVM environment to protect users from undesirable behavior by the program. Java's security manager feature mediates all access to system resources. Java still poses a minor security issue because it does not prevent a program from creating a denial-of-service condition nor does it prevent the exportation of a user's identity.

Active Server Pages (ASP and .NET)   Microsoft's operating system is written with C++ and C# (C Sharp). Microsoft's kernel supports user written programs in other programming languages including Beginner's All-purpose Symbolic Instruction Code (BASIC). The latest version is called *Visual Basic* and *Visual Basic Scripting Edition* (VBScript). Windows XP, Vista, and Windows 7 share the same programming language used in ASP. This programming commonality with the operating system is the root issue of security problems. Let's look at the security problems created when using Active Server Pages:

- Visual Basic and VBScript create interactive web pages under the nickname ActiveX.

- In theory, Microsoft's programming language was supposed to provide isolation boundaries to create a relatively secure environment. Implementation flaws and increased integration of the browser to the operating system have violated the barrier concept.

- Well-written ASP programs of a malicious nature can subvert Microsoft security by executing commands throughout the entire Microsoft operating system.

ActiveX places no restrictions on what the programmer can do. ActiveX software is digitally signed by the author via a technology scheme called *authenticode*. The publisher certificate for authenticode requires the publisher to pledge that they will not knowingly distribute harmful code; it does not ensure that the program is well behaved. Poorly designed programs can still do damage. ActiveX and authenticode place responsibility for security upon the user. You can see a comparison of risks in Table 6.1.

TABLE 6.1   Comparing security risks of mobile code

Low Risk	Moderate Risk	High Risk
Portable Document Format (PDF)	Applets	ActiveX
Adobe Shockwave Flash (SWF)	PostScript (PS)	
JavaScript	Visual Basic (VB)	

Mobile Code Security Policy

The mobile code security risk can be managed by using one of four basic concepts. Each of these will be determined by the organization's mission, capability, and value of data. The business unit and IT need to agree on which of these basic choices will be used:

- Disallow functionality (no benefit, no risk)
- Allow functionality only from internal servers (lower risk)
- Allow functionality from trusted external servers (moderate risk)
- Let the users do whatever they want from any server (high risk)

Choices made can be supported by the addition of technical controls using automated filters, application settings, digital signatures, isolation tools, and software behavior controls. Administrative controls are required to provide security audit, version control, user awareness training, and incident handling.

As an IS auditor, you will be interested in how the decision was reached regarding the use of mobile code. Particular areas of interest include available evidence supporting or challenging the decision, methods of detecting problems, and the implementation of corrective controls.

Maintenance Controls

Maintenance controls exist to ensure that hardware and software changes will have a minimum impact on processing schedules and system availability. All maintenance should be approved by the change control process before it occurs. It is not uncommon for an organization to issue blanket approval for small changes with low risk. Let's look at some of the issues that should be addressed prior to performing maintenance.

Backup and Recovery

System programs and data should be backed up before maintenance occurs. The backup tapes (or media) should be read/write verified. Verifying a backup ensures that the data copy matches the original. The backup provides a second copy of current data if something goes horribly wrong.

Project Management

Project management with a risk analysis should be performed prior to starting maintenance. Most maintenance is a mini project. As the scope of the maintenance increases, so should the project planning. Each project plan should include a provision for workarounds and fallback procedures. A fallback procedure will be executed if the change fails to deliver the desired result.

Dealing with change is so important that it deserves its own section. Let's talk about it with some additional detail right now.

Change Control Management

We discussed change management in Chapter 2 and Chapter 5. In terms of IT service delivery, change management concerns relate to hardware and software maintenance. The introduction of any change constitutes a risk to system integrity and availability. However, change is inevitable.

A flowchart of the change management process appears in Figure 6.4.

ISACA wants every CISA to be aware of four concepts that apply to change management in IT service delivery: change control review, configuration control, change authorization, and emergency changes.

Change Control Review

Everything changes in the normal course of life. Changes need to be reviewed to schedule the best time for implementation. Most vendors release changes to update security controls or fix malfunctions in the operation of software or hardware.

Configuration Control

The configuration of production systems must be controlled. The method of configuration control is similar to the one we discussed in Chapter 5 concerning software development. Each system configuration is written down and changes are tested before implementation into production. This is only possible with a separate test environment. Changes should not be made to a production system unless the change has undergone formal testing under the control of the change management process.

FIGURE 6.4   Change management process

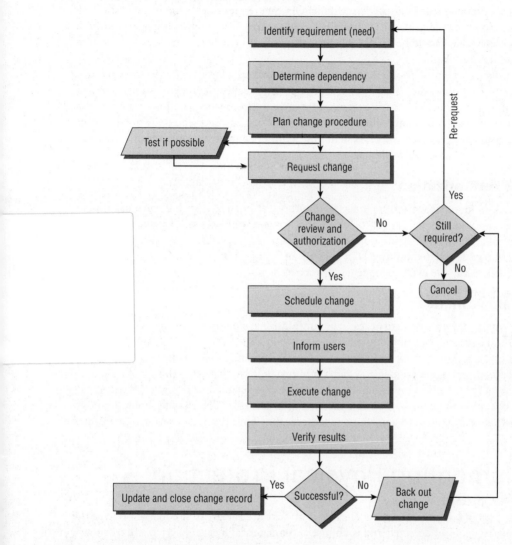

Separate Test Environment

The best way to prevent outages is through diligent testing. According to ISO 27002 item 10.1.4 and existing software quality assurance practices, testing should always occur in a separate test environment to ensure accuracy of the proposed change with integrity (completeness) of the software needed to make it work properly. Best of all, the separate test environment provides safety from malfunction. If the change blows-up, your regular daily processing is not interrupted.

Testing is executed by the software quality assurance tester to prevent any potential conflicts with programmers or IT operations. Remember that the testing should include functionality, interaction between programs (sociability), and security functions including penetration testing. Sanitary data should be used to eliminate the risk of breaching confidentiality requirements of actual user data.

Using a separate test environment saves money by preventing outages that would otherwise occur. The price of nonconformance (failure) provides an excellent financial justification. Use the price of downtime to demonstrate the need (price of nonconformance). Justifying a separate test environment will be more difficult if the auditee has misrepresented the organization's actual downtime metrics. Remember, system time is either counted as uptime for the user to operate at will, or it's counted as down.

Change Authorization

No change should occur without management authorization, and any changes must remain within the authorized scope. It is unfortunate that some technicians will attempt to implement additional changes at the first opportunity. These changes have consistently proven to be the source of a related failure. The objective of change authorization is to ensure that nobody bypasses the life cycle management process.

Emergency Changes

At times, emergency changes are necessary to minimize system interruption. This is when a separate test environment can really prevent a lot of serious headaches. A senior individual should be consulted for review and approval prior to implementing an emergency change. If the emergency change works, it may remain in production. If it fails, the change should be withdrawn (backed out) immediately. After an emergency change is implemented, the standard change control process will be invoked after the fact. The change should undergo formal testing and analysis to determine whether it may have created additional problems.

Implementing Physical Protection

The auditor should always remember electronic attacks are the greatest concern because the intruder usually goes undetected and is almost never caught. Physical barriers are frequently used to protect physical assets. Earlier in the chapter, we discussed the creation of a map displaying access routes and locked doors. After risk assessment, the next step is to improve physical protection.

Let's review a few of the common techniques for increasing physical protection:

Closed-Circuit Television   Closed-circuit television can provide real-time monitoring or audit logs of past activity. Access routes are frequently monitored by using closed-circuit television. The auditor may be interested in the image quality and retention capabilities of the equipment. Some intrusions may not be detected for several weeks. Does the organization have the ability to check for events that occurred days or weeks ago?

Guards Security guards are an excellent defensive tool. Guards can observe details that the computerized security system would ignore. Security guards can deal with exceptions and special events. In an emergency, security guards can provide crowd control and direction. Closed-circuit television can extend the effective area of the security guard. The monitoring of remote areas should reduce the potential for loss. The only drawback is that guards may be susceptible to bribery or collusion. It's a common practice for the guards to be monitored by a separate security staff in banks and casinos.

Special Locks Physical locks come in a variety of shapes and sizes. Let's look at three of the more common types of locks:

Traditional Tumbler Lock An inexpensive type of lock is the tumbler lock, which uses a standard key. This is identical to the brass key lock used for your home and automobile. The lock is relatively inexpensive and easy to install. It has one major drawback: Everyone uses the same key to open the lock. It is practically impossible to identify who has opened the lock. Figure 6.5 shows a diagram of the tumbler lock.

FIGURE 6.5 Tumbler lock

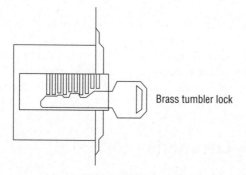

Brass tumbler lock

Electronic Lock Electronic locks can be used by security systems. The electronic line is frequently coupled with a badge reader. Each user is given a unique ID badge, which will unlock the door. This provides an audit trail of who has unlocked the door for each event. Electronic locks are usually managed by a centralized security system. Unfortunately, electronic locks will not tell us how many people went through the door when it was open. To solve that problem, it would be necessary to combine the electronic lock with a mantrap passageway, in which one door must be closed before the next door can be opened, and to use closed-circuit television recording to serve as an audit log.

Cipher Lock Cipher locks may be electronic or mechanical. The purpose of the cipher lock is to eliminate the brass key requirement. Access is granted by entering a particular combination on the keypad. Low-security cipher locks use a shared unlock code. Higher-security cipher locks issue a unique code for each individual. The FBI office in Dallas has a really slick electronic cipher lock using an LCD touchpad. The user touches a combination of keys in sequence on the LCD keypad. Between each physical touch, the key display changes to prevent an observer from detecting the actual code used. This is an example of a higher-security cipher lock.

Biometrics   The next level of access control for locked doors is biometrics. Biometrics uses a combination of human characteristics as the key to the door. We discuss this in Chapter 7.

Burglar Alarm   The oldest method of detecting a physical breach is a burglar alarm. Alarm systems are considered the absolute minimum for physical security. An alarm system may be installed for the purpose of signaling that a particular door has been opened. Remote or unmanned facilities frequently implement a burglar alarm to notify personnel of a potential breach. Burglar alarm systems should be monitored to ensure appropriate response in a timely manner.

 As a CISA, you are required to understand the fundamental issues of physical protection. Advanced study in physical security is available from ASIS International for the Certified Protection Professional (CPP) credential.

Environmental Sensors   Technology is not tolerant of water or contaminants. Environmental controls are used to regulate the temperature, humidity, and airflow. The failure of air-conditioning or humidity control can damage sensitive computer equipment. All the servers in the computer room would overheat and crash without continuous air-conditioning. Environmental sensors should be monitored with the same interest and response as a burglar alarm.

Data Processing Locations

We have discussed the need for security to restrict physical access. The data processing facility requires special consideration in its design. Data processing equipment is a valuable asset that needs to be protected from environmental contamination, malicious personnel, theft, and physical damage.

The data center location should not draw any attention to its true contents. This will alleviate malicious interest by persons motivated to commit theft or vandalism. The facility should be constructed according to national fire-protection codes with a 2-hour fire-protection rating for floors, ceilings, doors, and walls.

Some locations in a building are not suitable for a computer room. Basements are a poor choice because they are susceptible to flooding. In 1960, computers were placed behind glass windows to showcase them as a status symbol. A series of riots in the mid-1960s made it apparent that computers needed to be rapidly moved into fortified rooms. The most expedient location was an unused basement with no windows.

The preferred standard over the past 50 years is to place the data center on a middle floor in the building—preferably located between the second floor and one floor below the top floor. Basements can always flood, the first floor is susceptible to flooding and break-in, and the top floor is usually damaged in severe storms. Opaque windows are considered acceptable in some environments if the windows are shatterproof and installed by using a sturdy mount equal to the window rating.

Access to the data center should be monitored and restricted. The same level of protection should be given to wiring closets because they contain related support equipment. Physical protection should be designed by using a 3D space consideration: intruders should not be able to gain access from above, below, or through the side of the facility.

The physical space inside the data processing facility should be environmentally controlled. Let's move on to a discussion of environmental protection.

Environmental Controls

The first concern in the data center is electrical power. Electrical power is the lifeblood of computer systems. Unstable power is the number one threat to consistent operations. At a minimum, the data center should have power conditioners and an uninterruptible power supply.

You are expected to understand a few of the terms used to describe conditions that create problems for electrical power.

Figure 6.6 illustrates the different types of electrical power conditions.

FIGURE 6.6   Electrical power conditions

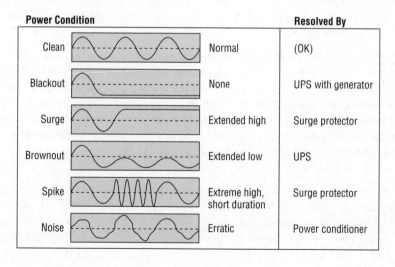

Emergency Power Shutoff

Electricity is both an advantage and a hazard. The national fire-protection code requires an emergency power off (EPO) switch to be located near the exit door. The purpose of this switch is to kill power to prevent an individual from being electrocuted. The EPO switch is a red button, which should have a plastic cover to prevent accidental activation. The switch can be wired into the fire-control system for automatic power shutoff if the fire-control system releases water or chemicals to disable a fire.

Uninterruptible Power Supply

The uninterruptible power supply (UPS) is an intelligent power monitor coupled with a string of electrical batteries. The UPS constantly monitors electrical power. A UPS can supplement low-voltage conditions by using power stored in the batteries. During a power outage, the UPS will provide a limited amount of battery power to keep the systems running. The duration of this battery power depends on the electrical consumption of the attached equipment. Most UPS units are capable of signaling the computer to automatically shut down before the batteries are completely drained. Larger commercial UPS systems have the ability to signal the electrical standby generator to start.

Standby Generator

The standby generator provides auxiliary power whenever commercial power is disrupted. The standby generator can be connected to the UPS for an automated start. The UPS will signal the generator that power is required, and the generator will start warming up. After the generator is warmed up, a transfer circuit will switch the electrical feed from commercial power to the generator power. The UPS will filter the generator power and begin recharging batteries. The standby generator can run for as long as it has fuel. Most standby generators run on diesel fuel or natural gas:

Diesel Generator   A diesel generator requires a large fuel-storage tank with at least 12 hours of fuel. Better-prepared organizations will store at least three days worth of fuel and as much as thirty days of fuel. Simple power failures will typically be resolved within three days. Power failures due to storm damage usually take more than one week to resolve. Smart executives would never trust the business to hollow promises from a fuel delivery service. When power stops, attitudes will flare because the business has been shut down. More fuel storage is cheaper than the outage or expense of a court battle with your supplier over late fuel delivery.

Natural Gas Generator   Natural gas–powered generators have the advantage of tapping a gas utility pipeline directly or using a connection through a storage tank. The natural gas generator does not require a fuel truck to refill its fuel tank. The local natural gas pipeline provides a steady supply of fuel for an extended period of time. The natural gas supply is a good idea in areas that are geologically stable.

Air-conditioning equipment is the Achilles' heel of generators. An enormous amount of fuel is consumed when running AC using generator power. It also takes a very big generator to run AC compressors. Realistic alternatives to AC include cycling cooler subsurface water from deep wells for convection cooling.

Dual Power Leads

The best way to prevent power outages is to install power leads from two different power substations. It would be extremely expensive to just pay someone to run special power cables. Instead, the location of the building housing the computer room should be selected according to area power grids. Power grids are usually divided along highways. Careful location selection will place your building within a quarter-mile of two power grids. This makes the cost of the dual connection affordable. Dual power leads should approach the building from different directions without sharing the same underground trench. A construction backhoe is extremely effective in destroying underground connections.

Power Transfer System

The power transfer system, known as a *transfer switch*, provides the connection between commercial power and UPS battery power in the generator. The transfer switch may be manual or computerized. It is not uncommon for the power transfer switch to fail during a power outage. Therefore, manual power-transfer procedures should be in place. Automated power-transfer switches may not be able to react to a pair of short power failures occurring within the same 30-minute window. After the first power failure, the generator will come online to produce electrical current. After commercial electrical power is restored, the power switch will transfer back to commercial electricity. At the same time, the generator will receive a signal to begin cooling down and finally shut off. If another power outage occurs during the generator cooling period, the power transfer switch will cycle to generator power while the generator is not producing electrical current. This condition may be resolved by increasing the battery capability of the UPS and adjusting generator start and stop times.

Figure 6.7 illustrates the basic electrical power system used for computer installations.

Heating, Ventilation, and Air-Conditioning

The computer installation requires heating, ventilation, and air-conditioning. Electronic equipment performs well in cold conditions; however, magnetic media should not be allowed to freeze. Ventilation is necessary for cooling computer equipment. Physical damage occurs if the computer circuitry sustains extended use at temperatures of 104 degrees or higher. Physical damage will also occur if the internal electronic circuitry exceeds 115 degrees during operation.

Air-conditioning is also used to control humidity. Humidity will control static electricity that could damage electrical circuits. The ideal humidity for a computer room is between 35 percent and 45 percent at 72 degrees. This will reduce the atmospheric conditions that would otherwise create high levels of static electricity.

FIGURE 6.7   Power system overview

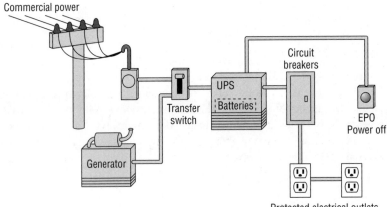

In certain climates, alternate methods of conserving power include pumping colder water from deep wells through a closed-loop condenser system (aka a chiller). During emergency situations, another method uses a stored tank of liquid nitrogen for temporary cooling over days or weeks. Liquid nitrogen is used by electronic manufacturers in environmental testing for component failure analysis. The same technique could be applied by venting small amounts of liquid nitrogen through a closed-loop condenser system, like the chiller concept. Air blowing across the condenser coils will help cool the room without burdening the power generator.

Fire, Smoke, and Heat Detection

The data center and records storage area should be equipped for fire, smoke, and heat detection. Unheated areas may need to be monitored for freezing conditions. There are three basic types of fire detectors, using smoke detection, heat detection, or flame detection:

Smoke Detection   Uses optical smoke detectors or radioactive ionization smoke detection

Heat Detection   Uses a fixed temperature thermostat (which activates above 200 degrees), or rapid-rise detection (which activates the alarm if the temperature increases dramatically within a matter of minutes)

Flame Detection   Relies on ultraviolet radiation from a flame or the pulsation rate of a flame

A fire-detection system activates an alarm to initiate human response. A fire-detection system may also activate fire suppression with or without the discharge of water or chemicals.

Fire Suppression

Fire suppression is the next step after fire detection. A fire-suppression system may be fully automated or mechanical. There are three basic types of fire-suppression systems:

Wet Pipe System   The wet pipe system derives its name from the concept of water remaining inside the pipe. Most sprinkler heads in a ceiling-based system are mechanical. Each sprinkler head is an individual valve held closed by a meltable pin. A fire near the sprinkler head will melt the pin, and the valve will open to discharge whatever is in the pipe. This type of system can burst because of a freeze, or leak due to corrosion, which would create an unscheduled discharge. Figure 6.8 shows a wet pipe system.

FIGURE 6.8   Wet pipe system

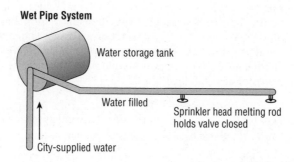

Dry Pipe System   The dry pipe system is an improvement over the wet pipe for two reasons. First, the pipe is full of compressed air rather than water prior to discharge. When the valve opens, there is a delay of a few seconds as the air clears from the line. The water will discharge after the air is purged. This leads us to the second advantage. The flow of rushing air can trigger a flow switch to activate the EPO switch to kill electrical power. Equipment will shut off during the few seconds before the water is discharged. This will reduce the amount of damage to computer equipment. Special computer cabinets are made to shed water away from electronic hardware mounted inside. Figure 6.9 shows a dry pipe system.

FIGURE 6.9   Dry pipe system

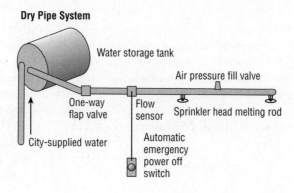

It's important to understand the difference between dry pipe systems, dry chemical systems, and gas-based systems. In dry chemical applications, such as a handheld fire extinguisher, an inert powder such as baking soda or sodium chloride is used to smother the fire or reduce the temperature below the minimum for combustion.

Gas Chemical System   Gas chemical systems are frequently used in computer installations because gaseous chemicals avoid the hazards created by water. The gas chemical system uses an inert gas such as FM-200 or NAF-S-3 to extinguish fire.

 Gaseous halon is no longer used because it is a chlorofluorocarbon (CFC) that destroys the Earth's ozone layer (1994 international environmental accord). The exception is for aircraft and ships. Fires occurring while in flight or at sea could be devastating with tragic loss of life. All former halon installations in computer rooms should have been converted to FM-200 or an equivalent gas chemical.

When electronic sensors detect a fire condition, the gas chemical system will discharge into the room. Figure 6.10 shows the basic design of a gas chemical system.

FIGURE 6.10   Gas chemical system

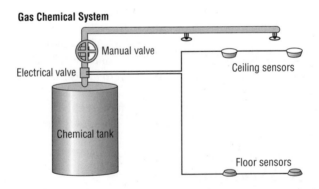

Special administrative controls are necessary with gas chemical systems. Maintenance personnel must never lift floor tiles or move ceiling tiles while the gas chemical system is armed. Floating particles of dust can activate a discharge of gas chemicals. Humans should not inhale the gas used in gas chemical systems because it may be lethal. A gas chemical discharge introduces a great deal of air pressure into the room within seconds. Fragile glass windows may shatter during discharge, creating a temporary airborne glass hazard.

You need to be aware that a water pipe system may be required even if a gas chemical system is installed. Fire safety codes can require wet pipe systems throughout the building, without exception. Some building owners will not allow the tenant to alter existing fire-control systems. The gas chemical system would then have to be installed in parallel to the existing water-based system.

Structured Premise Wiring

Poorly planned data centers can be a wiring nightmare. Industry reports state that 97 percent of all network performance problems can be traced to physical wiring problems. Modern building standards have been updated in the last 20 years to include structured premise wiring systems. Two areas of concern for the CISA are data/voice cabling and building automation systems (BAS).

It used to be a joke, but buildings themselves are becoming so automated that IT hardware is used even to operate the toilet (by using infrared proximity sensors to activate flushing). Most BAS installations are operated by facilities instead of IT for political reasons. Either way, the ceilings and underfloor areas are being used to run power and data cabling. Let's review three of the most important concepts required for ensuring safety and uninterrupted operation:

Suspended Cable Tray or Routing System   It's a very bad practice to allow cables to lie on the ground, floor, or across ceiling tiles. Wire cable trays protect the cables from water, physical abrasion, and accidental disruption. Tray systems are standard on all installations wired in accordance with EIA/TIA standards. Lack of a tray system indicates the work of amateurs.

Proper Color Coding   Over 30 years ago, the Building Industry Consulting Service International (BICSI) started publishing information for communication cabling covering the spectrum for voice, data, electronic security systems, and audio/video technology. With so many departments running cable, it's important for technicians to easily recognize which cables are under their control, which are not, and any safety issues.

Safety Isolation   Even low-voltage data cable carries serious risk of shorting, transferring dangerous voltages, and conducting lightning surges. Code-compliant safety isolation, disconnects, and electrical threats are not taught by Microsoft, Cisco, Nortel Networks, or other data/security communication vendors. This can pose a serious threat to life, safety, and valuable electronic equipment.

All installations by a Registered Communications Distribution Designer (RCDD) or BICSI-trained technician will recognize the need to keep data communications protected from stress and interference from power circuits. People who think surge suppressors will suffice are so far out of touch as to be part of the threat, too.

Water Detection

Water is discharged from air-conditioning or cooling systems and usually runs to a drain located under the raised floor. Water-detection systems are necessary under the floor to alert personnel of a clogged drain or plumbing backup. Water-detection sensors also may be placed in the ceiling to detect leakage from pipes in the roof above. It is common for water pipes to be located over a computer room directly above the ceiling tiles or higher floors. Water can even cascade down inside the building from the roof.

Figure 6.11 provides a simple overview of a data processing center and the various environmental control systems.

FIGURE 6.11 Typical computer room

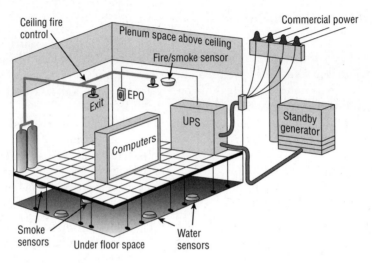

To minimize risk, the organization should have a policy prohibiting food, liquids, and smoking in the computer facility. Now it is time to discuss safe storage of assets and media records.

Safe Media Storage

Vital business records and computer media require protection from the environment, fire, theft, and malicious damage. Safe onsite storage is required. The best practice is to use fireproof file cabinets and a fireproof media safe. Standard business records are kept in the fireproof file cabinet. Computer tapes and disk media are stored in a special fire safe. The fire safe provides physical protection and ensures that the internal temperature of the safe will not exceed 130 degrees. Copies of files and archived records are transferred to offsite storage.

Offsite Storage

The offsite storage facility provides storage for a second copy of vital records and data backup files. The offsite storage facility should be used for safe long-term retention of records. The standard practice is to send backup tapes off site every day or every other day. The offsite storage location should be a well-designed, secure, bonded facility with 24-hour security. This site must be designed for protection from flood, fire, and theft. The offsite vendor should maintain a low profile without visible markings identifying the contents of the facility to a casual passerby. Most offsite storage facilities provide safe media transport.

Media Transport

Business records and magnetic media should be properly boxed for transit. The contents in the box must be properly labeled. An inventory should be recorded prior to shipping media off site for any reason. The tape librarian is usually responsible for tracking data media in transit. Backup tapes contain the utmost secrets of any organization. All media leaving the primary facility must be kept in secure storage at all times and tracked during transit. New regulations are mandating the use of encryption to protect the standing data on backup tapes. The tape librarian should verify the safe arrival of media at the offsite storage facility. Random media audits at the offsite facility are a good idea. The custodian must track the location and status of all data files outside the primary facility.

Media Asset Disposal

This is the seventh phase of the SDLC model. A formal authorization process is required to dispose of physical and data assets. Improper controls can lead to the untimely loss of valuable assets. A proper asset-disposal process contains procedures to ensure that data is purged (erased) from all equipment prior to disposal so that the data can never be recovered. Information and media will be disposed of at the end of its life cycle. Physical assets should be formally discharged from inventory. These assets can be destroyed, sold, or donated depending on the organization's desire.

All devices leaving the controlled environment must be purged of data by using disk-wiping utilities or degaussing methods. Disk reformatting is not an effective method because it will not destroy raw data that is accessible via special utilities that bypass the operating system. As an IS auditor, you need to determine whether the organization is following an acceptable asset-disposal process. Let's review the common disposal procedures for media:

Paper, Plastic, and Photographic Data   Nondurable media may be disposed of by using physical destruction such as shredding or burning.

Durable and Magnetic Media   Durable media may be disposed of by using data destruction techniques of overwriting, degaussing, and physical grinding.

> **Overwriting**   Data files are not actually deleted by a Delete command. The only change is that the first character of the file is set to zero. Setting the first character to zero indicates that the remaining contents can be overwritten whenever the computer system needs more storage space. Undelete utilities are operating system dependent, but a common method of reversing deletion is changing the first character back to a numeric value of one. This makes the file contents readable again. To destroy files without recovery, it is necessary to overwrite the contents of the disc. A file overwrite utility is used to replace every single data bit with a random value such as E6X, BBB, or other meaningless value.

Degaussing   Degaussing is a bulk erasing process using a strong electromagnet. Degaussing equipment is relatively inexpensive. To operate, the degaussing unit is turned on and placed next to a box of magnetic media. The electromagnet erases magnetic media by changing its electrical alignment. Erasure occurs within minutes or hours, depending on the strength of the device.

Physical Destruction (Preferred Method)   A significant amount of time and effort may be required for degaussing or overwriting obsolete media. Older hard drives have very little value, especially when you consider that the drive capacity is probably small by today's standards. The labor of overwriting or degaussing may exceed the financial value of the drive. In fact, labor costs may exceed the donation value of recycling disk drives to a charity. Physical destruction is accomplished by a commercial hard disk grinder, which also recycles the resulting debris. Hard disk destruction services may bring a mobile unit to your facility or offer mail-in service. Just remember the risk of standing data until you are certain that media is destroyed.

Federal Times reported that a random U.S. government audit test of over-written disk drives discovered 12 of 15 still contained recoverable data. Salvageable data existed even after all the procedures were performed correctly. This is why physical destruction is preferred. Auditors can verify that the destruction was actually performed by using a simple attribute test of weighing the disk before grinding and then weighing the resulting debris after grinding.

Now you have covered the major points of IT service delivery. Let's close with the summary and exam essentials.

Summary

The performance of information technology is ultimately interpreted by three fundamental business performance indicators: the IT budget, user satisfaction, and technical indicators. Technical indicators could include a combination of automated and manual metrics. You can gain a reasonable understanding of IT performance by reviewing these indicators.

IT management should conduct regular performance reviews of all the items discussed in this chapter. Management and staff should make provisions for an independent audit to review their work. The auditor's focus in IT service delivery will be to determine the effectiveness and efficiency of IT.

When reviewing IT service delivery, the paramount concern is that action items are identified, properly tracked, assigned to a competent individual, and resolved in a timely manner. IT's performance can be measured by a combination of metrics, budget performance, and user satisfaction.

The IT auditor evaluates the client's performance and effectiveness of their management techniques.

Exam Essentials

Know how to evaluate service-level management practices from internal and external providers.   Service-level management is based on an understanding between the provider and the user as to system availability, service definition, personnel qualifications, security requirements, and data integrity requirements. Service-level agreements (SLAs) need to include performance reporting, right to audit, SLA change procedures, and the cost of service.

Understand the principles of IT operations management to ensure that the service meets the business requirements.   IT operations management can be aligned to business requirements by using the traditional processes of mission, strategy, and metrics supported by policies, standards, and procedures. The alignment can occur by using the balanced scorecard methodology we discussed in Chapter 2.

Understand how the IT organization implements functional controls for service delivery.   Controls are established for system access, data files, input, application processing, output, maintenance, change management, asset control, capacity management, and problem management.

Understand the issues surrounding software licensing.   Software licenses are assets that need to be controlled, inventoried, tracked, and managed. Unauthorized installation of computer software is a violation of copyright law, which carries stiff penalties.

Understand production change control, release management, and configuration control.   Changes need to be carefully managed in a production environment to prevent an interruption or outage. Software may be released as a major release, an update, or an emergency fix. Emergency changes should undergo the standard change management process after implementation.

Understand the demands of ensuring processing integrity.   Data files must be protected from unauthorized access. Standing data is vulnerable to unauthorized copying. Application processing uses input controls, processing controls to ensure the completeness of processing, and output controls to ensure the confidentiality of the output.

Understand the purpose of valid backups and project management in maintenance controls.   Data backups are used to ensure that two copies of the data exist in case a failure occurs during maintenance. Project management is used with risk analysis to manage maintenance changes. The goal is to ensure that the maintenance occurs with the least possible impact to the system's availability and integrity.

Know the issues in problem and incident management.   Problem and incident management requires a timely response via predefined procedures and a method for escalating problems. The purpose of problem response is to correct a condition. Incident response determines the impact and the steps necessary for resolution. A concern is that the location of an incident may be a potential technology crime scene.

Understand the issues of maintaining evidence integrity during forensic investigations.   Forensics requires special handling procedures during the four phases of acquisition, examination, utilization, and review. Useful data may be scavenged from volatile RAM and nonvolatile temporary files on the hard disk in slack space or swap files. Data files should be obtained by using a write blocker to prevent the source media from being accidentally altered, which would taint the evidence.

Know the purpose of the environmental controls used in the IT environment.   Environmental controls are necessary to prevent an interruption to the system's availability and to protect assets from loss. Environmental systems include power, water detection, heating and air-conditioning, fire detection, fire control, and humidity to prevent the buildup of static electricity.

Review Questions

1. What type of control is representative of exception reporting?

    A. Processing

    B. Output

    C. Database integrity

    D. Service level

2. How should management act to best deal with emergency changes?

    A. Emergency changes cannot be made without advance testing.

    B. All changes should still undergo review.

    C. The change control process does not apply to emergency conditions.

    D. Emergency changes are not allowed under any condition.

3. What is one of the bigger concerns regarding asset disposal?

    A. Residual asset value

    B. Employees taking disposed property home

    C. Standing data

    D. Environmental regulations

4. Why is ongoing system monitoring important?

    A. For preventative control

    B. For historical logging and trend analysis

    C. To collect metrics for SLA reports

    D. To find inconsistencies and errors

5. What is the primary objective in problem escalation?

    A. Improve customer satisfaction

    B. Optimize the number of skilled personnel

    C. Ensure the correct response

    D. Prove that the IT staff is competent

6. Performance of a third party should be compared to the agreed-upon service-level metrics and must be

    A. supplied by an independent employee of the service provider.

    B. accepted at face value by the customer.

    C. reviewed by management.

    D. accepted; review is not necessary because it is a third party and outside the customer's control.

7.   What is the most important responsibility of the IT security person?

   A.   Controlling and monitoring compliance to data security policies

   B.   Promoting security awareness within the organization

   C.   Establishing procedures for IT and reviewing for legal accuracy

   D.   Assisting in system administration of the servers and database

8.   Segregation of duties may not be practical in a small environment. A single employee may be performing the combined functions of server operator and application programmer, for example. The IS auditor should recommend controls for which of the following?

   A.   Automated logging of changes made to development libraries

   B.   The hiring of additional technical staff to force segregation of duties

   C.   Preventing the operator login ID from making program modifications

   D.   Procedures verifying that only approved program changes are implemented

9.   Which of the following is a major issue facing incident response?

   A.   Location may be a technology crime scene

   B.   Scheduling of internal personnel

   C.   Developing appropriate help desk procedures

   D.   Compliance with current IT policies

10.   Which of the following functions should be separated from the others if segregation of duties cannot be achieved in an automated system?

   A.   Origination

   B.   Authorization

   C.   Correction

   D.   Reprocessing

11.   What is the primary concern regarding maintenance login accounts?

   A.   Computer systems have default user accounts for system setup.

   B.   Access to maintenance accounts must be restricted to a particular station address.

   C.   Maintenance accounts must be configured to use the hardware that was selected by the organization.

   D.   The default login ID used by maintenance accounts is often well known.

12.   An IS auditor is auditing controls related to an employee termination. Which of the following is the *most* important aspect to be reviewed?

   A.   Company staff are notified about the termination.

   B.   All login accounts of the employee are terminated.

   C.   The details of the employee have been removed from active payroll files.

   D.   Company property provided to the employee has been returned.

13. What are the three layers for scoring IT performance according to ISACA?

   A. Policy, standards, established procedures

   B. Budget, service-level agreement, problem management

   C. Mission, strategy, metrics

   D. Definition of service, internal controls, change management

14. What is one of the first concerns that the IS auditor should have when reviewing service-level agreements?

   A. The vendor can provide evidence that security controls are present.

   B. The services in the agreement are aligned to actual business needs.

   C. The client received the absolute best price for services offered.

   D. The contract guaranteed the right to audit the outsource vendor.

15. Which of the following statements about standing data is true?

   A. Standing data improves database performance. The data is standing ready for processing.

   B. Standing data is an operational requirement.

   C. Standing data is a security concern.

   D. Standing data is a normal occurrence in the database.

16. Which of the following is *not* an input authorization control?

   A. Signatures on source documents

   B. Sequence numbers

   C. Management review

   D. Separation of duties

17. Which of the following statements is true regarding the programmer?

   A. Is responsible for maintaining the production software currently in use by the user

   B. Should never have access to the production software library

   C. Makes changes to the production version of software under the supervision of a computer operator

   D. Is responsible for reviewing user change requests and implementing approved changes to the production library

18. Which of the following refers to providing verification of data values during different stages of processing for the purpose of completeness of the transaction?

   A. Run-to-run totals

   B. Job cost accounting

   C. Limit checks

   D. Validation checker

19. What is likely to be the biggest issue regarding log management?

   A. Systems need to be configured, and then someone needs to read the logs and respond to the findings.

   B. Log management is not required. It's considered a waste of time.

   C. Log files need to be configured, captured, read, and backed up.

   D. System log files consume valuable disk space and are used only by the auditor.

20. Why is a write blocker needed during the acquisition phase of digital forensics?

   A. To keep the hacker from changing or destroying evidence remaining on the hard disk, in order to preserve the chain of custody

   B. To prevent evidence from being altered, which destroys the chain of custody

   C. To disable the hacker's self-destruct utility from wiping the disk and destroying the chain of evidence

   D. To prevent activating a hidden keyboard-remapping utility that the hacker installed to destroy evidence and cover their tracks

21. What is an applet as compared to a servlet?

   A. An applet is a mobile program running on the workstation, and a servlet runs on the server.

   B. There is no difference, because both can run on the same computer.

   C. An applet is safer than a servlet.

   D. A servlet uses a Java Virtual Machine or ActiveX control to prevent crashing.

22. When separation of duties is not possible, what would be the terminology for forcing employees to take vacation, job rotation, reconciliation, and supervisor review?

   A. Preventative control

   B. Corrective control

   C. Compensating control

   D. Transaction control

23. Which of the following is the best definition of *slack space* on a hard disk?

   A. Unused space leftover after disk formatting

   B. Disk tracks and sectors marked as unusable

   C. Difference between space allocated and space actually used

   D. Uncompressed space remaining on the disk partition

24. Which of the following methods is used to make a backup copy of all the data files for a forensic investigation?

   A. Bitstream image backup

   B. Logical image backup

   C. Full disk backup

   D. Nonvolatile backup

25. Which of the following methods is designed to permanently destroy data on a hard disk?

   A. Reformatting the disk

   B. Deleting files

   C. Read blocker

   D. Disk wiping

Answers to Review Questions

1. A. Exception reporting is a processing control used to capture input errors before processing occurs. The exception may be held in suspension until the errors are corrected or rejected.

2. B. All emergency changes should still undergo the formal change management process after the fact.

3. C. Any standing data should be purged from the equipment prior to disposal.

4. D. Proper IT management focuses on proactive discovery of inconsistencies, errors, and processing failures. The results can be used for secondary value in trend analysis and SLA reporting.

5. C. Problem escalation is used to ensure that the problem is analyzed by a competent individual with the proper training.

6. C. All performance by a third party under the service-level agreement should be compared to the service levels that the provider and the user of the service agreed on.

7. A. The primary responsibility of the IT information security person is to ensure the proper implementation of data security policies and to monitor the level of compliance.

8. D. Compensating controls may be used when segregation of duties is not practical for a small staff. Procedures must exist to verify that only approved program changes are implemented.

9. A. The incident location may be a technical crime scene. The response should be preplanned and structured to ensure that the value of evidence is not diminished and confidentiality is maintained. The other points may be contributing circumstances but are not major issues.

10. B. Authorization for changes should be separated from other work if separation of duties cannot be achieved. Additional compensating controls would be required.

11. D. The default login ID used for maintenance accounts is frequently well known and commercially published. Login may be restricted to a particular station address. However, that is not the primary concern.

12. B. Employee access to information systems should be promptly terminated. The accounts for contractors no longer employed by the organization should be suspended. All accounts should be reviewed before the account is deleted.

13. C. ISACA defines the three layers for IT scoring as mission, strategy, and meaningful metrics for performance measurement.

14. B. The services provided should fulfill the organization's business objectives. The second concern would be the presence of security controls, followed by the right to audit. The last concern should be the absolute best price. Price would not matter if the services provided did not fulfill an actual business requirement.

15. C. Standing data is a security concern that requires additional controls such as storage in an encrypted format.

16. D. Separation of duties does not grant input authorization. The other three answers represent valid input authorization.

17. B. Software developers (programmers) should not have privileged access to production libraries. A programmer may have the same limited access as the user, but should never be allowed to move programs into production. Doing so would violate change control and separation of duties. The system operator is responsible for moving approved programs into the production library.

18. A. Run-to-run totals are used to ensure the completeness of a transaction during various stages of processing.

19. C. Log files must be backed up. The best practice is to export log files to a Syslog server. This helps protect the files from damage by moving them to another computer. Logs need to be configured to include the best possible data. Log files are used by IT operations staff for incident response. Auditors use log file data for audit evidence.

20. B. Write blockers are used during forensic bit-imaging backups to prevent evidence from being altered, which destroys the chain of custody.

21. A. Applets are small programs that download to the user's computer. Applets are considered mobile code. The equivalent program running on the server is called a servlet program running on the server.

22. C. Compensating controls are administrative controls used to detect problems that may be hidden by the person performing the work. Examples include audits, supervisor review, forced vacations, transaction logging, and account reconciliation.

23. C. *Slack space* refers to the remnant areas of the hard disk. The slack is the difference between space actually used by the file and the space allocated. Remnants of data files often remain in slack space until overwritten or until the drive is defragmented.

24. A. Physical disk imaging (also known as bitstream backup) copies the entire disk by using every data bit, including deleted files and residual data in slack space. A standard computer backup would copy only a logical image of files, skipping deleted data.

25. D. A disk-wiping utility is designed to prevent data from being recovered from a hard disk. Disk formatting simply maps available storage locations. Reformatting the disk is equivalent to tearing the index section out of a book and leaving all the other original pages intact. Disk wiping writes random characters across every data bit location on the disk by using multiple passes to ensure that no data is leftover that may be readable. As of 2009, the best choice is destruction by grinding because overwriting takes too much time and effort.

 Additional CISA practice questions are available on the author's website at www.certtest.com.

Chapter 7

Protecting Information Assets

THE OBJECTIVE OF THIS CHAPTER IS TO ACQUAINT THE READER WITH THE FOLLOWING CONCEPTS:

- ✓ Threats to security, perpetrators, and attack methods

- ✓ Perimeter security designs, firewalls, and intrusion detection

- ✓ Logical access controls for identification, authentication, and restriction of users

- ✓ Changes in wireless security, including the robust security network

- ✓ Encryption systems using symmetric and asymmetric public keys

- ✓ How encryption is used to provide confidentiality or authentication

- ✓ Understanding the differences of digital certificates, digital signatures, and digital rights management

- ✓ Controls and risks with the use of portable devices

- ✓ Security testing, monitoring, and assessment tools

In this chapter, you will study the implementation of access controls. These controls are implemented by using administrative, physical, and technical methods. The IS auditor is required to evaluate the implementation, processes, and procedures used by the client.

The goal of information asset protection is to ensure that adequate safeguards are in use to store, access, transport, and ultimately dispose of confidential information. The auditor must understand how controls promote confidentiality, integrity, and availability.

We will discuss a variety of technical topics related to network security, data encryption, design of physical protection, biometrics, and user authentication. This chapter represents the most significant area of the CISA exam.

The official ISACA exam topics represent a basic overview of concepts. Auditors are trained observers aware of the issues, not in-depth technicians. To attempt to implement these controls or claim expertise after CISA exam study would be a serious misstatement of the auditor's competence. Persons implementing these controls would need approximately 10 times the technical training compared to a CISA exam review. This is why auditors rely on the work of others to perform specific in-depth technical functions. The role of every auditor is to provide a systematic and consistent structure of analysis to produce a trustworthy audit report.

Understanding the Threat

Protecting information assets is a significant challenge. The very subject of security conjures up a myriad of responses. This chapter provides you with a solid overview of practical information about security. The unfortunate reality is that concepts of security have not evolved significantly over the last 2,000 years. Let me explain.

The medieval design of security is still pervasive. Most of your customers will view security as primarily a perimeter defense. History is riddled with failed monuments attesting to the folly of overreliance on perimeter defenses. Consider the castle walls to be equivalent to the office walls of the client's organization. Fresh water from the creek would be analogous to our modern-day utilities. The castle observation towers provide visibility for internal affairs and awareness of outside threats. The observation tower is functionally equal to network management and intrusion detection. A fortress drawbridge provides an equivalent function of the network firewall, allowing persons we trust to enter our organization. The castle courtyard serves as the marketplace or intranet. This is where our vendors, staff, and clients interact. During medieval times, it was necessary for our emissaries to enter and exit the castle fortress in secret. Confidential access was accomplished via a secret tunnel. Our modern-day equivalent to the secret tunnel is a virtual private network (VPN). Consider these thoughts for a moment while you look at Figure 7.1, concerning the medieval defensive design.

FIGURE 7.1   Medieval defensive design

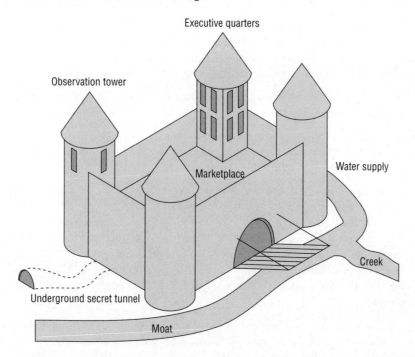

It is possible that security has actually regressed. In medieval times, royalty would use armed guards as an escort when visiting trading partners. In the modern world, the princess is given a notebook computer, PDA, cell phone, and airline ticket with instructions to check in later. Where is the security now?

Medieval castles fell as a result of infiltration, betrayal, loss of utilities such as fresh water, and brute force attacks against the fortress walls. This example should make it perfectly clear why internal controls need improvement. The only possible defensive strategy utilizes multiple layers of security with a constant vigil by management. Anything less is just another castle waiting to fall.

Let's take a quick look at some examples of computer crime and threats to information assets.

Recognizing Types of Threats and Computer Crimes

There is nothing new about the threats facing organizations. History shows that these threats and crimes date back almost 4,000 years (over 130 generations). Therefore, none of these should be a surprise. We need to take a quick review of the threats and crimes that shall be mitigated with administrative, physical, and technical controls:

Theft   The *theft* of information, designs, plans, and customer lists could be catastrophic to an organization. Consider the controls in place to prevent theft of money or embezzlement. Have equivalent controls in place to prevent the theft of valuable intellectual property.

Fraud   Misrepresentation to gain an advantage is the definition of *fraud*. Electronic records may be subject to remote manipulation for the purpose of deceit, suppression, or unfair profit. Fraud may occur with or without the computer. Variations of fraud include using false pretenses, also known as *pretexting*, for any purpose of deceit or misrepresentation.

Sabotage   *Sabotage* is defined as willful and malicious destruction of an employer's property, often during a labor dispute or to cause malicious interference with normal operations.

Blackmail   *Blackmail* is the unlawful demand of money or property under threat to do harm. Examples are to injure property, make an accusation of a crime, or to expose disgraceful defects. This is commonly referred to as *extortion*.

Industrial Espionage   The world is full of competitors and spies. *Espionage* is a crime of spying by individuals and governments with the intent to gather, transmit, or release information to the advantage of any foreign organization. It's not uncommon for governments to eavesdrop on the communications of foreign companies. The purpose is to uncover business secrets to share with companies in their country. The intention is to steal any perceived advancements in position or technology. Telecommunications traveling through each country are subject to legal eavesdropping by governments. Additional care must be taken to keep secrets out of the hands of a competitor.

Unauthorized Disclosure   *Unauthorized disclosure* is the release of information without permission. The purpose may be fraud or sabotage. For example, unauthorized disclosure of trade secrets or product defects may cause substantial damage that is irreversible. The unauthorized disclosure of client records would cause a violation of privacy laws, not to mention details that would be valuable for a competitor.

Loss of Credibility   *Loss of credibility* is the damage to an organization's image, brand, or executive management. This can severely impact revenue and the organization's ability to continue. Fraud, sabotage, blackmail, and unauthorized disclosure may be used to destroy credibility.

Loss of Proprietary Information   The mishandling of information can result in the loss of trade secrets. Valuable information concerning system designs, future marketing plans, and corporate formulas could be released without any method of recovering the data. Once a secret is out, there is no way to make the information secret again.

Legal Repercussions   The breach of control or loss of an asset can create a situation of undesirable attention. Privacy concerns have created new requirements for public disclosure following a breach. Without a doubt, the last thing an organization needs is increased interest from a government regulator. Stockholders and customers may have grounds for subsequent legal action in alleging negligence or misconduct, depending on the situation.

 Real World Scenario

Examples of Legal Repercussions

Life Time Fitness was the target of an investigation by the Texas attorney general for improperly discarding intact records of clients' membership applications. Life Time Fitness membership records were found in Dumpsters at more than a dozen of its fitness centers. This security breach exposed personal information, including driver's license data, credit card data, and other private information (2008).

Morgan Stanley incurred sanctions from the Security Exchange Commission for failing to maintain auditable records of all emails between the brokerage and its clients, as required under SEC rule 17a-4 (2006).

According to the U.S. Federal Bureau of Investigation (FBI), the top three losses in 2005–2009 were due to virus attack, unauthorized access, and theft of proprietary information. There is a trend of dramatic increase in unauthorized access and theft of proprietary information. So, the auditor may ask, who is doing this?

Identifying the Perpetrators

The perpetrators of crime may be casual or sophisticated. Their motives may be financial, political, thrill seeking, or a biased grudge against the organization. However, the damage impact is usually the same regardless of the perpetrator's background or motive. A common trait is that a perpetrator will have time, access, or skills necessary to execute the offense.

Today's computer criminal does not require advanced skills, although they would help. A person with mal-intent needs little more than access to launch an attack. For this reason, strong access controls are mandatory. The FBI reported that the number of internal attacks have been approximately equal to the number of external attacks since 2005. So, who is the attacker?

Hackers

The term *hacker* has a double meaning. The honorable interpretation of hacker refers to a computer programmer who is able to create usable computer programs where none previously existed. In this Study Guide, we refer to the dishonorable interpretation of a hacker—an undesirable criminal.

The criminal hacker focuses on a desire to break in, take over, and damage or discredit legitimate computer processing. The first goal of hacking is to exceed the authorized level of system privileges. This is why it is necessary to monitor systems and take swift action against any individual who attempts to gain a higher level of access. Hackers may be internal or external to the organization. Attempts to gain unauthorized access within the organization should be dealt with by using the highest level of severity, including immediate termination of employment.

Crackers

The term *cracker* is a variation of *hacker*, with the analogy equal to a safe cracker. Some individuals use the term cracker in an attempt to differentiate from the honorable computer programmer definition of hacker. The criminal cracker and criminal hacker terms are used interchangeably. Crackers attempt to illegally or unethically break into a system without authorization.

Script Kiddies

A number of specialized programs exist for the purpose of bypassing security controls. Many hacker tools began as well-intentioned tools for system administration. The argument would be the same if we were discussing a carpenter's hammer. A carpenter's hammer used for the right purpose is a constructive tool. The same tool is a weapon if used for a nefarious purpose.

A *script kiddy* is an individual who executes computer scripts and programs written by others. The script kiddy's motive is to hack a computer by using someone else's software. Examples include password decryption programs and automated access utilities. Several years ago, a login utility was created for Microsoft users to get push-button access into a Novell server. This nifty utility was released worldwide before it was recognized that the utility bypassed Novell security. The utility was nicknamed Red Button and became immensely popular with script kiddies. Internal controls must be put in place to restrict the possession or use of administration utilities. Violations should be considered severe and dealt with in the same manner as hacker violations.

Employee Betrayal

There is a reason why the FBI report cited the high volume of internal crimes. A person within the organization has more access and opportunity than anyone else. Few persons would have a better understanding of the security posture and weaknesses. In fact, an employee may be in a position of influence to socially engineer coworkers into ignoring safeguards and alert conditions. This is why it is important to recheck (recertify) employees' backgrounds annually for changes in their financial or criminal history and also to monitor internal employee satisfaction. The great medieval fortresses fell by the betrayal of trusted allies.

Ethical Hacker Gone Bad

An *ethical hacker* or *white hat* is one who is authorized to test computer hacks and attacks with the goal of identifying an organization's weakness. Some individuals participate in special training to learn about penetrating computer defenses. This will usually result in one of two outcomes.

In the first outcome, a few of the ethical white-hat technicians will exercise extraordinary restraint and control. Systems being tested are copies located in a separate test environment according to ISO 27002, as specified in item 10.1.4. Additionally, actual data of a sensitive nature should have been removed to prevent disclosure. The objective of ethical hacking is to exercise hacker techniques only in a highly regimented, totally supervised environment. White-hat technicians are required to operate from a prewritten test plan, reviewed by internal audit or management oversight. The slightest deviation is grounds for termination. Everything discovered must be reproducible by other individuals for follow-up tests.

This additional level of control is to protect the organization from error or personal agenda by the white-hat technician. If something went wrong, the use of so-called hackers in daily IT operations not only would sound bad to outsiders, including the news media, but also would make those individuals automatically suspect in any accusations of tampering. It may be difficult to sanction (punish) other employees who claim no wrongdoing, even if their alleged actions were in violation. Employees violating separation of duties or attempting unauthorized access may claim they are merely the hapless victims of the organization's own internal hacker/tester. Exhaustive evidence would be needed, because disproving reasonable doubt would be difficult, especially to outsiders sitting on a jury. Losing in wrongful job-termination lawsuits can be very expensive or even kill some organizations.

Security penetration testing should be under the job description of software testers or software QA testers under IS programming or an internal audit. Separation of duties requires the white hat (ethical hacker) to operate under the management of an internal audit or an equivalent audit role. Forced separation of duties provides evidence that protects both management and the technician. The ethical hacker must not have any operational duties or otherwise be involved in daily IT operations.

The second outcome is that a white-hat technician will direct their own efforts. Some individuals will demonstrate great pride in their ability to circumvent required controls. These self-directed hacking techniques create an unacceptable level of risk for multiple reasons including organizational liability. The series of movies about Jason Bourne, *The Bourne Identity* (2002), *The Bourne Supremacy* (2004), and *The Bourne Ultimatum* (2007) illustrate the risk of self-directed activity. After management loses control, there is no way back. These fictional movies are, in part, based on facts from real events.

As professional auditors, we've been engaged on several occasions to determine whether the internal staff has been using hacker techniques and tools without explicit test plans and executive approval. Proper test documentation requires keystroke-level detail combined with specific steps to capture corresponding evidence. In each event except one, the technician was fired for violating internal controls. Additional controls are necessary when a white-hat technician is employed by the organization. Honest people may be kept honest with proper supervision.

Third Parties

External persons are referred to as third parties. *Third parties* include visitors, vendors, consultants, maintenance personnel, and the cleaning crew. These individuals may gain access and knowledge of the internal organization.

 You would be surprised by how many times auditors have been invited to join the client in a meeting room with internal plans still visible on the whiteboards. The client's careless disregard is obvious by the words *important—do not erase* emblazoned across the board. You can bet this same organization allows vendors to work unsupervised. In the evening, the cleaning crew will unlock and open every door on the floor for several hours while vacuuming and emptying wastebaskets. We seriously doubt the cleaning crew would challenge a stranger entering the office. In fact, a low-paid cleaning crew may be exercising their own agenda.

Ignorance

The term *ignorance* is simply defined as the lack of knowledge. An ignorant person may be a party to a crime and not even know it. Even worse, the individual may be committing an offense without realizing the impact of their actions. Management may be guilty of not understanding their current risks and corresponding regulations. The statement "We/I did not know" is the fastest route to a conviction. Every judge will agree that ignorance of the law is not an excuse. Every manager is expected to research the regulations related to bear their business practice. There is no legal excuse for ignorance or apathy. Fortunately, ignorance can be cured by training. This is the objective of user training for internal controls. By teaching the purpose of internal security controls, the organization can reduce their overall risk.

Understanding Attack Methods

Your clients will expect you to have knowledge about the different methods of attacking computers. We will try to take the boredom out of the subject by injecting practical examples. Computer attacks can be implemented with a computer or against a computer. There are basically two types of attacks: passive and active. Let's start with passive attacks.

Passive Attacks

Passive attacks are characterized by techniques of observation. The intention of a passive attack is to gain additional information before launching an active attack. Three examples of passive attacks are network analysis, traffic analysis, and eavesdropping:

Network Analysis   The computer traffic across a network can be analyzed to create a map of the hosts and routers. Common tools such as IBM Tivoli, Cisco Works, HP Openview, Network Instruments Observer or open source equivalents like OpenNMS and OpsView are useful for creating live network maps. The objective of *network analysis* is to create a complete profile of the network infrastructure prior to launching an active attack. Computers transmit large numbers of requests that other computers on the network will observe. Simple maps can be created with no more than the observed traffic or responses from a series of ping commands. The network *ping* command provides a simple communications test between two devices by sending a single request, also known as a ping. The concept of creating maps by using network analysis is commonly referred to as *painting* or *footprinting*.

Host Traffic Analysis   *Traffic analysis* is used to identify systems of particular interest. The communication between host computers can be monitored by the activity level and number of service requests. Host traffic analysis is an easy method used to identify servers on the network.

Specific details on the host computer can be determined by using a *fingerprinting* tool such as the open source Nmap. The Nmap utility is active software that sends a series of special commands, each command unique to a particular operating system type and version. For example, a Unix system will not respond to a NetBIOS 137 request because NetBIOS is a nonstandard port used only by Microsoft. However, a computer running Microsoft Windows will answer. The exact operating system of the computer can usually be identified with only seven or eight simple service requests. Host traffic analysis will provide clues to a system even if all other communication traffic is encrypted. This is an excellent tool for tracking down a rogue IP address. The Nmap utility provides information as to whether the destination address is a Unix computer, Macintosh computer, computer running Windows, or something else such as an HP printer. This fingerprinting technique is also popular with hackers for the same reason.

Eavesdropping   *Eavesdropping* is the traditional method of spying with the intent to gather information. The term originated from a person spying on others while listening under the roof eaves of a house. Computer network analysis is a type of eavesdropping. Other methods include capturing a hidden copy of files or copying messages as they traverse the network. Email messages and instant messaging are notoriously vulnerable to eavesdropping because of their insecure design. Computer login IDs, passwords, and user keystrokes can be captured by using eavesdropping tools. Encrypted messages can be captured by eavesdropping with the intention of breaking the encryption at a later date. The message can be read later, after the encryption is compromised. Eavesdropping helped the Allies crack the secret code of radio messages sent using the German Enigma machine in World War II. Network sniffers are excellent tools for capturing communications traveling across the network.

Now let's move on to discuss active attacks.

Active Attacks

Passive attacks tend to be relatively invisible, whereas active attacks are easier to detect. The attacker will proceed to execute an active attack after obtaining sufficient background information. The *active attack* is designed to execute an act of theft or to cause a disruption in normal computer processing. Following is a list of active attacks:

Social Engineering   Criminals can trick an individual into cooperating by using a technique known as *social engineering*. The social engineer will fraudulently present themselves as a person of authority or someone in need of assistance. The social engineer's story will be woven with tiny bits of truth. All social engineers are opportunists who gain access by asking for it. For example, the social engineer may pretend to be a contractor or employee sent to work on a problem. The social engineer will play upon the victim's natural desire to help.

 Real World Scenario

Real-Life Social Engineering

There is a wonderful movie about social engineering titled *Catch Me If You Can* (2002), starring Leonardo DiCaprio with Tom Hanks and Christopher Walken. It is the story of teenager Frank Abagnale who successfully masqueraded for years as a doctor who actually practiced in a hospital, a commercial airline pilot who actually flew in the cockpit, and a lawyer with a genuine appointment to assistant district attorney. Abagnale at 19 was the youngest person to be on the FBI's most wanted list for forging over $6 million in fake checks passed worldwide.

Phishing   A social engineering technique called *phishing* (pronounced *fishing*) utilizes fake emails sent to unsuspecting victims, which contain a link to the criminal's counterfeit website. Anyone can copy the images and format of a legitimate website by using their Internet browser. A phishing criminal copies legitimate web pages into a fake email or to a fake website. The message tells the unsuspecting victim that it is necessary to enter personal details such as U.S. social security number, credit card number, bank account information, or online user ID and password. Phishing attacks can also be used to implement spyware on unprotected computers. Many phishing attacks can be avoided through user education.

Spear Phishing   One of the most effective attack techniques is known as *spear-phishing*. This attack targets a specific server, user, database, or network device. Spear-phishing is easier than it sounds. Target systems can be identified through traffic analysis, remnant metadata found in exported files, or simply by browsing a web page and right-clicking View Source. Dynamic pages, including user-submitted forms with HTML or Post HyperText Protocol (PHP) usually contain a POST or GET command that contains the exact address of your server, your database name, valid login ID of the program, and real password. These specific parameters must be disclosed (required) for programming the web page to get data out of your database, for web surfers to view content, or for users to save data submitted through online forms.

Object-oriented programming in Java is one method to help protect against spear-phishing by using object delegation. Separation of duties between programs isolates certain functions to another program out of the attacker's reach. But security works only if multiple layers of strong authentication are used between the programs. We will discuss this in more detail later.

Dumpster Diving   Attackers will frequently resort to rummaging through the trash for discarded information. The practice is also known as *Dumpster diving*. Dumpster diving is perfectly legal under the condition that the individuals are not trespassing. This is the primary reason why proper destruction is mandatory. Most paper records and optical disks are destroyed by shredding.

Persistent Electronic Threats

It's rare for modern hackers to physically enter building premises because they may be caught or apprehended. Physical facility controls have a limited purpose in information security, to simply provide a local barrier for physical intrusion. These localized barriers protect against common crimes by persons entering and leaving the facility. With the advent of the Internet, a smaller percentage of criminals will chance the risks of committing a physical crime. The new persistent threat is through electronic attacks. A hacker can commit the crime at a safe distance without fear of being physically caught. Attacks may originate from anywhere in the world or even be sponsored by a foreign government to gather intelligence data.

Technical controls to protect against electronic attacks are usually spotty and inconsistent because of a lack of awareness for specific threats or lopsided implementations. It is very easy for the technical staff to inadvertently focus on only a few areas, thereby neglecting serious threats that still exist in others. Technical threats against software are usually difficult for lay-persons to visualize in the physical world. The adage *out of sight, out of mind* also means outside of budget. Let's take a moment to understand how the electronic threat will manifest in our clients' environment.

Malware   This title refers to every malicious software program ever created, whether it exploits a known vulnerability or creates its own. There are so many different ones, it's easier to just call the entire group by the title of *malware*. The king of the malware threat is known as the Trojan horse.

Trojan Horse   A revised concept of the historical Trojan horse has been adapted to attack computers. In a tale from the Trojan war, soldiers hid inside a bogus gift known as the Trojan horse. The unassuming recipients accepted the horse and brought it inside their fortress, only to be attacked by enemy soldiers hiding within. Malicious programs frequently use the *Trojan horse* concept to deliver viruses, worms, logic bombs, and other root kits through downloaded files.

Virus   You may recall we mentioned the virus in a previous chapter. The goal of a *virus* is to disrupt operations. Users inadvertently download a program built like a Trojan horse containing the virus. The attacker's goal is usually to damage your programs or data files. Viruses append themselves to the end-of-file (EOF) marker on computerized files.

Internet Worm   An *Internet worm* operates in a similar manner to the Trojan or virus, with one major exception: Worm programs can freely travel between computers because they exploit unprotected data transfer ports (software programming sockets) to access other systems. Internet worms started by trying to access the automatic update (file transfer) function through software ports with poor authentication or no authentication mechanism. As mentioned previously in Chapter 5, "Information Systems Life Cycle," it is the responsibility of the

IS programmer to implement security of the ports and protocols. IT technicians for hardware and operating system support cannot fix poor programming implementations. For IT technicians, the only choice is to disable software ports, but that won't happen if the programmer requires the port left open for the user's application program to operate.

Logic Bomb   The concept of the *logic bomb* is designed around dormant program code that is waiting for a trigger event to cause detonation. Unlike a virus or worm, logic bombs do not travel. The logic bomb remains in one location, awaiting detonation. Logic bombs are difficult to detect. Some logic bombs are intentional, and others are the unintentional result of poor programming. Intentional logic bombs can be set to detonate after the perpetrator is gone.

Time Bomb   Programmers can install *time bombs* in their program to disable the software upon a predetermined date. Time bombs might be used to kill programs on symbolic dates such as April Fools' Day or the anniversary of a historic event. Free trial evaluation versions of software use the time bomb mechanism to disable their program after 30–60 days with the intention of forcing the user to purchase a license. Time bombs can be installed by the vendor to eliminate perpetual customer support issues by forcing upgrades after a few years. The software installation utility will no longer run or install, because the programmer's time bomb setting disabled the program. Now when trying to run the software, a message directs user to contact customer support to purchase an upgrade. Hackers use the same technique to disrupt operations.

Trapdoor   Computer programmers frequently install a shortcut, also known as a *trapdoor*, for use during software testing. The trapdoor is a hidden access point within the computer software. A competent programmer will remove the majority of trapdoors before releasing a production version of the program. However, several vendors routinely leave a trapdoor in a computer program to facilitate user support. Commercial encryption software began to change in 1996 with the addition of "key recovery" features. This is basically a trap door feature to recover lost encryption keys and to allow the government to read encrypted files, if necessary.

Root Kit   One of the most threatening attacks is the secret compromise of the operating system kernel. Attackers embed a *root kit* into downloadable software. This malicious software will subvert security settings by linking itself directly into the kernel processes, system memory, address registers, and swap space. Root kits operate in stealth to hide their presence. Hackers designed root kits to never display their execution as running applications. The system resource monitor does not show any activity related to the presence of the root kit. After the root kit is installed, the hacker has control over the system. The computer is completely compromised. Automatic update features use the same techniques as malicious root kits to allow the software vendor to bypass your security settings. Vendors know that using the term *root kit* may alarm users. Software *agent* is just another name for a root kit.

Brute Force Attack   *Brute force* is the use of extreme effort to overcome an obstacle. For example, an amateur could discover the combination to a safe by dialing all of the 63,000 possible combinations. There is a mathematical likelihood that the actual combination will be determined after trying less than one-third of the possible combinations. *Brute force attacks* are frequently used against user logon IDs and passwords. In one particular attack, all of the encrypted computer passwords are compared against a list of all the words encrypted from a language dictionary. After the match is identified, the attacker will use the unencrypted word that created the password match. This is why it is important to use passwords that do not appear in any language dictionary.

Denial of Service (DoS)   Attackers can disable a computer by rendering legitimate use impossible. The objective is to remotely shut down service by overloading the system or disable the user environment (shell) and thereby prevent the normal user from processing anything on the computer. *Denial-of-service (DoS)* attacks may look similar to the loss of service while your system is downloading and installing vendor updates. The message "please wait, installing update 6 of 41…" makes your system unavailable for an hour or more. That is exactly how DoS operates.

Distributed Denial of Service (DDoS)   The denial of service has evolved to use multiple systems for targeted attacks against another computer, to force its crash. This type of attack, *distributed denial of service (DDoS)*, is also known as the *reflector attack*. Your own computer is being used by the hacker to launch remote attacks against someone else. Hackers start the attack from unrelated systems that the hacker has already compromised. The attacking computers and target are drawn into the battle—similar in concept to starting a vicious rumor between two strangers, which leads them to fight each other. The hackers sit safely out of the way while this battle wages. Figure 7.2 illustrates the DDoS attack method.

FIGURE 7.2   DDos attack method

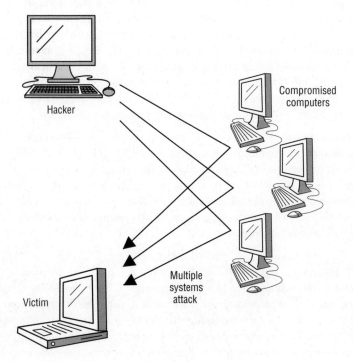

IP Fragmentation Attack   One of the common Internet attack techniques is to send a series of fragmented service requests to a computer through a firewall. This *IP fragmentation attack* is successful if the firewall fails to examine each packet. For this reason, firewalls are configured to discard IP fragments.

Crash-Restart   A variation of attack techniques is *crash-restart*. An attacker loads malicious software onto a computer or reconfigures security settings to the attacker's advantage. Then the attacker crashes the system, allowing the computer to automatically restart (reboot). The attacker can take control of the system after it restarts with the new configuration. The purpose is to install a backdoor for the attacker.

Maintenance Accounts   Most computer systems are configured with special *maintenance accounts*. These maintenance accounts may be part of the default settings or created for system support. An example is the user account named *DBA* for database administrator, or *tape* for a tape backup device. Vendors publish online user manuals containing examples of all the maintenance accounts on their system. Anyone can surf the Internet for a download of the information or spend a few dollars to buy a copy at the used bookstore with complete instructions on accessing maintenance accounts. All maintenance accounts should be carefully controlled. It is advisable to disable the default maintenance accounts on a system. The security manager may find an advantage in monitoring access attempts against the default accounts. Any attempted access may indicate the beginnings of an attack.

Robot Networks   By using malware programs such as a Trojan horse, hackers can build a remote-controlled *robot network* (aka. *bot-net*) composed of computers owned by unsuspecting users. This bot-net operates a distributed attack against other systems or delivers email spam messages against other systems. If the victim attacks back against the sender, the attack will harm only the unsuspecting user because the hacker is invisibly reflecting the attack off the compromised system. Robot networks are known to contain tens of thousands, if not millions, of compromised systems all under the remote control of the hacker. These compromised rogue systems may even be located behind your corporate firewalls. Figure 7.3 demonstrates the bot-net concept.

Programming Vulnerability   A significant number of computer programs contain multiple *vulnerabilities* due to poor programming practices, homegrown implementations with ineffective mechanisms, or inherent lack of security in the original design. This is why the industry has a push toward using Common Criteria certification of systems. The ISO 15408 Common Criteria toolkit is recognized as the worldwide evaluation model of program security mechanisms. Unfortunately, even a Common Criteria–certified system can be exploited if the user's application program is poorly written.

SQL Injection   The entire computing world depends on information kept in a database. As auditors, we talk about input validation, authentication, and data processing controls. One of the most fundamental techniques to integrate different computer programs is remote data submission. Data requests sent from untrusted sources can use command line instructions to read your database, modify the data using insert or delete, or change your shopping cart price from something like $195.00 to $1.95. This is now referred to as *SQL database injection*. One computer program sends data as input to another program operated by someone else, with or without their permission. An example is a utility program to automatically submit your website data to Internet search engines such as Yahoo!, MSN, or Google for better ranking in Internet search results, or a utility that automatically submits your bid to eBay in the last 3 seconds of an auction. Maybe it's a utility to automatically check you in on your airline and reserve your preferred seat. Each of these functions is a SQL injector. SQL injection is possible because of a lack of cryptographic authentication. Simply using static passwords for SQL data authentication will not work, because anyone could use or reuse the same password. Static passwords are probably visible to the trained eye through the operation of your website. That's why programmers have to implement cryptographic passwords which automatically change between every transaction or data submittal.

FIGURE 7.3   Bot-net concept of remote-control attacks

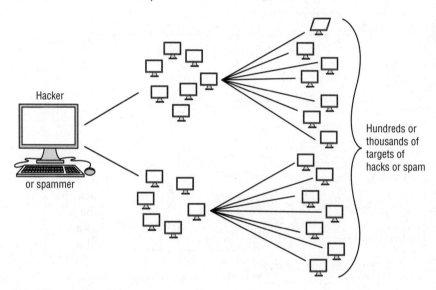

Cross-Site Scripting (XSS)   This is a common programming practice and backbone of 98 percent of all Internet commerce. *Crosssite scripting (XSS)* is a programming technique that enables one website, such as a shopping cart, to drive another website. The shopping cart sends an approval message to a different website, which then provides access or a file to download. This is how Digital River, Microsoft online sales, Apple iTunes, eBay, PayPal, and all airline ticket sales operate.

Unfortunately, most cross-site scripting implementations are poorly executed, use ineffective homegrown programming, or lack the cryptographic authentication that is always required. Once again, static passwords will be completely ineffective in protecting these systems from a hacker. Figure 7.4 shows an example of using reCAPTCHA for input validation to reduce the chance of programs submitting data into the client's database. Unfortunately, it's just one of a whole series of techniques necessary to protect the system. Defensive controls work only in layers of multiple controls.

FIGURE 7.4   Using reCAPTCHA for input validation to reduce automated submission

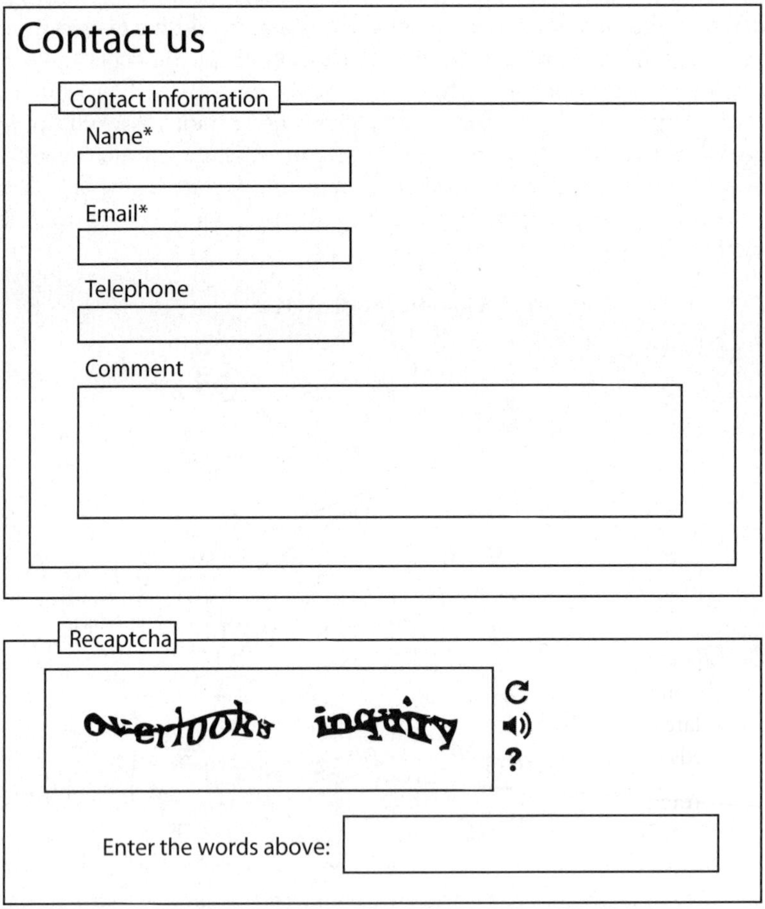

Middleware Attack   Computer programming is a complex process. Frequently the programmer will pass data between programs to create an invisible workflow for the user's benefit. Every program between the user and their data constitutes *middleware*, which are invisible programs in the middle of the processing flow. Each of these programs represents a potential vulnerability that a hacker can easily exploit.

Data passing between the programs is usually not authenticated, meaning we do not know exactly where it came from or if it's valid data acceptable as input. This is how SQL injection and XSS operate. The lack of true source authentication and input validation is a major risk in middleware attacks. Even worse, most middleware programs have privileged accounts or execute at the privileged level within the operating system. This frequently overlooked login account could be the super user, root user, or admin for the teeny software package. Hackers can exploit these middleware accounts in addition to any program vulnerabilities and thereby take control of the critical portion of the invisible workflow, completely undetected by the user.

Figure 7.5 illustrates how middleware is used in the majority of programming implementations to automate processing functions. Overall middleware attacks tend to be highly successful. Most intrusion in monitoring systems does not contain the complex programming necessary to detect the presence of a hacker compromise.

FIGURE 7.5   Typical implementation of middleware in computer programming

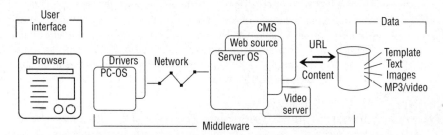

Zero-Day Attack   Computer programs are loaded with flaws and defects not yet known. This could be due to the programmer, software compiler, design problems, cross-compatibility issues, and middleware. Hackers work diligently to circumvent security controls by exploiting any vulnerability they can find. *Zero-day* refers to any attack that has not been seen before. Virus scanners and intrusion detection and prevention systems can't stop zero-day attacks because the hacker has discovered a new attack method that nobody has yet realized. After many successful attacks, the new zero-day method may be discovered. Then it's not a zero-day attack anymore. Months later there might be a patch or intrusion detection and prevention system (IDPS) update to block the attack, but only after it was successful hacking hundreds, thousands, hundreds of thousands, or even millions of unsuspecting users.

Remote Access Attack   Most attackers will attempt to exploit remote access. The goal of the casual attacker is often based on personal satisfaction or for political gain. Professional attackers will be motivated by financial gain. There is less personal risk involved in gaining remote access. The common types of *remote access attacks* are referred to as follows:

War Dialing   The attacker uses an automated modem-dialing utility to launch a brute force attack against a list of phone numbers. The attack generates a list of telephone numbers that are answered by a computer modem. The next step of the attack is to break in through an unsecured modem. This is why it's necessary for modems to reject inbound calls or to be protected by a telephone firewall such as TeleWall by SecureLogix. Remote access servers (RASs) provide better authentication than a modem. An RAS logging capability can be used to identify attacks, if properly configured. Using RAS modem pools combined with telephone-firewall products such as TeleWall reduces the chance of an attacker making a successful penetration.

War Driving/Walking   Wireless access is known to be insecure. Wireless manufacturers have seriously compromised security in an effort to improve Plug and Play capabilities for users. The trade-off of fewer user support issues for less security provides casual attackers the opportunity to gain remote access by walking or driving past wireless network transmitters. Previous attackers use symbols to mark the unsuspecting organization's property, to show other attackers that wireless access is available at that location. This marking technique is referred to as *war chalking*. War chalk maps of insecure access points are available for download on the Internet.

We discuss the latest standards in wireless security later in this chapter. Wired Equivalent Privacy (WEP) and Wi-Fi Protected Access (WPA) have been officially classified as insecure since April 2005 because of implementation failures. Existing equipment using WEP/WPA is designated as insecure. The current standard is IEEE 802.11i, known as Robust Security Network.

Cross-Network Connectivity Interconnected networks are effective in business. The connectivity across networks provides an avenue for more-efficient processing by the user. Computer networks are cross-connected internally, and even across the Internet. It is not uncommon for a business partner to have special access. All of these connections can be exploited by an attacker. Business partner connections can provide an opportunity for the attacker to remotely compromise the systems of a partner organization with little chance of detection. The purpose of internal and external firewalls is to block attacks. The implementation of internal firewalls is an excellent practice that dates back to the Great Wall of China. Better-run organizations recognize the need. Since 2005, the deployment of internal firewalls has accelerated. Figure 7.6 shows the threat of attackers entering through business partner connections.

FIGURE 7.6 Cross-network connectivity

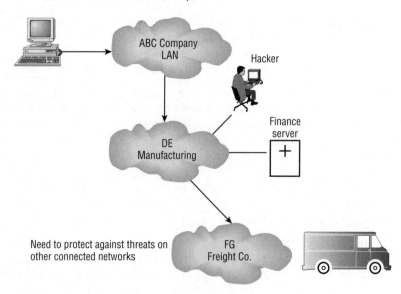

Source Routing   As stated earlier, useful system administration tools can be implemented as weapons. In the early days of networking, it was necessary to send data across a network without any reliance on the network configuration itself. Therefore, a special network protocol known as *source routing* was developed. Source routing is designed to ignore the configuration of the network routers and follow the instructions designated by the sender (the source). Source routing is a magnificent diagnostic tool for reaching remote networks. As you can imagine, source routing also is popular with hackers, because it allows a hacker to bypass routing configurations used for firewall security. For this reason, every firewall and most routers must be configured to disable source routing.

Salami Technique   The *salami technique* is used for the commission of financial crimes. The key here is to make the alteration so insignificant that in a single case it would go completely unnoticed—for example, a bank employee inserts a program into the bank's servers that deducts a small amount of money from the account of every customer. No single account holder will probably notice this unauthorized debit, but the bank employee will make a sizable amount of money every month.

Packet Replay   Network communications are sent by transmitting a series of small messages known as *packets*. The attacker captures a series of legitimate packets by using a capture tool similar to a network sniffer. The packets are retransmitted (replayed) within a short time window to trick a computer system into believing that the sender is a legitimate user. This technique can be combined with a denial-of-service technique to compromise the system. The legitimate user is knocked off the network by using denial of service, and the attacker attempts to take over communications. This can be effective for hijacking sessions in single sign-on systems such as Kerberos. We discuss Kerberos single sign-on later in this chapter.

Message Modification   *Message modification* can be used to intercept and alter communications. The legitimate message is captured before receipt by the destination. The content of the message, address, or other information is modified. The modified message is then sent to the destination in a fraudulent attempt to appear genuine.

This technique is commonly used for a man-in-the-middle attack: A third party places themselves between the bona fide sender and receiver. The person in the middle pretends to be the other party. If encryption is used, the middle person tricks the sender into using an encryption key known by the middle person. After reading, the message will be re-encrypted using the key of the true recipient. The message will be retransmitted to be received by the intended recipient. The man-in-the-middle is able to eavesdrop without detection. Neither the sender nor the receiver is aware of the security compromise.

Email Spamming and Spoofing   You are probably aware of email spamming. *Spamming* refers to sending a mass mailing of identical messages to a large number of users. Spamming occurs because it is profitable for the unethical business person. Spam is a multibillion dollar industry, selling the web traffic or generating buyers to visit a website. Anytime you see an advertisement offering a guarantee of 2 million people visiting your website for $199, it's probably from a spammer. The current laws governing email allow a business to send mass emails as long as the recipient is informed of the sender's legitimate address and the recipient is provided a mechanism to stop the receipt of future emails. Spammers frequently use Trojan horse attacks to distribute their remote-controlled spam program across unsuspecting users on computers scattered worldwide across the Internet. The poor unsuspecting user may notice their computer hard drive activity lights flashing and not realize why. In reality, their compromised computer is now the sender of spam being broadcast around the world.

Email spamming is a common mechanism used in phishing attacks. The term *spoofing* refers to fraudulently altering the information concerning the sender of email. An example of email spoofing is an attacker sending a fake notice concerning your bank account. The spoofed email address appears as if it were sent by your bank. Email spamming is illegal in many of the countries supporting world trade through the Organization for Economic Cooperation and Development (OECD), and email spoofing is usually prosecuted as criminal fraud and/or electronic wire fraud.

A variety of other technical attacks may be launched against the computer. A common attack is to send to the computer an impossible request or series of requests that cannot be serviced. These cause the system to overload its CPU, memory, or communication buffers. As a result, the computer crashes. An example is the old Ping of Death command (`ping -l 65510`), which exceeded the computer's maximum input size for a communication buffer.

The first step in preventing the loss of information assets is to establish administrative controls. Let's begin the discussion on implementing administrative safeguards.

Implementing Administrative Protection

Administrative control protections are people-based activities in the form of policies, standards, procedures, job roles, and responsibilities. These are considered the weakest form of control yet represent a necessary first step. Without a discipline of substantial monitoring, the violations of the administrative controls will go unnoticed. We already covered the basic concepts of administrative controls in prior chapters. Now it's time to discuss specific controls for protecting information through administrative methods. We'll start with the minimum information security policies that need to be formally sponsored by top executive management above all departments, not just the IT/IS function.

Management-Sponsored Controls

One of the primary objectives of the ISO standards is to remove self-discretion and doubt. Two decades ago, the ISO 9001 quality management standard emerged and forced itself upon organizations in the manufacturing and service industries. Organizations adopted ISO 9001 to keep up with a competitive market. The old saying *quality is free* is not correct. Quality along with any other compliance program can be very expensive overhead until the day you actually turn a reasonable profit.

The digital information economy is bearing pressure on organizations to demonstrate a minimum level of information security. There are more than 23 major information security standards ratified in the world today, with multiple standards targeting each organizational department function or major topic.

It is the absolute duty of executive management to identify the business rules with specific priorities. Top executive management specifies what is acceptable and unacceptable. Those rules will become known as their organizational culture. Normally the IT department is intentionally left out of the loop or remains unaware of several critical business functions and fluctuating priorities. Nonetheless, executive management has a duty to lead the organization and charter visible policies directing the use of organizational data and IT systems. At a minimum, the following policies support the IT mission and are specifically mentioned in regulations. These policies should be endorsed, adopted, and visibly advertised by executive management with a mandate for all personnel to comply:

- Formal organizational reporting structure with accurate job descriptions (maintained by HR for *all* personnel including contractors)
- Physical and environmental protection of IT assets
- Classification of data in the organization's possession (by value, type, or risk threshold)
- Records management policy (based on ISO 15489 with IT backup/restore functions)
- Access control policy (all data, all departmental functions across the organization)
- Personnel security policy (maintained by HR)
- Identification and authentication policy (authorized users, devices, program access)
- Security planning policy with capital budgeting (created by the steering committee with input from IT and Finance)
- Risk assessment policy focused on the likelihood of occurrence or consequence of loss
- System and services acquisition policy (by Procurement)
- System protection policy (by Legal, CFO, and IT for all computing devices)
- Communications protection policy (governing all connected networks, IT, ISP, and telcom provider)
- Configuration management policy (by Quality, mandatory change control)
- Acceptable use policy (maintained by HR)
- Computing/communications maintenance policy (for systems and devices)
- Media protection policy (print, electronic, CD, HDD, tape, portable drives, and so forth)
- Telecommuting policy (for remote workers)
- Network connection and data sharing with business partners (Legal, IT, internal audit)
- Contingency planning policy (driven by program office, business unit subcomponents)
- Incident response policy (HR, Legal, law enforcement, Facility, and IT components)
- Audit and accountability policy (executive audit committee, internal audit)
- Security assessment mandating use of specific technical certification procedures (prerequisite to management accreditation)

- Management accreditation policy (required for *all* systems at each SDLC phase during feasibility, requirements, design, build, and prior to entering production)
- Security awareness and required training policy (all users)
- General user awareness training and orientation policy (for all employees and all contractors)

Now we've covered 25 basic policies that the auditor should be looking for to evidence management's participation in specifying the minimum internal controls for their organization. Next we need to focus on classification of data. This is a fundamental point that provides the foundation of acceptable use.

Proper Data Classification

Fundamentally, there are only two types of protection for data:

Classified means that the data is ranked somewhere in a protection scheme (aka protection plan).

Unclassified is synonymous with public records or unprotected data. This type of design has been used for hundreds, if not thousands, of years in government, military, and commerce.

Unless confidential data is classified, users will not know how to handle it properly. But all data is not created equal. Your client may require several types of classification, each for a unique purpose. For example, credit card data requires special security with partial records destruction of account number segments and account authenticators in accordance with payment card industry (PCI) standards. To violate the PCI standards could bring forfeiture of merchant privileges plus civil and criminal liability. The same is true for health care records, employment records, and data on children. Don't forget confidential business records, contracts, customer lists, and research data and intellectual property such as unfiled patents, trademarks, or copyrights. Even if the data originated in the public domain, it's considered proprietary information if the organization paid money or consumed resources for special research, unique implementation, or modification.

Figure 7.7 demonstrates the basic process of records management classification. It does not matter whether the records are physical or electronic; somebody has to indicate to the user or librarian how to handle the data.

FIGURE 7.7 Records management classification process

Management's duty is to specify how each of those data records will be individually protected. This information protection classification plan (protection scheme) then becomes the foundation of all data controls used by the organization. Auditors need to remain aware that lack of a published classification scheme usually indicates a control failure. In bigger organizations, the risk of failure and consequence are substantially larger than with tiny organizations.

One of the major areas of concern is the self-directed use of encryption. Unless specific use of encryption is formally accredited by the classification scheme, it can cause substantial problems for the organization. The reason is simple: Individuals make mistakes, and their errors in discipline or understanding can result in accidental data leakage due to a poor encryption implementation or can lock out the organization from accessing the digital assets that it paid for using company resources. The goal of encryption is to lock out access. Users doing it on their own represent a serious operating risk. Officially sanctioned use of encryption includes formal discipline of daily management, burdensome key management, extra transaction record keeping, archiving, and weekly change control. This effort costs money and time to do it right. Just ask the question: "Who eats the bill for lost business opportunities, possible fines for missing records, plus costs for re-creating and recovering lost data?" I doubt it's the actual user. Beware of rogue users operating their own encryption. If encryption is so darn important, its use needs to be formally managed.

We already covered physical protection in previous chapters. Now it's time to move ahead into technical protection controls.

Using Technical Protection

Technical protection is also referred to as *logical protection*. A simple way to recognize technical protection is that technical controls typically involve a hardware or software process to operate. Let's start with *technical controls*, which are also known as *automated controls*.

Technical Control Classification

Technical protection may be implemented by using a combination of mandatory controls or discretionary controls. Technical controls are considered very strong *if* used in combination with administrative and physical controls. Technical controls should always be active, be monitored, and block unauthorized access attempts. Any unauthorized attempt should notify the security staff with both a log entry and matching alarm. Least privilege is supported by using additional controls based on a person's job role, job task, or specific attributes of the subject requesting access to the data involved. Let's discuss characteristics of each method:

Mandatory Access Controls   *Mandatory access controls (MACs)* use labels to identify the security classification of data. A set of rules determines which person (subject) will be allowed to access the data (object). The security label is compared to the user access level. The comparison process requires an absolute match to permit access. Here is an example:

```
(User label "subject" = Data label "object") = ALLOW
Label does not match = DENY
```

The process is explicit. Absolutely no exceptions are made when MAC methods are in use. Under MAC, control is centrally managed and all access is forbidden unless explicit permission is specified for that user. The only way to gain access is to change the user's formal authorization level. The government and military use MAC. In a MAC environment, its possible to consolidate all access control into a centralized, aka federated, system environment. This is preferred over decentralized methods because it enforces the maximum level of control.

Discretionary Access Controls   *Discretionary access controls (DACs)* allow a designated individual to decide the level of user access. DAC access is usually distributed across the organization to provide flexibility for specific use or adjustment to business needs. The data owner determines access control at their discretion. The IS auditor needs to investigate how the decisions concerning DAC access controls are authorized, managed, and regularly reviewed. Most businesses use discretionary access control.

Role-Based Access Controls   Certain jobs require a particular level of access to fulfill the job duties. Access that is granted on the basis of the job requirement is referred to as *role-based access control (RBAC)*. A user is given the level of access necessary to complete work for their job. The system administrator position is an example of role-based access control.

Task-Based Access Controls   Individual tasks may need to be performed for the business to operate. Whereas role-based access is used for job roles, *task-based access control (TBAC)* refers to the need to perform a specific task. Common examples include limited testing, maintenance, data entry, or access to a special report.

Attribute-Based Access Controls   The most selective control is attribute-based access. Attributes may be the time of day, role of the subject (person) or computer program requesting access (another form of subject), and content of the data (object) or anything else being tracked. *Attribute-based access control (ABAC)* is designed to tighten the controls as much as possible. It increases enforcement of least privilege for separation of duties. This is the preferred method in secure environments.

The type of access control used is based on risk, data value, and available control mechanisms. Now we need to discuss application software control mechanisms.

Application Software Controls

Application software controls provide security by using a combination of user identity, authentication, authorization, and accountability. As you will recall, *user identity* is a claim that must be *authenticated* (verified). *Authorization* refers to the right to perform a particular function. *Accountability* refers to holding a person responsible for their actions.

Most application software uses access control lists to assign rights or permissions. The access control list contains the user's identity and permissions assigned.

Database Views

Data within the database can be protected by using database views. The database view is a read restriction placed on particular columns (attributes) in the database. For example, Figure 7.8 illustrates using a personnel file to create a telephone list. Data that is not to be read for the telephone list has been hidden by using the database view. Unfortunately, the data may still be accessible to a skilled individual. A better method is to create a separate file extract without the field data you want to keep confidential.

FIGURE 7.8 Database views for security

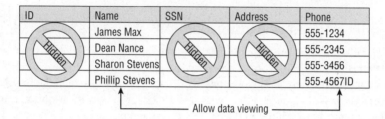

— Allow data viewing —

Restricted User Interface

Another method of limiting access is to use a restricted user interface. The restricted interface may be a menu with particular options grayed out or not displayed at all. Menu access is preferred to prevent the user from having the power of command-line arguments. The command line is difficult to restrict.

Security Labels

A major concern in security is the ability of users to bypass the security label. The *security label* is a control that specifies who may access the file and how the file may be used. The IS auditor should work with security managers to identify ways in which labels and security settings could be bypassed. Additional compensating controls are necessary to protect against the bypassing of labels and security.

Authentication Methods

The first step of granting access is identification of the user: A user presents a claim of identity. The second step is to authenticate the user identity claim against a known reference. The purpose of this authentication is to ensure that the correct person is granted access. Table 7.1 illustrates the difference between identification and authentication.

TABLE 7.1   Identification versus authentication

Concept	Function
Identification	A claim of identity *or* a search process of comparing all known entries until either a match is found or the data list is exhausted. Identification is known as a one-to-many search process.
Authentication	A single match of the identity claim against reference information. If a single attempt fails, the authentication failed. Authentication is a single-try process, also known as a one-to-one process (compare only, no search).

Understanding Types of Authentication

Three types of authentication are possible using discrete information. The most common type of authentication is the user password. The user password is expected to be a secret known only to the user. Unfortunately, many user passwords are poorly constructed or suffer from ineffective protection. When a user logs in with a password, the only information known is that someone has logged in with the password. That is no guarantee of who that person is. Let's take a look at the three types of information, or factors, that can be used to authenticate the user:

Type 1: Something a Person Knows   The login ID and password should be unique to each user. Unfortunately, the password may be discovered by observation or insufficient security by the user. Passwords should be considered weak authentication. Passwords can be forgotten, shared, discovered by observation, and broken by technical means.

Type 2: Something a Person Has in Possession   An improvement above the password is to authenticate the user based on a unique item in their possession. This requires the user to have a login ID with a password and the unique item at the time of login. Banks use type 2 authentication with your ATM card and PIN. Another example of type 2 authentication is the smart card. A smart card contains a microchip with unique information read by a card scanner. Figure 7.9 shows a drawing of a smart card.

FIGURE 7.9   Smart card with embedded microchip

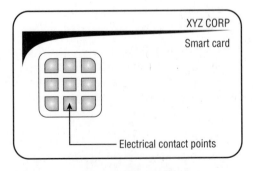

It is possible to use type 2 authentication without specialized hardware. Common techniques include using a hard token, USB token, or soft token.

User is required to read a key fob hard token like Figure 7.10. The user types a username and password combined with the number that appears on the token display screen. The number displayed by the token changes every 1 to 2 minutes, thereby making each password unique. The following shows a sample login and the password containing the code from the token:

```
Login ID = jmorris  Password = ******94328
```

Another method is to use a USB token. Authentication information is recorded in a microchip on a USB token device. The user plugs the USB token into the USB port when logging in to the computer. This type is popular in hospitals for use by doctors and nurse practitioners. Figure 7.10 shows a drawing of the two common types of hard tokens.

FIGURE 7.10   Hard authentication token

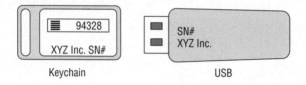

Another method of type 2 authentication is the use of software tokens (soft tokens), also known as *digital certificates*. Soft tokens are relatively inexpensive. The software token captures unique information, including the CPU's electronic serial number during the initial certificate-signing request. The resulting digital certificate contains this embedded information to prove the identity of the computer. Soft tokens are not portable because each is assigned to a specific computer.

Unfortunately, hardware and software tokens can be stolen or lost, and some can be secretly duplicated. These problems are what bring us to the third type of authentication.

Type 3: Physical Characteristic   The third type of authentication is based on a unique physical characteristic. The recording of physical characteristics and the matching process is known as biometrics. Let's investigate biometrics further.

Using Biometrics

Biometrics uses unique physical characteristics to authenticate the identity claimed by the user. This is accomplished by using either physiological characteristics or behavioral characteristics. You are expected to understand the different types of biometric data used for authentication.

Using Physiological Characteristics

These are considered strong authenticators of the user's identity because they are difficult to forge. A risk still exists in the management of the biometric sample and system implementation.

Fingerprint   Fingerprints have been used for many years to identify people, especially criminal offenders. In biometrics, the fingerprint is used to authenticate (not identify) the user. Information about the user's fingerprint is recorded into a biometrics database. Rather than the actual image, only summary lists of unique feature characteristics are recorded about the fingerprint. These features include curvature, position, ridge patterns, delta (separation), combined ridges (crossover), islands, and burification (ridge join). The feature data recorded in the database is called *minutiae*. When the user logs in, the minutiae are identified by the acquisition hardware and compared to the database. Authentication occurs when the acquired minutiae data from the biometric sensor matches the minutiae from the database. Using fingerprint minutiae instead of capturing the image allows a smaller file size to be stored. Minutiae file size is usually 250 bytes to more than 1,000 bytes. Figure 7.11 illustrates fingerprint minutiae.

FIGURE 7.11   Using fingerprint data (minutiae)

Fingerprint recognition

Palm Print   A person's palm print is as unique as a fingerprint. Like a fingerprint, the palm of the hand contains a significant number of unique minutiae plus additional wrinkle lines, blood vessel patterns, and scars. The palm offers a larger volume of data. Figure 7.12 illustrates the palm data.

Hand Geometry   The concept of hand geometry is to measure the details of a person's hand in a three-dimensional image. The usual technique is to put your hand into a machine of biometric sensors with your fingers spread between metal pegs. Another method in hand geometry is to grasp a metal knob or bar while sensors measure your knuckle creases or blood vessel patterns. Hand geometry is quite effective and inexpensive.

Retina Scan   The retina, located at the rear of the eyeball, contains a unique pattern of tiny veins that reflect light. The red-eye in photographs is the reflection of the retina. Changes in the retina occur during a person's life. Some of these changes may signal the onset of a new medical condition, such as stroke or diabetes. Users may be concerned about physiological issues or the possible invasion of privacy. Overall, retina scanning is very reliable. Figure 7.13 illustrates retina scanning.

FIGURE 7.12   Using palm print data

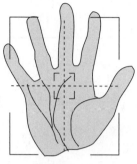

Palm of hand

FIGURE 7.13   Retina scanning

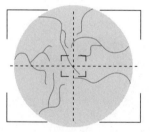

Retina

Iris Scan   Iris-scanning technology is based on visible features of freckles, rings, and furrows in the color ring surrounding the eye's pupil. The iris provides stable data from one year of age through a person's entire life. The visible features and their location are combined to form an iris-code digital template. To use an iris scanner, a person is asked to look into an eyepiece and focus on a displayed image. A biometric camera sensor records data of the iris and compares it to the biometric database to ensure that the viewer is a living person. Colored contacts would be detected because the iris would not change (or move) as the eye refocuses during the scan. Iris scanning is very dependable. Figure 7.14 illustrates iris scanning.

Face Scan   New face-scanning technology uses a series of still images captured by video camera. The technology uses three-dimensional measurements of facial features, including the position of eye sockets, nose, mouth openings, and heat pattern thermograph. The feature data is extracted from the image to form a digital facial template of 1,000 to 1,500 bytes. Major advances are occurring in facial recognition that reduce former problems of speed and accuracy. Figure 7.15 illustrates face recognition.

FIGURE 7.14 Iris scanning

Iris Scan

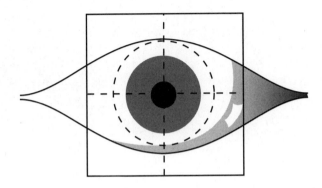

FIGURE 7.15 Face recognition

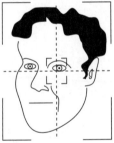

Face recognition

Using Behavioral Characteristics

Behavioral characteristics are considered a weak type of authentication because of concerns about their authenticity. Behavior is easier to forge than physical characteristics. For example, in my childhood, I taught my little brother how to speak. As a result, it's nearly impossible to distinguish even the slightest difference in our voices. My father's handwriting impressed me when I was learning to write in cursive. After much practice, my signature in sixth grade looked exactly like his. That illustrates the problem. Let's look at using signatures and voice patterns.

Signature Dynamics   Signature dynamics is a behavioral form of biometric data. The user's signature is monitored for time duration, pressure, and technique. The advantage is the low cost of implementation. The disadvantage is that many individuals do not write their signature consistently. Some individuals, such as celebrities and your author of this Study Guide, refuse to allow their signature to be digitally recorded because it is regularly used as the primary means of authenticating legal documents.

Voice Pattern   Voice pattern recognition is an inexpensive method of identifying a person by the way they talk. Voice pattern recognition is not the same as speech recognition. Speech recognition assembles sounds into words. Voice pattern analysis checks for characteristics of pitch, tone, and sound duration. A person's voice is analyzed for unique sound characteristics, tone, inflection, and speed. The typical method is to ask a user to repeat a particular passphrase. The characteristics of the passphrase are converted into a digital template. Voice pattern recognition is less expensive and less accurate than other types of biometrics. Voice authentication can be fooled by recorded audio playback of a person's voice. Figure 7.16 illustrates voice recognition.

FIGURE 7.16   Voice pattern recognition analysis in biometrics

Voice recognition

As a CISA candidate, you are expected to understand the older biometric techniques of signature dynamics and voice pattern analysis.

Managing Biometric Systems

Biometrics comprises technology-based systems and hence requires a disciplined approach. Each biometric system follows an SDLC life cycle, as discussed in Chapter 5. Auditors will encounter a growing number of clients using or planning to implement biometric systems. Remember that auditors don't need to be technicians. Our job as auditors is to witness whether executive managers did their job of selecting the right system and how it is governed. Let's take a walk through the basic life cycle.

Phase 1: Biometric Feasibility

Management determines the need, purpose, and function for biometrics. Are executives interested in using biometric technology because it looks cool? Real planning considers the following points:

- Analysis of regulations and classification of data to be protected.

- Physical environment, mission, and people. What problem is biometrics going to solve?

- Effect of biometrics on employees, customers, and business partners.

- Data collection may be difficult because of perceptions of intrusiveness, possible misuse, implications of system failure, and moral concerns.

- Return on investment (ROI) after analysis of initial cost, ongoing operation, maintenance, and comparison of alternatives.

> Proper encryption is required with full intrusion detection to protect the user's biometric data stored in the database. Otherwise, a hacker could swap biometric samples in the system, gain forged access using their own biometric sample under a legitimate user identity, and replace the original legitimate user's sample after committing the offense. Both biometrics and encryption require serious ongoing management to be considered as effective. Neither can be trusted; if the attitude is, "set it and forget it."

The results of management's feasibility study should be available for the auditor to review. Assuming that the decision was a good one, a formal review should occur to gain approval to proceed to phase 2.

Phase 2: Biometric Requirements

Before rushing out to buy a product, you'll need to consider the detailed requirements. These will come from a discovery exercise of intended use, unique needs, and the specific operating environment. Everyone knows you should not go shopping without a list. Doing so results in overspending or buying the wrong item. Independent consultants may assist with the requirements phase. The independent consultant shall be barred from bidding on or selling the biometric system to ensure that the consultant remains independent. Following the SDLC model, the requirements phase should include the following:

- Identification of the ownership roles, custodian duties, and users of the system.

- Executive support in the form of a signed biometrics policy, budget, and delegation of authority.

- Physical access restrictions covering both the biometric system and the area it will protect.

- Logical (technical) access needs to be restricted to prevent direct access into the data repository. Special methods such as single sign-on (SSO) are necessary for interfacing to other applications without risk of compromising the biometric repository.

- Solutions to design questions about biometric standards, data storage capacity, security, maintenance, backup, and restoration procedures.

- Functionality for the intended use. Will it do the job? Is additional functionality needed, such as the ability to export data for FBI background investigations? If so, the system needs to have that capability plus the implementation of a design using the Common Biometric Exchange Formats Framework (CBEFF) with the Electronic Fingerprint Transmission Specification (EFTS).

- Risk analysis for what happens *when* this system fails. The two most common failures are rejecting authorized people and mistakenly accepting an attacker. One technique for compromising biometrics is to substitute the attacker's biometric data for that of a legitimate user. After access is granted, the attacker will reload the original biometric data to hide the intrusion.

Assuming that your client did a good job, it's time for the phase 2 review. All the research and planning is presented to determine whether this project should continue into phase 3, return to the drawing board to rerun the discovery process, or be cancelled. If all the issues are addressed, the project may be granted formal approval to proceed to phase 3. Evidence of phase 2 research and formal approval to proceed is expected to be available for the auditor to review.

Phase 3: System Selection

We need to take a moment to explain the high-level technical concept of how a biometric system works. The two basic components in biometrics are the template generator and the template matcher. Everyone agrees that the vendor's product needs to be certified. The issue is how it's certified. Let's start with the template generator:

Biometric Template Generator   Biometric images are acquired during live enrollment of the user. A biometric sensor with special *template generator* software converts each image into a unique data template. This template data becomes the user's biometric reference. Template data sample is created every time the user activates the biometric sensor. A template generator must be laboratory tested by using very large data sets in repeatable evaluations. It will be tested offline to ensure that each unique user template is created by using the correct internal program procedures, so it is algorithmically correct and physically distinct from that of other users. Without this testing, the system would have no integrity and could accept the wrong person (false acceptance). Items 1 to 3 in Figure 7.17 show how the biometric system uses the template generator to create individual biometric data during user enrollment.

FIGURE 7.17   Template generator creates biometric data

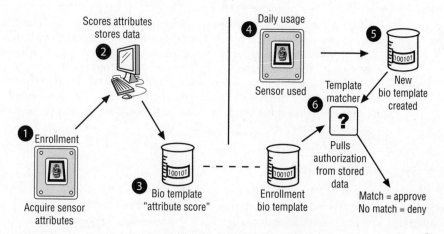

Biometric Template Matcher   A *template matcher* is used to compare sensor data against the user's reference template made during enrollment. Template matchers may compare multiple

samples against more than one template. The goal is to determine whether the new template data (created every time the user tries to gain access) and the user's reference template created during enrollment produce a similar score. Biometric template generators and template matchers must be tested and certified separately to insure accuracy. A template generator is certified as a software library. A match indicates personal identity verification (PIV). Items 4 through 6 in Figure 7.17 illustrate the template matcher being used to authenticate (match) sensor data against an individual's reference sample in the database.

Now let's return to the issues in phase 3 regarding system selection. A vendor's product has to be properly certified to be eligible for selection. Additional points to consider in this phase are as follows:

- Process for enrolling, re-enrolling, and removing users from the system
- Security protection to prevent tampering, sabotage, substitution of fake templates, and compromise of biometric data (templates)
- Available technical support and training materials
- Operational questions of user acceptance, maintenance, hygiene, backup, and restore functions
- Total cost of ownership (purchase, installation, maintenance) and the ROI
- Procurement method: bid, outsource, or straight purchase

Phase 3 concludes with a formal review. The selection criteria is presented along with alternatives. All the open issues need to be fixed, rejected, or withdrawn before formal approval can be given. With formal approval, the product can be purchased and the project proceeds into phase 4.

Untrained use of trial evaluations usually ends with the buyer getting stuck with unreturnable product unless the seller offers an unconditional 90-day "after installation" return policy. Most buyers don't realize what they really want until it's too late. It can be super beneficial to attend vendor-sponsored training during the final selection process, before making any purchase commitment. The purpose is to learn the hidden points of your intended use that don't match the vendor's sales literature. Consider it an educated tryout before you buy.

Phase 4: System Configuration

Some product training is helpful to ensure a proper installation. The auditee should be trained before the vendor sends the installation technicians out to configure the system. Too many times, the promise of knowledge transfer at a later date becomes just another failed promise. Points to consider in phase 4 include the following:

- Installing hardware and software
- Calibrating and recalibrating the system

- Following operating procedures for enrollment, security, transmission, processing, backup, and restoration
- Using transaction controls
- Monitoring the systems and logs
- Detecting system compromise plus use of corresponding incident response procedures
- Connecting the biometric system interface to other systems

Additional points may be added to suit the client's intended use. Let's assume that everyone did their job. The next step is to certify the system for production use by testing the people and the procedures.

Phase 5: Biometrics Implementation

Now the system is preparing to enter production. There are still a few steps to cover before announcing that the system is ready. Here's the short list:

- Formalize configuration management and change control into a system baseline.
- Train users.
- Enroll the user to populate the biometrics database.
- Manage the deletion of users removed from the system.
- Begin user testing.
- Determine whether the installed system met management's objective. Run technical tests to certify system performance.
- Determine whether the overall operation is acceptable to management. If so, formal accreditation is given in the form of a written sign-off to enter production. Management formally accepts the outcome and the responsibility for any possible failures. Accreditation may be for 90 days, for 180 days, or annual.

After management accreditation, the biometric system may now enter production use.

This may seem like a lot of work—because it is. The goal is to ensure that the right things happen for the right reasons. This biometrics example is one of our first opportunities to demonstrate how a system goes through the SDLC process. Now it's time to look ahead into the system's future.

Phase 6: Biometrics Postimplementation

Each year a system must be recertified and reaccredited. The purpose is to ensure that management has looked at its historical performance, ROI (if any), and changes in both regulations and attitudes. The question is whether the system is allowed to continue operation as is, is modified to keep up with changes, or is retired.

As auditors, we are interested in finding evidence of the post-implementation review, recertification process, and management's reaccreditation of the system for continued use in production for another 90 days, 180 days, or annually. The process repeats each year the system is in use.

Phase 7: Biometric System Disposal

This is the same process as in Chapter 5. A review is held to determine the implications of shutting down the system. Topics considered include regulations related to the system, record retention requirements, and ways to archive the data. Formal approval is requested to shut down the system. The decision should be based on a risk analysis of the impact. After formal approval, the system is shut down, media is sanitized, and hardware is removed from capital inventory. Equipment is resold, donated, destroyed, or recycled.

As auditors, we would like to see the evidence that this disposal was authorized and properly handled. Biometric systems have several technical advantages that must be balanced against the known problems. Let's discuss some of the known problems with biometrics.

Understanding the Drawbacks of Biometrics

Using biometric systems has some drawbacks. How will the biometric results be used? Is the biometric system expected to provide identification or authentication?

Biometric systems face issues of social acceptability. The users may have concerns about sanitary health issues regarding physical contact or about invasion of privacy. Biometric data must be managed to ensure the security of initial data collection, data distribution, and processing. A biometric data policy is required to specify the data life cycle and control procedures. Biometric data must always be protected for confidentiality and integrity.

Error rates exist in all automated systems, and biometric systems are no different. It is possible for an error to occur during data collection or data processing. The following are various types of errors that can occur in a biometric system:

Enrollment   Every user provides a sample for the biometric system during the *enrollment* process. The sample may fail to be accepted by the system. The typical enrollment process should take only 2 to 5 minutes; any longer could lead to user dissatisfaction.

Failure to Enroll   On rare occasions, the user's data will not be accepted by the system. This is referred to as *failure to enroll* (FTER). It could be due to image quality, calibration, system problems, or the scanner not interpreting a person's physical abnormalities.

False Rejection   A legitimate person could be rejected and fail authentication; the correct user fails to authenticate. This failure to accept a legitimate user is known as the *false rejection rate* (FRR) or type 1 error. The biometric system rejects a legitimate user. This is considered a type 1 error because it is the most common type of error.

False Acceptance   It is possible for the system to permit access to an individual who should have been rejected; the wrong person is authenticated. This is referred to as the *false acceptance rate* (FAR) or type 2 error. The biometric system inadvertently accepts an unauthorized user.

Equal Error versus Crossover Error Rate   Every system has a delicate balance of speed over efficiency. In biometrics, an equal balance of speed and accuracy is referred to as the *equal error rate* (EER); setting the biometric system to favor accuracy over speed or vice versa is known as the *crossover error rate* (CER). Figure 7.18 illustrates the differences between EER and CER. The biometric system is not perfect. An acceptable error rate will always exist. Figure 7.18 helps illustrate how CER represents the trade-off between favoring more speed or more accuracy.

FIGURE 7.18   Equal error rate versus crossover

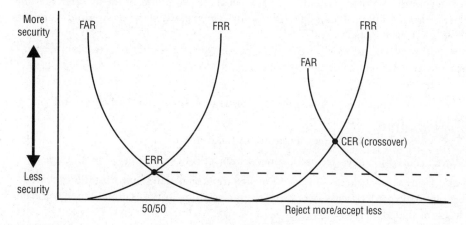

 Several websites, including those used by ISACA, have confused the difference between EER and crossover (CER). The difference of these settings is clear in national security directives. It's possible ISACA may contain in improperly worded reference mistakenly state EER and CER are the same.

Throughput Rate   How many people (samples) can the system process and still have reasonable accuracy? Lower throughput may be acceptable in situations of higher risk. Higher throughput may be better in low-risk situations such as the collection of visitors' fingerprints at turnstiles entering an amusement park.

We have discussed the methods for authenticating a user. Now it is time to discuss the types of access that could be granted on the network.

Network Access Protection

All computer networks are prone to access control problems. It is an ongoing challenge to provide access to legitimate users while blocking access from all others. Several methods have been developed to accomplish this goal. Computer users demand ease of use, while computer custodians strive for tighter controls. Unfortunately, network access is predominantly a perimeter defense. Better controls are sorely needed at the application level.

In this section, we discuss several technologies including firewalls. We will start with single sign-on. The CISA is expected to understand the concept of single sign-on. Its purpose is to improve network access controls by implementing a higher-security system that is easier for the user. One of the most common examples is Kerberos, developed by the Massachusetts Institute of Technology.

Kerberos Single Sign-On

The Kerberos single sign-on (SSO) system was developed to improve both security and user satisfaction. The name *Kerberos* refers to the mythical three-headed dog guarding the gates to the underworld. Kerberos provides security when the end points of the network are safe but the transmission path cannot be trusted—for example, when the servers and workstations are trusted but the network is not.

The concept of operation is for the user to log in once to Kerberos. After login, the Kerberos system authenticates the user and grants access to all resources. The process works as follows:

1. The user authenticates to the Kerberos workstation software. Authentication may be a password or a biometric method.

2. The workstation software authenticates to the Kerberos server.

3. Shared encryption keys are used. A network access ticket is created by Kerberos.

4. A Kerberos access ticket is sent to the workstation, signed in the workstation's shared encryption key. All other network servers receive a similar ticket granting the workstation access to shared servers.

5. The user is automatically signed in to all servers.

The belief is that a user with a strong password and strong encryption will improve overall security. Unfortunately, Kerberos works only with specially modified versions of software designed for use with Kerberos. Merely installing Kerberos will not improve security. There are compatibility problems with different versions of implementation.

Special skills and experience are required to make a Kerberos installation successful. First, a knowledgeable installer will understand how to use separate domains to partition Kerberos access for better security. Second, restoring data from tape backup is quite involved. The Kerberos system must be shut down and the date rolled back to the timestamp of the file being restored. As soon as the file is restored, the time clocks must be rolled forward again with the system resynchronized for the users. Any compromise of the key distribution center (KDC) means that the entire system is compromised and must be shut down. Using Kerberos requires highly experienced system administrators. Figure 7.19 illustrates a simplistic design of Kerberos single sign-on.

Network Firewalls

Computer networks can be protected from internal and external threats by using firewalls (FWs). The concept is that a specially configured firewall on the network will block unwanted access. However, this is a grossly misunderstood concept, and many organizations do not understand firewall capabilities and limitations. As a result, there can be a false sense of security. Let's consider the advantages and disadvantages of network firewalls:

Firewall Advantages   Reduces external access to the network.

FIGURE 7.19   Kerberos single sign-on

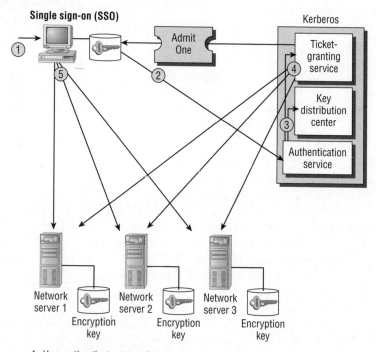

1. User authenticates to workstation.
2. Workstation authenticates to Kerberos.
3. Encryption keys are used, ticket granted.
4. Ticket sent to workstation and every server.
   Tickets encrypted with each computer's own key.
5. User is automatically logged in to all servers.

Firewall Disadvantages   There is always a hole for traffic to pass through—either good traffic or bad traffic or both. A firewall can control only the traffic that passes directly through it. It does not protect modems or other access points. A firewall can be misconfigured or technically circumvented. There is no such thing as a completely safe firewall. The firewall concept creates a false sense of security.

Network firewalls have undergone several generations of improvement. The first generation was simply a router with a primitive access control list (ACL) specifying the *to* destination and the sender's *from* network addresses. Attackers became more sophisticated, and so did the need for better firewalls. The following are the different generations of firewall technology:

First Generation: Packet Filter   The first generation was a packet filter. Filtering is based on the sending and receiving address combined with the service port (a packet). The advantage of this design is its low cost.

The first-generation packet filter design was prone to problems. The design was plagued with poor logging and granular rules that were difficult to implement effectively. Hackers were still able to get in. Figure 7.20 helps illustrate the concept of packet-filtering firewalls.

FIGURE 7.20 First-generation filter

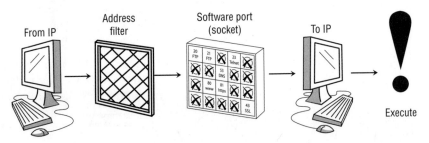

Second Generation: Application Proxy Filter A firewall application program was added to the first-generation design of packet filtering. The second generation uses an application proxy to relay requests through the firewall. The proxy checks the inbound request to ensure that it complies with safe computing in both format and type of request. Application proxies perform user requests without granting direct access to the target software. The application proxy is also referred to as a *circuit-level firewall*. This is because the application proxy is required to complete the circuit; otherwise, no connection exists. This design improved event logging; however, hackers were still able to get in. Figure 7.21 illustrates the concept of an application proxy testing the request before passing the data. Improper requests are usually discarded. This extra step of using a proxy program helps protect your system.

FIGURE 7.21 Application proxy with filter

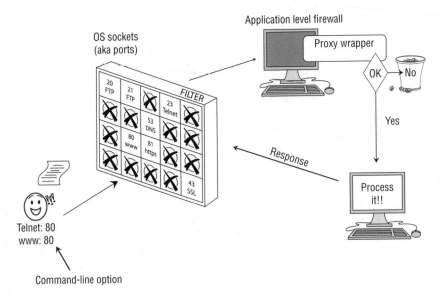

Third Generation: Stateful Inspection   Hackers were able to trick second-generation fire-walls by sending a request that was formatted to bypass the proxy design. Application proxy firewalls relied on open connections maintained with the user. Connectionless sessions such as the User Datagram Protocol (UDP) in IP were not protected. In the third generation, both TCP requests and UDP connectionless requests are recorded into a history table. The historic "state" of connectionless requests is now controlled by the firewall for better protection. This is referred to as *stateful inspection*. Stateful inspection is the de facto minimum standard for network firewall technology. However, there's still room for improvement.

Fourth Generation: Adaptive Response   Improvements in technology allow the firewall to communicate with an intrusion detection and prevention system (IDPS). This additional automation attempts to provide an adaptive response to network attacks. The firewall admin-istrator can configure stored procedures designed to rebut many types of firewall attack. The firewall can reconfigure itself to block ports or reset connections. This design is not bullet-proof because hackers will still get through and segregation of duties between systems is still required. One drawback is that a skilled attacker may masquerade as a critical device such as a necessary server. The fourth-generation firewall could accidentally disable the critical device, which would create a denial-of-service problem. It's possible that the exception rule to prevent self-denial will then be exploited by a stealthy hacker to quietly sneak through into your net-work. It's happened before during zero-day attacks.

Fifth Generation: Kernel Process   The fifth-generation firewall is actually an internal control mechanism designed into the operating system kernel. Individual processing requests are verified against an internal access control list. Those not on the list are rejected. Special military systems have been using fifth-generation firewalls for many years. Microsoft Windows XP and later operating systems such as Vista and Windows 7 have implemented a basic fifth-generation firewall. Figure 7.22 helps illustrate the fifth-generation method of embedding command filtering into the operating system kernel.

FIGURE 7.22   ACL in fifth-generation firewall in OS kernel

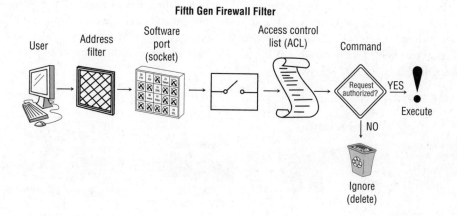

The network firewall is the best defense for protecting a network. Each generation provides different levels of cost and protection. Figure 7.23 illustrates the firewalls by generation in relation to the OSI model. We covered the OSI model in Chapter 4, "Networking Technology Basics."

FIGURE 7.23 Firewall generations compared to the OSI model

	Packet Filtering	Application Proxy w/ Packet Filter	Stateful Inspection w/ Proxy	Adaptive Response OS	Kernel
Application OSI layer 7	None	Varies	Varies	Varies	
Presentation OSI layer 6	None	None	Varies	Varies	Varies
Session OSI layer 5	None	Protected	Protected	Protected	Protected
Transport OSI layer 4	None	Varies	Protected	Protected	Protected
Networking OSI layer 3	Protected	Protected	Protected	Protected	Protected
Data-Link OSI layer 2	Protected	Protected	Protected	Protected	Protected
Physical OSI layer 1	None	None	None	None	None

Network firewalls can be implemented by using one of three basic designs. The first method is the screened host implementation. The screened host protects a single host through the firewall. The host computer is strongly defended. It is expected that this host may be attacked. Technical manuals may refer to this as the *bastion host*. Figure 7.24 illustrates the screened host implementation.

FIGURE 7.24 Firewall-screened host

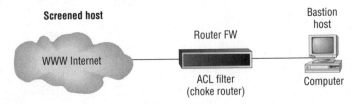

Screened host

Bastion host

WWW Internet

Router FW

ACL filter (choke router)

Computer

The next method of firewall implementation is to install two interface cards in the same host. This method is referred to as to *dual-homed*. The host computer is configured with the routing disabled. A special software application such as an application proxy relays appropriate communication between the two interface cards. This is the configuration of many Internet firewalls. Figure 7.25 illustrates the dual-homed host.

FIGURE 7.25   Dual-homed host

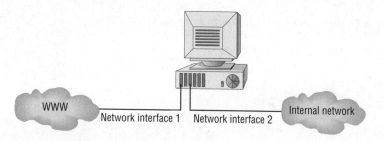

The third method of firewall implementation is known as the *screened subnet*, or *DMZ* design. DMZ is a term that refers to the demilitarized zone between enemy forces on a battlefield. The DMZ design allows for several computers to be placed in a protected subnet that is accessible from the outside and by systems inside the network. Any military veteran will tell you any DMZ must be regarded as semi-hostile territory where your systems can still be attacked and killed. The same applies to computers located here. Figure 7.26 illustrates the DMZ concept.

FIGURE 7.26   Screened subnet, also known as DMZ subnet

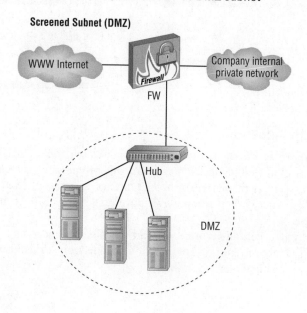

Firewall systems should be implemented to support a separation of duties. Separation of duties is just as important for machines as for personnel. The intention is to provide additional layers of control. Separate firewalls allow tighter access-control rules. Selected data is mirrored from internal production servers to a DMZ server for access by business partners or clients. This eliminates the dangers of direct access to an internal server. In addition, the redundancy improves overall availability. An outage would affect a smaller audience. Figure 7.27 illustrates the separation of duties using a firewall.

FIGURE 7.27   Separation of duties with firewalls

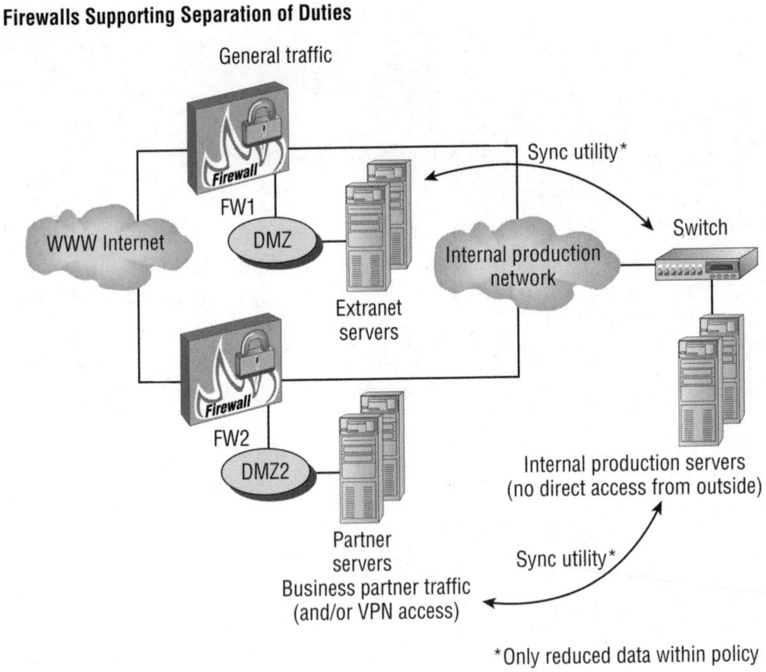

Firewalls Supporting Separation of Duties

General traffic

Sync utility*

WWW Internet

Firewall

FW1

DMZ

Extranet servers

Internal production network

Switch

Firewall

FW2

DMZ2

Partner servers

Business partner traffic (and/or VPN access)

Internal production servers (no direct access from outside)

Sync utility*

*Only reduced data within policy

Remote Dial-Up Access

Remote users can often access the network over standard telephone lines with modems. This method completely bypasses security mechanisms provided by the network firewall. The dial-up user may access the network through an access server modem bank or an individual modem on a networked computer. Figure 7.28 helps to illustrate the Remote Access server (RAS).

As an IS auditor, you need to determine whether the client has adequate safeguards to prevent this method of circumvention. Are the phone connections to modems properly managed considering the higher level of risk?

FIGURE 7.28   Remote Access Server (RAS)

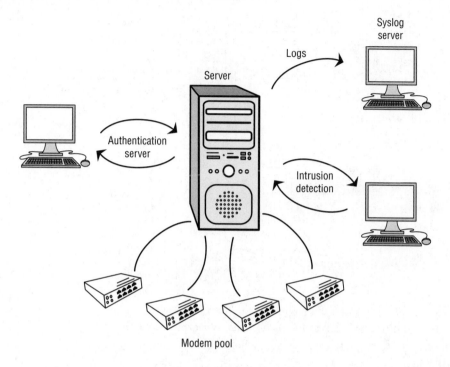

Remote VPN Access

Virtual private networks (VPNs) connect remote users over an insecure public network such as the Internet. The connection is virtual because it is temporary with no physical presence. VPN technology is cost-effective and highly flexible. A VPN creates an encrypted tunnel to securely pass data as follows:

- Between two machines (host-host)
- From a machine to a network (host-gateway)
- From one network to another network (gateway-gateway)

VPN connections will be using one of the these three methods shown in Figure 7.29. As an auditor, it's important to realize that host-based means there is no special software or just a single device with client-side license installed for communicating directly to the gateway (server). On occasion you may encounter a user laptop with the gateway version of the software installed. If the actual gateway software is used, consider the device a gateway with only one user.

FIGURE 7.29   Three common types of VPNs

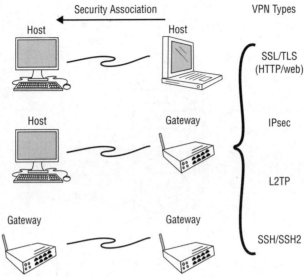

There are four types of VPN technology and protocol in use today. ISACA wants you to be familiar with the basic terms for each of the four types of VPN:

- Point-to-Point Tunneling Protocol, or PPTP

- Layer 2 Tunneling Protocol, or L2TP (OSI layer 2, Data-Link)

- Secure Sockets Layer, or SSL (OSI layer 5, Session)

- Internet Protocol Security, or IPsec (OSI layer 3, Networking)

SSL by Netscape and ISO standard Transport Layer Security (TLS) are commonly used for confidentiality and integrity in the session between the user and the server. Both SSL and TLS operate in a similar manner. TLS is the newer and preferred method because it implements certified and accredited security functions and stronger cryptographic algorithms following ISO standards. SSL is an outdated proprietary standard created by Netscape. SSL was great back in the day when nothing else existed, but contains a series of known weaknesses including simple handshakes and nonaccredited methods that are easily exploited. Both SSL and TLS design uses a digital certificate on the server to generate one-way authentication. If you add a digital certificate to the user workstation, a second one-way security association can be configured *from* the user back to the server. (Two opposite one-way security associations create an effect equal to dual authentication.) A secure login to the server can also be generated by using Secure Shell (SSH). Encryption occurs along the entire path between the sending and receiving computers. SSH provides end-to-end confidentiality and integrity in a terminal session with the host server.

IPsec VPN

The IPsec design is the newest development in virtual private networking. IPsec uses ISP gateways with two modes of creating a VPN. Let's start with two important differences in operation of the VPN gateway:

- IPsec VPN gateways are used for data that is entering or leaving the organization's local area network. These gateways use an external address from their ISP vendor (AT&T, Deutsche Telekom, BT Group, Verizon, and so forth).

- VPN encryption is occurring between the gateways. Data transmitted between the local VPN gateway and internal computer is not encrypted.

The difference between these two modes is illustrated in Figure 7.30. Notice that the encryption is occurring only between the gateways. Traffic on the LAN is not protected. This is because IPsec was designed to protect communications across the Internet rather than internal traffic.

FIGURE 7.30   IPsec VPN is designed to protect traffic crossing the Internet

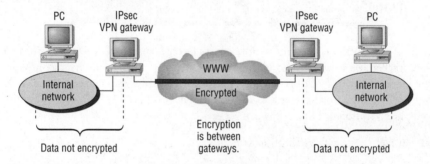

In IPsec virtual private networks, there are two specific operating modes:

Transport mode is used when there is no need to hide the network address of the sender or recipient. The message payload is encrypted for security; the address header is not.

Tunnel mode is used to hide the identity of the sender and recipient. Both address header and payload (message) are encrypted. A new address header is added to data traveling across the Internet. This new address header will use addresses of the sender's VPN-ISP gateway and recipient's VPN-ISP gateway.

Security is managed by the *authentication header (AH)* and *security parameter index (SPI)*. The authentication header uniquely identifies each packet and provides sequencing information. AH provides authentication, integrity, and nonrepudiation (nondenial).

The security parameter index provides information about encryption and special handling requirements. This design is based on the older X.25 communication standard you read about in Chapter 4. Figure 7.31 illustrates the IPsec design.

FIGURE 7.31 VPN using IPsec transport versus tunnel mode

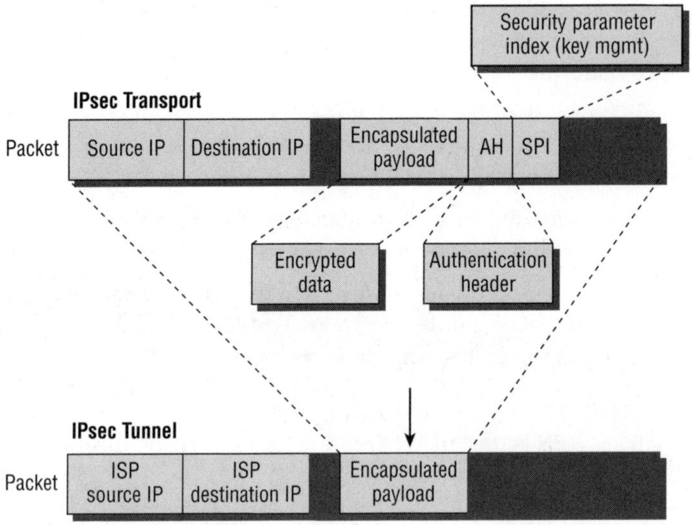

The goal of every VPN is to grant remote access to authorized users. Data can be shared across the Internet at a very low cost with relative safety if the proper internal controls are implemented. A VPN can be combined with a firewall DMZ by using a separation of duties between internal production servers and the external accessible server. Figure 7.32 illustrates a VPN with a separation of duties between servers.

FIGURE 7.32 VPN with separation of duties

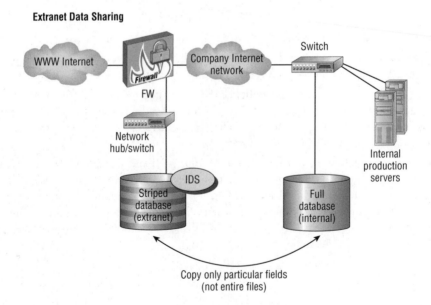

Wireless Access

User demands for wireless access to network resources increase every day. When you read the vendor ads, it appears that wireless can provide security equal to wired access. However, wireless access to networks represents an additional level of threat. Wireless security has been completely compromised by vendors to improve Plug and Play capabilities.

Setting Up a Wireless LAN

It's relatively simple to construct a wireless LAN. A wireless network can be peer to peer, which is known as *ad hoc mode*. Another type of wireless LAN is *infrastructure mode* with the access points (APs) connecting various stations. Several vendors offer low-cost wireless AP that is similar to a wireless hub or router. Each AP is connected to a wired network and broadcasts connectivity to handheld devices.

Usually the range of an AP is 300 feet, equivalent to 100 meters. Users can move freely within the 300-foot broadcast range without losing any connectivity. The individual broadcast area (range) is also known as a *cell*. This is comparable to the design of cellular telephone networks. Effective range can be increased by combining APs and their multiple cells (service range). WLANs are based on the IEEE 802.11 standard. Let's look at the basic components of a WLAN.

Station (STA)   The station is a wireless device, such as a PDA, notebook computer, or mobile phone that is accessing the network.

Access Point (AP)   A wireless transmitter/receiver that provides basic network services, usually within 300 feet, equivalent to 100 meters. Higher-power transmitters with longer ranges are entering the marketplace. The AP and STA compose a basic WLAN.

Cell   Individual AP broadcast range is known as the cell or span of coverage. Multiple AP cells are linked together to increase the range and to allow roaming within the building or between buildings.

Figure 7.33 shows the basic layout of a wireless network.

FIGURE 7.33   Basic wireless network

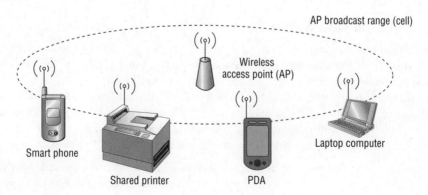

Usually the AP is connected to a distribution system such as the existing wired network to provide an infrastructure with greater services for the stations. This is the most common implementation of WLAN.

Obsolete IEEE 802.11 Wireless Standards

The original WLAN standard for wireless networks was very slow, operating at only 1 to 2 Mbps speeds. Three competing WLAN technology standards were established between 1999 and 2003. All three are considered obsolete because of security flaws:

802.11 a (1997)   Performance speeds were improved by increasing to 54 Mbps with transmissions in the 5 GHz frequency band.

802.11b (1999)   Transmitting at speeds up to 11 Mbps using the 2.4–2.48 GHz frequency band.

802.11g (2003)   Provided for transmission at either the 2.4 GHz or 5 GHz band, with speeds up to 54 Mbps.

The lack of effective security is an enormous drawback in wireless networking. IEEE's original design of Wired Equivalent Privacy (WEP) proved to be practically worthless. In response, IEEE issued a revised wireless standard.

Updated IEEE Wireless Standards

Technology is a constant series of evolving standards. IEEE helps drive technology by issuing new wireless standards offering better security or longer transmission range. Let's start with improving wireless security:

802.11i (2005)   Introduced the concept of a robust security network (RSN) with better implementation of encryption keys.

802.16 WiMAX (2003)   Mobile broadband using cellular-based networks. This standard allows roaming Internet access without any real data security. WiMAX is becoming increasingly popular because of its low-cost availability in metropolitan areas. WiMAX should always be considered an *insecure* network.

WLAN Transmission Security

Emerging demand for wireless connectivity is pushing the boundaries of information security. Moore's law states that computing power will double every 18 months, and at the same time the present methods of security will be reduced in effectiveness by 50 percent.

The challenge of protecting a WLAN can be solved only by a multilevel approach. Every subset of confidentiality, integrity, and availability (CIA) is at risk in WLAN implementations. There is no individual technology that will provide enough protection against the full spectrum of threats. WLAN security requirements can be summarized as follows:

Authentication   A third party must be able to authenticate the sender of a message as genuine. Authentication is the process of matching a claim to verify an exact match. There must be accurate methods of testing the claim to ensure that a legitimate match occurs. The worst method in WLAN authentication is the wireless device merely transmitting with the same shared key of the AP. The AP does not prove its identity to the wireless device, yet they are communicating to each other. This is why everyone should be worried about a rogue AP.

Three methods of WLAN authentication are as follows:

Shared Key (Poor Cryptographic Authentication)   A wireless client device transmits a copy of the shared symmetric key belonging to the AP. Typical implementations use a 128-bit key in an RC4 stream cipher. It may be called a preshared key, wireless-PSK, or WPA-PSK by the vendor to gloss over the problem. Overall, this design is very weak and should be considered rudimentary. It is not safe unless a separate VPN is used during transmission over any form of shared-key wireless equipment.

Open System (Default, No Authentication)   A wireless client device transmits the MAC address of the AP to establish communication. The open system method is notorious for falling victim to the infamous man-in-the-middle attack.

Robust 802.11i (Strong Cryptographic Authentication)   Uses 802.1x port-based access control with stronger key generation and authentication. This is also known as WPA2 dynamic security using cipher-block chaining with automatic key rotation.

> Only two methods are acceptable for security in wireless networks. The first choice is 802.11i (Robust Security Network). The second choice is a separate VPN implementation using strong authentication with digital certificates and tokens. All existing WEP equipment has been designated as unsafe under all conditions by current government standards and the information security industry at large. (Source: National Institute of Standards and Technology, April 2005.)

Wireless Nonrepudiation   To deny involvement is equivalent to repudiation. Nonrepudiation means the other person will not be able to deny their participation. This is used to prove the sender and receiver messages or participants in a transaction. You must have strong authentication to provide nonrepudiation.

Wireless Accountability   Individual actions must be traceable back to each unique individual entity. Accountability is difficult or impossible without strong authentication and nonrepudiation.

Wireless Integrity   Both sender and receiver need a method to ensure integrity for messages transmitted between the wireless client and AP. We need proof that contents of a message have not been tampered with or changed in transit. All versions of IEEE 802.11a/b/g specifications provided poor authentication between wireless devices.

The IEEE design prior to version 802.11i used a simple cyclic redundancy check (CRC) approach. A CRC-32 frame check sequence is computed on each payload prior to transmission. Then, the CRC-32 frame check is encrypted by using the RC4 stream cipher to create a ciphertext message. The message recipient decrypts the CRC-32 frame check by using a shared key. The CRC-32 results are compared, and messages are discarded if the CRCs are not equal. Unfortunately, the intrinsic flaw is that CRC is not as cryptographically secure as a hash message authentication code (HMAC).

WEP's integrity scheme is still considered vulnerable to certain attacks regardless of key size. RSN 802.11i networks use *temporal keys* for much stronger authentication. RSN is a trusted technology approved for government use.

Wireless Privacy   Many misleading advertisements claim that wireless systems have privacy equivalent to a wired connection. As noted earlier in this chapter, the term used is Wired Equivalent Privacy (WEP). The concept of WEP is to use the RC4 symmetric key in a stream cipher to generate a pseudorandom data sequence. WEP's operating technique is simply an exclusive OR (XOR) function using modulo 2 math for data transmitted in the Network layer and above. The XOR function is based on comparing two values for an equal match (for example, 1 and 1 match, so XOR will equal 0). Alternatively, the values don't match (for example, 1 and 0 will XOR to equal 1). It's a simple binary comparison for the computer. Using XOR for security functions is a primitive design.

Standard WEP   The 802.11 standard uses a 40-bit cryptographic key for WEP. Individual vendors offer nonstandard extensions of WEP keys at 128–256 bits. The intention was based on a theory that larger key sizes would be more difficult to break. Unfortunately, several attacks have been identified, which makes WEP vulnerable regardless of key size.

Enhanced WEP   An enhanced version of WEP was created in an attempt to overcome the original 802.11 security shortfalls. The enhanced version is still susceptible to several of the WEP subversion attacks.

802.11i Replaces WEP   All WEP implementations should be considered unsafe and obsolete. The current standard for wireless security is RSN. This may force the replacement of WEP/ WPA products with newer RSN 802.11i equipment. The only acceptable alternative is using end-to-end client VPN.

Figure 7.34 provides a simple depiction of the difference between WEP and 802.11i using 802.1x. Notice the changes improving our CIA objectives.

Achieving RSN Wireless Security

To secure wireless networks and their associated devices requires significant effort, coupled with proper resources and vigilance. It is imperative that management reassess wireless risks at least monthly. The only effective way to maintain security is by constant testing and evaluating systems' security controls when wireless technology is being deployed.

Firewall Protection for Wireless Networks

All wireless access points should traverse a network firewall for security reasons. Regulations such as the joint payment card industry (PCI) security policy governing Visa, MasterCard, Discover Card, and American Express have mandated that firewalls be used when merchant organizations process credit transactions on the network. The wireless firewall itself should be separate from the existing Internet firewall. It would be difficult or impossible to successfully combine the two functions into a single firewall. Figure 7.35 provides an overview of using a firewall with wireless access points.

FIGURE 7.34 Robust security compared to earlier versions

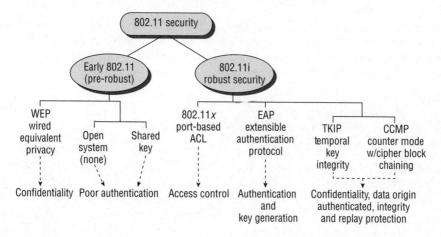

FIGURE 7.35 Firewall protecting against wireless access points

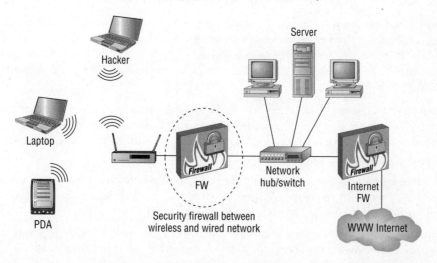

We've spent quite a bit of time discussing firewalls and wireless access controls. It is time to discuss methods for detecting intrusion to the network. Intrusion detection systems have been in the marketplace for more than 10 years. Every organization should have intrusion detection systems in place.

Intrusion Detection

A network *intrusion detection system (IDS)* functions in a manner similar to virus detection or a burglar alarm. The objective is to inform the administrator of a suspected intrusion or attack occurring. Constant monitoring is necessary in order to receive the benefit of intrusion detection; otherwise, intrusion detection is no more valuable than an audit log of past history.

An improved version of intrusion detection is the *intrusion prevention system (IPS)*. The IPS concept is to ensure that the attack is blocked immediately upon detection.

New standards refer to IDS and IPS systems as one combined *intrusion detection and prevention system (IDPS)*. There are two types of intrusion detection and prevention systems:

Host Based   The host-based system monitors activity on a particular computer host or device such as a router. Attacks on other devices will not be seen by the host-based IDPS. To avoid confusion, the host-based IDS (HIDS) is now referred to as a *host-based intrusion detection and prevention system (HIDPS)*.

Network Based   Network IDS systems observe traffic in a manner similar to a packet sniffer. Network-based IDS (NIDS) is referred to as a *network intrusion detection and prevention system (NIDPS)*. The network IDPS monitors activity across a network link. The IDPS can see attacks on promiscuous connections, but not across discrete switched network connections. The design of a network switch can prevent an IDPS system from detecting attacks occurring on systems connected to the other switch ports.

There are three technical methods of detecting a network intrusion:

Statistical   The statistical system uses a calculation of network traffic, CPU, and memory loading to determine whether an attack is occurring. Statistical systems are prone to false alarms because the traffic patterns of most networks are sporadic. The statistical system offers the advantage of being able to detect new attacks that might otherwise go unnoticed if a signature-based system were in use.

Signature   Signature-based IDPS relies on a database of attack techniques. The signature-based IDPS is similar in design to a signature-based virus scanner. The IDPS is looking for behaviors that indicate a particular type of known attack. Unfortunately, the signature-based IDPS cannot detect attacks that are not listed in its database.

Neural   Neural-based learning networks are being implemented on intrusion detection systems. The objective is to create a learning system that is a hybrid between statistical- and signature-based methods. Figure 7.36 illustrates an IDPS on the network.

Intrusion detection systems are helpful for identifying network attacks in progress. Auditors need to be aware that network hubs will pass 100 percent of the traffic, which ensures that all hacker activity is seen by the IDPS. Network switches are designed to filter traffic and even the best have trouble forwarding 100 percent of the activity on each port at full speed. Using a hub ensures that nothing is filtered from the IDPS monitoring sensor.

FIGURE 7.36 Intrusion detection and prevention system

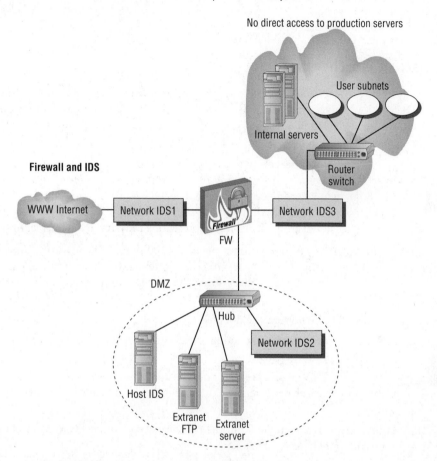

One of the more successful techniques to detect a hacker is to make a server or subnet appear as an enticing target for the attacker. The purpose of such a system is to be a decoy target. An attack of the decoy provides early warning to the appropriate personnel. The decoy can provide high interaction in a simulated production environment or low interaction of a static host. There are two basic styles of decoys:

Honey Pot The *honey pot* is a sacrificial server placed in such a manner as to attract the interest of the attacker. The honey pot server has no legitimate business value other than alerting the organization of an attack. The honey pot utilizes host-based IDPS or network-based IDPS.

Honey Net A *honey net* is a sacrificial subnet with a few machines designed to attract the interest of the attacker. All traffic from the honey net is considered suspicious because no real production activity is taking place. The purpose of this design is to allow security personnel the opportunity for advance notice of a potential attack against real production.

We have discussed firewalls, remote access, and intrusion detection. Now it is time to discuss the encryption methods used to hide data from prying eyes. Encryption provides a method of hiding data from other people.

Encryption Methods

Encryption systems provide a method of converting clear, readable text into unintelligible gibberish. Decryption converts the gibberish back into a readable message. Encryption and decryption systems have been in use for thousands of years. Encryption is used for two primary purposes: confidentiality or authentication.

Confidentiality by Encryption   Encryption is used to keep a secret by scrambling data into garbage. The secret to confidentiality is protecting the key from disclosure. Hopefully only an authorized user with the right key can decrypt the file. Each key represents a unique randomizer to scramble the message contents in different ways. Encryption is an application process designed to prevent the computer from displaying or presenting the data in a readable format.

Authentication Using Encryption   Used to test the user's ability to decrypt a file. If the user can decrypt the file properly, that user is believed to be legitimate. Once again, the secret to authentication is protecting the key from disclosure. The authentication function is used in the following:

- Digital signatures, to tell who sent the document, by a person's cryptographic identity.

- Digital certificates, to identify that the unique hardware profile represents the exact system we want to communicate with.

- Public-key decryption (PKI), to ensure that only the authorized recipient can open the file. This is how we can safely transfer files. It's also how digital rights management (DRM) operates.

As a CISA, you are expected to understand the two basic types of encryption systems: private-key systems and public-key systems.

Private-Key Encryption

Private-key encryption systems use a secret key, which is shared between the authorized sender and the intended receiver. Private-key systems contain two basic components. The first component is the mathematical algorithm for scrambling and unscrambling the message (encrypting and decrypting). The second component is the mathematical key used as a randomizer in the encryption algorithm. The longer the key length, the higher the security it will generate.

A single secret key is carefully shared between the sender and receiver. This is referred to as *symmetric-key* cryptography (see Figure 7.37). Symmetric-key cryptography is very fast, because the same key is used on both ends. The drawback is that the key must be protected with the highest possible diligence. Anybody who has a copy of the secret key can read the message. Examples of symmetric-key (secret key) cryptography include Data Encryption Standard (DES), which is now obsolete, and the new Advanced Encryption Standard (AES) designed by two Belgian researchers, Joan Daemen and Vincent Rijmen.

FIGURE 7.37   Symmetric-key cryptography

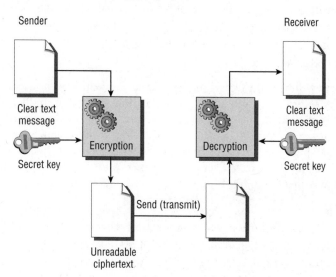

Because of the secret-key design of symmetric cryptography, encryption and decryption is very fast and efficient. The drawback is that the secret-key design cannot be used for digital signatures. To do so would expose the key to outsiders. Exchanging the secret key in symmetric cryptography is a major problem.

Public-Key Encryption

Asymmetrical cryptography is referred to as *public-key cryptography* (aka public-key interchange, or PKI). This design utilizes a separate pair of keys for encryption and decryption. The key pair is composed of a secret key protected by the owner and a second public key that is freely distributed. These two keys are mathematically related to each other. The secret key and public key are generated from a supersized prime number. It is practically impossible for a cryptographic hacker to derive the super prime number or related keys in use. Here is an example of an actual private key:

```
---- begin gnp private key ----
MX7ZBxzIQvSx1USk0tE5OY4rtaSg2VJbYGsHcmX8PipshS7IkW185kGwEQIDAQAB
FIVYQCNAWW6hh9RddMIICXQIBAAKBg6u3V3N5OVuv57nbqvaJJQCplcGSCBYgGop
fnnsjl21DHAatfpjDgRG6HWy7JJKqIjfxB717Rh/PbMiXu8Tjazc/dsRTxg5ACwD
kkY11u5Y9B/3ZexL2R4D+TmpdQfz0YtxB+5FJvhr5XGqnwsANk4bQCR2rGtAx4W6
0aTSk8D/3+e2wBCyr1z6zf9kGkHZSgzDDx5agKY1JhyxN2x1WUwcvtlW4b2Uol0/
pK6XMwWYU9BlgnMfW3n/q6qOUHfY dhRQZkONIZHbkdtaO1kWK8TA1bBAkEA26em
gNrW16W/tYjjKaTI98vOKsCesFPfKxxyV3ssnVqpJgt+eKd1awqq4JSfpK+xxDXw
r48CJuy1NuTaZCQDTPuTOv6gz6M1QJBAMW1MjpovBoddTnYon2d/DK3cXCKtZ4a1
DcOnhoLu1h9fFtVcgfbd6TjMMZfGf824IvHQQYE56dTtDUiBOxGBEOnNOyudbuib
```

SwpxAO+8giurCM4IdzTDfLPrpOqD9SWHnJ3NOeMDtBFpxfRxmp7AAJ8Z2vfjatW9
FMUCQHqwIO/SfwX4SlFxZsevY9QffZcnfFwYp9w9EAyOq9cZCOozAPLCI7TxqBDm
Dd8aval+Q8 DDL3K9e5ROG8BI+z7sh8XgTR5quBhJnjOwJDyEJsDZ4DO55MT/Vkt
1XkCQQDOEz9j+/kgb1LmZB5wKHPL/2jhSruZ5WFr2J6xjvL8GXu1I
---- end gnp private key ----

Most of the keys will have the begin and end headers to help prevent user confusion.
Truncating the key or using the wrong key will wreck the encryption. In PKI, the security
is based on nobody else having a copy of the private key. If someone manages to get a copy,
the security of your key-pair is 100 percent compromised; it's absolutely worthless. In PKI,
the second key is the public key, which can be shared with almost anyone. It would be reckless to expose the key unnecessarily. Every time an encryption key is used, the odds of security being broken will increase. Here is an example of the PKI public key:

---- begin gnp public key ----
MX7ZBxzIQAKBgQCuYO/OF/6Ih8p/hGU2isaKcttOGUMLxbjnfXtDMbky55SApEyf
c4jNqKG+Ng4/LoFuO6TlfzmaC/UT9QLufj8s9OMSZwJg37C22+/PUtEZPhM+foK9
C4PIj+v1WQQjr1vjQ1xC12V7p3jHrGbCNnBfS/4WoUNfFivOOCQQDWKcOjZXt44X
he4mxYNuqXZK7M829mi1yxnUtIr7LkEx9W7Bg bPZOEVVQnr4efy/28w2r93QIDA
QABAoGABSCWLHdw22WmJTCmGGgUxsI6o88rjDbIJxE2x7MAD2j9JQi7tAyPtI4rn
/D9ibLGovCQOWY681PV7IONMLJcOYatu2XPzSPuajQbHGkLNnfo/mgRZ6i+OJMGr
fLSM9rwpMXswgXQMOAQF5M+ouSz+11Zk/z8z3Jh/BzPZUx4lxsNO3F29k/OZ9Zmb
od7DMQgjAkEAOHF3cGbMUo+mMGmtOHEO9r2uf5semi+TJbhdvDfh81xTc5KBWURk
BRBg5B3oPUoICPw234CwJBAM9w/frjO ST8GjTpN4mq7iF Y4FF4quUFSaSfe8rg
51yGEhNkNmQN5/qu3GYdZNxT/AkB2qTeB7+QsDfRi/C9fvTUaNscROmM49CFFbR2
afgsm1epf98WdtGdBtovCGTUK6w1h8cxoCvo8TkGubdnrvDVb33prh5ViJTmCJXE
IKH9r9wPZtb1Tf/rf3AwHtwY3dHRnWXIDGHmzmdS/6/AoGBAJKdWmGDLYit7QQCV
ptzwiywjaGQMuSq9oyIBZ/LpXaexyUuiKp/kg13QLIblCbPZOEVrO
---- end gnp public key ----

Notice how both keys in the pair look very similar. The strength of public-key cryptography depends on the algorithm used and the encryption key length. To encrypt a message,
the sender would use their own "secret" private key and public key, plus the public key
of the intended recipient. Figure 7.38 shows the process of encrypting by using public-key
(asymmetrical) cryptography.

The process of decrypting the message returns it to readable text. To decrypt, the
recipient uses their secret key and public key, plus the public key of the sender. The basic
concept is that you need only three keys to unlock the data (decryption). If two values
were missing, decrypting the file would be impossible. Public-key systems offer three
major advantages because of the separate keys (key-pair). With a public-key system, you
can perform additional functions such as authentication, which are impossible in symmetric cryptography.

FIGURE 7.38   Encryption using public-key system

Sender keys

Private Public

Receiver keys

Public Private

Not used

To encrypt

Clear text
message

Sender
private key

Sender
public key

Receiver
public key

Encryption
algorithm

Ciphertext
message

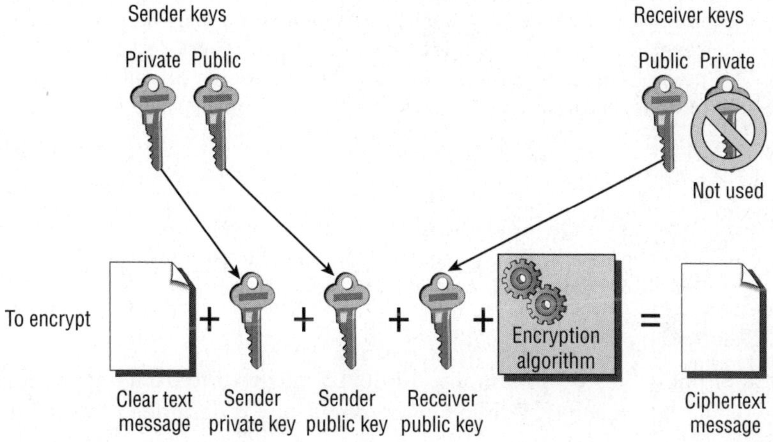

Let's look at how that works with PKI:

- Confidentiality: Encryption with a sender's key-pair and a recipient's public key creates confidentiality because the recipient's private key must be used to decrypt the message.

- Authentication: The recipient's public key is mathematically related to the recipient's private key. This means only our intended recipient can decrypt the message, unless the keys have been copied. Mismanagement and key copying are known problems.

- Encryption *never* provides availability. The goal of encryption is to prevent availability. Encryption is the art of destroying data in the hopes that only authorized users can reassemble (decrypt) the data.

Figure 7.39 shows the process of decrypting by using public-key cryptography.

FIGURE 7.39   Decryption using public-key system

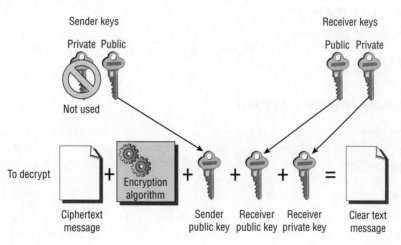

Sender keys

Private Public

Receiver keys

Public Private

Not used

To decrypt

Ciphertext
message

Encryption
algorithm

Sender
public key

Receiver
public key

Receiver
private key

Clear text
message

Although there are more complex systems, all it takes for confidentiality is to encrypt by using the sender's keys plus the receiver's public key (three keys). The receiver can decrypt by using the sender's public key with their own private key (both public keys plus their own private key). You *never* use, *never* need, all four keys to encrypt or decrypt.

Data in storage is seldom encrypted with public-key systems because it is 1,000 times slower. Symmetric (same key) systems are used for storage. Public-key systems are used during data transmission when authentication is necessary.

The design of public-key cryptography eliminates the need to exchange a secret key between the sender and receiver. Public-key cryptography is designed to allow digital signing of files.

Elliptic-Curve Cryptography

The newest method for encryption algorithms is the elliptic curve. The concept of an elliptic curve is to generate a three-dimensional space. The encryption key refers to a reference point within those dimensions. It would be extremely difficult to calculate keys generated from an elliptic curve. A small elliptic-curve key is exponentially stronger than one generated by linear math.

Elliptic-curve cryptography is used with wireless encryption. The implementation within wireless encryption is completely compromised; however, the concept of the elliptic-curve algorithm is essentially strong. Unfortunately, a 97-bit elliptic-curve encryption has been cracked from the Web by the same people who cracked the RSA 512-bit encryption key. It took twice as long, but the cracking attack was successful.

Quantum Cryptography

Quantum cryptography is based on polarization metrics of random photon light pulses. This promising technology is not available as a commercial product yet. However, the overall design appears to be quite strong.

Public-Key Infrastructure

The process of sharing encrypted files between various parties is referred to as *public-key interchange (PKI)*. You should have a basic understanding of this process for the CISA exam. Public-key interchange is designed to provide a level of trust and authentication between users. This infrastructure is built by using the public-key encryption system we discussed earlier in this chapter. Public-key infrastructure comprises four basic components:

Certificate Authority (CA)   A user contacts a certificate authority to procure a digital certificate. The digital certificate contains the owner's public key and user's contact information along with unique identifying characteristics. The certificate authority will vouch for the authenticity of the user after the certificate is issued. Certificate authorities typically follow the X.509 exchange standard.

Registration Authority (RA)   Some big customers such as IBM, Novell, and Microsoft issue certificates from a block of certificates acquired through a certificate authority, such as Entrust, Trustwave, or VeriSign. The RA is delegated bookkeeping and issuing functions from the CA. The certificate authority maintains the certificates that have been issued and verifies their authenticity.

Certificate Revocation List (CRL)   Digital certificates are checked to ensure that they are valid at the time of use. A certificate revocation list is maintained by the certificate authority to indicate that certificates have expired or are revoked. This process allows invalid certificates to be cancelled.

Certification Practice Statement (CPS)   A certification practice statement (CPS) is a disclosure document that specifies how a certificate authority will issue certificates. The CPS specifically states how PKI participants will issue, manage, use, renew, and revoke digital certificates. It does not facilitate interoperation between certificate authorities, but rather the practices (procedures) of a single certificate authority.

Figure 7.40 shows the concept of registering and acquiring a PKI digital certificate from the certificate authority.

FIGURE 7.40   Getting a PKI digital certificate

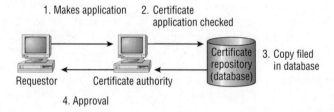

After acquiring a digital certificate, the user will present it during a transaction. The receiver will check the certificate against the certificate authority's database. If the certificate is valid, the transaction will continue. Certificates can be checked against other authorities, using a cross-verification process. Figure 7.41 shows the concept of presenting and using a PKI digital certificate.

FIGURE 7.41   Using a PKI certificate

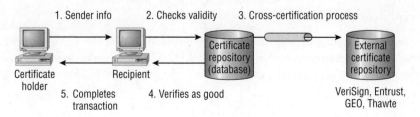

Digital Signatures

A digital signature is intended to be an electronic version of a personal signature. The purpose is to indicate that the message was sent by a uniquely identified individual. A digital signature created by running a hash utility against any size of file will generate a 128-bit, 160-bit, 256-bit, or 512-bit output. Hash file size is always a fixed length, so the output size is determined by the hashing utility being used. Figure 7.42 illustrates the process of generating a hash file and digital signature.

FIGURE 7.42   Generating a digital signature

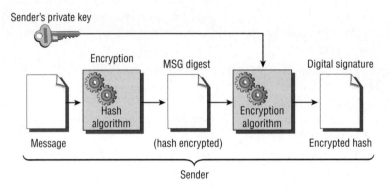

The digital signature is attached to the message file, and both are sent to the recipient. Digital signatures are portable, meaning they can be moved through different systems that accompany the file. Digital signatures are required to authenticate the sender as valid. The goal of a digital signature is to prove the cryptographic identity of the sender. Here is a sample of a real digital signature:

```
--- begin gnp signature ---
Version: GNP Universal 2.9.1 (Build 407)
Charset: us-ascii

OeUhwoQ59lp5kJhSOTjx15XKSzqzgX120X+Xq0H3kO5y9qUsS6gewnAO2q7SOGNq
wvi3NR8ie9TufslLZaajD1gU1CrQCPAIw+Dnv2QvwWT8+vooKco19luMqRS51Mfo
2IxN1LfIgtYKFQr4T8IFXtWulrsukXm8czrY1qcfIXpXyMIk42b3S8Vx5bWPcGa2
wsLbVz102FrlltumBVAwUBSYC5H/SYA8LbkPmy/hL6gu/7OEF5pzLXeG/RQHyUXN
IDW3t1XabOOXPraLj4wJXS819IMT6j5ai2YxtQdobMViwwJknUSJDEH3d5SdpzHb
MSq+VjYNjZ1M04veHy62ZYfzM3yjw==cp/JsGz86uwqAQj1mQgAgd89c=1oK5
--- end gnp signature ---
```

Notice how the signature file uses the same type of begin and end headers to prevent confusion. Each digital signature algorithm uses different techniques, so it's important to run the exact same method on both ends. PGP signatures require PGP on both ends, same with

GNP and all the others. To test the validity of the signature, the recipient must use all three items: a copy of the original message file, a digital signature file (just shown), and a copy of the sender's public key. The sender's private key is never used because disclosure would wreck confidentiality. Without testing the digital signature, there is absolutely no indication of its authenticity. Figure 7.43 illustrates the process of verifying a digital signature.

FIGURE 7.43   Verifying a digital signature

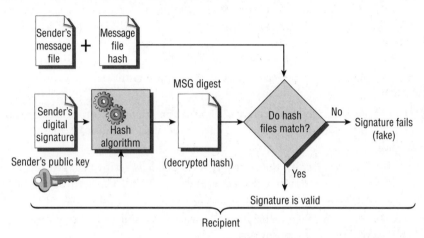

There is a method for sending an encrypted message and the key along with it. This process uses a digital envelope. A message is encrypted along with a session key. The session key is encrypted a second time, using the recipient's public key. After transmission, the recipient can decrypt by using their private key. Next the encrypted hash is decrypted using the sender's public key. The double-step encryption ensures that no one else is able to decrypt the key in transit. Figure 7.44 illustrates the process of using a digital envelope.

FIGURE 7.44   Using a digital envelope

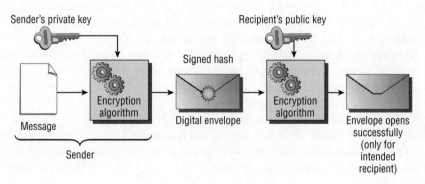

Practical Example of Using Digital Certificates

Consider the process for flying on an airline. The airline issues an electronic ticket to the buyer. The electronic airline ticket is a digital certificate in a human-readable form, while the computer's digital certificate is not readable by humans. Let's walk though the amazing similarity between processing an airline e-ticket and the computer using a PKI digital certificate:

1. The airline issues an electronic certificate, as long as the tickets are paid for and the buyer can prove their identity. This means that the airline is the certificate authority (CA).

    A travel agent may handle the transaction to get an electronic airline ticket issued (certificate). The travel agent is acting as a registration authority (RA) for the airline (CA).

2. The buyer receives an electronic copy of their airline ticket (electronic certificate). The original data is held by the airline in their certificate repository (database of tickets sold).

3. Prior to boarding the aircraft, the electronic ticket code is verified against the airline's database repository to determine whether the ticket is valid. The certificate is checked by the CA to see whether it is valid. If it checks out as valid, you board the airplane.

    Tickets issued through other airlines can be verified by using cross-certification between the two database repositories.

    Use of the electronic ticket is governed by the ticket revocation list and airline statement of policies. This is synonymous with the certificate revocation list (CRL) and certification practice statement (CPS).

Once again, the only real difference between the airline ticket example and your computer is the terminology—plus, a human can actually read an airline ticket.

Digital Rights Management

PKI encryption is helpful to slow the spread of bootleg copies of music, books, and original works on the Internet. Digital rights management (DRM) helps stop illegitimate copies by bootleggers. Just extend the use of encryption and digital certificates to identify computers authorized to open the files. By embedding DRM code into the file, it can be opened by only an authorized system capable of decrypting a special key. This is how iTunes, Microsoft, Amazon.com, and other sites protect their digital download products from redistribution. Every download contains a special piece of program code that is tested (decrypted) each time the file is opened or played. If decryption fails, the file will not work. This simple technique allows the copyright owner a method of protecting their intellectual property from the majority of common bootleggers. It may upset buyers who ignore intellectual rights. Remember, buyers get to enjoy individual usage under only limited license and never really own any rights. DRM helps to enforce the license. Figure 7.45 illustrates how DRM simply encrypts the file using PKI.

FIGURE 7.45   DRM uses public-key encryption to enforce digital rights.

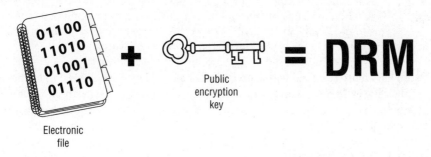

Secure Multipurpose Internet Mail Extension

Secure/Multipurpose Internet Mail Extensions (S/MIME) was developed so that people could send email across the Internet without having to worry about whether the recipient could read it. The original design was Privacy Enhanced Mail (PEM), developed in 1993. S/MIME was created in 1999 and incorporated several enhancements including support for the newer SHA-1 hash and MD5 hash. Additional support was added for the RSA encryption system and signing time attributes. S/MIME provides authentication of the sender and receiver and also verifies message integrity. S/MIME is the current standard for secure email and attachments. Figure 7.46 illustrates the reason why email security is so important.

FIGURE 7.46   Email security issues

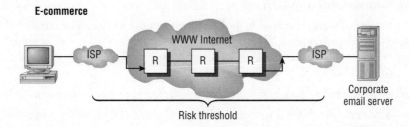

Encryption-Key Management

Encryption-key management is critical to ensure confidentiality and integrity of encrypted data. There are several risks with regard to encryption keys. First, the key itself must be protected from theft or illegal copying. Second is a requirement to use several different keys—one for each purpose. It's important not to overuse a key. This is to ensure integrity of the encrypted files. Each use exposes the key to compromise. Unfortunately, this multitude of keys also creates a significant administrative burden, which if mishandled can turn into a catastrophe.

Every auditor needs to investigate how management is controlling and governing the use of encryption. The critical success factor in encryption is to physically and logically protect the secret key. All keys undergo a full seven-phase life cycle, just like application software.

Encryption keys must be stored with a great deal of care. The keys will need to be managed throughout their life cycle. At a future date, a key will be marked for destruction. Creating, managing, storing, and destroying the keys is of particular concern to the auditor. Few organizations do a good job.

Control of Encryption Systems

The greatest vulnerability in encryption systems is the inherent lack of control. Encryption algorithms are well designed; however, their application or management may be poor. Encryption software and encryption keys should be managed as software applications under the SDLC. Here are a few tips:

- Use of encryption should be implemented for intellectual property and regulatory compliance.

- Each application of encryption (use) must be formally authorized by management. A user must never be allowed to encrypt files that management cannot decrypt without the user.

- Encryption keys must be individually managed and unique to each task.

- The encryption keys need to be generated on a system that is physically and logically isolated from other systems (separation of duties). Key transfer is via read-only media.

- Encryption keys should be stored in a different encrypted format. The term *key wrapping* refers to encrypting an encryption key by using a different algorithm. This concept is intended to prevent threats to the encryption key itself being exposed as standing data.

- Encryption keys need to be tracked, similar to checking out books at the library.

- The users should never have direct access to encryption keys (separation of duties).

- The use of specific encryption keys should be limited to prevent overexposure or violating the separation of duties. For example, the encryption keys used for data backups cannot be used for encrypting email correspondence.

- The use, archiving, and destruction of encryption keys requires a formal review. Destruction of encryption keys cannot occur without formal approval of management.

Just imagine what would happen if the organization was backing up data using encryption, and the encryption keys were lost. It could get even worse when you consider the implications to business continuity. Heaven forbid that the backup was required for disclosure under a court order for electronic discovery. Each of these conditions indicates a management failure in which integrity of the organization is lost. Failure to control the use of encryption leads to dramatic consequences.

Network Security Protocols

The world of safe e-commerce is built on a handful of network security protocols. These security protocols include the following:

- Pretty Good Privacy (PGP) for personal file encryption.

- Secure Sockets Layer (SSL), which is used by most Internet websites for HTTPS sessions. The newer implementation is called Transport Layer Security (TLS).

- Secure Hypertext Transfer Protocol (HTTPS), which uses SSL

- Internet Protocol Security (IPsec) using the authentication header (AH) and encapsulated security payload (ESP)

Without these protocols, it would be impossible for businesses, individuals, and the government to conduct confidential transactions. Figure 7.47 shows where these protocols fall within the OSI model.

FIGURE 7.47   Security protocols and where they fall within the OSI model

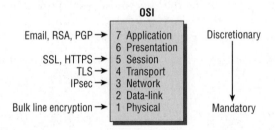

Using Digital Certificates for Secure Communication

Digital certificates provide a mechanism to verify that we are communicating with the correct server. But like all controls, they're not foolproof. Once again the secret to strong controls is using several different methods in layers of protection. Computers can use digital certificates issued by trusted certificate authorities to increase the odds that we are communicating with the right computer.

Let's look at the process of obtaining a digital certificate for communicating via Secure Sockets Layer (SSL) or the newer Transport Layer Security (TLS). The only difference is SSL is an older vendor standard with unapproved methods and algorithms. TLS is an official ISO standard using approved methods with FIPS-140 certified encryption algorithms. Both use digital certificates to create the encrypted session.

Step 1   Using our PKI private- and public-key pair, the system administrator creates a certificate signing request (CSR). This is just a digital certificate tied to our specific hardware CPU serial number, MAC address, IP address, and other data that should be unique to this particular system. The CSR is an encrypted file that will fail if moved (copied) to another system. This is what ciphertext looks like:

--- begin certificate request ---

```
VEFWSjCCAVMCAQAwgY0xCzAJBgNVBAYTAk1YMQ8wDQYDVQQIEwZDSFVBTEExETAP
BgNVBAcTCFBVVRBMxXIB6Q4wDAYDVQQKEwVaW1RTQTESMBAGA1UECxMJQ0FTQU1B
RFJFMRUwEwYDVQQDEwxjZXJ0dGGVzdC5vcmcxHzAdBgkqhkiG9w0BCQEWEFNTTEBD
QVNBTUFEUkUuTVowgZ8wDQYJKoZIhvcNAQEBBQADgY0AMIGJAoGBAK5g4wvFuOd9
eOMxuTLnlID/QX/oiHyn+EZTaKxopy2O4ZSkTJ/8P2Jssai8lw5hq27Zc/NI+5qN
BscaQs2d+j+aAJA5ZjrzU9XsjQ0wtFnqL44kwavibFg26pdkrszzb1s9nQRVVCev
h5/L/bzDav3eaLXLGdSOivsuQTH1bsGBAgMBAAGgHDAaBgkqhkiG9w0BCQcxDRML
dHlwZWhlcmUydHowDQYJKoZIhvcNAQEFBQADgYEAj2m/KLgk7z27KxAGIMaaHzTT
ClrbsYkH5jURPbtgDgmBw63UHvNsN4ORWJzhhba3HQnF+bG9gCQFO1WWj6TNo/57
z1icE/J7iNOpd3YBq8kmlkpxRqCMs1zCsVuoSAVNyzKN6UEafAdGxrmYaeI809Lo
oU9yO91PAPdcglOTNk4=
```

--- end certificate request ---

It would be impossible to decipher the contents yourself, so I printed out what is buried inside the encryption file about this computer so you can view it in plain text. Here is the actual content encrypted inside this particular CSR file:

--- begin csr data ---

```
Certificate Request:
    Data:
        Version: 0 (0x0)
    Subject: C=MX, ST=CHUALA, L=VITANOR, O=MICASA, OU=CASAMADRE,
    CN=casamadreorg.mx/emailAddress=ssladmin@casamadreorg.mx
        Subject Public Key Info:
            Public Key Algorithm: rsaEncryption
            RSA Public Key: (1024 bit)
                Modulus (1024 bit):
                    00:ae:60:e3:0b:c5:b8:e7:7d:7b:43:31:b9:32:e7:
                    94:80:ff:41:7f:e8:88:7c:a7:f8:46:53:68:ac:68:
                    a7:2d:b4:e1:94:a4:4c:9f:fc:3f:62:6c:b1:a8:bc:
                    97:0e:61:ab:6e:d9:73:f3:48:fb:9a:8d:06:c7:1a:
                    42:cd:9d:fa:3f:9a:00:90:39:66:3a:f3:53:d5:ec:
                    8d:0d:30:b4:59:ea:2f:8e:24:c1:ab:e2:6c:58:36:
                    ea:97:64:ae:cc:f3:6f:5b:3d:9d:04:55:54:27:af:
                    87:9f:cb:fd:bc:c3:6a:fd:de:68:b5:cb:19:d4:b4:
                    8a:fb:2e:41:31:f5:6e:c1:81
```

```
          Exponent: 65537 (0x10001)
     Attributes:
          challengePassword          :MyPassPhraseInClearText
     Signature Algorithm: sha1WithRSAEncryption
          8f:69:bf:28:b8:24:06:20:c6:9a:ef:3d:bb:2b:10:1f:34:d3:
          b1:5b:a8:48:05:4d:cb:32:8d:e9:41:1a:7c:07:46:c6:b9:98:
          0a:5a:db:b1:89:07:e6:35:11:3d:bb:60:0e:09:81:c3:ad:d4:
          88:d3:a9:77:76:01:ab:c9:26:96:4a:71:46:a0:8c:b3:5c:c2:
          1e:f3:6c:37:8d:11:58:9c:e1:85:b6:b7:1d:09:c5:f9:b1:bd:
          80:24:05:d3:55:96:8f:a4:cd:a3:fe:7b:cf:58:9c:13:f2:7b:
          69:e2:3c:d3:d2:e8:a1:4f:72:3b:dd:4f:00:f7:5c:82:53:93:
          36:4e
```

```
  --- end csr data ---
```

Step 2   The encrypted CSR file is emailed to the certificate authority. The level of trust is based on who is the certificate authority and whether the requester's identity was properly verified. Commercial organizations file tax returns, maintain charters with the secretary of state or other government entity, are listed in public records, and may hold special licenses. Therefore, the trail of records can be used to verify that the organization might be real. Once this claim of identity is verified, the CA will begin to issue a digital certificate. In higher-security situations, the CSR must be presented in person by a trusted representative to reduce the risk of fraud. It's also possible to create your own self-signed digital certificate, but outsiders will be hesitant to trust a self-generated certificate because it could easily be fraudulent.

Step 3   The CA uses your CSR to encrypt a unique digital certificate for your specific computer. This is emailed back with installation instructions and a copy of the CA's intermediate public key. Your digital certificate is encrypted with the CA private key. This provides a method to test the validity of your certificate. If it decrypts properly from the CA public key *and also* decrypts properly from your public key, the certificate is probably valid. Remember, nothing is trusted by itself; the whole process must be used with layers of additional controls to create any semblance of trust.

Step 4   Install the new digital certificate you received from the CA. The installation requires no more than copying the file to the correct location and adding a few lines to the SSL/TLS configuration file or your web server configuration file. The purpose is to identify the CA's intermediate encryption key (CA public key) for your system to use.

Step 5   Update your program to use HTTPS, SSL, or TLS for communication requests. This will vary according to your operating system and programming language.

Step 6   Now you are ready for preproduction testing. If the system is properly configured, when a user tries to access your system, the server will force a one-way security association (SA) to prove the identity of the server.

Hmm…but the one-way security association of SSL/TLS just proves the identity of only one server. What if you need to prove the identity of both ends, both computers in communication? Because a security association is only one-way, you will need to install unique digital certificates on both systems. Just repeat the CA issuing process a second time for the other computer. Each will make its own one-way security association. Then you have two one-way associations creating full authentication of both ends. With cross-certification between different CAs, either end can get their own certificate from a recognized vendor, and the process will still work.

Figure 7.48 illustrates the use of digital certificates to authenticate computers with SSL or TLS. This is one of the security backbones for e-commerce.

FIGURE 7.48 Using digital certificates to authenticate computers

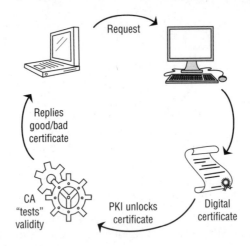

Using E-Commerce

E-commerce is becoming more important in today's IT landscape. Figure 7.49 illustrates several types of e-commerce in use today.

There is one special type of payment protocol that has been developed to protect credit card accounts. The Secure Electronic Transaction (SET) protocol provides a method for purchasing over the Internet without disclosing the credit card number to the merchant.

The merchant opens an account with a payment system such as PayPal's Payflow. A customer makes a purchase by using the merchant's shopping cart. At the appropriate time, the shopping cart passes the transaction to the SET payment gateway. The customer enters their credit card number on the SET gateway, completely out of sight from the merchant. The SET payment gateway sends to the merchant a transaction authorization to complete the purchase. The merchant uses the transaction authorization as authorization to ship the product. The SET gateway system deposits the funds into the merchant's bank account. This prevents a questionable merchant from being able to view a customer's credit card number. It also prevents credit card numbers from being retained in insecure shopping cart databases.

FIGURE 7.49   Types of e-commerce

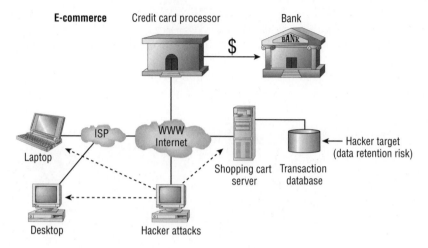

Design for Redundancy

There is more to protecting information assets than just encryption. Communication networks must be designed for redundancy. One method of improving redundancy is to use alternate telecommunications routing. We discussed meshed networks in Chapter 4. Alternate routing provides multiple communication paths in case the normal path fails. Alternate routing can be used in a local area network or a wide area network.

Another technique to ensure availability and integrity of information assets is the use of mirrored servers. Two servers acting as one are said to be *mirrored*. Mirrored servers are also known as *high-availability servers*. One of the servers acts as a primary server. The second server is the failover server, which runs in the background until the primary server dies. The second failover server assumes all processing responsibilities if the primary should fail for any reason. Figure 7.50 shows the basic design of a mirrored, or high-availability, server pair.

Computer disk systems are known to experience failures. The loss of a disk system could result in the loss of valuable data. A tape backup system can restore the data at the cost of additional downtime. A solution to this problem is the implementation of redundant hard disks. A Redundant Array of Independent—or Inexpensive—Disks (RAID) provides an excellent method of protecting information assets. Special software drivers copy the data files onto different hard disk controllers on two separate sets of hard disks. Either set of hard disks is capable of running the system without data loss. Figure 7.51 shows the basic layout of a RAID system.

FIGURE 7.50 Mirrored, or high-availability, servers

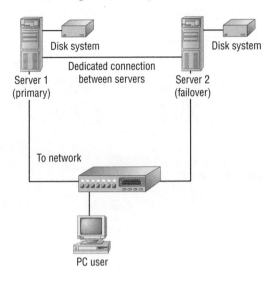

FIGURE 7.51 RAID system

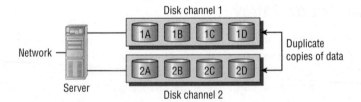

Telephone Security

The security of the telephone system is a major concern. Telephone hackers, known as *phreakers*, are notorious for attempting to steal telephone service.

The telephone PBX—which stands for Private Branch Exchange—needs to be protected by using the same techniques as those used to protect a network server or router. Care must be given to the life-cycle controls of the PBX. Maintenance accounts and unauthorized access are major concerns.

Newer phone systems use Voice over Internet Protocol (VoIP) networks to save money. This introduces the problems of network security controls to telephone systems. Newer VoIP phone systems inherit all the same problems of protecting computers over the Internet. As an auditor, you should be aware of the issues regarding IP networks for both data and voice. Figure 7.52 demonstrates the way VoIP systems connect to regular telephones over the Internet.

FIGURE 7.52   Voice over IP network

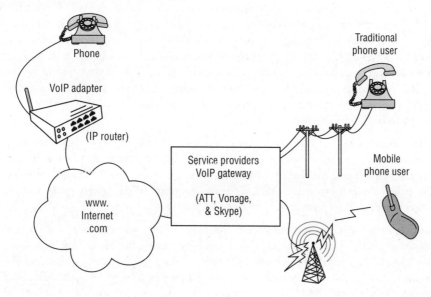

Technical Security Testing

Clients should undergo a regular schedule of security assessment by using the control self-assessment (CSA) and technical tools such as port scanners. We discussed the issue of how all tests must be performed under controlled procedures. You should recall that access to testing tools and authority to run the test must be tightly controlled.

Management needs to promote a regimented approach to discovery and resolution of vulnerabilities. Several types of testing are needed to ensure that security weaknesses are corrected. Let's look at the common types of tests:

Network Scanning   This is a fast method for discovering the hosts on the network, also called *host enumeration*. Most scanners are fully automated, yet they can also overload systems with service requests until they crash. Network scanning does not find vulnerabilities. Host enumeration should be conducted weekly to indentify any new hosts connected on your network. The next step is vulnerability scanning.

Vulnerability Scanning   Individual systems are first scanned for open ports. In the next step, automated attempts are made to exploit the open ports using various command line instructions. This is known as vulnerability scanning. It's not as effective as software code reviews, but vulnerability scanning is better than nothing. Unique attributes of different versions of software are tested, and particular types of service requests are sent by the scanning software to the target computer. This type of test usually triggers an intrusion detection alarm. Be advised a successful exploitation usually crashes the target computer or causes some software corruption. This is why ISO 27002 item 10.1.4 requires a separate test/development environment to prevent crashing production systems. This type of testing should be conducted monthly.

Password Cracking   A special tool is used to test the strength of user passwords. It works by creating a large set of passwords from dictionaries printed in every language. The hash output is matched against the system password file. When a match is found in the hash file, the word used to create the match will equal the actual password. Password-cracking utilities perform all the simple conversions, anagrams, palindromes, and common character substitutions just as a user would. Every known password can be easily cracked. This is why two-factor authentication with cryptography should be used. Care must be taken to ensure that only authorized people perform password-cracking tests under totally supervised conditions. Otherwise, password abuse will become a problem.

Log Review   All those great log files are useless if nobody reads the contents. Log reviews identify deviations in change control and security policies. This underrated jewel of data can be the auditor's best friend for determining whether operations are following their organizational policies. Unauthorized activities, security violations, and capacity problems can be quickly discovered. Log reviews should be continuous.

Penetration Testing   Penetration tests are commonly used by software testers in quality assurance or software certification roles to uncover vulnerabilities that may be discovered by an attacker. It may take minutes, hours, or days to penetrate the target. The U.S. National Security Agency created a certification program for Information Security Assessment Methodology (IAM) and Information Security Evaluation Methodology (IEM) to be used for all systems depended on by the government. This includes software developers, service providers, and prime contractors. Use in smaller areas of private industry is recommended but not required. The latest version is known as the Information Security Assessment Methodology (ISAM). This methodology provides the planning details and guidance for software tools to run a penetration test, and then report the results against a government-approved baseline. These techniques will be of significant interest to auditors and software developer testers in the quality assurance role involved in testing systems for regulatory compliance.

Summary

As an IS auditor, you should be extremely interested in the implementation of information asset protection mechanisms by the client. There are numerous threats that could compromise administrative, physical, and technical controls.

You should understand how these controls have been implemented by the customer and what level of monitoring is occurring. Implementing controls without constant monitoring would be a waste of effort. Without effective monitoring processes, the client would be negligent.

This chapter has covered several technical methods that the CISA is expected to know. Be sure to read this chapter at least twice and study the definitions carefully.

Exam Essentials

Be able to evaluate the effectiveness of technical (logical) access controls.   Technical controls include access control mechanisms, encryption, firewalls, and intrusion detection and prevention capabilities. Technical access control mechanisms include passwords, access control lists, and biometrics for authentication.

Understand the perimeter defense mechanisms.   The network security infrastructure must provide sufficient perimeter defenses along with mechanisms to minimize loss from hackers, viruses, and worms. But the network is susceptible to attack by hacking, spoofing, spamming, and denial of service, along with other threats such as social engineering.

Recognize the different types of technical attacks.   Passive attacks collect information to be used later in an active attack. Active attacks are designed to break down the defenses and execute the will of the attacker.

Understand the different motives of the malicious attacker.   Internal controls are used to prevent or detect most crimes committed by strangers and internal personnel. Remain aware that most theft is committed by someone known within the organization, because of access, motive, and time. The police refer to this concept as MOM: motive, opportunity, and means.

Understand how biometrics are used to test the authenticity of a user.   Biometrics use unique data about the user to test authenticity. It's absolutely critical to protect the biometric templates using encryption in the biometric database along with intrusion detection on the biometric server. Otherwise, a hacker can substitute their own biometric template data for a legitimate authorized user, access your system, and then put the original user's biometric template back, covering their tracks undetected. Biometrics can't be trusted unless the entire system is fully managed as an encryption system with constant electronic monitoring. Without detection monitoring, the system will be hacked.

Realize that technical controls offer a greater scope of protection than physical access controls.   Physical threats are real, yet represent a smaller percentage of all attack threats when compared with Internet attacks. Theft while staying safely out of your reach is more popular with professional thieves looking for your most valuable data. Professional attackers can secretly hack your systems for hours and even thousands of hours, usually without being detected. Physical access controls are still needed to enforce separation of duties.

Understand the need to implement technical access controls.   The weakest method of authentication is using a password (type 1 authentication). A better method is to use type 2 authentication with unique physical characteristics such as the possession of a device (ATM card, smart card, hard token) and combine possession with a password (secret). It is possible for legitimate users to be denied access by the system (type 1 error, or false rejection). Accordingly, illegitimate users may get access by mistake (type 2 error, or false acceptance).

Understand the differences between public-key and private-key encryption systems. The public-key interchange (PKI) provides authentication, integrity, and confidentiality between parties. A public-key system uses asymmetric cryptography with a public key that is shared and a secret private key that must be protected for disclosure. Secret-key systems use symmetric cryptography with a single shared secret key. The symmetric system is faster but fails to provide authentication. A compromised secret key will destroy confidentiality.

Recognize that management must exercise control over encryption. Encryption algorithms do not manage themselves. It is the responsibility of management to control the use of encryption and encryption keys under a System Development Life Cycle (SDLC) model. Special handling is required with encryption keys, including methods of safe storage with separation of duties.

Recognize technical mechanisms. Technical mechanisms such as server mirroring and RAID disk systems can be used to increase redundancy in order to promote better system availability. The redundant hardware increases fault tolerance for conditions involving hardware failure and possibly intruder attacks.

Understand the purpose of different VPNs to protect remote access. Virtual private networks use encryption for secure communication between systems on different networks. Secure Sockets Layer (SSL) and Transport Layer Security (TLS) implement fully encrypted sessions running from the sending computer to the receiving computer. SSL and TLS require the use of digital certificates. IPsec VPN uses VPN gateways for transmission over a wide area network. With IPsec, the encryption is between the gateways, not individual systems. IPsec gateways use the address of their ISP provider on the external interface.

Understand intrusion detection and prevention systems. Intrusion detection and prevention systems are designed to function as a computer-based hacker alarm. The system can be implemented by using either a host-based method or network-based method. An IDPS will react to only those perceived attacks that occur on the system with host-based IDPS installed or that are transmitted down a network link that is actively monitored by a network-based IDPS. Attacks on all other systems are invisible to the IDPS. The IDPS identifies attacks by using one of three methods: comparing a database of known attack signatures, comparing changes to a statistical baseline, or using a neural network with knowledge-based rules.

Review Questions

1. Digital signatures are primarily designed to provide additional protection with electronic messages in order to ensure which of the following?

    A. Provide verification of the sender's identity

    B. Prevent the message from being read by an unauthorized party

    C. Provide availability of the message

    D. Protect content of the message using encryption

2. Internet communication requires more security. To audit Internet security and access control, the IS auditor will first need to examine what?

    A. Validity of password changes

    B. Architecture of the client/server application

    C. Network architecture and design

    D. Virus protection and firewall servers

3. What is the best method for an organization to allow its business partners to access the company intranet across the Internet?

    A. Shared virtual private network

    B. Shared lease line

    C. Internet firewall

    D. Network router with MLSP

4. What is the primary purpose of a network firewall?

    A. Protect company systems from attack by external systems

    B. Protect downstream systems from all the internal attacks

    C. Protect all modem-connected systems from Internet attacks

    D. Protect attached systems from attacks running through the firewall

5. Which of the following is the least dependable form of biometrics?

    A. Hand geometry

    B. Facial recognition

    C. Signature analysis

    D. Iris scanning

6. What is the purpose of the DMZ (demilitarized zone) concept for Internet communications?

    A. *Demilitarized* refers to a safe zone that is protected from all Internet attacks.

    B. Subnet that is semiprotected and allows external access.

    C. Protected subnet implemented using a fifth-generation firewall.

    D. Safeguard control for communication allowing access to internal production servers.

7. An e-commerce website needs to be monitored to detect possible hacker activity. What would be the best security component to perform this function?

   A. Third-generation firewall

   B. Honey net ACL router with built-in sniffer software

   C. Elliptic data encryption for privileged files

   D. Statistical or signature-based detection software

8. The auditee organization decided to implement single sign-on (SSO) for all their users. Their implementation will be using logon ID and passwords for access control. What situation should they be concerned about?

   A. Password aging must be set to force unique password changes every 30 to 60 days using alphanumeric characters.

   B. The user's system access will have protection; however, password changes will be more difficult because of synchronization issues between servers.

   C. Unauthorized login would have access to the maximum resources available on the network.

   D. The servers will need memory and CPU upgrades to handle the extra workload generated by SSO.

9. Which of the following is the most appropriate method to ensure confidentiality in data communications?

   A. Secure hash algorithm (SHA-1)

   B. Virtual private network (VPN)

   C. Digital signatures

   D. Digital certificates with public-key encryption

10. Which of the following statements is true concerning asymmetric-key cryptography?

   A. The sender and receiver have different keys.

   B. The sender and receiver use the same key.

   C. The sender encrypts the files by using the recipient's private key.

   D. Asymmetric keys cannot be used for digital signatures.

11. What is the most important reason for management to control encryption by using a System Development Life Cycle model?

   A. To build better encryption algorithms.

   B. Poor management is the biggest threat.

   C. Encryption systems are complex.

   D. Cost overruns are common with encryption systems.

12. What is the function of a biometrics sensor?

   A. Create new biometric template data each time it's used

   B. Compare biometric data samples

   C. Detect intrusion into the biometric template database

   D. Check for the presence of an authorized user

13. What method provides the *best* level of access control to confidential data being processed on a local server?

   A. Writing a history of all transaction activity to the system log for auditing.

   B. Processing of sensitive transactions requires a separate login and password.

   C. Application software uses internal access control rules to implement least privilege.

   D. System login access is restricted to particular stations or hours of operation.

14. What is the primary purpose of intrusion detection and prevention systems (IDPS) when compared to firewall systems?

   A. A firewall blocks all attacks; IDPS informs us if the firewall was successful.

   B. IDPS will notify the system administrator at every possible attack that has occurred, whether successful or unsuccessful.

   C. A firewall reports all attacks to the IDPS.

   D. IDPS logs and notifies the system administrator of any suspected attacks but may not recognize every attack.

15. Besides confidentiality, what is another purpose of using encryption?

   A. Provide a method of authentication

   B. Provide a method for data integrity

   C. Provide a method for protecting from nondisclosure

   D. Provide a method to ensure availability for authorized users

16. Which of the following is the best definition of *minutiae*?

   A. Characteristics data

   B. Detailed log data

   C. High-definition scan

   D. Minutes of meeting

17. Which of the following techniques is used to prevent the encryption keys from being susceptible to an attack against standing data?

   A. Key wrapping

   B. Key generation

   C. Symmetric-key algorithm

   D. Asymmetric-key algorithm

18. Complete the following statement with the best answer: The _____ access controls are _____ managed with _____ approval requirements for the highest possible level of security.

    A. Mandatory, locally, manager

    B. Discretionary, centrally, formal

    C. Discretionary, individually, manager

    D. Mandatory, centrally, formal

19. Which of the following VPN methods will transmit data across the local network in plain text without encryption?

    A. Secure Sockets Layer (SSL)

    B. IPsec

    C. Transport Layer Security (TLS)

    D. Layer 2 Tunneling Protocol (L2TP)

20. Complete the following statement: The auditor can use _____ as a fast method for discovering the hosts on the network, and _____ to identify all available service ports.

    A. Vulnerability scanning, log review

    B. Penetration testing, host enumeration

    C. Host enumeration, port scanning

    D. File mount logs, vulnerability scanning

21. Which of the following VPN methods is used to transmit the payload and hide internal network addresses with encryption?

    A. IPsec tunnel

    B. Secure Sockets Layer (SSL)

    C. IPsec transport

    D. Transport Layer Security (TLS)

22. Which encryption system is primarily used in private industry and commerce for transportation rather than storage?

    A. Symmetric-key encryption

    B. Asymmetric-key encryption

    C. Secret keys

    D. Public keys

23. Complete the following statement with the best available choice: A _____ will subvert the kernel and bypass operating system security. This is _____ inside downloads and installs itself without the knowledge of the user.

    A. Root kit, hidden

    B. Worm, impossible to detect

    C. Denial of service, hidden

    D. Virus, impossible to detect

24. What is the best definition of *stateful inspection*?

    A. History and nature of connectionless requests

    B. Packet-filtering firewall with application proxy service

    C. Internal control mechanism designed into the operating system kernel

    D. History and nature of connection-oriented requests

25. Which of the following access control models is used for distributed management?

    A. Discretionary

    B. Mandatory

    C. Explicit

    D. Formal

Answers to Review Questions

1. A. Digital signatures provide authentication assurance of the email sender. Digital signatures use the private key of the sender to verify identity. The signature is encrypted; whether the message is still in plain text or encrypted is not related. Digital signatures do *not* encrypt the message content; instead, they help prove who sent the message. If the message content is a secret, that content must be encrypted separately.

2. C. The IS auditor will need to understand the network architecture and design before being able to evaluate the security and access controls. Later, the architecture of the client/server application and virus protection will be of interest.

3. A. The virtual private network (VPN) is the most flexible and least expensive solution for accessing company resources across the Internet.

4. D. The network firewall can protect only those systems that route communication through the firewall. The firewall cannot protect systems attached via modem. Insecure wireless networks are also a major threat.

5. C. Signature analysis is the most undependable form of biometrics. Hand geometry and iris scanning are very dependable. Facial recognition is improving.

6. B. The DMZ is a subnet that is semiprotected by the firewall and allows for external access.

7. D. An IDPS with statistical or signature-based detection software would be the best choice.

8. C. In simple SSO implementations, any unauthorized logon would have access to all the server resources on the network. Passwords are the *least* effective authentication method of controlling access. Two-factor authentication should be used to reduce the threat of compromised passwords, cracked passwords, and password guessing.

9. B. The virtual private network (VPN) would ensure data confidentiality. A secure hash algorithm would identify that a file has been changed but will not provide confidentiality. Digital signatures are used to assess the identity of the sender but do not provide confidentiality.

10. A. The sender and receiver each have their own public and private (secret) key-pair. All the other statements are false. Asymmetric keys are definitely used for creating digital signatures. The sender would never use the recipient's private key, only the recipient's public key.

11. B. The System Development Life Cycle is used to control the use of encryption and encryption keys. Poor management is the number one cause of failure.

12. A. Biometric sensors create a new data template every time the sensor is used. During initial enrollment, the user's unique biometric data template is saved to the biometric database. In subsequent use, the sensor creates a brand new data template, which is compared to the database by the template matcher. If it matches, the user is believed to be correctly authenticated.

13. C. Application controls should use internal access control lists to implement least privilege. System login restrictions are of less importance by comparison.

14. D. The IDPS keeps the transaction log and alerts the system administrator of any suspected attacks. The IDPS can use statistical behavior or signature files to determine whether an attack has occurred.

15. A. Encryption is frequently used for authentication. If the user is able to decrypt the message, it is believed that the user is genuine. However, if the encryption keys are poorly managed, an unauthorized user may be able to get in by using unauthorized copies of the encryption keys.

16. A. Minutiae is the collection of characteristics used in biometric data about a specific user (a user's biometric template). The process converts a high-resolution scan into a tiny count of unique characteristics. Minutiae must be protected for unauthorized substitution using encryption to protect each user's template file.

17. A. Key wrapping is used to protect encryption keys from disclosure. Otherwise, encryption keys would be susceptible to the same attacks as standing data.

18. D. Mandatory access controls are always centrally managed, with formal approval required to increase that individual's level of access.

19. B. IPsec uses encryption between the VPN gateways. Data transmitted from the gateway to the local computer is not encrypted.

20. C. Host enumeration provides a fast method for discovering all the hosts on the network. Vulnerability scanning will identify all the available service ports on the host computers. Neither of these processes should be performed during production hours. These scanning methods will activate intrusion detection alarms. Vulnerability scanning may crash the target computer.

21. A. The tunnel mode of IPsec will encrypt both the payload and local network addresses. This hides the messages and prevents identification of the sender and recipient while the messages travel across the public Internet.

22. B. Asymmetric-key encryption, also known as public-key encryption, is typically used for the transmission of data (electronic transportation). The other options are closely related distractors.

23. A. Root kits are malicious software designed to subvert the operating system security. Software agents such as auto-update utilities are the same as root kits. Both can compromise system security and use stealth to hide their presence. After a root kit is installed, the system is completely compromised.

24. A. Connectionless UDP requests were almost impossible to track in older firewalls. Stateful inspection collects the history and nature of connectionless requests to determine whether the remote request should be transmitted to the destination computer or discarded as hazardous.

25. A. Distributed security uses discretionary access control. Decisions are based in the local assessment of requirements and intended use. Distributed security is notorious for having consistency problems.

Additional CISA practice questions are available on the author's website at www.CertTest.com.

Business Continuity and Disaster Recovery

THE OBJECTIVE OF THIS CHAPTER IS TO ACQUAINT THE READER WITH THE FOLLOWING CONCEPTS:

- ✓ Debunking common myths about focusing on facilities and information technology

- ✓ Distinguishing between disaster recovery, business continuity, emergency management, and continuity of operations

- ✓ Understanding how to set up the ongoing business continuity program

- ✓ Using the business impact analysis for low-level mapping of existing processes

- ✓ Using the risk analysis to guide planning

- ✓ Determining strategy based on time windows

- ✓ Creating a strategy without any dependency on the vendor's technology

- ✓ Introducing the international Incident Command System (ICS)

- ✓ Using emergency invocation processes and known problems with leased alternate sites

- ✓ Developing a plan

- ✓ Understanding human resource management

- ✓ Improving plan-testing strategies

- ✓ Creating a communication and media plan

- ✓ Integrating with other plans

This chapter focuses on an organization's ability to recover from a disaster and to continue minimum acceptable operations. Your CISA exam maintains a very narrow focus of disaster recovery as it relates to an organization's ability to restore IT services. The focus is record retention. However, we feel that to be a successful IS auditor, you should be taught a broader reference, even though this chapter represents only about 5 percent of the executive body of knowledge.

The chapter starts by debunking myths and presenting the five conflicting disciplines that share the name *business continuity*. Then we progress into the expanded scope of actual business continuity as well as the principles of disaster recovery.

We compare the CISA exam's ISACA material to business continuity best practices. We also introduce some of the terminology ISACA wants every CISA to know as it relates to disaster recovery and their IT services view of business continuity.

Debunking the Myths

In a holistic view, business continuity is a modern evolution of executive scenario planning. Consider this analogy: In the ocean, a shark has to continually be on the move or it may die. The same could be said of business in this world of increased competition. Executives are forced to focus on generating new opportunities whether the market is up or down. Choices at the executive level boil down to two options: increase revenue or cut costs. The revenue pressures and contract performance issues exist 365 days a year in contrast to physical disasters, which occur far less frequently.

To accomplish revenue goals, a savvy executive is willing to pursue more business than the organization has previously managed to deliver. Would a 30 percent surge in business create roughly the same magnitude of challenge as a 30 percent reduction in capability? At the executive level, the answer is yes. Executives crave the opportunity to grow. They adapt market positioning, product lines, people, facilities, equipment, and time schedules to pursue higher revenues. While employees plan their retirement, executives sweat the monthly and quarterly financial reports as if they were an intergalactic asteroid bearing down on them, because executive-level jobs are temporary and based on the financial numbers reported to Wall Street. Substantial investments in infrastructure weigh heavy on the profit margin, unless the investment will generate additional incremental revenue. If the executives are unable to generate enough revenue, the next choice is to cut costs, usually through downsizing, product discontinuation, and layoffs. Let's look at the common myths that have been busted in lessons learned and showcased in the news.

Myth 1: Facility Matters

New rules of operating in the international business world pay little respect to heavy investments in your current facility. Sinking a bunch of money into the infrastructure may limit options more than solve problems. For example, would you relocate your office to be across the street from a major client's manufacturing plant to win their business? Does it matter if the office survives when the homes of your workers are destroyed? What can you do if the economic market in your neighborhood collapses, as in New Orleans after Hurricane Katrina, or in Las Vegas after President Obama's 2009 press conference slamming General Motors executives by saying companies getting bailout money shouldn't be going to Las Vegas on the taxpayer's expense. The New Orleans and Las Vegas business economy crashed for different reasons, but both represent major business continuity situations. In both cases, the businesses began to die, people were laid off, companies relocated to better markets, and the local economy crumbled. Even the military will abandon a facility when faced with a high-risk situation. Revelation: It's not the facility that matters.

Myth 2: IT Systems Matter

Information technology is tasked with being a record keeper. IT's primary goal is to make records available to the business unit whenever users need access. IT doesn't work when important records are stashed in someone's desk drawer. Redundant systems that could be impacted by the same event don't make any sense either. Depending on the identified risk, the cost of equipment duplication may prevent generating a reasonable profit. And no matter how redundant your systems, it is unlikely that you're going to earn any revenue without the skilled people from your business unit. Their unique know-how and customer relationships make the business unit staff practically impossible to outsource. IT systems, on the other hand, may be outsourced at any time. Like facilities, IT systems aren't what really matters. It's the skilled business people in key roles that are the most critical. That's why Wall Street analysts cringe and shout orders at investors to sell when key executives leave.

From Myth to Reality

A stark realization for many professionals is that the most important elements to protect are the people with the right knowledge and access to records. Location, technology, and a particular vendor don't matter. A skilled IT professional who has no loyalty to a specific vendor and instead focuses on adapting to the detailed workflow requirements within the business unit, enhances the organization's value.

Being able to relocate your business is a major advantage in today's market. It makes no difference whether the relocation is due to economic constraints, geographic opportunity, or an unfortunate disaster.

Understanding the Five Conflicting Disciplines Called Business Continuity

Depending on your industry, level of authority, or objectives, *business continuity* is an overused term representing five conflicting disciplines. Let's take a moment to review a brief summary of the conflict. We present each discipline in more detail throughout this chapter.

Business "Revenue" Continuity (BC)   This is the most accurate definition of an executive's interest in both the business world and government agencies. An organization would be unable to survive without revenue or funding. Money buys time and provides options.

Continuity of Operations (COOP)   The goal is to continue uninterrupted operations with or without funding. This is frequently the objective of social services or essential life-support utility providers. Electricity providers and telephone services are prime examples of essential services. Information technology may find itself split between different priorities depending on whether IT is simply the record keeper or whether IT directly generates 24-hour revenue through high volume e-commerce sites such as Travelocity, Amazon.com, eBay, and Apple iTunes. What about mission control at NASA? Not all systems are created equal.

Emergency Management (EM)   Rescue assistance may use offensive (fight) or defensive (protect) strategy with medical aid. Emergency management is based on halting normal operations and shutting down utilities while evacuating persons in the hope of saving lives. Its objective is to halt all activity when something goes wrong. The primary goal is to rescue those who could not get out on their own. So why would you ever wait to evacuate if the risks are increasing? Government's continual prayer is that business will be able to restart after enduring a major interruption, but industry reports show that four out of five businesses never reopen after a major disaster. Their brand name is resold, but the original executives and staff are elsewhere.

Continuity of Government (COG)   This discipline allows using or commandeering all available resources to prevent the failure or overthrow of the existing government. Even if you buy extra telcom lines, fuel, generators, and satellite frequencies, the agency official can take it away for use by the government under COG authority. This is a very serious risk to business operations.

Disaster Recovery (DR)   This is the process of rebuilding what was damaged to its previous historical condition, or of absorbing the damage impact in the case of business resilience. Frequently the scope of disaster recovery ignores the disruption to people's lives, financial hardship, and irreplaceable loss of customer revenue. Sadly, this is the scope of most government recovery organizations such as the U.S. Federal Emergency Management Agency (FEMA). Most investors and several key personnel will abandon organizations at the onset of a disaster condition. This is what led to the redefinition of business continuity as the uninterrupted stream of revenue or funding.

Defining Disaster Recovery

During the 1980s, the term *disaster recovery (DR)* became popular as a definition for rebuilding and recovery following a natural disaster. The entire focus of disaster recovery could be summed up with a one-word definition: *rebuilding*.

In 1988, the Disaster Recovery Institute International (DRI International) was founded using information gathered from FEMA to produce a list of professional practices for disaster recovery planning. Its objective was to help organizations with their planning efforts to ensure that they could rebuild and recover their facilities and equipment following a natural disaster. Even after efforts to rebrand itself, DRI remains focused on disasters—and just like FEMA today, it ignores the actual economic challenges facing business executives as they try to keep their organizations afloat every single day.

In 1992, Hurricane Andrew proved that disaster recovery lacked a critical element for survival. We could survive the storm, protect the people, and rebuild the facilities. However, without a steady stream of incoming revenue, organizations might recover only to find they were forced out of business by bankruptcy, or a lack of money. Granted, facilities and IT systems are important for an organization to conduct business. Unfortunately, those elements alone are not enough for any organization's existence to continue. The scope of disaster recovery needed to be expanded to include revenue and customers.

Let's discuss three issues that lead into defining business continuity.

Surviving Financial Challenges

The greatest threats to the survival of any organization center on financial concerns of continued existence. One needs to be sure that under all conditions special measures have been taken to ensure the following:

- The organization does not breach any significant contractual commitments.
- The banker does not call business loans due, rerate available credit lines, or increase the interest rate.
- Investors do not back out or dump their stock in a rapid sell-off.
- Clients continue to do business without hesitating or canceling their orders.
- Business partners continue to perform under the original terms of contract without placing new demands or suspending services.

The loss of any of these items can structurally weaken the organization and management's ability to continue operation. In fact, the loss of any of these items would probably be a showstopper. The organization would grind to a halt and cease to function.

Valuing Brand Names

Let's consider for a moment the subject of brand names. Brand names include well-known corporate names such as Gulf Oil, Frontier Airlines, and Holiday Inn. Few people realize that each of the aforementioned brands was once shut down or sold off. Brand names represent the recognition of goodwill established after years of successful advertising. If advertising is successful, the brand name alone brings about recognition and a perception of value in the consumer's mind. Successful advertising generates revenue from 5 times to 30 times the cost of the advertisements. In fact, the established brand name may be one of the most viable assets of the organization.

You may ask, "What does this have to do with disaster recovery?" The answer is simple. Business continuity planning focuses on maintaining the public image of the corporate entity—in order to ensure survival of the organization.

In 1994, a new airline was started by former Frontier Airlines executives. The Frontier brand name had reverted to public domain during eight years of disuse and was available again. Many consumers never realized that the original airline had ceased operation. The brand's value had continued to survive.

Rebuilding after a Disaster

Even the mightiest of organizations can be brought down by a variety of events. Every day in the *Financial Times* or *The Wall Street Journal*, you can find an example of operational failure, leadership failure, or a mishandled incident that became a man-made disaster.

As you may recall, a simple definition of *disaster recovery* is *rebuilding*. Almost all activities under disaster recovery focus on rebuilding to match a previous historical configuration. It would be futile to rebuild without your customers and the flow of revenue created by their purchases.

Most businesses are very sensitive to any changes which reduce the profit margin. Increased operating costs or a reduction in sales will rapidly convert a profitable business into a nonprofitable mess.

The largest problem is that DR plans are departmental in nature. No doubt the two most important functions in business are making sales and receiving payment, even if the product is not required to be delivered yet. Keeping the revenue stream functional takes skilled people from all areas of the enterprise working in coordination. Therefore cross-coordination between departments is necessary for survival. Both DR planning and BC planning require the CEO or COO to be the leader. It's the only way to overcome internal politics.

Even the greatest of businesses could be reduced to a fraction of themselves or be taken over by new management. Brand names may survive, but the people running the organization are different. Just consider the long delays in rebuilding New Orleans after Hurricane Katrina. Customers and investors are not interested in waiting through long delays. Lack of sales deprives the organization of the world's most important asset... incoming money. The undeniable result is either sucking money from somewhere else, shutdown, or sell the organization to another group.

US Airways experienced a software problem in December 2004 that was created by a failure in change control. The programmers involved attempted to make a poorly timed change during the peak of holiday travel. The result was a logistical nightmare. US Airways' manifest system could no longer coordinate flight schedules, airplanes, passengers, or their baggage. IT restored operations, but customers were furious. This problem became an unrecoverable disaster because of lost sales and spot increases in operating costs as a result of the original failure. Investors abandoned the airline within days. Regional competitor America West Airlines (AWA) took over US Airways for pennies on the dollar. AWA's first action was to discharge all the original executives and replace US Air managers with America West people. In its first year under new leadership, US Airways earned a half billion dollars. The US Airways brand name continues under new ownership.

Both customers and investors are notorious for abandoning organizations during their rebuilding phases. People favor undamaged vendors. Few people will wait for the rebuilding to be completed; instead they take their money elsewhere. It doesn't take much of an interruption to cause layoffs, tumbling stock prices, and even permanent shutdowns. This leads us to the evolution from disaster recovery to business continuity.

Defining the Purpose of Business Continuity

Unlike DR, *business continuity (BC)* focuses on *revenue*. As long as the organization has time and money at its disposal, the organization can continue to function. Money can take the form of capital, credit lines, investors, and payments from customers. Business continuity focuses on putting more money in the bank, even if the business is not delivering a product. A perfect example is the age-old "fire sale." The objective of a fire sale is to increase the amount of capital on hand in order to allow the business time to continue operation and possibly fund rebuilding activities.

The purpose of business continuity is to ensure that core business functions continue with minimal or no interruption. When focusing on business continuity, you may choose not to return to the past and to instead focus all endeavors toward new opportunities. The objective is to ensure that the organization will survive and continue to generate revenue. Uninterrupted revenue equals money that provides the luxury of time and opportunity.

An organization can use the principles of business continuity to accomplish the following:

Survive Man-Made or Natural Disaster   Survival means sustaining control while ensuring that enough money is flowing to the bank to keep the organization running during and after the event.

Acquire or Divest Business Units   The business continuity planning process creates an incredibly valuable set of documents, including a current risk analysis and a low-level blueprint of business processes currently in use. This information would be invaluable for outsourcing or insourcing.

Organizations can be affected by events that disrupt the daily operation of their business. Consider, for example, AOL (formerly called America Online), which suffered a change management crisis in which configuration of the routers and servers was lost. The result was an operational disaster in 1994 with a complete blackout of AOL's Internet services for more than three days. As a result, AOL suffered a negative public perception and negative publicity. This operational mistake ultimately led to the sale of the business. In 2003, while AOL was owned by Time Warner, AOL was again the subject of much controversy and rapidly falling stock prices. The issue this time centered on the management team refusing to sign for the integrity of the company financial statement. Their failure to sign created a legal requirement for the organization to notify the entire world that their record keeping was questionable and that there was no assurance of integrity in any statements made. AOL management was aware of the consequences but did not want to accept personal liability for signing a potentially false integrity statement. The resulting news stories led many investors to dump stock at a fraction of its previous value.

Change to a Different Market   Some markets are no longer profitable because of changes in consumer attitude, cost/competition, or increasing regulatory law. Management may find a more profitable market for their efforts. As an example, consider Daisytek International. Daisytek started business as a distributor of office supplies and later became a hardware manufacturer for Hewlett-Packard. After several years, the management team decided to quit manufacturing hardware and refocus on the more-profitable market of distributing office supplies. Recently the supplies portion of the business was sold because of low profit margin, and the remaining organization was renamed PFSweb. Now PFSweb operates as a contract fulfillment and distribution vendor, providing fulfillment services for other organizations. Many of the original executives and staff remain.

Improve Market Position by Demonstrating a Potential for Surviving or Profiting   One of the reasons an organization participates in business continuity planning is to attract better financial terms from investors and to attract more clients. A good business continuity plan could attract new contracts and revenue opportunities by demonstrating an organizational plan to fulfill contractual commitments.

Gain Advantage over a Competitor in the Marketplace   An organization might gain advantage by demonstrating an ability to help their customers in spite of whatever may occur. We can use the example of FedEx and their "absolutely positively overnight" reputation to demonstrate this point. Customers pay a premium for this level of commitment.

Other examples of gaining an advantage are as follows:

To Service a Surge in Business   An organization may execute business continuity plans to undertake a higher-than-normal business volume. The organization sheds low-profit tasks to make resources available for the increased volume. A dramatic surge in demand creates a survival challenge comparable to an equivalent reduction in capacity. Apple's iPhone on the AT&T cellular network is a prime example, with more than 35 million subscribers switching to iPhone in less than three years.

To Lead an Aggressive Campaign against a Faltering Competitor   The competitor may be facing temporary delivery problems, an unfavorable media image, labor issues, or a man-made or natural disaster. Consider the number of new cars sold when gas prices were high and the United States offered a government-subsidized trade-in allowance. Import car makers unleashed a marketing campaign with compelling offers to entice clients to abandon the American auto competition. Depending on the offer, in the past, customer swings have been recorded as high as 20 percent to 55 percent of market share during a 16-hour period.

To Be Available for Your Customer's Needs   Consider the story of the Bank of Italy during the California earthquake of 1906. The earthquake lasted only 30 seconds, but the city of San Francisco was destroyed by the earthquake and subsequent fires. All the banks were ordered closed to prevent a run on the banks. The tiny Bank of Italy set up temporary operations in a wooden horse cart at the wharf. While the other banks were closed, the Bank of Italy made small loans to help people rebuild. Many individuals wanted to make deposits to this little bank in a horse cart. The customers wanted their money from coffee cans and from under mattresses to be protected. Serving $10 depositors, the little Bank of Italy took in more than $800,000 during the next few years. This was an incredible sum of money during that period. Multiple divisions were formed under other names, and ultimately these were combined under one new name: Bank of America.

Survive a Runaway Marketing Campaign   Do you remember the fabulously successful "Where's the beef?" campaign by Wendy's Hamburgers? It is a marketing legend. It also illustrates how a runaway marketing campaign can place excessive strain on an organization's resources. Dave Thomas, the founder of Wendy's, told the story as follows:

> Wendy's had run a series of advertising campaigns which never really seemed to catch on. Other competitors were able to attract customers using lower-priced products with less meat. Wendy's "Where's the beef?" marketing campaign was based upon a commonsense observation and was well timed to the marketplace. Wendy's advertisement caught on like wildfire. Aspiring politicians used the "Where's the beef?" slogan against competitors for coattail publicity during campaign rallies. The campaign was enormously successful beyond everyone's expectations. This one campaign created so much attention, new customers were lining up at their door. The ad also brought the attention of Wendy's larger competitors. Wendy's was forced into a rapid national expansion or face losing their marketplace. Wendy's opened over 500 new stores during a one-year period at the rate of two or more stores per workday.

(Source: Discovery Channel)

Could your organization have done the same? Wendy's is not the only company facing this type of challenge. United Parcel Service (UPS) and FedEx are involved in the same type of competition for expansion. UPS purchased Office Depot. Next, UPS purchased the MailBoxes Etc. chain to increase the number of UPS drop-off locations. FedEx purchased Kinko's in a race to see who would dominate the market. FedEx Office, formerly Kinko's, opened more than 250 stores in the first year of acquisition, with plans to open 2,000 additional stores over the next five years. This type of rapid expansion requires good continuity planning to ensure that your customers stay happy customers. It requires a strong leader like FedEx CEO Fred Smith to pull this off.

Uniting Other Plans with Business Continuity

As we have said, business continuity is the next level beyond disaster recovery. Business continuity is double-sided. One side protects what a business already has, while the other offers the opportunity to generate more revenue than ever before.

A good continuity plan defines a strategy and details for supporting a business with fewer resources. After the business has learned how to make more money, there is no need to wait for a disaster. The business can begin to execute the revenue-enhancement plans immediately, and will be prepared for both disaster and market opportunity.

Business continuity planning integrates and coordinates the narrow scope of smaller plans. It would be impossible for a single department to provide the broad-level support necessary to be successful. Figure 8.1 shows this integration.

Business continuity spans departmental and political boundaries. Whereas DR is based in facilities and IT plans, BC plans focus on what it takes for the business to resume generating revenue. Business continuity is frequently led by the chief operating officer or program management office. Plans include media handling and campaigns to retain customers, vendors, and investors that would otherwise be tempted to switch to a competitor.

Identifying Business Continuity Practices

It is the executive above the business continuity/disaster recovery planner who determines whether the focus will be disaster recovery for rebuilding or business continuity for revenue. Auditors can quickly identify the focus of the client's business continuity plan by looking at who's in charge. Table 8.1 illustrates the differences in planning are dependent on the job focus of the leader.

FIGURE 8.1   Business continuity integrates smaller departmental plans.

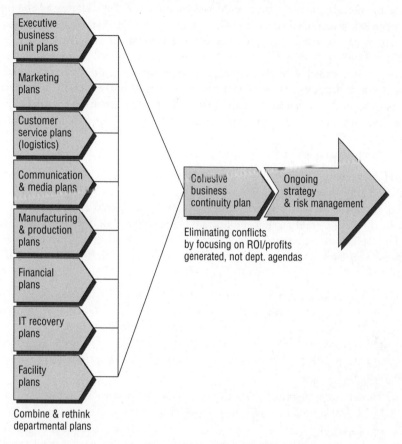

TABLE 8.1   Leader indicates the organization's focus

Focus	CEO/COO	Facilities	Government Authorities	CFO/CIO
Revenue (business unit)	X			
Product lines	X			
Disaster rebuilding (resilience, recovery)		X		X
Emergency management			X	
Continuity of operations				X
Continuity of government			X	

Depending on who you listen to, there are several common practice areas in the business continuity rebuild-recovery models. Most governments, U.S. DRI, and the international Business Continuity Institute (BCI) are focused on disaster recovery aspects. None of these offer any advice outside emergency management and disaster-related preparation.

Executives use continuity vehicles to generate new revenue on a daily basis, which means your business unit executives will be yawning with disinterest on disaster-centric plans, unless IT is unable to maintain good data backups. Pay attention to our BC program approach because it will increase your market value far beyond just passing this portion of the CISA exam.

Business continuity requires two things:

Training and Awareness   Planning is a wasted effort unless you teach individuals the necessary roles and skills to perform the required functions of the BC/DR plan. Educate the organization about the plan's existence, job duties, and anticipated areas of coverage. It's important for the staff to realize that the business continuity plan does not cover everything. In fact, the key to success is to limit coverage to only the highest-value processes. Everything else may be shut down for a period of time or indefinitely. We cannot afford to protect everything.

Integration with Other Organizations   No organization can exist by itself. A good plan will integrate with supply-chain plans of business partners, suppliers, clients, and government agencies. You may need to rely on them, or they may need to rely on us during critical functions. Often a prime contractor will incorporate the plans of a subcontractor into their own. Good integration adapts the relationship from one based on price to one based on being a true partner.

Figure 8.2 shows an overview of the best practice areas in business continuity planning based on the FEMA emergency management model.

Real World Scenario

Best Practices Compared to the CISA Exam

Remember that your CISA exam and ISACA have a narrow view of business continuity and disaster recovery as it relates to IT records management as service. ISACA reflects only the tiny portion of the entire body of knowledge relating to IT COOP and records recovery. You are expected to know the terminology used by ISACA for the exam. Each organization uses similar terms of reference but may not know all the terminology.

The focus of this chapter is to introduce an overview of best practices in business continuity to increase understanding of real-life situations. Each of the examples presented should help increase your value as an IS auditor.

FIGURE 8.2   The best practices in business continuity planning according to FEMA

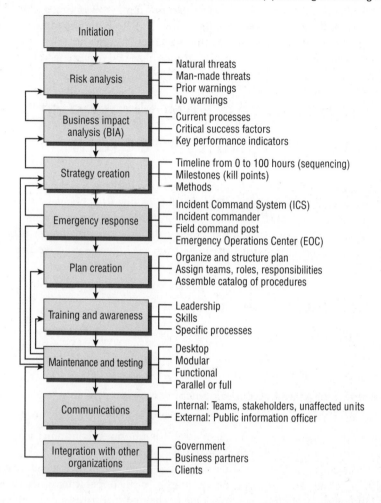

 It is important to remember that the number one priority is your customer and your customer interface. Without the customer, there is no revenue. Without revenue, business continuity would be difficult or impossible. Without a steady stream of happy customers, the investors will bail out too.

Following a Program Management Approach

In Chapter 2, "Managing IT Governance," we covered the basics of program management. As a quick refresher, it's important to remember that a program is an ongoing sustaining operation that may generate several temporary projects. Whereas a team member will outlive a project, a program will outlive the team members. This means we are constantly recruiting and training new members in order to keep the program running. Running a business continuity program is slightly different from running an ISO 9001 quality program.

Now let's explore how the practices of business continuity apply in a little more depth. Our goal is to provide you with a basic understanding that you can use in your audit work.

Understanding the Five Phases of a Business Continuity Program

Real business continuity reflects a natural evolution of executive scenario planning. The goal is for the organization to survive, even if that means divesting business units, selling product lines, downsizing the staff, or closing less-profitable operations. Programs are sustaining operations, which are intended to last longer than the careers of most people. The first step is to set up the program with a mandate from the highest executive and rally key people to the cause.

Phase 1: Setting Up the BC Program

Every program undergoes an initiation phase with the objective to secure the following:

- A sponsor to pay for the project
- A charter to grant responsibility and authority
- A defined scope (for a particular geographic site, division, product, or client)
- Specific business objectives (critical success factors, management direction)

After executive management has chosen to establish a business continuity program, the first course of action is to establish a BC leadership council.

Executive management needs to provide two critical components. First is active leadership participation by the chief executive officer (CEO) or chief operating officer (COO) to provide credibility with a genuine direction. One of the first directives may be to increase gross profit margin by 2 percent annually, for example. This profit increase may be accomplished by working together to figure out how to increase business through new efficiencies.

The BC council is composed of senior staff workers from each of the functional areas, regardless of their interest or lack thereof in business continuity. The ideal appointee would be a person whom other staff members rely on when they really need a problem solved. These are your go-to people. It is an excellent practice to have that person's manager on the council as well, to ensure that at least one of them is always available for meetings.

Members of the council provide a way to fulfill two major objectives. One is to bring ideas with a can-do attitude from each member's area of expertise. The other is to sponsor business continuity as a representative in their work center.

The second component provided by the executive management team is identification of the first target. It could be an existing business process or new market opportunity. It should be something significant, but maybe not your number one revenue line because the first pass may involve a learning curve. A common technique to identify the first target is a simple feasibility study based on the profit-and-loss statement.

We need to introduce the simple definition of three important terms:

Critical Success Factor (CSF)   A critical success factor represents an objective or task that absolutely must be accomplished. The CSF must function correctly every single time. To fail a CSF would be a real showstopper. Let's use an example of a student in school. Scholarship requirements would be a type of CSF. If you don't meet all the requirements, you won't get the scholarship. For public corporations, the timely filing of quarterly financial results is a CSF because failure to file will attract fines from the government. Worse yet, delayed filing will trigger stock analysts to spread a bad performance report that, in turn, drives down the stock value regardless of the truth.

Key Goal Indicator (KGI)   These identify the organization's goals and define the smaller departmental goals. Key goals are those objectives that are important, but not as threatening as failing a CSF. Goals can include customer satisfaction and quality levels. For comparison: KGIs can slip without creating a showstopper. Key performance indicators are used to determine whether the goal will be reached.

Key Performance Indicator (KPI)   Metrics are created based on a variety of sources. These lower-level metrics are similar to player statistics in sports (batting average, points scored, speed or distance covered). Unfortunately, KPIs may not indicate a problem until it's too late. Think of KPIs as comparable to report-card grades in school.

During the initiation phase, specific discussions are held between the BC council and executive management. Avoid using the technique of doom and gloom to threaten a variety of negative consequences. This technique is intended to intimidate executives with liability if they fail to cooperate. A more favorable technique would be to provide clippings of related news articles to generate awareness. A person could ask, "If this event happened to us, would we have a similar outcome?"

The majority of BC programs are floundering because of a shortsighted approach that business continuity or disaster coverage is similar to insurance. Far too many professionals have such a narrow scope: their only goal is to protect the business from a future loss. Unfortunately this narrow thinking results in missing a great opportunity for advancement since the real problem is the majority of executives are more worried about generating revenue than maintaining comprehensive insurance.

Brands and goodwill affiliated with a company name contain significant "real" value. Most marketing campaigns are built up year after year using anywhere from 15 percent to 25 percent of product gross revenue to pay for advertising. It is common to expect strong ad campaigns to earn returns that are 5 times to 30 times the cost of the campaign itself. Years of happy customers create brand loyalty. A hard-earned image can be destroyed by adverse publicity or disaster. Approach value by calculating the amount of money invested in advertising and public relations over the past years. The BC planners need to communicate with an understanding of the multiple categories of risk that face their organization. Consider this to be the short and broad list in discussions with management. Each of these situations could rapidly surface and get out of control during a crisis or even cause a disaster.

The threat categories include the following:

Strategic (Plans)   Poor marketing strategy, changes in laws, consumer attitudes

Financial (Controls)   Fraud, poor record keeping, failed reconciliation, poor cash/credit management, treasury problems, Securities and Exchange Commission (SEC) reports, Gramm-Leach-Bliley bank performance rules

Operational (Human)   Human error, apathy, wrong procedures, poor judgment, communications conflict, politics, lack of up-to-date training

Commercial (Relationships)   Loss of key supplier/customer; supply-chain failure; scandal involving partner, supplier, or significant customer

Technical (Assets)   Equipment breakdown, natural disaster, destruction, loss of use, other perils

Figure 8.3 shows that business continuity can be focused on protecting a variety of business processes.

FIGURE 8.3   Selecting the business process to protect

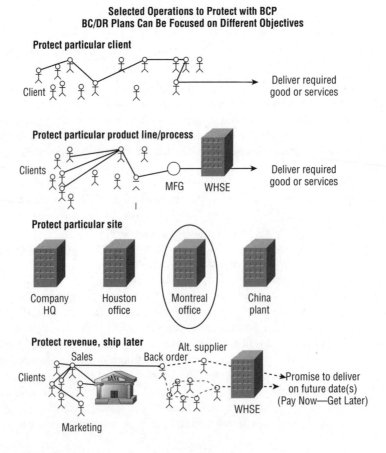

Selected Operations to Protect with BCP
BC/DR Plans Can Be Focused on Different Objectives

An incredibly effective technique is to tie business continuity objectives into plans for revenue and market share. Earlier, we touched on a few examples of using business continuity planning to generate revenue. Funding is less of an issue when you include marketing plans in the objectives. This lends itself to acquiring a significant amount of funding from the advertising budget—far less money than advertising would miss and far more money than most DR plans would ever acquire.

Some of the possible deliverables from the business continuity/disaster recovery planning process include the following:

- Verification of capabilities (efficiency, inefficiency, deficiency, overreliance, unused capacity)

- Identification of new revenue opportunities

- Functional blueprint of current business processes with mapping of interrelationships and sequence

- Definition of risk and performance strategy

- Documentation of specific required tasks for business survival

- Strategy to increase revenue

- Fulfillment of a business interest or executive business desire

NOTE People agree to fund and support projects for a variety of reasons. The goal of the initiation phase is to determine what the sponsor will pay for and why, and to document the desired result.

As an IT auditor, you will focus on whether the IT functions will be able to support the business objectives. Planning for business continuity/disaster recovery will be successful only when sponsored from the top down. It is the responsibility of senior executive management to ensure that this planning occurs. With a target identified, it's time to move into phase 2 for the discovery process.

Phase 2: The Discovery Process

No two organizations are exactly alike, even in the same industry, and neither are their business processes. The *business impact analysis (BIA)* is the singular most important component of every business continuity plan. It is impossible to have a business continuity plan without performing a current BIA. Without the BIA, the best you could hope for would be basic disaster recovery.

The goal of the discovery process is to identify the company's sequence of steps and timing. It is very important to pay close attention to those details during this phase because this research will be the foundation for our strategy. Usually it is beneficial to begin with the BIA before running a risk assessment. This will lend a tangible value because risks will change depending on which step of the business process you're in at any given time. Besides, staff members may find it difficult to do a risk assessment before the BIA because the risks would be out of context.

Business Impact Analysis

You'll need a data-gathering project plan with five major components:

- Access authority to the M4 (methods, manpower, machinery, materials)
- End-to-end work-in-process map with time intervals
- Identification of any known alternative work-in-process (WIP) methods.
- Records register (for recording M4, identifying work-in-process records and all associated risks)
- Evidence sampling plan

It's easy to be sidetracked while gathering data. As a rule of thumb, you want to follow the invisible route traveled by money from a customer's pocket into the organization's bank account. As long as you're following the money trail, you'll be on the right track. Go step-by-step, from how an order enters the system all the way through to delivery and post-sale follow-up. Along the way, you're looking for an indication of unique activities that add value versus common commodities that everybody can get from competitors.

The BIA process offers substantial benefits to an organization. The resulting information is invaluable for business process reengineering, outsourcing activities, resizing plans, acquisition or divestiture activities, and business continuity planning.

In Figure 8.4, you can see the relationships among business processes.

FIGURE 8.4   Relationships among business processes

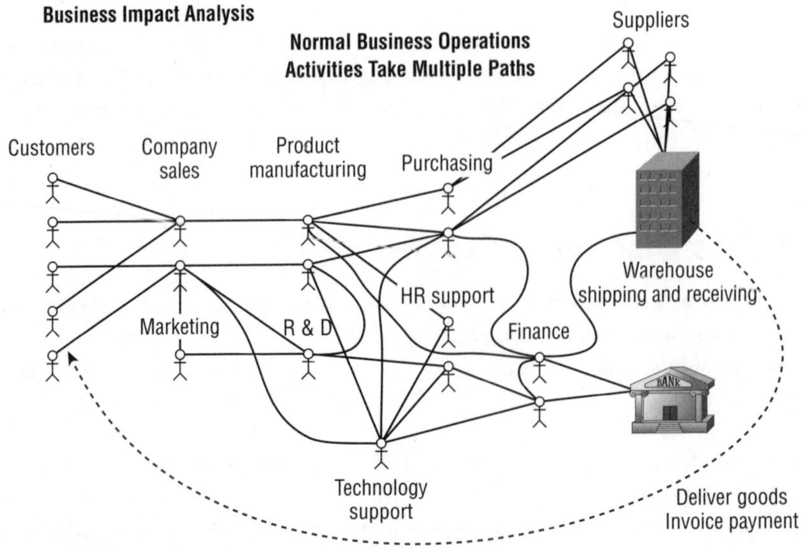

A BIA documents current low-level process dependencies and discovers new opportunities.

A BIA is a specialized project designed to uncover the inner workings and vulnerabilities of an organization. The value of this phase cannot be overstated. In Chapter 3, "Audit Process," we discussed using both qualitative and quantitative assessment for planning. The same qualitative and quantitative techniques can be used in the BIA. Proper execution of the BIA process entails a series of discovery exercises, including the following:

- Asking a series of questions similar to those used in business process reengineering (BPR). These questions would focus on identifying trigger events and the current sequence of the organization's workflow.

- Interviewing key personnel.

- Reviewing existing documentation.

- Collecting data by observing actual processes.

- Possibly observing personnel performing actual tasks. The auditor should recall that using surveys creates issues of inaccuracy and inconsistency.

- Looking for existing workarounds and alternate procedures. Many times, the client's personnel may be aware of workarounds that could prove valuable during a business continuity situation.

- Verifying critical success factors (CSFs).

- Identifying vital materials and records necessary for recovery. This would include numerous items: data backups, vendor list, inventory records, customer list, employee records with contact data, bill of materials, procedure documents, BC plan, banking information, copies of all contracts, and legal documents.

Collecting and organizing this information is a formidable task. All the disciplines of project management are invoked during the execution of the BIA. Later, during the business continuity planning process, the BC planners use the risk analysis and BIA information to guide the formulation of the BC strategy. Almost every organization would be unable to properly sequence business continuity activities if they failed to collect the correct information during the BIA phase.

All the data collected from the BIA and risk analysis should be properly archived and protected with the highest level of security available. This archive creates a central repository of all the organization's plans, secrets, and capabilities—hence effective security controls are paramount. The contents of this archive will be reused in subsequent planning sessions that should occur at the following times:

- At least annually

- Upon addition or loss of key customers

- Upon change of current business processes

- Whenever the organizational structure changes

- Upon change in the management direction

The business users must always be involved in the planning of business continuity. Without their input, it would be impossible to align the plans with real-world requirements.

Keeping users involved is the secret to attaining buy-in.

Risk Assessment

Now from your BIA records register you will have the information necessary to perform a valid risk assessment. Start with a strength, weakness, opportunity, and threat (SWOT) analysis. Consider the impact of events with prior warning versus no warning to help you identify likely emergencies.

Many people see this phase as a well-known requirement but then proceed to skip right past it without any regard for its impact. In Chapter 3, we provided a flowchart detailing the methods for performing risk analysis.

The starting point in risk analysis entails listing the individual steps and matching threats, and then assigning a potential score. Risk managers are similar to gamblers: They want to calculate the present odds and see what can be done to improve them. Your goal at this stage of the planning process is to accurately document the present state of each threat. After you have identified all of the risks, the planner will focus efforts on the threats of the highest priority. Priority may be determined by frequency, consequence, or dependency.

A sense of order is necessary to manage the list of potential threats. Your sponsor and executive management team will have little interest in wading through volumes of spreadsheets. The easy way to deal with this is to create a summary sheet and related detail sheets. Each item on the summary sheet will relate to an entire page or pages of detail sheets.

Figure 8.5 illustrates risk assessment worksheets. Shown are the summary and related detail reports.

The higher-level summary sheet will include a list of threats related to the following:

- Various natural disasters
- Man-made disasters
- Operational and technology failures
- Vendor failures
- Current site failures
- Alternate site failures
- Relocation threats

Each of these line items will be broken down into individual components listed on a detail sheet. From the detail sheet, the planner will create a composite score that will appear on the summary sheet.

A well-documented threat and opportunity listing will note where the evidence was acquired or where the evidence can be found. All risk analysis worksheets represent a tremendous value in time, effort, and informational detail. These worksheets should be preserved and protected. Every intelligent risk manager will review them on a regular basis.

Let's take a moment to discuss the often neglected area of selecting an alternate site and potential threats to relocation. Far too often the alternate site is selected by the service vendor providing the alternate facility for rent. In some cases, this could prove to be an absolute killer.

FIGURE 8.5   Risk assessment worksheets for summary and detail

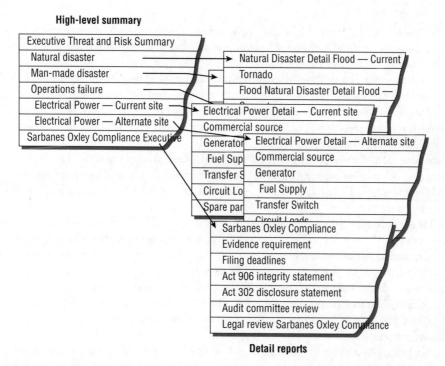

High-level summary

Executive Threat and Risk Summary
Natural disaster
Man-made disaster
Operations failure
Electrical Power — Current site
Electrical Power — Alternate site
Sarbanes Oxley Compliance Executive

Natural Disaster Detail Flood — Current
Tornado
Flood Natural Disaster Detail Flood —
Electrical Power Detail — Current site
Commercial source
Generator   Electrical Power Detail — Alternate site
Fuel Sup   Commercial source
Transfer S   Generator
Circuit Lo   Fuel Supply
Spare par   Transfer Switch
Circuit Loads
Sarbanes Oxley Compliance
Evidence requirement
Filing deadlines
Act 906 integrity statement
Act 302 disclosure statement
Audit committee review
Legal review Sarbanes Oxley Compliance

Detail reports

Suppose you were looking for an alternate site. What would be the geographic location requirements? Hopefully, the geographic selection process would include consideration of the following:

- General area hazards. Ask questions about the neighbors, crime rate, and previous events in the area.

- Downwind hazards from military targets and nuclear power plants.

- Known storm tracks for severe weather, including hurricanes and tornadoes.

- Potential flood areas.

- Geophysical data concerning potential earth movement.

- Access to telecommunications.

- Nearby airports, helpful for regular visits and necessary for rapid relocation.

- Roadway access. Remember September 11, 2001. Who says airplanes will be flying the day you need to fly? Some major city airports may be closed.

- Proximity. You need to be close enough to drive, yet not so close that you are affected by the same regional disaster.

- Railway access for shipping heavy loads or volume goods.

- Municipal services, including fire, police, and hospital.

- Expedited services and mail services.

- Safe accommodations.

All this data is readily available, including maps of military targets and nuclear materials. Contrary to myth, worldwide military targets and nuclear materials maps are still available on the Internet at the time of this writing.

Figure 8.6 shows a simple map illustrating basic geographic threats for the state of Texas. Any country or state could have been used for this demonstration; however, the Texas map does a nice job of illustrating our objective. The northeastern United States is considered a more likely terrorist target; however, we still need to consider technical failure no matter where the business is located.

Notice how each of the elements of the selection process overlay the state. The major cities of Dallas, Fort Worth, Houston, Austin, and San Antonio contain multiple area threats. An upwind biological or nuclear hazard could affect each of the cities by carrying contaminants downwind.

Now take a look on the left side of the state. The Rio Grande River is the western border between Texas and Mexico. Notice the town of Del Rio, Texas, along the Rio Grande River. Del Rio is outside most of the severe weather zones. It has no significant upwind biological or nuclear hazard. The town is located within 175 to 300 miles of the major Texas cities. This is the recommended safe distance of separation from regional disasters. At a closer location, the same event or collateral disruption could impact both the primary and alternate sites.

The highway to Del Rio could fulfill the minimum access requirement. An organization could transport their staff by car, bus, or truck within 8 hours of normal driving time. Del Rio is a switching point along Union Pacific Railroad's main line. Rail access is good for heavy shipments but could represent a concern regarding possible transportation of hazardous materials. Amtrak provides regular passenger rail service. The Del Rio airport offers regularly scheduled flights and supports private aircraft operations. The organization can charter a full-sized commercial jet for about $8,500 an hour to move a large group of people in a hurry. The jet's cargo bay can be loaded with the freight needed for recovery. It is usually cheaper to charter rather than buy a handful of last-minute airline tickets.

All major air freight carriers operate from the Del Rio airport, including DHL Express, UPS, and FedEx. That will provide reasonable levels of logistical support. There are practically no geophysical concerns regarding earth movement. Fiber-optic access for communication is available. Land is relatively cheap. The crime rate is low. A seasonal rain may bring light flooding in low-lying areas, indicating that the recovery site needs to be in an elevated area of town. Based on this information, Del Rio, Texas, scores well as an alternate site location.

  Successful planners will go to this level of detail when selecting an alternate site.

FIGURE 8.6   Geographic threat map for Texas

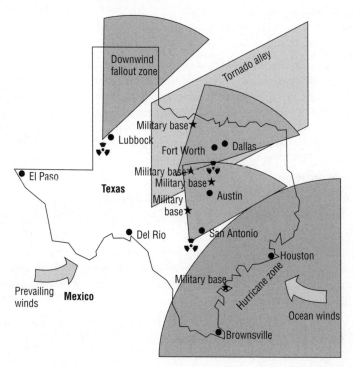

Phase 3: Plan Development

This area of planning involves two major components: implementing the executive strategy based on criticality and documenting subcomponent plans for various areas of activity.

In using information from the first two phases, you can begin the process of selecting a business survival strategy. This strategy may be one of protection, growth, or change. It is unfortunate, but a number of uninformed individuals in all job roles may immediately jump ahead into technology solutions without having exercised a proper strategy selection process.

Strategy selection should take into account the management directives from initiation as well as the identified risks and documented process dependencies. The BIA process will furnish a blueprint that can provide a critical path sequence.

The next step in planning is to create a priority-based timeline of activities necessary to support the critical path. A great deal of discussion and politics may enter into this otherwise simple process. Effective business continuity planning will categorize everything into one of three areas of interest:

Core Process   Those activities that are specifically required in the critical path and related directly to production of revenue. These are the rock-bottom must-do functions without any extras or add-on activities.

Supporting Process Supporting functions that are necessary to fulfill revenue-direct activities. These may include an alternate mechanism for delivering invoices to the customer for prompt payment, for instance. Common examples include mail rerouting, invoicing, and payment processing, regardless of whether it's done in-house or by an alternate contractor.

Discretionary Process Everything else that is not part of core or direct revenue supporting processes. These activities are not used in critical business functions and do not feed or process data for critical or supporting systems. These activities would cost more to protect than the value of work that the system produces. Most of the IT service platforms are discretionary. For example, email is a supporting process, but the system it runs on is discretionary because substituting Unix servers, mainframes, or other mail platforms doesn't really matter as long as it works. It will be necessary to unbundle low-priority discretionary tasks to streamline the core processes.

With this information, a working timeline is created for the targeted process activities. This timeline references multiple levels of time and service delivery metrics. We identify these as follows:

Recovery Target (RT) These are the critical assets necessary for the business process to run. Recovery targets are individual items - nouns (person, place, or thing) identified during the cataloging of M4 resources. Each target is numbered in order of priority to prevent confusion (RT1, RT2, and so forth).

Current WIP Cycle (WIP) The current as-it-is-today baseline will be used for identifying likely scenarios to be used in strategy planning. Two additional work-in-process metrics will also be implemented:

Lost Work in Process (LWIP) Identification of potential lost work in process. This work will need to be recovered or discarded for whatever reason.

Recovered Work in Process (RWIP) This is existing work at the time of interruption that we can salvage. The work would be undamaged and therefore acceptable by the customer to process through to completion.

Recovery Priority (RP) It's very important for ALL effort to remain focused on the correct sequence recovery of shared priority. Effort, time and resources are wasted if a user, department, or custodian attempts to recover any asset out of sequence. Every auditor must understand some assets (systems, records, jobs, people) will remain shut down with no priority. Recovery is based on highest direct source of revenue or mission value; everything else comes much later if it's restarted at all.

Service Delivery Objective (SDO) The level of service available at a particular point in time. We use this reference to indicate the level of reduced or suspended service (SDO1, SDO2, SDO3, and so forth). Our final SDO (SDOx) would be full service in normal operation.

Legal Deadline (LD) Any legal or regulatory deadline we have to meet to keep the organization afloat. This is used like a timer for filing extensions, reports, or mandated performance metrics. In the banking industry, an example of the first legal deadline may be an SDO (SDO1) for allowing customers to deposit money, withdraw money, and check balances within 59 minutes of an outage. The next legal deadline might be an SDO (SDO2) allowing the execution of financial stock trades, be it manual or automated.

Recovery Time Objective (RTO)   The point in time at which a particular system is recovered to specific levels of operation. Consider a phone system that may be recovered in stages of increasing functionality. RTOs are assigned for each stage. RTOs are measured by when the business resumes use, not when IT restored the system. That's why it's called business continuity rather than IT continuity. Multiple RTOs will exist (RTO1, RTO2, RTO3, and so on).

Maximum Acceptable Outage (MAO)   The maximum time the systems can be offline before breaching a deadline or causing damage to the organization. The MAO is factored into creating recovery time objectives (RTOs). This may also be referred to as *maximum tolerable downtime (MTD)*. It's simply that people with positive attitudes use the word *acceptable*. Both terms are similar in purpose.

Recovery Point Objective (RPO)   The defined level of recovery for a particular item. Processing that occurs between the RPO and the incident will be lost work. An example is recovery of last night's backup tape or recovery to completed database transactions that occurred 5 minutes ago (based on a redundant high-availability system). Multiple RPOs may exist.

Work in progress will be lost at the time of disruption. The business continuity/disaster recovery planner should review the risk and plan according to the criticality. Each RPO should take into consideration the following:

Critical Function   These must occur to fulfill the minimum requirements to accomplish *core processes* (mission). Critical functions will be very time-sensitive and might not be recoverable by manual operation.

Vital Function   These are less critical, with somewhat more time before recovery is necessary. Vital functions may be able to run manually depending on volume and duration of work.

Sensitive Function   These can be delayed for several days and might be performed manually or outsourced to another vendor.

Noncritical Function (Everything Else)   These may be discontinued for extended periods of time, and may or may not be restarted in the future. The recovery point objective (RPO) may be "none" for noncritical stuff.

Revenue Objective (RO)   Just how long can the organization last before it passes the financial point of no return? The revenue objective identifies throughout the timeline how much money needs to be earned to keep the organization afloat (financially solvent). Failing the revenue objective may indicate a need to halt current activities before wasting any more capital on a failing business process.

For a real-world example of revenue objectives, the Steak and Ale Restaurant chain shut down abruptly in 2008 because the founding executives realized attempts to continue operation for another 90 days would just waste money that could be paid to the investors as dividends. Their competitive business market had changed with increased cost pressure and stronger competition. Conditions were not likely to improve, so reorganizing the chain was not expected to generate enough money. It was inevitable that staff workers would have to find employment elsewhere. The executives' goal was to take care of investors so those people would invest their money in the executives' next venture.

> At CertTest, we teach business continuity planners to organize and illustrate these objectives by using a visual timeline. Our initial PERT timeline begins at 100 hours in the past and proceeds to 100 hours in the future. This will cover approximately four calendar days before and after the event. It is well documented that an organization that does not recover by the fourth day will likely fail during the coming year. Unfortunately, some organizations may fail in fewer than four days. Either way, our timeline will accomplish its purpose.

One of the most important objectives of business continuity planning efforts is to identify what constitutes the zero hour. In most organizations, nobody wants to be the person who cried wolf, nor the person who activated the plan before its designated time. So just what is that zero hour? Is it when the client is indicating a desire to switch to another vendor, when the company receives bad press coverage, when the founder dies, when the labor union strikes, when a competitor suffers a setback worth exploiting, or when smoke comes billowing out of the building? Management holds the responsibility for identifying situations that would mandate activating the continuity plan. The senior manager on duty would be under orders to execute the plan whenever the predetermined conditions were met. Otherwise, the plan may be executed too early or too late to save the organization. The zero hour may be defined based on the level of physical damage, marketing failure, degraded media image, loss of production capability, or the runaway success of a marketing campaign.

By using this information, a variety of strategies may be selected. The IT strategy selection is based on the unique needs of individual departments, available personnel, facilities, capital management, technology, and business processes. An effective strategy will fit within the requirements of each RT, LWIP, RTO, RWIP, RPO, SDO, and RO. In highly regulated industries, the target objectives may be clearly defined by regulatory law.

After you identify the proper sequence of objectives, you need to decide the best method of implementation from the IT perspective. Available options include the following:

Do Nothing   This is often unacceptable and creates the potential for catastrophic liability. Executives will normally choose this route if the planning justification or financial return on investment is weak.

Use Redundant Hardware   A redundant hardware strategy may be used for equipment within the facility. The concept of redundancy could be to have spare systems online, or to stock an in-house supply of replacement parts. The following are examples of redundant hardware:

Mirrored Servers   Mirrored high-availability servers are an example of redundant online systems. Two servers operate as one machine. If functioning correctly, a secondary server takes over processing when the primary server fails.

Mirrored Disk Drives   Using RAID technology, the data on disk drives can be mirrored. We discussed mirrored servers and RAID in Chapter 7, "Protecting Information Assets."

Redundant Communication   Network routers can be set up in a redundant configuration to ensure maximum uptime. This effective design utilizes communication services from more than one communication provider—for example, Internet connections from both AT&T and Verizon.

Unfortunately, purchasing the redundant hardware strategy might be too expense when compared to using an external subcontractor. The auditor should investigate if the decision was driven by a verifiable business payback or politics of the IT staff's desire for the organization to "own" everything. While management recognizes purchasing locks up money and reduces flexibility of change, employees usually feel comfort knowing the organization is locked into a specific technology platform. The locked-in situation often provides self-centered employees an illusion of job protection.

Use an Alternate Processing Location   Alternate sites are used for processing in the event that the organization is unable to use a regular location. Alternate sites may be owned by the organization or leased by subscription. The leased site by subscription is rather expensive after calculating all the costs of usage and rehearsal exercises. Unfortunately, some leased sites have more customers than space available for recovery (oversubscription). Alternate sites are usually one of the following types:

Redundant Site   This location contains either duplicate mirror facilities that are online at all times, or computing facilities of a reduced capacity that can process at the acceptable SDO requirement. The data is live—no delays waiting for files to be restored. All necessary personnel are already present and on the job. The redundant site is in full operation and able to take over processing within seconds or minutes. A redundant site can offer a competitive marketing and operational advantage. Redundant sites can be located in the same geographic region or across the country. A location should be selected that is not subject to disasters in the same proximity as the primary site. The two sites should be geographically separated. The dominant issue of operating a redundant site is the cost.

Hot Site   This is similar to a redundant site except that it is offline when not in use. Hot sites can be obtained by subscription (rented) or by capital investment (owned). All necessary facilities, equipment, and communication lines are ready to go without delay or setup time. Basically, a hot site is fully operational and gathering dust until it is ready to be used. Data files will need several hours to load from backup tapes before the systems can go live. A hot site is fully equipped and capable of being in operation within hours. A delay may occur as personnel are traveling to the site. Hot sites may be elaborate for use in executive marketing to attract key investors and clients. Hot sites are ideal for supporting IT functions and live customer communication.

Real World Scenario

A Lesson in Hot Site Declaration Criteria

During the fall of 2005, several hurricanes impacted the southeastern United States. A handful of business continuity/disaster recovery planners complained that they were placed in a dangerous situation of being denied access to a hot site that they had paid to use by subscription. The vendor gave excuses that other customers from prior hurricanes were still using the facility. Another customer was told by the big hot site vendor that they would not be allowed to declare hot site activation because their city had not been hit by the hurricane nor was it designated a disaster area yet. Their vendor allocated hot site space based on a *first to declare* criteria rather than guaranteed access. Stories verifying the situation appeared in newspapers and on the Internet.

Warm Site   This location offers significantly less opportunity for success. Warm sites are typically shell buildings with basic utility services and require extra time to make ready. Computer equipment may not be on site yet, or may require configuration before it is ready to use. After several hours of system configuration, additional delays will occur as data files are loaded. Communication lines will need to be activated and traffic rerouted before the voice and data can go online. This type of site will be operational in a matter of days or weeks. The location may be a branch office of the same organization.

Cold Site   This option offers the lowest possibility of success. Cold sites are typically building shells without any computing equipment, and offer no more than a street address and basic shelter. Examples include a hotel conference room. A cold site is the cheapest of all alternate site options and is unacceptable for IT functions. A cold site may be acceptable for recovery of noncritical systems as time permits.

Mobile Site   Very popular with vendors selling alternate site solutions, the mobile site is usually a trailer configured so that it is equivalent to the level of a hot site or warm site. These are popular for extended use on site while buildings and facilities are reconstructed. Unfortunately, mobile sites may be restricted by building permit delays, mandatory evacuations, or inaccessible regions due to roadway damage or roadblocks. A handful of customers affected by hurricanes Charley, Katrina, and Wilma reported that their mobile sites did not arrive as promptly as promised because of travel restrictions and fuel shortages. Many professionals consider the mobile site to be a derivative of the cold site, with no guarantee of timely service. If a mobile site can be reliably obtained, a practical application may be to use the site as an interim facility for the months after leaving a hot site, but before reoccupying a permanent site.

Table 8.2 shows the basic differences between the types of alternate site options.

TABLE 8.2 Comparison of recovery site types

Type	Recovery Time	Basic Advantage
Redundant	Seconds	Always online and processing. Staff is in place and working. Perfect for high-priority processing that cannot be interrupted.
Hot site	Hours	Preconfigured, just restore data files. Designed for rapid 4- to 24-hour recovery of applications.
Warm site	Days	Cheaper. Will need to assemble equipment and activate communication lines.
Cold site	Weeks	Cheapest. Provides a building shell without equipment. Used for noncritical recovery or staging of salvaged assets.
Mobile site	8+ hours to days	Can supplement damaged facilities at original site. Can be configured with equipment equal to hot, warm, or cold site depending on customer's interest.
Outsource	Minutes to weeks	Shift operations to a subcontractor. This buys time for the organization to focus all efforts on making revenue. Operations may return in-house or not. Overall cost/benefit needs to be determined outside the affected departments to prevent bias over job loss.

Create a Fortification in Place It may be determined that an acceptable option is to create a fortress out of an existing facility. Fortifications can be made to compensate for minor natural disasters and varying degrees of man-made disasters. The fortification process requires a significant investment in structural reinforcement. Unfortunately, the fortification may not survive acts of terrorism, airborne contaminants of chemical or biological nature, flood, or mandatory evacuation. History is riddled with thousands of years' worth of failed fortifications.

Reciprocal Agreements This option is based on the belief that two organizations could render mutual aid to each other to save money. Unfortunately, often neither organization has the free space or excess capacity to support the other. Two organizations in the same geographic area could also be affected by the same event. Issues of security and noncompetition will also exist. Traditionally, reciprocal agreements are both unenforceable and unrealistic.

Data Backup Strategy Every recovery strategy requires data to be kept on backup tapes. The tapes need to be managed by a librarian, as discussed in Chapter 2 and Chapter 6, "System Implementation and Operations." The speed of recovery (RTO) is affected by the time needed for the restoration process to run. When selecting the data backup strategy, it is important to consider the time necessary for data restoration. Care should be given to ensure that the RTO and RPO are met. The typical data backup strategy implements one of the following methods:

Full Backup   Creates an entire copy of each file on the system. This is the most effective backup method and requires a significant amount of time. It's common for a full backup to be run at least once per week, but the frequency of your backup should depend on the value of your data. To restore data, the computer operator loads the latest full backup, usually from tapes. Next, the most current data is loaded by using files from a subsequent incremental or differential backup tape. *System-State Imaging* is the newest method of making a complete electronic backup of everything to extra hard disks immediately prior to writing data to a fast tape drive. Only tape is dependable enough to restore data from a specific point in time. Good tape cartridges will last for years.

Cooperative recovery sites in banking are an exception for reciprocal agreements. Small banks in the financial industry frequently operate a shared hot site as a cooperative venture. Banking laws require even the smallest bank to prove its continuity strategy on a quarterly basis. Several smaller banks will form a cooperative to rent or purchase the necessary recovery site facilities. If a smaller bank fails to prove an effective recovery capability, federal regulators will reassign all of the small bank's accounts to a larger bank.

Don't assume the same backup strategy is the right approach for everyone. Listen to the RTO and RPO requirements from the BIA. For example, CertTest's internal servers run a full backup twice a day for everything related to our customers and seminar classes. CertTest's internal servers have an RPO of 4 hours with 2-hour RTO. Full backups will restore a complete system faster than any other method of restoration.

Incremental Method   Copies only the files that have changed since the last backup. The incremental method is commonly used for backups on weekdays. This method requires less time than a full backup. Unfortunately, the file restoration process takes longer because it is necessary to restore the full backup and each version of incremental backup. An incremental backup resets the archive bit (backup flag) to indicate that a file needs to be backed up. If any of the tapes or disks in incremental restoration fail, the RPO will also fail. Incremental recovery requires using more tapes.

Differential Method   Copies every file that has changed between full backup runs. Differential is the preferred method for business continuity. This method ensures that multiple copies of daily files should exist on multiple tapes. A differential backup is very fast on the first day after a full backup, and then takes longer each day as more files are copied. A differential backup works because the backup software does not change the archive bit (backup flag).

Insurance   Most business continuity/disaster recovery planners review insurance during the risk assessment phase. Insurance carries several risks, including significant delays in receiving payments, likelihood of claims being denied, and difficulties proving financial loss within the policy limitations. Insurance is commonly used for durable goods, property, and life or casualty. Most policies pay for only a percentage of loss and do not include lost income, increased operating expenses, or consequential loss.

WARNING   Some insurance claims are never paid. Businesses in the World Trade Center at the time of the 1993 bombing in New York City have yet to receive any financial settlements for damages or the extended utility service outages. Similarly, it's doubtful any business will receive payment for Sept 11, 2001. Acts of war are excluded from insurance policies.

Insurance is available for a variety of situations. Let's look at a few of the types of insurance available:

Property Insurance   Property insurance provides financial protection against the loss of or damage to physical property—for example, burglary, plate glass damage, and fire. It may include coverage for the loss of income-producing ability.

Casualty Insurance   Casualty insurance revolves around legal liability for losses caused by injury to other people. Examples include robbery and workers compensation insurance.

Fidelity Insurance or Bonding   This protects the employer from theft caused by a dishonest employee. This type of insurance also covers embezzlement and fraudulent acts. To collect on this policy, the employer may need to prosecute the employee and win each court trial to a final conviction. Final conviction usually takes two to four years.

Omissions and Errors Insurance   A special policy covering administrative omissions and errors by corporate executives. This is commonly referred to as O&E insurance.

Machinery Insurance (or Boiler Insurance)   Covers accidental loss to machinery and equipment. It is called *boiler insurance* for historic reasons from 100 years ago. This type of insurance can cover almost any mechanical or electrical device.

Business Interruption (BI) Insurance   A policy that covers consequential losses of earnings due to property loss. Business interruption insurance typically pays a historical average of earnings during the coverage period. This type of insurance typically covers the fixed operating cost while business operations are suspended. The cost of premiums may be high.

The number one concern with insurance is that potential loss decisions have been transferred to the insurance company. The insurance company may decide that salvage is inevitable. The cost of salvage is usually less than 15 percent of the cost of replacement. Salvage operations may take weeks and place the organization in a bind. Costs of salvage may be reimbursed for only a particular amount of services from a preauthorized vendor.

Stockpile of Supplies   It is a common practice to stockpile supplies in preparation for recovery. These include common office supplies, items with long lead time, and spare parts. Stockpiling supplies is in direct conflict with just-in-time (JIT) inventory practices. A rule is to stockpile 30 days' worth of consumable supplies at the offsite or alternate storage facility.

Figure 8.7 shows the various recovery strategies compared to the amount of time it would take to resume processing.

FIGURE 8.7   Recovery options compared to time

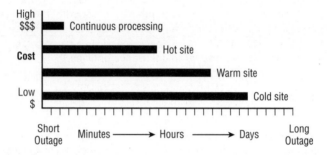

Incident Command System

Command and control function in emergency response is considered part of the "foundation" information that every business continuity/disaster recovery professional is expected to know early in planning for the project. An *incident* is defined as a negative or harmful event that involves people, property, or assets. After the event occurs, regaining control over the situation is a challenge. Advance planning is necessary to ensure that personnel are properly trained. Each response activity needs to be coordinated to ensure timeliness and the safety of personnel. The number one priority in an emergency response is the safety of life. Nothing has a higher priority.

To develop emergency response procedures and document them as part of the plan, the business continuity/disaster recovery planner needs to understand how to fulfill the following objectives:

Set Activation Criteria   Management needs to create a set of criteria for declaring a business continuity emergency. The criteria should clearly state a set of conditions that would dictate activation of the plan. Nobody wants to be the one who is accused of crying wolf and activating the plan too early. As a result, management will delay activating a plan that compromises the recovery window. If you wait too long, it may become impossible to recover. Use easy-to-understand criteria. For example, set criteria to be based on the following:

- Major injury to persons.
- Time. If it appears that the business operation will be interrupted for more than 4 hours for any reason, the plan should be activated.

- Unknown severity. If you don't know the severity of the impact, it's time to declare.
- Management response using the activation criteria. A rule should be instituted that if the criteria are met, the senior manager is required to declare plan activation. This removes uncertainty from the process.

Identify Potential Emergencies   What are the types of emergencies and the appropriate responses necessary? Consider, for example, fire, hazardous materials leak, collapse, terrorism, and medical emergencies. Each event contains unique response requirements; however, all events include the following:

- Reporting procedures for communicating information during the emergency. This information will be necessary after the event to justify actions taken and to provide evidence for legal challenges, insurance claims, and personnel training.
- Pre-incident preparation, making plans for responding to the crisis situation with equipment, planning, and training.
- Emergency actions to be taken to protect life, provide safety, minimize loss, and contain the situation.

Emergency Response Procedures   Identify the existence of, or develop, appropriate emergency response procedures. Most organizations have varying degrees of plans under different departments. Plans would include the following:

- Personnel protection procedures
- Emergency declaration process with procedures designed to contain the incident
- Procedures to assess the situation
- Procedures for communicating with responders, employees, customers, vendors, and the media
- Procedures for providing emergency response and triage
- Salvage and restoration procedures

Invocation Procedures   Establish invocation procedures to activate the alternate site. The decision to activate the alternate site will cascade into a variety of tasks necessary for recovery or relocation. The hot site vendor will accept an activation request from only a list of preauthorized individuals. The activation process will cost the organization a significant sum of money for exercising the declaration. This is how the hot site vendor ensures that the client is serious about activation. Activation costs may be $50,000 to $500,000 each time. It depends on the scope of your need.

Use Preplanned Decision Trees to Minimize On-the-Spot Decisions   Establish written procedures with decision trees to lead management and others in determining the best actions to take in response to a specific situation. A decision tree is a logical process of questions and answers, often in the format of a flowchart. As you ask the question, the answer will lead you through the decision tree until a final decision is reached. If you can't agree before the stress induced by the emergency, you can bet that decisions during the emergency will be questionable. Now is the time to work out the decision criteria—before you need it.

Integrate Separate Plans into One Comprehensive Plan   Integrate disaster recovery/business continuity procedures with emergency response procedures, creating one comprehensive plan. Everyone must be executing the same objectives and agreed-upon procedures in order to combat conflicting efforts and time delay in recovery. The last thing you need is someone attempting to push their own agenda ahead of predefined priorities. Changing sequence or emphasis is a sure sign of a pending failure by interrupting the recovery sequence.

Use the Incident Command System   The international Incident Command System (ICS) is used worldwide by first responders to identify who's in charge and coordinate all the various teams of people working on the problem. An expanded version is called the Unified Command System (UCS) and is included within the U.S. National Incident Command System (NIMS: 2007). It would be unrealistic to expect public authorities to conform to your leadership method; therefore, you need to conform to theirs. ICS outlines roles and duties regarding the following:

Incident Commander (IC)   The first person on the scene is the incident commander until relieved by a more qualified individual. The incident commander is in charge, leading on-scene activities in the field during the emergency response. All response team leaders report to the incident commander. A field command post is established to off-load logistical tasks from the IC. Incident commanders direct emergency teams and communicate to the field command post. Field command provides support services and coordination for the IC. Field command keeps the Emergency Operations Center (EOC) updated with the current status of the crisis control efforts. Figure 8.8 shows the roles and reporting structure of the Incident Command System.

FIGURE 8.8   Roles in the Incident Command System

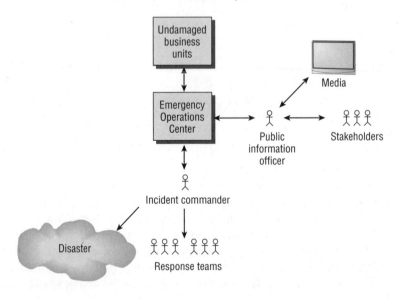

Emergency Operations Center (EOC)   The Emergency Operations Center (EOC) serves as command headquarters for the emergency management team (EMT). This team of executives makes decisions and takes actions based on reports from the IC. The EMT uses procedures outlined in the business continuity plan to provide crisis communication with stakeholders regarding support recovery plans. The EOC handles all communications with the undamaged portions of the business still in operation. A designated public information officer (PIO) handles all media communications. Some key investors may want to see the EOC in operation, and a degree of caution is urged before you agree to allow financially interested observers in a crisis. Negative observations could rattle investor confidence.

Document Command and Decision Authorities   Multiple authorities may respond to your emergency, and each will carry the full authority of their position. You can gain their trust and cooperation by demonstrating your ability to provide leadership. This can buy you time and grace to extend your business continuity efforts. You will be pushed aside if you fail to attain or maintain their confidence. This can get confusing, and the time to work out conflicts is before the crisis.

Create Procedures for Opening the EOC and Providing Extra Security   The media and competitors will likely have great interest in your situation. Details could make an interesting news story or competitive battle. To survive the situation, you must remain in control.

Create Explicit Definitions of Authority Roles   Recommend and develop command and control procedures to define roles, authority, and communications processes for managing an emergency.

Incident Management Plan

By now the individual strategies have been converted into an overall incident management plan for the targeted business unit process under protection. This incorporates the BIA M4 requirements (methods, manpower, machinery, materials), risk activation triggers, activity response plans, communications, and resources. One of the major subsets is the communications plan component.

Our stakeholders and clients are always interested to hear how an organization has succeeded or failed miserably in their endeavors. The planner needs to design an uninterruptible communications system with access via multiple delivery methods. Controlling communications with the public and the company's stakeholders is essential to surviving a crisis.

Buy-in from the highest level of the company needs to be obtained to enforce a policy that improper and unauthorized communications during a declared disaster is a terminating offense with possible legal repercussions.

Support plans need to be created for employees and their families. Be aware that trauma counseling may be required for employees, their families, and even corporate management during a crisis.

The business continuity planner must make sure that all stakeholders, key customers, critical suppliers, and owners/stockholders are kept informed as appropriate during the crisis to avoid confusion or distrust. The time to build confidence is before the event occurs. During the event, the focus is to communicate status information and immediate needs. People need to feel that the situation is under control and being properly handled. Without timely communication, it is human nature to grow restless and distrustful. Let's look at some of the more common techniques for better communication:

Employee Check-In Aids   Provisions should be made for employee check-in after the declaration has been made. Individuals may attempt to check in and provide information concerning their status. Failure to account for personnel would be a serious problem. A common solution is to use 800 numbers answered by an operator in a message center. This could easily be outsourced to a telemarketing firm. The operator asks questions concerning the employee's status and whether the employee requires additional aid. Business travelers also can be accounted for through an 800 service. Another method is to implement a secure website database for check-in.

Prioritized Calling List (Call Tree)   Outbound notification can be executed through a combination of live personnel and automated systems. Telephone numbers are sequenced according to the priority of the individual. Senior executives and recovery team leaders are, of course, a high priority. A scripted message is delivered to each individual with a short explanation of the situation. The message should conclude with instructions explaining what the organization is requesting the individual to do.

Alternate Communications   All business continuity planning exercises incorporate a worst-case scenario. The loss of communications would definitely be the worst possible scenario. It is important to plan for alternate communication methods. Each communication method needs to be properly implemented and monitored during a crisis. Alternate methods can be accomplished via private radio, wired Internet access, cellular voice/data communications, and satellite voice/data communications.

A satellite phone with voice and data capability makes communication easy. For example, my satellite phone was purchased used for less than $300 on eBay. The satellite phone was the only dependable method of communication for several days in remote areas or following a disaster. The satellite phone data kit made it possible to access the Internet in less than 1 minute when normal cellular service was inoperable.

Public Information Officer (PIO)   As previously discussed, controls are necessary to prevent damage or loss to the organization. A public information officer should be appointed as the sole media contact. This individual is the spokesperson for the organization through the entire crisis. A public information officer should be a well-spoken individual with a professional voice for radio and a presentable appearance for television. This role may be fulfilled by the vice president of marketing or another senior executive. Occasionally, the PIO is contracted through a public-relations vendor.

The time to communicate actions is before the crisis. Then the staff will face a lesser challenge of communicating the level of success or status attained under the plan. All communications should be based in prewritten templates that have been vetted for proper effect. Don't make the company look foolish to the public.

Communicating with our team members, public authorities, vendors and influential stakeholders is a key element to success. It is essential that accurate information is available to investors, clients, and proper authorities.

Writing the Plan

Nothing goes out-of-date faster than a big book of plans. The written plan must be clear, intuitively organized, and easy to read. The business continuity plan is usually a multi-volume set. The best practice is to use a modular design to enhance security and updating.

Full sets are kept at offsite storage and at the EOC. Security and version control are paramount concerns. This set of plans contains all the organization's secrets, process blueprints, and documented priorities.

Figure 8.9 shows the content outline for creating the plan.

FIGURE 8.9   Creating the plan structure and content

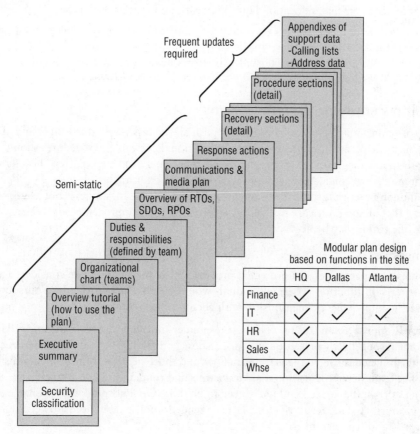

The plan should be organized for quick and easy location of personnel duties and specific procedures. A suggested layout includes sections for the following:

- Executive summary to provide a brief overview of the plan's purpose, scope, and assumptions.
- Command and control instructions to identify who is actually in charge.
- Life safety procedures. Protection of life is the highest priority.
- Emergency response activities, including incident containment procedures and environmental protection plans.
- Asset protection strategy and procedures. A copy of inventory and vital materials will be useful.
- Recovery plans to support restoration and resumption efforts. What are some alternate site provisions? Did you include a copy of the risk analysis?
- Administration and logistics designed to keep appropriate records of the event, maintain the emergency budget, and provide support to the recovery effort. Logistics include transportation requirements, relocation housing, meals, and sanitation needs.

The plan is intended to provide everyone with clear instructions on where each person is to report for work and what they will be working on at various time intervals. The business will not be running business as usual. All efforts need to focus on the predetermined priorities in assigned sequence.

Assigning People to Specific Teams

Alternate personnel may be necessary to accomplish all the tasks within the RTO and SDO requirements. The plans should account for the additional personnel. Procedures should contain easy-to-follow diagrams, photographs, maps, flowcharts, and step-by-step checklists. A significant number of concurrent activities will need to be coordinated.

The common practice is to divide into teams. The number of personnel is not as important as ensuring that all job duties are fulfilled. A risk management approach needs to be used. The following teams may be needed:

Core functions

The business unit personnel of a protected process within the BC plan are considered a core revenue or mission function. These individuals would be extremely difficult to outsource due to specific knowledge or relationship with clients and investors.

Emergency Response Team (ERT)   The first responders internal to the organization. This team has the responsibility of accounting for personnel and rendering aid. The emergency response team includes fire wardens for each floor and those persons trained in administering first aid. The team may provide initial aid to victims and route injured personnel to the hospital. During a crisis, the injured will likely need to be routed to a hospital with available capacity, not necessarily the nearest hospital. The emergency response team needs to keep track of the location of injured personnel.

Emergency Management Team (EMT) Executives and line managers able to make tough decisions at the Emergency Operations Center. This team coordinates the managers still operating undamaged areas of the business. The EMT makes decisions about the allocation of personnel necessary to support the response and recovery effort. The leaders of each team report to the emergency management team.

Business Unit Recovery Team Each business unit will have its own recovery team to focus on restoring its operation. This team may comprise the power users in a particular business unit. The business unit plan may be of a smaller or larger scale than the plan of the head office.

Communications and Media Relations Team Poor communications is frequently more damaging than your actual disaster. Clients, investors, partners, employees, and stakeholders need to be kept informed and feel comfortable with the information they receive. Internal and external messages need to be properly vetted by the PIO's staff to convey the intended message. A schedule of communications and scripted messages needs to be developed by the BC marketing team in advance. Plans need to include an uninterruptible communication system, which is not prone to the same outages as cell phones or land lines.

This team works with the PIO to deliver communication via radio, phone, fax, and TV. The team uses preapproved scripts from the PIO and EMT for communication to employees, stockholders, clients, and the media. Provisions are made for both inbound and outbound communication. All outbound communication to the media is handled by a designated PIO. Media relations involve issuing news releases, scheduling press conferences, and providing a controlled release of information to the news. News reporters will get the story one way or another, so stories should be released in a manner that demonstrates the organization's care, concern, and control of the situation. The media team needs to be aware of local and national broadcast deadlines. The plan will be needed to communicate with the appropriate personnel and each of the news agencies.

Marketing and Customer Support Team It is imperative to maintain communication with customers. The customer support team provides communication and reassurance to customers. Key customers will want to know that their needs will be met by the organization. Some customers may be impacted by the same event and may require the assistance of the organization—for example, customers may need to reschedule airline tickets because of a hurricane, while the airline is evacuating its own headquarters to a safer location. The customer support team may be a combination of in-house personnel and services contracted through an external vendor. The business does not want customers to switch vendors or cancel orders. The goal is to ensure that the organization continues to receive revenue even if the organization is not shipping a product.

External Agency Team This team coordinates with fire, police, the Federal Emergency Management Agency (FEMA), the FBI, and other government agencies. At least one dedicated liaison equivalent to organizational vice-president authority should be assigned for each agency expected to respond. Leaving a government official waiting is high on the list of bad ideas.

Supporting Functions:

These teams provide services directly required to support collection of revenue. Supporting functions might be outsourced.

Logistics Team   This team handles administrative support activities necessary to relocate personnel and equipment. The team facilitates resumption efforts by providing meals and rest locations for workers. The team also is responsible for transportation, mail rerouting, and a thousand other administrative details necessary to support the recovery effort.

Personnel Team   Human Resources will be a busy place. Employees and their families will need assistance with benefits. Time and attendance tracking will be necessary for the workers. A process for rapid staff augmentation will be required.

Damage Assessment Team   Works with structural engineers to assess damage to the facility. This team is trained to provide accurate analysis and estimates of the impact. This team works with the safety team for matters of safe reentry to the facility.

Finance Team   This team provides budget control for recovery and accurate accounting of costs. It would be a shame to overspend on the recovery effort and later fail due to insolvency. The recovery costs may qualify for special financial aid. It is often necessary to file claims early, before recovery funding disappears. Special tracking may be implemented to identify the response and recovery costs.

Legal Team   The organization's lawyers may be able to provide assistance and advice to the emergency management team. This advice could include dealing with regulators, government bureaucracy, extensions on filing deadlines, and confidential matters.

Discretionary Functions

Discretionary functions may be a hybrid of internal or outsourced to improve response time while obtaining the best recovery time objective (RTO). These functions provide commodity level support outside of the core business unit activity. Discretionary functions normally do not generate direct revenue by themselves. These functions can be provided by any competent provider.

IT Recovery Teams   They may be deployed on site at the incident and/or the alternate site depending on the situation. The IT recovery teams typically comprise several smaller teams, each with a unique specialty. Each of these functions would be operating in parallel to save time. The smaller teams include the following:

> **IT Hardware Recovery**   The hardware recovery team focuses on getting the hardware up and running as rapidly as possible in accordance with the RTO and SDO. Hardware recovery may be split into two categories: server hardware and user workstations.

> **Software Loading**   As hardware is recovered, a software-loading process begins. This may be from a tape backup, disk image, or program CDs.

> **Server Applications**   Application programs and data from tape are loaded onto servers as the hardware becomes available. This process may be dependent on the IT hardware

recovery function. After software loading is complete, the systems administrator or database administrator verifies that the application is functioning correctly. After the application is up and running, users may log in and begin using it. Complex databases may require the dedicated attention of several technical personnel.

Network Communications   This group ensures that computer and telephone communication are back online. The process may entail verifying that redundant circuits are functioning correctly, installing new connections as needed, or working with a recommended vendor to expedite changes in order to restore service.

Data Entry   The data entry personnel focus on reloading the most recent transactions and executing manual procedures during recovery. This may be an in-house or outsourced function.

User Support   This team assists users in restoring individual workstations. It provides special assistance for workarounds to help persons with the greatest impact on the recovery effort. Normal user support may be suspended during the recovery effort. The help desk focuses on finding user support necessary to achieve the stated RTO and SDO.

Salvage Team   The salvage team is responsible for onsite cleanup and recovery of assets. This team inventories, stages, and coordinates the salvage of assets. This team also is responsible for creating documentation to be used for insurance filings, legal actions (lawsuits), and future training exercises. The team will need provisions for site security during the salvage effort.

Safe Operations Team (Safety Team)   The safety team supervises activities to ensure that nobody is placed in a hazardous work situation. This team can terminate any activity that is deemed to endanger personnel. The safety team ensures that workers are adequately protected from hazards, including potentially hazardous material or precarious work environments. The objective is to ensure that no additional injuries occur after the initial impact.

Property and Insurance Teams   The property team assists with locating or rebuilding the office. An inventory of each facility, including space requirements and furniture needs, is used to help guide the selection of suitable offices for the interim need and long-term requirements. The insurance team works to get claims processed and paid. Insurance loss consultants may be hired to help increase the dollar amount of the insurance settlement.

Vendor Team   This team provides coordination with key vendors. The organization may need to make special requests of vendors to facilitate recovery. It will also be necessary to ensure that the vendor does not close the line of credit or delay shipment of product.

Phase 4: Plan Implementation

Training programs need to be implemented to educate staff about the plan, its limitations, and the procedures they will be expected to execute. Training can take many forms, including seminars, workshops, video presentations, and individual training sessions.

The training plan is designed to increase the proficiency of every individual. Some individuals will require specialized training for assertiveness, crisis resource management, and medical procedures. An individual who is unable to fill a role for any reason should be moved to another support area. If it is a senior manager, the best use may be to fulfill an advisory role. Some individuals will not be mentally capable to lead under the heavy burden of crisis command.

Successful planners know how to set up training exercises for individual components of the plan each week. The training is combined with modular testing to build both awareness and skills. Training exercises should be designed to reinforce the following:

- Plan objectives (scope)
- Work procedures (RT, RPO, SDO)
- Technical details (LWIP, RWIP)
- Administrative personal skills (activities and communications)
- Realistic scenarios

Which do you think is better: a doctor aware of your condition or a doctor skilled in actually doing the work? Failing to train indicates a management failure.

Successful execution of the business continuity plan will depend on training with thorough testing. Without testing, the plan is sure to fail. Testing should begin with small processes and gradually build into testing larger functional processes. You need to focus on tests that support the core processes first. Every training exercise should be timed and witnessed by a qualified observer. The objective is to record lessons learned and record data for an accurate estimate of the actual recovery time. By tracking the metrics of the PERT timeline, RT, RTO, RPO, SDO, and LWIP/RWIP, you will be able to benchmark improvement or reengineer the strategy:

Desktop Review (Paper Exercise)   The simplest test is a desktop review. All the plans and documentation are laid out across the table and reviewed for obvious errors in consistency. Participants from each major area walk through the plans for a general review of accuracy. The purpose of the desktop review is to groom the document and eliminate obvious errors. After the errors are corrected, the next step is a functional test.

Functional (Modular Exercise)   In the functional test, actual procedures are executed by staff members. This provides an opportunity for hands-on training. During this training process, it is possible to view the effectiveness of both the procedure and actions by personnel. Functional testing is an extremely important component of preparedness. A functional test of the calling list, for example, could be used for notification of a company party. Another example is to use the business continuity procedures to train new staff members for their regular jobs. When you think about it, there are a number of opportunities for executing a small-scale functional test. An evaluator should grade the test exercise and make any recommendations for improvement. The first functional tests will start small, and then incorporate other functional tests with a growing scope. The final objective is to ensure that the full-scale business processes are properly supported.

Preparedness Simulation   In the preparedness simulation, the staff is asked to react to a particular scenario as if it were a real event. The preparedness of each team is judged as well as the overall preparedness of the organization to respond. A preparedness simulation consumes resources and supplies. The objective is to carry out each activity to ensure that the staff is capable of responding properly. The next step after preparedness simulation is to perform a full operation test.

Full Operation Exercise   Testing should be planned and structured to ensure that the test does not create injury to persons or damage to the organization. Tests should be announced with warning to prevent panic. A well-known provision needs to exist to cancel the test if a real emergency occurs during the drill. Each drill needs to be preplanned, staged, executed, and subjected to a review. The lessons learned are recorded.

Figure 8.10 shows the life cycle of testing and exercising the plan.

FIGURE 8.10   The life cycle of testing and exercising the plan

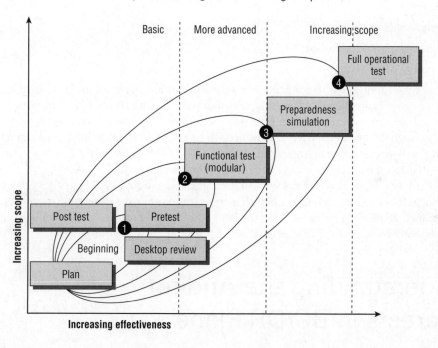

I strongly advise all professionals to adopt the terminology of *exercising* business continuity plans, rather than testing plans. The word *test* denotes passing or failing. A failing score will usually demoralize or alienate staff members. Nobody wants to be associated with a failure. A simple solution is to build on the concept of exercising for improvement. Athletes exercise to prepare to run marathons. The organization is no different.

The results of test exercises are used to gain support from management and buy-in from the team members. Testing is like auditing: You don't have to do it all at once. Failure to test indicates a management failure.

Phase 5: Maintenance and Integration

People have to practice their roles to gain proficiency, and a change control system will be needed to improve the documentation. It is impossible to keep plans current without structured exercises to improve skills and identify deficiencies.

After all this work, the performance data from training exercises and observations is reincorporated into planning revisions. The executive strategy may need to be revisited if the recovery times are too long. It's important to confirm the objectives, because they will change over time due to organizational changes and new market opportunities.

Four basic areas to reconsider at least annually are as follows:

- Clients

- Operational changes

- Marketing/public relations

- Planning assumptions

Each organization needs to reach out to its clients, business partners, and government agencies to coordinate the organization's plans and strategy with theirs. No organization is an island. Every business depends on someone else for revenue, investment, and support. The business continuity/disaster recovery plans need to be reviewed and modified to incorporate cooperation between different organizations. An annual GAP analysis (good, average, or poor) will help focus attention on areas in need of improvement.

It is extremely likely that your plans will need to change to support key vendors and your most valuable clients. The strategies between organizations may be different, or priorities may conflict. Depending on the scale of the issue, this may require you to rerun the entire process in order to create the next generation of planning.

Understanding the Auditor Interests in BC/DR Plans

Let's summarize with the points of interest that an IS auditor should look for. We have discussed the basic objectives to be fulfilled by management. It is the auditor's job to determine how well those objectives have been served. The auditor can use the following points for evaluation:

- Compare the results of the business impact and risk analysis to the various strategies selected for each activity in the overall process timeline. Do the BIA research and work flow based risk assessment support management's strategy?

- Time delays are an absolute killer of business continuity plans. Has the client done a good job of documenting the RTOs? Are the recovery time objectives well founded and realistic? Does the organization have the hardware and skills necessary to recover data in sufficient time to meet each RTO?

- Ask whether the organization's document outlines a 0- to 100-hour timeline. This type of timeline sequences and prioritizes the recovery by using RT, RP, RTO, RPO, LWIP, RWIP, SDO, and RO. The presence of this document is a powerful statement in favor of the client. Absence of this document foretells a questionable future.

- Work backlogs exist every day in business. How does the organization intend to handle the backlog when the processing capability is significantly diminished? Manual methods are usually proposed because of the low cost; however, substantial testing would be required to prove that the organization could manually keep up with the volume of work.

- An audit of the vital records inventory will tell an interesting story. Well-organized vital records foretell the future of a successful recovery.

- When was the most recent training exercise? It would be valuable to review the exercise plan, the results, and the schedule of future exercises. Plans must be exercised regularly to remain effective.

Summary

Business continuity planning is an involved process of preparation. The focus of this preparation could be to exploit new revenue opportunities, or, in a more limited plan, to simply rebuild in response to a disaster. The organization may be more concerned about protecting a particular line of business or a highly prized customer.

This concludes our chapter on disaster recovery and business continuity for CISA candidates. The subject is far deeper and broader than you will encounter for your CISA exam. Just remember that the next step after a control failure is a business continuity situation. According to the stories in the news, there is plenty of room for improvement.

Exam Essentials

Know the difference between business continuity and disaster recovery.   Disaster recovery is focused on rebuilding the organization. After obtaining the disaster recovery plan, the organization can upgrade plans to include business continuity. Business continuity ensures that critical revenue-producing processes continue.

Understand the requirements for business process resumption.   It is not necessary for all the business processes to be resumed immediately. The core business processes that generate revenue will be recovered first; supporting processes are recovered second. Noncritical, or discretionary, processes will be recovered last if they are recovered at all.

Know the business impact analysis and the value it represents.   The business impact analysis will generate a blueprint of the current business processes. The BIA is used to define the recovery priorities and sequence timing of activities in the plan. Without the BIA, it would be impossible to generate a business continuity plan. Without the BIA, the best one could hope for would be a disaster recovery plan.

Understand the key terms describing business priorities.   The recovery targets (RTs) represent the priority during recovery. The recovery time objective (RTO) defines the target time when the system will be back online. The recovery point objective (RPO) defines the amount of acceptable data loss (lost work in progress) that will occur because of the interruption. The service delivery objective (SDO) specifies the level of service at a particular time in the recovery plan. Re-created or salvaged data transactions are known as recovered work in process (RWIP). The recovery plan will specify multiple RTs, RTOs, RPOs, and SDOs during the recovery timeline. Ultimately, the goal is to recover fast enough to reach your executive's revenue objective (RO) before shutting down the business unit because of financial instability.

Understand how the business continuity plan is developed.   The business continuity plan should be developed in a modular format. The business continuity planning exercise coordinates development of a clear and well-defined set of steps to accomplish the strategic objectives. Individual procedure plans will be created by the team leaders representing the key stakeholders. An ongoing series of revisions will groom the plan to become the best possible response to almost any event, whether it's a disaster or sudden surge in business volume. The plan will require special security controls because of the sensitive nature of its contents.

Understand providing for personnel management.   In the business continuity plan and the disaster recovery plan, it is imperative that procedures exist to ensure the direction and control of personnel. Temporary personnel and contractors will be joining the recovery effort. Human resources will need to provide support for employees and employee benefits.

Know the emergency plan invocation process.   The emergency plan needs to be designed with simple, easy-to-understand invocation criteria. The most effective method is based on the level of destruction or the estimated magnitude of the outage. A senior executive is responsible for invoking the recovery process.

Know the types of alternate sites.   A recovery strategy may include redundant sites, hot sites, warm sites, and cold sites. The redundant site is always parallel to normal production and available within seconds. The hot site is preconfigured, just waiting for the backup to be restored before resuming processing, and is available within hours. The warm site will require equipment to be set up and shipped in and is available for processing within days. A cold site is no more than the building and requires everything to be shipped in and set up. The cold site will be available for processing within weeks.

Understand how to control communications and the media during the emergency.   All communications must be predefined and vetted before distribution. The public information officer (PIO) should be the only spokesperson to the media. Stakeholder communication should occur in a confidential manner. All communication must occur at regular intervals to promote trust and confidence.

Review Questions

1. Which of the following acronyms refer to the expected level of service during recovery?

    A. RTO

    B. SDO

    C. RPO

    D. ITO

2. A critical success factor is defined as which of the following?

    A. A measure or score of efficiency

    B. An asset to be planned

    C. Something that must occur perfectly every time

    D. A factor that is calculated for insurance purposes

3. Which of these is the most significant issue to consider regarding insurance coverage?

    A. Salvage may be dictated rather than replacement.

    B. Premiums may be very expensive.

    C. Coverage must include all business assets.

    D. Insurance can pay for all the costs of recovery.

4. The ultimate obstacles to business continuity are threats that may include which of the following?

    A. Natural disasters

    B. Missed targets

    C. Loss of profit

    D. All of the above

5. When planning team assignments, it is more important to remember which of the following?

    A. Nobody should hold more than one team assignment.

    B. The number of people or number of teams is not as important as making sure all the duties are performed.

    C. A single key person can be assigned to all teams for consistency.

    D. The number of duties is the same for each team.

6. What is the principal reason you might use a hot site?

    A. Expensive, but already configured for our use

    B. May not be available during a crisis

    C. Expensive, but we will have to install and configure new equipment

    D. Expensive and prevents us from using other warm or cold site alternatives

7. What does the term *MAO* stand for?

   A. Minimum acceptable outage

   B. Maximum acceptable outage

   C. Minimum available on-hand

   D. Maximum available overnight

8. In business continuity, why it is important to replicate every process?

   A. To ensure 100 percent full operational capabilities

   B. Market pressures

   C. Not important, only select processes will continue

   D. To protect the company reputation

9. Name one of the purposes of creating the business continuity plan.

   A. To maximize the number of decisions made during an incident

   B. To minimize decisions needed during a crisis

   C. To lower business insurance premiums

   D. To provide guidance for federal regulations

10. What does the acronym *EOC* represent?

   A. Emergency Office Complex

   B. Evacuate Office Center

   C. Emergency Offensive Controls

   D. Emergency Operations Center

11. News media attention should be

   A. Directed to a single designated spokesperson

   B. Used to create awareness of the crisis and warn the public

   C. Restricted to prevent any information from being released

   D. Allowed full access to interview staff

12. When can continuity planners create BC plans without the business impact analysis (BIA) process?

   A. When business impact analysis is not required.

   B. When management already dictated all the key processes to be used.

   C. It's not possible; critical processes constantly change.

   D. If risk assessment is acceptable.

13. What should signal that the business continuity plan needs to be updated?

   A. Time and market conditions

   B. Personnel changes

   C. Significant changes in business objectives or direction

   D. All of the above

14. Why is plan testing important?

    A. To prove that the plan worked the first time

    B. To find and correct problems

    C. To show the team that is not pulling their own weight

    D. To verify that everyone shows up at the recovery site

15. What are the best examples of vital records and media?

    A. Specialized forms, financial records, how-to manuals, backup tapes

    B. Past annual reports, last year's cancelled checks, vacation forms, HR policies

    C. Preferred vendor lists, personal desk files, extra blank paper for copy machine

    D. Customer lists, office supplies, maintenance manuals, corporate seal

16. Which of the following should be considered when setting your business continuity strategy?

    A. Recovery time objectives

    B. Alternate sites available

    C. Testing time available at alternate sites

    D. All of the above

17. What is the process to activate the business continuity plan?

    A. Members of the organization call the recovery site to activate.

    B. Management designates decision criteria and appoints authorized personnel.

    C. The facility manager receives a severe threat warning.

    D. The senior manager on duty makes the decision.

18. What is the fundamental difference between disaster recovery and business continuity?

    A. Disaster recovery is focused on natural disasters; business continuity deals with man-made events.

    B. Business continuity is focused on ensuring that none of the services are interrupted; disaster recovery deals with restoring services.

    C. Disaster recovery is focused on rebuilding; business continuity deals with revenue to continue in the market.

    D. Business continuity is focused on protecting the IT investment; disaster recovery applies to the entire organization.

19. What indicators are used to identify the anticipated level of recovery and loss at a given point in time?

    A. RPO and RTO

    B. RTO and SDO

    C. RPO and ITO

    D. SDO and IRO

20. What are the five phases of business continuity planning according to ISACA? (Select the answer showing the correct phases and order.)

A. Analyze business impact, develop strategy, develop plan, plan testing, implement

B. Analyze business impact, develop plan, implement, plan testing, write the plan

C. Analyze business impact, write the plan, test strategy, develop plan, implement

D. Analyze business impact, develop strategy, develop plan, implement, plan testing

21. When can a warm site be used for recovery?

A. When the downtime is acceptable to the business without breaching any legal requirements

B. When it's not profitable to operate a hot site

C. When the recovery is of high priority

D. When the actual recovery exceeds the recovery time objective

22. Which of the following methods of testing BC/DR plans is not acceptable?

A. Desktop

B. Modular

C. Full interruption

D. Unannounced

23. Which of these is the primary output from the business impact analysis (BIA)?

A. Identification of alternate revenue opportunities

B. Analysis of dependencies and areas of overreliance

C. High-level understanding of definitions

D. Low-level blueprint of the business process

24. Which of the following definitions is the best example of an RTO?

A. Target point of optimum data recovery

B. Target time for the user to be processing again with all work recovered.

C. Target service level at a particular point in time

D. Target for recovery to be completed

25. What is the biggest difference between disaster planning and business continuity planning?

A. Disaster plans are usually specific to a department.

B. Business continuity plans are run by IT.

C. Business continuity plans span department boundaries.

D. Disaster planning is an extension of facility plans.

Answers to Review Questions

1. B. The service delivery objective (SDO) illustrates the expected level of service during recovery. The organization may have several SDO targets based on the different phases of recovery. RTO is the recovery time objective, and RPO is the recovery point objective. ITO is a distractor.

2. C. A critical success factor is also known as a showstopper. Critical success factors must go right every time in order for recovery to be successful. A key performance indicator (KPI) is a numerical score.

3. A. The insurance company may dictate salvage to save money. Salvage will increase the delay before recovery. Any replacement purchases by the organization may not be covered under reimbursement.

4. D. The concerns in business continuity include natural disasters, missed targets, and loss of profit. The goal of continuity is to ensure that important targets are not missed and revenue is not interrupted.

5. B. The most important point to remember when planning team assignments is that all the duties are performed, regardless of the number of people. In major incidents, the organization may need to hire hundreds of extra personnel to ensure that all the duties are performed.

6. A. The hot site is expensive but offers a better chance for recovery because it is already configured for use and ready to go.

7. B. MAO is the maximum acceptable outage that can occur before critical deadlines are missed or recovery is no longer feasible because of the amount of time lapsed. MAO also may be referred to as maximum tolerable downtime (MTD).

8. C. Only critical processes will continue. The other processes will be interrupted while the organization focuses efforts to restore critical processes. Plans will sequence recovery by using service delivery objectives (SDOs), recovery point objectives (RPOs), and recovery time objectives (RTOs). A noncritical process might be shut down and never restarted.

9. B. The plan minimizes decisions needed during the crisis. Possible options would have been researched and decisions made in advance by management. The recovery staff is expected to follow the directions contained in the plan.

10. D. The EOC is the Emergency Operations Center, staffed by the emergency management team during a crisis.

11. A. All inquires and statements should be from the designated public information officer (PIO), the spokesperson for the organization. The PIO uses predefined scripts to deliver messages that have been vetted to ensure a positive image for the organization.

12. C. It is not possible to create business continuity plans without a current business impact analysis (BIA). The BIA will identify critical processes and their dependencies. The critical processes will change as the business changes with new products and customers.

13. D. The plan should be reviewed quarterly and updated at least annually. Updates should occur after each test, changes in personnel, or changes in business direction. Plans are often updated for changes in key customers and products.

14. B. Plans are tested to train the staff in carrying out their work. The intention is to find problems and correct any mistakes. A secondary benefit is to demonstrate improvement in the response and recovery efforts.

15. A. Financial records and backup tapes are extremely important. How-to manuals will help aid the recovery effort.

16. D. The strategy will be selected based on information obtained during the risk assessment and business impact analysis. All options should be considered when selecting the business continuity strategy.

17. B. The purpose of planning is to establish decision criteria in advance. After the criteria are met, the plan will be activated by the appointed personnel. The alternate site invocation process allows a preauthorized manager to activate the alternate site. Invocation of the alternate site will cost money and should occur only when it is required.

18. C. Business continuity is intended to ensure that critical processes are restored in a timely manner and that revenue is not interrupted. With revenue, the organization will acquire the money necessary to survive.

19. A. The recovery point objective (RPO) indicates the fallback position and duration of loss that has occurred. A valid RPO example is to recover by using backup data from last night's backup tape, meaning the more recent transactions have been lost. The recovery time objective (RTO) indicates a point in time that the restored data should be available for the user to access.

20. D. Notice that analyzing the business impact is always the first step. Then criteria are selected to guide the strategy selection. A detailed plan is written using the strategy. The written plan is then implemented. After implementation, the plan and staff are tested for effectiveness. The plan is revised, and then the testing and maintenance cycle begins.

21. A. The warm site is acceptable to the business when the downtime is acceptable without breaching any legal requirements. Making a profit is not the reason for using a warm site.

22. D. Unannounced testing is not acceptable because of the potential to create additional harm. Some people are not able to deal with the extra stress or may exercise the wrong response and create a real emergency.

23. D. A workflow featuring a low-level blueprint (or schematic) of the business process is the primary output from the business impact analysis (BIA). If performed correctly, the BIA will provide high-quality supporting detail for the other possible answer choices.

24. B. The recovery time objective (RTO) is the deadline for when the user must be processing again. IT is expected to have completed the necessary level of technical recovery. The user is able to resume processing work unless that RTO has failed.

25. C. Business continuity plans are focused on the processes for generating revenue. This is the biggest difference when compared to rebuilding in disaster recovery. Plans of the various departments such as IT, facilities, manufacturing, and sales may become smaller components of the final BC plan. All decisions and activities are determined by the revenue generated, not by the desires or goals of the department. The only agenda that matters is the CEO's agenda.

Additional CISA practice questions are available on the author's website at www.CertTest.com.

Appendix
A

About the Companion CD

IN THIS APPENDIX:

✓ What you'll find on the CD

✓ System requirements

✓ Using the CD

✓ Troubleshooting

What You'll Find on the CD

The following sections are arranged by category and summarize the software and other goodies you'll find on the CD. If you need help with installing the items provided on the CD, refer to the installation instructions in the "Using the CD" section of this appendix.

Sybex Test Engine

The CD contains the Sybex test engine, which includes the two bonus exams.

Electronic Flashcards

These handy electronic flashcards are just what they sound like. One side contains a question, and the other side shows the answer.

PDF of the Book

We have included an electronic version of the text in PDF format. You can view the electronic version of the book with Adobe Reader.

Adobe Reader

We've also included a copy of Adobe Reader so you can view PDF files that accompany the book's content. For more information on Adobe Reader or to check for a newer version, visit Adobe's website at www.adobe.com/products/reader/.

System Requirements

Make sure your computer meets the minimum system requirements shown in the following list. If your computer doesn't match up to most of these requirements, you may have problems using the software and files on the companion CD. For the latest and greatest information, please refer to the ReadMe file located at the root of the CD-ROM.

- A PC running Microsoft Windows 98, Windows 2000, Windows NT4 (with SP4 or later), Windows Me, Windows XP, Windows Vista, or Windows 7
- An Internet connection
- A CD-ROM drive

Using the CD

To install the items from the CD to your hard drive, follow these steps:

1. Insert the CD into your computer's CD-ROM drive. The license agreement appears.

 Windows users: The interface won't launch if you have autorun disabled. In that case, click Start ➢ Run (for Windows Vista or Windows 7, Start ➢ All Programs ➢ Accessories ➢ Run). In the dialog box that appears, type D:\ Start.exe. (Replace *D* with the proper letter if your CD drive uses a different letter. If you don't know the letter, see how your CD drive is listed under My Computer.) Click OK.

2. Read the license agreement, and then click the Accept button if you want to use the CD.

The CD interface appears. The interface allows you to access the content with just one or two clicks.

Troubleshooting

Wiley has attempted to provide programs that work on most computers with the minimum system requirements. Alas, your computer may differ, and some programs may not work properly for some reason.

The two likeliest problems are that you don't have enough memory (RAM) for the programs you want to use or you have other programs running that are affecting installation or running of a program. If you get an error message such as "Not enough memory" or "Setup cannot continue," try one or more of the following suggestions and then try using the software again:

Turn off any antivirus software running on your computer. Installation programs sometimes mimic virus activity and may make your computer incorrectly believe that it's being infected by a virus.

Close all running programs. The more programs you have running, the less memory is available to other programs. Installation programs typically update files and programs; so if you keep other programs running, installation may not work properly.

Have your local computer store add more RAM to your computer. This is, admittedly, a drastic and somewhat expensive step. However, adding more memory can really help the speed of your computer and allow more programs to run at the same time.

Customer Care

If you have trouble with the book's companion CD, please call the Wiley Product Technical Support phone number at (800) 762-2974.

Glossary

A

Acceptable use policy (AUP)   A formal statement of policy signed by management and acknowledged by the user with their signature. This policy typically is enforced by the Human Resources department. The policy should state that computing resources are for company business only and that noncompany activities, including those related to religion or topics of questionable use, are prohibited. The AUP should state that possession of administrative system utilities and related system tools not specifically authorized are prohibited as contraband. This eliminates any excuses or misunderstanding and enforces separation of duties.

Access control list (ACL)   A table of user login IDs specifying each user's individual level of access authorized to use computer resources. The access control list tells the computer which files the user is allowed to access.

Access rights   The level of permission granted to an individual user for the purpose of reading data, writing data, or executing specific programs. Access does not ensure any form of integrity or confidentiality.

Accountability   Responsibility, liability. To be accountable is to be liable for the final result or to be held responsible for one's actions.

Accreditation   A formal approval by management based on perceived fitness of use. Approval may be granted for a system, site location, or function. Accreditation occurs after system certification for a period of 90 days, 180 days, or one year. Systems must be reaccredited prior to expiration of their current accreditation period.

ACID principle   ACID stands for *atomicity* (write all or nothing), *consistency* (data is restored to its original state if the write fails), *isolation* (each transaction is independent), and *durability* (completed data is retained in the database).

Activation criteria   Conditions which, when met, dictate the activation of disaster recovery or business continuity plans. Any delay or failure to activate indicates negligence. Typically, the criteria are based on impact, anticipated duration of outage, or immediate lack of sufficient information to calculate the actual impact. It's always better to overreact when compared to the consequences of an inadequate response.

Active attack   An overt attack against the system or system data files. Active attacks are usually detected during routine monitoring.

ActiveX   A program applet designed by Microsoft with access throughout the entire system. ActiveX is more dangerous than Java applets. ActiveX applets can be digitally signed using authenticode, but this does not provide any protection from malware. Malicious programmers can design ActiveX programs to circumvent or defeat the security of Microsoft Windows. As a safeguard, firewalls should always be configured to prevent the downloading of ActiveX programs. Individual computers should have ActiveX disabled.

Address binding   Creating a software link (association) between the hardware MAC address of a network interface and the administratively assigned IP address.

Administrative audit   Verifies that appropriate policies and procedures exist, and that they have been implemented as management intended. This audit focuses on operational effectiveness and efficiency.

Administrative controls   The use of administrative policies and procedures in the implementation of preventative, detective, and corrective controls.

Advanced Encryption Standard (AES)   Symmetric-key encryption system designed by Belgian mathematicians. Also known as the Rijndael, Advanced Encryption Standard (AES) replaces the outdated Data Encryption Standard (DES) previously used by the U.S. government. This is the de facto standard for many applications because AES is approved by the U.S. National Institute of Standards and Technology (NIST) for unclassified and certain classified information.

Adware   A tiny, downloaded software program that intentionally displays or promotes advertising directly on the user's computer. This is a variation of spam or malware disrupting the user's time and attention.

After-image   Changes to data in the database are held in a temporary file called the after-image journal. The transaction can be reversed (discarded) until the program writes the change into the master file. Also see *before-image* and *ACID principle*.

Agile development   A micromanagement methodology to force development within a series of short time boxes. Agile is used for the development of prototypes. The focus is on tactile knowledge in a person's mind, rather than the use of formal SDLC design and development documentation.

Antivirus software   A specialized software program used to detect viruses based on a database of known behavior (signature) or an attempt to append to a file.

Applet   A small, downloaded program using ActiveX, Java, XML, or a similar programming language.

Application   Computer software program designed for a particular purpose. Application software provides functions and stored procedures to solve a problem on behalf of the user.

Application controls   The lowest level of control, usually governing system use or internal program controls. Application controls are easily subverted if higher-level controls governing the operating environment are missing or ineffective. Higher controls include *general controls*, *pervasive controls*, and *detailed controls*.

Application layer   The highest layer of the OSI model is layer 7. The Application layer runs problem-solving software for the user. This layer provides the interface between the user and the computer program.

Application programming interface (API)   A software interface designed to allow communication between different programs. APIs are used to specify the procedural rules, type, and format of data to be passed between programs. Proprietary APIs are referred to as closed. Nonproprietary APIs are called open. The API design is used by programs in both open-system and closed-system architecture for cross-compatibility.

Application service provider (ASP)   See *software as a service (SaaS)*.

Artificial intelligence (AI)   An attempt to simulate human reasoning by using a computer program with a knowledge database and abstract procedures to measure cause-and-effect relationships.

Assessment   A less formal process used to determine value or relevance to the intended use. Assessments may be internal or external. The results of an assessment are of low to moderate value. The results are used for internal purposes only. See *audit* and *independent audit* to compare the differences.

Asset   Anything of value. May be tangible or intangible in the form of information, skilled people, money, physical goods, products, resources, recipes, or procedures.

Assurance   A promise with supporting evidence given in a declaration or activity designed to instill confidence.

Asymmetric-key encryption   An encryption system using two different keys. Both keys are mathematically related. Asymmetric-key encryption is not time sensitive. The private key is kept secret by the sender, and the public key is freely distributed to anyone who desires to communicate with the owner. Also known as public-key cryptography.

Atomicity   A process used for database transaction integrity to ensure that the entire transaction is correctly processed or all the changes are backed out of the database.

Attestation   An affirmation by the signer that all statements are true and correct. The purpose is to certify that a declaration is genuine.

Attribute   In computer programming, an attribute is equivalent to a column in a database table. The attribute refers to a specific characteristic of a database entry.

Attribute sampling   A technique used to estimate the rate of occurrence for a particular attribute within the subject population. In compliance testing, attribute sampling answers the question, "How many?"

Attribute-based access control (ABAC)   The most detailed level of access control, which matches the combined security of subject (user or program), object (data), and context of usage (need or purpose) to determine whether a request should be approved or denied. ABAC is used in mandatory access control, which also requires a centralized control approach.

Audit   A formal and systematic process of collecting evidence to test or confirm a statement or to confirm a record of transaction. Also see *internal audit* and *independent audit*.

Audit charter   A formal document issued by management to designate audit responsibility, authority, and accountability. The absence of a formal audit charter document would indicate a control weakness.

Audit committee   A committee of the board of directors composed of financially literate executives. The purpose of the audit committee is to challenge the assertions of management by using internal and external auditors.

Audit evidence   Samples collected by the auditor to prove or disprove the audit findings. Every audit must use relevant evidence of dependable quality in sufficient quantity to generate a score of success or failure.

Audit objective   Specific goal(s) to be accomplished by the audit. This is the reason for the audit.

Audit plan   Detailed project plan containing a list of objectives, specific tasks in proper sequence, skills matrix, written copy of data collection procedures, written audit test procedures, and the forecast illustrating scope time and cost estimates. The audit plan is an essential document to be archived with the resulting audit report for proving integrity of the corresponding results.

Audit risk   The possibility that material errors may exist that the auditor is unable to detect.

Audit scope   The boundaries and limitations of the individual audit. Normally, particular systems or functions that will be reviewed during the audit.

Audit subject   The target to be audited. The audit subject may be a particular system, process, procedure, or department function.

Audit trail   Evidence that can be reassembled in chronological order to retrace a transaction or series of transactions.

Auditee   The persons and organization being audited.

Auditing standard   The mandatory examination procedures to be executed during an audit to ensure consistency of findings. The auditing standard specifies a minimum level of performance. Any deviations must be well documented, with justification as to why the standard was not followed.

Auditor   The person(s) performing the audit by gathering evidence, testing, and reporting the findings. Auditors should not be related to the subject of the audit, to prevent bias. Also see *independence*.

Auditor's opinion   An overall score generated by the sufficient collection of evidence, effective testing, observations, and findings from the test results. It's actually a score based on the relevance of the test results rather than an opinion.

Authentication   The process of verifying a user's identity. The user's claim will be tested against a known reference. If a match occurs, the user is authenticated and allowed to proceed. A mismatch will deny the request.

Authentication header (AH)   Used in the IPsec protocol to provide integrity, authentication, and nonrepudiation by means of encryption. The authentication header contains the security associations (SAs), which are used for covert tunneling mode. The AH works with the encapsulated security protocol to both hide the internal IP address and encrypt the data payload.

Authenticode   Microsoft's technique for software developers to digitally sign downloadable ActiveX applets. The authenticode design fails to provide any security from poorly written programs and does not protect the user from malicious programs designed to intentionally cause harm.

Authorization   The granting of a right or authority.

New terminology is created all the time by individuals wanting to portray an illusion of intelligence, by salespeople attempting to make their product appear different from those of competitors, and by a very small number of people who actually have something new to convey. A person of intelligence and genuine understanding will have absolutely no trouble explaining concepts by using a handful of small words. A good explanation will include a simple test that the listener can duplicate to verify the meaning.

Availability   A term that refers to the accessibility and proper functioning of a system at the time frame required by the user.

B

Backdoor   A hidden software-access mechanism that will bypass normal security controls to grant access into a program. A *root kit* is the most powerful type of backdoor because it creates covert access paths into the system. Also see *trapdoor.*

Backup and recovery capability   The culmination of software, hardware, procedures, and data files that will permit timely recovery from a failure or disaster.

Balanced scorecard   A management tool that aligns individual activities to the higher-level business objectives.

Baseband   A single channel for data transmission. Coax cable is an example of a baseband technology.

Baseline   An agreed-upon reference point. Also see *software baseline.*

Bastion host   A gateway host fully exposed to an external connection such as the Internet. Bastion hosts are special-purpose systems designed with their own protection to withstand normal (average) attacks. Examples include a proxy server or firewall. If compromised, the bastion will be shut down.

Batch controls   Used to ensure the accuracy and correct formatting of input data. The batch controls include sequence numbering and run-to-run totals. The batch count will count the number of all the items to ensure that each transaction is processed. Batch totals can be used to verify the values within the transactions.

Before-image   A temporary record of work in progress. This database journal file contains the original data before a new transaction is written. A copy of the original data is retained in this "before" journal file in case the transaction fails. If the transaction fails, the change is discarded and the original data is kept. Related to the *ACID principle* and *after-image* transaction journal.

Benchmarking   A test to evaluate performance against a known workload or industry-accepted standard. Using the Capability Maturity Model (CMM) is a form of benchmarking.

Best evidence   Refers to evidence that specifically proves or disproves a particular point. The best evidence is both independent and objective. The worst evidence is subjective or circumstantial evidence.

Black-box testing   Tests the functionality of compiled software by comparing the input and output, without understanding the internal process that creates the output. The internal logic is hidden from the tester. The term *black box* refers to the software being in nonreadable machine format (compiled code). Almost all commercially available software is tested by using the black-box technique.

Blackout   The complete failure of electrical power.

Biometric management   Management isn't a policy; management is the enforcement/overseeing of the policy concerning the intended use of biometric data with corresponding standards and procedures. Management includes identifying how data is collected, stored, protected, transmitted, used, and disposed of.

Biometric sensor   Special acquisition device used to create unique minutiae data representing an individual user. Sensors convert physical attributes into electrical signals, which are recorded as attribute scores for each individual user.

Biometric system   A combined assembly of hardware and software that uses biometric templates, acquisition sensors, a biometric template generator, an encrypted database of biometric template data, and a complete matcher to determine whether an individual is actually a legitimate authorized user.

Biometric template   Minutiae data created by the biometric system's acquisition sensor, it represents unique characteristics of the legitimate authorized user that are trustworthy enough to be used for authentication.

Biometric template generator   The system sensor that acquires a biometric image and converts it into biometric minutiae for digital storage or comparison.

Biometric template matcher   Compares a biometric image template just acquired by the sensor to the biometric minutiae already stored inside the biometrics database. A match between the two templates will authenticate the individual, allowing access through the physical door or barrier.

Biometrics   A technical process to verify a user's identity based on unique physical characteristics.

Bitstream imaging   A special bit-by-bit backup of physical media, which records all the contents, including deleted files and current contents of swap space or slack space. Also known as physical backup. Bitstream backups are used in forensic analysis and may be used in electronic discovery. Also see *logical backup*.

Boot strapping (boot)   The initial loading of software to start a computer. Also see *initial program load (IPL)*.

Bot-net   Remote-controlled robot network created from compromised computers owned by unsuspecting users. Unsuspecting victims may even be located behind a firewall on a corporate network. This bot-net operates a distributed attack against other systems or delivers email spam messages against other systems. Bot-nets are known to be as large as hundreds of thousands or even millions of systems.

Bridge   A network device or software process that connects similar networks together. Network switching is based on a bridging process to join users into logical network segments. A standard bridge will forward all data packets to the other users in the subnet. A bridge operates at the OSI Data-Link layer (layer 2).

Broadband   Multiple communication channels that are multiplexed over a single cable. DSL is an example of broadband transmitted on a different frequency and sharing the same physical wire with the voice telephone circuit.

Broadcast   A network transmission by one computer to all computers on the network. Ethernet uses broadcast technology to transmit data packets, which are seen by all the computers on the network.

Brownout   Low voltage for an extended period of time.

Brute force attack   An attempt to overpower the system or to try every possible combination until access is granted.

Buffer   A temporary memory location used to stage data before or after processing.

Bus   A shared connection used in common by other devices. Examples include the power bus and the computer data bus.

Bus topology   An early type of networking in which all the computers were connected on a single cable in a linear fashion.

Business continuity (BC) manager   A specific manager with the authority of a vice president or director assigned to lead planning and exercises. Usually this person reports to the chief executive officer (CEO), chief operating officer (COO), or holds a leadership position in the program management office. Unlike departmental managers, the BC manager has authority across departmental boundaries.

Business continuity plan (BCP)   An organizational plan to continue core revenue-generating operations following a crisis or disaster. The objective of business continuity planning is to ensure uninterrupted revenue for business survival.

Business impact analysis (BIA)   The process of determining the actual steps to produce the desired product or service, as in use by the organization. The intention is to provide management with accurate information about how the business processes are performed.

Business performance indicators   Business performance can be measured by a variety of indicators, including return on investment (ROI), gross profit margin (GPM), capital gains, market share, production cost, and debt ratio.

Business process reengineering (BPR)   The process of streamlining existing operations in an effort to improve efficiency and reduce cost. Benefits may be derived by eliminating unnecessary steps as the organization has progressed through the learning curve, or by expanding capability for more work.

Business risk   The inherent potential for harm in the business or industry itself, as the organization attempts to fulfill its objectives. Business risks may be regulatory, contractual, or financial.

Bypass label processing   An attempt to circumvent mandatory access controls by bypassing the electronic security control label. Examples include writing data to a read-only file, or accessing a file that would be off-limits because of its higher security rating.

Bytecode   See *pseudocode*.

C

Cable plant   A physical collection of network cables contained inside the building.

Cache   A high-speed buffer used to temporarily stage data before or after processing.

Candidate key   Rows of data used with search attributes to find all matching records within the database. For example, searching the database to find the name of every hotel in Grapevine, Texas.

Capability Maturity Model (CMM)   Developed by the Software Engineering Institute to benchmark the maturity of systems and management processes. Maturity levels range from 0 to 5. Level 5 is completely documented and optimized for continuous improvement.

Capacity monitoring   The process of continuously monitoring utilization in the environment against existing resource capacity. The objective is to ensure optimum use and expansion of services before an outage occurs.

Certificate   A written assurance or official record representing that an event has or has not occurred. Certificates can be stored as electronic records or physical documents, signed by the party providing a declaration of authenticity.

Certificate authority (CA)   The trusted issuer of *digital certificates* using public- and private-key pairs. The certificate authority is responsible for verifying the authenticity of the user's identity.

Certificate revocation list (CRL)   A list maintained by the *certificate authority*, of certificates that are revoked or expired.

Certification   A comprehensive technical evaluation process to establish compliance to a minimum requirement.

Certification practice statement (CPS)   A detailed set of procedures specifying how the *certificate authority* governs its operation.

Chain of custody   Refers to the mandatory security and integrity requirements used in the evidence life cycle. The custodian of evidence must prove that the evidence has been kept secure with a high degree of *integrity* and has not been tampered with.

Change control board (CCB)   A management review process to ensure awareness and control of changes in the IT environment. A change control board provides separation of duties.

Change control process (CCP)   A formal review of proposed changes using a systematic *methodology*.

Ciphertext   An encrypted message displayed in unreadable text that appears as gibberish. The message is displayed in cipher form.

Circuit switching   All communications are transmitted over a dedicated circuit such as a T1 leased line telephone circuit. Circuit switching is the opposite of *packet switching*.

Circuit-level gateway   Refers to a *proxy firewall*. No data packets are forwarded between the internal and external network, except by the proxy application. The proxy application is required to complete the data transmission circuit.

Classified information   Data is ranked somewhere in a protection scheme (aka protection plan) that has been clearly identified to the users and includes handling procedures on how the information should be controlled. Also see *unclassified information*.

Clear text   A message that is completely readable to a human. The message can be clearly read.

Client   A person or organization with the authority to request an audit. The auditor's report of findings is presented to the client at the conclusion of the audit. The client may be internal or external to the *auditee*.

Closed system   Software containing methods and programming of a proprietary design, which remains the property of the software creator. Most commercial software is closed system. Closed systems can exchange data to other programs by using a specific *application programming interface (API)*. Microsoft Windows is an example of a closed system containing proprietary design.

Cloud computing   Application software hosted by remote vendor and offered across the Internet to subscribers. Cloud computing is a variation of the *application service provider (ASP)* and *software as a service (SaaS)* models. Security issues are a major concern because specific details of the communications network, network servers, internal software application, and vendor's operation may not be known by the user. Auditors need to remain aware that cloud computing may cut operating expense, bypass IT controls, fuel an individual's political agenda, circumvent management, or violate data control requirements.

Cold site   A physical location that can be used for disaster recovery of noncritical processes. The cold site is no more than a building with basic utility service. The entire computing environment must be shipped in and then assembled. The cold site will be ready for production use in weeks or months.

Committee of Sponsoring Organizations (COSO)   A voluntary association of governments (members) engaged in regulating the integrity of financial transactions worldwide. COSO is based on London's banking system for investment, stock trading, and transaction controls. COSO represents the foundation of auditing laws and audit controls worldwide. ISACA represents a narrow derivative of IT-specific controls attempting to implement an IT-only portion of the COSO control model. COSO controls are used in conjunction with those of the International Organization for Standardization (ISO) and the Organization for Economic Cooperation and Development (OECD), which specify the details and interpretation of laws each country needs to adopt in support of world trade.

Common Criteria   An international standard (ISO 15408) for testing criteria of computer security controls. All ISO member countries are expected to use the Common Criteria standard with testing performed by an ISO 17025–certified laboratory testing facility. Common Criteria is currently in use by Canada, France, Germany, the Netherlands, the United Kingdom, and the United States.

Compensating control   An internal control that reduces the potential for loss by error or omission. Supervisory review and audit trails are compensating controls for a lack of separation of duties.

Compile   An automated process used by software developers to convert human-readable computer programs into executable machine language. Compiled computer software runs faster than interpreted program scripts. Compiled computer programs cannot be read by humans.

Compliance audit   A type of audit that determines whether internal controls are present and functioning effectively.

Compliance testing   The testing of internal controls to determine whether they are functioning correctly.

Computer console   Physical access to the computer's primary input/output terminal, usually the video display and keyboard. Access to the computer console is a security risk that must be controlled.

Computer-assisted audit tools (CAAT)   The family of automated test software using a computerized audit procedure with specialized utilities.

Confidence coefficient   The quantified probability of error. A confidence coefficient of 95 percent is considered a high level of confidence in IS auditing.

Confidentiality   The protection of information held in secret for the benefit of authorized users.

Configuration management   An administrative process of being able to prove the documented design as built, by verifying the correct version of all the individual components used in final construction. The three elements of configuration management are control, accounting, and reporting.

Constructive Cost Model (COCOMO)   An early software project estimation technique used to forecast the time and effort required to develop a software program based on size and complexity.

Continuity of operations   Preemptive activities designed to ensure the continuous operation of core processes, utilities, and lifeline services. Vendors involved in lifeline medical services, power utilities, communications, national infrastructure supply-chains, or food and water are expected to provide their services without interruption regardless of whether they generate revenue or not.

Contraband software   Any system utility or special software not required in the specific performance of a person's job duties. A tightly controlled software policy prevents any excuses for violating separation of duties. Examples of contraband software include password crackers, network discovery tools, CAAT software, traffic generators, disk-wiping utilities, or known hacking software. Violations should be grounds for immediate termination following the conclusion of an investigation.

Control   The power to regulate or restrict activities. IS controls are used as a safeguard to prevent loss, error, or omission.

Control environment   A space designed to protect assets by using sufficient physical and technical controls to prevent unauthorized access or compromise. The computer room is a control environment.

Control group   Members of the operations staff responsible for collecting data from users for input to the computer system.

Control risk   The risk that errors may be introduced, or not identified and corrected in a timely manner. The risk of losing control.

Control self-assessment   A formal review executed by the user to assess the effectiveness of controls. The purpose of the control self-assessment is to induce ownership by the user and to facilitate improvement.

Corrective control   A control designed to minimize the impact of an error by repairing the condition or executing an alternative procedure. Examples of corrective controls include data restoration from tape backup, hot sites, and automated failover systems.

Cost of asset   The capital expense of an asset may be measured as total ownership cost (TOC). The cost of the asset is the cumulative total expense based on purchase price, delivery cost, implementation cost, and effective downtime.

Cracker   A malicious computer attacker who attempts to break into a system. Synonymous with the term malicious *hacker*.

Crash dump   A special diagnostic file created when a computer system crashes. The contents represent the data being processed at the time of the crash, including contents of the memory registers and tasks running when the crash occurred. Crash dump files vary according to the operating system. Contents of this file are extremely valuable in forensic analysis.

Critical Path Methodology (CPM)   The path of execution that accomplishes the minimum, yet most important objectives of the project. The critical path is the longest single route through a network diagram and the shortest time to accomplish the main objectives. Critical path items represent mandatory tasks that, if not accomplished, would wreck the project.

Critical success factor (CSF)   A process that must occur perfectly every single time in order to be successful. To fail a critical success factor would be a showstopper.

Crossover error rate (CER)   In biometrics, crossover error rate refers to adjusting sensitivity of the system to specifically favor either speed or increased accuracy. The most common error in biometrics is false rejection (type 1 error, aka. FRR), which poses little risk to an organization's security requirements. The greater risk of breach occurs when an illegitimate user is accepted in error (type 2 error, aka FAR, or false acceptance rate). The crossover rate indicates the level of favoritism protecting against either FRR or FAR. Also see *equal error rate*. Note that ISACA may confuse the terminology of CER and EER in documentation and on exam questions. These are definitely different settings.

Cross-site scripting (XSS)   Very common programming technique that allows one program, such as a shopping cart, to drive another website. The shopping cart sends a transaction approval message to a different website, which provides access or a file to download. XSS creates a serious vulnerability unless strong cryptographic controls are used to authenticate that the request is actually valid. Static passwords will not protect against XSS attacks.

Cryptographic system   The implementation of a computer program using a cryptographic algorithm and keys to encrypt and decrypt messages.

Cryptography   The theories and methods of converting readable text into undecipherable gibberish and later reversing the process to create readable text. The purpose of cryptography is to hide information from other people.

Crystal-box testing   See *white-box testing*.

Cyclic redundancy check (CRC)   A simple error-detection process whereby the contents are divided by a number prior to transmission. After transmission, the process is rerun to determine whether an error occurred. A value of zero indicates that the transmission was successful.

D

Data classification   A process of ranking information based on its value or requirements for secrecy.

Data custodian   The individual charged with protecting data from a loss of availability, loss of integrity, or loss of confidentiality. The data custodian implements controls appropriate to the desires of the data owner and data classification.

Data dictionary   A standardized reference listing of all the programmer's data descriptions and files used in a computer program.

Data Encryption Standard (DES)   A cryptographic symmetric-key algorithm implemented by the U.S. government from 1972 to 1993. The DES standard was modified to use a triple process of encryption and decryption in an attempt to improve confidentiality (triple DES). DES was replaced by the *Advanced Encryption Standard (AES)*. DES is commonly used in older devices.

Data integrity controls   Procedures to ensure the appropriateness and accuracy of information.

Data mart   A group of data selected from a data warehouse for analysis. The data selected is of particular interest to a group of people.

Data mining   The process of analyzing volumes of data to determine correlations that may be useful.

Data owner   The individual or executive responsible for the integrity of information. The duties of the owner include specifying appropriate controls, identifying authorized users, and appointing a custodian.

Data retention   See *records management*.

Data set   A set of related data files.

Database   A collection of persistence data items that are maintained in a grouping.

Database schema   The data structure and design of the database that represents a logical layout or schema.

Data-Link layer   The transmit-and-receive protocol between networked devices. Data-Link operates on OSI layer 2.

Data-oriented database (DODB)   A data collection designed around relevant information in a known format. The database and the program methods operate separately from each other.

Decision support system (DSS)   A database information system with scenario models designed to convey important facts and details to aid the decision process.

Decryption   The process of reversing encryption to convert unintelligible ciphertext into human-readable clear text.

Default gateway   The address of a router used to communicate with systems located on a different subnet or different network.

Defense-in-depth (DID)   A process of building layers of defensive controls for protective assurance. Also known as a layered defense strategy.

Defuzzification   To sharpen the details of an average population by using a stratified mean (for example, demographics) to further define the data into small units.

Deleted files   Computer files remain on the hard disk after deletion. To conserve processing, space occupied by deleted files is simply marked as eligible for overwriting. Deleted files that have not been overwritten may be recovered by using a simple recovery utility or forensic analysis. Use of an overwriting utility or physical destruction is necessary to prevent unauthorized disclosure of deleted files.

Demilitarized zone (DMZ)   See *screened subnet*.

Denial of service (DoS)   An attack designed to prevent the user from accessing the computer system.

Detailed controls   Lower-level controls placed on specific procedures.

Detection risk   The risk that an auditor will not be able to detect material error conditions (faults) that exist.

Detective control   A control designed to report items of concern including errors, omissions, and unauthorized access.

Dictionary attack   An attack used to discover system passwords by loading all the words found in a language dictionary into a password-cracking utility. The password-cracking utility will encrypt each word by using the same method as the operating system. Matching encrypted passwords are identified, and the originating word is displayed to the attacker as the unencrypted password.

Differential backup   A file backup method that copies every file that has been added or changed since the last full backup. A differential backup does not set the final archive bit flag.

Digital certificate   An encrypted computer file containing unique information about the identity of the individual and the issuer of the certificate. Digital certificates are used to verify the authenticity of a remote system. Digital certificates are required to enable *Secure Shell (SSH)* and *Secure Sockets Layer (SSL)*.

Digital rights management (DRM)   Uses encryption and/or digital certificates to enforce licensing of electronic files (music, movies, e-books, and so forth). DRM is used to help prevent bootlegging of illegal copies. The electronic file contains a special DRM interface that uses the vendor's public key to unlock the product for authorized users. Depending on the vendor's implementation, DRM may or may not use digital certificates as part of the protection mechanism.

Digital signature   An encrypted hash of an electronic file. The subject file is processed by using a hash algorithm such as MD5 or SHA-1. The resulting hash output file is encrypted with the sender's private key. This encrypted hash file is known as a digital signature that is related to both the sender and the subject file. The signature is verified by using the sender's public key to decrypt the hash.

Disaster recovery plan (DRP)   A set of procedures for providing an emergency response following a disaster. The objective is to rebuild the organization to a state equal to that prior to the disaster. Disaster recovery does not provide for losses of market share and revenue. Business continuity is the next step above disaster recovery.

Discovery sampling   The process of searching 100 percent of the available records for specific attributes to determine the probability of occurrence. Used when the likelihood of evidence is low or extreme accuracy is required. The intention is to discover whether a particular situation has occurred. Common examples include fraud, forensic investigations, and identifying correlations from unexpected events.

Discretionary access control (DAC)   A type of access control in which a person of authority decides to grant or revoke access for an individual. The decision may be based on need or desire.

Disk imaging   See *bitstream imaging*.

Disk mirroring   See *mirrored*.

Disk strings   The orderly connection of multiple disk drives in a storage array. Strings of individual disks are connected for use in *RAID* subsystems.

Disposal (SDLC phase 7)   The manner in which hardware and software assets are authorized for retirement without the loss of data records. Data must be archived according to legal commitments and regulations. No one in the organization should profit from the disposal process.

Distributed denial-of-service attack (DDoS)   A particularly vicious form of denial-of-service attack that is launched concurrently from multiple systems.

Domain   A kingdom or political territory of direct influence.

Domain Name System (DNS)   An Internet protocol that looks up the server's IP address by using the server hostname, such as www.certtest.com. The Internet domain names and IP addresses are loaded into a server running the domain name service.

Downtime   A resource or system being unavailable to the user for any reason whatsoever. Downtime may be the result of a planned outage for maintenance or backups, or an unplanned outage due to a failure.

Dry pipe   A type of fire-suppression system in which the pipes remain dry until seconds after the release is required. Most dry-pipe systems utilize compressed gas to minimize the chance of leakage due to corrosion or freezing conditions.

Due care   The level of care that a normal, prudent individual would give in the same situation.

Dumpster diving   The process of digging through trash in a dumpster to recover evidence or improperly disposed-of records. The same process is frequently used by government agents and law enforcement to gather evidence; therefore, it's legal unless the person is trespassing. Trespassing is unnecessary if the refuse is going to be unloaded at the public waste dump. A hacker or investigator can pick through the trash after it's unloaded at the dump or recycler.

E

Electromagnetic interference (EMI)   Magnetic waves of interference generated by electricity.

Electronic Data Interchange (EDI)   Used for e-commerce between two organizations for communicating purchases and payment. EDI mapping converts the names of data elements (data fields) between two trading organizations. Traditional EDI transmits data through a value-added network (VAN) operated by a service provider. Web-based EDI transmits data across the Internet.

Electronic discovery (e-discovery)   The process of searching electronic records to gather evidence. The legal discovery process allows another party the right to investigate records for the purpose of compiling evidence relevant to their claim. Electronic discovery may include recovery of *deleted files* and the search of *standing data* on offline media, including backup tapes. Persons accused of obstructing the discovery process face serious criminal charges.

Electronic vaulting   A process of transmitting data to a remote backup site. This ensures that the most recent files are available in the event of a disaster. A common implementation is to transmit live data files to a remote server.

Elliptic curve cryptography   A new type of encryption using specific points on a three-dimensional random curve as the encryption key.

Emergency management (EM)   Provides organizational control for evacuation and rescue assistance during an emergency, crisis, or disaster. The focus of emergency management is to preserve life regardless of the disruption it will create to the business, disruption to the economy, or inconvenience to an individual's objective. Saving lives or preservation of life is always the exclusive top priority.

Emergency management team (EMT)   Senior executives with full delegation of authority to make decisions on behalf of the entire organization without additional delays or approval by other executives. During business continuity events or disaster recovery, this team will make the best possible decisions necessary for the survival of the organization.

Emergency Operations Center (EOC)   Alternate command post that houses the *emergency management team (EMT)* during business continuity events or disaster recovery.

Emergency power off (EPO)   A switch that shuts off computer room power in an emergency. The national fire protection act requires an emergency power disconnect to protect human life from electrocution. The EPO switch is located near the exit door.

Encryption   The process of converting human-readable clear text into decipherable gibberish. The objective is to hide the contents of the file from other people.

Encryption algorithm   A mathematical transformation procedure used to encrypt and decrypt files.

Encryption key   A unique randomizer used by the encryption algorithm to ensure confidentiality. Strength of *symmetric-key encryption* and the *PKI* private key is based on the absolute secrecy of the secret/private key. Secrecy is dependent on limiting use of the key, isolating the key, and regular rotation (changing the key). Also see *key wrapping*.

End state   A description of the anticipated final outcome. The end state explains the attributes of the finished product.

Enterprise resource planning (ERP)   An integrated database used for planning resource requirements of multiple departments.

Entity-relationship diagram (ERD)   A diagram of data elements and their relationship to other data. The ERD specifies data names and data attributes to be used by the software program being developed. The ERD is created in the requirements and design phase to build a database schema.

Equal error rate (EER)   A setting used in biometrics, when adjusting sensitivity of the system, that creates a 50/50 compromise between the false acceptance rate (FAR, authorized user is refused, and authorized user is refused) and the false rejection rate (FRR, illegitimate user is accepted). Also see the opposing definition of *crossover error rate (CER)*. Note that some ISACA documents and exam questions may mistakenly confuse EER and CER as synonyms. EER and CER are very different settings.

Ethics   Discipline of following forthright and honest conduct without impropriety, deceit, or conflicting agenda.

Evidence   A collection of verifiable information that is used to prove or disprove a point. The best evidence is both independent and objective.

Evidence timing   The timely disclosure of evidence relevant to the situation. Evidence timing in computer systems also refers to the time window in which data is available before being lost or overwritten during normal processing.

Evolutionary development   See *iterative development.*

Exception report   A report identifying data and transactions that may be incorrect and may warrant additional attention. Exception reports can be manual or automated.

Expert   An individual with a significant amount of direct experience, or special training with direct experience, and the ability to deduce a correct conclusion when everyone else would form an incorrect conclusion.

Expert system   Specialized computer database software used to provide a recommendation based on the knowledge recorded from an expert. Expert systems possess between 50,000 and 100,000 discrete points of information. The system uses an inference engine to identify possible conditions relating to the problem and their meaning.

Exposure   The adverse consequence that will occur if a potential threat becomes reality.

Extensible Authentication Protocol (EAP)   A newer security protocol used in wireless networks with automatic encryption-key generation and authentication. EAP is a component of the new 802.11i standard known as *Robust Security Network (RSN).* EAP replaces the seriously insecure method of using a preshared encryption key in the outdated *Wired Equivalent Privacy (WEP)* protocol.

Extensible Markup Language (XML)   A universal program architecture designed to share information between different programming languages. XML uses three underlying programming specifications: SOAP (originally called Simple Object Access Protocol) is used to define APIs; Web Services Description Language (WSDL) identifies the format to use; and Universal Description, Discovery, and Integration protocol (UDDI) acts as an online directory of available web services.

External audit   An audit performed by an external party, including business partners. External audits may be biased if the auditor is related to the auditee through a trading partner relationship (client, vendor, and subcontractor). Also see *independent audit.*

Extranet   An Internet communication server used to exchange files between the organization and external business partners.

F

Failure to enroll (FTE)   An error in the collection of biometric data that prevents the information from being recorded.

False acceptance rate (FAR), type 2 error   An error condition in *biometrics* that grants an unwanted user with permission to access the system by mistake. This is a less common error since falsely granting access to an unauthorized person is supposed to be rare.

False positive   Generating an alert by mistake or error.

False rejection rate (FRR), type 1 error   Used in *biometrics*, false rejection means to reject access to an authorized user by mistake. This is the most common type of biometric authentication error.

Fault-tolerant   A system that can continue to operate after a single failure condition has occurred. RAID systems are designed to be tolerant of individual disk failures. The success of the fault-tolerant system depends on the system being able to identify that the fault has occurred.

Feasibility study (SDLC phase 1)   An initial study to determine the benefits that will be derived from a new system and the payback schedule for the investment required.

Financial audit   A review of financial records to determine their accuracy.

Fire-control system   A fire-suppression system using water or chemicals to extinguish a fire in the data processing facility.

Firewall   According to *The American Heritage Dictionary*, a fireproof wall used as a barrier to prevent the spread of fire. In information systems, the term refers to a combination of hardware and software used to restrict access between public and private networks.

Firmware   The solid-state memory chips on a circuit board containing a read-only program designed to operate the hardware.

Flowchart   A systematic diagram that details the procedures for data manipulation and data transformation in a computer program. The program flowchart is developed during SDLC design in phase 2.

Foreign key   Data in the database is stored in separate tables to improve speed. A foreign key is the link between data in different database tables. When the links are valid, the database has *referential integrity*.

Formal   Documented in writing and authorized by management.

Fourth-generation language (4GL)   An English-like programming language with integrated database support. 4GL programming tools allow the forms and database to be generated by using a drag-and-drop functionality. The 4GL does not create the data transformation procedures necessary for business functionality.

Full backup   The process of copying every file that exists onto backup media such as a tape cartridge. The full backup is used in combination with incremental or differential backup strategies to restore the most recent copy of data. The ability to restore files from a full backup is used to calculate the recovery point objective (RPO). Files that cannot be restored are lost.

Function point analysis (FPA)   A software estimation method used to forecast development, based on the number of system inputs, number of outputs, and complexity. FPA is used in the SDLC feasibility study to calculate resources and time required. FPA can be used as a baseline to measure the progress of software development.

Function testing   Tests run during software development to determine the integrity of specific program functions.

Fuzzification   Reducing the detail in an average by using an unstratified mean to roll the details into a larger lump-sum value.

G

Gateway   A device running software to transfer data between two networking protocols. The gateway is an OSI layer 7 application. Examples include a mainframe gateway converting TCP/IP to 3,270 sessions.

General controls   Higher-level policies, standards, and procedures used across the entire organization to govern everyone's behavior.

Generally Accepted Accounting Principles (GAAP)   A well-recognized set of agreed-upon procedures for auditing financial records and information systems.

Guideline   A list of recommendations to follow in the absence of an existing standard.

H

Hacker   A malicious attacker of a computer system. A secondary meaning in computer programming is a programmer able to generate usable applications where none existed previously.

Halon   A chlorine-based gas previously used in fire-suppression systems. Production of gaseous Halon 1301 has been banned since 1994 because of the damaging effects of chlorine products on the earth's ozone. Halon is still used on aircraft because of the severity of fires while in flight. Computer room halon has been replaced by FM-200, NAF-S-3, and other products.

Hand geometry   Used in *biometrics* to verify a user's identity based on the unique three-dimensional geometry of the human user's hand. Common examples include checking wrinkle patterns, measuring joints, and analyzing blood-vessel patterns.

Hash file   A mathematical value generated from the original message file for verifying integrity. The sender runs their original message through a hash algorithm to produce a unique hash value. The sender sends their message and hash file to the recipient. The recipient reruns the same hash process and compares the sender's hash file against the hash generated by the recipient. The purpose of a hash file is to determine whether any changes have occurred to the original message file. Matching hash files indicate that no changes occurred; different hash values indicate that the message has been altered.

Hash message authentication code (HMAC)   A hashed message file is used to verify message integrity (to prove no changes occurred) and is also encrypted to provide authentication of the sender. The more common hashing algorithms with encryption are MD5 and SHA-1 (also known as SHA-160). Newer HMAC versions include SHA-256 and SHA-512. The format is [HMAC name] dash [output size]. SHA-512 means SHA algorithm with 512 output size.

Hashing algorithm   The mathematical formula used to reduce the contents of any size message file into a smaller output file representing a unique value that is very difficult to duplicate. The hash algorithm creates a unique output file that can be used like a tamper seal. If the source message is altered, the hashing algorithm generates a different hash value when regenerated by the recipient. Both sender and recipient must use the same hash algorithm.

Heuristics   Programmed rules inside the database used to evaluate data by sorting for possible correlations. Used in *expert systems*, *decision support systems*, email spam filters, and many common business applications. *Antivirus software* and *intrusion detection and prevention systems* use heuristics to determine which requests to accept or discard.

Honey net   A fake network created to entice a hacker to attack. The purpose is for the attack to generate an alarm signaling the early warning of a hacker's presence.

Honey pot   An individual system set up to entice a hacker and generate an early warning alarm of the hacker's presence.

Host based   Software that is installed on an individual host for the purpose of monitoring activity on that specific host.

Host enumeration   Automated software discovery of all the active hosts on a network.

Hot site   An alternate processing facility that is fully equipped with all the necessary computer equipment and capable of commencing operation as soon as the latest data files have been loaded. Hot sites are capable of being in full operation within minutes or hours.

Hub   See *network hub*.

Hybrid sourcing   A combination of using in-house workers and *outsourcing* selected processes.

I

Identification   The process of determining a user's identity based on their claim of identity. The identity claimed by the user must be verified with an authentication process before access is granted.

Immunization   See *inoculation*.

Impact   The level of damage that will occur.

Incident   Any disruptive event, especially those that may cause harm.

Incident Command System (ICS)   ICS is the internationally recognized, government-mandated standard for crisis command during disaster recovery and business continuity events.

Incident commander (IC)   Under the international Incident Command System (ICS), the incident commander is the first person to arrive on the scene regardless of training or experience. Even a four-year-old child calling 911 for help is the initial incident commander until relieved by a more qualified person. The incident commander directs the emergency response activities.

Incident handling   The systematic process of responding to an incident in order to determine its significance and impact. Proper incident handling will prevent negligent activities that could destroy meaningful evidence. A computer incident always has the potential of being a cyber crime scene.

Incremental backup   The process of backing up only the files that have changed since the last backup was run. An incremental backup uses the file archive bit flag to signal files that should be copied to the backup tape.

Independence   Independence in an audit refers to the auditor not being related to the audit subject. The desire is for the auditor to be objective and free of conflict because they are not related to the audit subject.

Independent audit   Independent audits are conducted by an auditor who is not related to the auditee. These audits therefore represent a high value of assurance that can be used for external purposes, including regulatory licensing.

Information assets   Data that has a value.

Information processing facility (IPF)   The building that houses the data center.

Inherent risk   The natural or built-in risk that always exists.

Initial program load (IPL)   Computer systems are susceptible to compromise while the system is loading and before the security control front end becomes active. Computer software is vulnerable to configuration changes during the initial program loading. A system in IPL mode is in supervisory mode.

Inoculation   A technique used by antivirus software to replace the original end-of-file (EOF) marker with a new EOF marker generated by the antivirus program. Anything attempting to attach itself to the new EOF marker indicates a virus attack.

Integrated audit   A type of audit that combines financial records review with an assessment of internal IS controls.

Integrated development environment (IDE)   An advanced software development tool used for writing programs. The IDE provides built-in functions for capturing the software design, commands, and macros for creating program code and debugging testing.

Integrity   Unbiased honesty by a person dealing with other people or in the records of transactions.

Interface   A specification of physical characteristics, electrical signals, format, and procedures used to communicate between systems.

Internal audit   Internal audits are used to help the auditee improve their score. Reports from internal audits may be used only for internal purposes. The reports contain a known bias, which reduces their corresponding value of representations to low or moderate.

International Organization for Standardization (ISO)   A voluntary organization of 160 governments (members) participating in world trade. The objective is to create a universal standard of measurement adopted by each member country. The United States membership is represented by the American National Standards Institute (ANSI) while the United Kingdom is represented by British Standards (BS). Each country cooperates to create the proper conversion of proprietary standards into one worldwide ISO standard to be followed by everyone. ISO measurement standards are used in conjunction with Committee of Sponsoring Organizations (COSO) controls over financial transactions and Organization for Economic Cooperation and Development (OECD) standards for the creation and interpretation of laws within individual countries.

Internet   The shared public communications network.

Internet layer   The equivalent to OSI layer 3, the Networking layer, in the TCP/IP model.

Internet Protocol (IP)   The de facto communications protocol and addressing standard used on the Internet. IP is implemented with TCP for connection-oriented data transmission or UDP for connectionless transmission.

Interoperability   The ability for hardware and software systems from different manufacturers to communicate with each other.

Intranet   A private internal business network.

Intrusion detection and prevention system (IDPS)   A technical system designed to alert personnel to activity that may indicate the presence of a hacker. An intrusion detection system is a type of network hacker alarm. The *IDS* term has been officially updated by the government to *intrusion detection and prevention systems (IDPS)*. Preprogrammed response procedures activate stored commands to modify the IDPS to block an attack before it can penetrate (prevention activity).

Intrusion detection system (IDS)   See *intrusion detection and prevention system (IDPS)* for updated terminology.

IPsec   A security-based implementation of the Internet Protocol. IPsec offers encryption during data transmission or the tunneling of encrypted packets through network routing with an ISP.

Iris scan   A type of biometric technique that uses the unique characteristics found in the iris of the human eye.

Irrelevant   Having no significant bearing on the final outcome. Irrelevant, or trivial, information will not change the results.

IS steering committee   A committee composed of business executives for the purpose of conveying current business priorities and objectives to IT management. The steering committee provides governance for major projects and the IT budget.

IT governance   A clearly stated process of leadership to lead and control the performance expected from the IT function. The focus of IT governance is control over the technology environment.

Iterative development   The progressive development of software through a succession of multiple versions.

J

Java   A very portable object-oriented programming language created by Sun Microsystems. Java can run on cellular phones, iPods, and most computing devices. Java has very good security mechanisms.

Java Virtual Machine (JVM)   An internal processing environment for running a Java program inside of another Java program session, also known as a virtual machine. The partitioning of resources creates a secure environment to protect the rest of the computer system from harm.

Joint venture   Two or more obligators (persons or organizations) bind themselves without actual partnership or corporate designation in a specific venture with the risk, liability, and potential profits shared between the parties. All parties participating in the venture share a communal liability for the failure of the other party.

Just-in-time inventory (JIT)   A process of scheduling the minimum amount of inventory to arrive shortly before it is required in the manufacturing process. The objective is to reduce inventory on hand. The opposite of JIT is stockpiling inventory. JIT practices create a quandary with business continuity plans.

K

Key distribution   The safe process of exchanging keys to be used in a cryptographic system for encryption and decryption.

Key goal indicator (KGI)   The KGI identifies a specific goal to be reached. KPI (historical score) is used together with KGI (goal) in planning and forecasting.

Key performance indicator (KPI)   A historical score of business process performance. Unfortunately, the score may indicate that a failure has occurred before corrective action can be taken.

Key wrapping   Encryption keys must be stored and transmitted in a different encrypted format to protect them from harm. A user should not have direct access to encryption keys. Encryption keys are re-encrypted with a different algorithm that uses a different key to obscure the original key. This key wrapping technique protects the real key from harm. It's extremely difficult to tell where the wrapping stops and the key inside begins.

Keyboard remapping   Changing the normal function of keys on the keyboard to execute different commands.

Knowledge base   A database of information derived from the knowledge of individuals who perform the related tasks. Knowledge-base systems are used for decision support systems.

L

Leased line   A dedicated communications line between two locations, such as a T1 circuit. Also known as a circuit-switched connection. This type of connection is charged by distance covered regardless of volume of data transmitted.

Least privilege   Granting only the minimum access necessary to perform the job function or role. Least privilege is implemented to improve confidentiality.

Legal deadline (LD)   Used in business continuity and disaster recovery planning to identify potential violations that must be avoided or that require special handling to minimize penalties. Examples include mandatory government filings, required legal disclosures, specific performance, and contract breaches. Also see *lost work in process (LWIP)*.

Lessons learned   A best practice for recording the analysis of problems and improvements that worked. The purpose is to avoid repeating mistakes while improving the technique used.

Local area network (LAN)   A computer network with boundaries that match the physical building.

Logic bomb   A programmed function inside of a computer software application designed to damage the system or data files on the occurrence of a particular event, date, or time. Logic bombs are extremely difficult to locate.

Logical access   Electronic access to a system without being physically present.

Logical backup   The process of copying current data files for records retention (safe keeping). Logical backup will ignore *deleted files* and temporary system data in *swap space*. Also see *bitstream imaging*.

Lost work in process (LWIP)   Work tasks and data processing that were lost by a disaster, disruption, or failure. All work since the last backup is lost and must be re-created. LWIP may cause a violation of a *legal deadline (LD)*. LWIP needs to be calculated by the organization when planning their *recovery point objective (RPO)* and *recovery time objective (RTO)*.

M

MAC address   A unique serial number burned into the network interface card by the manufacturer. The Media Access Control (MAC) address operates in the Data-Link layer (layer 2) of the OSI model. The MAC address is used to tie the TCP/IP address to a particular computer.

Mainframe   A large-scale, traditional, multiuser, multiprocessor system designed with excellent internal controls.

Major software release   A new generation of software or a major design change resulting in a new version. Major releases tend to occur in 12- to 24-month intervals.

Malware   A family classification of computer programs designed to intentionally cause malicious damage.

Management oversight   A committee or reporting hierarchy to convey questionable situations involving management to the highest level of authority, often the board of directors.

Mandatory access control (MAC)   An access control system, based on rules that require the user to have an explicit level of access that matches the appropriate security label. The only way to increase access is by a formal promotion of the user ID to the next security level.

Mantrap   A physical location between doorway barriers that is designed to trap an unauthorized individual between the closed doors. Fully caged turnstiles can provide a mantrap to capture potential intruders.

Manual reconciliation   The process of manually verifying that records match.

Manufacturing requirements planning (MRP)   A computer database designed to schedule the requirements of manufacturing design, purchasing, scheduling, and the manufacturing production process.

Masquerading   Pretending to possess an identity under false pretense.

Materiality   Materiality applies to evidence. Evidence is materially significant if it will have enough bearing to change the final outcome.

Maximum acceptable outage (MAO)   The longest period of *downtime* that an organization can survive from a specific outage involving a system, process, or resource.

Maximum tolerable downtime (MTD)   Synonym for *maximum acceptable outage* (MAO), used as a negative connotation.

Meshed network   Connection of redundant links.

Message digest   A hash file of a fixed length created by a source file of any length. The purpose of the message digest is to indicate whether the source file has changed.

Message modification   The alteration of a message to change its contents.

Methodology   A systematic process of procedures to generate a desired outcome.

Metropolitan area network (MAN)   A type of limited-area network in which the boundary is equal to the city's metropolitan area.

Middleware   All software programs, interfaces, and utilities that operate invisibly between the user and their data. Middleware performs an intermediary service to create an invisible workflow connecting various programs. Examples include the database application running on your server, SQL/ODBC drivers, print formatting utilities, communication gateways, operating system, and all device drivers.

Minor software update   Small corrective update issued by the software developer to fix problems found in a major version previously released. Also known as a software patch or minor software release. Also see *major software release*.

Minutiae   A special template of biometric data converted into a count of specific characteristics that is unique to each user.

Mirrored   Duplicate or redundant components operating in parallel.

Multicast   To transmit data across the network to several specific stations concurrently.

Multiprocessing   Using multiple processors.

Multitasking   Running multiple tasks concurrently in a time-sharing mode by allocating a specific amount of resources.

Multithreading   Running several instances of a program concurrently for multiple users.

N

Netmask   An overlay setting used to parse the IP address into two distinct portions representing the unique network address and unique host address. Without this setting, the computer will be confused and unable to communicate on the network.

Network based   A hardware or software device that is watching the communications traffic flowing across the network to other systems.

Network File System (NFS)   A method of sharing disk systems across the network by using remote procedure calls. NFS was invented by Sun Microsystems to share hard disks with multiple users across the network.

Network hub   An OSI layer 1 device designed to relay electrical transmissions and receive signals between computers.

Network layer   The OSI layer 3 functions of network addressing and routing.

Network monitoring   The process of monitoring communications, traffic, performance, and events by using a packet analyzer (sniffer), *Simple Network Management Protocol (SNMP),* and the Remote Monitoring Protocol (RMON).

Network switch   An intelligent bridge running on OSI layer 2. The network switch converts shared traffic from all ports into filtered discrete traffic for an individual port. The purpose is to reduce network congestion by eliminating traffic that does not involve the specific station.

Neural network   A type of decision-making system that uses weights and the simulation of human synapses to make a decision.

Nondiscretionary access control   A method of access control based on job role and required tasks.

Nonrepudiation   A technical process designed to eliminate the opportunity for a person to reject or renounce their participation. Intended to protect the recipient from claims of denial by the other party.

Nonvolatile data   Persistent data retained on the hard disk and other storage media after system shutdown.

Normalization   The process of removing duplicate, redundant data from a database.

O

Object   In object-oriented programming, the program object contains both data and procedural methods. Program objects are able to delegate to another program object.

Object class   An administrative grouping of program objects with similar attributes or related behavior. Similar to the classification of insects by their shared attributes, or classification of manned spacecraft versus unmanned spacecraft. Programming objects are classified by similarity of their attributes and operating methods.

Object code   The machine-executable instructions that are output from the programmer's compiling process. Object code is designed to run on the computer and is unreadable to humans.

Objective   A specific goal or target.

Objectivity   Impartiality, fairness. This term is used in relation to fair and unbiased information used in an audit. An auditor who acts in a manner that is fair and unbiased has objectivity.

Object-oriented database (OODB)   A database designed for data with an unknown format and structure. OODB is very flexible and may be quite complex. OODB is good for organizing information such as MP3 files with photographic images and other programs as items inside the database.

Open system   Software that is readily available by using nonproprietary programming methods in its design. The recipient receives the human-readable *source code* with the ability to make any internal changes they desire. An open system can exchange data with a *closed system* by using a specific *application programming interface (API)*. The Apache web server, Linux operating system, OpenOffice.org application, and SugarCRM software are examples of open systems.

Open Systems Interconnect (OSI)   An international reference model used to explain the functions in network communications.

Operating system (OS)   A computer software program that interfaces between hardware devices and the user's application. Operating systems provide the coordination of resources and the user interface.

Operational audit   A type of audit that reviews the internal controls used in daily operation.

Organization for Economic Cooperation and Development (OECD)   A voluntary organization of governments participating in world trade. OECD provides the framework of laws and interpretations for each country to adopt support of world trade. Since 1992, the OECD guidelines serve as an agreed-upon reference for a total information security framework. OECD guidelines are used in conjunction with Committee of Sponsoring Organizations (COSO) for financial controls and international standards of measurement provided by the International Organization for Standardization (ISO). All three combined create the World Trade Organization (WTO).

Output controls   A combination of physical and administrative controls used to protect the confidentiality of system output. Examples of output controls include report distribution lists and physical security of specialized output such as payroll checks.

Outsourcing   The contractual arrangement to transfer ongoing operations to an external service provider.

P

Packet replay   An attack that replays a series of previously recorded legitimate network messages in an attempt to fool the recipient into believing that the attacker is a legitimate user.

Packet switching   A method of transmitting data through a variety of different paths en route to its destination. The user is billed by the data packets sent and not the route or distance traveled.

Packet-filtering firewall   A primitive type of network firewall that filters traffic based on source and destination addresses.

Paper test   A desktop review of printed documentation.

Parallel testing   Running two systems in parallel to verify the integrity of transactions and minimize risk during the system migration process.

Passive attack   Eavesdropping and other covert techniques used to collect information.

Password   A short sequence of characters used in single-factor (weak) authentication. Most user passwords are usually six to eight characters in length. Passwords should be changed every 30 to 90 days. The password itself should not be a word printed in any language, but instead a set of alphanumeric characters that is memorable to the user.

Patch   See *minor software update.*

Patch management   A planned method of testing and tracking *minor software updates* prior to implementation in production. Minor updates (or *patches*) are known to have unexpected consequences that can alter or disable other controls. All changes should be installed in a separate test environment and *regression tested* before being installed in production. The cost of separate testing can be justified by using the price of failure (*price of nonconformance*).

Patent   A public record of a unique design or function to which the author/inventor is granted exclusive rights for a limited period of time. Patents require the inventor to furnish a complete and functional blueprint of the design for anyone to reproduce a working replica with the exact same functionality. This is why intellectual trade secrets shall never be patented. Future patent applicants must show how their new design does not infringe on existing patents. Also see *trade secret.*

PDCA cycle   Walter Shewhart's quality planning cycle of Plan, Do, Check, Act. The PDCA model may be mistakenly referred to as the Deming PDCA cycle because W. Edwards Deming was a student of Shewhart. Origins of PDCA date back to Alexander the Great of Macedonia.

Penetration testing   A type of test designed to gauge possible penetration through the system security mechanisms by exploiting known vulnerabilities. Penetration testing should be conducted only under the supervision of software quality control technicians or trained auditors with formal approval of executive management. Separation of duties must be enforced.

Persistent electronic threat   Continuous threat of breach through electronic attacks. A hacker can commit the crime at a safe distance without fear of physical capture. Attacks may originate from self-directed hackers anywhere in the world. Well-organized attacks are known to be sponsored by a foreign government to gather intelligence data.

Pervasive controls   Specific mid-level controls over any technology shared across multiple departments. IT systems exist in almost all departments, and therefore IT-type controls must also exist in each department regardless of who is in charge.

Phishing   A social engineering technique designed to trick the user into divulging confidential information such as user ID, password, bank account information, and social security number. Also see *spear-phishing*.

Physical control   A type of control implemented by using barriers to prevent unauthorized access.

Physical layer   The lowest layer of the OSI model, which deals with physical cabling and electrical signals.

Ping test   Submarines detect other objects by using a single broadcast transmission and waiting for the sound reflection (ping) to bounce back. Similarly, computers use ping commands on the network to request that all machines on the same subnet respond with a ping-reply transmission.

Policy   A high-level statement by management specifying an objective that requires mandatory compliance for all persons of lower authority.

Portfolio management   Selecting projects based on the principles of "highest and best use" of available resources for generating the best return on investment (ROI). Projects are selected or cancelled according to which ones will generate the best return under the current circumstances. Similar to trading stock investments or baseball cards to improve the overall value of your collection.

Postimplementation review   A review of the system after it is placed in operation to determine whether it has fulfilled its original objectives. New objectives may be identified that require the system to be modified to attain compliance with the new requirements.

Presentation layer   This layer of the OSI model deals with screen formatting and display properties. Presentation runs on OSI layer 6.

Preventative control   A type of control that seeks to stop a particular type of event from occurring. Preventative controls may be implemented by using administrative methods, technical methods, and physical methods.

Price of conformance (POC)   The cost savings for doing it right the first time. Proper training and planning is a POC expense that conserves money and time by avoiding the additional costs of failure.

Price of nonconformance (PONC)   Represents the added costs of failure for not doing it right the first time. Added costs include penalties, redoing work, and uncompensated warranty repair. PONC usually exceeds the original profit margin.

Primary key   A unique entry into a database record that is required for the record to be valid. The primary key for user information might be the login ID. Without the login ID, the user's details would be invalid. Primary keys can be user ID numbers to prevent conflicts from using last names for people. Last names can change as users get married or divorced.

Private Branch Exchange (PBX)   The telephone switch that creates virtual private extensions for the users in the organization. The telephone switch is a technology resource that must be protected from hackers.

Private key   A file used as a randomizer in encryption algorithms. The private key must be kept secret from all other users in order to protect the confidentiality of encrypted files.

Procedure   A mandatory set of steps used as a cookbook recipe for a desired result. Procedures provide the day-to-day low-level execution necessary to support a standard.

Process audit   Evaluating the process method by measuring the inputs, sequence of activities, and output to determine whether the process meets the published requirements (specifications).

Product audit   Checks the product attributes against design specifications to determine whether the product meets the intended requirements. Attributes may include connectivity features, audit logging, security controls, and the quality of documentation.

Program Evaluation Review Technique (PERT)   A project management technique used to determine the critical path and to forecast the time and resources necessary to complete the most important elements of a specific project.

Program management   Managing a series of individual projects to create an ongoing operation, also known as a functional support program. Examples include maintenance, customer service, auditing for annual compliance, and new product development.

Project management   A management methodology used to plan and control the execution of a unique project to maximize its outcome based on limitations of time, resources, and scope.

Protection profile (PP)   A defined list of testing objectives applicable to the intended use of the system under evaluation (*target of evaluation*, or TOE). Different protection profiles exist in the *Common Criteria* (ISO 15408) depending on whether the system's role will be a workstation, file server, database, or security device.

Protocol   A formal specification of rules for interfaces and procedures used in communication.

Protocol stack   Different layers of services provided inside a communication protocol, also known as stack of protocol services.

Prototyping   A system development technique used to create initial versions of software functionality. The prototype is focused on proving a method or gaining early user acceptance. Prototypes seldom have any internal controls.

Provisioning   Administrative process of dividing services for allocation to the user.

Proxy firewall   A type of firewall that prevents direct access to network resources. The user request is rerouted through a proxy application that will filter the request for security compliance and present the filtered requests to the desired application on behalf of the user.

Pseudocode   A set of commands and macros developed into a custom template inside of an *integrated development environment (IDE)* programming tool. The software engineer designs the structure and function of the software inside the IDE for ease and maintainability. The IDE tool converts the pseudocode into actual programming code for the machine to use. Most fourth-generation programming tools use pseudocode templates to write programs.

Public key   A variable used in the encryption algorithm that is mathematically related to the private key. The public key is freely distributed by the sender to parties interested in communicating with the sender. A sender and recipient would exchange public keys in order to encrypt the files for transmission.

Public-key interchange (PKI)   See *asymmetric-key encryption*.

Q

Qualified opinion   The auditor has placed restrictions on the nature, use, or content of their findings. The audit may have encountered problems in scope, time, and thoroughness of tests, or content of available evidence. Also see *unqualified opinion*.

Quality   Development of well-defined specifications while ensuring adherence to those specifications. Quality is created in the planning and design phases, not by postinspection. Quality provides a cost savings when compared to the added costs of failure (*price of non-conformance*).

Quality assurance (QA)   A process of measurement standards designed to ensure product integrity.

Quality control (QC)   The process of planning, testing, and reviewing to ensure that the product meets the minimum acceptable performance specifications (level of quality).

R

Radio frequency identification (RFID)   Insecure method of reading radio signals to identify products, people, or physical items. Any RFID tag that can be read can also be duplicated.

Rapid Application Development (RAD)   A software development methodology that automates portions of the SDLC process. RAD does not provide the enterprise-level requirements planning necessary for a business system. RAD is designed to speed coding time in smaller software modules.

Reciprocal agreement   An agreement between two parties to help each other in the event of a disaster. Most reciprocal agreements are ineffective and unenforceable. The concept is popular because it does not bear any direct cost to either party. The reciprocal agreement ignores inherent conflicts that exist between two organizations. An exception exists regarding cooperative ownership of hot sites between financial organizations.

Records management   Collective process of classifying information to ensure proper safe-guards and control with the goal of providing complete integrity. Records must be created, labeled for proper handling, kept in safe storage, have controlled distribution, and ultimately be retired with proper disposal. Records of real property transactions are required to be kept forever. All record management and criminal penalties are judged by comparison to the ISO 15489 standard for records management.

Recovered work in process (RWIP)   Work tasks and data processing interrupted by a disaster or system failure. Recovered work is reprocessed according to the designated *recovery time objective (RTO)*.

Recovery point objective (RPO)   Refers to a point backward in time to which the loss of data is acceptable. This means that work in progress since the last data backup will be lost.

Recovery time objective (RTO)   The estimated time to recover a system based on the organization's capabilities and maximum acceptable outage.

Redundant Array of Independent—or Inexpensive—Disks (RAID)   A technical method of providing redundant disk storage space by using multiple disk drives. Previously known as Redundant Array of Inexpensive Disks until hardware vendors discovered the opportunity for a price increase.

Referential integrity   When information contained in two or more data tables is valid across the links inside the database (*foreign-key* relationship). A failure of referential integrity indicates a failed program or corrupt database.

Registration authority (RA)   A delegated representative of the *certificate authority* (CA) with the ability to issue a valid *digital certificate*. For example, a travel agent is the registration authority for selling airline tickets. The airline is the certificate-issuing authority and issues an electronic ticket (a type of digital certificate).

Regression testing   The process of retesting a system after changes to ensure that the change does not create any additional undesired complications.

Regulatory controls   Controls placed on industry by the government.

Relational database structure   A type of database that splits information between multiple tables while maintaining a link between the data for related entries. A relational database keeps a relation between different data elements.

Remote access server (RAS)   A service that provides security and authentication for remote users.

Remote Procedure Call (RPC)   A program method in client/server computing that allows a computer to request services from another computer without having to develop specific procedures for each program.

Residual risk   The amount of risk that remains after all controls have been implemented and mitigation efforts have been completed.

Retina scan   A biometrics technique that maps the unique pattern of veins in the back of the human eyeball.

Revenue objective (RO)   Used in business continuity planning to demonstrate the minimum revenue necessary for survival at various stages of recovery. Also used in business process reengineering as a claim of the expected benefit for reengineering a process.

Reverse engineering   An engineering technique used to steal the secrets of a competitor for the purpose of developing your own product. Reverse engineering is usually a violation of the software user license agreement.

Right to audit   The contractual rights of an organization to audit a third-party service provider. The right to audit must be clearly defined in the contract along with the expected terms of the audit.

Ring topology   A networking topology that creates two paths between the senders and receivers. The most common implementation is an IBM token ring for a local area network. The public telephone company uses a fiber ring topology for a redundant connection between central offices.

Risk   The likelihood that an unfortunate event will occur and cause a loss of assets.

Risk assessment   The process of reviewing risks, threats, and vulnerabilities to determine appropriate controls.

Risk management   The process of assessing risks in determining the organization's response. Acceptable responses could be mitigation, avoidance, acceptance, or transference.

Risk-based audit   The technique to determine the high-risk areas of an organization. Priority would be given to audit the high-risk areas first, before low-risk areas.

Robot network   See *bot-net*.

Robust Security Network (RSN)   A new 802.11i standard for security on wireless networks (2005). Mandated by the U.S. government to replace network equipment using the outdated and insecure *WEP* method of preshared encryption keys. RSN uses *Extensible Authentication Protocol (EAP)* with temporal keys and port-based access control.

Role-based access control (RBAC)   A type of nondiscretionary access control based on job duties.

Root kit   A malicious hacker program designed to unsuspectingly install a backdoor without the consent of the system user. A root kit will subvert the operating system kernel security and operate in stealth to hide its existence. Normal system utilities are usually unable to detect the presence of a root kit.

Router   A networking device that uses traffic routing to forward a message to its intended destination. Network routers operate on OSI layer 3.

Routing protocol The procedure and formula used to direct communications across the available path. Static routing will always follow the same path. Dynamic routing will use a formula of metrics to redirect communications along the best available route at the present time.

Run-to-run totals A process that tracks the total number of submissions to ensure that all transactions have been processed.

S

Scenario approach Planning exercises center around solving the problems presented in a simulated event (scenario). This lends a credible purpose bearing on reality in the exercise. Scenario exercises are used in planning to uncover previous assumptions and interesting quirks used in the decision process. Assumptions may no longer be valid. You may discover additional defects in the decision criteria.

Screened host A single computer host protected by a firewall and accessible by both internal and external users.

Screened subnet A subnet of multiple computer hosts protected by a firewall and accessible by both internal and external users. A screened subnet is also known as a *demilitarized zone (DMZ)*. War veterans will tell you that you can still get killed in a demilitarized zone.

Script kiddies Individuals who execute scripted programs or utilities without comprehensive knowledge of the internal mechanisms being executed. Your author is a script kiddy, every time I run a macro or setup script that I didn't write. Script kiddies also refer to novice hackers using automated attack tools downloaded from the Internet.

Secure Shell (SSH) An encrypted terminal session providing additional security for the user.

Secure Sockets Layer (SSL) Session-layer security and encryption between a user and a server. SSL is a common form of security for virtual private networks (VPNs). This method uses private-key encryption with a digital certificate on the server.

Security parameter index (SPI) A security specification used in the header of the IPsec protocol to identify encryption keys used in communication.

Security policy A formal statement by management of the importance in implementing proper security controls. A second definition is a set of rules implemented to protect the organization.

Security target (ST) Security targets represent the chosen *Common Criteria* standard of performance acceptable from the system under evaluation (TOE). To fail this target would result in a lower assurance rating. Also see *protection profile (PP)* and *target of evaluation (TOE)*.

Segregation of duties The separation of transaction authorization from other normal work activities. The purpose of segregation of duties is to ensure that no changes are executed without being observed by another individual. The purpose of the control is to minimize fraud, error, and omission.

Server mirroring See *mirrored*.

Service delivery objective (SDO) The level of service to be available at a particular point in time. This may be full-service for all users or service for a particular core process only.

Service-level agreement (SLA) A contractual agreement between the user and the service provider that outlines an acceptable level of support for business processing.

Servlet A web-based program that runs on the server, also known as server-side includes (SSI). This type of program does not download to the PC as an applet would. However, applets can access servlets for better performance by using distributed processing.

Session layer Layer 5 of the OSI model, which manages service communication requests between systems.

Shell A technical name for the user's display session on the computer.

Signature based A technical method that relies on the database of known software behavior. Signature files indicate a particular type of attack for virus protection or intrusion detection.

Simple Network Management Protocol (SNMP) An automated process for managing devices across the network by transmitting remote commands with passwords. The SNMP passwords are referred to as *community strings*. The management value of SNMP is high, and security usually is very poor. If properly configured, SNMP version 3 contains some security, provided all the devices are using version 3 and not the older versions of 1 and 2. Running mixed versions of SNMP indicates a security failure. SNMP can remotely reconfigure or reboot a device.

Simple Network Management Protocol (SNMP) console A dedicated system used by IT operations to actively monitor all the SNMP alerts generated by all the network devices. Examples include the original HP OpenView. and open network management system (Open-NMS). IS security usually has its own SNMP monitoring console for separation of duties.

Single sign-on (SSO) A technical method that uses encryption to allow the user to simultaneously log in to all the network servers. The objective is to increase security with stronger passwords and to make the network easier for the user. Unauthorized access under single sign-on may allow the compromise of all network resources.

Single-factor authentication A type of authentication that uses passwords alone or tokens alone to authenticate a user. There is no real assurance that the user is the intended party. Single-factor authentication is known as weak authentication regardless of the constructive strength of passwords used. The password indicates only that somebody known or unknown has logged in by using that password string.

Skills matrix   An administrative planning tool used to ensure that each task is assigned to the right person with the correct skills. Data in the matrix will demonstrate skill gaps and help justify training needs. This discourages the assignment of untrained personnel (or any warm body).

Slack space   Refers to the difference between space currently used by files compared to the remnant space previously allocated on a hard disk. Slack space is the leftover space that may contain old deleted data that has not yet been overwritten.

Sniffer   A packet analyzer that can decode data transmissions across the network. A sniffer can also display passwords in transit.

SOAP   Used in XML programming to define the *application programming interface* (API) being used. Originally known as Simple Object Access Protocol.

Sociability testing   Software tests to determine how well a program can operate with other programs (social behavior).

Social engineering   The process of gaining access by tricking a user into cooperating.

Sockets   Special software buffer used for communication between programs across the network.

Software as a service (SaaS)   Online vendor provides the use of commercial software through subscription agreement. Software is hosted and supported remotely for the benefit of the subscriber and their users. This is simply a name variation of an outsource service bureau, application service provider (ASP), or productivity software supplied via cloud computing.

Software baseline   A document recording all the design features agreed to be included in the software. Progress and changes are reported against this baseline to indicate actual performance in the development phase. Any variance in the development needs to be approved by the user and management.

Source code   The original version of computer programs that are still in human-readable form. Programmers write program in source code. The source code is fed into a compiler that generates object code to run on the machine. Source code needs to be protected for integrity. The source code represents the original set of instructions and a tremendous amount of work.

Source lines of code (SLOC)   An older style of estimating the complexity of a program or of measuring progress of new development. SLOC is still used in software estimation. The value of this calculation is lost whenever you combine the SLOC count from different generations of programming tools.

Source routing   An old diagnostic protocol that allows the sender to specify the communications path to be used in spite of the network router settings configured by the network administrator. Source routing can circumvent firewalls and should be disabled on network devices.

Spamming   Replying to more people than necessary when you respond to an email message (also known as email flaming). It also refers to sending a large number of unsolicited email messages. Sending unsolicited commercial email advertisements is usually legal if the sender is fully identified and offers a working mechanism for the recipient to opt out of (stop receiving) future messages. Opt-out may be automated or offer the option of using a manual process.

Spear-phishing   Very effective attack technique used to target a specific system. This attack targets an individual server, user, database, or network device.

Spiral model   A software development planning model that demonstrates the life cycle for multiple versions of software.

Split horizon   A network routing algorithm used to prevent communication loops by breaking the loop through the creation of an artificial horizon. Similar to the concept of creating the earth's international dateline.

Spoofing   Committing fraud by masquerading as a legitimate user or another system.

SQL injection   One computer program sends data as input to another program operated by someone else, with or without their permission. SQL injection techniques represent the most common method of integrating between programs, especially e-commerce across the Internet. SQL injection is possible due to input authentication failure by the receiving program. Using strong cryptographic controls instead of passwords is one method to discourage unauthorized SQL injection.

Standard   Specifies a minimum level of mandatory compliance to ensure uniform consistency with *integrity*.

Standing data   Information stored on the hard disk and other storage media. This information is "standing still" on the media and susceptible to attack, disclosure, or compromise.

Star topology   Uses a dedicated connection from the hub/switch to each node on the network. Star topology is the most flexible topology and has a higher cost due to the redundant use of cabling.

Stateful packet inspection   The technique used in third-generation firewalls to maintain a table of session connections including connectionless communications, also referred to as the state. Communication requests are monitored against the table to ensure that the request is in character with the transaction and is not a hacking attempt.

Statement on Auditing Standards (SAS)   A list of accounting standards put forth by the American Institute of Certified Public Accountants.

Stop-and-go sampling   A simple test used to prove that the likelihood of errors is low. It is used when errors are expected and allows the auditor to stop at the earliest possible opportunity.

Storage area network   A special type of network used to connect various storage devices to servers. Storage area networks are usually attached by fiber optics.

Strategic objective   Describes a fundamental method or change used to direct the organization toward an objective. Strategic objectives are usually in a time frame of three to five years.

Strong authentication   See *two-factor authentication*.

Subject   The target of the audit or control mechanism.

Subnet   A small group of computers and devices sharing the same broadcast domain. Subnets are connected to larger networks via routers. Also known as a subnetwork.

Substantive testing   A type of test that seeks to verify content and its integrity. Substantive tests include verifying count balances and performing physical inventory counts. Technical methods include executing detailed system scans to detect the effectiveness of a particular security configuration.

Swap space   A special area on the hard disk designated as a temporary location for data to be "swapped" out of RAM (electronic working memory). This improves system performance by moving selected tasks out of the way while other data is processed. Also known as *virtual memory*.

Switch   See *network switch*.

Symmetric-key encryption (secret key)   An encryption algorithm that uses the same secret key shared between the sender and the receiver. Symmetric-key encryption systems are time sensitive and will operate only while both ends are using the same key. Symmetric-key systems are faster than asymmetric encryption because the key does not have to be derived through mathematical calculation.

Syslog   A program designed to send system event logs to a remote system log server (also known as syslogging). A copy of all the log events is safely stored on a separate server. Log files are protected from the attacker, and the extra copy of log files enforces separation of duties.

System audit   Evaluates the management of a system, including its configuration. The purpose is to determine how well the system is managed by collecting evidence indicating its specific configuration settings.

System Development Life Cycle (SDLC)   A series of seven phases that represent the life cycle of software development. The phases are as follows: feasibility study, requirements definition, system design, development, implementation, postimplementation, and disposal.

Systems Network Architecture (SNA)   Early hierarchical design created by IBM for connecting different computers.

T

Tactical   Describes the application of a procedure or method, hopefully in support of an organizational objective.

Target of evaluation (TOE)   A computer system or network device to be evaluated under the *Common Criteria* standard (ISO 15408). Also see *protection profile (PP)* and *security target (ST)*.

TCP/IP   Transmission Control Protocol running on the Internet Protocol. This has become synonymous with the Internet Protocol and accessing data across the network. Transmission Control Protocol is used for connection-oriented sessions on the Internet.

Temporal key   A temporary and uniquely generated encryption key. Also see *Robust Security Network (RSN)*.

Threat   A potential danger that, if realized, will have a negative effect on assets.

Throughput   Effective speed metric for processing a complete set of specific transactions. Overall throughput speed usually varies according to the input, processing, and output requirements of particular transactions.

Time bomb   Instructions written by the programmer in computer software to disable the functionality of the program based on a specific date or event. Time bombs are used by programmers to disable evaluation periods, force license upgrades, or cause damage on a particular date such as April Fools' Day.

Top-down structured programming   A methodical design breaking down the high-level functions into an orderly design of smaller distinct program modules. Individual modules perform unique functions and can be updated or replaced with relative ease. Modules are linked together to form the finished program. In top-down programming, more time is spent on formal planning of functional specifications versus code development.

Tort damages   An injury or wrong inflicted upon another party and created by a violation of duty. It can be created by deprivation of a legal right, by violation of a private obligation with or without a contract, or by infraction of a duty to the public. Special damages will accrue. Examples include negligence or breach of an agreement in bad faith. The victim may be eligible for up to 20 times the actual damages.

Trade secret   A unique process, tool, formula, pattern, or knowledge possessed by its creator and hidden from everyone else for the purpose of obtaining an advantage in the market. The owner must provide extensive protection to prevent disclosure, or risk forfeiting their claim. Trade secrets cannot be patented.

Traffic analysis   A technique used by an intruder to monitor communications and determine the most significant systems on the network. The objective is to build a map of network devices to be used for launching future attacks.

Transaction processing (TP) monitor   A software process that monitors the performance and health of the hardware running a database application. The purpose is to throttle back requests when necessary to avoid overloading the hardware. TP monitors help to prevent overloading or "crashing" the server with too much work.

Transborder data   Data crossing a political border. This data requires special handling. Transborder risks include legality of the data, differences in legal requirements, and extra protection necessary to prevent unauthorized disclosure. Examples include data transmission between countries or between trading partners in business.

Transport layer   Layer 4 of the OSI model, responsible for the delivery of data transmissions across the network. Two common methods are the Transmission Control Protocol, which guarantees delivery, and the User Datagram Protocol, which does not provide any assurance of delivery.

Trapdoor   Secret point of entry into a system. Usually a hidden access technique left in the software by the developer for future use by the developer's technical support staff.

Trojan horse   Malicious software that is intentionally hidden inside of a normal program. The concept is analogous with the Trojan horse story of ancient times.

Tuple   A row in a database, also known as the attribute of a particular data record.

Two-factor authentication   The processes of basing a decision regarding the user's identity on two pieces of information—usually, the user password and a unique physical characteristic of the user. Two-factor authentication is also known as strong authentication.

U

Unclassified information   *Unclassified* is synonymous with public records or unprotected data. This type of design has been used for hundreds, if not thousands, of years in government, military, and commerce. Anyone may have access to the contents.

Unicast   A technical method used to transmit data to a single destination on the network.

Uninterruptible power supply (UPS)   An intelligent device that monitors commercial power and delivers supplemental battery power when necessary. The purpose of the UPS is to provide supplemental electricity for a brief period of time until the systems can be shut down. The UPS may have the capability to start an electric generator for extended runtimes during a power outage.

Unit testing   A testing technique to verify the functionality of an individual program module.

Universal Description, Discovery, and Integration (UDDI) protocol   An online directory used in XML programming to identify available web services.

Unqualified opinion   The auditor has no reservations about their findings, and there are no special restrictions on the use of the audit report. Also see *qualified opinion*.

Uptime Refers to the system or resource being available for the user whenever they care to use it. Uptime is reported in simple comparison to all forms of downtime. Service-level agreements need to specify how uptime is reported and the specific operating hours that each system must be up and available for the user.

User acceptance testing (UAT) A formal process of verifying that the system meets the user's requirements during the SDLC implementation phase.

User Datagram Protocol (UDP) Provides for connectionless sessions with lower overhead by using Internet Protocol. UDP sessions are a best effort and will not ensure delivery to the destination.

V

Variable sampling Used to designate a prorated dollar amount or weight of effectiveness to an entire subject population.

Version control Tracking the details of tiny changes inside of software versions and revisions. Version control is the foundation of *configuration management*. Each change introduces the likelihood of unexpected consequences.

Virtual Synonym for *fake* or *not real*. May appear as simulated computer, server, or user. It could be simulation software to make another program pretend to be a server.

Virtual local area network (VLAN) An artificial grouping of systems into a common broadcast domain, also known as a subnetwork. Similar to a conference call between computers instead of people.

Virtual machine A software partition simulating private processing, memory, and computer interfaces. The design was created for service bureaus using mainframes with different users running their own programs in time-sharing mode. Each partition is protected by isolation from the other partitions to prevent any disruption. The virtual machine concept has been copied for use in small computers by VMware, Parallels, and *Java Virtual Machine*.

Virtual memory See *swap space*.

Virtual private network (VPN) The method of providing secure access to the network for a remote user by means of encryption.

Virus A malicious, self-replicating computer program that spreads itself through the system as infected computer programs are executed. Viruses can destroy data or program files.

Volatile data Information in the computer's working memory (RAM) that will be lost when power is shut off. Also see *nonvolatile data*.

Vulnerability The weakness or path that can be exploited by a threat to damage an asset.

Vulnerability assessment The process of reviewing risks and vulnerabilities to determine the organization's current level of exposure.

W

Walk-through testing   Used in disaster recovery testing to simulate the basic recovery process in order to clean any errors from the procedure.

War chalking   Process of physically marking insecure wireless access points to the Internet. Most war chalking has evolved into downloadable maps available on the Internet.

War driving   Process of driving through a neighborhood with technical tools to detect insecure wireless access points.

War walking   Similar purpose as *war driving*.

Warm site   A facility that has basic utility services installed and some computer equipment but lacks other computer equipment necessary for recovery. A warm site needs to be built out before it can be used. It can be ready in days or weeks. A warm site offers a lower chance of success than a hot site.

Waterfall model   An early software development model that cascades the completion of each phase into the next phase.

Weak authentication   See *single-factor authentication*.

Web Services Description Language (WSDL)   Identifies the format used in the programming of XML objects.

Wet pipe   A fire-suppression system with water stored in the pipes at all times. This type of system is susceptible to corrosion and freezing.

White hat   An honest software tester working in the security or audit department under a formal, structured test procedure to determine system vulnerabilities by using known hacker techniques. This individual never has any staff responsibilities in IT operations, to preserve the separation of duties.

White-box testing   Testing that checks the integrity of transactions while allowing the programmer to view the logical paths through the software. Also known as program code review. Internally developed software-programming scripts and *pseudocode* templates in human-readable form (not compiled) may be subjected to white-box tests. Conversely, compiled software is not readable and must use *black-box testing* techniques.

Wide area network (WAN)   A computer network providing user access in multiple cities.

Wiping utility (memory wiping)   A special utility designed to overwrite the contents of storage media and RAM memory. This prevents any recovery of data from system memory or the hard disk. Wiping utilities can sanitize a system prior to redeployment, or be used by an individual to destroy evidence. Possession of wiping utilities should be a violation of the *acceptable use policy* unless specifically authorized in writing as a job requirement.

Wired Equivalent Privacy (WEP)   A *symmetric-key* (preshared key) encryption protocol originally designed to promote wireless security. The U.S. government published a declaration in April 2005 that all WEP installations are now considered totally insecure. Security was compromised by the industry vendor's poor choice of implementation that favors Plug and Play access over security. A radio beacon advertises the entire key to any listening device.

Wireless Application Protocol (WAP)   Loosely based on the OSI model and designed to display data on small screens with the limited resources of handheld devices.

Work in process (WIP)   Work tasks or data currently being processed at the time of disruption. Business continuity and disaster recovery plans need to identify how work in process will be recovered. The *recovered work in process (RWIP)* must be reprocessed in a timely manner to avoid violating a *legal deadline (LD)*.

Working papers   The auditor's notes, checklists, audit procedures, and results of audit testing. These documents must be kept secure via electronic file backup. The auditee is not permitted to see the working papers.

Worm   A malicious computer program that can travel independently through the network and infect systems.

Write blocker   A device used in forensic investigations to prevent any changes to the original data on the hard disk or media during *bitstream imaging*. Without a write blocker, the original media is considered tainted, tampered, or contaminated by any form of unintentional change that occurs during the investigation.

X

XML   See *Extensible Markup Language (XML)*.

Z

Zero-day attack   Any attack that has not been seen before. Virus scanners, firewalls, and intrusion detection and prevention systems can't stop zero-day attacks because the hacker has discovered a new attack method that nobody realized. Most zero-day attacks exploit vulnerabilities in middleware or default settings.

Index

Note to the reader: Throughout this index **boldfaced** page numbers indicate primary discussions of a topic. *Italicized* page numbers indicate illustrations.

T

The Best CISA Book/CD Package on the Market!

Get ready for your CISA certification with the most comprehensive and challenging sample tests anywhere!

The Sybex Test Engine features:

- All the review questions, as covered in each chapter of the book.

- Challenging questions representative of those you'll find on the real exam.

- Two full-length bonus exams available only on the CD.

- An Assessment Test to narrow your focus to certain objective groups.

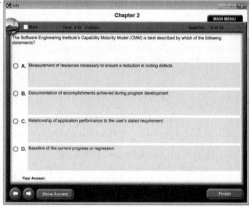

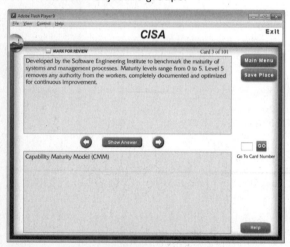

Use the Electronic Flashcards to jog your memory and prep last-minute for the exam!

- Reinforce your understanding of key concepts with these hardcore flashcard-style questions.

- Now you can study for the CISA anytime, anywhere.

Search through the complete book in PDF!

- Access the entire *CISA: Certified Information Systems Auditor Study Guide, Third Edition* complete with figures and tables, in electronic format.

- Search the *CISA: Certified Information Systems Auditor Study Guide, Third Edition* chapters to find information on any topic in seconds.

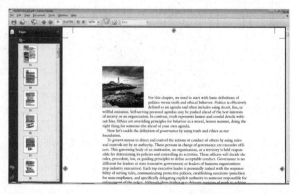